Lexicology and Corpus Linguistics

Open Linguistics Series

Series Editor
Robin Fawcett, University of Wales, Cardiff

This series is 'open' in two senses. First, it provides a forum for works associated with any school of linguistics or with none. Most practising linguists have long since outgrown the unhealthy assumption that theorising about language should be left to those working in the generativist–formalist paradigm. Today large and increasing numbers of scholars are seeking to understand the nature of language by exploring one or other of various cognitive models of language, or in terms of the communicative use of language, or both. This series is playing a valuable part in re-establishing the traditional 'openness' of the study of language. The series includes many studies that are in, or on the borders of, various functional theories of language, and especially (because it has been the most widely used of these) Systemic Functional Linguistics. The general trend of the series has been towards a functional view of language, but this simply reflects the works that have been offered to date. The series continues to be open to all approaches, including works in the generativist–formalist tradition.

The second way in which the series is 'open' is that it encourages studies that open out 'core' linguistics in various ways: to encompass discourse and the description of natural texts; to explore the relationships between linguistics and its neighbouring disciplines – psychology, sociology, philosophy, cultural and literary studies – and to apply it in fields such as education, language pathology and law.

Recent titles in this series

Lexicology and Corpus Linguistics

An Introduction

M. A. K. Halliday, Wolfgang Teubert, Colin Yallop
and Anna Čermáková

continuum
LONDON • NEW YORK

Continuum

The Tower Building	15 East 26th Street
11 York Road	New York
London SE1 7NX	NY 10010

British Library Cataloguing-in-Publication Data
A catalogue record for this book is available from the British Library.

ISBN: 0–8264–4861–5 (hardback)
ISBN: 0–8264–4862–3 (paperback)

Library of Congress Cataloguing-in-Publication Data
A catalogue record for this book is available from the Library of Congress.

Typeset by YHT Ltd, London
Printed and bound in Great Britain by MPG Books Ltd, Bodmin, Cornwall

Contents

1 Lexicology

M. A. K. Halliday

1.1 What is a word?

To many people the most obvious feature of a language is that it consists of words. If we write English, we recognise words on the page – they have a space on either side; we learn to spell them, play games with them like Scrabble, and look them up in dictionaries. It ought not to be difficult to know what a word is and how to describe it.

Yet when we look a little more closely, a word turns out to be far from the simple and obvious matter we imagine it to be. Even if we are literate English-speaking adults, we are often unsure where a word begins and ends. Is *English-speaking* one word or two? How do we decide about sequences like *lunchtime (lunch-time, lunch time), dinner-time, breakfast time*? How many words in *isn't, pick-me-up, CD*? Children who cannot yet read have little awareness of word boundaries, and often learn about them through word games, like 'I'm thinking of a word that rhymes with . . .'.

Even more problematic is whether two forms are, or are not, instances of the same word. Presumably if they sound alike but are spelled differently, like *horse* and *hoarse*, they are two different words. But how about pairs such as:

like 'similar to'	*like* 'be fond of'
part 'portion'	*part* 'to separate'
shape 'the outline of'	*shape* 'to mould'
content 'happy'	*content* 'that which is contained'

– not to mention *shape* as the old name for a kind of solid custard pudding?

We know that there is no single right answer to these questions, because different dictionaries take different decisions about what to do with them.

Then, what about variants like *take, takes, took, taking, taken*: are these five different words, or is there just one word *take* with many forms? Or

go, goes, went, going, gone? Are *book* and *books, friend* and *friendly* one word
or two? Are *big, bigger, biggest* three forms of a single word *big*? If so, what
about *good, better, best*? Or *four* and *fourth, three* and *third, two* and *second*?

All these are problems within English, a language where the words
are fairly clearly bounded. In Chinese it is much harder, because words
are not marked off in writing; Chinese characters stand for **morphemes**, which are components of words. (For example, if English was
written with Chinese characters then a word like *freedom* would be
written with two characters, one for *free* and one for *dom*.) The Chinese
are very conscious of morphemes, even before they are literate,
because each one is pronounced as one syllable and hardly ever varies;
but they have much less intuition about what a word is. Many other
writing systems also, such as Japanese, Thai, Arabic and Hindi, give no
very consistent indication of word boundaries. When Ancient Greek
was first written down, all the words were joined together without any
spaces, and it was a few centuries before the word emerged as a clearly
distinct unit.

So writing systems do not always identify words: partly because there
are different kinds of writing system, but partly also because the languages themselves are different. There is no universal entity, found in
every language, that we can equate with what in English is called a
'word'. And in unwritten languages the 'word' can be a very elusive
thing.

Nevertheless there is a general concept underlying all this diversity;
that is the **lexical item**. Every language has a **vocabulary**, or 'lexicon',
which forms one part of its grammar – or, to use a more accurate term,
one part of its **lexicogrammar**. The lexicogrammar of a language
consists of a vast network of choices, through which the language
construes its meanings: like the choices, in English, between 'positive'
and 'negative', or 'singular' and 'plural', or 'past', 'present' and
'future'; or between 'always', 'sometimes' and 'never', or 'on top of'
and 'underneath'; or between 'hot' and 'cold', or 'rain', 'snow' and
'hail', or 'walk' and 'run'. Some of these choices are very general,
applying to almost everything we say: we always have to choose between
positive and negative whenever we make a proposition or a proposal
(*it's raining, it isn't raining*; *run! don't run!*). Others are very specific,
belonging to just one domain of meaning; these arise only when we are
concerned with that particular domain. The choice between rain and
snow, for example, arises only if we are talking about the weather.
Choices of this second kind are expressed as lexical items: e.g. *hot/cold*;
rain/snow/hail; *walk/run*.

If we are using the term 'word' to mean a unit of the written language, i.e. 'that which (in English) is written between two spaces', then ultimately all these choices are expressed as strings of words, or **wordings**, as in *it always snows on top of the mountain*. But teachers of English have customarily distinguished between **content words**, like *snow* and *mountain*, and **function words**, like *it* and *on* and *of* and *the*; and it is the notion of a content word that corresponds to our lexical item. Lexicology is the study of content words, or lexical items.

The example sentence in the last paragraph shows that the line between content words and function words is not a sharp one: rather, the two form a continuum or cline, and words like *always* and *top* lie somewhere along the middle of the cline. Thus there is no exact point where the lexicologist stops and the grammarian takes over; each one can readily enter into the territory of the other. So dictionaries traditionally deal with words like *the* and *and*, even though there is hardly anything to say about them in strictly lexicological terms, while grammars go on classifying words into smaller and smaller classes as far as they can go – again, with always diminishing returns.

This gives us yet a third sense of the term 'word', namely the element that is assigned to a **word class** ('part of speech') by the grammar. So the reason 'word' turns out to be such a complicated notion, even in English, is that we are trying to define it simultaneously in three different ways. For ordinary everyday discussion this does not matter; the three concepts do not in fact coincide, but they are near enough for most purposes. In studying language systematically, however, we do need to recognise the underlying principles, and keep these three senses apart. The reason our lexicogrammar is divided into 'grammar' and 'lexicology' (as in traditional foreign language textbooks, which had their section of the grammar and then a vocabulary added separately at the end) is because we need different models – different theories and techniques – for investigating these two kinds of phenomena, lexical items on the one hand and grammatical categories on the other. This is why **lexicology** forms a different sub-discipline within linguistics.

1.2 Methods in lexicology: the dictionary

There are two principal methods for describing words (now in our sense of **lexical items**), though the two can also be combined in various ways. One method is by writing a **dictionary**; the other is by writing a **thesaurus**.

The difference between a dictionary and a thesaurus is this. In a thesaurus, words that are similar in meaning are grouped together: so, for example, all words that are species of fish, or all words for the emotions, or all the words to do with building a house. In a dictionary, on the other hand, words are arranged simply where you can find them (in 'alphabetical order' in English); so the place where a word occurs tells you nothing about what it means. In the dictionary we find a sequence such as *gnome, gnu, go, goad*; and *parrot* is in between *parlour* and *parsley*.

In a dictionary, therefore, each entry stands by itself as an independent piece of work. There may be some cross-referencing to save repetition; but it plays only a relatively small part. Here are some typical entries from a fairly detailed dictionary of English, the two-volume *New Shorter Oxford English Dictionary*, 1993. (The full entries are much longer and omissions are indicated by ... in parentheses; the abridged entries given here serve to show the general structure and to illustrate the kind of detail included.)

bear /bɛ:/ *n.* [OE *bera* = MDu. *bere* (Du. *beer*), OHG *bero* (G *Bär*), f. Wgmc: rel. to ON *bjǫrn*.]

1. Any of several large heavily-built mammals constituting the family Ursidae (order Carnivora), with thick fur and a plantigrade gait. OE.

b With specifying wd: an animal resembling or (fancifully) likened to a bear. E17.

2. *Astron.* the Bear (more fully *the Great Bear*) = URSA *Major*; the Lesser or Little Bear = URSA *Minor*. LME.

3. *fig.* A rough, unmannerly or uncouth person. L16.

(...)

3. LD MACAULAY This great soldier ... was no better than a Low Dutch bear.

(...)

Other phrases: **like a bear with a sore head** *colloq.* angry, ill-tempered.

(...)

bear /bɛ:/ *v.* Pa. t. **bore** /bɔ:/, (*arch.*) **bare** /bɛ:/. Pa.pple & ppl a. **borne** /bɔ:n/, BORN. See also YBORN. [OE *beran* = OS, OHG *beran*, ON *bera*, Goth. *bairan* f. Gmc f. IE base also of Skt *bharati*, Armenian *berem*, Gk *pherein*, L *ferre*.]

I *v.t.* Carry, hold, possess.

1 Carry (esp. something weighty), transport, bring or take by carrying; *fig.* have, possess. Now *literary* or *formal.* OE.

(...)

2 Carry about with or upon one, esp. visibly; show, display; be known or recognized by (a name, device, etc.); have (a character, reputation, value, etc.) attached to or associated with one. OE.

(...)

1 CHAUCER On his bak he bar ... Anchises.

R. HOLINSHED This pope Leo ... bare but seauen and thirtie yeeres of age.

SHAKES. *Macb.* I bear a charmed life, which must not yield To one of woman born.

E. WAUGH Music was borne in from the next room.

(...)

2 SHAKES. *Wint. T.* If I Had servants true about me that bare eyes To see alike mine honour as their profits.

STEELE Falshood ... shall hereafter bear a blacker Aspect.

W. H. PRESCOTT Four beautiful girls, bearing the names of the principal goddesses.

A. P. STANLEY The staff like that still borne by Arab chiefs.

(...)

Phrases (...)

bear fruit *fig.* yield results, be productive. (...)

bear in mind not forget, keep in one's thoughts. (...)

cut /kʌt/ *v.* Infl. **-tt-**. Pa. t. & pple **cut.** See also CUT, CUTTED *ppl adjs.* ME [Rel. to Norw. *kutte,* Icel. *kuta* cut with a little knife, *kuti* little blunt knife. Prob. already in OE.]

I *v.t.* Penetrate or wound with a sharp-edged thing; make an incision in. ME.

b *fig.* Wound the feelings of (a person), hurt deeply.

(...)

1 N. MOSLEY The edge of the pipe cut his mouth, which bled. *fig.*: ADDISON Tormenting thought! it cuts into my soul.

b F. BURNEY He says something so painful that it cuts us to the soul.

(...)

Phrases: (...)

cut both ways have a good and bad effect; (of an argument) support both sides.

cut corners *fig.* scamp work, do nothing inessential. (...)

These entries are organised as follows:

1. the headword or **lemma**, often in bold or some other special font;
2. its pronunciation, in some form of alphabetic notation;
3. its word class ('part of speech');
4. its etymology (historical origin and derivation);
5. its definition;
6. citations (examples of its use).

Most dictionaries follow this general structure, but variations are of course found. For example, etymological information may come at the end of the entry rather than near the beginning. Let us look more closely at each item in turn.

1.   The **lemma** is the base form under which the word is entered and assigned its place: typically, the 'stem', or simplest form (singular noun, present/infinitive verb, etc.). Other forms may not be entered if they are predictable (such as the plural *bears*, not given here); but the irregular past forms of the verbs are given (irregular in the sense that they do not follow the default pattern of adding -*ed*) and there is also an indication under *cut* that the *t* must be doubled in the spelling of inflected forms like *cutting*. An irregular form may appear as a separate lemma, with cross reference. This dictionary has such an entry for **borne** *v*. pa. pple & ppl a. of BEAR *v*., indicating that *borne* is the past participle and participial adjective of the verb **bear**. In a language such as Russian, where the stem form of a word typically does not occur alone, a particular variant is chosen as lemma: nominative singular for nouns, infinitive for verbs, etc.

2.   In most large and recent dictionaries, the pronunciation is indicated, as here, by the International Phonetic Alphabet in a broad, phonemic transcription. Some older dictionaries use a modified alphabet with a keyword system, e.g. *i* as in 'machine', i as in 'hit', u as in 'hut'; and some dictionaries, especially those intended for use by children, simply use informal respellings, e.g. **emphasis** (EM-fa-sis) or **empirical** (em-PIR-ik-uhl).

3.   The word class will be one of the primary word classes (in English, usually verb, noun, adjective, adverb, pronoun, preposition, conjunction, determiner/article). To this class specification may be added some indication of a subclass, for example count or mass noun, intransitive or transitive verb. The senses of the verbs illustrated here, for example, are identified as transitive verbs (*v.t.*). Some dictionaries, especially those compiled for learners of English, give more detailed word class information, showing for example the functional relations into which verbs can enter.

4.   The etymology may include, as here, not only the earliest known form and the language in which this occurs (e.g. Old English, OE for short) but also cognate forms in other languages. Some dictionaries may also include a suggested 'proto-' form, a form not found anywhere but reconstructed by the methods of historical linguistics; proto-forms are conventionally marked with an asterisk. The various forms of the noun *bear*, for example, suggest an ancestral form **ber-*, pre-dating the differentiation of languages such as Old English and Old High German. For many words, little or nothing is known of their history, and a common entry is 'origin unknown' (or the more traditional 'etym. dub.'!). This edition of the *Oxford* also indicates the first recorded use against each (sub)definition: OE means the word (or an earlier form of

it) is attested in this sense in Old English texts, E17 means this sense is first recorded in the early seventeenth century, L16 that the sense is first recorded in the late sixteenth century.

5. The definition takes one or both of two forms: description and synonymy. The description may obviously need to include words that are 'harder' (less frequently used) than the lemmatised word. Some dictionaries, such as the *Longman Dictionary of Contemporary English* (first published in 1978), limit the vocabulary that they use in their descriptions. With synonymy, a word or little set of words of similar meaning is brought in, often giving slightly more specific senses. All definition is ultimately circular; but compilers try to avoid very small circles, such as defining *sad* as *sorrowful*, and then *sorrowful* as *sad*.

6. Citations, here grouped together under numbers referring back to definitions or senses, show how the word is used in context. They may illustrate a typical usage, or use in well-known literary texts, or the earliest recorded instances of the word. There may also be various 'fixed expressions' (idioms and cliches) and what the *Oxford* here calls 'phrases', where the expression functions like a single, composite lexical item (e.g. *bear fruit, bear in mind*).

The dictionary will usually use a number of abbreviations to indicate special features or special contexts, for example *fig.* ('figurative'), *Astron.* ('Astronomy') and so on. With a common word such as *bear* or *cut* there are likely to be subdivisions within the entry, corresponding to different meanings of the word.

Compound words, like *cutthroat* (as in *cutthroat competition*), and derivatives, like *cutting* (from a plant) or *uncut*, are often entered under the same lemma; in that case, compounds will appear under the first word (*cutthroat* under *cut*, *haircut* under *hair*), derivatives under the stem (both *cutting* and *uncut* under *cut*). But dictionaries adopt varying practices. In some dictionaries, compounds are given separate lemmata; and sometimes a derivational affix is used as lemma and derivatives grouped under that (for example *antibody, anticlimax, anti-dote*, etc. all under *anti-*).

1.3 Methods in lexicology: the thesaurus

In a thesaurus, by contrast, there is no separate entry for each word. The word occurs simply as part of a list; and it is the place of a word in the whole construction of the book that tells you what it means.

Thus if we look for *cut* in Roget's *Thesaurus of English Words and Phrases* we will find it (among other places) in the middle of a paragraph as follows:

v. cultivate; till (the soil); farm, garden; sow, plant; reap, mow, cut; manure, dress the ground, dig, delve, dibble, hoe, plough, plow, harrow, rake, weed, lap and top, force, transplant, thin out, bed out, prune, graft.

This may not seem to have very much organisation in it; but it is actually the final layer in a comprehensive **lexical taxonomy**.

A lexical taxonomy is an organisation of words into classes and sub-classes and sub-sub-classes (etc.); not on the basis of form but on the basis of meaning (that is, not grammatical classes but semantic classes). The principal semantic relationship involved is that of **hyponymy** (*x* is a hyponym of *y* means *x* 'is a kind of' *y*, e.g. *melon* is a hyponym of *fruit*). There is also another relationship, that of **meronymy** ('is a part of'), which may be used for classification. Such taxonomies are familiar in the language of everyday life, where they tend to be somewhat irregular and variable according to who is using them. Many of us might organise our shopping around taxonomies such as the one for *fruit* shown in Figure 1, perhaps according to how things are arranged in our local shop or market.

The taxonomies of living things on which biological science was founded in the eighteenth century are systematic variants of the same principle: the five kinds (classes) of *vertebrates* are *fishes, amphibia, rep-tiles, birds* and *mammals*; the eight kinds (orders) of *mammals* are *pachyderms, carnivores, cetaceans* ... Here each rank in the taxonomy is

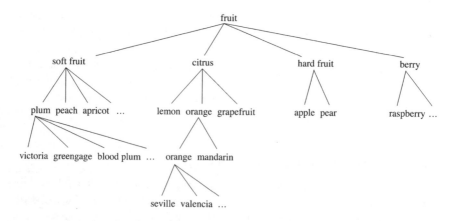

Figure 1 A partial taxonomy for *fruit*

given a special name: *kingdom, phylum, class, order, family, genus, species, variety.*

A thesaurus takes all the lexical items that it contains and arranges them in a single comprehensive taxonomy. Roget's original *Thesaurus,* compiled over four decades from 1810 to 1850, was in fact conceived on the analogy of these scientific taxonomies; in his Introduction, Roget acknowledged his debt to Bishop John Wilkins, whose *Essay towards a Real Character and an Universal Language,* published in 1665, had presented an artificial language for organising the whole of knowledge into an overarching taxonomic framework. Roget's taxonomy started with six primary classes: I, Abstract relations; II, Space; III, Matter; IV, Intellect; V, Volition; VI, Affections. Here is the path leading to one of the entries for the word *cut.* Starting from *Matter,* the path leads to *Organic* Matter, then to *Vitality* and *Special* Vitality (as opposed to Vitality in general); from there to *Agriculture,* then via the verb *cultivate* to the small sub-paragraph consisting of just the three words *reap, mow, cut,* which has no separate heading of its own. Thus there are eight ranks in the taxonomy, the last or **terminal** one being that of the lexical item itself. This path can be traced in the schematic representation shown in Figure 2.

Figure 2 is not how *cut* appears in the thesaurus of course; but we can reconstruct the path from the way the thesaurus is organised into chapters, sections and paragraphs. This particular example relates, obviously, only to one particular meaning of the word *cut,* namely cutting in the context of gardening and farming. But there is no limit on how many times the same word can occur; *cut* will be found in twenty-six different locations, each corresponding to a different context of use. There is an alphabetical index at the end of the book to show where each word can be found.

Thus a thesaurus presents information about words in a very different way from a dictionary. But although it does not give definitions, it provides other evidence for finding out the meaning of an unknown word. Suppose for example that you do not know the meaning of the word *cicuration.* You find that it occurs in a proportional set, as follows:

> animal : vegetable
> :: zoology : botany
> :: cicuration : agriculture

The proportion shows that *cicuration* means 'animal husbandry'.

We cannot always construct such proportionalities. But the fact that a word is entered as one among a small set of related words also tells us a lot about what it means. Such a set of words may be closely

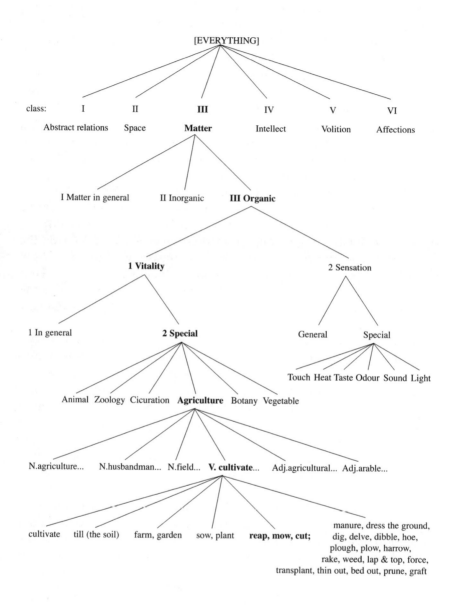

Figure 2 Schematic representation of a thesaurus entry. (Based on Roget's *Thesaurus of English Words and Phrases*, 1936)

synonymous, like *reap, mow, cut* – although not necessarily so; rather, they are **co-hyponyms**, or else **co-meronyms**, of some superordinate term. Thus *reap, mow, cut* (*cut* in this special sense) are co-hyponyms of *cut* in its more general sense; and the items in the next sub-paragraph (*manure, dress the ground ... prune, graft*) all represent stages in the cultivation process – that is, they are co-meronyms of *cultivate*. When we use a thesaurus to search for synonyms, as an aid to writing for example, what we are really looking for are words that share a common privilege of occurrence; they do not ordinarily 'mean the same thing', but they share the same address, as it were, within our overall semantic space.

Another way of thinking about this shared privilege of occurrence that unites the words in one paragraph of the thesaurus is in terms of **collocation**. Collocation is the tendency of words to keep company with each other: like *fork* goes with *knife*, *lend* goes with *money*, *theatre* goes with *play*. Of course, if words do regularly collocate in this way, we shall expect to find some semantic relationship among them; but this may be quite complex and indirect. Collocation is a purely lexical relationship; that is, it is an association between one word and another, irrespective of what they mean. It can be defined quantitatively as the degree to which the probability of a word *y* occurring is increased by the presence of another word *x*. If you meet *injure*, you may expect to find *pain* somewhere around: given the presence of the word *injure*, the probability of the word *pain* occurring becomes higher than that determined by its overall frequency in the English language as a whole. The words that are grouped into the same paragraph in a thesaurus are typically words that have a strong collocational bond: either with each other or, more powerfully, each of them with some third party, some common associate that forms a network with them all.

1.4 History of lexicology: India, China, the Islamic world, Europe

When did lexicology begin? Like all systematic study of the **formal** patterns of language, lexicology depends on language being written down. Many oral cultures have developed highly elaborated theories of speech function and rhetoric; but it is only after writing evolves that attention comes to be focused on grammar and vocabulary. This typically began as a way of keeping alive ancient texts whose meanings were beginning to be lost as the language continued to change. In India as early as the third to second century BC, glossaries were drawn up to explain the difficult words in the Vedas, which by that time were already a thousand years old. These glossaries gradually evolved into what we would recognise today as dictionaries. In the seventh century

AD, the scholar Amera Sinha prepared a Sanskrit dictionary, the *Amera Kosha*. More than ten centuries later this was still in use – it was translated into English by Colebrooke, and Colebrooke's translation, published in Serampur in 1808, is acknowledged by Roget as one source of ideas for his *Thesaurus*. Hamacandra's great dictionaries of Sanskrit and of Prakrit, the *Abhidhana Kintamani* and the *Desinamamala*, date from the twelfth century. By this time Indian scholarship in grammar and phonology had reached a high degree of sophistication, and dictionary-making took its place as part of the systematic description of language.

In China the earliest extant lexicological work is in fact a thesaurus, the *Er Ya* 'Treasury of Fine Words'. Compiled in this form in the third century BC, it is a list of about 3,500 words found in ancient texts, arranged under nineteen headings: the first three sections contain words of a general nature – nouns, verbs and figurative expressions; the remaining sixteen being topical groupings, headed Kin, Buildings, Implements, Music, Sky (i.e. calendar and climate), Land, Hills, Mountains, Water (rivers and lakes), Plants, Trees, Insects and Reptiles, Fishes, Birds, Wild Animals and Domestic Animals. Each word is glossed, by a synonym or superordinate term, or else briefly defined. The Chinese paid little attention to grammar: since Chinese words are invariant, the question of why words change in form, which was what led the Indians, Greeks and Arabs to study grammar, simply did not arise. But their study of vocabulary developed in three directions: (1) recording dialect words, as in the *Fang Yan*, by Yang Xiong, in the first century BC; (2) investigating the origin of written characters, in *Shuo Wen Jie Zi*, by Xu Shen, in the first century AD; and (3) describing the sounds of words, classifying them according to rhyme, notably in the *Qie Yun* (AD 600) and *Tang Yun* (AD 750). By the time of the Ming and Qing dynasties, large-scale dictionaries and encyclopaedias were being compiled: notably the *Yongle Encyclopaedia* (1403–9) in 10,000 volumes, few of which however survive; and the *Kangxi Dictionary* (1716), containing some 50,000 characters together with their pronunciation and definition.

Both the Arabic and Hebrew traditions are rich in grammatical scholarship, and the earliest Arab grammarian, al-Khalil ibn Ahmed (died AD 791), is known to have begun work on an Arabic dictionary, using a phonological principle for ordering the words. But the leading lexicographers in the Islamic world were the Persians. The first dictionary of Farsi-dari, the Persian literary language, written by Abu-Hafs Soghdi in the ninth to tenth centuries, is now lost; but the eleventh-century *Lughat-e Fars* (Farsi dictionary), by Asadi Tusi, is extant. Persian scholars also produced bilingual dictionaries, Persian–Arabic (*Muqad-dimat al-adab* 'Literary Expositor', by an eleventh-century scholar from Khwarezm, Abul-Qasim Mohammad al-Zamakhshari) and, from the fifteenth century onwards, Persian–Turkish.

It is known that the Egyptians produced thesaurus-like topically arranged wordlists from as early as 1750 BC, although none has survived. In Greece, as in India, the earliest studies of words were glossaries on the ancient texts – Homeric texts, in the case of Greece. Apollonius, an Alexandrian grammarian of the first century BC, compiled a Homeric lexicon, but both this and the later glossaries by Hesychius are lost. Perhaps the greatest work of the Byzantine period was the *Suda*, a tenth-century etymological and explanatory dictionary of around 30,000 entries from literary works in Ancient, Hellenistic and Byzantine Greek and in Latin.

The development of dictionaries in the modern European context was associated with the spread of education and the promotion of emerging national literary languages. From about 1450 onwards bilingual dictionaries were being produced for use in schools, at first for learning Latin (Latin–German, Latin–English, etc.), but soon afterwards also for the modern languages of Europe. Many of the nation states of southern and eastern Europe then set up national academies, and these were responsible for establishing norms for the definition and usage of words: for example the Italian *Vocabulario degli Academici della Crusca*, 1612; the *Dictionnaire de l'Académie française*, 1694 (the lexicographer Furetière was expelled from the Academy because he published his own dictionary, the *Universal Dictionary Containing All French Words*, in 1690 before the official one had appeared); the dictionary of the Spanish Academy in 1726–39, and that of the Russian Academy in 1789–94. By the nineteenth century the great publishing houses were bringing out extended series of lexicological works: notably in France (Littré, *Dictionnaire de la Langue française*, in four volumes plus supplement, in 1863–78; and Larousse, *Grand Dictionnaire Universel du XIXe siècle*, an encyclopaedic dictionary in 15 volumes, 1865–76) and in Germany (Meyer's *Great Encyclopaedic Lexicon* in 46 plus 6 supplementary volumes, 1840–55). Each of these major works was followed by a large number of 'spinoff' publications of various kinds.

1.5 Evolution of the dictionary and the thesaurus in England

As an illustration of how twentieth-century dictionaries have evolved, we will take the example of English. But it is important to bear in mind that English dictionaries did not evolve in isolation from other traditions; they were influenced from elsewhere in Europe and even from further afield. Lexicography in England began in the form of glossaries on 'difficult' words in manuscripts of Latin texts: at first these were given in Latin, using simpler words for the purpose, but by the seventh century they were appearing in English (e.g. in the Épinal manuscript preserved at a monastery in France). Next, such glosses were taken out and arranged in a list (a 'glossary'); and then various lists, especially of technical terms, for example in agriculture or in medicine, were collected together into a 'vocabulary'. In the eighth and ninth centuries compilers started arranging the words in alphabetical order. By the thirteenth century the term 'dictionary' had come into use; the collections of words were becoming considerably larger, and English–Latin lists began to be compiled. The *Promptorium Parvulorum sive Clericorum* 'Repository for Children and Clerics', by Geoffrey 'the Grammarian' of Norfolk, dated about 1440, contained some 12,000 words. It was during this century that printing was introduced into Europe; the *Promptorium* was printed in 1499, and from then on the scope and variety of published dictionaries grew rapidly. Sir Thomas Elyot's *Latin–English Dictionary* appeared in 1538; R. Howlet's *Abecedarium Anglico–Latinum* in 1552. Bilingual dictionaries of modern languages began with Palsgrave's English–French dictionary of 1530, and this was soon followed by dictionaries of English–Spanish and English–Italian. The arrangement of words by their strict alphabetical order had now become established practice; and lexicographers began introducing citations from literary works to illustrate usage in the foreign language.

The first monolingual English dictionary was published by Robert Cawdrey in 1604; this was *A Table Alphabeticall of Hard Usuall English Wordes*, which gave the spelling and meaning of about 2,500 terms. In 1616 John Bullokar's *An English Expositor* appeared, and in 1623 Henry Cockeram's *The English Dictionarie*. Cockeram's dictionary contained two parts: one of hard words, one of ordinary words, with words of each group being used to explain those of the other. The first dictionary which set out to include all words, and to define their meanings, was John Kersey's *A New English Dictionary* of 1702; shortly after this, in 1720, Nathan Bailey published his *Universal Etymological English Dictionary*, in which he added a new dimension to lexicography by including the history ('etymology') of each word. This work, along with other publications by Nathan Bailey, was the immediate precursor to Samuel Johnson's *Dictionary of the English Language*, which appeared in 1755. Dr Johnson's dictionary was a landmark not only in setting high professional standards in lexicography but also in establishing the role of the lexicographer as an authority on the 'correct' spelling, pronunciation and definition of words.

This normative function of a dictionary was a distinctive feature of two major American lexicographers of the first half of the nineteenth century, Noah Webster and Joseph Worcester. Webster in particular, in *An American Dictionary of the English Language* published in 1828, sought to codify American English as a distinct tongue, marked out by its own orthographic conventions; the modifications of spelling which he introduced in his dictionary, while much less radical than his original proposals, became accepted as the American standard.

In nineteenth-century lexicology in England, four achievements stand out.

(1) One was Roget's *Thesaurus*, referred to earlier (1.3). Peter Mark Roget was a doctor who became a leading member of the Royal Society; his work of arranging the words and idiomatic phrases of the English language into one comprehensive semantic taxonomy occupied him for some forty years. As already noted, he was influenced both by his predecessors in the Royal Society of 150 years earlier, in their construction of an artificial language for scientific taxonomy, and by the Indian tradition of lexicology that he knew from Colebrooke's translation of Amera Sinha's seventh-century Sanskrit dictionary.

(2) Another was the *New English Dictionary on Historical Principles*, at first edited by James Murray and published in 12 volumes over the period 1884 to 1928 (by the Oxford University Press; hence its more familiar designation as 'Oxford English Dictionary' or *OED*). This dictionary incorporated both extensive textual citations, a practice established in Charles Richardson's (1837) *New Dictionary of the English Language*, and detailed historical information about each word, following the principle established by Jacob and Wilhelm Grimm in their large-scale historical dictionary of German (begun in 1852, although not finally compiled and published until 1960). The *OED* contains over 400,000 entries and a little under two million citations. Four supplementary volumes appeared between 1933 and 1986, and a revised edition of the entire dictionary was published in 1989 as *The Oxford English Dictionary*, second edition, in 20 volumes. The *Shorter*, *Concise* and *Pocket* Oxford dictionaries are all 'spinoffs' from this venture, and have been through numerous editions since the 1930s (one of which has been used for illustration in 1.2 above).

(3) The third achievement was Joseph Wright's *English Dialect Dictionary*, published in 6 volumes in 1898–1905. This followed the tradition of dialect glossaries that had arisen earlier in various European countries, notably in Germany. Wright assigned each word to the

localities where it was used, county by county; and detailed dialect surveys in the mid-twentieth century confirmed the comprehensiveness and accuracy of his lexicographical work.

(4) Finally, the nineteenth-century dictionaries of the classical languages, Lewis and Short's *Latin–English Dictionary* and Liddell and Scott's *Greek–English Lexicon*, set a new standard that all subsequent bilingual dictionaries, classical or modern, have had to acknowledge.

In English-speaking countries in the twentieth century, dictionaries became a significant proportion of all publishing activity. In general the practices developed in nineteenth-century lexicography continued, but there was further expansion in three main areas: technical dictionaries, both monolingual and bilingual; learners' dictionaries, of English as a foreign or second language; and dictionaries of varieties of English other than those of England and America – principally Scots, Australian, Canadian, New Zealand and South African. In the latter part of the twentieth-century, dictionaries of the so-called 'new varieties of English' also began to appear, for example a *Dictionary of Jamaican English*, first published in 1967 and revised in 1980, and a *Dictionary of Caribbean English Usage*, 1996.

1.6 Recent developments in lexicology

Towards the end of the twentieth century significant changes were taking place in the theory and practice of lexicology, largely brought about by the new technology available for data-processing and text-based research. The two critical resources here are the computer and the corpus. Existing lexicographical techniques have of course been computerised. For example, lexicographers can now check their list of dictionary entries against other lists of words – say a list of words occurring in recent editions of a newspaper – and can run such a check electronically in a fraction of the time that it would take to do this manually. But the computer does much more than speed the processes up – it shifts the boundaries of what is possible. For example, the total content of the 1989 edition of the *OED* is now available on compact disc (CD) to anyone whose computer has a CD drive. It thus becomes a database such that lexical information of all kinds can be retrieved from its half-million entries, with the entire search under any chosen heading usually taking less than one minute.

At the same time, lexical research can now be based on very large corpora of written and spoken language. Corpus work in English originated in the late 1950s, with the Survey of English Usage at the University of London and the Brown University Corpus in Providence,

Rhode Island. The two universities each compiled a corpus of one million words of written text, in selected passages each five thousand words long. By the 1990s lexicographers could draw on massive resources such as the British National Corpus, the International Corpus of English, and the 'Bank of English' at the University of Birmingham in England; and indefinitely large quantities of text, from newspapers to transcripts of enquiries and parliamentary proceedings, began to be accessible in machine-readable form (for further details, see Chapter 3, especially 3.5).

The effect of these resources on dictionary-making is already apparent: the dictionary can now be founded on authentic usage in writing and speech. This means that, in an innovative corpus-based venture such as the Collins COBUILD series of English dictionaries, not only is every citation taken from real-life discourse, but the way the different meanings of a word are described and classified can be worked out afresh from the beginning (instead of relying on previous dictionary practice) by inspecting how the word is actually used – what other words it collocates with, what semantic domains it is associated with, and so on. Here is an example of an entry from the first edition of the *Collins COBUILD English Language Dictionary*. The format of the entry has been changed slightly for presentation here, but the wording and sequence of information are exactly as in the 1987 edition of the dictionary. (A later edition of the dictionary has different wording.)

sturdy /stɜːdi[1] /, **sturdier, sturdiest**.
Someone who is **sturdy**
1.1 looks strong and is unlikely to be easily tired or injured.
e.g. *He is short and sturdy...*
... Barbara Burke, a sturdy blonde.
sturdily
e.g. *She was sturdily built.*
1.2 is very loyal to their friends, beliefs, and opinions, and is determined to keep to them, although it would sometimes be easier not to do so.
e.g. *With the help of sturdy friends like Robert Benchley he set about rebuilding his life.*
sturdily
e.g. *He replied sturdily that he had only followed her orders.*
2 Something that is **sturdy** looks strong and is unlikely to be easily damaged or knocked over.
e.g. *... sturdy oak tables...*
... a sturdy branch.

In the *Collins COBUILD English Language Dictionary*, an 'extra column', beside the entry, adds the information that *sturdy* is a qualitative adjective, in all its senses; and that, in sense 1.2, it is usually used attributively, that is before the noun, as in *sturdy friends*. (This pattern is clearer in an example such as *they are sturdy supporters of the club*, where *sturdy* goes with the verb *support* (= *they support the club sturdily*). If the adjective is used predicatively, that is, after the noun, the sense will typically shift to 1.1: *the club's supporters are sturdy* = 'strong robust people'.)

The extra column also gives, in sense 1.1, the synonym *robust*; in sense 1.2, the synonym *steadfast* and superordinate *dependable*; and in sense 2, the synonym *tough*. This entry may be contrasted with the more traditional entry in another dictionary of approximately the same size, the 1979 *Collins Dictionary of the English Language*. (Again, the presentation here has been slightly changed, with more generous spacing than is normally possible in a large dictionary; and there are later Collins dictionaries than this edition.)

> **sturdy** ('st3:dɪ) *adj.* **-di-er, -di-est**.
> **1.** healthy, strong, and vigorous.
> **2.** strongly built; stalwart.
> [C13 (in the sense: rash, harsh): from Old French *estordi* dazed, from *estordir* to stun, perhaps ultimately related to Latin *turdus* a thrush (taken as representing drunkenness)]
> – 'stur-di-ly *adv.*
> – 'stur-di-ness *n.*

We said at the beginning that lexicology – the study of words – is one part of the study of the forms of a language, its **lexicogrammar**. Lexicology developed as a distinct sub-discipline because vocabulary and grammar were described by different techniques. Vocabulary, as we have seen, was described by listing words, either topically (as a thesaurus) or indexically (as a dictionary), and adding glosses and definitions. Grammar was described by tabulating the various forms a word could take (as **paradigms**, e.g. the cases of a noun or the tenses of a verb) and then stating how these forms were arranged in sentences (as **constructions**, or **structures** in modern terminology). But vocabulary and grammar are not two separate components of a language. Let us borrow the everyday term **wording**, which includes both vocabulary and grammar in a single unified concept.

When we speak or write, we produce wordings; and we do this, as we suggested in 1.1 above, by making an ongoing series of choices. Usually, of course, we 'choose' quite unconsciously, although we can also bring conscious planning into our discourse. We also noted that some of these choices are between two or three alternatives of a very general kind, like positive versus negative (e.g. *it is / it isn't; do it / don't do it*); likewise singular versus plural number, first / second / third person, past / present / future tense, and so on. These 'closed systems' are what we call grammar. Of course, such choices have to be expressed in the wording, and sometimes we have specifically grammatical words to express them ('function words') like *the* and *of* and *if*. But often these general choices are expressed in a number of different ways, some of them quite subtle and indirect; so we tend to label them as **categories** rather than by naming the words or parts of words that express them. For example, we refer to the category 'definite' rather than to the word *the*, because (1) *the* is not in fact always definite, and (2) there are other ways of expressing definiteness besides the word *the*.

Other choices that we make when we use language are choices among more specific items, the 'content words' that we referred to at the beginning. These are not organised in closed systems; they form open sets, and they contrast with each other along different lines. For example, the word *cow* is in contrast (1) with *horse, sheep* and other domestic animals; (2) with *bull;* (3) with *calf* and some more specific terms like *heifer;* (4) with *beef,* and so on. So we refer to it by itself; we talk about 'the word *cow*', and define it in a dictionary or locate it taxonomically in a thesaurus.

We could describe *cow* using the techniques devised for dealing with grammar. We could identify various systems, e.g. 'bovine / equine / ovine', 'female / male', 'mature / immature', 'living organism / carcass', and treat *cow* as the conjunct realisation of 'bovine + female + mature + living'. In this way we would be building the dictionary out of the grammar, so to speak. This may be useful in certain contexts, especially when different languages have to be interfaced as in machine translation – different languages lump different features together, so their words don't exactly correspond. Equally, we could build the grammar out of the dictionary, treating grammatical categories as generalisations about the words that express them: instead of the category of 'definite' we could describe the various meanings and uses of the word *the*. Again there are contexts in which this might be helpful: teaching foreign learners who want only to read English, not to speak or write it, for example.

In general, however, each technique gets less efficient as you approach the other pole: you have to do more and more work and you achieve less and less by doing it (as we put it in our initial summary, there are diminishing returns in both cases). What is important is to gain an overall perspective on lexicogrammar as a unified field – a continuum between two poles requiring different but complementary strategies for researching and describing the facts. This perspective is essential when we come to deal with the regions of the language that lie around the middle of the continuum, like conjunctions, preposi- tions and many classes of adverb (temporal, modal, etc.) in English. But it is important also in a more general sense. With our modern resources for investigating language by computer, namely 'natural language processing' (text generation and parsing) and corpus studies, we can construct lexicogrammatical databases which combine the reliability of a large-scale body of authentic text data with the theore- tical strengths of both the lexicologist and the grammarian. The user can then explore from a variety of different angles.

One topic that has always been of interest to lexicologists is the recording of neologisms – 'new' words, not known to have occurred before. Earlier dictionary makers depended on written records, which are increasingly patchy as one goes back in time; the first occurrences cited for each word in the *OED* obviously cannot represent the full range of contemporary usage. The huge quantity of text that flows through today's computerised corpora (while still comprising only a fraction of what is being written, and a still smaller fraction of what is being spoken) makes it possible to monitor words occurring for the first time. But the concept of a 'neologism' is itself somewhat mis- leading, since it suggests that there is something special about a 'new word'. In fact a new word is no more remarkable than a new phrase or a new clause; new words are less common, for obvious reasons, but every language has resources for expanding its lexical stock, no matter how this is organised within the lexicogrammar as a whole. It is a mistake to think of discourse as 'old words in new sentences'. The chance of being 'new' clearly goes up with the size of the unit; but many sentences are repeated time and again, while on the other hand quite a number of the words we meet with every day were used for the first time within the past three generations.

1.7 Sources and resources

The best source of information about lexicology is the dictionary or thesaurus itself. It is important to become familiar with these works, which are now fairly common within the household. (In English- speaking countries at least, most large dictionaries and thesauruses are bought either for family members as Christmas gifts or for the children of the household to help them with their schoolwork.) You can **consult** dictionaries, to find out the meaning and usage of a particular word or phrase; and you can **read** them, dipping in at random or wherever your fancy takes you. They can be unexpectedly entertaining. Samuel Johnson's 1755 dictionary is famous for several entries that betray a certain personal perspective, such as

> **excise**, a hateful tax levied upon commodities, and adjudged not by the common judges of property, but wretches hired by those to whom excise is paid.

Or you might come across a definition such as the following, from *Chambers Twentieth Century Dictionary*:

> **ranke**, *rangk*, *n.* (Shak., *As You Like It*, III.ii.) app. a jog-trot (perh. a misprint for **rack**(6)): otherwise explained as a repetition of the same rhyme like a file of so many butterwomen.

Nowadays dictionaries and other works of this kind are compiled for a wide range of different purposes. Naturally therefore they vary, both in the information they contain and in the way the information is presented. Consider for example an English–Chinese dictionary, one with English words listed and translated into Chinese. This might be compiled for Chinese students of English; or for English speakers studying Chinese; it might be for use in natural-language processing by computer (e.g. in multilingual text generation), or in the professional work of technical translators. It will be different in all these different cases. It soon becomes apparent that there is no single model that we can set up as the ideal form for a dictionary to take; nor are dictionaries totally distinct from other types of publication such as technical glossaries or travellers' phrasebooks.

This kind of indeterminacy is nothing new in the field. There is no clear line between a dictionary of a regional variety of a language (a dialect dictionary) and a dictionary of a functional variety of a language (a technical dictionary), or of a part of a language, such as a dictionary of slang, or of idioms, or of compounds. Nor is there any clear line between explaining the meaning of a word (dictionary definition) and explaining a literary allusion, or a historical or mythical event. The little dictionaries of hard words for children that used to be produced in various countries of Europe, like the Russian *azbukovniki* ('little alphabets'), included a great deal of useful information besides. In this respect they belong in the same tradition as *Brewer's Dictionary of Phrase and Fable* (first published in 1870, subtitled 'giving the Derivation, Source, or Origin of Common Phrases, Allusions, and Words that have a Tale to Tell') – and are only one or two removes from the great encyclopaedias of China and the encyclopaedic dictionaries of

European countries referred to in 1.4 above. The line between a dictionary and an encyclopaedia has always been uncertain, and has been drawn differently at different times and places throughout the history of scholarship. Equally indeterminate is the line between a dictionary and a scholarly monograph: a dictionary may be conceived of purely as a work of linguistic research, like an etymological dictionary (typified by August Fick's *Comparative Dictionary of the Indo-European Languages* first published in 1868), or dictionaries of the elements that are found in personal or place names.

Finally we might mention the comic dictionaries, like Douglas Adams' *The Meaning of Liff*, which consists of imaginary – and highly imaginative – definitions of place names treated as if they were English words. These in turn are part of the general tradition of lexical humour, which is found in some form or other in every language (the 'play on words' like punning by speakers of English). Related to this are various forms of word games, both traditional and codified: those in English include both competitive card or board games like Lexicon and Scrabble, and individual games such as plain and cryptic crosswords. In quite a few languages people play informal games in which they invert or swap syllables: rather as if in English we were to make *village* into *ageville* or *elbow* into *bowel*. And Indonesians sometimes create an 'explanation' for a word by pretending that its syllables are shortenings of other words; if we tried something comparable in English we might say that an 'expert' is someone who is 'EXpensive' and 'PERTurbing'. These games often fit a particular language – different patterns of phonological word structure lend themselves to different kinds of playful manipulation – but all of them provide insights into the way words work; and the special word games played with children, like 'I'm thinking of a word that rhymes with –', have an important developmental function in giving children a sense of what a word is, and how words arc classified and defined.

Standard works written in English on lexicology include Chapman (1948), Hartmann (1983), Hartmann (1986), Householder and Saporta (1962), Landau (1989), McDavid *et al.* (1973) and Zgusta (1971). A more recent general introduction to the field is Jackson and Ze Amvela (1999). Green (1996) is a comprehensive history of lexicography, and Cowie (1990) is also a useful overview, from which much of the information in 1.5 above is drawn.

2   Words and meaning

Colin Yallop

2.1 Words in language

People sometimes play games with words. People may also recite or memorise lists of words, for example when trying to learn the words of another language or to remember technical terms. And they may occasionally leaf through a dictionary looking at words more or less randomly. These are legitimate activities, enjoyable or useful as they may be. But they are not typical uses of words. Typically, human beings use words for their meaning, in context, as part of communicative discourse.

As Halliday has made clear (see especially 1.6 above), vocabulary can be seen as part of lexicogrammar, a lexicogrammar that represents the choices which users of a language make, a lexicogrammar that represents our ability to *mean*. For, ultimately, language is about meaning. The main function of language – and hence of words used in language – is to mean.

This part of the book is particularly concerned with exploring the semantics of words. Section 2.2 offers some comments on meanings as presented in dictionaries. This is followed by brief discussion of potentially misleading notions about 'original meaning' (2.3) and 'correct meaning' (2.4). In 2.5 we try to explain what we mean by a social perspective on language and meaning, followed by some background on the theorising of Saussure and Firth (2.6) and Chomsky and cognitive linguists (2.7). We then look at the implications of our theorising for language and reality (section 2.8) and, to open up a multilingual perspective, we talk about the diversity of languages in the world (section 2.9) and about the process of translating from one language to another (2.10).

2.2 Words and meaning

A dictionary seems the obvious place to find a record of the meanings of words. In many parts of the English-speaking world, dictionaries have achieved such prestige that people can mention 'the dictionary' as one of their institutional texts, rather in the same way that they might refer to Shakespeare or the Bible. Such status means that a printed dictionary may easily be seen as the model of word-meanings. We may then, uncritically, assume that a dictionary in book form is the appropriate model of words as a component of language or of word-meanings stored as an inventory in the human brain or mind.

In fact a dictionary is a highly abstract construct. To do the job of presenting words more or less individually, in an accessible list, the dictionary takes words away from their common use in their customary settings. While this is in many respects a useful job, the listing of words as a set of isolated items can be highly misleading if used as a basis of theorising about what words and their meanings are.

There is of course no such thing as 'the dictionary'. For a language such as English there are many dictionaries, published in various editions in various countries to suit various markets. The definitions or explanations of meaning in a dictionary have been drawn up by particular lexicographers and editors and are consequently subject to a number of limitations. Even with the benefit of access to corpora, to large quantities of text in electronic form, lexicographers cannot know the full usage of most words across a large community, and may tend to bring individual or even idiosyncratic perspectives to their work.

In the past, dictionaries were quite often obviously stamped by the perspective of an individual. We have already mentioned Samuel Johnson's definition of *excise* as 'a hateful tax' (1.7 above), and, as another example, here is Johnson's definition of *patron*:

patron, one who countenances, supports or protects. Commonly a wretch who supports with insolence and is paid with flattery.

Modern lexicographers generally aim to avoid this kind of tendentiousness. Certainly today's dictionaries tend to be promoted as useful or reliable rather than as personal or provocative. Nevertheless, despite the obvious drawbacks of a dictionary that represents an individual editor's view of the world, it is regrettable that dictionary users are not reminded more often of the extent to which dictionary definitions are distilled from discourse, and often from shifting, contentious discourse. In any event, lexicographers can never claim to give a complete and accurate record of meaning. A team of expert lexicographers may by their very age and experience tend to overlook recent changes in meaning; or they may tend to write definitions which are elegant rather than accurate or simple; or they may follow conventions of definition which are just that – lexicographical conventions – rather than semantic principles.

Dictionaries often tend to favour certain kinds of technical identification, definitions that describe *dog* as *Canis familiaris,* or *vinegar* as 'dilute and impure acetic acid'. While this kind of information may sometimes be precisely what the dictionary-user is looking for, it is debatable whether it constitutes a realistic account of meaning. Many of us communicate easily and happily about many topics, including domestic animals, food, cooking, and so on, without knowing the zoological classification of animals or the chemical composition of things we keep in the kitchen. Perhaps people *ought* to know information like the technical names of animals or the chemical composition of things they buy and consume, whether as general knowledge or for their health or safety. But it would be a bold move, and a semantic distortion, to claim that people who don't know such information don't know the *meaning* of the words they use.

In general, it is unwise to assume that meaning is captured in dictionary entries, in the definitions or explanations given against the words. Dictionary definitions can and should be informative and helpful, and, when well written, they provide a paraphrase or explanation of meaning. But the meaning is not necessarily fully contained or exhaustively captured within such a definition. This is not to say that meanings are vague or ethereal. Within the conventions of a particular language, meanings contrast with each other in established and often precise ways. Speakers of the same language can convey meanings to each other with considerable precision. Words do not mean whatever we want them to mean, but are governed by social convention. Nonetheless, we cannot assume, without qualification, that the wording of a dictionary definition is an ideal representation of what a word means.

Extending this point, we normally use and respond to meanings in context. As users of language we know that someone's mention of a recent television programme about big cats in Africa implies a different meaning of *cat* from a reference to the number of stray cats in the city of New York. And if someone talks about 'letting the cat out of the bag' or 'setting the cat among the pigeons', we know that the meaning has to be taken from the whole expression, not from a word-by-word reading of *Felis catus* jumping out of a bag or chasing *Columbidae.* Any good dictionary recognises this by such strategies as listing different senses of a word, giving examples of usage, and treating certain combinations of words (such as idioms) as lexical units. But it is important to recognise that this contextualisation of meaning is in the very nature of language and not some unfortunate deviation from an ideal situation in which every word of the language always makes exactly the same semantic contribution to any utterance or discourse.

For reasons such as these, we should be cautious about the view that words have a basic or core meaning, surrounded by peripheral or subsidiary meaning(s). For example, the very ordering of different definitions or senses in a dictionary may imply that the first sense is the most central or important. In fact there are several reasons for the sequence in which different senses are presented. Some dictionaries, especially modern ones intended for learners of the language, may use a corpus to establish which are the most frequent uses of a word in a large quantity of text, and may list senses of a word in order of frequency. Some lexicographers follow a historical order, giving the oldest recorded senses first (even if these are now obsolete and largely unknown). Or a compiler may order the senses in a way that makes the defining easier and more concise (which is probably of help to the reader, even though it intends no claim about the centrality of the first sense listed).

For instance, the word *season* is commonly used in phrases like *the football season, the rainy season, the tourist season, the silly season, a season ticket, in season, out of season.* These uses taken together probably outnumber what many people may think of as the fundamental meaning of *season* as 'one of the four seasons, spring, summer, autumn and winter'. But the lexicographer may judge it sensible to begin the entry with the 'four seasons of the year' sense, not only because this is perhaps what most readers expect, but also because the subsequent definitions of *season* as 'a period of the year marked by certain conditions' or 'a period of the year when a particular activity takes place', and so on, may seem easier to grasp if preceded by the supposedly basic sense.

To take another example, consider the first four senses listed for the noun *rose* in the *Macquarie Concise Dictionary* (1998). Some of the definitions have been abbreviated for this example:

1. any of the wild or cultivated, usually prickly-stemmed, showy-flowered shrubs constituting the genus *Rosa* ...

2. any of various related or similar plants.

3. the flower of any such shrubs ...

4. an ornament shaped like or suggesting a rose ...

The sequence of these senses is not random and the entry has been written or edited as a whole. The second sense, using the words 'related' and 'similar', assumes the reader has read the first definition;

the third ('any such shrubs') presupposes the first and second; and so on.

The *Macquarie Concise* entry for *rose* also demonstrates that dictionaries are obliged to order items at more than one level. There are of course two quite distinct *roses*, the one we have just been talking about, and the one which is the past tense of *rise*. The *Macquarie* numbers these distinct meanings, as many dictionaries do, with a superscript [1] and [2], giving all the senses of the flower or bush (and the rose-like objects) under the first *rose*, and then simply indicating that the second *rose* is the past tense of *rise*. Probably most dictionary users find this the sensible order. Perhaps nouns seem more important, especially ones which have several different senses. Perhaps the second *rose* seems as though it is here accidentally – it really belongs under *rise*. Evidence from corpora suggests that the verb form *rose* (as in 'the sea level rose by 120 metres' or 'exports rose 2 per cent' or 'the evil genie rose from the jar') is used far more frequently than the noun; but this greater frequency does not seem to give priority to the verb in the minds of dictionary compilers and users.

It sometimes seems to be mere convention to list certain meanings first. Definitions of the word *have* often begin with the sense of 'possess' or 'own', and many people may indeed think of this as the fundamental or ordinary meaning of the word. In fact, corpus evidence indicates that the uses of *have* as an auxiliary verb (as in 'they have shown little interest') and in combinations like *have to* (as in 'we have to do better next time') are more frequent than uses like 'they have two cars' or 'we have a small house'.

Notions of what is a basic or central meaning of a word may thus be encouraged and perpetuated in a variety of ways, including common beliefs about words (which may or may not match actual usage) as well as lexicographical tradition. Sometimes such notions may be given formal recognition. For example, it is common to distinguish denotation from connotation. If taken as a serious semantic or philosophical claim, the distinction tends to separate what a word refers to from the associations that the word conjures up in the mind. More popularly, and sometimes simplistically, the distinction becomes a way of separating a core meaning from peripheral or variable aspects of meaning. But the distinction is by no means straightforward. It is complicated by the fact that what a word refers to in a particular context (as when talking to you I mention 'your cat') is not what is usually intended by *denotation* (which is more like 'any cat' or 'the class of cats'). The notion of denotation also runs the risk of identifying meaning with a class of objects or some idealised version thereof, as if meaning can be

anchored in a world of concrete objects. This is clearly not very helpful
in the case of many words, such as abstract nouns in general or verbs
like *believe, dream, think, worry* or epithets like *good, kind, mysterious, poor.*
And even where a denotation can be satisfactorily identified, it is not
self-evident that this is an appropriate way of characterising *meaning.*

The term *connotation* tends to slip awkwardly between something like
'peripheral meaning' and 'emotive meaning' and 'personal associations'. The notion of peripheral meaning simply raises the question of
what is central or core meaning and why it should be so. It is clear from
examples already given that the most frequently used sense of a word is
not always the one that strikes most people as the core meaning. And it
is equally clear that the older senses of a word are often neither the
most frequent in current usage, nor the most basic by any other con-
ceivable criterion.

Even 'emotive meaning', which might seem a good candidate for the
margins of meaning, cannot always be considered peripheral. If I say to
you 'Did you hear what happened to poor Sid?', the semantic contribution of *poor* must surely be 'emotive': the word says nothing about
Sid's lack of wealth, but seeks to establish and elicit sympathy towards
Sid. And this is hardly peripheral, since my question to you is most
probably intended to introduce, and engage your interest in, a story of
Sid's misfortune. Similar things can be said about the use of adjectives
like *lucky* and *unfashionable,* which commonly serve to signal the
speaker's attitude, and even about the verb *think* when used in utterances like 'I think the meeting starts at noon' (in which the words 'I
think' serve to make the message less authoritative or dogmatic) or 'I
think these are your keys' (as a polite way of telling someone they are
about to leave their keys behind). Thus what might be termed 'emotive
meaning' or 'attitudinal' meaning may sometimes be an integral part
of discourse.

On the other hand, if 'associations' really are personal or idiosyncratic, then they hardly qualify as meaning at all, since they cannot
contribute to regular meaningful exchanges. Suppose, for example, I
have a fondness for a particular kind of flower, say, carnations, perhaps
because of some valued childhood memory of them or other such
personal experience. This may well have some consequences in my
behaviour, including my discourse: I may often buy carnations, whereas
you never do, I may mention carnations more than you do, and so on.
But does it follow from any of this that you and I have a different
meaning of the word *carnation?* Both of us, if we speak English,
understand what is meant when someone says 'carnations are beautiful
flowers', 'carnations are good value for money' and 'most people like

carnations', whether we agree with the truth of these claims or not. Indeed, to *dis*agree with these statements requires an understanding of what they mean, just as much as agreeing with them does.

Of course to the extent that an association is shared throughout a community, it does contribute to discourse and becomes part of meaning. If a name like *Hitler* or *Stalin* is not only widely known but widely associated with certain kinds of evil behaviour, then it becomes possible for people to say things like 'what a tragedy the country is being run by such a Hitler' or 'the new boss is a real Stalin'. And if people do say things like this, the names are on their way to becoming meaningful words of the language, along a similar path to that followed by words like *boycott* and *sandwich*, which had their origins in names of people associated with particular events or objects. (Note how *boycott* and *sandwich* are now written with initial lower-case letters rather than the capitals which would mark them as names. We might similarly expect to see the forms *hitler* and *stalin* appearing in print, if these names were to become genuine lexical items describing kinds of people.)

There may also be differences of experience and associations within a community which have systematic linguistic consequences. If, for example, some speakers of English love domestic cats while others detest them, this *may* well remain marginal to linguistic systems. But there may be small but regular linguistic differences between the speakers: for example some people may always refer to a cat as 'he' or 'she' while for others a cat is always 'it', and some people may use *cat* as the actor of processes like *tell* and *think* (as in 'my cat tells me when it's time for bed' or 'the cat thinks this is the best room in the flat') whereas others would never use this kind of construction. To that extent we may have (slightly) different linguistic systems, say one in which a cat is quasi-human in contrast to one in which a cat is firmly non-human. In that case, it is legitimate to recognise two somewhat different meanings of *cat* and two minor variants of English lexicogrammar.

For meaning is ultimately shaped and determined by communal usage. A dictionary definition of a word's meaning has authority only in so far as it reflects the way in which those who speak and write the language use that word in genuine communication. In this sense, meaning has a social quality, and while it is sometimes convenient to think of the meaning of a word as a concept, as 'something stored in the human mind', this is legitimate only to the extent that the concept is seen as an abstraction out of observable social behaviour.

An overview of issues to do with word meaning, and references to classic discussions such as Lyons (1977), can be found in the first two sections of Chapter 3 of Jackson and Ze Amvela (1999). We will return to the issues in the following sections of this chapter, both to elaborate our own views of language as social behaviour and of meaning as a social phenomenon, and to contrast our views with others.

2.3 Etymology

In this section we look briefly at the relevance of historical development. Changes in language – specifically changes in meaning – are inevitable, but they are sometimes decried, as if language ought to be fixed at some period in time. In fact, attempts to fix meanings or to tie words to their 'original' meanings deny the social reality of linguistic usage. (In the following section, 2.4, we will look more generally at attempts to prescribe and regulate meaning.)

Warburg tells the story of a lawyer who disputed a witness's use of the word *hysterical* (Warburg 1968, pp. 351–2). The witness had described a young man's condition as 'hysterical'. But, the lawyer pointed out, this word was derived from the Greek *hystera*, meaning 'uterus' or 'womb'. The young man didn't have a uterus, so he couldn't possibly be 'hysterical'.

Would a good lawyer really expect to score a point by this kind of appeal to etymology? Few of us are likely to be persuaded to change our view of the current meaning of the word *hysterical*. It is true that the word is based on the Greek for 'uterus' (and the Greek element appears in that sense in English medical terms such as *hysterectomy* and *hysteroscopy*). But it is also true that words may change their meaning and that the modern meaning of *hysterical* has more to do with uncontrolled emotional behaviour, by men or women, than with the uterus as a bodily organ.

Sometimes an older sense of a word survives in limited contexts, while the most frequent meaning has changed. The word *meat*, for example, now has the common meaning of 'animal flesh used as food', but its Old English antecedent was a word that had the more general meaning of 'food'. Traces of the older more general meaning can be seen in phrases and sayings like *meat and drink* (i.e. 'food and drink') and *one man's meat is another man's poison* (i.e. 'one man's food is another man's poison'). The word *sweetmeat* also demonstrates the older sense. Other than in these restricted contexts, the older meaning of the word has become not only obsolete but irrelevant to modern usage. If you ask today whether a certain supermarket sells meat, or talk about the amount of meat consumed in Western Europe, or have an argument about what kind of meat is in a meat pie, no one who speaks English pauses to wonder whether you really intend *meat* to mean 'food in general' rather than 'animal flesh'.

Indeed, older meanings become lost from view, and phrases and sayings may even be reinterpreted to suit the new meaning. The word *silly* had an older sense of 'happy' (compare German *selig*, 'blessed') but this sense has been ousted by the current meaning of 'foolish' or 'absurd'. A phrase sometimes applied to the county of Suffolk in eastern England, *silly Suffolk*, dates from the days when Suffolk was one of the wealthier counties, and therefore 'happy' or 'fortunate'. But if the saying is quoted at all these days, either it has to be explained, as we have just done here, or it is taken to be an allegation of foolishness or backwardness.

The word *prove* once had the sense of 'try' or 'test' but the most common modern meanings are of course 'show beyond doubt' (as in 'we all suspect him of corruption but no one has been able to prove it') and 'turn out' (as in 'the book proved to have lots of useful information in it'). The saying that *the exception proves the rule* shows the older sense – an exception indeed 'tests' whether a rule is really valid or needs to be reformulated. But the saying is often reinterpreted, with *prove* taken in its modern sense, to mean that an odd exception actually confirms a rule. This is clearly not true – an exception doesn't support a rule, it challenges it – but such is the power of current meaning to efface the old.

There is a long history of interest in etymology, in 'where words have come from', and many large dictionaries of English include etymological information (see McArthur 1992, pp. 384–6, Landau 1989, pp. 98–104, Green 1996, esp. pp. 337–48). Unfortunately, until the development of methodical historical linguistics in the nineteenth century, much etymology was highly speculative and often erroneous. Misguided guesswork about the origins of words can be found in ancient Europe, for example in the work of Varro, a Roman grammarian active in the first century BC (Green 1996, p. 41), and the practice of trying to relate as many words as possible to a relatively small number of allegedly simple or basic words was common until the mid-nineteenth century. Green cites a classic example from the late eighteenth century, in which a whole array of English words were claimed to be derived from or based on the word *bar*: thus a *bar* is a kind of defence or strengthening, and a *barn* is a covered enclosure to protect or defend what is stored in it, a *barge* is a strong boat, the *bark* of a tree is its protection, the *bark* of a dog is its defence, and so on (Green 1996, p. 353). In fact, careful historical research indicates that the word *bar*, as in the bars in a fence or across a window, came into English from Old French, while *barn* is from an Old English compound meaning 'barley store', *barge* is related to an Old French word for a kind of boat, the *bark* of a tree is a word of Scandinavian origin, and the *bark* of a dog goes back to the Old English verb *beorcan*, 'to bark', which is not related to the other *bark*. These various words are of different origins, there is no evidence that they are all based on *bar*, and the idea that they are all clustered around the notion of defence is pure speculation.

Occasionally, an erroneous origin has become enshrined in the language by a process of 'folk etymology', in which the pronunciation or spelling of a word is modified on a false analogy. The word *bridegroom*, for example, has no historical connection with the *groom* employed to tend horses. The Old English antecedent of *bridegroom* is *brydguma*, where *guma* is a word for 'man'. The word ought to have become *bridegoom* in modern English, but as the word *guma* fell out of use, the form *goom* was popularly reinterpreted (with a change in pronunciation and spelling) as *groom*. A similar process of trying to make the odd seem familiar sometimes applies to words adapted from other languages. The *woodchuck*, or 'ground hog', has a name taken from a North American Algonquian word which, in its nearest anglicised pronunciation, might be something like *otchek* or *odjik*. The word has nothing to do with either *wood* or *chuck*, but was adapted to seem as if it did.

There is nothing wrong with being interested in where a word has come from, and many people who use modern dictionaries expect historical or etymological information to be included. For much of the nineteenth and twentieth centuries, most dictionaries gave considerable prominence to historical information. The first complete edition of what is now commonly referred to as the 'Oxford dictionary' was entitled *A New English Dictionary on Historical Principles*, and it set out to record the history of words, not just their current meanings (see 1.5 above; but not all subsequent Oxford dictionaries, including various abridged editions and dictionaries for learners, have had the same historical priority). It hardly needs to be said that modern professional lexicographers try to avoid speculation and guesswork and to give only information based on good research.

It is indeed often interesting to know something of a word's history and its cognates in other languages, and many (though not all) modern dictionaries still include etymological information. English happens to share with most European languages a reasonably well-documented Indo-European heritage. Languages like Greek, Latin and Sanskrit, as well as a 'proto-Germanic' language ancestral to modern English, German and other Germanic languages, can be shown to be historically related within an Indo-European 'family' of languages. The entry for *bear* (in the sense of 'carry') in the *New Shorter Oxford*, as cited earlier in 1.2, illustrates the way in which some dictionaries list cognates: the etymology includes not only forms considered to be ancestral to the modern English, in this case Old English *beran*, but also forms from other Germanic languages which are parallel to Old English rather than ancestral to it, such as Old Norse *bera* and Gothic *bairan*. The *Oxford* also lists forms that are parallel to Germanic, including Sanskrit *bharati*, Greek *pherein* and Latin *ferre*. As the *Oxford* entry implies, linguists hypothesise that there was an Indo-European form from which the Sanskrit, Greek, Latin and Proto-Germanic forms were separately derived.

Sometimes there have been intriguing changes of meaning. The word *town*, for example, can be traced back to an Old English form *tun* (with a long vowel, pronounced something like modern English *oo* in *soon*). We can connect this form with related words in other modern Germanic languages, notably *tuin* in Dutch and *Zaun* in German. There are regular patterns of sound change which (partly) explain how the forms have become different: modern English *out, house, mouse*, all pronounced with the same diphthong as in *town*, can be related to Old English *ut, hus, mus* (all with a long *u*) as well as to Dutch *uit, huis, muis* and German *aus, Haus, Maus*. But in the case of the forms related to *town*, Dutch *tuin* means not 'town' but 'garden' and German *Zaun* means neither 'town' nor 'garden' but 'fence'. There was also a similar word in Celtic languages, namely *dun*, meaning something like 'citadel' or 'fortified town'. This element is evident in some Roman place names incorporating Celtic elements, like *Lugdunum*, modern *Lyons*, and in names such as *Dunedin*, an old Celtic name now generally replaced in Scotland by the anglicised form *Edinburgh*, but still the name of a city in New Zealand. Thus the word must once have referred to fortified settlements. By modern times the English word *town* has generalised in meaning to refer to any substantial urban centre (between a village and a city in size and importance) while the Dutch word *tuin* has come to mean 'enclosed cultivated land', that is 'a garden', rather than an enclosed town, and the German *Zaun* has narrowed to the enclosure itself, or 'fence'.

Such information is not only interesting to many readers, it is often valuable as an accompaniment to historical and cultural research. Moreover, modern European languages not only have a certain shared heritage, they have continued to draw on it in various ways. Latin words can still be found in uses as diverse as the English translation of Freud (the *ego* and the *id*) and the mottoes of army regiments (such as *Ubique* 'everywhere', the motto of the British Royal Artillery). Some Latin phrases are indeed everywhere, even if no longer fully understood. Notable examples are *etc.*, the abbreviated form of *et cetera*, 'and the rest'; *e.g.*, short for *exempli gratia*, 'for (the sake of) example'; and *a.m.* and *p.m.* (*ante meridiem, post meridiem*). Latin has been regularly used in anatomical description (*levator labii superior*, the 'upper lip raiser' muscle, or *corpus callosum*, the 'callous (hard) body' in the brain), and in botany and zoology (*quercus* 'oak' for a genus of trees, or *felis* 'cat' for the genus of animals that includes domestic cats and some closely related species). Latin phrases such as *de facto, in camera, sine die, sub judice* and *ultra vires* are known in legal contexts, and some of them have a wider currency (such as the Australian use, even outside legal contexts, of the phrase 'a de facto' to mean 'a common-law spouse').

Greek and Latin have also provided a rich source of modern coinage. Words like *altimeter, electroencephalogram, hydrophone* and *telespectroscope* are obviously not themselves classical words: they have been built from Latin and Greek elements to deal with relatively recent technological innovation. Indeed, it has become so customary to use such elements as building blocks, that Latin and Greek are often combined in hybrid forms, as in Greek *tele-* with Latin *vision*, or Latin *appendic-* with Greek *-itis*.

But it is by no means just new items of technology, like cardiographs and synthesisers, that attract classical naming. Greek and Latin elements are integral to our standardised systems of calculating and measuring (*centigrade, centimetre, kilogram, millisecond, quadrillion*). Concepts like *social security, multimedia, globalisation* and *privatisation*, though essentially twentieth-century concepts, are conceived in classical forms. A classical heritage similarly underlies terms like *interdisciplinarity* (which I heard used at Macquarie University in discussions about creating links among different academic 'disciplines' or areas of learning) and *interdiscursivity* (which I have seen on a whiteboard in a university lecture theatre but not yet understood). And terms formed with Greek and Latin elements like *intra, non, post, pseudo, ultra* are used as much in administration or business or politics as in science or technology (*intrastate, noncompliance, postdated, pseudo-solution, ultraconservative*).

Nevertheless, as we have already argued, the history of a word is not the determinant of its current meaning, and the greatest persisting drawback of etymological studies is that they may be misused to support assertions about what words 'ought' to mean. No modern dictionary (including Oxford's *New English Dictionary*) seriously misuses historical information in this way. And, for the greater part of English vocabulary, no one seriously proposes that an older meaning of a word is the only correct meaning. But where a shift in meaning is relatively recent, and particularly where a newer sense of a word is evidently competing with an older sense, some people may deplore the change and attempt to resist it. Thus in the seventeenth century, the English word *decimate* was used to mean something like 'take or remove one tenth from', as in 'tithing', that is taxing people one-tenth of their income or property, or in the sense of killing one in ten. (Executing one in ten of a group of soldiers was a punishment sometimes used in the ancient Roman empire.) Nowadays the word is most commonly used to mean 'destroy most of', as if the 'decimation' now means reducing to one-tenth, rather than reducing to nine-tenths. Some people, especially those who have had a classical education and are aware of the ancient Roman punishment, condemn the modern usage as loose and unwarranted.

Whatever our feelings about respecting tradition or preserving history, it has to be said that such attempts to resist changes in general usage are rarely if ever successful. What usually happens is that by the time a shift is in progress, a majority accepts or doesn't notice the change, and only a minority condemns or resists the change. At this point, the minority may claim that their usage is educated or correct, and that the majority usage is careless or mistaken. But the minority usage is at risk of seeming unduly conservative and pedantic, and the situation is usually resolved by the disappearance of the minority usage. Over the years, people have deplored the changes in meaning of words like *arrive, deprecate* and *obnoxious* and have been able to argue that the older meaning was more faithful to the etymology. Thus *arrive* used to mean 'to reach a shore' rather than to reach anywhere (and the older meaning could be justified by appeal to the French *rive* 'shore, riverbank'); *deprecate* once meant 'to pray against, pray for deliverance from' rather than the modern 'to disapprove of, criticise' (and this too could be justified etymologically, given the Latin *deprecatus* 'prayed against'); and *obnoxious* meant 'liable to criticism or punishment' (Latin *obnoxius* 'exposed to harm') whereas the modern meaning is 'unpleasant, offensive'. Needless to say, the older meanings are now virtually unknown – except to those who find them in dictionaries and other records of the past.

Finally, we should note the need to be cautious about the idea of 'original meaning'. Sometimes we can identify the origin of a word – as for instance with the word *boycott*, which is believed to have come from the name of a land agent in nineteenth-century Ireland, who was 'boycotted' by tenants. But in many cases, there is no justification for calling an earlier meaning 'original'. The most common current meaning of *nice* – pleasant or enjoyable – has probably come from an earlier meaning, something like 'delicate' or 'dainty'. But this meaning can scarcely be called original. It probably came from earlier use of the word to mean 'finely differentiated' or 'requiring care and discrimination' (compare a traditional legal phrase 'a nice point'), which must in turn have come from the Latin *nescius* 'ignorant'. But even the Latin word and its meaning are only original relative to modern English. Latin is also a language with a history. It descended from something spoken previously, just as much as modern Italian came from Latin or modern English from old English. In short, however interesting and instructive the past may be, not all of it is accessible to us and not all of it is relevant. The past is not the present, nor is the history of a word its meaning.

2.4 Prescription

The idea which we have been looking at in the previous section, that a word ought to mean what it used to mean, is just one instance of what can be called a prescriptive approach to language. More generally, there have been many and various attempts to prescribe how language ought to be – prescriptions about pronunciation, for example, or rules about correct grammar, as well as claims about the proper meanings of words. Many of these attempts have been misguided if not perverse, and it became axiomatic in twentieth-century linguistics to reject prescriptivism. A common slogan of linguists was that 'linguistics is descriptive, not prescriptive'.

As a commitment to scientific method and ethical research, the slogan is exemplary. Whether investigating the physiology of speech production, recording what people say to each other in specific situations or examining the frequencies of words in printed texts, linguists, like all scholars and researchers, are under obligation to describe what they find. Even allowing that complete objectivity is unattainable, and that there will always be controversy about what exactly constitutes 'describing what you find', there is an indisputable obligation to aim to describe what is there, rather than to describe what you would like to be there or what you think ought to be there.

The slogan also represents a justifiable reaction to some of the prescriptivism of the past. In seventeenth- and eighteenth-century Europe, for example, some scholars and writers believed that it was necessary to regulate language and to set up academies for this purpose, such as the Académie Française, founded in 1634 and charged with compiling a French dictionary and with ruling on matters of grammar, vocabulary and usage. Though no academy was ever set up in Britain, there were certainly calls to refine and reform the English language. To some extent, these ambitions were motivated by a desire for regularity and consistency. Since it is important both to understand the weakness of prescriptive approaches to language and to recognise the genuine normativity inherent in language, we will consider two examples in some detail, first the history of comparative forms like *(more) bigger*, and second the proposal that prepositions shouldn't end sentences.

In English grammar, by the seventeenth century, the old pattern of forming comparative and superlative adjectives by endings (as in *big, bigger, biggest* or *tall, taller, tallest*) had begun to blend with a newer pattern using the words *more* and *most* (as in *evil, more evil, most evil* or *corrupt, more corrupt, most corrupt*). In Shakespeare's writings, for example, we can find the two patterns combined, as in *more better, more corrupter, most unkindest, most coldest*. But eighteenth-century grammarians began to criticise this practice, apparently on the grounds that only one of the two devices (either the ending or the *more/most*) is logically necessary to convey the meaning. Modern English usage has been partly influenced by these grammatical strictures. People nowadays quite often say things like *more kinder* or *most earliest*, but they tend to avoid them in writing, and editors are likely to delete the *more* or *most*. Written usage is still not exactly regular, however, since the tendency is to use the endings on monosyllabic words (*colder, coldest, higher, highest, later, latest*) and to use *more* and *most* with polysyllabic words (*more difficult, more interesting, most intelligent, most troublesome*). But this is only a generalisation: some monosyllabic words do take *more* (*more tired*, for instance) and for some words of two syllables it seems perfectly acceptable to go either way (*shallower* or *more shallow, commonest* or *most common*). There are also the 'irregular' forms *better, best, worse, worst*. (For an overview of usage see Biber *et al.* 1999, pp. 521–5, and for details of past as well as more modern usage, see Fries 1940, pp. 96–101.)

Despite some variation in usage, forms such as *more bigger* and *most highest* are usually disapproved of by editors and teachers. While there may be a superficial appeal in simplifying such phrases to the single words *bigger* and *highest*, there are two difficulties to be noted. The first is that users of language will rarely if ever be bound by the dictates of individuals and academies, however educated or well informed those authorities may be. Many speakers of English continue to say things like *more kinder* and *most earliest,* even after they have been told not to. And imagine the reaction (or indifference) of the community at large if linguists or teachers were to recommend that we regularise the language by saying *gooder* and *goodest* rather than *better* or *best,* or *badder* and *baddest* rather than *worse* and *worst.* Whatever arguments might be put forward, that forms like *gooder* are simpler, more regular or more logical than what we actually say, most people would continue to follow their customary practice and would consider the recommendation absurd. With few exceptions, language does not change because of regulation, it changes according to its own communal patterns.

The second problem in making language more logical or regular is that it is not at all self-evident what constitutes logic or regularity in linguistic matters. It is somewhat clearer, and rather more carefully discussed, what logic means in thinking and reasoning, or what regularity means in the study of natural phenomena. But linguistic systems generate their own logics and regularities. Is it really illogical to say *more kinder*? If it is the redundancy that is illogical, then by similar argument, we might claim, for example, that plural forms are redundant and illogical after numerals. A numeral already signals that the noun must be understood as plural, and we could therefore write *five dollar, a hundred student, a thousand spectator.* (And some languages, such as Welsh, do indeed use the singular form of a noun after a numeral.) In fact if we look dispassionately at the patterns of languages, we find a variety of ways of organising the lexicogrammar to express meaning, and it is not at all obvious why any of them should be regarded as more or less logical than others. Is it more logical for adjectives to precede nouns (as they mostly do in English, German or Japanese) or to follow nouns (as they mostly do in French, Italian or Indonesian)? Is there any reason why we should express contrasting verb meanings by suffixes (as English does with, say, *walk, walked, chase, chased*) rather than by auxiliary verbs (as English does with, say, *will walk, might walk, will chase, might chase*)? Is it neater or more regular to signal meanings like 'for', 'in' and 'on' by separate words preceding a noun (as English and most European languages do) or by suffixes on the noun (as languages as diverse as Finnish, Turkish and Australian Aboriginal languages mostly do)? What is logical and regular is the way in which each language underlies the linguistic behaviour of its speakers, the way in which each language builds a system out of its systems. The positioning of adjectives, the mechanics of the verb system, the use of prepositions or noun suffixes are not just trivial and isolated features of a language but are woven together in a complex, coherent and powerful lexicogrammar.

To return to the point about attempts to reform English, our second example is a rule sometimes imposed on English that sentences should not end with prepositions. According to the severest version of this rule, prepositions belong before a noun or pronoun, as in *for Uncle Leo, for me, in Singapore, in the afternoon, on Fridays, on the table*. A sentence in which a preposition appears other than before a noun or pronoun, like 'that's the book which I've been looking for', should be rephrased as 'that's the book for which I've been looking'; and a question like 'what is she looking at?' should be rephrased as 'at what is she looking?' This rule seems to have been invented by Dryden in the seventeenth century (Strang 1970, p. 143) and since then it has been often promoted, possibly beyond Dryden's intentions, and widely ignored or ridiculed.

In modern grammars, a preposition such as the 'for' in 'what are you looking for' is sometimes said to be 'stranded' (see e.g. Biber *et al.* 1999, pp. 105–8). The reasons for wanting to avoid 'stranded' prepositions probably include the fact that prepositions do not occur at the end of sentences in Latin (and Latin has often been held up as a model which other languages should conform to) and the very name *preposition*, which might seem, etymologically, to imply that these words should always be 'pre-posed' before another word.

But Latin grammar is not the same as modern English grammar, and the etymology of the name *preposition* does not impose any requirement on well-established English usage (any more than *premises* must mean '(things) sent beforehand' or *prevent* must mean 'come before'). While many writers, having been schooled in Dryden's rule, may now prefer to avoid sentence-final prepositions in formal English, most of us continue to ask questions like *what were you looking for?* and *who did you give it to?*, and find the rephrased versions awkward or pompous. Indeed, the strength of communal resistance to arbitrary regulation is seen in the way in which the rule is mocked by pronouncements such as 'a preposition is a bad word to end a sentence with' or the witticism ascribed to Winston Churchill 'this is a form of pedantry up with which I will not put'.

While it may sometimes seem desirable to make language more logical or consistent, the fundamental challenge to regulators is that the patterns of language emerge as a matter of social convention. Regularity and consistency are important factors in this process, but not the only ones or the pre-eminent ones. As we have already suggested, the complexity of language and its processes of acquisition and change are such that it is not always clear what exactly logic and consistency mean in linguistic practice. If *most coldest* ought to be simplified or regularised, should it be to *coldest* or to *most cold*? And if this reform is important, why is it not equally important to get rid of redundant plural forms after numerals or to tidy up the English verb system? Why not get rid of the irregular and redundant word *am*, and simplify *I am* to *I are*, on the analogy of *you are* and *we are*? (We already say *aren't I?* rather than *amn't I?* which takes us some of the way towards this regularisation.) Why not make all verbs regular, replacing *ran* with *runned*, *wrote* with *writed*, and so on? The absurdity of trying to impose some externally conceived general notion of logic and simplicity on language puts a harsh spotlight on the odd details that are on reformist agendas.

Indeed, many people have tried to reform or regularise a language or to stop it from changing, but few have had much success. In general, languages change as societies and cultures do: as we differ from our grandparents, whether radically or not, in our beliefs, our perspectives, our social behaviour, our hobbies, our dress, so we differ from them, significantly or trivially, in our accent, in our idiom, in the words we use and the meanings we exploit. Changes in language do not happen uniformly across the world, and perhaps not even at a constant rate – there may be periods of rapid change and periods of relative stability. But change is observable, everywhere where the history of languages can be studied.

We should nevertheless be clear that an argument against regulation and prescription is not an argument against normativity in principle. The social nature of language brings a normativity of its own. As children we learn our linguistic patterns in the community in which we function, from our peers and from the adults with whom we interact. We learn the conventions of the written language which our community has inherited. And the patterns and conventions that underlie linguistic behaviour around us exert a strong pressure to conform: as human beings we are powerfully motivated, not only to understand and be understood, but to belong.

As we enter places of formal education and employment, we may be subject to specific linguistic norms, the kinds of norms that govern the writing of university essays or press releases or product information or government reports. Here we may well be in relatively circumscribed domains, where norms may be imposed more directly and more authoritatively. Thus a commercial company may have rules about the structure and wording of the memorandums written by its employees, a journal may have requirements about the style and presentation of papers which it is prepared to publish, a government department may follow conventional guidelines about the format and style of its documentation, and so on. (For more discussion of 'controlled' language, especially nomenclatures, see 2.8 below.)

It is in such domains that arbitrary prescriptions of the kind that tell us to write *shallower,* not *more shallow,* or to avoid ending sentences with prepositions, may have some measure of success. To some extent, arbitrary rulings in well-defined contexts are necessary, simply to yield consistency in, for example, the way in which dates are written or bibliographies compiled or reports presented. Hopefully the focus of those who write the relevant style guides or otherwise determine conventions in such settings is on clarity and consistency and efficiency, and on meaningful rather than empty traditions.

Moreover, even in society at large, it is important, even essentially human, to bring moral perspectives to bear on social and cultural changes. Social and cultural changes can, and should be, evaluated for their effects on human wellbeing, on the distribution of resources, on fairness and justice, difficult and contentious though the processes and criteria of evaluation may be. And to the extent that language reflects and supports behaviour and social structures, it is open to moral evaluation. Without such evaluation there would be no debate about sexism and racism in language, no possibility for argument about clarity and truth in language. Thus most of us do accept style guides that promote inclusive or egalitarian language, guidelines that provide for a certain degree of consistency of format in journals and bibliographies, courses that teach report writing, and so on.

The argument against prescription is not an argument against normativity in principle. But linguistic norms must be founded in social agreement on issues that matter to people – in a recognition by most people that we ought to eliminate racist words from the language, or that it is worth some effort to make instruction manuals as clear as possible, or that bibliographies are much easier to use if they follow standard conventions. This kind of commitment does not constitute justification for prescriptions about whether you can end a sentence with a preposition, and it gives no support to rulings based on individual interpretations of what might make language more regular, nor to arguments that language should be fixed once and for all in some supposedly golden age.

2.5 A social view of language and meaning

In this book we take the view that language is social behaviour and meaning a social phenomenon. By this we mean that language is more than an individual possession or ability, that language 'exists' because of its life in social interaction, that meaning is shaped and negotiated in social interaction and that meaning must be studied with due recognition of its social setting.

The concept of meaning itself is difficult to define and it is no exaggeration to say that modern linguistics has failed to formulate a widely agreed theory of meaning. But the fact that there is something elusive and mysterious about meaning need not embarrass us, any more than humans should be embarrassed by the difficulty of understanding and defining exactly what we mean by time, number, life and other fundamental concepts of our existence. Most of us readily acknowledge that we cannot give a snappy definition of what time is, but we are still conscious of what we call the passing of time, we know the difference between yesterday and tomorrow, we even make it possible for ourselves to measure and quantify time by counting the alternations of daylight and darkness, constructing a twenty-four-hour day, and so on. Similarly, it is hard to give a technical definition of life. Dictionaries resort to phrases like 'the state of being alive' or to descriptions of what distinguishes living beings from dead ones or living beings from inanimate objects. In so doing they demonstrate both the difficulty of what they are trying to do and the good sense of drawing on our experience: we know that some things (people, animals, plants) live, that other things do not, that living beings sooner or later die. We will try to take a similar approach to meaning: it may be hard to define, but we all experience it; we negotiate meanings in our daily life; we (mostly) know what we mean and what others mean.

In societies with well-developed literacy and a tradition of publishing and using dictionaries and other reference books, there is always a danger that a language will be equated with some written account of the language. We have already referred to the dangers of assuming that a dictionary of English *is* the vocabulary of English (2.2 above), and a book describing the grammar of English may likewise seem to *be* the grammar of English. But dictionaries and grammar books are only representations of the language (and limited representations of certain aspects of the language). If they have value, it is because they represent, in some generalising abstract way, what people do linguistically. The meanings of words or the rules of grammar have not been laid down by some expert or authoritative decree at some point in the past and then enshrined in print. Dictionaries and grammar books are not legislation enacted by a linguistic parliament, nor are they the official manuals issued by people who created the language. If dictionaries and grammar books have authority, it is because they reflect general usage. Thus a language exists or lives not because it is described or recorded but because it is in use among people who know the language.

We say that people 'know' a language. And this, perhaps as well as images of language as recorded rules and inventories, may imply that language exists in the human mind. While it is obviously true that adult speakers of a language have large resources of knowledge – including for example knowledge of words and meanings and experience of using and understanding them – it would be misleading to suggest that an individual's linguistic knowledge is a complete and adequate version of 'the language'. For an individual, taken in isolation, is just that, an isolated individual. We cannot really speak of a language unless individual human beings are communicating with each other, bringing the language to life. Our individual knowledge of language comes from interaction with others, at first particularly with parents and family, later also with other children with whom we spend time, with schoolteachers, and so on. Some bases of our linguistic behaviour seem to be established relatively early and firmly. Most people acquire their accent or patterns of pronunciation fairly early and seem to change very little, even if they move to an area where people speak differently (although some people do make substantial changes in their pronunciation, for example at secondary school or at university). People similarly tend to maintain basic vocabulary and idioms that they have used frequently in their early years, although again they may yield to strong pressures to change, for example if they realise there are substantial social and economic advantages in making changes, or if they move to an area where some different words and idioms are customary. But even those whose language seems to change little during their lifetime are still using and experiencing language. For most of us, in most parts of the world, language is realised – actualised, made real – in a wide range of settings, such as homes and schools and workplaces and shops among many others. Our sense of what is normal usage, of what words mean, is constantly shaped by such experience.

Consider for example the word *stakeholder*. Until the latter part of the twentieth century, the meaning of the word was something like 'the person who holds the stakes in a bet'. English-language dictionaries published before the 1980s record only that sense. By the end of the 1980s, however, the word was being used in a commercial sense, as in an Australian newspaper's reference to 'the best interests of the company taking into account the stakeholders'. From this kind of use in commercial and financial contexts, the word extended into other institutional uses, so that we find, during the 1990s, a university talking about its 'accountability and information provision to external stakeholders' and a water supply authority talking about workshops attended by 'stakeholders, managers and scientists'. A website relevant to the construction industry speaks of the importance of the 'collabora-tive efforts of all stakeholders' and then helpfully specifies stakeholders as designers, engineers, property consultants, technologists and clients 'among many others'. From uses such as these it is clear that *stakeholder* can no longer be taken in the sense of someone who is holding or directly investing money.

While it would be unwarranted to attach too much significance to a single word, the shift and extension of *stakeholder* not only illustrates how words and our understanding of them can change, but also how changes in words reflect social movements, in this case the widening scope of *stakeholder* going hand in hand with an increasingly commer-cialised perspective on services such as education and health through the 1990s and the extension of many commercial or financial terms into general administrative discourse.

The word *gender* has also shifted in recent years, again reflecting social changes. Until quite recently English-language dictionaries gave as the main use of *gender* its meaning in grammar, as in talking about the two genders (masculine and feminine) of nouns in French or Spanish, or the three genders (masculine, feminine and neuter) of nouns in Latin or German. Some dictionaries also recorded a technical biological use of the word, as in talking about gender differentiation within a species, and an informal, possibly jocular or euphemistic use, as in talking about people 'of the opposite gender'.

By the end of the 1980s, dictionaries are recording *gender* as having a significant and formal use for something like 'the fact of being male or female'. The word has largely replaced *sex* in this sense, for *sex* has increasingly been used as shorthand for 'sexual intercourse'. At the same time the word *gender* has increasingly appeared in various kinds of official and academic discourse. A corpus search suggests that in for-mal written discourse in the 1990s, references to grammatical gender were now vastly outnumbered by the use of the word in phrases like 'redefining gender roles' or 'gender balance (in the workforce)' or 'gender and sexuality'. Thus demographers can refer to the 'age/ gender profiles' of population groups and a trade union can raise the question of 'gender inequities in the existing staff structure', while universities offer courses with titles such as 'Gender and Policy' and the 'Politics of Culture and Gender'. Readers may like to ask themselves what they would take to be the current difference in meaning between 'the politics of gender' and 'the politics of sex'.

There is a sense in which the meaning of (most) words is constantly being negotiated. Our notion of what words like *stakeholder*, *gender* and *sex* mean is dependent on our discourse, on our experience of these words, on our experience of how others use these words in real situations. Older readers may remember uses that are now archaic or obsolete, like 'the gentle sex' and 'the second sex'. Even phrases that are current may reveal a certain competition between different senses: note for instance how we understand the word *sex* in 'sex discrimination' compared with 'safe sex', or 'sex stereotyping of women' compared with 'gratuitous sex scenes'. (Compare examples given earlier of meanings which may be associated with particular contexts, or of meanings which may disappear other than in a few phrases, such as *meat* in the sense of food in general, 2.3 above.)

The word *patron* comes from a Latin word that meant something like 'protector' or 'guardian'. In English, the word has had a similar meaning, still evident in the phrase 'patron saint' for example. When we read about the eighteenth-century lexicographer Samuel Johnson and his need for patrons (and see his biting definition of *patron*, 2.2 above), we also understand the word against a background of benefactors and their dependants. Current corpus evidence shows continuing use of *patron* in this kind of meaning ('galleries which were trustees of public art, with local government as their major patrons') but also shows the word with a meaning that is closer to *customer* or *client*, especially a customer in a hotel or restaurant ('most diners want privacy ... some patrons, however, do not mind being observed'). Meanwhile the French word *patron* has come to be used in the sense of 'manager'. Thus in a restaurant in France, someone who asks for *le patron* is looking for 'the boss', not any of the customers. That two words of one origin can end up with contrasting, almost opposite meanings demonstrates again that meanings are negotiable and negotiated.

In the following section, we will further develop this perspective by looking briefly at the contribution to linguistic theory of the Swiss linguist Ferdinand de Saussure and the British linguist J. R. Firth. Saussure is widely considered to be the founder of modern structural linguistics and Firth a leading figure in mid-twentieth-century British linguistics. While these are by no means the only two linguists whose ideas we respect and draw on, they are both influential and explicit theoreticians who have shaped the way many linguists talk about meaning.

2.6 Saussure and Firth

Saussure

Ferdinand de Saussure was a francophone Swiss, born in Geneva in 1857. He seems to have had a great talent for languages and at the age of 15 was said to be already competent in Latin, Greek, German and English (as well as French, his mother tongue, of course). He came from a family with a tradition of scientific achievement – his father was a well-known naturalist, for example – and he entered the University of Geneva as a student of physics and chemistry in 1875. But his talents and enthusiasm were focused on language, and after a year of studying science in Geneva, he persuaded his parents to send him to Germany to study Indo-European languages.

Saussure studied in Germany for four years, mixing with learned and creative scholars, acquiring extremely useful experience in the research methodology of the times. He then taught for ten years in Paris, where he seems to have been highly regarded and influential, before returning, in 1891, to a professorship in Geneva. He taught mostly the linguistics of the time – Sanskrit, comparative and historical linguistics – but there is some evidence from his correspondence that he was dissatisfied with general linguistic thinking, that he thought there was need to reform the jargon and terminology of the day, and that he thought linguists needed to think more about what they were doing.

In 1906, the University of Geneva asked him to take over the responsibility for teaching general linguistics, and from then until 1911 he gave a series of lectures in alternate years. In 1912 he fell ill and he died in 1913. (For a concise account of Saussure's life and work, see Culler 1976.)

He had written a substantial amount about Indo-European languages and historical reconstruction, by which he had maintained his high reputation, but he had written nothing about his ideas on language in general. His colleagues and his students were so impressed by what they had heard from him that they thought they should try to preserve the lectures from the last years of his life. Two of his students put together what they could, from Saussure's own lecture notes and their and other students' notes, and created a book now known as Saussure's *Cours de Linguistique Générale* or *Course in General Linguistics*. The *Cours* was first published in Paris in 1916 and has been through several editions since then. A critical edition of the French text, prepared by Tullio de Mauro, was published in 1972 (Saussure 1972) and includes copious background and notes on the text. An English translation (translated by Wade Baskin) was published in 1960 and another (translated and annotated by Roy Harris) in 1983. Harris has also written a critical commentary on the text (Harris 1987).

Saussure is now famous for various points which are developed in the *Cours*. He made a clear distinction, for example, between describing the history of a language and describing how it is at any particular point in its history, a distinction between a historical (or diachronic) perspective on language and a current (or synchronic) perspective. If that distinction seems self-evident to us nowadays, that is partly because Saussure firmly established it.

Saussure devotes considerable attention to the nature of the linguistic sign, which he describes as an inseparable combination of a *signified*, a concept or meaning, and a *signifier*, the spoken or written form which conveys or represents that meaning. This view contrasts with a long and continuing tradition in philosophy and linguistics in which it is assumed or claimed that you can separate form and meaning. This difference of theoretical stance has many consequences – for example for one's view of what translation is (see 2.10 below). We will therefore be returning to this point, but for the moment we note that Saussure says you can no more separate the signifier from the signified than you can separate the front and back of a sheet of paper.

Saussure's *Cours* also emphasises the point that linguistic signs are arbitrary (although he elaborates and qualifies the point in ways that make a simple summary difficult). Arbitrariness is not just a matter of the lack of logical or natural connection – in most instances – between the meaning of a word or phrase and the spoken sounds or written form which represent that meaning. Arbitrariness is also evident when we compare languages and find that their signs and meanings do not neatly match each other. The Dutch *slak* could be either 'snail' or 'slug' when we translate it into English. English *blue* is two different colours in Russian. And in some Australian Aboriginal languages, what looks like the word for 'father' is a term referring not just to an individual but to a range of male persons, not only one's biological father but also to brothers of one's father, parallel cousins of one's father and even certain great-grandsons.

Thus to speak of arbitrariness in language is not only to say that one concept in one language can become two in another, or that two can be collapsed into one. More than that, languages often see the world very differently. They divide reality up differently, they focus on different criteria, they structure experience in different ways. In the case of kinship terms like 'father' and 'mother', English highlights biological relationships, whereas Australian Aboriginal languages focus on social structure in such a way that a word which English speakers might expect to refer to a unique individual refers rather to a group of people who share a similar place or role in the system.

In the kind of linguistics promoted by Saussure, it is important to do justice to the structures and systems which language itself generates or embodies. If you want to understand the kinship terms of an Australian Aboriginal language, don't try to set up some universal transcendental framework, try to get inside the language itself. If there's a word that looks as though it means 'father' but evidently does not correspond with English *father*, the questions to ask are: what are the other kinship words in this language? How do they contrast in meaning with each other? How do they appear in discourse? What kind of systems and structures do they form or enter into?

These meanings may be arbitrary in the sense that there is no pre-determined framework that says all languages must make this or that distinction, but they are certainly not arbitrary in the sense that individuals can play freely and randomly with the language. While there is of course scope for creative excursions, whether in the strikingly unusual turn of phrase of a poet or in the entertaining zaniness of a comedian, what holds a language together, what makes it work as a language, is the social convention or agreement that undergirds it. A word means what it means because that is what people here and now in this community take it to mean. At its heart, language rests on social convention.

For reasons such as these, Saussure is considered a modernist and sometimes compared with figures like Freud (born the year before Saussure) and Durkheim (the 'founder' of modern sociology, born the year after Saussure). The three of them, among others, were leaders in a powerful movement that brought into the twentieth century new kinds of science and scholarship, behavioural and social sciences with their own thinking and methods.

Despite the fact that the Saussurean approach is not universally approved (see the following section for some brief comments on Chomsky's criticism of Saussure), it has shown its strength in its continuing appeal to substantial numbers of linguists and social scientists.

Firth

John Rupert Firth was born in England in 1890 and taught at the University of the Punjab from 1919 until 1928. Returning to England, he held posts in London, first at University College, then at the School of Oriental and African Studies, where he was the Professor of General

Linguistics from 1944 to 1956. Much of Firth's work was in phonology, a field in which he was descriptively and theoretically innovative. (For introductory overviews of this work, see for example Robins 1979, pp. 214–21, or Sampson 1980, pp. 215–23.) But Firth wrote also about meaning and about language in general. Unlike many of his European contemporaries, Firth had extensive experience outside Europe. (In phonology, for example, he was alert to the dangers of assuming that a European alphabetic writing system was a good model of the organisation of spoken language: while it is possible to draw an analogy between the letters of an alphabet and the phonemes or sounds of spoken language, there are significant differences as well as similarities.) Firth also read the work of anthropologists like Malinowski, whose charmingly entitled *Coral Gardens and their Magic* (1935) gave an account of the culture of the people of the Trobriand Islands, in what is now Papua New Guinea. Malinowksi stressed the importance of understanding language in its context and spoke of language as activity, explicitly rejecting the notion that language was a means of transferring thoughts or ideas from one person's head to another's.

For Firth, meaning is function in context, and, consistently with this broad claim, not only words but also grammatical structures and even the sounds of language have meaning. At times Firth seems to equate meaning with use (a word, for example, is meaningful because it serves some purpose in genuine contexts) or with context itself (a word's meaning is the range of contexts in which it occurs). While this has struck – and still strikes – many people as an unusual if not perverse extension of the notion of meaning, what is significant here is Firth's attention to what could be observed, and to genuine usage. Firth takes a theoretical stand not only against the kind of linguistic description which deals with invented examples considered outside any real context, but also against the kind of theoretical mentalism which presents speculations about the contents and workings of the human mind as if they were scientific observations.

The influence of Firth's views is evident in much of British linguistics: he was a major influence on Halliday, and hence in the development of modern systemic functional linguistics (see for example Sampson 1980, pp. 227ff., Martin 1992, p. 4, Eggins 1994, pp. 51–2), and on Sinclair and the development of corpus linguistics (to be explored in detail in Chapters 3 and 4). The development of corpora – the large electronically accessible collections of textual material – has made Firth's seemingly bizarre statements about meaning as use and meaning as context far more believable. Now that it has become possible to track thousands of occurrences of words and phrases, in their real settings, linguists have begun to see just how informative a record of use in context can be – and how wrong our intuitions sometimes are. As we will see in Chapters 3 and 4, modern corpus linguistics brings a new seriousness to observation of actual usage.

2.7 Cognitive linguistics

In contrast to Saussure and Firth, many linguists writing in the latter part of the twentieth century have been avowedly 'mentalist' or 'cognitivist'. The most famous of these is Noam Chomsky.

Chomsky was born in Philadelphia in 1928. He studied linguistics, mathematics and philosophy and qualified for his doctorate at the University of Pennsylvania, before taking up an academic post at the Massachusetts Institute of Technology, where he became famous not only as a theoretical linguist but also as an outspoken critic of the war waged by the USA in Vietnam in the 1960s and 1970s, and as a writer and speaker on US foreign policy, politics and the mass media. Encyclopedias and dictionaries describe him variously as 'a linguist, writer, and political activist', 'a political observer and critic' and 'one of the leading critics of American foreign policy [since 1965]'. His published books include not only widely read works on linguistics but also political works such as *Manufacturing Consent: the Political Economy of the Mass Media* (with Edward S. Herman, 1988) and *Rethinking Camelot: JFK, the Vietnam War, and US Political Culture* (1993). The titles of these works already give some idea of Chomsky's stance: *American Power and the New Mandarins* was dedicated to 'the brave young men who refuse to serve in a criminal war'; and the phrase 'manufacturing consent' is often quoted by critics of the modern 'free enterprise' mass media.

As with Saussure and Firth, it will be impossible to do full justice here to an influential and widely discussed scholar. (A brief but useful evaluation of the earlier years of Chomsky's contribution to linguistics, psychology and philosophy can be found in Lyons 1970; a later and more critical account is Chapter 6 of Sampson 1980; and Chomsky's more recent views can be found in Chomsky 2000.) Our concern here is with approaches to meaning, and in particular with twentieth-century mentalism and cognitivism, rather than with an overall assessment of Chomsky's work. And it is Chomsky's *Cartesian Linguistics* (1966) which offers us a classic defence of mentalism: the book is significantly sub-titled 'a chapter in the history of rationalist thought' and it seeks to draw on and continue the work of the seventeeth-century philosopher Descartes.

In this view, there is a 'fundamental distinction between body and mind' (Chomsky 1966, p. 32) and the mind and its structure and processes are deemed to be a proper object of study. It is assumed 'that linguistic and mental processes are virtually identical, language providing the primary means for free expression of thought and feeling, as well as for the functioning of the creative imagination' (Chomsky 1966, p. 31). Thus the human mind has a certain structure and certain ways of operating, which in some sense determine – or even *are* – the structures and processes of language itself.

The programme of cognitive linguistics initiated by Chomsky and his colleagues in the 1950s and 1960s proposed a distinction between 'deep' and 'surface' structure in language. At least in the early stages of this programme, deep structure was assumed to have a mental reality closely related to meaning: 'It is the deep structure underlying the actual utterance, a structure that is purely mental, that conveys the semantic content of the sentence' (Chomsky 1966, p. 35). It was also suggested that this deep structure might be universal: 'The deep structure that expresses the meaning is common to all languages, so it is claimed, being a simple reflection of the forms of thought' (Chomsky 1966, p. 35). Those who followed Descartes 'characteristically assumed that mental processes are common to all normal humans and that languages may therefore differ in the manner of expression but not in the thoughts expressed' (Chomsky 1966, p. 96). This universalism is itself tied to the mentalism: 'The discovery of universal principles would provide a partial explanation for the facts of particular languages, in so far as these could be shown to be simply specific instances of the general features of language structure ... Beyond this, the universal features themselves might be explained on the basis of general assumptions about human mental processes or the contingencies of language use ...' (Chomsky 1966, p. 54).

As Chomsky himself sees it, his late-twentieth-century mentalist linguistics thus revives the concerns and perspectives of the rationalists of the seventeenth and eighteenth centuries and links them with modern psychology: 'it seems that after a long interruption, linguistics and cognitive psychology are now turning their attention to approaches to the study of language structure and mental processes which in part originated and in part were revitalized in the "century of genius" and which were fruitfully developed until well into the nineteenth century' (Chomsky 1966, p. 72).

Judged in this cognitivist light, the kind of linguistics which builds on the work of Saussure and Firth (2.6 above) is too sceptical about the mind and mental processes, and too oriented to what is observable 'on the surface'. In Chomsky's own words:

From the standpoint of modern linguistic theory, this attempt to discover
and characterize deep structure and to study the transformational rules that
relate it to surface form ... indicates lack of respect for the 'real language'
... and lack of concern for 'linguistic fact'. Such criticism is based on a
restriction of the domain of 'linguistic fact' to physically identifiable sub-
parts of actual utterances and their formally marked relations. Restricted in
this way, linguistics studies the use of language for the expression of
thought only incidentally, to the quite limited extent to which deep and
surface structure coincide; in particular, it studies 'sound–meaning
correspondences' only in so far as they are representable in terms of surface
structure. From this limitation follows the general disparagement of Cartesian and earlier linguistics, which attempted to give a full account of deep
structure even where it is not correlated in strict point-by-point fashion to
observable features of speech.

(Chomsky 1966, p. 51)

This focus on mind and thought, backed by a dualistic perspective on
mind and body, tends to assume that meanings are mental concepts
which have real existence in the mind (as opposed to being convenient
or theoretical abstractions or constructs). Previous sections of this
chapter have already indicated that our view is somewhat different.
Like the linguists whom Chomsky criticises, we take it that the distinction of mind and body is an assumption, not a proven fact, and we
are indeed sceptical about how much can be discerned within the
mind. In fact the mind–body dichotomy represents a particular conception of humanity, a conception that is by no means self-evident and
universal.

Firth was clear on this point: 'As we know so little about mind and as
our study is essentially social I shall cease to respect the duality of mind
and body, thought and word ...' (Firth 1957, p. 19). For Firth and
many other linguists of the twentieth century (see Hasan 1987, esp. pp.
117ff., Halliday 1994b), the postulation of mental entities is not well
justified and too easily takes linguistics away from its proper concerns
with the physical, biological, social and semiotic character of language.

This section has given no more than a thumbnail sketch of some of
the theorising of Chomsky and cognitive linguists, and it is certainly
not intended as a thorough review of this theorising. Nevertheless it
serves no good purpose to avoid or disguise serious differences in
theoretical stance which affect modern linguistics. We hope that some
indication of the differences between Saussurean and cognitivist linguistics helps to clarify our approach as well as to remind readers that
in linguistics, as in most human enquiry, there is no one theoretical
position which is taken for granted by everyone. Chapters 3 and 4 will
expand and illustrate further the theoretical stance of this book.

2.8 Language and reality

It seems an obvious and necessary truth that language connects with reality, that language is in some sense grounded in reality. Words seem to refer to things that have an existence independent of human language, discourse somehow relates to actions and situations, language at large must be grounded in a world at large.

The fact that it seems self-evident to talk about a 'real world' to which language refers or relates actually has more to do with traditions and habits of talking and thinking than it does with objective necessity. It is customary to talk about words referring to things and about language connecting with reality; this does not mean that this is necessarily the best way of thinking about language and reality. We have already mentioned (2.2 above) the awkwardness of treating meaning as reference, of assuming that all words refer to things. For some words, it does seem quite reasonable to make a connection with a reality that is 'external' to language. But for many others, such a connection is speculative.

Part of being human is to try to make sense of the world and our place in it, and part of this endeavour is ordering and classifying the world, as we perceive and experience it. To a large extent, our language does the job for us. As children learn their first language, they learn categories and classes, usually without being at all conscious of it. We learn words for objects which we see and talk about, and these words imply categorisation: a stick is different from a stone, a hill different from a mountain, a flower different from a fruit, a sheep different from a goat, a pen different from a pencil, a book different from a magazine, and so on. We learn words for colours, which give us a division of the colour spectrum, we learn words for human relationships, such as *aunt* and *cousin*, which bring with them ways of structuring our kinship, we learn verbs like *say, speak, stand, stay, steal, stumble*, among many others, which imply all kinds of distinctions and judgements relevant to human actions and behaviour.

It may be convenient for us to assume that this categorisation is natural and universal. But this assumption will be constantly disturbed, as our experience becomes wide enough to realise that not all human beings live in the same environments, that there is more than one way of defining what flowers and fruits are, that some languages don't have a simple lexical distinction between hills and mountains or between sheep and goats, that some books look more like magazines and some magazines more like books, that communities have different ways of describing kinship, and so on.

Indeed, the more we widen our experience – for example by learning new languages or by empirical scientific investigation of the nature of reality – the more we are forced to recognise that what we call 'reality' or 'the real world' is by no means as natural and self-explanatory as we sometimes like to believe. Consider, for example, the scientific discovery that colour is a spectrum, not a set of discrete colours, combined with the observation that different languages divide the spectrum differently. Descriptions like 'green' or 'blue' and properties like 'greenness' and 'blueness' cannot be considered part of an objective reality: they are at least as much due to the English language as they are to the 'physical' world. Or consider an example already mentioned in 2.6, the difference between the English word *father* and what looks like the equivalent word in some Australian Aboriginal languages: the Aboriginal word refers not just to the person we call *father*, but also to brothers of one's father, and even to male parallel cousins of one's father. There are many other related differences between the English and Aboriginal ways of seeing kinship. In general, the English terms highlight genetic relationships, while the Aboriginal terms focus on social structure. From the English-speaking point of view, my father and mother are individuals who are biologically or genetically related to me. From the Aboriginal point of view, my fathers and mothers are groups of people who are related to me communally or socially, by a structure of obligations and responsibilities.

At least as far back as Aristotle, human beings have also tried to describe their world more deliberately and self-consciously, in ways that might transcend or improve upon 'ordinary' language or 'naïve' thinking. Attempts like these underlie much of what we now call a scientific description of the world. We now have, for example, elaborate classifications of plants and animals that extend – and in some respects clash with – our everyday vocabulary. Thus most Australian speakers of English have a notion of what a 'pine' tree is, based largely on the nature of the foliage (evergreen needle-shaped leaves) and the overall appearance of the tree (with a relatively straight trunk and long branches bending out from it) and perhaps also on its smell and its sticky resin. The word *pine* is part of an informal classification of trees implied by the (Australian) English lexicon: pine trees are different from gum trees, wattle trees, palm trees, and so on. But in modern discourse we also have access to a far more elaborate classification of plants, the naming system sometimes called botanical nomenclature or the Linnean system (after the Swedish botanist usually credited with introducing the system in the 1750s, Carl von

Linné, or in the Latinised version of his name, Carolus Linnaeus). In the Linnean system, pine trees belong to a genus known as *Pinus*, and particular kinds or 'species' of pine are identified in a standard way, by putting the name of the species after the genus, as in *Pinus radiata* (radiata pine) or *Pinus palustris* (longleaf pine).

Now the 'scientific' way of naming plants is not simply a refinement of 'ordinary' vocabulary. For a start, the Linnean classification is based largely on observation of the stamens and pistils of plants, features which are significant in plant reproduction but not nearly as relevant in 'ordinary' discourse as the overall shape and appearance of a plant or its usefulness to humans. Partly for that very reason, there are trees which are not scientifically classified as *Pinus* species but which are nevertheless popularly known as pines – for example the Huon pine (scientific name *Dacrydium franklinii*) and the Norfolk Island pine (scientific name *Araucaria heterophylla*). Similarly, there are 'gum' trees which do not belong to the *Eucalyptus* genus (such as the Sydney red gum, *Angophora costata*) and lilies which do not belong to the *Lilium* genus (such as the belladonna lily, *Amaryllis belladonna*).

Since the eighteenth century there has been an enormous expansion of taxonomies. The nomenclature of plants and animals are just two of the most widely known examples. Other fields in which classificatory naming systems have been developed include geology and mineralogy, anatomy (names of muscles, nerves and so on), medicine (names of diseases, surgical procedures, and so on) and chemistry (names of chemical compounds). Indeed, many large industries have created their own nomenclature, such as an organised set of names for tools and procedures, or a systematic classification of products, components and spare parts.

Many of these taxonomies are supervised and regulated, by a company or an industry or by some international body like the International Union for Pure and Applied Chemistry, in ways that are unthinkable for everyday discourse. (Compare our earlier remarks on prescription and regulation in 2.4 above.) In the twentieth century, terminography or terminology processing (see e.g. Sager 1990, Pavel and Nolet 2002) became a field in which people could train and work. Terminologists may collect information on specialist terms, may provide information, whether in published glossaries or terminological databases or through an advisory service, and may provide advice and recommendations on terms and their use. They may be employed by companies and industries who maintain databanks of technical terms, or by publishers, or by bodies such as the European Union or the government of Canada who maintain large terminological resources particularly to support translation work. (If we include the many people working in non-English-speaking countries in agencies that coin and promote indigenous terminology, there must be far more people now employed in terminological work than in conventional lexicography.)

The classification enshrined in a taxonomy is (in theory at least) rigorous, and the naming conventions are precise and strict. For example, any species of plant can be placed within the 'Plant Kingdom' which is in turn divided into phyla, classes, orders, families, genera and species. The example below shows the classification of one species of pine tree mentioned earlier. The use of Latinised forms ('Plantae', not 'plants', 'Coniferales', not 'conifers') is conventional and highlights the distinction between scientific description and everyday language. Note also the conventions governing the mention of a species: both genus name and species name are written in italics, the species name follows the genus, and the genus name takes an initial capital, while the species name is always given a lower-case initial letter.

Kingdom	Plantae (plants)
Phylum	Tracheophyta (plants with a vascular system)
Class	Pteropsida (plants with leaves with branched venation)
Order	Coniferales (trees and shrubs producing bare seeds, usually on cones)
Family	Pinaceae (trees with needle-shaped leaves, including firs, larches and spruces, as well as pines)
Genus	*Pinus* (pine trees, comprising about a hundred species)
Species	*Pinus radiata* (radiata pine, also known as insignis pine or Monterey pine)

Here are two more examples, first another plant, the musk rose (*Rosa moschata*) and then, from the animal kingdom, the silver gull, the common seagull of Australia (*Larus novaehollandiae*).

Kingdom	Plantae
Phylum	Tracheophyta
Class	Angiospermae (plants with their seeds enclosed in ovaries; flowering plants)
Order	Rosales (families of flowering plants incl. cherry, plum, strawberry, as well as roses)
Family	Rosaceae (flowering plants with typically five-petalled flowers)
Genus	*Rosa* (roses)

Species   *Rosa moschata* (musk rose)

Kingdom   Animalia (animals)
Phylum   Chordata (animals with vertebrae or a notochord)
Class   Aves (birds)
Order   Charadriiformes (families of gulls, puffins and waders such as curlews and plovers)
Family   Laridae (gulls and terns)
Genus   *Larus* (gulls)
Species   *Larus novaehollandiae* (silver gull, in Australia usually referred to as gull or seagull)

Conventions such as we have just mentioned – the use of italics and so on – are by no means obvious. They can be enforced reasonably successfully, however, precisely because the nomenclature is used mostly in professional writing, subject to careful editing, as in scientific journals, technical reports and textbooks.

The discrepancies between such taxonomies and everyday language may be considerable. We have already mentioned pine trees which are not species of *Pinus*, gum trees which are not eucalypts and lilies which are not *Lilium*. In general, taxonomies serve to identify and classify large numbers of items: many of these items may be rarely if ever talked about by most people and the criteria by which they are classified in the taxonomy may also be marginal in daily discourse. Thus roses belong botanically in the genus *Rosa*, within the family *Rosaceae*. This family happens also to include blackberry and strawberry plants as well as the (often decorative and ornamental) herbs and shrubs of the genus *Spiraea*. But this scientifically established family of plants does not have any relevance in everyday discourse. Indeed, most people find it surprising that such a diverse group of plants should form one family. Similarly, it goes against habitual discourse to say that, botanically, a tomato is a fruit rather than a vegetable, or indeed that nuts are fruits.

This brings us back to the question of an objective description of reality. It is clear that nomenclatures of the kind developed for describing and classifying animals and plants and chemicals serve an important purpose: they are generally more comprehensive than everyday language, they are based on careful and often highly detailed observation, and they may bring with them valuable insights from empirical research. To that extent, a scientifically validated taxonomy may be closer to reality, or more revealing of reality, than everyday language.

Nevertheless, this does not justify the further step of claiming that everyday language is defective, misleading or in need of reform. In daily life, the categories of everyday language are likely to be more useful than a scientific nomenclature. The everyday English distinction between fruit and vegetables may not be entirely scientifically 'correct', but it is highly relevant to our eating habits and shopping practices. If I am planning meals and making up a shopping list, thinking perhaps about salads as light meals, or about cooked vegetables to accompany other food, or about desserts of fresh fruit, then it makes sense to think, as speakers of English habitually do, in terms of everyday categories. For my purposes, fruits do not include tomatoes or nuts, and it would be foolish and inefficient to suppose that they ought to. If I am asking a friend about fruit currently available at the market, or looking for fruit in a greengrocer's shop, or offering my guests a choice of fresh fruit to eat, none of us should feel any need to defer to a botanical classification based on careful investigation of plant reproductive systems.

Moreover, it should not be assumed that scientific taxonomies, once developed, reveal objective truth once and for all. The botanical and zoological nomenclatures, for example, are always open to revision and some areas of the taxonomies remain controversial. Sometimes a simple renaming has proved necessary: when the Australian platypus was first described scientifically, in 1799, it was given the species name *Platypus anatinus*; but it turned out that the term *Platypus* was already in use for a group of beetles, and a new genus name *Ornithorhynchus* was devised, so that the platypus is now described as *Ornithorhynchus anatinus*. Sometimes the taxonomy itself has had to be extended. Linnaeus and his contemporaries in the eighteenth century probably believed that species of plants were invariant and invariable; subsequent research, including the development of evolutionary theory and empirical studies of diverse environments around the world, has led to a more flexible view. The plant taxonomy now includes subcategories (such as subspecies) as well as varieties within species. And sometimes, as a result of further research, a particular plant is relocated in the system, say from variety to subspecies or from subspecies to species. (The example given above, of the place of the silver gull in the animal kingdom, should actually include a suborder Lari, below the order Charadriiformes and above the family Laridae, and a subfamily Larinae, below the family Laridae and above the genus *Larus*. For further discussion of the provisional nature of scientific taxonomies, see 3.4.)

The terms of a scientific taxonomy are in some ways more like a naming system than a vocabulary. In the Linnean plant nomenclature, for example, it is normal to refer to genus and plant 'names', and the typical genus species name, say *Pinus radiata*, is sometimes likened to a surname plus given name. Nomenclatures also tend to be recorded and explained in encyclopaedias and technical publications rather than in general-purpose dictionaries. Tendencies such as these inspire a tradition of distinguishing between encyclopaedic knowledge and linguistic knowledge, between 'knowledge of the world' and 'knowledge of language'. Thus, it may be argued, knowing the names of individual people, knowing historical facts and knowing about particular objects are all part of knowing about our world, and not part of our language. And it has to be said that there are things we know which are, on the face of it, quite outside language: telephone numbers, addresses, names of people and places, historical dates, and so on. Obviously, it is possible to be a fluent and competent speaker of English without knowing who the premier of Tasmania is, which is the largest city in California or when the kingdoms of England and Scotland began to be ruled by one and the same monarch.

But the line between factual knowledge and linguistic knowledge cannot be drawn sharply. We have referred earlier to the way in which names can become words (e.g. *boycott, sandwich,* 2.2 above). Some names of people and places – and 'facts' about them – are so well known in a community that users of the language do assume that everyone knows them. An old Australian idiom, *to do a Melba,* 'to keep saying goodbye, to make repeated farewells', drew on common knowledge of the singer Dame Nellie Melba and her several 'farewell' appearances. Legendary figures may figure in discourse as if they were common nouns, like King Canute, who is supposed to have commanded the tide to turn, unsuccessfully of course, but deliberately so, in order to demonstrate to his followers that there were limits to human power, even the power of a king. Thus a fiction writer says of a character that he was 'Canute controlling the waves' and assumes that readers will know the story of Canute so that they grasp the ironic meaning. In fact, the meaning of 'Canute' may have generalised to anyone who resists or denies evidence – or even to the act of resistance itself, as in the phrase 'doing a Canute'. On 24 July 2002, the Melbourne *Age* had a headline in its business section 'Bush does a Canute with falling US stockmarkets'. The article reported President George W. Bush's claim that the future was 'going to be bright', despite, in the words of the article, 'much evidence to the contrary'.

It may not be essential to one's ability to speak English to know who the first president of the USA was or who the prime minister of England was in 1945. But discourse does sometimes assume such knowledge in its meaningful progress. Some historical figures do carry meaning. An American writer refers to 'George Washington's cherry

tree': according to the story, the young George chopped down a cherry
tree and when questioned by his father, confessed to the misdeed,
saying that he was unable to lie. The writer assumes that most or all
readers will know the background story. Or, to take the example of the
British wartime prime minister, a search of a few corpora for references
to Churchill naturally produces many references to the man – in historical accounts, political discussions, and so on – but also yields some
uses where the name is used descriptively, again presupposing that
author and audience have some shared understanding or image of the
man. For example, someone is described as 'of Churchillian mien'; a
politician is recorded as having told reporters that a recent 'stirring'
speech was 'his Churchill speech'.

In fact there is no way of drawing a principled distinction between
knowledge of the language – the lexicogrammar – and extra-linguistic
knowledge. Not long ago I was walking out of a particularly complicated car park in Canberra when a car pulled up beside me. The driver
asked me if I could point him towards the exit – *any* exit – and added
that he'd been driving round the car park for some time and had
'done more miles than Burke and Wills'. Now I'm not sure whether I
have ever heard that phrase before, and I don't recognise this as a
familiar Australian idiom; but I do know (as probably most Australians
do without having to look them up) that Burke and Wills were
explorers who undertook an ambitious journey across Australia from
south to north and then back again, but died of starvation before
completing their expedition. Presumably the man assumed I knew that
much, to be able to share in his self-deprecating joke about arduous
and fruitless travels across a car park. (The Bank of English corpus
records a couple of idiomatic uses: 'She's seen more Australia than
Burke and Wills' is similar to the phrase I heard, while 'Waugh and
Healy [Australian cricketers] are as much an Aussie institution as
Burke and Wills' at least implies that Burke and Wills are well known in
Australia.)

An example like this illustrates the uncertain edges of social discourse. Perhaps the man who spoke to me came from an area of
Australia where his turn of phrase was a familiar idiom to most people.
I might have simply been ignorant of his usage, just as any of us can
easily find ourselves out of our depth when we move into a community
where we are not accustomed to local usage. Perhaps he was simply an
individual with a liking for a certain kind of Aussie imagery, and I will
never hear the phrase again. Perhaps the phrase is in fact more widely
used than I realise, and it's just that I have failed to come across it.
Perhaps even my mention of it in this book might cause it to be quoted

more often. Whatever the possibilities might be, the eventual status and meaning of the wording will depend on further usage, on uses which bring the phrase into play as an increasingly well-known idiom, or on absence of use which will ensure that the phrase does not enter a pool of linguistic resources nor find its way into dictionaries and phrase books.

For words are first and foremost elements of text, elements occurring in actual discourse, not isolated items listed in a dictionary (2.2 above). Traditional lexicographers have separated linguistic knowledge from encyclopaedic knowledge by a process of decontextualisation, trying to describe the meaning of words in isolation from their contexts. In this view, if we could detach from a word all its links to relevant contexts, we should be left with the isolated unadulterated meaning. But access to modern corpora has made it possible to study texts far more intensively, and corpus linguists are now able to show the semantic cohesion of textual segments. If we are no longer limited to single words detached from their contexts, if we do away with decontextualisation, we need not insist on the distinction between linguistic and encyclopaedic knowledge.

What we normally call encyclopaedic knowledge is in fact almost always discourse knowledge. For most of us nowadays, everything we know and are able to know about King Canute, George Washington, the explorers Burke and Wills, and Winston Churchill, is based on texts. Even photos and film and video mean relatively little without accompanying text. If we consider how much our encyclopaedic knowledge owes to our discourse knowledge, the distinction virtually disappears. This too is a topic we will revisit in Chapters 3 and 4.

2.9 Language and languages

The diversity of human languages is an inescapable truth. Some languages, such as those of Western Europe or the group of languages sometimes called the 'dialects' of Chinese, do show similarities, because of common ancestry or a history of contact, but many languages are strikingly different from each other. Even where languages have much in common – as English and German do, two languages which are historically related and which show many cultural similarities, including a long tradition of being influenced by Latin and French – differences are still of some consequence. Modern English and German are not mutually intelligible and it takes considerable time and effort for adult speakers of the one language to learn to function reasonably well in the other.

Taking a wider sweep across the world, languages differ more radically than English and German do. Phonetically, some languages have sounds and patterns of pronunciation which seem quite impossible to speakers of other languages. The click sounds of some languages of southern Africa seem odd and difficult to those who have not grown up speaking such a language; needless to say, there is nothing difficult or bizarre about these sounds to those who do habitually use them. The dental fricative consonant at the beginning of English words like *thin* and *thorn* is a constant challenge to those whose mother tongues do not have the consonant, while the various uvular and glottal consonants of Arabic strike a speaker of English as impossible to pronounce.

Grammatically, the patterns of one's own language become so habitual that alternatives seem perverse and sometimes beyond learning. Hence we hear people who have learned English as a second language saying things like 'you like coffee, isn't it?' (instead of 'you like coffee, don't you?') or 'I'm working here since 1995' (instead of 'I've been working here since 1995'). In so doing, they are simply following the patterns of another language and failing to follow those of English. And of course speakers of English learning other languages make other – but comparable – errors. The patterns of one's own language are 'natural', ingrained enough to interfere systematically with the learning of different patterns.

What is true of pronunciation and grammar is also true of meaning. Even related words which look or sound similar often differ in meaning. An example is a word already referred to more than once in this chapter (2.2 and 2.5), namely *patron*. Commonly used in English to refer to the customers in a hotel or restaurant, the seemingly equivalent word in French means 'boss' rather than 'customer'. Other deceptive differences between French and English include French *large*, which corresponds to English 'broad' or 'wide' rather than to 'large', and French *sensible*, which is closer to the meaning of English 'sensitive' than to 'sensible'. In French, 'sensitive skin' is *peau sensible*, and a sensitive or tender spot might be described as *l'endroit sensible*. But note how the words and meanings of different languages do not line up as perfect equivalents across languages: when the French *endroit sensible* is used metaphorically it is probably better translated into English as 'sore point' rather than 'sensitive spot'.

To take an example from Dutch, the word *serieus* looks and sounds to an English speaker as though it ought to correspond to English 'serious'. And in a sense it does, in some contexts, particularly where a contrast is implied with humorousness or lightheartedness, as in a person looking a bit serious or a happy occasion turning out to be too serious. But this word is not used of, for example, a 'serious problem' or 'serious illness'. Here the relevant Dutch word is *ernstig*. You might shrug off a minor injury as *niet ernstig*, 'not serious', or you might be accused of *(iets) niet ernstig nemen*, 'not taking (something) seriously'.

More seriously, whole areas of meaning are differentiated and elaborated in some languages but seemingly unimportant in others. Some languages, like Dutch and Italian, have morphological devices for expressing diminutives which are used to signal not just smaller size of an object but also (sometimes) endearment and informality. Compare Dutch *kast* 'cupboard, wardrobe', *kastje* 'little cupboard, locker', *kop* 'mug', *kopje* 'cup', *hand* 'hand', *handje* 'little hand'. But these so-called diminutive forms may be used in various ways: for example *handje* may be used in talking about a young child's hands but it is also the appropriate form in the metaphorical 'lend a hand' with a job. The informal or casual effect of diminutives is also evident in a request like *mag ik een sigaretje van je?* 'may I (get) a cigarette from you?', where the diminutive form *sigaretje* of course does not indicate that the speaker is asking for a small cigarette but is rather a device to downplay the request (somewhat as an English speaker might ask, strictly inaccurately, to 'borrow' a cigarette, or might add the word 'just', as in 'could I just ask you …'). Some languages have similarly extensive use of diminutives – Czech and Italian, for example – but while English does have some comparable morphology, as shown by *book* and *booklet* or *dog* and *doggie*, it is not nearly as widely used, nor used with the same elaboration of interpersonal meaning.

A language like English has an infinitely expandable set of numerals and considerable resources for talking mathematically – ways of talking about addition and multiplication and solving equations and so on. By contrast Australian Aboriginal languages have relatively few terms for numerals and little comparable resources (although with the arrival of a more technologically-oriented culture in Australia they have started to acquire such resources). And so one could go on, comparing the more elaborate semantics of Australian Aboriginal kinship and clan structure with the simpler resources of English, among many other possible examples.

Languages do influence each other semantically, and this is an important observation for two reasons. First, it underlines the point that languages differ from each other, for if they were not significantly different, there would be nothing significant for other languages to imitate or acquire. Second, it is a reminder that while differences are real enough, languages are not always separated by impenetrable boundaries or yawning chasms. Just as individuals can learn foreign languages, so cultures can acquire the characteristics of other cultures – although it must be said that they never seem to end up identical.

In Australian Aboriginal languages there is usually a verb which refers to hitting or striking with an implement, potentially hurting or even killing, as in clubbing or spearing an animal. (A different verb is used of hitting someone or something with a missile such as a stone.) In Aboriginal English, the word *kill* is now used regularly not with the sense of causing to die or ending life, but with the sense of attacking or hitting or beating up. The history of languages is full of such semantic readjustments, often in conjunction with major cultural changes. When Christianity came to England in the seventh century, not only did Old English adopt Latin words already in Christian use (such as *maesse* 'mass' from Latin *missa*, and *scrin* 'shrine' from Latin *scrinium*) but Old English words took on new meanings. The Old English word for 'build' started to be used to mean 'edify', on the analogy of Latin *aedificare*, which already had the sense of 'build up' or 'edify' as well as 'build' in a more material sense. The Old English *halig* 'holy' was probably derived from a word to do with health or wellbeing (compare Modern English words like *hale* and *whole*) but it came to be used in a specifically Christian way. In fact in the Old English period, the plural of the word was used to translate the Biblical 'saints', i.e. 'the holy ones'. This usage survives in certain names such as 'Allhallows' (All Saints) and most notably 'Halloween' (Allhallows Eve), but, in another semantic adjustment, the word 'saint' (Old English *sanct*, from Latin *sanctus*) has now taken on the Christian sense of 'a holy one'.

Just as Latin has influenced English, so elsewhere languages which were in one way or another dominant or prestigious, like Arabic as the language of Islam, or English as the language of the British Empire, have left their mark on many other languages. Thus Arabic has influenced Malay (now Indonesian and Malaysian) and Urdu, and English has influenced many languages of sub-Saharan Africa.

When the Netherlands ruled what is now Indonesia as the Dutch East Indies, the Malay that was widely used in the area took over many words from Dutch, many of them still evident in modern Indonesian, from *rem* for the brakes of a vehicle to *bank* for the financial institution, from *dokter* for a medical doctor to *gang* for a lane or passageway. As English words extended their meaning in the Christianisation of England, so Indonesian words acquired wider uses in the period of Dutch colonial rule, as illustrated by the word *pusat* which refers to the navel or to the centre of a (more or less) circular pattern like a thumbprint, but now also has a far wider range of uses for abstract and institutional 'centres' such as 'centre of gravity' or 'language centre'. As always, the semantic patterns of language shift and adjust. To take another example, the Indonesian word *rumah* 'house' now enters into a series of specialised combinations such as *rumah penatu* 'laundry' and *rumah sakit* 'hospital' (compare Dutch *washuis* 'laundry', *ziekenhuis* 'hospital', based on the Dutch *huis* 'house').

Given the evident diversity of human languages and cultures, and the ways in which they interact, often influencing each other and copying from each other, but never quite ending up the same, it makes sense to say that languages have their own semantic strengths, their own areas of richness and elaboration. It is this that often makes learning another language a rewarding experience, an experience which changes one's horizon and opens up new views of the world. And this may make it seem all the more surprising that anyone has ever entertained the notion of universal grammar or universal semantics. In fact there have been a number of attempts to generalise across languages, to find a kind of ideal model or to find something that could be said to underlie all human languages. An arrogant but not unknown way of denying or minimising language differences is to focus on one or a few languages and to regard any language that is not similar to them as deviant or degraded. European respect for Latin has sometimes led to this kind of view, especially when accompanied by an imperialistic willingness to dismiss many non-European languages as not really fully-fledged languages. But there have also been more thoughtful and more scholarly attempts to define some kind of universal grammar or universal semantics. We have referred earlier (2.7) to Chomsky's postulation in the 1960s of a 'deep structure' that might be common to all languages. Chomsky looked back to those who had thought along similar lines – for example the grammarians working at the convent of Port Royal in France in the seventeenth century, who theorised that the categories and structures of grammar could be related to universal logic or universal thinking.

Universalism, as a theoretical position on language, usually rests on one of two strategies. One is to postulate something which is actually not observable, like a set of 'universal concepts' or Chomsky's 'deep structure'. Universal concepts, for example, could exist only in human minds, or perhaps in some common human consciousness, if there is such a thing. We cannot observe and record what is in the human mind in the same way that we can observe and record human behaviour, in particular what people say or write. This is in itself no objection to universalism as a belief, since most of us have beliefs of one kind or another, whether belief in God or in fellow humans or in ghosts or in good or bad luck, or beliefs about the future or about what is valuable and significant in human living. But it is important to recognise the role and nature of belief here. Those who do believe in universal concepts, underlying the semantics of all languages, will argue that one can only put forward theoretical postulates and then check their explanatory power or test them against the evidence, for example by looking for their consequences in observable behaviour. It then becomes necessary to face questions about what exactly constitutes a valid check or test of one's theoretical position, and not simply to begin to take theoretical hypotheses as probable or self-evident. Of course one can live by faith – as we all do to a greater or lesser extent – but faith needs to be acknowledged as faith, not presented as indisputable scientific finding.

The other strategy found in universalism is, in one way or another, to set up a supposedly universal framework or inventory from which all languages make some kind of selection. Thus one might claim that there is a vast inventory of universal concepts or components of meaning, including presumably very general ones like 'human' and 'animate' and 'concrete' (which might be semantic components of many words in many languages) as well as much more specific ones that would differentiate (semantically) a snail from a slug, a mountain from a hill, saying from telling, hitting with an implement from hitting with a missile, and so on. The fact that languages differ from each other semantically – for example Dutch makes no lexical distinction between 'snail' and 'slug', just as English does not have separate lexical items for 'hit with an implement' and 'hit with a missile' – is then allowed for by saying that each language makes its own selection from the universal inventory. This is an interesting ploy. On the one hand it recognises the difficulty of the universalist position, for the 'universal' inventory is no longer genuinely common to all languages. On the other hand it raises the question of what kind of existential status this inventory has. Since the inventory is by definition larger or more comprehensive than the semantics of any one language, it must exist beyond or above specific languages. If it resides in human minds, then part of it is redundant or irrelevant to the language(s) known to any individual mind, which must surely put that part of it well beyond any kind of empirical verification. And if it is not confined within individual minds, where is it to be found and how can we access and study it?

Much has been written about languages and their differences and similarities. What we have said here goes only some way towards justifying our reluctance to postulate universal grammar and universal concepts and our preference for a more cautiously descriptive approach to linguistic behaviour. We emphasise again that we are not suggesting that languages are so different from each other that they constitute totally different worlds, cut off from each other. We do acknowledge that languages show similarities. But except where languages happen to be quite closely related, their similarities cannot be grounded in a core vocabulary or an underlying and invariant set of concepts or anything as temptingly concrete or specific as that. Rather, the similarities are better understood in terms of functions and general design rather than in terms of inventories of items or components or rules.

The analytical and theoretical problem here is not unique to linguistics or semantics, for it affects most of our study and understanding of humans and their behaviour and institutions. It is rather as if we set out to see what was common to wedding ceremonies around the world; or what was universal about food and eating; or what was common to all the world's practices of religious worship. We might try to find the objects common to weddings (such as rings or flowers or special clothing) or we might look for a universal underlying structure (for example with people arriving, participating and departing in a certain typical sequence). But if we really pursued such a project along these lines, we would soon find it futile. Rings and bouquets and wedding cakes are indeed part of many weddings in many countries but they are not universal. They were certainly not part of most marriage ceremonies in Australia or Papua New Guinea or the Amazon Basin before the arrival of white colonists and their culture. In fact, the very notion of 'wedding ceremony' already suggests a European perspective on the event. If we wanted to assess universality in a more open-minded and realistic way, we would do better to step back from our immediate experience of weddings and to start to think in a more broadly functional way: how human beings form alliances or partnerships for sexual intercourse and parenting, how these partnerships are integrated into wider social structures, whether and how these partnerships need to be endorsed or recognised by other members of the larger society, and how these partnerships are entered into and characterised, in theory or in practice, by commitment and loyalty. Even here, we are still talking in English, using modern English words like *parenting* and *partnership*, which already project a certain light on what we think we are looking for and talking about. But at least at this point we have lifted our sights above a mere search for shared objects and entities, a search which is bound to fail, and we have started to think in a more general and productive way about what it is that characterises people and their social behaviour as human. The wording used here may not satisfy everyone – I can think of several lines of objection to the phrase 'partnerships for sexual intercourse and parenting' – but if it is hard even to frame what we are studying, that is precisely because we are facing the genuinely rich complexity and diversity of humankind.

Much the same could be said about food and eating, or about religious worship. There are few if any foodstuffs which are truly universal. Even if certain items such as sandwiches and hamburgers are now obtainable in some kinds of hotels and restaurants around the world, they are definitely not consumed by everyone everywhere. Even items that are very widespread – say bread – take different forms and shapes and are eaten in different ways. (Indian bread typically has a different appearance and function from French bread, for example.) What might be universal is rather the human need to eat, the need for substances such as starch and sugar, human enjoyment of eating, and so on. Likewise with the practice of worship in settings as diverse as the mosque, the synagogue, the temple, the church and the chapel: universals are found not in the objects and components that are present in worship but in the ways in which humans function as worshipping beings.

So also with language. If there are universals of language, they are best approached from the perspective of how language functions in human life and how it serves human purposes. All languages seem to be systems for making meanings, meanings encoded in wording which is expressed in spoken form (or, in the case of many languages, spoken and written form). All languages seem to provide ways of talking about things or entities and, by contrast, ways of talking about events or processes or relationships. (This distinction is often related to the grammatical distinction between nouns and verbs, but the relationship is by no means a direct and simple one.) All languages seem to project both experiential or representational meanings (relating to what can be said about the world and facts and events and so on) and what can be called interpersonal meanings (relating to how speakers or writers are interacting with hearers or readers). This is a quite different approach to universals from one which seeks to find a common core vocabulary or a universal set of concepts. (For more detailed exposition of this kind of functional perspective on language, see Eggins 1994, esp. Chapter 1, or Halliday 1994a, esp. pp. xvii–xx, xxvi–xxxv.)

2.10 Translation

Translation from one language to another is sometimes described as if it were a process of rewording the same meaning, a process of finding new words to express the same meaning. While this may sometimes be a convenient way of describing the process, and good translators do have a commitment to what we might call loyalty to the original, there are several objections to conceptualising translation as if it were a process of taking meaning out of the words of one language and re-expressing it, unchanged, in the words of another language.

In the first place, most translators know from experience the rashness of claiming that they are preserving meaning unchanged. As we have seen in the previous section of this chapter, meaning is not isomorphic across languages. To take a simple example, if you translate the English word *sister* into the Australian Aboriginal language Pitjantjatjara, you have to choose between a word meaning 'older sister' and one meaning 'younger sibling'. (There is of course another Pitjantjatjara word meaning 'older brother', but there is no lexical distinction between 'younger sister' and 'younger brother'.) You cannot simply transfer 'the same meaning'. Information about the relative age of the sister may be implicit in the English text or may be entirely unmentioned and irretrievable. And even if you can establish that the sister is in fact a younger sister, you still won't be expressing exactly the same meaning in the relevant Pitjantjatjara word, since the sex of the sibling will now become as invisible as relative age is in English. Of course you can make a special effort to bring information to the fore, in both English and Pitjantjatjara: for example in English it is perfectly possible to use expressions like 'older sister' or 'younger sibling', as we have just done above; but the words are still not exactly equivalent. English *sibling* is not a word which is normal in the English-speaking world in the same way as the Pitjantjatjara words in the Pitjantjatjara community. It belongs to anthropological or sociological discourse (or to discussions of translation!) rather than to talk of family and friends. I sometimes heard my father talk about his brother and sister, but never about his 'two siblings'; and I have sometimes heard my wife refer to her sister and (two) brothers but never to her 'three siblings'. In fact, even at this point, we have not exhausted the problem of translation, since the Pitjantjatjara words actually refer not only to brothers and sisters but also to parallel cousins (children of mother's sisters and children of father's brothers). But enough has been said to indicate that even apparently simple words cannot be assumed to match each other across languages.

This example has been a little too abstract. In real translation work, one has a context and purpose (say translating a service manual or interpreting in a court of law or assisting in a land claim) and problems have to be solved in their context. Let's take another example and place it in context. Suppose I want to send a letter to a number of people around the world. Let's say it is a letter inviting them to contribute a paper to a journal. As I draft this letter in English I will have to make a decision on how to begin it. There are quite a few options. If I know all the names and can adapt each letter, I might begin each letter with a personal address, choosing among options like 'Dear Professor Jones' or 'Dear Susan' or 'Dear Sue'. If I am unable or unwilling to make each letter specific in that way, and am prepared to be rather formal, I can choose among options like 'Dear Colleague' and 'Dear Sir or Madam'. I can even take the option of omitting such an opening entirely. Without going through all the reasons why some people dislike letters beginning 'Dear Sir or Madam' and some dislike letters without any salutation at all, let us say that I opt to begin my letter 'Dear Colleague'.

Now I want to translate my letter, and I want it to be 'the same letter' in several languages. If I translate the letter into Dutch, I now have options which were not available in English. At the point where 'Dear' occurs in the English there are two possibilities in Dutch: *Beste*, which is appropriate for friends, and *Geachte* which is typical of official or business correspondence. (There is actually a third option, *Lieve*, but this is familiar and affectionate and not an option to consider in this context.) Thus there is no simple way to match the generality of English 'Dear ...', which can be used quite intimately ('Dear Susie') as well as very formally ('Dear Madam'). The Dutch version of the letter forces a choice between a more familiar option and a more formal one. Even in this small detail, we cannot claim that the Dutch letter will have exactly the same meaning as the English one.

In the second place, it is not at all clear that we have any way of separating meaning from wording. To hark back to Saussure's classic metaphor, a linguistic sign is like a sheet of paper, with 'thought' (or a concept or meaning) on one side and its expression (the form or actual word) on the other (2.6 above). One cannot isolate either side from the other (Saussure 1972, p. 157). What translators actually do when 'discovering' or 'analysing' the meaning of a text involves paraphrasing within the relevant languages rather than thinking in any genuine sense 'outside' the languages. Thus, when translators ponder what the text really means or search for the right words in the translation, they range over words of similar or contrasting meaning, over phrases that might expand the meaning or words that might condense the meaning, both in the language of the text in front of them and in the language into which they are translating. What they do not do, as far as we can understand the process, is to engage in some kind of abstract thinking that is independent of both languages. Consider the example we have just been through, of translating 'Dear Colleague' into Dutch. The translator, aware of the context, runs through options in both languages and thinks about what sort of equivalence might be achieved. It seems highly unlikely that translators engage in any sort of higher level abstraction in which they categorise kinds of 'dearness' (whatever that might be) independently of both Dutch and English.

Third, suppose that we could somehow separate meaning from wording. How could we then express meaning, other than through language itself? The suggestion that we can extract meaning from the words of one language and then put it into the words of another, poses the question of where this meaning is and how it is represented when it is, so to speak, in between the two languages. In some cases, depending on the kind of text they are translating and its meaning, translators may be able to visualise objects and situations that are referred to, but even here it is doubtful whether they do this in a way that is independent of language. Is it really desirable, let alone possible, for a translator to imagine an agricultural tractor or a fluorescent lamp or a voicemail system without thinking of descriptions of it in language?

The examples that we have considered should make it clear that scepticism about metaphors of 'extracting' and 'transferring' or 'rewording' meaning is not the same as saying that translation is impossible. Experienced translators work quickly and skilfully with their linguistic material but they do not deceive themselves that they handle meaning detached from texts, nor do they claim to translate in such a way that their output is a perfect semantic match of the original text.

As Haas puts it

> The translator ... constructs freely. [A translator] is not changing vehicles or clothing. [A translator] is not transferring wine from one bottle to another. Language is no receptacle, and there is nothing to transfer. To produce a likeness is to follow a model's lines. The language [the translator] works in is the translator's clay.
>
> (1962, p. 228).

3 Language and corpus linguistics

Wolfgang Teubert

3.1 Are all languages the same?

'According to Chomsky, a visiting Martian scientist would surely conclude that aside from their mutually unintelligible vocabularies, Earthlings speak a single language' (Pinker, 1994, p. 232). Indeed, if we discount the meaning of words, sentences and texts, our natural languages share many characteristics. They are linear. Utterances have a beginning and end, and between beginning and end we find a string of sounds or of characters, perhaps ideographic as in Chinese, or alphabetical as in most European languages. This is, of course, also the case for sign languages. An utterance in a sign language is again a string, in this case of signs such as hand and finger movements and facial expressions.

Utterances differ from pictures. Utterances are one-dimensional, pictures are two-dimensional. Even if we try to describe a picture, the description will be inherently one-dimensional. Linearity would also be a characteristic of the language of the visiting Martian scientist. All languages are systems for signifying content. Each utterance has a content. But the content is not the utterance. The utterance is a sequence of signs which represent the content, which stand in place of the content. The utterance 'a Martian scientist visits Earthlings' can be said to represent an image, a photograph or a mental image which is two- or even three-dimensional. But the utterance is always a one-dimensional string of signs. John Sinclair, one of the pioneers of corpus linguistics, is fond of repeating what he believes to be a quote of the grammarian E. O. Winter that 'grammar is needed because you cannot say everything at the same time'. This is certainly the reason why all natural languages need grammar, and perhaps also why these various grammars can be described if not in identical, then in very similar terms.

Is this what Noam Chomsky meant (Chomsky 1957)? Not quite. Chomsky argues that all humans share the same language faculty, an innate faculty that regulates the ways signs are to be organised so that they become utterances. This is what is called grammar. In Chomsky's view, the innate language faculty shapes the grammar. This is not to say that all languages share the same grammar, not even on a deeper level. Today, in his minimalist programme, Chomsky sees the language organ as an apparatus that gives limited options. Adjectives, for example, can precede the noun they modify, or they can follow it. But all languages have adjectives and nouns and several other parts of speech. They are universal, they are shared by all human languages. So, and this is the important point, the language faculty is contingent, i.e. it happens to be the way it is, but it could have been different (and the language faculty of Martians might be different). The philosophical problem connected with this stance is that its credibility depends on conceiving of a convincing language, a language that could exist but does not exist – a language that does not comply with the settings of the language organ but is otherwise, in functional terms, equivalent to existing natural languages.

Chomsky's views on universal grammar (in a more recent version than referred to earlier in 2.7) are found in his book *New Horizons in the Study of Language and Mind* (Chomsky 2000, pp. 7–15). Whether he has succeeded in presenting his case convincingly is a matter of contention. Geoffrey Sampson (1997) in *Educating Eve: The 'Language Instinct' Debate* shows that there is evidence to the contrary in respect of many of the language features that Chomsky and Pinker claim as universals.

Traditional linguistics has been good at describing how syntax, morphology and inflection work. There is a set of basic assumptions, most of which have been around since classical times and which are used for describing any language that linguists stumble across. These assumptions include the facts that there is an entity we call a sentence, another entity we call a clause, that there are subjects, objects and predicates, and that there are words. There are different kinds of words, so-called parts of speech (from Latin *partes orationis*), featuring prominently among them: nouns, adjectives, verbs and adverbs (the big four), and less prominently others, such as pronouns, determiners, prepositions, and depending on the language or the particular grammatical theory, a few more or many more. In a language such as English, a word can come in different forms. The noun *table*, for example, can be a singular form (*table*) or a plural (*tables*). In many European languages a finite verb can be characterised by the properties person and number (e.g. first-person singular as in English 'I laughed', or first-person plural 'we laughed'), tense (e.g. past tense, present tense), mood (e.g. indicative, subjunctive) and voice (active, passive). Words can be combined to form larger units such as noun phrases, or verb phrases, or other kinds of phrases, and several phrases can be put together to form a clause, or even a sentence.

There are of course differences in the details of grammatical description and theory, and all these entities form sets with fuzzy edges. For instance, some English -*ing* forms are usually described as verb forms ('she was laughing'), others as nouns ('laughing uses quite a few muscles'). Different linguistic schools tend to define these entities in different ways, and they give them different names. For example, in the sentence 'I enjoyed the concert', many linguists would call 'the concert' the object (of the verb 'enjoy'); but a more general term such as 'complement' may also be used, while some linguists would differentiate various kinds of 'objects', distinguishing for example between the material goal of verbs like 'hit' and 'break' and the object of behavioural or attitudinal verbs like 'enjoy' and 'dislike'.

The basic entities and categories of grammar are nevertheless common ground for many linguists. Whatever a specific school of linguists may call them, they are to a large extent translatable into each other. Noam Chomsky also subscribes to them. They are used to describe not just English, or other Indo-European languages, but, in principle, all languages. Some languages may display features that others do not have: for example, many Australian Aboriginal languages have a dual category in contrast to the singular and the plural, to indicate that there are exactly two, or a pair of entities; compare Pitjantjatjara *ngayulu* 'I', *ngali* 'we two', *nganana* 'we three or more'. Some languages, like Indonesian, do not have categories of the verb such as tense and mood. But principally it is the same finite set of entities and properties that we use to describe any of the Earthlings' languages, and it wouldn't be surprising if we used them also for all the Martian dialects once we come across them.

Smaller entities can be combined to form larger entities. Syntactic rules tell us which combinations are grammatical, and which are not. For many linguists, the smallest syntactic entities are words. For some, the morpheme is the smallest unit. Morphemes are parts of words, the smallest linguistic elements to which we can assign a meaning or a function. The word form *singing* consists of two morphemes: *sing* and -*ing*. The morpheme -*ing* can occur in most other verbs, as well; we find it in certain syntactic constructions, e.g. after a certain set of verbs like *help, see, hear*: 'he heard her singing in the rain'. Because its occurrence may be said to be caused by syntax, some linguists take morphosyntax to be part of syntax, and for them, morphemes are part of syntax. But generally, if syntax is held to be something different from the rest of the lexicogrammatical systems, it is understood to describe how words can be assembled to form a grammatical sentence.

Seen in this light, words are the basic tissue of syntax. They make up the vocabulary, the lexicon of a language. Linguists, including Chomsky, agree that the lexicon is a more or less finite list of lexical entries. Each lexical entry consists of the word, an indication of the part of speech it belongs to, and the syntactic and semantic properties it has. The entry for *boy* would tell us that it is a noun, that it is countable (hence there is a plural *boys*), and that it fits, according to specifiable rules and constraints, into a slot (i.e. a terminal element of the syntactic structure of a given sentence), which asks for a word denoting a human being (such as the subject and the object position of the verb *love*). The sentence 'Big boys love intelligent girls' could be described as having the structure: adjective + noun + (transitive) verb + adjective + noun. Each noun and the verb exemplifies a slot into which we can insert a suitable lexical element taken from the lexicon.

Entities, properties and rules: this is the stuff that, according to Chomsky, constitutes each language. Therefore Chomsky's claim about the similarity of languages is not totally implausible. Languages resemble each other because their phonology, syntax, and morphology can be described in the same – or at least similar – terms. For mainstream linguists, languages are all more or less the same. They may follow different rules, but they are made up of the same entities and share many properties.

But does this mean that entities, property types and rule types are language universals? This is not a question to which there is an easy answer. When we describe language, what kind of a reality are we describing? There are sound sequences, or chains of alphabetic characters (or other kinds of characters in languages that have non-alphabetic writing systems), which we are accustomed to interpret (successfully) as language. Linguists cut these strings into little bits and pieces and assign various functions to them. Certain bits (say in English those that can be preceded by a determiner, that can serve as heads of noun phrases or prepositional phrases, and that can be modified by an adjective phrase or a prepositional phrase) we call nouns. But does that mean that nouns are more than bundles of properties that we construe in our theory? In the sentence 'This is a fake diamond', is *fake* a noun or an adjective? Obviously it is modifying the indisputable noun *diamond*. In this sense, it shares the properties of adjectives. But usually adjectives are gradable (*big, bigger, biggest; short, shorter, shortest*), whereas *fake* is not. And usually adjectives can be used predicatively, as in 'the house is big, but the garden is small', or 'isn't his hair short!' The word *fake* can occur predicatively ('this diamond is fake') but many people might prefer to say 'this diamond is a fake'. Grammatical description would seem to require that we say that *fake* is an adjective in 'this diamond is fake', but a noun in 'this diamond is a fake'. So it may be up to the linguist or the lexicographer to decide whether they describe *fake* as a noun that can be used as an adjective, or as an adjective that can be used as a noun. Observations like these should throw some doubt on the widespread belief that entities or categories such as nouns exist independently of their description, in the way that apples and pears would still exist, even as something categorically different, if there was no one trying to categorise them.

Linguistics, Chomsky tells us, should describe the human faculty of generating an unlimited number of different grammatical sentences. This is why he and many of his followers are opposed to an empirical study of language (where empirical means the analysis of existing texts). No amount of text, Chomsky claims, can account for the competence to distinguish non-grammatical structures from grammatical structures. If we accept the premise that we can always utter a (grammatical) sentence that has never been uttered before, then the criterion of grammaticality is not something that can be found in texts. Rather, it is a feature of our language faculty. It is the application of the rules that can generate endlessly new, never heard before, sentences, all of which are grammatical, because they comply with the rules. This competence to produce new grammatical sentences is something (ideal) native speakers have.

The language faculty is therefore a feature of the mind. If we want to find out how language works, we have to look at the mind, and not at texts. Let us, for a moment, return to the sentence 'Big boys love intelligent girls'. This sentence structure can demonstrate the generative power of the language faculty. We can say that this sentence structure consists of two parts, the noun phrase *big boys* and the verb phrase *love intelligent girls*. This verb phrase consists of a transitive verb (*love*) and another noun phrase (*intelligent girls*). Noun phrases must have a head, usually a noun (such as *boy* or *girl*), either in the singular or in the plural, which can be preceded by a determiner (*a* or *the*), and modified by an adjective (such as *big* or *intelligent*). Now, this structure can easily yield a seemingly endless amount of different sentences, by the insertion of other nouns and verbs into the respective slots ('little girls hate spiteful boys', 'intelligent women admire intelligent men', and so on). Some verbs may not go well with some nouns as in: 'Fake diamonds hate eternity'. It seems we must therefore apply other rules as well that make sure that only those nouns are selected which go together with a particular verb. (For Chomsky, those so-called sub-categorisation rules are part of syntax, not of semantics, a position that is arguable.)

Chomsky's revolution in linguistics is about the generative power of rules. Rules, he says, do not describe what is there but what is possible. This focus on the generative aspect of language has changed the agenda of linguistics. The role of linguistics is no longer to interpret what we find in existing texts, but to describe the language faculty, or, in abstract terms, the competence of a speaker to produce new grammatical sentences. While rules were once formulated by language experts in order to facilitate the understanding of existing texts, or to help us to learn a foreign language, the task for a Chomskyan linguist is to discover the rules we follow as native speakers without even being aware of them, i.e. the rules which constitute the language faculty of human beings. In traditional linguistics, entities or categories like nouns, or tense, or person, were useful constructs in the framework of a theory. Rules were expressions of the linguist's ingenuity to make sense of the language evidence. Under the new agenda, language is like a game of chess. We are born with the capability to follow the rules without ever having to learn them. Chomskyan linguistics thus changes the status of linguistic rules. Rather than being tools for language analysis, they now become the metaphysically real essence of language.

Pre-modern linguistics in Europe was not concerned with the productivity of language. From the Middle Ages well into the nineteenth century, linguists were philologists, which was, at the time, more or less synonymous with classicists. Their research was on 'dead' languages: Latin, Greek and Hebrew. Their aim was not to produce new texts in these languages; they wanted to understand the texts we had inherited from ancient times. The rules they came up with were rules to help us make sense of the sentences. The rules were meant to describe what we were confronted with in the texts; they were not designed to empower us to become competent speakers of ancient Greek. The grammatical rules philologists were interested in were those that explained the specificity of Greek as compared to other languages, those that helped to understand their texts. Philologists were not interested in what was universal. Their rules were descriptive; they had to facilitate the analysis of textual evidence.

The philologists may not have had a scientific method. And yet we inherited from them the academic editions of classical and oriental texts we are still using today, together with comprehensive dictionaries, or rather glossaries, citing each noteworthy occurrence of any word embedded in its contexts and still providing an irreplaceable aid in understanding these texts.

Hermeneutics was the philosophical basis not of linguistics as we know it today but of philology. Hermeneutics is the art (or craft) of interpretation. In the early Middle Ages, this meant interpretation particularly of the Bible, but later also of the other classical texts. The goal of hermeneutics is to find out what a text means. What, indeed, does a text mean? Do we have to find out what the authors *thought* was the meaning of their texts? The authors might not tell us that explicitly, or they might tell us but be deceiving us in one way or another. Whatever they say, it is not the meaning of their texts. Or is the meaning of a text what the text means to me? Then meaning is something subjective, individual, something that cannot be validated by other readers. Meaning must be something else. When we encounter the word *love* in a medieval text, can we find out what the word meant then? Is there a methodology to answer this question? Is there a possibility of coming to an understanding that is shared by our fellow linguists? This is the key question hermeneutics is concerned with.

Particularly in the English-speaking countries, hermeneutics and philology have lost much of their earlier appeal. Since the first years of the twentieth century, British empiricism has given way to the new paradigm of analytic philosophy. This brand of philosophy, dating back both to Cambridge and connected with names such as Bertrand Russell, and equally to the Vienna circle and connected with names such as Mach, Carnap and (the young) Wittgenstein, is concerned with truth and reality. The question that is at the core of the current mainstream paradigm of the philosophy of language is not what a text, a sentence, a word means but how we can know whether it is true, whether it truly reflects the discourse-external reality or not. This is not a question hermeneutics, or philology, is concerned with. Philologists do not want to know under which conditions the sentence 'Mary, the mother of Jesus, was a virgin' is true; they content themselves with the exploration of the meanings of words, for example with questions such as whether the English word *virgin,* Latin *virgo,* Greek *parthenos* are appropriate translations of Hebrew *almah,* a word which usually just means 'young woman'.

Today, hermeneutics and philology are often considered dull, continental and old-fashioned. Edward Said, the famous Lebanese-American orientalist, is a noble exception. For him, philology is 'the extraordinarily rich and celebrated cultural position' that (not only) gave classics and orientalism their methodological basis. The philologist is the interpreter of bygone texts on the horizon of our own modernity. The philologist makes us understand cultural and intellectual history. This act of understanding is two-directional. Our understanding of these texts always also presents a challenge to the way in which we understand ourselves. Thus, 'philology problematises – itself, its practitioner, the present'. Said quotes Ernest Renan, a nineteenth-century orientalist: ' "The founders of the modern mind are philologists". And what is the modern mind ... if not "rationalism, criticism, liberalism [all of which] were founded on the same day as philology" ' (Said 1995, p. 132). What has made philology so unattractive in the twentieth century? Perhaps it is the sense of arbitrariness, of subjectivity, the lack of a truly scientific method. Interpreting a text is always an act, as opposed to a process that follows clearcut rules. The art of hermeneutics, the craft of philology always involves making decisions. It means choosing between alternatives, without unambiguous instructions on how to select one of the options.

In the nineteenth century we find a novel interest in languages, different from traditional philology. It was the century when the enlightenment finally bore fruit and nature began to be understood in terms of the laws of nature. The main foundations of the sciences as we know them today were laid. All the academic glamour now rested with the sciences; and the liberal arts, including the humanities, were relegated to backstage. The hermeneutical approach to language was not interested in immutable, eternal laws or rules. But that did not necessarily mean that there weren't any. The first domain of this new 'scientific' approach to language was the study of relationships among languages. That became the starting point of modern linguistics. It seemed that many languages spoken in Europe, in the near East and even as far away as India, were somehow related to each other, some closer, like Gaelic and Breton as Celtic languages, Lithuanian, Latvian and Old Prussian as Baltic languages, or Czech, Polish and Russian as Slavonic languages. There was Sanskrit, there were the Romance languages, there were the Germanic languages and many more, dead or alive. They all seemed to descend from one single language, Indo-European, and in the course of history they seemed to have become more and more separated from each other. Over the course of their existence, all these languages underwent change. What was *patēr* in Greek and *pater* in Latin became *padre* in Italian, *père* in French, *Vater* in German and *vader* in Dutch. English *father* developed from Old English *fæder*. All of them share, ultimately, the same ancestor. Similarly we can work out that the English word *rich* is related to the German *reich*, that early Germanic took the ancestral form of these words from Celtic, and that they are also related to the Latin *rex*, 'king'; or that the English word *glamour* is borrowed from Scots, while, in turn, the Scots word is derived from English *grammar*, which is, in turn, taken from Latin *(ars) grammatica.* (For more examples of historical changes, see 2.3.)

To the linguists of the nineteenth century who studied these phenomena, it seemed that the phonetic changes these words underwent in the course of history were governed by laws. The new linguists were less concerned with interpreting the meanings of texts, sentences, or words; they wanted to discover the laws of phonetic change. They were so confident in their scientific powers that they did not shy away from reconstructing ancestral languages, like Indo-European, even though no texts had survived. For the first time, it had become possible to describe language in terms of rules; rules that did not involve any decision-making on the part of the linguists, rules that produced results that had to be objectively correct once you accepted the premises. And if there were laws in phonetic change, there must also be laws for grammar. Therefore we can find, from the middle of the nineteenth century, a surge of literature on grammar, coinciding with a relegation of linguistic literature dealing with the vocabulary and the meaning of words to a less prominent position. This is still the situation in which we find ourselves today.

The modern linguists who succeeded the philologists saw themselves as scientists. However, from Ferdinand de Saussure (2.6 above) and the structuralists of the Prague school, to Louis Hjelmslev and Roman Jacobson, these linguists were not interested in the mental processes linked to language. They wanted to investigate the structure of language, based on analyses of texts, in order to understand the language system behind it, what Saussure called *la parole.* They wanted to describe a system of rules and means that existed independently of its individual speakers and its historical development (language synchrony) – although this system could also be studied from the historical point of view as a system gradually undergoing change according to language laws (language diachrony).

Thus the preoccupation with rules and laws characterises both non-Chomskyan modern linguistics (henceforth: standard linguistics, preoccupied with the idea of the system) and the Chomskyan variety of language studies (less interested in the system). Both varieties look at language as a system, which can be described in terms of rules, entities, categories and properties. From the structural point of view, these laws, entities and properties are, on a general level, more or less identical for all human languages, though rather, and at times profoundly, different in particulars.

Yet while Chomsky insists on the fundamental sameness of all languages (on a biological level), he also points out something very important: the vocabularies of all these languages across the world are (mostly) mutually unintelligible. People do speak different languages, and we do not understand each other. Doesn't this contradict the claim of sameness? In general, Chomsky's interest in the lexicon is, contrary to structuralists, only marginal. But, how important is the lexicon? How important is it to find out about the meanings of words?

3.2 Standard linguistics and word meaning

Even if Chomsky is technically wrong in positing an innate mechanism that determines, by a minimum of external input, the grammar of the language we grow up with, it still remains a fact that we seem to have much less difficulty in learning the syntax of a foreign language than its vocabulary. It is not always too difficult to construe grammatically correct sentences in a second language. But unless we are acquainted with it very thoroughly, we will make mistakes when we try to put our thoughts into words or to translate a text from our native language. We can follow rules easily. But how can we do the right thing if it seems all but impossible to teach us what is the right thing? This is indeed the impression if we attempt to let ourselves be guided by bilingual dictionaries. They offer many choices but few instructions.

The difference between grammar and vocabulary is largely a matter of perspective or method (1.6). For vocabulary, at least at first sight, there seem to be few rules which we can follow. Rules we can learn, and instructions we can follow. But no bilingual dictionary seems to be big enough to tell us how to translate an apparently quite simple word, like *grief*, into French. There are, according to the *Collins–Robert French Dictionary* (1998, repr. 2001), two main options: *chagrin* and *peine*. We are, however, not clearly told which of the alternatives to choose when. In the absence of clear instructions, even the most comprehensive bilingual dictionaries let us down when we want to translate a text into a non-native language.

The same dictionary gives us, as the equivalents for *sorrow*, the same two words it has given us for grief, *peine* and *chagrin*, plus another word, *douleur*, which is preceded by the ominous comment: '(stronger)'. It is not quite clear what this means: is this the word to use if your grief is stronger than average grief, or is *douleur* a stronger word than *peine* or *chagrin*? From the French perspective the two equivalents *sorrow* and *grief* appear to be synonyms. However, most native speakers of English agree that in these two sentences 'Grief gave way to a guilt that gnawed at him' and 'A magic harp music made its listeners forget sorrow', *grief* cannot be replaced by *sorrow*, and vice versa, so that, at least from the

monolingual English perspective, they cannot be regarded as synonyms. Things get even more confused when we look up, in our
bilingual dictionary, the English equivalents for the French word *chagrin*.
For *chagrin* we find: '(= affliction) grief, sorrow', and thus we become
curious what French *affliction* means in English. The only English
equivalent we are offered, though, is *affliction*. The French equivalents
of English affliction are *affliction* and *détresse*, while *détresse* is, we are
told, *distress* in English. As the English equivalents of *peine* we find
sorrow and *sadness*, but not *grief*. Our analysis thus reveals a distressing
absence of systematicity, and we are left wondering whether this is due
to the languages as they are or due to our inability to describe them
properly. (And it has to be said that the *Collins–Robert* is not just any
French–English dictionary. Together with the *Oxford–Hachette French
Dictionary*, it represents the apogee of modern bilingual lexicography.)

The meaning of words, as compared with the regularities of phonetic
change and sentence construction, is generally fuzzy and vague, not
only when we compare one language with another, but also from a
monolingual perspective. Words, single words, may be the ideal core
units when it comes to describing the working of grammar. But they
are much less the appropriate core units when we are interested in
meaning. Single words are commonly ambiguous. Dictionaries capture
this ambiguity by assigning two or more word senses to a word. As
shown above, we are confronted with the ambiguity of single words
whenever we want to translate into a foreign language. Then we have to
choose between several options, only one of which is acceptable. But
when we read a sentence or text we are not fooled, under normal
conditions, by any ambiguity. Usually we have no problem understanding what a sentence means. This is because we do not look at the
words in isolation, but embedded in a context. We read a word together with the words to its left and to its right; we have no problem in
knowing what a word means. Ambiguity is a consequence of our misguided belief that the single word is the unit of meaning. Units of
meaning are, by definition, unambiguous; they have only one meaning. While some words are units of meaning, many are not.

This enquiry into meaning makes the case that meaning is an aspect
of language and cannot be found outside of it. It is entirely within the
confines of the discourse that we can find the answer to what a unit of
meaning means, be it a single word or, more commonly, a collocation,
i.e. the co-occurrence of two or more words. A unit of meaning is a
word (often called the node or keyword) plus all those words within its
textual context that are needed to disambiguate this word, to make
it monosemous. As most of the more frequent words are indeed

polysemous, they do not, as single words, constitute units of meaning. As any larger dictionary tells us, for example, the word *fire* is ambiguous. It is therefore not a unit of meaning. In combination with the noun *enemy* it becomes a part of the collocation *enemy fire*, meaning 'the shooting of projectiles from weapons by the enemy in an armed conflict'. This collocation is (under normal circumstances) monosemous, and therefore a unit of meaning.

In the venerable field of phraseology, people have always been aware that language is full of units of meaning larger than the single word. When we hear 'She has not been letting the grass grow under her feet', we do not expect that to be literally true. Rather we have learned that the phrase 'not let the grass grow under one's feet' is an idiom, a unit of meaning which, according to the *New Oxford Dictionary of English* (*NODE*), means 'not delay in acting or taking an opportunity'. Indeed, the idiomaticity of language is a favourite topic of the discourse community. People like to talk about idioms; we feel that they are an important part of our cultural heritage. There is many a book explaining their origins, and there is hardly a dictionary that would dare to leave them out. Over the last century, we have come up with ever more refined typologies of idioms. Rosamund Moon's excellent study *Fixed Expressions and Idioms in English* (1998) provides a thorough corpus-based analysis of the phenomenon of idiomatic language. While some idioms are more or less inalterable ('it's raining cats and dogs'), others are somewhat ('a skeleton in the closet', 'a skeleton in the cupboard'). Most idioms oscillate between the two extremes of invariance and alterability. If we probe too deeply, our 'intuition' will often desert us. Are 'figments of imagination' an idiom, or can there be other figments? Does figment have a meaning of its own? We have to look in a corpus (here the British National Corpus) to find that there are indeed other figments, namely 'figments of linguistic bewitchment' and 'figments of fiction'. In the singular as well, there are some deviations from the prototypical collocate *imagination*: 'a figment of his own mind; a figment of my neurosis; a figment of its leaders' fantasies; a figment of his own name'. But these are four instances (i.e. less than 5 per cent) out of fifty-eight occurrences.

Idioms have found their way into bilingual dictionaries as well. The *Wildhagen Héraucourt German–English Dictionary* tells us that the English equivalent of *wie ein Blitz aus heiterem Himmel* [literally: like a bolt from a serene sky] is 'like a bolt from the blue'. Idioms feature rather prominently in foreign-language learning – with the result that speakers of English as a second language tend to overuse those they have learned, such as 'it's raining cats and dogs' (an idiom not greatly used by native speakers).

Modern linguistics has taught us that there is, indeed, a range of lexical constituents that can lay claim to being a unit of meaning. There are bound morphemes which have a meaning only by virtue of being part of a larger constituent (as the plural -s in English); there are free morphemes whose meanings seem to be rather invariable; there are words; and there are idioms including proverbs making up a full sentence. We have also learned that the borderlines between them are areas of contention. But while we would never doubt that morphemes are linguistic constructs, we have come to accept the ontological reality of the word (1.1).

Today, when we hear 'word', we normally think first of 'an element of speech', as the second sense given in the *OED* is circumscribed. If we believe Jack Goody (Goody 2000), this concept is foreign to oral societies. That is not so astonishing. In spoken language we normally do not insert a pause between words. Neither were the Greeks and Romans of antiquity in the habit of putting spaces between their written words. Where the space is inserted is largely a matter of convention, and not always well-established convention. Look in any large English dictionary for entries beginning with *half*. One dictionary has *half brother* as two words, another gives it a hyphen: *half-brother*. One has *halfback* as a single word, another has it with a hyphen. And so on. What is *linguistique de corpus* in French is *corpus linguistics* in English and *Korpuslinguistik* in German. There is no cogent reason other than tradition why there should be no space between the elements of German compounds, i.e why it is *Korpuslinguistik* rather than *Korpus Linguistik*.

Other modern languages missed the chance to define words by spaces. When it was recognised that in most cases it did not make sense to define a single Chinese character as a word and it became accepted that most Chinese words would consist of two or even three characters, it became a problem to identify words in a sentence. It is often the case that Chinese sentences can be cut up into words in different ways as long as we apply nothing but formal rules and leave out what they mean. Thus, in Chinese-language processing, there is still no segmentation software that is entirely reliable. How could it be different? We find cases of doubt in practically all Western languages. The problem of where there should be spaces and where not featured prominently in the German spelling reforms introduced in the mid-1990s.

Listening to foreign languages which we do not understand makes us even more aware of this problem. How do we know where a word begins and where it ends? Normally, people do not mark word boundaries phonetically. How do we know if two occurrences of the same concatenation of phonemes are occurrences of the same word (e.g. *no* versus *know*)? How can someone who does not speak English find out that *a* and *an* are two variants of the same word, the indefinite article, or that *the* in *the enemy* and *the* in *the friend* are variants of the same definite article, even though they are usually pronounced differently?

Languages in written form seem, at first, to simplify matters for us, particularly if they are written in the Latin alphabet. There we find spaces between the words. But how reliable are they? We have already seen some variation with words beginning with *half*. Is *half time* the same as *halftime* and *half-time*? Some dictionaries distinguish the musical term *half tone* from the printing term *halftone*. If *corpus linguistics* is one word in German (*Korpuslinguistik*), why is it two words in English? Or is it not? Do compounds consist of two words, or are they, in spite of the space between the two elements they consist of, just one word? Are words in languages as Hungarian or Welsh, which often seem to consist of a rather large number of elements, words in the same sense as English words? One Finnish word *talossanikin* means 'also in my house', which is translated as four words in English. In Chinese, we find the same spaces between all characters and there is no special indicator telling us which characters belong together or where a word begins or where it ends. In order to identify words we have to rely on wordlists and dictionaries. But they are the more or less arbitrary results of lexicographers at work. What are we left with once we take away the spaces between words?

We have always known that there are units of meaning larger than the single word. From early childhood, we are made aware of them. A phrase like 'to turn a blind eye to something' has become part of our cultural heritage. It is an idiom, and idioms have always been listed in our dictionaries. Yet we are not so readily aware that large portions of our texts are also made up from larger, often rather complex units of meaning, like *weapons of mass destruction* or *friendly fire*. For the most part, these are absent from our dictionaries. With our ingrained focus on the single word, that is not surprising. The larger units escape the attention of even experienced and well-trained lexicographers. They do not catch the eye when we come across them. Before the advent of corpora and of corpus linguistics, we did not even have a methodology to detect them. Neither standard linguistics nor Chomskyan linguistics can identify these units of meaning.

What is it then that makes the single word continue to be such an attractive unit in linguistics? Words seem to be almost ideal units for grammars, particularly grammars that do not touch on meaning. Noam Chomsky's *Syntactic Structures* (1956) is a good example. Here we find sentences (S), non-terminal symbols such as noun phrases (NP) and verb phrases (VP), and terminal symbols such as nouns (N), adjectives (Adj), determiners (Det), verbs (V), etc. Grammatical rules, starting with the S-symbol, generate strings of terminal symbols. In principle, we can insert the corresponding lexical elements in the slots provided by these symbols. Those lexical elements are single words. Up to a point, such a grammar seems to work, particularly for non-inflecting languages with a strict word order. We run into real trouble only when we demand that the sentences generated by this grammar make sense, that the sentences can be interpreted semantically. For a meaning-free grammar, the single word seems to be indeed the lexical element *par excellence.* In language learning, meaning-free grammars are good enough for constructing grammatical sentences in the target language, regardless of what they mean.

It is meaning, not grammar, that casts a shadow over the single word. A glance at any monolingual or bilingual dictionary confirms that the main problem of single words, from a semantic perspective, is their polysemy, their ambiguity and their fuzziness. For the verb *strike,* the *NODE* lists eleven senses. One of them is 'make (a coin or medal) by stamping metal'. As a sub-sense of this we find 'reach, achieve, or agree to (something involving agreement, balance, or compromise): the team has struck a deal with a sports marketing agency'. Though we might, upon consideration, come to accept this sense as a metaphorisation of striking coins, the actions seem to have hardly anything in common. The *strike* in *strike a deal* means something else than the *strike* in *strike coins,* and something different from the other ten senses ascribed to it in the dictionary entry. Indeed one could easily maintain that it has no meaning of its own; together with *deal* it does mean something, namely 'reach an agreement'. This is the gist of John Sinclair's article (1996) 'The empty lexicon'. Once we have identified semantically relevant collocates of words like *strike* (*a blow, a deal, oil,* etc.), their ambiguity and fuzziness disappears. The collocation *strike a deal* is as monosemous or unambiguous as anyone could wish. Even though neither the *NODE* nor the *Longman Dictionary of English Idioms* (1979) list *strike a deal* as an idiom, it seems to belong in this category. In the British National Corpus (BNC) there are twenty-five occurrences of *struck a deal.* The absence of *strike a deal* from larger dictionaries and specialised idiom dictionaries illustrates that the recognised lists of idioms, those we are aware of as part of our cultural heritage, represent no more than the tip of an iceberg. Time and again, corpus evidence suggests that there are many more semantically relevant collocations than dictionaries tell us.

What about the sense of *strike* described in the *NODE* as 'discover (gold, minerals, or oil) by drilling or mining'? In the Bank of English, there are 23,096 occurrences of *struck*. In a random sample of 500 occurrences, we find 7 instances for this sense of *strike*, 4 of 'struck gold', 2 of 'struck oil', and 1 of 'struck paydirt'. All of these citations represent metaphorical usage. Here are two examples:

> Dixon, who, together with the unfailing Papa San, struck gold with 'Run The Route'.

> telephone franchises. No one has struck paydirt yet, although the Bells have captured business

The example of *strike* 'discover by drilling or mining' shows that there is no obvious feature to tell us whether we should analyse a phrase as consisting of two separate lexical items (*strike* and *gold*) or whether we should analyse it as a collocation, i.e. as one lexical item (*strike gold*). It is not a question of ontological reality, of what there is, but a question of expediency. Carrying things to extremes and replacing most single words in our dictionaries by collocations would mean that these dictionaries would have to become much more voluminous. We would have to account for *strike a chord, strike a balance, strike a blow, strike a pose, strike a note, strike fear, strike terror, strike home, strike someone (as)* and possibly some others. If we leave things as they are, we find *strike a coin* and *strike a deal* belonging to the same sense category. Expediency alone, however, seems to be unsatisfactory. Aren't there any more plausible arguments?

3.3 Words, idioms and collocations

Let us look at another example in more detail. Some grammatical patterns are particularly prone to form collocations, such as nouns modified by adjectives. This fact has not escaped the attention of lexicographers. However, without the application of the methodology developed for corpus linguistics, it seems to be left to the whims of dictionary-makers what they decide to include. For the adjective *false*, the *American Heritage Dictionary* (4th edition, 2000) lists these collocations: *false alarm, f. arrest, f. consciousness, f. fruit, f. imprisonment, f. indigo, f. ipecac, f. memory syndrome, f. miterwort, f. pregnancy, f. pretense, f. rib, f. Solomon's seal, f. spikenard, f. start*. The *NODE* lists these collocations: *false acacia, f. alarm, f. bedding, f. card, f. colour, f. coral snake, f. cypress, f. dawn, f. economy, f. face, f. friend, f. fruit, f. gharial, f. helleborine, f. memory, f. move, f. oxlip, f. pretences, f. rib, f. scorpion, f. start, f. step, f. sunbird, f. teeth, f.*

topaz, f. vampire. Even if we acknowledge the differences between American and British English, there are surprisingly few overlaps: *f. alarm, f. fruit, f. memory, f. pretense/pretences, f. rib, f. start.* A random sample of 50 citations from the BNC attests *false alarm, f. dawn, f. pretences, f. start, f. teeth,* but in addition many other collocates of *false: assumptions, cheerings, claims, complaints, confidence, declarations, decisions, denial, distinctions, echo, enquiries, expectations, formastation* (!), *hopes, idea, information, market, money, position, proportion, readings, reasoning, report, take, testimony, theory, tradition, understanding, witness.* Which of these co-occurrences should be described as two separate lexical items, which as a single lexical item? How many senses should we ascribe to *false*? Does *false* in *false alarm* mean something different from *false* in *false echo* or *false witness*? Or would it make things easier to say that it does not really matter what *false* means in these instances and we should rather try to describe what *false alarm, false echo* and *false witness* mean? Which cases should we describe as collocations, which as a combination of (one meaning of) *false* with (one meaning of) the noun in question?

Within the confines of one language it is impossible to come up with clear criteria. But once we bring in a second language, we suddenly find the arguments we have been looking for. The *Wildhagen–Héraucourt* dictionary tells us that these are all possible German equivalents of *false*: 1. *falsch, unrichtig, irrig; ungesetzlich, widerrechtlich;* 2. *unwahr, trügerisch, täuschend; verräterisch, treulos; untreu;* 3. *falsch, gefälscht; unecht, nachgemacht; vorgetäuscht; blind; vorgeblich; Falsch-, Schein-; irrig, so genannt.* How helpful is such an entry? The senses are being distinguished by the different sets of equivalents. But some of the equivalents occur in more than one set. Does that mean that the equivalents themselves are polysemous, or just that the sense categories are fuzzy? (Note that *falsch* is the first and, implicitly, most significant equivalent for both sense 1 and sense 3!) For those who know some German it is also immediately obvious that the words we find within a given sense are far from synonymous; we cannot simply substitute them for each other in various contexts. Why then are we given three senses, and not one, or maybe ten or twenty? If we speak German well, the list of words will help us to choose the one that fits best into a given context. If we do not know German that well, how are we to choose the appropriate equivalent?

Naturally, the lexicographers are aware of their predicament. If they want to cater to native-English speakers with a cursory knowledge of German they have to deliver more. They have to give the translation equivalents not of *false* but of *false* in combination with the nouns it co-occurs with. They have to provide the translations for the collocations of *false*. Some of these collocations are listed as additional information within a given sense category. For sense 1 we find: *false quantity, false arrest, false imprisonment*. For sense 2 we find: *false mirror, false oath* [the equivalent given is *Meineid*], *false pretences, false swearing*. For sense 3 we find *false coin, teeth, hair*; and the idiom *to sail under false colours*. There is also a subsequent section called *Verbindungen* ['collocations'] with more phrases: *false alarm, f. bottom, f. cap, f. door, f. key, f. ogive, f. shame, f. report, f. step, f. take-off*.

Looking at the *Oxford–Duden* (compiled 1990, i.e. *c.* 50 years after the first edition of the *Wildhagen*), *false* is again divided up into three senses. Again slightly abridged, sense 1 is *falsch; Fehl-* (*Fehldeutung, ...*); *Falsch-* (*Falschmeldung, ...*); *treulos; gefälscht;* sense 2: (*sham*) *falsch; künstlich; geheuchelt; gekünstelt;* sense 3: (deceptive) *falsch; unberechtigt; trügerisch*. There is no way to map these three senses on to the three senses of the *Wildhagen–Héraucourt*. The users are left in doubt whether the division into senses in either of the dictionaries reflects the way *false* is being used in English or the hypothesis that there are three different main translation equivalents of *false* in German. Neither claim seems to be particularly helpful or supported by evidence. It just happens that *Cobuild* (the *Collins Cobuild English Language Dictionary*) also divides *false* up into three senses, identified as (1) 'incorrect', (2) 'artificial' and (3) 'insincere'. The *Oxford–Duden treulos* (sense 1), however, does not sail under 'incorrect'; neither does *geheuchelt* (sense 2) travel under 'artificial', nor *unberechtigt* (sense 3) under 'insincere'. As to German ways of negotiating word meanings, it would be next to impossible to claim that *treulos* and *gefälscht* belong to the same category, or *künstlich* and *geheuchelt*, or *unberechtigt* and *trügerisch*.

However, this dictionary entry could give us some ideas on how to be more helpful to its users. For translating into our own native language we might welcome a list of all relevant equivalents (in order of frequency or alphabetic order) so that we might choose among them on the basis of our linguistic competence. For translating into a language other than our own, a language where we do not have a comparable competence, we would, first of all, need a default translation. In the case of *false*, that is easy. According to the *Oxford–Duden*, the first equivalent in each of the three sense categories is *falsch*. This is no doubt the most common equivalent, being closely related to it etymologically. This translation equivalent should be used whenever *false* is not followed by a noun that is given in a subsequent list of collocations. In bilingual lexicography, we can define a collocation as a phrase that cannot be translated using the default translations offered for its components. Thus, users do not need to be told that the equivalent of *false teeth* is *falsche Zähne,* because that would be the default translation anyway. (Actually the German is more commonly *Gebiss,* a word used more often than *dentures* is in English.) But they do need to know that the equivalent of *false coin* is *Falschmünze* (as opposed to *falsche Münze*). How do we arrive at such a list of collocations? If we compare the lists we find in the *American Heritage Dictionary,* in the *NODE* and in the *Wildhagen–Héraucourt* there is only a relatively small overlap.

This is an indication that without suitable corpora, lexicographers are at a loss when it comes to collocations. Even though they are aware of the problem, their findings will be always accidental. Leaving aside, for the moment, the problem of identifying semantically relevant collocations in a monolingual context, we can sketch now what we have to do from a bilingual perspective. We have to look at a corpus. It should be big enough to mirror the kind of language we find in books, newspapers and 'educated speech', i.e. the kind of language we tend to teach in language teaching, and it would yield many more collocations than lexicographers can think of. We would then have to find translations for them. All of those for which the default translation of its elements would be wrong would be entered into the dictionary. We will certainly end up with different sets for each language. In German, a *false alarm* is a *blinder Alarm* (not a *falscher Alarm*); thus this phrase counts as a collocation and belongs in the dictionary. In French, however, it is *alarme fausse,* i.e. the default translation of *alarm* and *false*; and we do not have to treat it as a collocation. If, due to size, not all collocations can be entered into the dictionary, frequency would be an important parameter. We might do without the *false Solomon's seal* and without the *false coral snake.* They seem to be more part of terminology than of the general vocabulary, anyway. *False dawn,* on the other hand, is relatively frequent and would count as a collocation, from a German perspective. The *Oxford–Duden* tells us that its equivalent is: *Zodiakallicht;* (fig.) *Täuschung.* But is *false dawn,* from a monolingual perspective, really a unit of meaning, a single lexical item, or just the combination of two separate lexical items? Can we apply the default meaning test in a monolingual environment?

The *NODE* describes *false dawn* as 'a transient light which precedes the rising of the sun by about an hour, commonly seen in Eastern countries'. According to this definition, *false dawn* seems to be a single lexical item. For we cannot deduce from the meaning of *false* (or from any of the senses a monolingual dictionary may give) and from the meaning of *dawn* (or any of its dictionary senses) that it precedes sunrise by about an hour and that it is specific to Eastern countries (whichever might be meant). But are these really essential or just ornamental features? If they are essential, then *false dawn* is a unit of meaning. For users of the *American Heritage Dictionary*, *false dawn* is described as 'resembling but not accurately or properly designated as the time each morning at which daylight first begins'. This is something that I would be able to deduce from my knowledge of *false* and *dawn*. Here, we are not told that it precedes the real dawn and that it is more commonly found in Eastern countries than elsewhere. If *false dawn* is nothing else, then it is not a unit of meaning. For in this definition, a false dawn resembles a dawn. It is an 'incorrect' dawn. To resolve the issue of the two definitions, let us have a look at the BNC. In the BNC, we find eighteen occurrences of *false dawn*. Just two of them refer to a meteorological situation:

> ... it was not until another hour had passed and the moon was paling in the night of the false dawn that they were at last among strange scattered rocks...

> It was a false dawn, replaced soon after by a now starless night that was blacker than the previous hours.

Neither of these citations mentions an Eastern country, and neither refers to a sunrise occurring an hour later. If these instances are representative, then the *American Heritage Dictionary* seems more reliable, and *false dawn* is not a lexical item. But what about the other occurrences? All of them refer to situations in social life that initially seem to be better than is recognised later. Most commonly these situations refer to economic enterprises. These are some typical citations:

> It is our belief that Christmas will prove to be yet another false dawn as far as reawakening consumer confidence is concerned.

> The organisation's chief executive was optimistic that the latest figures did not merely represent another false dawn.

> Unhappily, it was a false dawn.

Google confirms the BNC evidence. It lists 14,000 hits for the expression 'false dawn'. Among the first 40 hits there is not a single instance where *false dawn* means what the *NODE* says. The first four citations refer to an economic entity called False Dawn. The subsequent instances refer again to situations that appear to be better than later recognised, e.g. the headline: 'Another false dawn for Africa?'. Of course, this meaning of *false dawn* can easily be explained as a metaphor of the *American Heritage Dictionary*'s *false dawn*. Important as this issue of metaphorisation is for lexicography, this is not the place to pursue it. Dissatisfied with either of the two definitions, we again checked Google, this time for ' "false dawn" night morning'. Under www.space.com/spacewatch/zodiacal_light/ we found this definition, which ties in nicely with the German equivalent *Zodiakallicht*:

> At certain times of year in the right locations, a faint cone of light appears in the predawn sky for lucky viewers in dark locations. This eerie glow is the Zodiacal Light.
>
> It is best seen before daybreak, generally two to three hours before sunrise in the eastern sky. But it's also visible in the west at certain times of year. Over the centuries countless individuals have been fooled into thinking the Zodiacal Light was the first vestige of morning twilight. In fact, the Persian astronomer, mathematician and poet Omar Khayyam, who lived around the turn of the 12th Century, made reference to it as a 'false dawn' in his one long poem, The Rubaiyat.

If this is what false dawn means, then it is a unit of meaning that cannot be reduced to a combination of any of the dictionary senses of false and dawn. It is a unit of meaning in its own right, a collocation not just on the basis of the frequency of co-occurrence of its elements, but also on the basis of semantic relevance.

When it comes to word-meaning, we are in dire straits. Native speakers understand the meanings of (the more frequent) words of their language. But they are less competent in describing these meanings. This incompetence seems to be shared, to some extent, by the lexicographers. Whatever the reason may be, this may explain why linguistics as we know it has been preoccupied with grammar. Rules are more elegant than the intricacies of meaning. Rules have explanatory power, they create clarity and understanding, and they provide us with instructions on what to do. There is, however, no rule which could tell us how many senses a word has. The decisions taken are arbitrary. At first glance, it is hard to decide whether it is simply that linguistics has never developed a satisfactory method for dealing with the meanings of words, or whether the situation we are confronted with defies any methodology. Worst of all, the division into different senses seems not to reflect properly how people understand these words when they read them in a text. Experiments have shown that neither lay native speakers nor speakers for whom English is a second language nor trained linguists can easily agree which dictionary sense they should assign to the word in question (Fellbaum 1998; cf. also Edmonds 2002).

How does it come about that highly reputable dictionaries leave such a lot to be desired? There might be a better explanation than incompetence. When we encounter an ambiguous word in a sentence, we normally do not ask ourselves which sense it is used in. Perhaps our understanding of fuzzy words such as *friendly* does not imply putting a given usage into a given pigeonhole. Perhaps our understanding of words is mostly based not on our capacity to categorise, but on our faculty to draw on analogies and to discover resemblances.

Standard linguistics and Chomskyan (or post-Chomskyan) linguistics have not been strong in lexicography. With the demise of philology, the study of the meanings of words has more or less ceased to be a serious academic topic. There is still academic lexicology, and there is semantics; but lexicology has never questioned the categorical approach to word meaning. Rather than describing the meaning of a lexical item as a whole, it has sought to decompose it into more basic semantic features or categories. Many lexicologists still insist that once we get our categories right, better dictionaries will emerge. Semantics, these days, is predominantly cognitive semantics. Cognitive semantics wants to extend Chomsky's claim of the sameness of all languages to meaning as well. These semanticists say that, in principle, we all share the same language, the so-called language of thought, these days often called 'mentalese' (Fodor 1975, Pinker 1994). When we speak, they say, we translate an expression in mentalese into a natural language, and as hearers, we re-translate the natural language expression we hear back into mentalese. This is how Steven Pinker describes this universal mental language:

> People do not think in English or Chinese or Apache; they think in a language of thought. This language of thought probably looks a bit like all these languages; presumably it has symbols for concepts, and arrangements of symbols ... [C]ompared with any given language, mentalese must be richer in some ways and simpler in others. It must be richer, for example, in that several concepts must correspond to a given English word like stool or stud. ... On the other hand, mentalese must be simpler than spoken languages; conversation-specific words and constructions (like a and the) are absent, and information about pronouncing words, or even ordering them, is unnecessary.
>
> (Pinker 1994, pp. 81–2)

Pinker does not tell us, however, how many different concepts correspond to *friendly*, and so we are not told what the universal solution to the categorisation of word meanings would look like. It seems that the universality of mentalese is achieved by getting rid of everything which is language specific. There are many languages that do not feature articles, so mentalese does not have them; and languages come up with different word orders, so mentalese does not have information about word order. Pinker is by no means alone in his putting his faith in mental representations. He is supported by, among others, Dan Sperber and Deirdre Wilson who discuss the following options: '[T]here are fewer concepts than words', 'there is roughly a one-to-one mapping between words and concepts', and '[m]ost mental concepts do not map into words' (Sperber and Wilson 1998, pp. 186–7). Concepts are more angelic than the earthly words of our natural languages; they seem to avoid the unpleasantness of dealing with the many unpredictable idiosyncrasies of words we find in all the human languages. For cognitive linguists, a word has as many senses as there are concepts into which it translates. Unfortunately there is no dictionary of concepts that lexicographers can consult. Rather, it is the other way around. The so-called conceptual ontologies, which are still popular in artificial intelligence, should be, as their proponents claim, in theory language independent. How would that be possible? How could we describe the content of a concept without using language? As it is, conceptual ontologies borrow heavily from dictionaries, and there is little hope that it could ever be the other way around. Semantics and lexicology, as they are practised today in the academic world, contribute very little towards an improvement of our dictionaries.

Standard linguistics has brought about better grammars. While it has also brought about a noticeable improvement of dictionaries, particularly of bilingual dictionaries, modern lexicography still falls short of answering our enquiry into the meanings of words in a satisfactory way. The vast majority of people, however, who listen to other people or read their texts, or who try to tell something to other people, do this because they want to understand or be understood. They do not analyse a sentence for the beauty of its syntactic construction, or because they are hunting for a rare species of a verb form. They may not even know that the sentence they have just uttered was in the passive voice. All they want to be sure about is that they, or their listeners, got the meaning right. And here the linguists seem to be unable to help them. They can tell you that 'Paul loves Mary' is (roughly) equivalent to 'Mary is loved by Paul'. But when asked what love means, linguists will refer Mary and Paul to their poor cousins, the lexicographers, who write in the dictionary (in this case the *Cobuild English Dictionary for Advanced Learners*): 'If you love someone, you feel romantically or sexually attracted to someone' or: 'You say that you love someone when their happiness is very important to you, so that you behave in a kind and caring way to them.' If Mary is being told by Paul that he loves her, she finds it important to know what he means by love. She does not have to be aware that the dictionary could inform her about the many senses of this word, which for her is just fuzzy. For her the question is: does Paul only want to go to bed with her, or is he also willing to do the dishes? If Mary grew up in a Western country where English is the native language, she perhaps would not have a problem understanding Paul. But if she came from an Islamic or Hinduistic culture, she might not be acquainted with our kind of love talk. Standard linguistics will not be able to help her. Something new is needed. When we want to find out how language is being used, what words, sentences, texts mean, we have to analyse texts. Looking at the scripts of soap operas, Hollywood movies, novels and magazines read by young people, we can find out what normally happens after a lad says 'I love you'. It is from these soaps, movies, stories, alongside the examples set by his peers, that Paul has learned when to use the phrase himself.

3.4 Corpus linguistics: a different look at language

What is language? Is it the miraculous language faculty we all are born with, which, once it is awakened by verbal contact with native speakers, empowers us to become native speakers as well, and which requires but minimal input to tune the innate mechanism to the specifics of that language? Is it our competence to come up with grammatical sentences that have never been said or heard before? Is there an innate language organ, just as there is an innate capability to see and distinguish colours? If this is what language is, then we have to study it as a feature of the human mind and we do not have to be aware of the rules. They are wired into our brain, and we follow them unconsciously. We also do not have to learn what words mean. Once we are exposed to a word, we relate it to the mental concept into which it translates.

Or is language an acquired skill enabling us to take an active part in verbal communication? Can we learn a language in the same way as we learn to tie our shoelaces, to play chess or to solve equations? This is how we learn to speak a foreign language. We are taught the grammatical and inflectional rules, we are taught the equivalents of the words of our own language in that new language, and vice versa, and in the end we can produce utterances in the new language that comply with what we have learned. It does not really matter if the language we learn really exists, in the sense that there are native speakers. Learning French is hardly different from learning Esperanto, and, in principle, it should not be too different from learning a programming language. If this is what language is, then we take it to be the accumulation of all the instructions needed to speak it competently. If this is what language is, language is not a feature of the mind. Once we have accumulated all the instructions, then there is nothing new to learn about the language.

Or is language something tangible, namely the accumulation of all the acts of communication that took place in a language community, in the same way that British architecture can be seen as the sum of all the buildings that were built in Britain and that we know about? Is the language of the Etruscans or of the Mayans what remains of their texts, or is it the sum of all the acts of communication that ever took place in Etruscan or Mayan? If we accept the latter position, then we can never hope to understand Etruscan or Maya fully. If English is the totality of all acts of communication of the English-language community, of all the texts that exist or have existed at a given time, then language is not a feature of the mind. It is something that exists, in some physical way, something that remains of the recent and the more remote past, something that keeps on growing and developing. If this is the English language, then most of it is lost – most spoken texts, except the very few that were recorded, and many written texts, except those that survive in libraries or in some kind of accessible archive. If we have to restrict our study of English to what is still accessible because it was recorded and preserved, then our picture of English will certainly be much larger than we can ever hope to come to terms with; but it will never be the full picture.

Language is a human faculty which children acquire naturally without being given instructions; it is a set of rules we have learned, from forming plural nouns, to using words in the appropriate order, to following the conventions of letters or essays or reports, and it is a long list of words we have learned (from the simplest of everyday vocabulary to learning that 'an apophthegm is a concise maxim, like an aphorism'). It is also the sum of all texts in that language. In *Macbeth*, IV, iii, 220, Shakespeare uses the verb *dispute* in the sense of 'revenge'. Nobody uses the word like that any more. But this usage has not exactly disappeared. Shakespeare's texts are still a part of our discourse. We read them, we watch his plays, we discuss his language. Thus there are different ways to look at language. It is up to us to decide how we want to study it. It depends on which aspect of language we are interested in. If we want to find out what is common to all languages, we should embrace Chomskyan linguistics. If we want to find out if a French sentence is structured grammatically, we should rely on standard linguistics. If we want to find out what words, sentences and texts mean, we should opt for corpus linguistics.

Corpus linguistics sees language as a social phenomenon. Meaning is, like language, a social phenomenon. It is something that can be discussed by the members of a discourse community. There is no secret formula, neither in natural language nor in a formal calculus, that contains the meaning of a word or phrase. There is no right or wrong. What I call *a weapon of mass destruction* differs probably a lot from what President George W. Bush calls *a weapon of mass destruction*. What I call a *baguette* is not the same as what many supermarkets sell as a *baguette*. What I call *love* may not be what my partner calls *love*. Different people paraphrase words or phrases in different ways. They do not have to agree. In a democracy, everyone's opinion is as good as anyone else's.

Meaning is what can be communicated verbally. If you do not know what *apophthegm* means, you can ask your fellow members of the English discourse community. Many may not be quite sure themselves, and they may refer you to the dictionaries. Someone may quote Samuel Johnson's famous apophthegm 'Patriotism is the last refuge of a scoundrel', and perhaps from then on you will not forget what the word means. The meaning of *apophthegm* for you, then, is the sum of all you have heard from the people you have asked plus all of what you have found in the dictionaries. There is certainly more to the meaning of *apophthegm*. There are more dictionaries that you could consult, there are more people you could ask, there are more texts you could find in libraries and archives containing the word embedded in various contexts. The full meaning of the word is only available once all occurrences of the word in the texts of the English discourse community have been taken into account. All citations together (plus what people tell you when you ask them) are everything one can know about the meaning of *apophthegm*. There is nothing else that could tell us what this word means. And all of it is verbal communication.

The perspective of Chomskyan and cognitive linguistics represents a very different view of language. In that perspective, language is a psychological, a mental phenomenon. Both views are, of course, legitimate, and they are complementary. Corpus linguistics deals with meaning. Cognitive linguistics is concerned with understanding. Meaning and understanding can easily be confused, but it pays to keep them apart. Understanding is something personal, an act that we carry out, both as speakers and as hearers. For cognitive linguists, understanding means translating a word, a sentence, a text into the language of thought, into mentalese. But there remain many unsolved questions. Are all mental concepts universal, including 'bureaucracy' and 'carburettor', which seem to be rather culture specific? Chomsky thinks there are good arguments to believe that all concepts, including those we are not yet aware of (like future neologisms) are innate (Chomsky 2000, p. 65). Others, like Anna Wierzbicka, think that only a limited number of basic or primitive concepts are universal and that culture-specific concepts are compositional, in the sense that they are composed of basic concepts. These complex concepts are not universal (Wierzbicka 1996). Jerry Fodor, however, rejects the idea of compositionality (Fodor 1998; Fodor and Lepore 2002) (see also 2.9).

The unresolved question of the nature of mental concepts is only one of the problems cognitive linguists are confronted with. The other main problem is that of the Aristotelian qualia. Daniel Dennett defines qualia as 'the way things seem to us'. Qualia are 'ineffable' (i.e. they cannot be described), they are 'intrinsic' (internal to the mind) and 'private' (known only to oneself) (Dennett 1993, pp. 65, 338ff.). The image the word *primrose* evokes in my mind is different from the image the same word evokes in your mind. The affective qualities that go with it, i.e. what you feel when you hear the word *primrose*, is something you cannot fully convey to other people. It is difficult to see how the assumption of a universal conceptual basis can be reconciled with the view that understanding is a first-person experience that defies communication. But even if there were a consensus among cognitive linguists about how understanding works, it would still be necessary to set it apart from meaning. Meaning is what we trade in when we communicate; by exchanging content we share it. Thus, cognitive linguistics and corpus linguistics have a different focus of interest. The cognitive sciences are concerned with what happens in the mind in the process of encoding and decoding a message. Corpus linguistics is concerned with the message itself.

Corpus linguistics can tell us more about meaning than either Chomskyan linguistics or standard linguistics. Even so, corpus linguistics can never give us the full picture. If meaning is not a formula, an unambiguous expression in some symbolic calculus (which was what many of the adherents of analytic philosophy were hoping for), if meaning is neither a mental image informed by ineffable qualia, nor a universal concept in a language of thought we know nothing about, if meaning is what can (and must be) conveyed verbally, then meaning is something we can talk about only in natural language. In all probability, we know what the word *school* means not because at some point in our past we looked it up in the dictionary. We know what it means because someone, or, more probably, a number of people, must have told us, in the course of our childhood, what it meant. The people who told us must have learned it the same way. This process, or rather activity, of conveying the meaning has been repeated generation after generation ever since there were schools. If we assemble everything that has been said, in this discourse, about schools, then we have the meaning of *schools*. Not everyone will paraphrase the word *school* for us in the same words. It could well emerge that the common denominator is very small. A good collection of quotations will show this diversity. The following citations are a selection taken from the Bank of English, a 450-million word corpus of English language:

```
           and offers an after- school club. There are infant and
    them in detention after school. Yet pupils in adjoining
        having a tough time at school and came home in tears again
          as they can, because school fees are so unpredictable.
    he was sent to boarding school in England, where he was a
             small private day school in California. There were
       children's camps during school holidays, which include
         at eleven to a grammar school. The rest stayed on at
           And, I'm still in high school!'' While rewarding the first
           university medical school but it could be rented or
      Oxford, said that more school sport is the answer to the
career after leaving music school to start the family, saw it
       we are a caring sort of school that looks after everybody's
            written by Head of School, Heather Dixon. 'The two-day
         like some kind of prep school, with its Standing Committee
  currently still at primary school, later gained a place at
          I'll have to go to public school. Iz and Jude say the teachers
     The boy, now 15, skipped school for a year as he took orders
        is practical: 'In Sunday School they told us what you do.
last night demanded that the school council and head nun Mother
      teenagers. The four go to school, do homework and finish
          said: 'I used to walk to school with Lisa and her children.
```

Corpus linguistics studies languages on the basis of discourse. English discourse is the totality of texts produced, over centuries, by the members of the English discourse community. Even if we confine ourselves to the texts that have been preserved, this discourse is much too large to make it, *in toto*, the object of our research. It will never be possible to study all extant texts. All corpus linguistics can do is to work with a (suitable) sample of the discourse. Such a sample is called the corpus. Because we can never access the whole discourse and not even all extant texts, we can never be sure that what we have assembled as the meaning of a word like *school* will be the full picture. Even more important is the fact that the picture we can deduce from the corpus is full of contradictions. Some like school; others hate it. Some find it useful; for others it is a waste of time. For all lexical items that are worth thinking and talking about, there is hardly a common denominator, there is little agreement. The discourse is not nearly as streamlined as dictionaries want to make us believe. Some lexicographers seem to think that because what we find in our corpus is nothing but an arbitrary and accidental collection of occurrences, this evidence has to be checked by what *school* is in reality, that it is dangerous to rely only on discourse evidence. But if there is a reality outside of the discourse, it has to be turned into a text, it has to become a part of the discourse, so that it can be communicated.

We should not, therefore, believe that, if we import information which is not found in our corpus, we are importing discourse-external, factual knowledge. We must not mistake for reality what is outside of our corpus. It is still the discourse. We find, for example, in many dictionaries the custom of adding the Latin name of plant species. Thus the *NODE* tells us the species name of the elm tree is *ulmus*. This has nothing to do with reality. It is information copied from other texts, from Linnaeus's classification of plants and animals (2.8 above). This taxonomy is actually a part of discourse and can be discussed in discourse. But isn't this classification, as many people believe, including philosophers of language, a mirror of reality? Isn't a species the same as the natural kind these philosophers (and many cognitive linguists with them) take for granted? Isn't it a fact that there is a species called *elm* or *ulmus* which would still exist even if there were no humans to give it a name? Isn't it true that a tree either is an elm or it is not, regardless of what you or I happen to believe? Is the category species a concoction of the members of the discourse community, or are there, out there in whatever reality may be, entities that can be classified as belonging to this species or that?

Ernst Mayr, a leading biologist and evolutionist, is deeply sceptical about the reality of natural kinds. He recalls, in his recent book *What Evolution Is*, the history of the species concept:

> Traditionally, any class of objects in nature, living or inanimate, was called a species if it was considered to be sufficiently different from any other similar class ... Philosophers referred to such species as 'natural kinds' ... This typological concept is in conflict with the populational nature of species and with their evolutionary potential.
>
> (Mayr 2002, pp. 165–8)

It seems that the concept of species is, after all, being discussed in uncountable contributions to the discourse. A query in Google for 'definition + species' yields 735,000 hits. The concept of species or category allows us to put items into a pigeonhole because they share features we think are important. It is a useful device. But we must not forget that we decide which features are so important that the items sharing them belong in the same pigeonhole. George Lakoff, a cognitive linguist widely known for his work on metaphors, gave one of his books the title *Women, Fire, and Dangerous Things*, because one of the four noun classes in the Australian language Dyirbal includes females, fire and dangerous animals (among other things; see Lakoff 1987, pp. 92–104).

The discussion about whether there are elms because we have agreed on calling something an *elm*, or whether we call something *elms* because elms exist in reality goes back to a disagreement between Plato and Aristotle. Platonic realism tells us that there are natural kinds, and we cannot do better but acknowledge them and give them names. According to this view, we would not be able, in the long run, to cope with reality, unless we find out and accept what nature really is. This nature exists independently of our giving names to the entities that it comprises. Aristotelian nominalism disagrees. It holds that people are free to put some things into one pigeonhole and other things into another pigeonhole. It is humans who invent categories to make sense of reality; it is not that they discover categories when they investigate reality. We find it important to distinguish oranges from lemons. Yet for some of us, mandarins, satsumas, tangelos and tangerines are all the same. Do they belong to different categories? Is a morello just a kind of cherry or is it a different fruit?

Wherever in the world analytic philosophy prevails, it seems to go hand in hand with some version or other of realism. Actually, this is not surprising. For analytic philosophers, the important question is this: what has to be the case to make a sentence such as 'this is an elm' or 'this is a morello' true? What makes such a sentence coincide with reality? But to ask this presupposes that there are things out there that are elms. We would have to redefine our concept of truth if elms could be anything that we agree on calling *elms*. Cognitive linguistics holds that if not words then certainly concepts are locked onto things out there in what is called reality (Fodor 1994). Thus cognitive linguistics shows itself to be an offspring of analytic philosophy.

For realists it is therefore very important that the things words stand for really exist and are not just chimeras like the Nazi concept of race. John Searle, a highly distinguished scholar within the philosophy of mind community, tells us in his recent book *Mind, Language and Society*: 'Among the mind-independent phenomena in the world are such things as hydrogen atoms, tectonic plates, viruses, trees and galaxies. The reality of such phenomena is independent of us' (Searle 1998, pp. 13–14). Can we be sure of this? Two hundred years ago, people had never heard about hydrogen atoms, tectonic plates or viruses. But they thought they knew, as a fact, that there was phlogiston, a combustible matter that escapes into the air whenever something is burning. Will we, in another two hundred years, still be happy to describe certain macromolecular structures with an ability to replicate as viruses? Or, for that matter, can we be so sure about the reality of trees? Are there irrefutable criteria to distinguish trees from shrubs or bushes? The *NODE* calls the hazel 'a temperate shrub or a small tree', for the *Cobuild* it is only 'a small tree'. For Germans, it is either a bush (*Haselnussbusch*) or a shrub (*Haselstrauch*), but never a tree. What we call a tree depends, it seems, more on decisions taken by the language community than on facts.

In the Middle Ages a meeting of bishops declared rabbits to be fish. This gave them permission to have rabbit on their Friday menu. Today we are wiser. We know that rabbits belong to the category of rodents. But is this category more real than a category grouping together things that a good Catholic could eat on a Friday? That rabbits belong to the category of rodents seems to be scientifically true, whereas the category of things permitted as food for Fridays is entirely arbitrary and no longer widely accepted. But the Linnean system of classifying plants and animals in terms of relationship and ancestry is not perennial; it became accepted in the Western world in the course of the nineteenth century, and perhaps it will be superseded one day by a new classification based on DNA. Which categorial systems refer more directly to reality, if it is possible to ask such a question?

So if we do not find in our corpus something that tells us what a word means, where are the facts that determine that word's meaning? Facts, as we have seen, only become facts once they are introduced into the discourse. They may be, for all we know, external to the discourse. But it is up to the members of the discourse community to introduce into the discourse what they deem to be facts. The vast majority of things we think are facts, or what we think we know to be true, are things that we have never encountered or investigated personally but have been told about in discourse. Some people say they know, as a fact, that there are weapons of mass destruction in Iraq. They have never been there; they have never investigated the existence or non-existence personally; and they are relying on texts that are part of the discourse. For any one of us (perhaps other than a leader like the president of the United States of America) it is quite impossible to establish a fact without having it negotiated by the discourse. It is the discourse that decides whether a phenomenon is real or not. There may be plenty of facts outside the discourse, but the only facts we can talk about are the ones that have been introduced into the discourse.

It therefore seems obvious that the only source we can ever hope to access about the meaning of a word is the discourse. We cannot hope to make the discourse as a whole accessible to our lexicographic enquiries, but we can compile larger and larger corpora, and we can also use the ever-growing Internet as a virtual corpus. Nevertheless, as new words and phrases are coined day by day, it is conceptually impossible to come up with a corpus that comprises the whole vocabulary of a discourse community. There will always be words which are not contained in our corpus. And there is always the chance to add to our corpus the texts in which these words occur. When it comes to the meaning of words, corpus linguists have to consult their corpus, amend it, consult it again, and so forth, in a Sisyphean effort. What corpus linguists make out as the meaning of words, can, thus, never be more than an approximation. A different, a larger corpus can always come up with new paraphrases that were missing from the original corpus.

All communication acts together constitute the discourse of a given discourse community. There is, you could say, a discourse community of all people speaking English. It has existed for centuries, ever since English was around. In it we have the texts written by Geoffrey Chaucer, William Shakespeare, Elizabeth Gaskell and Sylvia Plath, and all the other texts we find in our libraries and archives. We have lost, of course, all the oral communication acts (with the exception of some recent ones) because they could not be recorded, and we have lost most of the unprinted written material, because it was thrown away. All those texts are part of the discourse. We can never study all of it, not even what is extant.

Noam Chomsky and many of his followers have dismissed the corpus as the source of our linguistic knowledge. Language, they say, is productive. With limited means, a finite vocabulary and a manageable set of rules, our language faculty empowers us to generate an infinite number of utterances. All the time things are being said that have not been said before. Corpus research, they claim, will only tell us what people have said so far. It will not tell us what people are going to say tomorrow. That is certainly true. Corpus linguistics cannot predict language change any better than meteorologists can predict the weather of tomorrow or of next week. When Ted Levitt used *globalization* in the title of an article 'The globalization of markets' he published in the *Harvard Business Review* in 1983, he could not have known, and linguists were not able to predict, that globalisation would become a keyword of the 1990s.

Generative linguists, however, are not, as we have seen, very much concerned with semantic change. They are interested in grammar. Of course, grammar also changes over time. If we regard quotatives as part of grammar and not of the lexicon, then it is an example of grammatical change that it is now possible to say: 'He comes into the room and he is like "It's much too hot for me in here", and he turns on the air'. Our old grammars do not list the construction *be like* + direct speech. But is this what the generative grammarians have in mind? What they mean by the generative force of grammar is that using the very same grammar (the grammar of the ideal native speaker) we can produce an infinite set of sentences. This is certainly a true claim, even though Chomsky also admits that 'expressions of natural languages are often unparseable (not only because of length, or complexity in some sense independent of the nature of the language faculty)' (Chomsky 2000). Whatever conforms to rules (some expressions apparently do not) will not be better confirmed by looking at data. More empirical evidence will not make us wiser. Once we have found out that sound travels in standard air at a speed of 330 metres per second, there is no point in examining ever more sound events. If you have learned to inflect Lithuanian nouns with their seven cases correctly, there is absolutely no need to study the inflections of Lithuanian nouns in a corpus. If you know for sure that split infinitives are 'illegal', no amount of split infinitives in your corpus will make them legal. Corpus linguistics should keep its hands off grammar, to the extent that the rules we find in our grammar books are indisputable. (They are not always, though.)

Therefore, in this sense, corpus linguistics is no help when it comes to studying the grammar of a language of which the rules have already been 'discovered'. (However, are these 'discovered' rules always adequate?) But it can tell us more about the meaning of words than standard or Chomskyan linguistics. It extracts from the discourse all that we can find out about meaning. Natural human language is unique in this respect. It is the discourse community that negotiates how words should be used and what they mean. The result of these negotiations is not always agreement. Some people may say that *weapons of mass destruction* is a neutral and unbiased expression; others may say it is derogatory because you only use it for the weapons of your enemy. There seems to be no common understanding what these weapons of mass destruction exactly are, and, consequently, what the phrase *weapons of mass destruction* means. Do cluster bombs belong in that set? What about depleted uranium? We only have to look at the recent discourse to find numerous citations in which people are keen to tell us what they think weapons of mass destruction are. A search in the Bank of English on weapons of mass destruction shows us that they stand against the conventional weapons and most commonly mean biological, chemical and nuclear weapons, as in the following citations:

Terrorists were seeking weapons of mass destruction: chemical, biological and nuclear.

...Bush's policy goal of regional security and stability meant eradicating Iraq's capability to build weapons of mass destruction – chemical, biological, and nuclear –...

The Security Council is still not satisfied that all weapons of mass destruction, notably biological and chemical arms, have been purged from Iraq...

The evidence that it is assembling biological, chemical and other weapons of mass destruction is overwhelming.

But the corpus tells us much more than that, it shows us how black and white our world picture is. It tells us that indeed when we talk or write about the weapons of mass destruction, we often mean Iraqi (or other enemy) weapons, that it is very often Iraq or Baghdad that is developing, producing, building, acquiring these weapons, and that it is the United Nations who is banning or trying to eliminate them from the Middle East.

The discourse is full of paraphrases of words and of comments concerning their meaning and the connotations that come with them. Aren't these explanations the kind of information we would like to find when we look up a word or a phrase in the dictionary? Once we take the view that the meaning of words is what members of the discourse community proffer as their meaning, the distinction lexicographers have become attached to, namely the distinction between lexical knowledge and encyclopaedic knowledge, dissolves. Encyclopaedic knowledge is part of our discourse just as much as whatever dictionaries offer as word meanings. The meaning of the phrase *weapons of mass destruction* is what people tell us *weapons of mass destruction* are. Similarly, the true meaning of *water* is not, as the famous American philosopher Hilary Putnam wants us to believe, what water is 'in reality', but what people tell us water is (Putnam 1975, pp. 215–71).

Corpus linguistics questions the position of the word as the core unit of language. The word is not inherent to language. The Greek word *logos* which we usually believe to be the equivalent of *word* means primarily 'speech' or the 'act of speaking', then 'oral communication', and also an 'expression'. Where it does mean 'word', it means first of all the 'spoken word' (as opposed to *rhema* or *onoma*). Latin *verbum* also means first of all 'expression', 'speech' and 'spoken word'. When we think today of *word*, it seems to be much less a transitory sound event than the written word, something that can easily be identified because it is preceded and followed by a space, a space we normally do not speak or hear. Spaces between written words are a relatively recent invention. It was the monks in the medieval *scriptoria* who introduced them because it made it easier to copy texts. Words are what constitute dictionary entries, and because *weapons of mass destruction* is not a single word, it is hidden away in the dictionary, if it occurs at all. In the *NODE*, the phrase is found under the entry for destruction: 'the action or process of killing or being killed: weapons of mass destruction'.

3.5 A brief history of corpus linguistics

Corpus linguistics is a fairly new approach to language. It emerged in the 1960s, at the same time as Noam Chomsky made his impact on modern language studies. His *Syntactic Structures* appeared in 1957, and while it quickly became a widely discussed text, it was only the publication in 1965 of his *Aspects of the Theory of Syntax* and the subsequent reception of this work that provoked the revision of the standard paradigm in theoretical linguistics. Yet while language theory became increasingly interested in language as a universal phenomenon, other linguists had become more and more dissatisfied with the descriptions they found for the various languages they dealt with. Some of the grammar rules in these descriptions were so obviously violated in all (written) texts that they could not be adequate. Certain features of the language were insufficiently described. For example, there had always been a distinction between transitive verbs and intransitive verbs. This is not enough, however, to describe the number and quality of objects or complements that can depend on a verb. These objects include the direct object, various kinds of indirect objects, prepositional objects and clausal objects, among others. They have to be properly kept apart if we want to describe grammatical structure accurately. For instance, if a verb is turned from active into passive voice, some objects can disappear while others will become subjects. In the 1950s, details such as these raised empirical questions which could not be answered by introspection alone. Real language data were needed.

In the English-speaking world, the first large-scale project to collect language data for empirical grammatical research was Randolph Quirk's Survey of English Usage which later led to what became the standard English grammar for many decades: *A Comprehensive Grammar of the English Language* (Quirk *et al.* 1985). The project kicked off in the late 1950s. It formed a reference point for anyone interested in empirical language studies, including the Brown Corpus to be mentioned below. But at the time, the Survey did not consider computerising the data. This happened much later, in the mid-1980s, in Quirk and Greenbaum's subsequent project now known as the International Corpus of English (ICE) (http://www.ucl.ac.uk/english-usage/ice/).

Quirk's Survey was a mixture of spoken and written data; there were about 500,000 words of spoken English within a total of one million words. The spoken component was actually the first to be put on a computer, by Jan Svartvik, and became, in the late 1970s, the London Lund Corpus. It was transcribed in an elaborate way, with much phonological and even phonetic information. It became the first spoken corpus widely available for use, published as a book, though unfortunately still not available as a soundtrack (Svartvik 1990).

The Survey was mostly interested in grammar, not in meaning. Nevertheless, it was one of the very few projects working on empirical data. Due to the pervasiveness of the Chomskyan paradigm, it became increasingly difficult in the 1960s to find acceptance of this kind of data-oriented language research. The Survey was the exception in Britain at that time. Later, in the 1970s, this strand of research was to be taken up by a number of Scandinavian linguists, most of them based in Bergen, Lund and Oslo.

The second data-oriented project in the 1960s was the Brown Corpus, named after Brown University in Providence, Rhode Island, where it was compiled by Nelson Francis and Henry Kučera. The corpus consists of one million words, taken in samples of 2,000 words from 500 American texts belonging to 15 text categories as defined by the Library of Congress. The Brown Corpus was a carefully organised corpus, very easy to use, and proofread until it was almost free of mistakes. So is the similarly composed corpus of British English, the LOB (Lancaster–Oslo–Bergen)–Corpus from the 1970s (Johansson *et al.* 1978). Later, both corpora were manually tagged with part-of-speech information. While it was at first hoped that these corpora would answer questions concerning both the grammar and the lexicon, it was soon realised that a corpus of one million words cannot contain more than a tiny fraction of the whole vocabulary. After the Brown Corpus was compiled and the proofreading was completed, it seemed that linguists, at least in America, lost interest in it. It hardly played a role in transatlantic linguistics, even though it became a popular resource in European linguistics. The LOB–Corpus was exploited in subsequent corpus studies, for research into grammar and, more importantly, into word frequency, but not into meaning, mostly in co-operation between British and Scandinavian scholars, including Geoffrey Leech, Knut Hofland and Stig Johansson.

It seems it was Nelson Francis who was the first to apply the term *corpus* to his electronic collection of texts. John Sinclair believes this is how the new usage may have originated:

> There is a story that Jan Svartvik tells about him [Nelson Francis] coming to London with a tape containing the Brown Corpus or part of it and meeting Randolph Quirk there in the mid sixties. Nelson threw this rather large and heavy container, as tapes were then, on Quirk's desk and said: 'Habeas corpus'. Francis also uses *corpus* in the title of his collection of texts, i.e. the Brown University Corpus, and as such it is referred to in the OSTI Report.
> (Interview with John Sinclair in Krishnamurthy 2003)

A third, and certainly most important, early corpus project was English Lexical Studies, begun in Edinburgh in 1963 and completed in Birmingham. The principal investigator was John Sinclair. It was he who first used a corpus specifically for lexical investigation, and it was he who took up the novel concept of the collocation, introduced in the 1930s by Harold Palmer and A. S. Hornby in their *Second Interim Report on English Collocations* (1933), and then taken up by J. R. Firth in his paper 'Modes of meaning' (Firth 1957). This project investigated, on the basis of a very small electronic text sample of spoken and written language, amounting to not even one million words, the meaning of 'lexical items', a term that included collocations. John Sinclair's final report, *English Lexical Studies* (often referred to as the OSTI-Report), was distributed in no more than a handful of typewritten copies in 1970. It was often referred to in later studies, but has only recently been published properly for the very first time, by the Birmingham University Press (Krishnamurthy 2003). At the time, Sinclair had not yet completely abandoned the notion of the word as the unit of meaning, but he was keen to modify the traditional view of the word as the core unit. Still, while the project participants explored the relationship between the word and the unit of meaning, there was no clear appreciation of semantic units as multi-word units with their variations stretching across the phrases. A beginning had nevertheless been made.

Unfortunately, in the 1970s, 1980s and even 1990s, the quest for meaning all but disappeared from the agenda of the newly established corpus research. This is not as astonishing as it sounds. After all, compiling corpora, particularly larger ones, posed a host of problems, mostly technical ones, but also the still popular question of representativeness. Was there a corpus that could be said to represent the discourse? Was it possible to define text types, domains or genres in general terms? Was there a recipe for the composition of what came to be called a reference corpus? How important was size? What was the role of special corpora?

Standardisation also became an issue of overriding importance for the 1980s and 1990s. How should corpora be encoded? Was it permissible to add corpus-external information in the form of annotation or tagging? Could there be a common tag-set for all languages? Wouldn't using annotated corpora mean that you only extract from them what you first added to them, thus perpetuating possible misconceptions?

Then there is the question of frequency. With corpora, it was, for the first time, possible to come up with lists of the most frequent words accounting for the basic vocabulary. Everything could be counted and compared: verb–complement constructions, the distribution of the various relative pronouns, or the position of adjectival modifiers in late Middle English noun phrases. Register variation of different Englishes is still a common topic of many corpus studies. Frequency information could also shed new light on grammatical rules. It became possible to investigate the relationship between rare events and a decrease of linguistic competence, of what one could say and what one would say. In this sense, frequency data could be used to revise our view of syntax.

If we look at the papers from the 13th and 14th International Conferences on English Language Research on Computerised Corpora (Aarts *et al.* 1992; Fries *et al.* 1993), organised by the venerable ICAME association, these were very much the topics presented there. The papers deal with creating corpora, with corpus design questions, with annotation, with language varieties and with parsing techniques. Among the thirty-eight papers presented at the two conferences, perhaps four or five focus on collocational aspects of language and only one explicitly deals with semantic issues: Willem Meijs on 'Analysing nominal compounds with the help of a computerised lexical knowledge system'. Here, too, then, we learn very little about extracting meaning from the corpus, and more about assigning predefined semantic features from a conceptual ontology to collocations found in the corpus.

It is not astonishing that the final report *Towards a Network of European Reference Corpora* (finally published in 1995) of the 1991/92 European Commission project talks about user needs, corpus design criteria, encoding, annotation and even knowledge extraction, but does not touch on meaning as a possible focus of corpus research (Calzolari *et al.* 1995). Even the introductions to corpus linguistics which appeared in the 1990s refrain from devoting much space to the corpus-oriented study of meaning. Tony McEnery and Andrew Wilson

(McEnery and Wilson 1996) may serve as one example. Forty pages of their book are devoted to encoding, twenty pages deal with quantitative analysis, twenty-five pages describe the usefulness of corpus data for computational linguistics and thirty pages cover the use of corpora in speech, lexicology, grammar, semantics, pragmatics, discourse analysis, sociolinguistics, stylistics, language teaching, diachrony, dialectology, language variation studies, psycholinguistics, cultural anthropology and social psychology. The final twenty pages present a case study on sub-languages and closure. In Graeme Kennedy's introduction to corpus linguistics (Kennedy 1998) thirty pages out of three hundred are devoted to 'lexical description', including twelve pages on collocation. Unsurprisingly, for Kennedy lexical description seems to be more or less synonymous with frequency information. In their book of similar size *Corpus Linguistics: Investigating Language Structure and Use* (also 1998) Douglas Biber, Susan Conrad and Randi Reppen again have about thirty pages on 'lexicography'. The two basic questions they address are: 'How common are different words? How common are the different senses for a given word?' (Biber *et al.* 1998, p. 21). This looks like frequency analysis together with the belief that word senses are somehow discourse external and can be assigned to lexical items. But at least they mention, on two pages, the relevance of the context for determining senses. The rest of the section is devoted to an investigation into the distribution of the word *deal,* with its various senses, over the registers of different text genres. In the absence of an introduction dealing explicitly with matters of meaning, John Sinclair's *Corpus, Collocation, Concordance* (1991) filled the gap, until Michael Stubbs' *Words and Phrases: Corpus Studies of Lexical Semantics* was published in 2001.

There was, however, a large corpus-based dictionary project, the *Collins Cobuild English Language Dictionary,* conceived and designed in the mid-1970s and published in 1987, under the guidance of John Sinclair. The story of this venture is told in *Looking Up: An Account of the Cobuild Project in Lexical Computing,* also published in 1987. This was the first ever general language dictionary based exclusively on a corpus. Therefore, the corpus had to be big enough to include all the lemmas and all the word senses the dictionary assigned to these lemmas. A consequence is that rare words, like *apo(ph)thegm,* are missing. They were not in the corpus. However, except in cases of doubt the lexicographers did not use corpus information to carve up the meaning of a word into its senses; rather, the corpus was used in the first place to validate the lexicographers' decision and to provide examples. More could not be done with this corpus of 18.3 million words (Birmingham

Collection of English Text), then the largest general language corpus in the world. From today's point of view, collocations are not given the prominence they ought to have. Dictionary publishers have not been keen on collocation dictionaries. In many ways, the *Cobuild* dictionary is still unique. While it encouraged other dictionary makers to include more corpus evidence, there is still no other dictionary exclusively based on a corpus.

Elena Tognini-Bonelli distinguishes between the corpus-based and the corpus-driven approaches (Tognini-Bonelli 2001). Linguistic findings (including the contents of dictionaries) are corpus based if everything that is being said is validated by corpus evidence. Findings are corpus driven if they are extracted from corpora, using the methodology of corpus linguistics, then intellectually processed and turned into results. This is a crucial distinction. The corpus-based approach will deliver only results within the framework of standard linguistics. It can show that one of the five senses normally listed for *friendly* does not occur at all in the corpus, and that in addition to the five senses, there is another usage that has been overlooked by other dictionaries. It will not show that you can get rid of most of the ambiguity by identifying the collocates of *friendly* and making these collocations your lemmas. If corpus linguistics is really going to complement standard linguistics rather than just extend it, it must follow the corpus-driven, not the corpus-based approach. This is what we aim to demonstrate in the following chapter.

4 Directions in corpus linguistics

Wolfgang Teubert and Anna Čermáková

4.1 Language and representativeness

Ever since linguists started using corpora they have been thinking hard about how corpora should be composed. The corpus should represent the discourse, or some predefined section of it. What the Brown Corpus represented was the English language of the year 1961, in print, as catalogued by the Library of Congress. In this corpus, each publication is assigned to one of fifteen content categories. The catalogue for the publications of 1961 represents this discourse. It tells us how many texts were published within each of the categories, and these figures were used as guidelines to select the texts. From each of the 500 texts chosen, a 2,000-word sample was then entered into the corpus. This selection process can be operationalised, turned into unambiguous, clear instructions, and is therefore objective. But is the corpus representative?

It represents, in a rather loose way, the Library of Congress catalogue. That is not the same, though, as the discourse constituted by all the printed publications of the USA in 1961. The fifteen categories into which the catalogue entries are divided are arguable. You could have more or fewer, and the subject fields could be defined quite differently. A few centuries ago, there would have been a category for alchemy and one for astrology, but none for economics. The whims of people change. Depending on the number and content of these basic categories, one might come up with an entirely different selection of texts for our corpus, a selection which was in every respect as objective as that of the Brown Corpus.

Then there is the question of readership. In a catalogue, a newspaper with a circulation of several million copies has an entry comparable to a book printed in 120 copies. But is the number of readers important? What really determines the importance of a text: who wrote it? How many copies circulated? How many people read it? Is it right to include only printed and published texts and thus to exclude perhaps more than 90 per cent of what makes up the discourse of any given year: informal conversations within the family, in schools, in bars, cafes and clubs, with friends on an outing, at the workplace; the letters we receive, the advertisements we read, the reports, minutes and memos we find on our desks, to name but a few?

There are wider questions. Are English texts published outside of the USA, but found on the shelves of the Library of Congress, part of the American discourse? What about books published by Americans who live outside the USA? Does American English include, for example, the English spoken by immigrants in the USA or the English of Puerto Ricans? What exactly is the discourse?

A language, a discourse, consists of the totality of verbal interactions that have taken place and are taking place in the community where this language is spoken. This community we call the discourse community. Language communities can be small. Some are so small, in fact, that their languages have become endangered, or even extinct as with many of the Uralic (Finno-Ugrian) languages. There are (or were) languages spoken by only a dozen people or even less. Manx, for example, died out a few decades ago; at the end, there was only one (native) speaker left, conversing in Manx only with the handful of linguists specialising in this Celtic language. Other language communities are so large and diverse, like the community of English-language speakers, that it does not seem proper from a sociological perspective to call them communities at all.

The totality of the verbal interactions of a specific language community includes idiolects, sociolects, dialects, regional variants, languages for special purposes, eighteenth-century language and contemporary language, female language and male language, slang and jargon, and innumerable other kinds of language we can sometimes distinguish.

Languages and discourse communities do not exist as such. They are social constructs. We construe them to suit our purposes. Until the dissolution of the old Yugoslavia, most of us believed there was a language called Serbo-Croatian. Now there are books telling us that such a language never existed, and that Serbian and Croatian were always distinct languages. Nowadays words considered to be originally Serbian (or even Turkish) are purged from Croatian and replaced by newly coined words built from 'purely' Croatian morphemes. Half a century ago the Northern Indian lingua franca Hindustani (a pidgin that become a Creole) was replaced by Hindi and Urdu. Both of these were originally at least as artificial as Hindustani, yet today, thanks to massive political intervention, they are irrefutably natural languages in their own right and to a large extent mutually incomprehensible. Germans normally do not understand spoken Swiss German, but tradition has it that it is the same language. Slovaks and Czechs do not need interpreters to understand each other, but historical and political circumstances have enforced the notion that they are two separate languages. There is no formula telling us what a language is and what a language community is. It is up to us to design our formula in agreement with our intentions. We define languages and language communities according to experience, according to what seems useful at a given time.

Discourse communities may be social constructs, but we do experience them as real. The members of a discourse community negotiate who belongs to it and who does not. There are thousands of texts telling us, as a 'fact', how many speakers there are for English, or Chinese or Manx. The discourse itself is unfathomable, inexhaustible, and as a whole, inexplorable. Perhaps we can approach the conundrum of representativeness more easily if we approach it from the other end, from the corpus.

In the words of John Sinclair (1991) a corpus is 'a collection of naturally occurring language text, chosen to characterize a state or variety of a language'. The texts are all samples, cross-sections of the discourse. But sampling the discourse can mean different things. If we look at the discourse of written English texts, we could, if we chose to, say that a representative corpus is one that reflects the frequencies and proportions of all the twenty-six letters plus the special characters like punctuation marks and the space in between words. Is that what we should call a representative corpus?

Perhaps, though, we are interested not so much in the frequency of letters as in the frequency of words. Let us assume, again, that there are half a million words in English (the number does not matter, really, because we will not agree on the definition of word). Some of these half-million words are very frequent, such as the function words (a, the, to, etc.; see 1.1); some of them are quite frequent (say, the 20,000 or so headwords you would find in a typical pocket dictionary); and the rest of them are rather less frequent. The most frequent word in English is the definite article the and nearly all of the most frequent hundred words are function words such as pronouns and prepositions. Among the most frequent words there are only a very few nouns and verbs which can be said to have a meaning of their own, and all of these words are highly ambiguous or fuzzy (words like thing or set). All words are part of the discourse; they all have been used at least once. But no matter how large our sample of the discourse is, we will miss most of them. There is no occurrence of my favourite word apophthegm in the

450-million-word Bank of English. This is purely accidental. There are, on the other hand, many thousands of other words nobody has ever heard of, words occurring only once in the corpus, for example *abelch*, *airpad*, *eurocrisis* and *keyphone*. Such a word, for which we have no more than one citation, is called a *hapax legomenon* (Greek: 'read only once'). Some of these words may be misspellings but many may be real words.

Therefore, talking about the frequency of words, we just may be able to say that a corpus represents a discourse, inasmuch as the 10,000 most frequent words of the discourse are also the 10,000 most frequent words of the corpus. The presence or absence of words less frequent is as unpredictable as the winning numbers in a lottery. But even if we only consider the most frequent part of the vocabulary we find ourselves at a loss.

In whatever way we look at the question of representativeness, we will always have to define what it is that our corpus is to represent. As long as we have not defined what the discourse is which we want to represent, we just do not know what the 10,000 most frequent words are. Nor do we know how different domains (such as politics, gardening, property law or rugby) are distributed over the discourse. The same is true for genres, based on text-external classification (fiction, newspaper language, academic writing, appliance instructions, poetry), or text types, based on text-internal features (containing first person singular, past tense, passive, quotations, etc.), and for registers (e.g. formal, informal, technical, derogatory, vulgar language).

There have been many attempts to define the discourse, and the catalogue of the Library of Congress is just one example. You might want to compile a corpus representing the discourse of Australian English of the year 2000. Since we cannot hope to have easy access to spoken texts, let us restrict our discourse to written texts. Let us also exclude, for the moment, unpublished written texts. We thus narrow our definition of the discourse for which we want to compile a corpus down to the totality of written English texts, published in Australia in the chosen year. Is that what we want? Let us further assume we have agreed on what to do with texts by Australians published outside Australia and texts by non-Australian English writers published within Australia, and that we have agreed upon the relationship of writing texts (sampling authors) to reading texts (sampling readers). There are still other parameters such as gender, educational background and age of writer and/or of reader. Probably for a country like Australia, some linguists are also interested in the ethnic backgrounds of the writers/readers of texts. These are parameters defining the discourse community, and not the discourse. Are these parameters we should be interested in?

In any case, we are only justified in claiming that a given corpus is representative of a discourse, however we have defined it, if we have, at least in principle, access to all the texts the discourse consists of. Only then will we have all the relevant information concerning the parameters mentioned above, and only then can we be sure that the corpus we compile as a sample of this discourse is representative, at least in respect to the parameters mentioned above. But if this utopia came true, we could well do without the corpus. We would already have the discourse as a whole and would not need to sample it. We would have no need to work with a sample. We could work with the whole discourse. Perhaps in a decade or two it will be possible to access all the written texts published in Australia in a given year. But presumably it will never be possible to enumerate all the spoken and written texts of the Australian discourse of a given year as a whole. This is why it does not make much sense to talk about representativeness.

4.2 Corpus typology

However, this might not be at all what we mean when we discuss the representativeness of a corpus of British, Australian or American English. Fortunately, these discourse communities have discussed at length what they mean by standard English. There is a good measure of agreement about what kind of English we should teach to foreigners. Of course, these attitudes have changed in the course of history. A century ago, languages were mostly taught on the basis of 'good' literature, including novels and non-fiction books on certain cultural and historical topics. Today we think the register to be taught should also include the kind of spoken language used by the educated middle classes. This is not the most numerous segment of society, but, in the eyes of the discourse community, it is the most prominent or significant. We could also define as standard English the private annual reading load of educated middle-class citizens. This might consist of a larger share of broadsheets and a smaller one of tabloids, amounting to probably 50 per cent of the total, perhaps another 10 per cent consisting of the weekly and monthly periodicals we subscribe to, perhaps 25 per cent consisting of fiction and non-fiction books we read through the year, and the remaining 15 per cent an odd mixture of brochures, instruction leaflets and sundry printed material we come across, from tax forms and telephone bills to tourist brochures and theatre programmes. We could include, in proportion, children's literature. There is no cogent reason to exclude our professional reading load, but many people, including many linguists, would think that these texts are too diverse and too far away from what we usually read that they would not belong to any common ground. The language of a medical journal, of aircraft maintenance manuals or the customs regulations, for example, is not part of my linguistic repertoire. Our corpus thus comes to consist of what the members of the discourse community have agreed to be representative of standard (British, Australian or American) English. For the reasons discussed above, we should not call a corpus which represents such a socially accepted standard a representative corpus. These days, corpus linguists prefer to call such a corpus a reference corpus.

Today, corpus linguists would expect a national language reference corpus to comprise between 50 and 500 million words, if not more. There are perhaps one or two dozen languages for which reference corpora of this (or larger) size already exist or are under construction. For German, there is the IDS (Institut für Deutsche Sprache) corpus with more than a billion words; there is the Språkbanken Swedish corpus of 75 million words and the Czech National Corpus of 100 million words; and there are two large reference corpora for English, the 100-million word British National Corpus and the 450-million word Bank of English. Reference corpora of different languages are comparable if they are similar in size and if their composition is similar in respect to genres and/or other parameters. The PAROLE corpora of all official EU languages, for example, are comparable in this sense, but, given today's standards, they are rather small – not more than 20 million words per language.

Reference corpora are being used for a multitude of purposes. Reference corpora contain the standard vocabulary of a language. They are the corpus linguist's main resource to learn about meaning. If they are large enough, they reveal the contexts into which words are usually embedded, and with which other words they form collocations. Only in corpora of this size can we detect these units of meaning that are so much more telling than single words, with their ambiguities and fuzziness. We need reference corpora, the larger the better, for investigating lexical semantics. A typical reference corpus will represent what the discourse community agrees to be what a fairly educated member of the middle class would read outside of work, mostly in printed form, but also handwritten or typed; and, in principle at least, it should also contain a sample of what they would hear, in conversation, at more formal social events, or on the radio. It is carefully construed, with a deliberate composition. The British National Corpus of 100 million words, compiled in the early 1990s, is a good example (http://www.hcu.ox.ac.uk/BNC/).

Reference corpora, however, also serve another purpose. They can be used as benchmarks for special corpora. Whenever we do not want to look at standard language as a whole but at some special phenomenon we happen to be interested in, we usually have to compile a corpus that fits our research focus. Such a corpus is called a special corpus. Special corpora are sometimes quite small, under a million words, though they can be much bigger of course. Let us assume, for the moment, we are interested in the collocation *friendly fire*. Our research questions are: how quickly did this neologism spread after it was first coined in 1976? How was it paraphrased? Are people aware of the inherent irony? Are there different usages? Does it occur only in talking about the military, or are there other domains in which we now use *friendly fire*? When did the expression pick up in British English? What was *friendly fire* called before the expression was coined? What happened to that word? If this is the set of questions to which we want to find answers, we have to compile an appropriate corpus. It must include texts from 1976 onwards. In order to find out the frequency over longer periods of time, we must set up subcorpora for different phases, say for 1976–8, 1980, 1985, 1990 and 2000. These subcorpora have to be identical in size and in composition so that it really makes sense to compare frequencies. The easiest way to come up with such a set of comparable subcorpora is to take newspapers. So perhaps we should take *USA Today*, the *Washington Post*, the *Los Angeles Times*, the *Burlington Intelligencer* and the *Springfield Examiner*, for the years we want to look at. Where do we find these newspapers and their text files? Some papers publish all the year's texts in annual CDs, which can be bought. In other cases, we may have to contact the publisher. If we cannot get a paper, we must find a suitable substitute. We should look around for databanks on the Internet containing this kind of material. Do we need the whole newspaper? In fact, we could reduce the size of the corpus by selecting only those articles in which the phrase occurs. Or should we just take the sentences containing *friendly fire*? Better not, for it may well be that relevant semantic information may be found in the wider context. Can we leave out certain sections, such as sport? Not if they contain the phrase. We then have to compile a very similar corpus of British newspapers, to be able to find similarities and differences. If our British corpus includes the (London) *Times* of 2 November, 2001, we will find the following citation:

> Blair's war effort is put under friendly fire. Labour rebels, disgruntled backbenchers, forced the first Commons vote on the conflict in Afghanistan.

This citation tells us a number of things: first of all, *friendly fire* is also used in British English. Second, the phrase is also used in the political domain. Third, if used outside of the military domain, we also find a metaphorical usage. These backbenchers do not use guns or missiles; they use their right to vote. And finally, there is a semantic difference that comes with metaphorisation: this friendly fire is no longer accidental; it is intentional.

There is no standard recipe for the composition of a special corpus. All we have to do is to draw up a set of hypotheses that will guide us in defining the special corpus we need. It may well turn out that in the course of our inquiry, our hypotheses have to be modified. This may mean it becomes necessary to extend our corpus. It is always possible to add to it. Corpora are by no means sacrosanct. They are the corpus linguists' creation, and they can do with them whatever they deem reasonable.

An alternative to the reference corpus is the opportunistic (or cannibalistic) corpus. The opportunistic corpus does not claim to represent a language or to mirror a discourse; an opportunistic corpus is based on the assumption that each and every corpus is imbalanced. Once we take for granted that corpora are inherently imbalanced, we are free to tackle the problem of representativeness or balance from a different angle. This new perspective is the strict separation of corpus compilation from corpus application. The opportunistic corpus is the result of collecting all the corpora one can lay hands upon. Almost all of these corpora will be special corpora; but there may also be a few that call themselves reference corpora. The larger the opportunistic corpus is, the better it is. But the best opportunistic corpus is also the one that is documented in the most comprehensive way.

Therefore we first have to define the genres, domains and text types, and in doing so we have to take into consideration two aspects. One aspect is what possible users of our opportunistic corpus might want to look for. What are the genres, domains and text types that have been discussed and analysed by linguists? This should be the starting point of our own classification. The other aspect is what kind of information we can hope to find in any corpus we want to add to our opportunistic corpus. Will there be any genre/domain/text type information, either in the texts or attached to them, that we can retrieve automatically and include in the documentation files? This is an important question because the integration of a new corpus into an existing opportunistic corpus should be done as automatically as possible. What we also need is, for each text, the date of its publication, the name and details of the author, its title and all the other information one would like to put into a bibliography. An ideal opportunistic corpus is a corpus in which this kind of information is available for each text of each of the corpora it is composed of.

Once there is a sufficiently large opportunistic corpus available, people who want to use corpora for their research can query the documentation in order to identify the texts they would like to use. Someone working on the vocabulary of Victorian novels would select all the relevant novels they would find in the opportunistic corpus, and leave the rest aside. Another project might be an exploration of the special language of sport. Opportunistic corpora will contain a lot of newspaper material, and again the thorough documentation of all texts will make it very simple to select the ones we are interested in, i.e. the sport sections of the newspapers, plus whatever other material is classified as belonging to the domain of sports. There will always be research topics for which an opportunistic corpus does not provide the basis. The larger it grows, however, the wider will be the variety of research purposes it fits. Indeed, whenever people maintaining an opportunistic corpus come across some special corpus which could be useful for a future research agenda, it should be added. Opportunistic corpora are principally open-ended. The corpus holdings of the Mannheim Institut für Deutsche Sprache, now running at more than two billion words and still growing rapidly, are currently the largest opportunistic corpus.

The monitor corpus is a corpus that monitors language change. It is, in principle, regularly updated and open-ended. Corpus linguistics is particularly interested in lexical change, such as:

- the change of frequency of words or other units of meaning (compounds, multi-word units, collocations, set phrases), which is often indicative of a change in meaning or a change in the domains in which words are used;
- the occurrence of new words;
- the occurrence of new larger units of meaning;
- changing context profiles, i.e. changes in the frequencies of words occurring in the contexts of words or other units of meaning.

The introduction of new words into the discourse is the most obvious, but not the most frequent lexical change. Studies undertaken for a German newspaper (the *Süddeutsche Zeitung*, Munich) have shown that the majority of new character strings in between blanks, i.e. strings that have not been previously registered, are first typing errors and then names of persons, organisations and geographical units, then abbreviations. The small remainder (about fifteen items per day) consists of previously unrecorded forms of words already registered, ad hoc compounds (which are written in one word in German) and every now and then a true neologism.

Monitor corpora should, as much as possible, adhere to the same initial composition. As far as they consist of newspapers and periodicals, this should not be difficult. Newspapers tend to develop their own unique styles, and this style manifests itself in a specific vocabulary. Comparing this week's *Daily Telegraph* with last week's *Guardian* yields unreliable evidence. What is new for one paper may have been another paper's common usage for a long time. A corpus of nothing but newspapers and periodicals seems to be somewhat unsatisfactory. We would like to include other genres, as well. But what do we achieve, in terms of documenting lexical change, by randomly selecting, say, ten fiction and ten non-fiction books per annum? Novels as well as popular science or history books tend to have a specific topic. A single book on tennis would change the frequency of tennis terminology for this monitor corpus year to such an extent that it would bias the results. Such a slant could be set off only if we added not ten but hundreds of books per year. A compromise would be to include a book review journal like the *Times Literary Supplement.* A book review will normally contain the new vocabulary that comes with the book, but not to such an extent that it will bias frequency counts. Unfortunately, large-scale monitor corpora reflecting what is seen as standard written language are still not available. However, this situation will change over the next few years.

A parallel corpus, sometimes also called a translation corpus, is a corpus of original texts in one language and their translations into another (or several other languages). Reciprocal parallel corpora are corpora containing original texts and translated texts in all languages involved. Sometimes parallel corpora contain only translations of the same texts in different languages, but not the text in the original language. Such a corpus can tell us how the English we find in translations differs from authentic English. Sometimes it is not known – or it is thought to be irrelevant – which text is the original and which text is the translation. For example, we are not told in which language legal documents issued by the European Commission are drawn up. It used to be mostly French, but more recently the final version has often been in English, and it can well happen that previously working versions were drafted in other languages. The same is true for texts issued by the Vatican. These days a long time has passed since Latin was the original version. The languages are mostly Italian and French but also

English, Spanish and German, and the Latin version is added at a later stage. These parallel corpora cannot tell us how French texts are translated into English, but they can show in which cases the word *travail* (or its plural *travaux*) is equivalent to *work*, and in which cases to *labour* or other expressions.

Parallel corpora are repositories of the practice of translators. The community of translators from language A to language B and vice versa know a lot more about translation equivalence than can be found in any (or all) of the bilingual dictionaries for these languages. Even the largest bilingual dictionary will present only a tiny segment of the translation equivalents we find in a not too small parallel corpus. Because the ordering principle of printed dictionaries is alphabetical, based on mostly single-word entries, bilingual dictionaries do not record larger and more complex units of meaning in a methodical way. Neither do they tell us which of the equivalents they offer belong in which contexts. This is one of the reasons why bilingual dictionaries do not help us to translate into a language we are not very familiar with. The user is left with many options and hardly any instructions for selecting the proper equivalent. From parallel corpora we can extract a larger variety of translation equivalents embedded in their contexts, which make them unambiguous. This is what makes parallel corpora so attractive. Working with parallel corpora lets us do away with ambiguity, with being given alternatives between which we have to choose. We will identify monosemous units of meaning in one language and find the equivalents in the other language(s). Now, when we have to translate a given word, we will compare this word with the words we find in its company, with the words in the units of meaning we have extracted from the parallel corpus. The closest match usually renders the correct translation equivalent.

For most applications, parallel corpora will have to be aligned so that a unit in one language corresponds to the equivalent unit in another language. The standard unit of alignment is still the sentence. In the beginning, parallel corpora were sentence aligned by hand. For alignment is not a trivial task. First, it is not always easy to identify sentence endings automatically. Full stops can also designate abbreviations, some of which can occur either within a sentence or at the end, such as *etc.* In some languages, full stops can also indicate ordinal numbers (2. = 2nd). Second, sentences are by no means stable units. One sentence in the source language can correspond to two or more sentences in the target language; or two source language sentences can be subsumed in one target language sentence. Anyone who has closely compared texts and their translations will have noticed that sometimes sentences are plainly omitted in the translation, or that new sentences are introduced, it seems almost at the translator's whim. This is why, even though there are various tools available to align corpora on the sentence level, alignment is a time-consuming process involving substantial human intervention. This is one of the reasons why there are still only a few parallel corpora of considerable size (say, more than 5 million words per language).

It is even trickier to align corpora on the lexical level. Ideally, one would like to see each unit of meaning in the source corpus linked to the equivalent unit in the target corpus. (Source and target, in this context, do not refer to the language of the original and the translated text; rather, the source language is the language which we choose as our point of departure, while the target language is the one in which we want to find equivalents.) Our results will, to a certain extent, depend on this directionality. It is well known that bilingual dictionaries are not reversible. Whether the results extracted from a parallel corpus are reversible, and to what extent, is still unknown. Lexical alignment uses statistical procedures and/or lexicon look-up. Neither is very reliable. It is because bilingual dictionaries (and the lexicons derived from them) are not very instructive that we turned to parallel corpora in the first place. Hence the lexical alignment we start with is only tentative; and all it tells us is what could be an equivalent of the source unit. We will still be given both *work* and *labour* and also some other words like *employment* or *job* as equivalent of French *travail*. If we want to find out more, we have to look at the contexts in which *travail* is embedded when it is translated as *work*, as opposed to the contexts in which *travail* is embedded when it is translated as *labour*. Thus, if we have to translate *travaux* followed by the adjective *préparatoires*, our parallel corpus tells us that this phrase is never translated as *preparatory labours* but always as *preparatory work* (with a singular phrase in English corresponding to the French plural phrase).

Recently it has become quite common among corpus linguists to consult the Internet as a virtual corpus. This is particularly useful when we want to find out if a word or a phrase we have heard really exists and in which kinds of texts it occurs. Whenever we cannot find evidence of words or units of meaning in our classic corpora, we can turn to the Internet. There are many commercial browsers we can use, like Altavista or Google, and they all have their advantages and disadvantages. The Internet is larger than any existing library, and if a word is in current use, we are bound to find it there. What we do not know, however, is how the Internet is composed in terms of the parameters mentioned earlier. Frequencies of occurrence have to be carefully interpreted. The Internet can be seen neither as a sample of a middle-class person's private reading load nor as a sample of text production *in toto*. So far, there are hardly any transcripts of spoken language on the Internet, and the written language we find is a reflection of what kind of texts different people put on the Internet. Some texts exist only there; others are copied from other written material. And here too we must be careful; not all copies are perfect clones of the original texts.

For practical purposes, the Internet, even if we restrict ourselves to the freely accessible websites, is, at any given time, if not infinite then certainly inexhaustible. No browser can claim to cover more than a selection. Such a selection is usually so big that by the time we have extracted all citations for a given keyword (or larger unit of meaning), some texts queried will already have been taken from the servers they were on, while others, new ones, will have been added. The Internet is a virtual corpus, and, like the discourse of any language community, we cannot expect to access it as a whole. Normally, if someone wants to use the Internet as a source, they should, therefore, download all the texts they are working with, and compile them in a special corpus; and they should document them with their web addresses and other bibliographic information and the date of the download.

4.3 Meaning in discourse

'When I use a word,' Humpty Dumpty said in a rather scornful tone, 'it means just what I choose it to mean – neither more nor less.'

'The question is,' said Alice, 'whether you can make words mean so many different things'.

'The question is,' said Humpty Dumpty, 'which is to be the master – that's all'.

(Lewis Carroll, *Alice Through The Looking Glass*)

It is not Humpty Dumpty as an individual but the discourse community as a whole (or at least sufficiently significant fractions of it) that decide what a word means. Individual members of this community who want to say something but are dissatisfied with the words they find and how they are being used, have two options. They can either introduce a new word (e.g. *Eurotrash*, the name of a popular series on British television) into the discourse – which happens relatively rarely – or they can try to change the meaning of an existing word, by using it in a new context. Shifts in the meaning often start off in slang: today's slang use of *wicked* means 'good', while the 'proper' meaning is quite the opposite. The meaning of the word *tart* as 'woman of loose morals' has become so dominant that bakeries and cafes sometimes see themselves pressed to use new (and no doubt more elegant) names like *gateau* and *torte*. Another example is the *cold caller* (most neologisms appear to be collocations of some sort or other), who is not a caller in the cold, but someone who is paid for calling people they do not know to try to sell things to them. This new usage is now beginning to be registered in the dictionaries.

To show how meaning is constituted in discourse we will present one word in detail. We want to show that there is no magic formula, inside or outside of the discourse, no concept or no feature of 'reality' that we can identify as the thing the word stands for. Words are symbols. But they do not stand for something unequivocally assigned to them by some infallible deity for a shorter or longer eternity. A word in a text refers to (or is a trace of) previous occurrences of the same word, in the same text, or in all previous texts to which the present text, sometimes explicitly, but mostly implicitly, refers. It refers to all that has been said about that word previously. As we know, people do not always agree with each other. For corpus linguists, this is good news. For then we find a discussion going on in the discourse community, with various factions making different claims about what they consider to be reality. If this controversial feature can be subsumed under one concept, then each faction will try to define this concept as it suits their views. They will volunteer to present their views in the form of paraphrases of the linguistic expression in question to the linguists on silver trays.

The word we have chosen for the investigation here is *globalisation* (or in its alternative spelling, *globalization*). This word is a derivation from the adjective *global*, which has been part of the English language for many centuries without changing its meaning in a noticeable way. From this adjective, it was always possible to form the word *globalisation*, and, though not very frequently, it happened now and then. Not all dictionary-makers have registered that somewhere in the 1990s this word suddenly embarked on an unprecedented career. Thus, the relatively recent *NODE* has only a very short entry for *globalize*:

> **globalize** (also **-ise**) verb
> develop or be developed so as to make possible international influence or operation.

In the same entry, *globalization* is mentioned only as a derived noun, meaning nothing more than 'the process or activity of making something global'. Globalisation was not always as popular as it is today. In 1983, the economic scientist Ted Levitt entitled one of his articles for the *Harvard Business Review* 'The globalization of markets'. This journal is obligatory reading for all leading experts, and Ted Levitt is a well-known figure. There are only nine sentences with the actual word *globalization* in his ten-page article. The article does not define *globalization* as a term, nor does it introduce it as a new word, rather it is used assuming everyone understands it. It seems to have been this very article that determined the current usage of *globalisation* that has made the term a household word in disciplines such as economics and social and political studies. As terms need to be defined, specialised terminological dictionaries do so, and give us a host of definitions. However, in general language lexicography, *globalisation* is not recognised as a new word by a number of reference dictionaries. We have already mentioned *NODE* but we do not find *globalisation* in *The Oxford Dictionary of New Words* (1997) either. The *Macmillan English Dictionary for Advanced Learners* (2002), however, tells us that *globalization* is 'the idea that the world is developing a single economy and culture as a result of improved technology and communications and the influence of very large MULTINATIONAL companies'.

What does the corpus tell us about the meaning of *globalisation/ globalization*? First of all, it tells us that most citations in British sources of the Bank of English use the form with *s*, while almost all citations in the US part of the sources use the form with *z* (although *z* is also the preferred form for some British publishers). It is useful to look at them separately, because it just may happen that British *globalisation* has a meaning that differs from American *globalization*.

But before we look at this example in more detail, we will explore the notion of meaning as usage and paraphrase.

4.4 Meaning as usage and paraphrase

How does corpus linguistics deal with meaning? Meaning, as has been said before, is in the discourse. But how do we look for it there? How do we find it? There are two main aspects to meaning. Meaning is usage and paraphrase. Usage and paraphrase reflect the two ways we deal with language. We can participate in the discourse as speakers and as hearers.

Knowing the usage of a word or other lexical item lets us participate successfully in discourse. To make ourselves understood as speakers we must use linguistic items according to the expectations of hearers. These expectations are based on what has been said before. Since everybody has heard time and again the phrase 'the increasing globalisation of the financial markets', it will offend no one if we use *globalisation* with *increasing* as an adjectival modifier, and with *of the financial markets* as a genitive or prepositional modifier, depending on what you prefer to call it. There are other adjectives that often modify *globalisation,* and there are other nouns we frequently find in the genitive phrase modifiers. We also find that *globalisation* can be part of a genitive phrase modifying another noun, such as *the effects of globalisation.* This kind of contextual data determines the usage of a word. For nouns such as *globalisation,* we should also know of which verb phrases it can be the subject, and which verbs it can complement. Not all the information we find is relevant for establishing the usage of a lexical item. But the words, together with their phrasal positions, which occur with a satisfactory frequency and with a defined statistical frequency in the context of the lexical item in question (i.e. *globalisation*), make up its usage. As long as we, as discourse participants, stick to the established usage, we cannot go wrong. But once we say 'the green globalisation of our forgotten noses' we will have lost our audience. Nobody will listen to us, and we will be told we are talking nonsense. There is nothing remotely similar to this phrase in established usage that could serve as an analogy for interpreting it. Usage is something that can be established by a computer. That means in order to deal with the usage of a lexical item we do not necessarily have to understand it, in the sense that we would be able to paraphrase it. Computers can create texts fully complying with the established usage of all the lexical items that form the text. They might be indistinguishable from texts of certain politicians, but this does not imply that the computers knew what they were saying. In this sense, usage is meaning only in a very twisted way.

Usage, however, is what we have to learn as discourse participants. It is what comes naturally to native speakers, it seems. Those who are striving to acquire English as a second language have to learn consciously that bereavement in the context of guilt is expressed by *grief,* while bereavement in the context of sadness is always felt as *sorrow,* and not the other way around. Usage is therefore something we have to cope with as members of the discourse community, as little as it may help us with the understanding of a lexical item.

Determining the usage of lexical items and coping with it are essential to the methodology of corpus linguistics. It is as close as computational methods can hope to approximate the mystery of meaning. Whenever we want the computer to identify a word as part of a unit of meaning in a corpus, it will be done through established usage. The profile of usage generated by the computer (which itself is incapable of understanding, incapable of what is sometimes called 'interpreting symbols') is like the fingerprint of a word as part of a unit of meaning: it identifies the person without telling you who the person is. The usage profile is the device in computation that can resolve ambiguity.

Meaning, we have said, is usage and paraphrase. The computer can give us the usage profile of a unit of meaning without knowing what it means. But the computer does not know and cannot know what it means. Indeed it seems as if humans are the only species of the kingdom of machines or animals who have a tendency to think about what something is about. When they see, in springtime, bees flying from blossom to blossom, they believe they know that this is about making honey, and has the additional fortuitous effect that the blossoms get fertilised. They see these two aspects as the meaning of why bees fly. The bee does not know why it is flying (and probably does not care about it). And while a computer, programmed for this task, may have no problem in translating the sentence 'Bees fly from flower to flower to produce honey' into the French sentence '*Les abeilles volent de la fleur à la fleur pour produire le miel*' (translation produced by the Altavista browser) we would not believe for a minute that this machine or the program it runs on has any idea about bees, flowers or honey. Only humans can appreciate aboutness. Only they can deal with signs. For something like flying bees is 'about' something else only when we take this something (flying bees) as a symbol for something else (producing honey). But is not the flower then a symbol for the bee signifying that it will find sugar there? I don't think it is. I don't think the bee will reason along the lines of 'oh, over there I can see (or smell) a flower – I take this to mean that I'll find sugar there'. An appreciation of aboutness presupposes consciousness, awareness. Only humans can be conscious in this sense. This unique human mental ability to find out consciously (rather than randomly) what something is about is called intentionality. In the philosophy of mind there has been a long debate about whether intentionality really is a human trait or perhaps just an illusion. If it were nothing but an illusion, then we could say the human mind is, in principle, the same as a computer, only more complex. But if intentionality exists, computers will never become like humans, and we will always be able to pull the plug when we feel like it. The issue of intentionality is very skilfully discussed in John Searle's book *Intentionality* (Searle 1983).

Only something that is a sign can mean something, because only a sign can signify something other than itself. We can say that our life has a meaning only if we take it to be a sign, a symbol for something else. Things, events, processes which we do not interpret as signs do not mean anything. However, there are different kinds of signs: symptoms, icons and symbols in the narrow sense. What we have mentioned above, the flying bees as signs that they are on their way to produce honey, is a symptom. It is something we can figure out, not because flying bees bear some resemblance to a honey jar, but because the discourse is full of stories about bees flying around to produce honey. What we did, when we saw those bees, was to remember those stories and to use our common sense to infer that they were up to honey-making. The second kind of sign are icons, signs that somehow give you a visual (or oral or tactile) clue of what they, as signs, stand for. A big picture at the roadside representing a honey pot will probably mean that there is someone there who wants to sell their honey. Icons are signs that we interpret in terms of their resemblance to whatever is indicative of some thing, act or event. Interpreting icons is, again, largely an application of common sense, together with memory of other instances to which this instance may be analogous. Finally, symbols in the narrow sense are signs to which a meaning has been assigned arbitrarily. The vocabulary of a language is commonly seen as a set of such symbols. Some people may speak as if it is the dictionary or lexicographers who assign meanings to words. But the lexicographers only document the meanings that are already assigned. It is the dis-course community that assigns meanings to words (or, rather, to lexical items). Members of this community may not always be happy with the meanings they find assigned, and they are free to change the assign-ments, for the sign, the lexical item, does not resemble what it stands for. If, in England, the word *robin* stands for one kind of bird, that does not prevent Americans from deciding that in their variety of English the word stands for quite a different bird. It is not particularly sur-prising that words such as *beech, bream, grasshopper* and *magpie* have different meanings in different parts of the English-speaking world. With icons, of course, it cannot be so simple. A placard representing a jar of honey can hardly indicate that you can buy green asparagus. Flying bees will never signify that coal is being mined. A good guide to signs is Rudi Keller's book *A Theory of Linguistic Signs* (1998).

Meaning is an aspect of signs, of symptoms, icons and symbols. Meaning is one of the aspects, form being the other. Meaning and form are inseparable. Once you take away the form, the meaning vanishes. This is why it is wrong to look at language as a system into which you can encode a message and from which you can decode a message. There is no message without form. Thus it is wrong to say the text contains a meaning; the text is the meaning.

There are many theories about meaning, and almost all claim that the meaning of a linguistic unit is something outside of the discourse.

Some say the meaning is what the linguistic unit refers to, out there in some discourse-external reality; others say that the meaning corresponds to some representation we have in our minds; some say meaning is represented by semantically interpreted logical calculus or some other formal system. Reality will hardly do, as we have pointed out above. It is, before it is ordered and structured by language, amorphous and chaotic. Mental representations only multiply our problems. For either these representations are also signs, in which case their meaning is inseparable from their form, and to get at their meaning, we would have to come up with yet another representation, and still another one on top of that, and so on. (John Searle, in his book *The Rediscovery of the Mind*, 1992, refers to this phenomenon as the 'homunculus' problem, while for Daniel Dennett, in his book *Consciousness Explained*, 1993, it is the problem of the 'central meaner'. Both scholars agree that translating the meaning of a linguistic unit into a mental representation is nothing but a fallacy.) Or, if mental representations are translations of meaning into an expression of some formal system, we are still no better off. For how would we know what the expressions of such a formal system mean? We could only explain them in natural language, and then we are back at square one. Of course we can translate any sentence or text into an artificial language such as Esperanto. But to understand that Esperanto sentence or text we would have to re-translate it into a language we are familiar with. We just cannot escape the prison of natural language. All these attempts to approach meaning are like burning wood in a stove: if we succeed, we are left with nothing. Once the form is burnt, the meaning has vanished.

Our point of departure was that a sign is something that stands for something else. But if, as we have been arguing, it does not stand for something in some reality not affected by the discourse, if it does not stand for a representation in the mind, if it does not stand for some expression in a formal linguistic system, then what does it stand for? When you are asked what a cantaloupe is, or a unicorn, what comes to your mind? You may remember market stalls where you have seen heaps of cantaloupes, you may remember eating cantaloupe, and the taste and texture of the fruit perhaps come to your mind. You may remember stories you were told about unicorns, or you may have read about them. You may also remember what you have told other people about them. You may remember a picture in a children's book, or a Burgundian wall hanging, or a little illustration in a medieval manuscript, depicting a unicorn. Isn't that what meaning is, what the linguistic signs *cantaloupe* and *unicorn* stand for?

If we were to take these memories to be the meaning of lexical units, then we would adopt the position of cognitive linguistics. Our mental representations would not be as orderly as Anna Wierzbicka (1996) would like them to be, and certainly these representations would not be anything like universal, because everyone's memories are unique, and they would contain ineffable qualia like your or my taste experience of cantaloupes. Your memories form your understanding of cantaloupes and unicorns, and they would be reflected in your response to the question what these items are. But these memories are private and individual, and therefore they cannot be the meaning of the signs *cantaloupe* and *unicorn.*

Language is a social, not a psychological phenomenon, and so is meaning. The meaning of *cantaloupe* and *unicorn* is what is said about them in the discourse. Your response to the question what these items are will be a new contribution to the discourse, and it may well contain statements that have not been said before. If your audience is happy with them, they may remember them, and they may even repeat them in suitable situations. In ten or twenty years, you might even find traces of it in new editions of dictionaries. On the other hand, your audience will also compare what you say with what they have heard before. If what you say disagrees with their memories, they will ask other members of the discourse community. Unless they quote from dictionaries, it is highly improbable that those who volunteer their view of cantaloupes and unicorns will repeat anyone else's statements *verbatim,* word for word. If your audience is still unsatisfied with what they are being told, they might resort to querying libraries, archives and even the Internet. In the end, they will come up with a host of reports on cantaloupes and on unicorns. Some of these reports look more or less like definitions; some like more technical explanations; many are just stories. A lot will overlap each other, while some reports will not be supported by any others. There could be a lot of disagreement. Should we trust Caesar when he claims there were real unicorns in the Teutonic forests, for example? Many of the statements will in fact not be directly about cantaloupes and unicorns but about what other people have said about them, about how reliable or credible their claims are.

We call all these statements, definitions, explanations, and stories that focus on cantaloupes or on unicorns, paraphrases. What all the paraphrases of the word *unicorn* will definitely have in common is that they paraphrase the word *unicorn.* That alone is what keeps them together. Otherwise they may be as different as they come. This set of paraphrases then is the meaning of the lexical item *unicorn.* It cannot be reduced to a simple formula. It is fuzzy, vague, full of contradictions;

some of it may be true and some of it may be wrong. It is not the linguist's task to filter out what they think is right. This is what the linguistic sign *unicorn* stands for: the set of paraphrases dealing with unicorns. This is what the word *unicorn* is about.

Meaning as paraphrase thus shows us another way of identifying units of meaning. In this perspective, a unit of meaning is whatever we find paraphrases for in the discourse. Usage profiles can be handled efficiently by computers. Paraphrases, on the other hand, have to be interpreted. They have to be understood. This is something computers cannot do. Therefore they will never know what cantaloupes and unicorns are.

After these rather lengthy remarks about usage and paraphrase, we can finally return to the case study of the meaning of the word *globalisation*. In the following section, we show how a computer can create a usage profile for us.

4.5 Globalisation

To start, we have analysed a sample of 200 citations (from the Bank of English) of *globalisation*, and asked the computer to give us the most frequent collocates of the word. Among the most frequent collocates are the following words: *anti, world, against, means, economic, international* and *business*, as illustrated by the following concordance lines:

```
      Forum, the main anti- globalisation umbrella group at the
    defended against anti- globalisation protesters by one of
  than we used to. Despite globalisation, the world has at the
    debate, related to the globalisation of the world economy,
    of the protest against globalisation is, however, mistakenly
      has held our against globalisation of culture for a long time
    is the argument that globalisation means economic problems
   artistic strategies. Globalisation here means the same old
          and economic globalisation was kidding themselves
  economic policy is the globalisation of markets. If economic
  change in the wake of globalisation, international competi-
    related has been the globalisation of international manu-
        in business law globalisation will cause even worse
 illogical attacks on the globalisation of business
```

As we have said before, it is useful in this case to look separately at the spelling variant with *z* in order to establish whether *globalization* is used differently. Already the total number of actual occurrences in the Bank of English is quite different: *globalization* occurs 468 times, while the total number of the citations for *globalisation* is 1,447. This can be easily explained by the fact that the data in the Bank of English are 'biased' towards British English in which the spelling with *s* is more common. But that is not the whole truth. If we look at the sources of the citations, we can see that citations for *globalisation* come mainly from newspaper texts and citations for *globalization* are mainly from books, many of them American (but also some British. The most frequent collocates for *globalization* (based on a sample of 200) are only partly the same as above. We do find such collocates as: *economic, markets, world, investment, financial, international* but we do not find *anti* or *against*.

To find some of the paraphrases of *globalisation* we looked up a sample of what the corpus tells us about 'what globalisation is':

```
              degradation. But globalisation is a fact and, by
     rapidly changing world. Globalisation is a much overused word
        on the world stage.'' Globalisation is a trend that many
     technological change. Globalisation is a catch-all to
       and access to capital. Globalisation is a redistribution
    conventional wisdom on globalisation is a relic of the
     war and the economics of globalisation is a story which gets
         the poor even poorer. Globalisation is a fancy euphemism
       problem in particular. Globalisation is a market-led process,
          in inverted commas. Globalisation is a term that Giddens
      at Conduit, explains: 'Globalisation is a trend that everyone
          major issues. Still, globalisation is a process that has
              you realise that globalisation is an accepted phenomenon
        and benefiting from, globalisation is an open society, in
            may be in danger. Globalisation is an opportunity and a
       apreciation is that globalisation is an unstoppable force,
    lot of the criticism of globalisation is based on ignorance
             Mr Rubin argues globalisation is both good and inevi-
        Precisely because globalisation'' is demonised as an
         Etzioni argue that globalisation is destroying communities
    euro's arrival is that globalisation is here to stay as
       the allegation that globalisation is inherently harmful.
       those who say that globalisation is just a bigger market,
      - with mixed results. Globalisation is like a giant wave,
        The reality is that globalisation is not inevitable, it is
    tourists. All the same, globalisation is not to be resisted,
      best way to deal with globalisation is not to fight it but
           however, that globalisation is not a painless exercise
    trend towards increasing globalisation is not easily
       past few months show, globalisation is not a one-way street.
    must demonstrate that globalisation is not just a code word
       a sounder basis for globalisation is required. If neither
```

```
voiced an anxiety that globalisation is robbing nations
     left in the age of globalisation is tearing apart even
   the global economy. Globalisation is the big issue of our
humbly born. To be anti- globalisation is to march, under the
```

As we can see globalisation 'is' and 'is not' lots of things. The discourse takes notice of the fact that, if there is a relationship between
the word *globalisation* and some discourse-external reality, it is not an
easy one. We are told that *globalisation* is a much overused word, a
story, a fancy euphemism, a term, and not just a code word or a one-
way street. This shows how we can use natural language to talk about
language. It is something we cannot do in formal languages like
mathematics, logical calculi, or programming languages. There you
have to move outside the system to be able to talk about it. But where
should we move from our language? Indeed every other language,
every formal language, can be defined only by natural language. There
is no formal algorithm, no calculus that would not need this kind of
definition or explanation in a natural language. And therefore we
have to use our own language to discuss it. If we look at the context
left to *globalisation*, we see that people discuss the way in which other
people use *globalisation*. Someone explains, you realise, there is an
appreciation and also a criticism, people argue, demonstrate or say
that *globalisation* is this or that.

But what is the thing behind the word? Globalisation is: a fact, a
trend, a process, a phenomenon, an opportunity, an unstoppable
force; it is both good and inevitable; is here to stay; is inherently
harmful; is like a giant wave; is not inevitable; is not to be resisted; is
not a painless exercise; and is the big issue. This looks confusing. Is it
not inevitable, or is it here to stay? Is it harmful, or is it good? For
whom is it an opportunity, for whom is it a painful exercise? Can we
understand the word on the basis of these citations? Can we define it?

Our corpus is the Bank of English, with about 450 million words.
The texts it contains were spoken or written mainly in the last twenty
years and it is strongly biased towards British English. When we go
through the concordance lines of *globalisation* we notice there is a lot of
debating, worrying and talking about globalisation; there are many
protests, demonstrations and campaigns against globalisation, and we
find many instances of anti-globalisation and anti-globalisation pro-
testers; globalisation is economic and increasing, there is an ongoing
globalisation process; people talk about an age or era of globalisation,
about the benefits, the challenge, the impact, the pressures, the forces
and effects of globalisation. This all sounds familiar. Globalisation is
often also connected with emotions, and these are predominantly

negative ones. About one-third of the citations are of neutral tone and only about one-tenth of them can be considered to have a positive tone. This occurs mainly in the context of business, politics and new technology.

We get a slightly different picture if we look at *globalization*. Not all of these instances are American English, for the *OED* prefers the spelling with *z*. Here is a sample of the citations:

```
  the impact of economic globalization on the world of work
overwhelmed by the rapid globalization of economic
   trends, including the globalization of markets.
us a picture of how this globalization of financial markets
elsewhere in the world, globalization holds the promise of
This is the world of new globalization of borders easily
   itself a result of the globalization of investment. While
illustrates cost of the globalization of investment. It also
technology and increasing globalization challenging the way
 Third, there has been a globalization of the international
      In this new form of globalization, the international
```

The most apparent differences from the previous citations are the matter-of-fact tone and the different genre from which these citations come.

Let's compare our corpus evidence with Ted Levitt's use of the word *globalization* in 1983. The following are the citations from his article:

The **globalization** of markets is at hand.

Nor is the sweeping gale of **globalization** confined to these raw material or high-tech products, where the universal language of customers and users facilitates standardization.

The theory holds, at this stage in the evolution of **globalization**, no matter what conventional market research and even common sense may suggest about different national and regional tastes, preferences, needs, and institutions.

Barriers to **globalization** are not confined to the Middle East.

It orchestrates the twin vectors of technology and **globalization** for the world's benefit.

The differences that persist throughout the world despite its **globalization** affirm an ancient dictum of economics – that things are driven by what happens at the margin, not at the core.

To refer to the persistence of economic nationalism (protective and subsidized trade practices, special tax aids, or restrictions for home producers) as a barrier to the **globalization** of markets is to make a valid point.

Two vectors shape the world – technology and **globalization**.

Given what is everywhere the purpose of commerce, the global company will shape the vectors of technology and **globalization** into its great strategic fecundity.

Levitt's first use of the word *globalization* in his article (apart from the title) is in the following sentence: *The globalization of markets is at hand.* In the Bank of English there are eleven occurrences of *globalisation of markets* and five of *globalization of markets* as illustrated by the following lines:

```
of stocks. Also, as globalisation of markets continues to
a mystery where the globalisation of markets is taking us. Its
   adjustment to the globalisation of markets and the influence
     into account the globalisation of markets and of the features
       because of the globalisation of markets, which will have
           rapidly with globalisation of markets. Kevin Bales reports
```

Levitt talks about 'the globalization of markets' being 'at hand'. All the evidence from the Bank of English shows that 'globalisation of markets' is now an established notion. It tells us what is happening with the 'globalisation of markets' presently: it 'grows' and we have to take it 'into account'.

Levitt mentions *globalization* for the second time when he talks about how 'globalization' influences world business; the expression he uses is the 'gale of globalization'. In the Bank of English we find no occurrences of 'gale of globalisation'. If we look up what comes as a 'gale of', we find it is mostly 'giggles' and 'laughter' and 'wind', but we do also find *gale of economic change, energy* or *modernity*, notions closely related to globalisation.

The third occurrence of *globalization* in Levitt's text is in the phrase 'the evolution of globalization', which has no occurrences in our corpus. This may correspond to our earlier finding that 'globalisation' in our contemporary language use is an established notion. Levitt mentions 'barriers to globalization' twice in his text. There are no citations for exactly the same wording in our corpus, but if we look up 'barriers to' we can see that most frequently we talk about 'barriers to entry' and 'barriers to trade', again facts closely related with globalisation. Levitt strongly associates 'technology and globalization' (three occurrences in his text); and indeed, judging from the evidence from Bank of English, globalisation is still very much associated with technology both directly and indirectly.

```
     pressure from technology and globalisation 'the half-life
  benefit from new technology and globalisation than others,
  arthritic. When technology and globalisation demanded changes
     INFORMATION technology and globalisation are the driving
     arguing that technology and globalisation are tending to
        of clothes. Technology and globalisation mean that every-
     the impact of technology and globalisation, where business
              needs. Technology and globalisation have revolu-
Why? 'Because of technology and globalization, everyone has
```

The last occurrence of 'globalization' in Levitt's text is the following:

> The differences that persist throughout the world despite its globalization
> affirm an ancient dictum of economics – that things are driven by what
> happens at the margin, not at the core.

A search for 'globalisation' and 'despite' yielded the following lines:

```
     insular despite the globalisation that affects
  But, despite all of this, globalisation has been the source
 despite the drift towards globalisation, national policies
    despite the increasing globalisation of the capital
      despite pressures of globalisation, it will take a
```

What we present here is based on insufficient evidence. We do not know if there are differences between American and British usage, as we do not have a comparable corpus of American English. Our citations are not classified according to domain, genre, text type or publication date. We cannot see if there was a change of meaning, and we do not know whether *globalisation* is used differently in texts written for the public at large from texts addressed at a professional audience. The structure of the Bank of English makes it hard to extract the information needed for this kind of classification. But the evidence we have for example clearly suggests there is a difference in tone, depending on the genre: texts from newspapers often have a sceptical tone, while the tone of professional and academic writing is more 'matter of fact'. This is not surprising; in fact it could have been expected and it is most probably also true of many other words.

This, then, is how and what corpus linguistics can contribute to the meaning of the word *globalisation*. It is the evidence of the corpus citations of *globalisation* within their contexts, condensed and brought into some kind of contingent order. It is much more than we would find in any dictionary, and, at the same time, it does not have the coherence of an encyclopaedic article. It is obviously in many points contradictory; it is nothing like a definition. Is this the meaning of *globalisation*? Globalisation has become such an important fact of our society that social scientists have felt the need to define it. 'Globalisation' has thus established itself as a term. Let's have a look at its complex definition in the *Oxford Dictionary of Sociology* (1998). Is it so very different from some of our citations?

globalization, globalization theory

Globalization theory examines the emergence of a global cultural system. It suggests that global culture is brought about by a variety of social and cultural developments: the existence of a world-satellite information system; the emergence of global patterns of consumption and consumerism; the cultivation of cosmopolitan life-styles; the emergence of global sport such as the Olympic Games ... the spread of world tourism; the decline of the sovereignty of the nation-state ... More importantly, globalism involves a new consciousness of the world as a single place. ... Perhaps the most concise definition suggests that globalization is 'a social process in which the constraints of geography on social and cultural arrangements recede and in which people are becoming increasingly aware that they are receding' (Malcolm Waters, Globalization, 1995) ... Contemporary globalization theory argues that globalization comprises two entirely contradictory processes of homogenization and differentiation; and that there are powerful movements of resistance against globalization processes ... It is undoubtedly true that, on a planet in which the same fashion accessories (such as designer training-shoes) are manufactured and sold across every continent, one can send and receive electronic mail from the middle of a forest in Brazil, eat McDonald's hamburgers in Moscow as well as Manchester, and pay for all this using a Mastercard linked to a bank account in Madras, then the world does indeed appear to be increasingly 'globalized'. However, the excessive use of this term as a sociological buzzword has largely emptied it of analytical and explanatory value...

As globalisation is a worldwide phenomenon, we need not restrict ourselves to the English-language evidence. There are also some interesting data available about *Globalisierung*, its German equivalent, based on the analysis of one single newspaper, the *Tageszeitung*. It was only in the year 1996 that *Globalisierung* gained ground. From 1988 until the end of 1995 we find altogether about 160 citations. Then, suddenly, for the year 1996 the figure jumps up to 320, and from then on remains more or less on the same level. Before 1996, *Globalisierung* was used as an *ad hoc* formation derived from *global*, without any specific meaning other than 'the action or process of something turning global'. In each instance, it was necessary to specify what was being globalised, and therefore *Globalisierung* never came alone, but was always in the company of modifiers (such as in *die Globalisierung der modernen Lebensweise*, the globalisation of the modern way of life). For the year 1996, when the word suddenly made a jump in frequency (indicating, among other things, that a change of meaning, from something more general to something more specific, had occurred), we find a large number of citations in which *Globalisierung* comes without modifiers, but with explanations or paraphrases (*in der Tat bedeutet Globalisierung Amerikanisierung*, indeed, globalisation means Americanisation). By the time that everyone is supposed to understand what *Globalisierung* means, this percentage goes down again, and we find again many modifiers. Before 1996, the modifiers appeared to be a random lot – everything could be connected to *Globalisierung*. After 1996, the same modifiers recurred time and again; the new meaning of *Globalisierung* associated the word mostly with finance, trade, technology, the economy at large, and the workforce, indeed remarkably similar to the modifiers we find with *globalisation* in the Bank of English.

We deliberately chose the word *globalisation* as a neologism. Must we not assume that all words once were neologisms? Before Lucullus brought the cherry (*cerasus*) from Persia to Rome, there was no need for a name for it. It makes sense to assume that the introduction of neologisms into the discourse always occurs along the same lines. As long as the word (or larger unit of meaning) is still new, it needs to be explained. Not everyone understands the word in the same way. Explanations also serve the purpose of negotiating the meaning of a word within the discourse community. It can take a while before the larger part of the audience has come to some kind of tacit agreement. From then on, only those discourse participants who object to the agreement will come up with new paraphrases. In principle, we can say that once the meaning of a new word has become uncontroversial it can be used to paraphrase other units of meaning.

The word *globalisation* shows nicely that the discourse community is not at all homogenous. The discourse community is, it should be remembered, identical with the society whose language we are dealing with, and it is as multifaceted as this society is. So while for one section of the discourse community the meaning of *globalisation* has become established and accepted, there are other sections still in disagreement. This is why the paraphrases and explanations we find in the corpus do not have a common denominator and why, at times, they even contradict each other. Contradictory evidence, however, is not what we have come to regard, in traditional lexicography, as the meaning of a word. Now, once we have presented the citations, we must sift the evidence and write up a coherent, concise definition that we can put into the dictionary. Now we must find the magic formula.

There is no secret formula; and there is no overt formula, unless we leave it to a committee of experts (on what?) to define *globalisation* once and for all, so that anyone who thereafter uses *globalisation* differently will be reprimanded. But if this were to happen, *globalisation* would have ceased to be a natural language word; it would have become a term in a formal system of terminology. Corpus linguistics has nothing to contribute to standardised terminology. No contribution to the discourse will ever change the meaning of a standardised term, because it has no other meaning than the definition assigned to it. *Ascorbic acid, DNA* or *electrolytic rectifier* are terms with relatively fixed meaning, hardly variable in any imaginable context.

Why do new words occur? Why do other words disappear? Will *globaloney* be as widely used in twenty years' time as *globalization* is today? In December 2002 *Newsweek* published an article 'The new buzzword: globaloney'. The article begins: 'So far as we can tell, congresswoman Clare Boothe Luce coined the term "globaloney" in 1943 to trash what Vice President Henry Wallace liked to call his "global thinking" ...' (Miller 2002).

There are only five citations for *globaloney* in the Bank of English and they all are from British sources.

```
      in impressive-sounding globaloney are provided by
and more earlier. For all the globaloney to be found in modern
     LSE lecture last week – is globaloney. Much of the talk about
  nosed divi, talkin a load o' globaloney (Fings ain' t what they
       Business, 1993. Hirst, P. Globaloney in Prospect,
```

It is only recently that *globaloney,* as in the example below from the *Mail on Sunday* (22 July 2001), has started appearing more frequently in the press as a reaction to the phenomenon of globalisation. We have to wait to see whether it catches on.

These 'anti-globalist' demonstrators are globalists themselves. Whether they
are hippy-dippy groups concerned with peace, the environment and Third
World debt, or old-fashioned leftie groups with a tradition of small-scale
violence, they all want to replace the present globalisation with their own
form of globaloney.

Words are different from terms. A word we find in the text resonates
with an infinite number of previous citations, many of them shared
between the speaker and the hearer, because they have grown up in the
same discourse community and have been exposed to many of the same
texts. It is in the light of these previous citations that the speaker uses
the word and that the hearer will understand it. It is linguists who define
the discourse community. They decide how deeply they want to dig into
the past, and they define where the lines are drawn at the fringes. But
even given these limitations, this discourse is just not available *in toto*,
neither to the linguists nor to any members of the discourse community.
None of them will ever be able to capture the full meaning of a word (or
a larger unit of meaning). When we read or listen to texts we have not
previously encountered, we may well be confronted with citations
showing new semantic aspects. What we find out about the meaning of a
word will never be more than an approximation.

4.6 What corpus linguistics can tell us about the meaning of words

In 1976, a relatively unknown author by the name of Courtlandt D. B.
Bryan writes a novel about an American soldier in Vietnam killed
accidentally by fire from American forces, and he calls this novel
Friendly Fire. This phrase immediately catches on, and now, also due to
two wars against Iraq, there is hardly anyone left in the English-
speaking world who does not know what *friendly fire* means. During the
last war against Iraq, journalists started using more widely another
expression for 'friendly fire': *blue on blue*. During the war, the *Guardian*
featured a series of articles on 'The language of war'. *Blue on blue* had
an entry of its own explaining its meaning and origin:

> Blue on blue, which made its debut yesterday after the downing of an RAF
> Tornado by an American Patriot missile, comes from wargaming exercises
> where the goodies are blue and – in a hangover from cold war days – the
> baddies are red. Replaces the older term 'friendly fire' which, as Murphy's
> Laws of Combat eloquently note, isn't.
>
> (Stuart Millar, *Guardian*, 24 March 2003)

This is nothing that could have been predicted by linguists. As we have
seen for *globalisation*, there is no rule that can predict the emergence of

new expressions. And there is no rule which tells us whether an expression will catch on or not. *Friendly fire* is a fairly recent addition to our vocabulary. The title of this 1976 novel quickly entered the general discourse. It replaced the military term *fratricide*, which we also find in French. But *fratricide* is a word meaning 'the killing of one's brother (or sister)'. As such, it is rare and smacks of erudition. *Friendly fire*, on the other hand, has a familiar ring, in spite of being a neologism. With each subsequent war, it became more popular. In the 450 million words of the Bank of English, there are 267 occurrences of this phrase. Here are a few citations:

```
    those men died from friendly fire, a phenomenon which he said
   Author C.D.F. Bryan < Friendly Fire> came to the five-day
may have been killed in friendly fire. General Johnston also said
       Relatives of the friendly fire victims are angrily accusing
   mistakes, accidents 'friendly fire' , including Private Errol
```

Do lexicographers regard *friendly fire* as a unit of meaning? The largest online English dictionary is WordNet, an electronic database that has been compiled for some years now – and is still being compiled – at Princeton University under the guidance of Christiane Fellbaum. WordNet is more than a traditional dictionary. It systematically lists relations between each entry and other entries, such as synonymy, hyponymy, meronymy and antonymy. It organises the senses which it assigns to its entries as 'synsets' (sets of synonyms), where each synset is defined as a list of all entries sharing this particular meaning. All synsets or senses come with glosses and often also with an example. For several years now, WordNet has been listing collocations as well. But we did not find an entry for *friendly fire*. There could have been several possible reasons. The phrase was too new, or it was not frequent enough, or it was thought not to be a unit of meaning. The third of these reasons turned out to be the case.

The adjective *friendly* has four senses in WordNet:

1. friendly (vs. unfriendly) – (characteristic of or befitting a friend; 'friendly advice'; 'a friendly neighborhood'; 'the only friendly person here'; 'a friendly host and hostess')
2. friendly – (favorably disposed; not antagonistic or hostile; 'a government friendly to our interests'; 'an amicable agreement')
3. friendly (vs. unfriendly) – ((in combination) easy to understand or use; 'user-friendly computers'; 'a consumer-friendly policy'; 'a reader-friendly novel')

4.   friendly (vs. hostile) – (of or belonging to your own country's forces or those of an ally; 'in friendly territory'; 'he was accidentally killed by friendly fire')

This entry shows that a deliberate decision was made not to enter *friendly fire* as a collocation. For the compilers of WordNet, the phrase is a combination of two units of meaning. Are they right? Is there a separate sense of *friendly* accounting for cases such as *friendly fire* and *friendly territory*? Are there other phrases where we find this sense of *friendly*, such as *friendly houses, friendly planes, friendly newspapers*? Friendly houses seems to belong to synset 1 (cf. *friendly neighbourhood*), *friendly newspapers* seems to belong to synset 2 ('favourably disposed'). So perhaps there are really only two instances for the fourth synset. The antonym of *friendly territory* (Google: 5,130 hits) is sometimes *hostile territory* (Google: 27,800 hits), but more often *enemy territory* (Google: 239,000 hits). The antonym of *friendly fire* (Google: 150,000 hits) is sometimes *hostile fire* (Google: 30,300 hits), but again more often *enemy fire* (83,300 hits). Both antonyms should be mentioned in the entry. The question is whether it makes sense to construe a sense that is limited to two instances.

Let us now have a look at *fire* in WordNet. The noun *fire* has eight senses in WordNet.

1.   fire – (the event of something burning (often destructive); 'they lost everything in the fire')
2.   fire, flame, flaming – (the process of combustion of inflammable materials producing heat and light and (often) smoke; 'fire was one of our ancestors' first discoveries')
3.   fire, firing – (the act of firing weapons or artillery at an enemy; 'hold your fire until you can see the whites of their eyes'; 'they retreated in the face of withering enemy fire')
4.   fire – (a fireplace in which a fire is burning; 'they sat by the fire and talked')
5.   fire, attack, flak, flack, blast – (intense adverse criticism; 'Clinton directed his fire at the Republican Party'; 'the government has come under attack'; 'don't give me any flak')
6.   ardor, ardour, fervor, fervour, fervency, fire, fervidness – (feelings of great warmth and intensity; 'he spoke with great ardor')
7.   fire – (archaic) once thought to be one of four elements composing the universe (Empedocles))
8.   fire – (a severe trial; 'he went through fire and damnation')

The sense we are interested in is, of course, sense 3. Here we find the phrase *enemy fire* in an example. Adding up the glosses for sense 4 of *friendly* and sense 3 of *fire*, we obtain, *mutatis mutandis*, 'the act of firing weapons … at our own or our allies' forces'. This is an appropriate definition. Is WordNet right to deny *friendly fire* the status of a unit of meaning? While other dictionaries have nothing equivalent to Word-Net sense 4 of *friendly*, some of them list *friendly fire* as a separate entry, recognising the phrase as a unit of meaning, e.g. *NODE*: [Military] 'weapon fire coming from one's own side that causes accidental injury or death to one's own people'. Both options seem legitimate. The disadvantage of the first alternative is that it introduces a polysemy which does not exist if we accept the unit of meaning as a solution. In the context of *fire*, *friendly* can only mean sense 4, and in the context of *friendly*, *fire* can only mean sense 3. But multiplying the four senses of *friendly* with the eight senses of *fire*, we end up with thirty-two combinations, out of which we have to select the only one possible. So, if we accept Ockham's razor as the underlying principle for constructing a semantic model ('Entities are not to be multiplied without necessity'), the interpretation of *friendly fire* as a unit of meaning is obviously preferable.

From a methodological point of view, it makes sense to put *friendly fire* down as a unit of meaning because it simplifies the linguist's task to account for what a text, a sentence, a phrase mean. It is more convenient to treat the phrase as a collocation than to describe it as the contingent co-occurrence of two single words. This aspect is particularly important for the computational processing of natural language, for example for machine translation. Computers do not ask whether the meaning of *friendly fire* (or of *false dawn*) is something that cannot be inferred from the meaning of the parts they are constituted of. We use computers that do not understand what people talk about. We want them to facilitate the translation of sentences in which we encounter these and comparable phrases. The above meaning has been discussed in terms of usage and of paraphrase. Usage is something computers can cope with. If *friendly fire* is used in a unique way and not in any of the other thirty-one ways suggested by WordNet, then it is simpler to deal with it as a unit in its own right, as a lexical item that just happens to be composed of two words. But usage does not tell us how we understand the phrase. When we want to communicate with other members of the discourse community about how we understand *friendly fire*, we have to paraphrase it. Whether a given paraphrase, i.e. the interpretation of a phrase, is acceptable to the discourse community has to be left to the members of that community.

The question is, therefore, whether *friendly fire* is a unit of meaning also from the perspective of meaning as paraphrase. The answer to this question is simple. It is a unit of meaning if we find paraphrases telling us how others understand it, and thus, how we would do better to understand it as well. In the *NODE*, we have already found one paraphrase. That this is more than the concoction of an assiduous lexicographer is confirmed by a glance at the Bank of English. Among the citations of *friendly fire* there are about a dozen that comment on the phrase, try to explain it, circumscribe it or downright paraphrase it, for example:

> The United States Defence Department says an investigation has shown that about one out of every four Americans killed in battle during the Gulf War died as a result of '**friendly fire**' – in other words, they were killed by their own side.

> Whether called fratricide, amicicide, blue on blue, **friendly fire**, or – as in official U.S. casualty reports from Vietnam – 'misadventure', the phenomenon had become all too commonplace on twentieth-century battlefields.

> In Vietnam, the Americans coined the phrase '**friendly fire**', a monstrous use of the language, as if any such fire could be regarded as friendly.

> And the other problem, low visibility increases the risk of **friendly fire** – a term that means mistakenly shooting at your own side.

We learn that friendly fire is a 'phrase', a 'term', that it constitutes a 'monstrous use of language', that the Americans introduced it into the discourse in their Vietnam war, and that it means your troops are 'killed by their own side'. Paraphrases of this kind abound when a new unit of meaning, be it a single word or a collocation, enters the discourse. Then people must be told about it. As we have seen, the first evidence of *friendly fire* is probably the title of the 1976 novel. Unfortunately there are no corpora that could verify an assumption that, during that and the subsequent year, there was an abundance of paraphrases. Here again, a bilingual perspective might prove useful. What happens when translators are confronted with a lexical item for which they cannot find a translation equivalent because it has not been translated before?

Corpus linguistics tells us that translation equivalence is not something that latently always exists and just has to be discovered. Translation equivalence has to be construed. As with meaning, this construal is a communal activity, only it does not involve a discourse community of a specific language such as English, but the community of bilingual speakers of the two languages involved. One translator will come up with a proposal, which is then negotiated with the other members of that community, until agreement is reached and every translator starts using the same equivalent, or until several equivalents are considered acceptable and translators choose among them. It seems as if in the case of *friendly fire* translators had to start from scratch. Apparently there was never a fixed expression in German as an equivalent of *fratricide, blue on blue* or *friendly fire*.

Friendly fire is a phrase which is worth looking at from a bilingual perspective. What does the bilingual perspective add to the issue? This relatively new expression became more frequent only in the course of the first Gulf war, when more British soldiers were killed by friendly (mostly American) fire than by enemy fire. It was only then that the phrase began to be translated into other languages, German among them. How was it translated?

The second edition of the *Oxford–Duden*, published in 1999, acknowledges *friendly fire* as a single lexical item and gives it a separate entry. The translation equivalent it proposes is *eigenes Feuer* ('own fire'). Other translation equivalents which we find in Google and in various corpora are *freundliches Feuer, befreundetes Feuer* and the English collocation *friendly fire*, as a borrowing into German. Most of the texts we find there are texts originally written in German, not translations from the English. Still we have to assume that the concept 'friendly fire' did not exist before it was introduced into the German discourse via translations. For neither of the German equivalents mentioned above occur in the older texts of our corpora. Thus all four German options have to be seen as the results of translations.

It is noteworthy that there is, in Google, only one occurrence of *durch befreundetes Feuer* ('through/by fire of our friends'). We might have expected more, given that *befreundet* is the standard translation for the fourth meaning of *friendly* in WordNet, where we find *friendly fire* together with *friendly territory*. Indeed, *friendly territory* is *befreundetes Territorium* in German. This is a first indication that translators understand *friendly fire* as a collocation and not as a contingent combination of two single words. We can be sure that *befreundetes Feuer* will never become the default equivalent of *friendly fire*. For the phrase *durch freundliches Feuer* we find forty-eight occurrences in Google. This is a second indication that translators see *friendly fire* as a true collocation. For *freundliches Feuer* (*freundlich* being the default translation of *friendly*) would normally – without English influence – never mean 'soldiers killed by their own side' but something quite different, as in this singular Google citation:

Ihre nachtschwarzen Augen leuchteten jedoch in freundlichem Feuer, als sie in die Runde ihrer Amazonenkriegerinnen sah. ('Yet her nightblack eyes glowed in a friendly fire, as she was glancing at the round of her Amazon warriors.')

(www.silverbow.de/kilageschichte.htm)

As a single lexical item, as a unit of meaning, however, *freundliches Feuer* can mean anything the discourse community accepts. Before this can happen, however, people have to do a lot of explaining. This becomes evident from the two examples taken from Google:

Es gab 120 Verletzte durch 'freundliches Feuer' – also Treffer durch die eigenen Leute. ('There were 120 wounded from "friendly fire" – i.e. hits by one's own people.')

(www.stud.uni-goettingen.de/~s136138/ pages/read/depleted.html)

Natürlich haben die amerikanischen Militärs auch einige elektronische Mittel erfunden, um den 'Fratrizid', wie der Tod durch 'freundliches Feuer' im offiziellen Jargon auch genannt wird, möglichst auszuschließen. ('Of course, the American military have invented some electronic gadgets to rule out "fratricide", as death by "friendly fire" is often called in official jargon.')

(www.ish.com/_1048075934919.html)

In the first example the audience is told explicitly, in the form of a paraphrase, what *friendly fire* means. In both instances we find *freundliches Feuer* in quotation marks, making the audience aware that it is a new expression, and that this expression has to be understood as a unit of meaning. The next few years will show whether *freundliches Feuer* will become the default translation of friendly fire.

More frequent is *eigenes Feuer*, with 107 hits in Google for the phrase *durch eigenes Feuer* ('through/by own fire'). Two examples are presented which show that this phrase is the result of English interference:

Das Verteidigungsministerium in London hat Berichte bestätigt, nach denen durch 'eigenes Feuer' in der Nähe von Basra ein britischer Soldat getötet und fünf weitere verletzt worden sind. ('The Ministry of Defence in London has confirmed reports that near Basra one British soldier was killed and five more were wounded by "friendly fire"'.)

(www.tagesschau.de/aktuell/meldungen/
0,1185,OID1725410_TYP1_THE1687956_
NAVSPM3~1664644_REF,00.html)

Man kann es sich leicht vorstellen, dass es für die Moral eines militärischen Verbandes die schlimmste Erfahrung ist, wenn ein Kamerad durch eigenes Feuer, durch friendly fire, ums Leben kommt. ('It is easy to imagine that it is the worst experience for the morale of a military unit when a comrade dies from one's own fire, from *friendly fire*.')

(www.dradio.de/cgi-bin/es/neu-kommentar/609.html)

It seems strange indeed that the expression *eigenes Feuer*, which is very easy to understand, is put in quotation marks, but it shows that the speaker uses it as a translation of *friendly fire*. This becomes even more evident in the second example where the perfectly transparent *eigenes Feuer* is paraphrased by the much less familiar *friendly fire*. There seems to be a certain uneasiness to represent the concept expressed in English by a single unit of meaning, by a decomposable adjective+noun phrase, i.e. by two separate words. Therefore it is still doubtful whether *eigenes Feuer* will become the German default equivalent. Even though it seems to be more common, its other disadvantage is that it sounds less like *friendly fire* than the option *freundliches Feuer*.

However, the most frequent equivalent we find is the borrowing *friendly fire*. There are, in Google, 459 hits for '*durch friendly fire*'. Again we notice that in most citations, the collocation is put into quotation marks, indicating the novelty and strangeness of the expression. Here are two examples from the Österreichisches Zeitungskorpus (ÖZK; 'Austrian Newspaper Corpus'), a 500-million word corpus covering the 1990s:

Und fast schon ans Zynische grenzt jene Bezeichnung, welche die Militärsprache für den irrtümlichen Beschuß der eigenen Leute kennt. Man nennt das friendly fire – freundliches Feuer. ('And that name borders almost on cynicism which military jargon uses for mistaken fire on one's own people. They call it friendly fire – *freundliches Feuer*.')

An dieser Frontlinie beobachten wir auch immer wieder das, was die Militaristen 'friendly fire' nennen, nämlich Verluste in den eigenen Reihen durch fehlgeleitete Geschosse aus den eigenen, nachfolgenden Linien. Was die Haider-Diskussion anlangt, hat sich dieses Phänomen sogar zu einer Art intellektueller Selbstschußanlage verfestigt. ('At this frontline, we keep seeing what the military call "friendly fire", i.e. losses in one's own lines from badly aimed shots from one's own rear lines. As for the discussion about Mr Haider, this phenomenon has become firmly established as a kind of intellectual automatic firing device.')

Paraphrases reveal whether a phrase has become a fixed expression, a collocation, a unit of meaning. The paraphrases in these two examples do not tell us what *friendly* means, they explain what *friendly fire* is. While we have learned above to establish, whenever expedient, collocations or fixed expressions on the basis of usage, paraphrases will tell us whether indeed they are understood as units of meaning. There is one more indicator for a true collocation: its availability for metaphorisation processes. The second example demonstrates that friendly fire in German can now be used to refer to internecine warfare. As a metaphor, *friendly fire* loses the feature of 'accidental fire'; instead it refers to consciously hostile actions within a group. Here is another example, taken from Google:

> *Nicht alle 'Liberalen' sind eingeschwenkt. Aber das friendly fire schmerzt besonders. Merkels Kandidatur ist streitbesetzt.* ('Not all "liberals" [within the Christian Democratic Party] could be won over. But the friendly fire is particularly painful. [Party chair] Merkel's candidature is controversial.')
> (www.zeit.de/2001/51/Politik/print_200151_k-frage.html)

The same metaphorical usage is also found in English texts. Here is an example taken from Google:

> Defence Secretary Geoff Hoon faced questions about the deployment, why it happened so quickly, what his exit strategy was and how long it would last – all of which he had answered in previous exchanges.
> But his opposite number, Bernard Jenkin, offered his overall support for the operation.
> There was not even much friendly fire from Mr Hoon's own benches.
> (news.bbc.co.uk/hi/english/uk_politics/ newsid_1884000/1884226.stm)

In this section we have explored *friendly fire* in a monolingual and a bilingual context with the aim of finding criteria that set apart statistically significant, but contingent co-occurrences of two or more words from semantically relevant collocations, also called fixed expressions. There are two approaches. If we look at meaning from the perspective of usage, we find that there are good reasons of simplicity to assign collocation status to those expressions which, taken as a whole, are monosemous. The phrase *friendly fire* belongs here; a collocation analysis will reveal that it (almost) always occurs in comparable contexts. This perspective is decisive for the computational processing of natural language; as we will see, it facilitates computer-aided translation.

From the perspective of language understanding, the prime criterion for assigning collocation status to lexical co-occurrence patterns is paraphrase. If we find that a phrase is repeatedly paraphrased as a unit of meaning, we have a reason to assume that it is a single lexical item. A supporting criterion is that the phrase, as a whole, can be used in a metaphorical way. This is, as we have seen, the case for both *false dawn* and *friendly fire*. A third criterion is specific to a bilingual perspective. It seems that the translation equivalent of a true collocation is not what would be the most appropriate translation if each of the elements were translated separately. If it were, we would expect, as the equivalent of *friendly fire*, the German phrase *befreundetes Feuer*, for which we found only one occurrence. Rather, collocations are translated as a whole, and it does not seem to matter whether the favoured equivalent makes any sense if interpreted literally as a combination of the elements involved. The phrase *freundliches Feuer* is, if taken literally, seriously misleading. For a new unit of meaning, this does not matter; the unit will mean whatever is acceptable to the discourse community. Finally, the high frequency of the English phrase *friendly fire* in German texts suggests that there is no acceptable autochthonous German equivalent and that the English phrase therefore has to be imported.

Is *friendly fire* a true collocation? 'True' collocations can be shown to be not only statistically significant but also semantically relevant. Semantic relevance can be demonstrated both for the methodological approach and for the theoretical approach to the definition of units of meaning. The analysis presented here has demonstrated that the concept of the unit of meaning as the criterion for fixed expressions is not arbitrary. Corpus linguistics can make an enormous impact on lexicography. It can change our understanding of the vocabulary of a natural language. We can overcome the unfortunate situation that most of the (more common) lexical items in the dictionaries are polysemous. The ambiguity we had to deal with in traditional linguistics will disappear once we replace the medieval concept of the single word by the new concept of a collocation or a unit of meaning. Instead of choosing among four senses for *friendly* and eight senses for *fire*, we end up with one single meaning for the fixed expression *friendly fire*.

4.7 Collocations, translation and parallel corpora

In this section, we will address the methodological aspect of working with collocations. Our aim is to demonstrate the impact which the appreciation of the collocation phenomenon can have on translation. As empirical bases, we will produce evidence from several parallel corpora. To work with these corpora, we have to align each text and its translation first on a sentence-to-sentence level and then on the level of the lexical item, be it a single word, or an idiom, or a 'true' collocation, in short, on the level of the unit of meaning.

All those who have ever translated a text into their own or a foreign language know that we do not translate word by word. Nevertheless, our traditional translation aid is the bilingual dictionary. Most entries, by far, are single words, and for most of the words we find many alternatives for how to translate them. In most cases, the dictionary cannot tell us which of the alternatives we have to choose in a particular case. This is why bilingual dictionaries are not very helpful when the target language is not our native language. We do not translate single words in isolation but units that are large enough to be mono-semous, so that for them there is only one translation equivalent in the target language, or, if there are more, then these equivalents will be reckoned as synonymous.

We call these units translation units. Are they the same as units of meaning? Not quite. Natural languages cannot be simply mapped onto each other. The ongoing negotiations among the members of a discourse community lead to results which cannot be predicted. Languages go different ways. They construe different realities. According to most monolingual English dictionaries, the word *bone* seems to be a unit of meaning, described in the *NODE* as 'any of the pieces of hard, whitish tissue making up the skeleton in humans and other verte-brates'. This accurately describes the way *bone* is used in English. From a German perspective, however, *bone* has, traditionally speaking, three different meanings; there are three non-synonymous translation equivalents for it. In the context of fish (or any of its hyponyms), Germans use the word *Gräte*. In the context of non-fishy animals, dead or alive, and of live humans, they call a bone *Knochen*. In the context of the bones of the deceased, the German word is *Gebeine*. For translating into German, the relevant unit of meaning therefore is *bone* plus all the context words that help to make the proper choice among the three German equivalents. What we come up with in our source text is (probably) not a fixed expression, a collocation of the type *false dawn* or *friendly fire*, but rather a set of words (collocates) we find in the close vicinity of *bone*. Thus in Google we find:

> The poor were initially buried in areas in the churchyard or near the church. From time to time, the bones (*Gebeine*) were dug up and then laid out in a tasteful and decorative manner in the charnel house.
> (death.monstrous.com/graveyards.htm)

> Then place trout on a plate and run a knife along each side of ... Sever head, fins and remove skin with a fork. All you have left is great eating with no bones (*Gräten*).
> (www.mccurtain.com/kiamichi/troutbonanza.htm)

> We expect a person to say she feels terrible after breaking a bone (*Knochen*).
> (www.myenglishteacher.net/unexpectedresults.html)

The word in italics indicates the appropriate German translation in each case. A suitable parallel corpus would give us a sufficient number of occurrences for each of the three translation equivalents. Once we have found all the instances of *Gräte(n)* we can then search for *bone(s)* in the aligned English sentence and set up the collocation profile of *bone* when translated as *Gräte*. Such a collocation profile is a list of all words found in the immediate context of the keyword (*bone* in our case), listed according to their statistical significance as collocates of the keyword. The collocation profile of bone as the equivalent of *Gräte* will contain words like *trout, salmon, eat, fin, remove*, etc. A dictionary of translation units would give, for each keyword which is ambiguous relative to the target language, the collocation profile going with each of the equivalents. The users then have to check which of the words contained in the collocation profiles occur in the context of the word they are about to translate, and the choice can then be made almost mechanically. These combinations of a keyword together with their (statistically significant) collocates are also called collocations. Thus we find two kinds of collocations: those which can be described as fixed expressions and to which a grammatical pattern can be assigned (*false dawn*: adjective + noun) and those of which we can say only that the collocates are found in the immediate context of the keyword (e.g. *trout* in the context of *bone*). Both kinds of collocations have in common that they are monosemous, either in a monolingual or in a bilingual perspective, and that they therefore represent units of meaning or translation units.

The parallel corpora we are working with have been compiled from selections of the legal documents issued by the European Commission and excerpts from the proceedings of the European Parliament, together with some reports issued by them. They do not talk much about bones. This is why we chose another keyword, French *travail/travaux*. We have included the plural *travaux* in our analysis, because the plural is often rendered as a singular when translated into English. The default translation is *Arbeit* in German, while for English there are two main translation equivalents: *work* and *labour*. When do we translate *travail/travaux* as *work*, when as *labour*? The parallel corpus allows us to set up the relevant collocation profiles, on the basis of an analysis of a context span of five words to the left and five words to the right of the keyword:

Travail/travaux translated as *work*	*Travail/travaux* translated as *labour*
Programme (410)	Marché (747)
Commission (255)	Ministre (170)
Conseil (212)	Marchés (151)
Cours (123)	Sociales (125)
Organisation (122)	Affaires (117)
Préparatoires (113)	Emploi (88)
Vue (109)	Forces (65)
Groupe (108)	Normes (60)

Temps (99)   Femmes (60)
Sécurité (97)   Sociale (50)

For each of the collocation profiles, we have selected the ten most frequent words (other than grammatical words like articles and prepositions) found in the context. The frequency of each item is given in brackets. The most amazing finding is that there is no overlap at all between the two profiles. This is striking evidence that *travail/travaux* occurs in different contexts when it is translated as *work* from those when it is translated as *labour*. Do the collocation profiles help with translation? Here are two French sentences, one in which *travaux* corresponds to *work*, one in which *travail* corresponds to *labour*:

> *WORK: La réforme du fonctionnement du Conseil soit opérée indépendamment des travaux préparatoires en vue de la future conférence intergouvernementale.*

> *LABOUR: Le Comité permanent de l'emploi s'est réuni aujourdhui sous la présidence de M. Walter Riester, ministre fédéral du travail et des affaires sociales d'Allemagne.*

Indeed, the collocation profile approach to translation seems to work. This has little to do with our human understanding of meaning. In the first example, we find *vue*, part of the fixed expression *en vue de*, a prepositional expression meaning 'in the face of'. This is in no way semantically connected with *travaux* meaning 'work'. That it is part of the profile is contingent to our corpus. Also, there seems no sound reason why *travaux* in the context of *Conseil* should be translated as *work* and not as *labour*. It just happens to be that way.

Again, in the second example there is no obvious reason why *emploi* would necessitate the equivalent *labour*. It just so happens that in eighty-eight cases where we find *emploi* close to *travail/travaux*, we find *labour* and not *work* in the translation. The real reason is a different one: *le ministre du travail* is a named entity in the form of a fixed expression for which the equivalent in English is 'Minister of Labour' or 'Secretary of Labour'. What we learn here is that the methodological approach to collocation analysis, the approach based on usage rather than on paraphrase, is a technical operation whose results do not map well onto human understanding.

Investigations of translation equivalence based on parallel corpora are still very much in their infancy. The collocation profiles have to become more refined. The goal is to increase their significance by allocating positions in grammatical patterns to the lexical elements they contain. For the time being our parallel corpora are too small for that. Once they can compare in size with our monolingual corpora we may well find out that the kind of collocations which are not fixed expressions (like *travail/travaux* and its collocates as they appear in a collocation profile) can be better described as 'true collocations' conforming to a specific grammatical pattern. Thus, in the first sentence, we find *travaux préparatoires*. This phrase can be seen as a monosemous fixed expression, a unit of meaning, conforming to the adjective + noun pattern, and indeed it is (almost) always rendered as *preparatory work* in our parallel corpus.

Parallel corpora monitor the practice of translation. Because they often cannot rely on bilingual dictionaries, translators have to acquire a competence that is the result of experience and interaction with other members of the bilingual discourse community of which they are a part. In their work, they aim to reflect the conventions upon which this community has agreed. The methodology of corpus linguistics enables us to tap this expertise. Our goal is, as we have said above, to replace the single-word entries of current bilingual dictionaries with entries of translation units. The results can be impressive. In a final example, we will use a small French–German parallel corpus. The word we have chosen is *exclusion*, meaning roughly the same as its English counterpart. For the single word we will find an astonishing variety of equivalents. But this diversity disappears once we replace the single word by a collocation of which it is a part. In our example, the fixed expression is *exclusion sociale*. For it, we find only one German equivalent: *soziale Ausgrenzung*. From our bilingual perspective, this proves that *exclusion sociale* is, indeed, a 'true' collocation. It is monosemous; it is a unit of meaning.

To begin, here are some corpus extracts, in the form of a KWIC (key word in context)–concordance, demonstrating the diversity:

extraites pour la vente, à l'exclusion des activités de transformation
den Verkauf mit Ausnahme der Tätigkeiten zur Weiterverarbeitung
['with the exception of activities']

qui résulte de leur travail, à l'exclusion de l'irradiation résultant
wobei Bestrahlung durch Grundstrahlung unberücksichtigt bleiben
['remain ignored']

roïde, la peau ou le tissu osseux, à l'exclusion des extrémités désignées
so Bestrahlung anderer Organe oder Gewebe als Extremitäten
['other organs or tissues than']

des concertations qui débouchent sur l'exclusion de ceux qui sont
deren Ergebnis die Arbeitslosen ausgeschlossen werden
['are being excluded']

il nous manque le combat contre l'exclusion des travailleurs plus âgés
uns fehlt die Bekämpfung der Ausgrenzung von älteren Beschäftigten
['exclusion']

de viandes de gibier sauvage à l'exclusion des viandes de porcin sauvage
von Wildfleisch, ausgenommen Wildschweinfleisch, aus Drittländern
['except boar meat']

This is only a small selection of the variety encountered; all citations are taken from the first ten instances. All translations are perfectly viable. Within their contexts, they are certainly appropriate. Only one of them, we should add, features in the largest French–German dictionary, the *Sachs–Villatte* (1st edition 1979): *mit Ausnahme von/der* as the equivalent of the phrase *à l'exclusion de*. In our few lines, we have four occurrences of this French phrase; and each time it is translated differently. We also find *Ausschluss, Ausschließung, Verweisung*, but no *Ausgrenzung*. Traditional bilingual dictionaries also tend to overlook the fact that it often makes sense to translate a noun phrase (*sur l'exclusion de ceux*) by a verb phrase (*ausgeschlossen werden* ['are being excluded']).

Once we move on to the collocation *exclusion sociale*, the result is straightforward. In 29 of the total of 31 occurrences in our small corpus, we find *soziale Ausgrenzung* as the German equivalent. In the remaining two instances, the adjective has been turned into an adverb modifying the verb. This is a representative selection of our findings:

```
    diese Opfer sozialer Ausgrenzung für immer ausgeschlos
 und der Gefahr sozialer Ausgrenzung entgegengewirkt wird.
 Kampf gegen die soziale Ausgrenzung in ihren verschiedenen
das Problem der sozialen Ausgrenzung junger Leute
 Vermeidung der sozialen Ausgrenzung, sind in einer
   von Armut und sozialer Ausgrenzung ist.
Bekämpfung der sozialen Ausgrenzung.
 Armut und der sozialen Ausgrenzung. In der EU leben
```

4.8 Conclusion: from meaning to understanding

From a corpus linguistics perspective, the meaning of a unit of meaning is what we can glean from the discourse. It is what we can find out about how a unit of meaning is being used. More important than the plain usage data are the paraphrases of a unit of meaning. They explain to us what this unit means; they attempt to define it; they tell us how this unit is semantically related to other units of meaning. A whole book can be a paraphrase. All those books about globalisation try to explain to their audiences what *globalisation* means. Indeed, the conflation of linguistic knowledge with encyclopaedic knowledge is one of the major axioms of corpus linguistics.

It is impossible to compile the complete meaning of a unit of meaning. We cannot have access to more than a tiny fraction of the discourse. Therefore we will never capture all the paraphrases that the discourse contains for a given unit of meaning. Corpora, be they as large as we might imagine, will only ever provide a glimpse of what has been said. This shouldn't deter us. The relevance principle of corpus linguistics assures us that whatever is thought to be important will be repeated in other texts. Once our corpus is large enough to display a certain saturation of paraphrases we can rest assured that what is missing is at least not the mainstream understanding of our unit of meaning.

It is unlikely that any two persons have been exposed to exactly the same discourse events. Once they discuss the meaning of a unit of meaning, their views are bound to differ. They may have heard some identical paraphrases or some that are similar, but each of them will also have heard paraphrases that the other person hasn't. Each of them will subscribe to some paraphrases and will object to others. This is why it is highly unlikely that two people will ever entirely agree on what a unit of meaning means. There is no one description that will completely cover what the unit means. The discourse community is a community of autonomous members. So if two persons want to achieve an agreement on what a unit of meaning such as *globalisation* means, they have to negotiate. The result of their negotiation won't necessarily be that there is only one way to paraphrase *globalisation*; they could also agree that there are two or three competing paraphrases, partially overlapping, partially contradicting each other.

Wouldn't that mean that such a unit of meaning has not one, but two, or three, or many meanings? Wouldn't that contradict our claim that units of meaning have only one meaning, and that, therefore, linguists shouldn't be concerned about lexical ambiguity? Whether a chunk, a conglomerate of words (or, for that matter a single word) is a unit of meaning is not a matter of identical paraphrases, it is a matter of usage. There might be a dozen different paraphrases for *globalisation*; as long as all occurrences of *globalisation* display the same usage pattern, it will continue to be counted as one unit of meaning. Only if two (or more) usage patterns emerge is there ambiguity. Then we are forced to add more lexical elements to the chunk or conglomerate, until again for this larger unit we find only one usage pattern.

Even if there are no two people for whom a unit of meaning means exactly the same, meaning is still a social and not a mental phenomenon. All the paraphrases of a unit of meaning are part of the same discourse. But no member of the discourse community will have been exposed to all of them. If we ask any member of the discourse community what *globalisation* means, they might provide us with yet another paraphrase, and this paraphrase would, of course, also become part of the discourse and thus be available to other members of the discourse community. They would probably attempt to describe as closely as they could how they understood *globalisation*. But a paraphrase can never be more than one voice among many.

Paraphrases are exclusively verbal. They are part of the discourse. My understanding of a unit of meaning, however, is private. It normally involves a lot of what is not verbal and what cannot be easily verbalised. Your understanding of *globalisation* will originate from the paraphrases you have heard, but it will not stop there. As all these paraphrases tell you something different, you're forced to make up your own mind. While trying to make sense of these paraphrases, you'll use your own judgement. When some people paraphrase *globalisation*, you may have more or less strong reservations. When they tell you that globalisation leads to prosperity, you may associate that with an image of the poor in some underdeveloped country. Or you might think of Enron managers and of how they ruined the indigenous economy of the countries they did business with. However, you'll never be able to verbalise all the associations, all these flashes of memory that come to you whenever someone uses the word *globalisation* in your company. How one understands a unit of meaning will always remain a first-person experience, accessible only to that person, in the same way as emotions are. Only I can really know how I feel grief, no matter how hard I try to explain what I feel to others. Only I can know how I experience globalisation, when I am confronted with the word. People aren't machines. Even if they are fed with the same input they can come up with different conclusions.

The interesting question, then, is how do people develop their understanding of units of meaning? There was a time when we hadn't heard of the word *globalisation*. Today, when we hear it, we think we understand it, and our understanding of it encompasses a lot more than what any dictionary definition would contain. Where do these associations come from? How did we arrive at this complex, fuzzy network of associations and images?

We would like to investigate this quandary by probing into the word *truth*. What does it mean, and how does its meaning relate to our understanding of this word? We will start with the definition we find in the *NODE* (here, and in subsequent quotes, leaving out technical details, examples and further senses):

the quality or state of being true; that which is true or in accordance with fact or with reality; a fact or belief that is accepted as true

What does *true* mean?

in accordance with fact or reality; real or actual

How are *fact* and *reality* defined?

fact: a thing that is indisputably the case; the truth about events as opposed to the interpretation
reality: the world or state of things as they actually exist, as opposed to an idealistic or notional state of them

What does *be the case* mean?

be so

Finally, what is the meaning of *actual(ly)*?

existing in fact, typically as contrasted with what was intended, expected or believed

The definitions are, as we can see, to a large extent circular. This, in itself, is not surprising. All dictionary definitions have to be circular; they are using the words which also have to be defined in the dictionary. What is surprising is the close circuit. *Truth* is defined by *true* and by *fact* and *reality*; *true* is defined by *fact* and *reality*, and by *actual*; *fact* is defined by *be the case* (i.e. 'be so'), and by *truth*; *reality* is defined by *actual(ly)*; and *actual(ly)* is defined by *fact*. So *truth* is defined by *fact*, and *fact*, in turn, is defined by *truth*. Lexicographers normally try to avoid definitions with such close circles because they do not really help the user to understand the lexical item in question. However, in the case of words like *truth*, *fact* and *reality*, there seems to be no other way to proceed.

This set of definitions is not (and is not intended to be) equivalent to my (or anyone else's) understanding of the concept 'truth'. Truth, we no doubt all feel, is something immensely important and goes far beyond just being the case. Truth is a moral value, it is something people owe to each other, it is something very deep which needs to be explored responsibly, and it is not something we come across or appeal to when we deal with the mundane facts of everyday life like asking for a pint of ale.

Fortunately, the *NODE* gives us some hints that truth is not quite as simple as we have made it look in our summary of the dictionary definitions. This gives credit to the exceptional quality of this dictionary. *Truth,* we are told, can also mean a 'belief that is accepted as true', *truth* stands in opposition to *interpretation,* and it refers to reality as opposed to 'idealistic or notional' things, while *actual(ly)* refers to facts as opposed to 'what was intended, expected or believed'. So truth is opposed to what is just 'notional' or 'believed', or a subjective 'interpretation', and it can also be a 'belief' that is accepted (by whom?) as the truth. So *truth* is more than 'what is the case'. People can have conflicting ideas about what is true. There is a tension that seems to go along with this word; and the dictionary makes us aware that truth is a contentious issue. This is shared by my understanding of *truth.*

A look at the American *Random House College Dictionary* of 1975 (two-thirds of the size of *NODE*) shows definitions for the words in question that are, on the surface, very similar to the *NODE*. This is what we find for *truth* (here again, and in subsequent quotes, we leave out technical details, examples and further senses):

> 1. true or actual state of the matter. 2. conformity with fact or reality; verity. 3. a verified or indisputable fact, proposition, principle. 4. state or character of being true.

These are the definitions for *fact* and *reality*:

> *fact*: 1. the quality of existing or being real. 2. something known to exist or have happened. 3. a truth known by actual experience or by observation. 4. something said to be true or to have happened.
> *reality*: 1. the state or quality of being real. 2. resemblance to what is real. 3. a real thing or a fact.

It seems we also have to take into consideration the adjective *real*:

> 1. true, not merely ostensible or nominal. 2. actual rather than imaginary, ideal or fictitious. 3. having actual, rather than imaginary, existence. 5. genuine, authentic.

The other two words asking for definitions are *verity* and *verify*:

> *verity*: 1. the state or quality of being true. 2. something that is true, as a principle, a belief, or statement.
> *verify*: 1. to prove the truth of, confirm. 2. to ascertain the truth, or correctness of. 3. to act as ultimate proof or evidence of; serve to confirm.

On the whole, the Random House definitions seem to profess a stronger realism than the *NODE* ones. The 'true or actual state of a matter' is much more straightforward than 'the quality or state of being true; that which is true or in accordance with fact or with reality; a fact or belief that is accepted as true'. Something is true, or it is not. We are not made aware of the tension connected with *truth*. Where it comes in is in the first definition of *real*: 'true, not merely ... nominal'. But this allusion to the medieval battleground of realism versus nominalism presupposes an acquaintance with philosophy few people can claim; on others it is mostly lost. The discourse is brought in by the phrase 'indisputable fact', reminding us of the *NODE* phrase of something being 'indisputably the case'. It comes in much stronger in the definition 'something said to be true or to have happened'. But should we subscribe to this definition? Would we really say that a UFO incident was true because it is said by some people to have happened? The Random House definitions do not let us feel the tension that the *NODE* conveys, for instance with its definition for *actual*: 'existing in fact, typically as contrasted with what was intended, expected or believed'.

When we ask ourselves how we understand the word *truth*, or what *truth* means to us personally, the mundane dictionary definitions with their close circular definitions will be about the last thing that comes to our mind. Truth, we feel, is something very important, something that is frequently at stake. It is a moral value. The way we will have first learned about truth may easily have been in the context of lying. Our parents, rightly interested in our whereabouts, wanted to make sure we would tell them the truth, and this is why they taught us lying is wrong. It is strange that neither of the dictionaries mentions *lies* in their definitions of truth. It certainly plays a very prominent role in my understanding of *truth*. In the Catechism of the Catholic Church we read:

> (2483)   Lying is the most direct offence against truth. To lie is to speak or act against the truth in order to lead into error someone who has the right to know the truth.

This is a somewhat jesuitical way of putting it, in spite of being the received wisdom. Parents, we are told, do have the right to know the truth; children don't. Again tension comes in. Truth is never simple.

Understanding is a first-person experience. We will never be able to convey fully, verbally or in any other way, to other people how we understand a unit of meaning, just as we are not able to let anyone else know exactly what kind and intensity of pain we suffer. Our understanding of any unit of meaning is not something static that could be put into words. When we hear a unit of meaning, or a text sequence, or when we want to use a unit of meaning within a textual sequence, there are memories that come up, memories of events to which we were a witness or in which we played a part. Often what we think are genuine memories of an event itself are recollections of subsequent verbalisations of the event. All these memories involve images or other sensations, and while some of them refer to actual sensual data, others are largely imaginary. Another part of these memories will be memories of other people's contributions to the discourse, things we heard people say themselves, or things that were reported. These texts again, as we remember them, will evoke memories. It is our memory that forms our understanding. But we have little control over what we remember. Remembering is a combination of intention and randomness. It is not the result of an algorithmic procedure. Our understanding of a unit of meaning is nothing fixed. It depends on the situation, on how we feel, on what we want to do, and on innumerable other factors. Any new input will change our understanding. We never can understand a text when we read it a second time in the same way as we understood it as we read it the first time.

We would not know about truth without other people telling us what it is. It is the paraphrases, the explanations, the instructions we received from them that we remember and that evoke the memories of events we associate with them. These paraphrases are what constitutes for us the meaning of a unit of meaning. As we have said often before, we have all been exposed to different sets of such paraphrases, and therefore a word such as *truth* may mean different things to different people. But what is worth remembering is also worth repeating. Therefore many of the paraphrases will strike a familiar chord even if we have never read the texts in which they occur.

To find paraphrases of the unit of meaning *truth*, we searched the Bank of English (BoE), with its 420 million words, for sentences beginning with 'Truth is'. This is a very common pattern for opening up a paraphrase. Altogether, we found 159 occurrences of this phrase. Compared to the total number of occurrences of the word *truth* in the BoE, 34,645, this is only a tiny fraction. As it turned out, about half of the citations were not paraphrases at all. They were sentences like: *Truth is most of us have mediocre souls.* However, the remaining paraphrases still represent something of a common denominator of what truth means to all of us. At first glance it seems amazing that so few of them refer to what the dictionaries tell us. Perhaps it's not so strange, though. The definitions we find in the dictionaries are normally not controversial. So there is no point discussing them in the discourse community. Here, now, is a selection of paraphrases for truth, ordered loosely into seven pigeonholes. We've left out from these corpus citations what we deemed to be accidental and irrelevant.

(1) Truth is an emotional phenomenon
Truth is a force which pierces your heart, Vysotsky said.
Truth is mostly subjective and that's good when you are talking about music.
Truth is an attribute of love. Love is not complete without truth.
The truth never hurts another person.

(2) Truth is a spiritual phenomenon
Truth is a totem to Murphy: artistic and spiritual truth, rather than mere accuracy.
Truth is always before us: the truth of God is bigger and smaller than all our formulations, however precious they may be.
Truth is one of the first casualties of secularism.
Truth is our king, the rest is nothing.
'Truth is our king.' Truth was holy, and cloud-cuckoo-land was silly, and blasphemy too.

(3) Truth is ugly
Truth is full of warts, and worse. It is a heap of dirt, sucked dry by Ariadne's kiss.
Truth is horrible. We live in an empty and meaningless cosmos where we can only expect to suffer.
Truth is not Beauty. It is something to be hidden in the deepest depths of one's inmost being.

(4) Truth is elusive
Truth is a black cat in a darkened room and justice is a blind bat, said Bertolt Brecht.
Great Britain spent centuries making modifications to the ancient system of trial by combat. Truth is immaterial and, often, so is justice.
Truth is the most fragile of ideas.

(5) Truth is relative
Truth is always relative.
Truth is an immensely personal matter – what is true for me is not necessarily true for you.
Truth is, in fact, a product of dispute.
Truth is sought in a joint quest and effort.
Truth is a victim of time.
Truth is something complicated, something to be sought out.
Truth is provisional, Mr Rushdie seems to be saying.

(6) Truth is absolute
Truth is absolute.
Truth is blindingly obvious once you've recognised it.
Truth is established rationally, by proof.

Truth is normatively consonant with warranted assertability.
Truth is truth, in Malaysia or in Manchester.
(7)   Truth is a many splendoured thing
Truth is a difficult concept.
Truth is a problem.
Truth is at stake.
Truth is the main thing. Lenin said: More light! Let the party know everything!
Truth is the foundation of trust.
Truth is manly.
Truth is often stranger than fiction.
Truth is what the masses like.
Truth is not a priority.

All these statements are part of the meaning of truth. We could not have heard them all. But all are part of the discourse. Many of them will sound familiar. Google has 33,000 hits for *truth* + '*stranger than fiction*'. Similar figures would be found for many other paraphrases. Even the phrase 'Truth is normatively consonant with warranted assertability' is not as singular as it looks; Google has 292 hits for '*truth consonant warranted assertability*'. What has caught the attention of people will be endlessly repeated in the discourse. It will leave traces in many texts.

As we see it, understanding a unit of meaning is a feature of our memories. Part of it is verbal input, what we have gleaned from the discourse. This is the part that constitutes what the unit means for each of us individually. It is what we can convey verbally, by repeating it verbatim or by rephrasing it. The other part of understanding is con-stituted by the memories that are evoked by hearing or saying a unit of meaning in a given situation. These memories are fuzzy and instable, they are full of holes and constantly shifting. They are true first-person experiences. Try as we can, we will never be able to relate them faith-fully to others. This doesn't mean they cannot be verbalised. We will refer to them whenever we discuss truth with other members of the discourse community. These textual sequences will enrich the dis-course on truth, and they may well change what *truth* means, for those who hear them and for ourselves. The third part of our understanding of a unit of meaning is our rationalisation of the verbal input and of the memories it evokes. We don't have to accept everything we're being told. We can form our own opinion, and that can differ more or less from the mainstream meaning of that unit. We can contribute our own paraphrase of *truth*. If it differs a lot from what others believe, they will probably reject it. Then it won't leave traces in subsequent texts. But our understanding of paraphrase may just differ modestly from what *truth* means to other people. If it catches their attention, if it expresses an idea that lies in the air, if it reverberates the Zeitgeist, then it may be picked up by others, and it may even change the mainstream meaning.

For corpus linguistics, meaning is a social phenomenon. It is the members of the language community who negotiate what units of meaning mean. What a unit of meaning means is the result of a democratic process. Everyone has, or should have, a voice in it. Meaning is not a matter for experts, self-appointed or otherwise. We do not have to accept that the meaning of *murder* includes abortion. There is no truth in the matter of meaning, and there is no legitimate coercion to agree on a definition. We do not have to accept that *property* is an inviolate right. We can also say that all *property* is theft. Both views are equally legitimate. What we have to learn is what it takes to make our paraphrases palatable to the other members of the discourse community. Education is about learning to exercise one's rights as a free citizen in a responsible way. Corpus linguistics puts us into a position where we can inform ourselves what use others have made of language. This knowledge empowers us to contribute successfully to the discourse of which we are members.

Glossary

affix
a meaningful element which is typically found attached to a stem or base; for example, in English the word *unwanted* contains two affixes, the prefix *un-* and the suffix *-ed*.

alignment
the process of aligning equivalent units in bilingual or multilingual **parallel corpora**, so that a unit in one language corresponds to the equivalent unit in another language and both of them can be accessed or displayed at the same time.

annotation
corpus-external information added to a **corpus**, such as **tagging** or information identifying the origin and nature of the text.

antonymy
the relationship of oppositeness in meaning, as in English between the words *good* and *bad* or *buy* and *sell*.

cognate, cognate word
(1) a word related to one or more other words in the same language by derivation, as in English *thought* is a cognate of *think*.

(2) a word which shares a common ancestor with one or more other words, as with English *sleep*, Dutch *slaap* and German *Schlaf*, which are all considered to be descended from an ancestral Germanic form.

cognitive linguistics
a branch of linguistics or cognitive science which seeks to explain language in terms of mental processes or with reference to a mental reality underlying language.

collocate
a word repeatedly found in the close vicinity of a node word in texts; for example, in English the words *partial, lunar, solar* are collocates of the word *eclipse*.

collocation

the habitual meaningful co-occurrence of two or more words (a node word and its **collocate** or **collocates**) in close proximity to each other; as a lexical relationship, **collocation** can be defined quantitatively as the degree to which the probability of a word y occurring in text is increased by the presence of another word x.

collocation profile

a computer-generated list of all the **collocates** of a node word in a **corpus**, usually listed in the order of their statistical significance of occurrence.

concordance

a list of lines of text containing a node word, nowadays generated by computer as the principal output of a search of a **corpus** showing the word in its contexts and thus representing a sum of its usage; see also **KWIC**.

connotation

the emotional or personal associations of a word, often contrasted with **denotation**.

content word

a word with a relatively clear meaning of its own, in contrast to a **function word**.

corpus

a collection of naturally occurring language texts in electronic form, often compiled according to specific design criteria and typically containing many millions of words.

denotation

the central or core meaning of a word, sometimes claimed to be the relationship between a word and the reality it refers to, and often contrasted with **connotation**.

discourse

the totality of verbal interactions and activities (spoken and written) that have taken place and are taking place in a language community.

etymology

an account of the historical origin and development of a word.

fixed expression

a co-occurrence of two or more words which forms a unit of meaning.

function word

a word with a relatively general meaning serving to express functions such as grammatical relationships, as in English the words *for, to, the,* in contrast to a **content word**.

generative

(of a grammar or a finite set of formal rules) capable of generating an infinite set of grammatical sentences in a language.

hapax legomenon

a word or form found only once in a body of texts, for example in a **corpus** or in the works of a single author.

hyponymy

the relationship of meaning between specific and general words; for example, in English *rose* is a hyponym of *flower*

idiom

a type of **fixed expression** in which the meaning cannot be deduced from the meanings or functions of the different parts of the expression, as with the English idiom *kick someone upstairs* meaning 'move someone to what seems to be a more important post but with the motive of removing them from their current post'.

KWIC (short for **key word in context**)

a computer-generated set of **concordance** lines in which the node word is in the centre of each line.

lemma

a form which represents different forms of a lexical entry in a dictionary, as with the English lemma *bring* representing *bring, brings, bringing* and *brought.*

lexical item

a word understood as a unit of meaning rather than as a written or spoken form.

lexicogrammar

the **lexicon** and grammar of a language, taken together as an integrated system.

lexicon

the vocabulary or word stock of a language, usually understood as a lexical system or as part of **lexicogrammar**.

lexicology

the study of the **lexicon**.

lexicography

the art and science of dictionary-making.

mentalism

the belief in the reality of the human mind and in the possibility and importance of systematically investigating its nature.

meronymy

the relationship of meaning between part and whole, as in English between the words *arm* and *body* or *sole* and *shoe.*

monitor corpus

a **corpus** which contains specimens of language taken from different times (and is ideally regularly updated) and which thus assists the study of language change.

morpheme

the smallest element of language which carries a meaning or function, including **affixes** such as *pre-* or *-ed* as well as irreducible words such as *want* or *white*.

neologism

a new word, form, construction or sense introduced into **discourse** and ultimately into the language.

opportunistic corpus

a **corpus** which makes use of existing and readily available resources, does not claim to be representative, and reflects the assumption that every corpus is inevitably imbalanced.

paradigm

a set of forms, usually grammatically conditioned, based on a single **lexical item**, as in English the set *chase, chasing, chased* or *want, wanting, wanted*.

parallel corpus

a **corpus** which contains equivalent and usually **aligned** texts in two or more languages; it is sometimes called a **translation corpus** but does not always include the original text as well as translations of it.

parsing

grammatical analysis of a text, usually with the principal aim of identifying elements as subjects, nouns, verbs, and so on.

part of speech = word class

qualia

the felt qualities associated with experiences, such as the feeling of a pain, or the hearing of a sound, which are expressed by specific words.

reference corpus

a **corpus** which aims to be balanced and to reflect the contemporary language.

semantics

the systematic study of meaning in language.

special corpus

a **corpus** built for a special research purpose.

synonymy

the relationship of identity (or more realistically of near identity) in meaning, as in English between *dentures* and *false teeth* or *often* and *frequently*.

tagging

attaching grammatical labels, usually indicating **word classes**, to words in a **corpus**, usually by automatic methods.

term

a word with a meaning that is relatively precise and independent of the context, often subject to some special convention or regulation, as for example with technical terms defined by standards associations.

thesaurus

a reference work in which words are grouped by meaning rather than listed alphabetically.

translation corpus

a **corpus** which contains an original text and at least one translation of it into another language; see also **parallel corpus**.

word class

a small set of grammatical categories to which words can be allocated, varying from language to language but usually including such classes as noun, verb and adjective; also known as **part of speech**.

References

Aarts, J., P. de Haan and N. Oostdijk (eds), 1992, *English Language Corpora: Design, Analysis and Exploitation,* Papers from the Thirteenth International Conference on English Language Research on Computerized Corpora, Rodopi, Amsterdam.

Adams, Douglas, 1983, *The Meaning of Liff,* Pan Books, London.

The American Heritage Dictionary, 2000, (4th edn), Houghton Mifflin, Boston.

Béjoint, Henri, 2000, *Modern Lexicography: an Introduction,* Oxford University Press, Oxford. (First published as *Tradition and Innovation in Modern English Dictionaries,* 1994.)

Biber, D., S. Conrad and R. Reppen, 1998, *Corpus Linguistics: Investigating Language Structure and Use,* Cambridge University Press, Cambridge.

Biber, Douglas, Stig Johansson, Geoffrey Leech, Susan Conrad and Edward Finegan, 1999, *Longman Grammar of Spoken and Written English,* Pearson Education, Harlow, England.

Brewer's Dictionary of Phrase and Fable, 1999, Cassell, London (millennium edition, revised by Adrian Room, originally compiled by Ebenezer Cobham Brewer and published 1870).

Calzolari, N., M. Baker and T. Kruyt (eds), 1995, *Towards a Network of European Reference Corpora,* Linguistica Computazionale Vol. XI–XII, Giardini Editori e Stampatori, Pisa.

Carroll, Lewis, 1994, *Alice Through the Looking Glass,* Penguin Popular Classics, London.

Catechism of the Catholic Church, 1995, available online (www.christusrex.org).

Chambers's 20th Century Dictionary, 1983, edited by E. M. Kirkpatrick, Chambers, Edinburgh.

Chapman, R. W., 1948, *Lexicography,* Oxford University Press, London.

Chomsky, Noam, 1957, *Syntactic Structures*, HarperCollins Publishers, New York and Glasgow.

Chomsky, Noam, 1965, *Aspects of the Theory of Syntax*, MIT Press, Cambridge, Massachusetts.

Chomsky, Noam, 1966, *Cartesian Linguistics: a Chapter in the History of Rationalist Thought*, Harper & Row, New York and London.

Chomsky, Noam, 1993, *Rethinking Camelot: JFK, the Vietnam War, and US Political Culture*, South End Press, Boston.

Chomsky, Noam, 2000, *New Horizons in the Study of Language and Mind*, Cambridge University Press, Cambridge, Massachusetts.

Chomsky, Noam and Edward S. Herman, 1988, *Manufacturing Consent: the Political Economy of the Mass Media*, Pantheon Books, New York.

Collins COBUILD English Language Dictionary, 1987, editor-in-chief John Sinclair, HarperCollins, London.

Collins Dictionary of the English Language, 1979, edited by Patrick Hanks, William Collins, Glasgow.

Collins–Robert French Dictionary, 1998 (5th edn), HarperCollins, London.

Cowie, A. P., 1990, Language as words: lexicography, in N. E. Collinge (ed.), *An Encyclopedia of Language*, Routledge, London and New York.

Culler, Jonathan, 1976, *Saussure*, Fontana Modern Masters, William Collins, Glasgow.

Dennett, D. C., 1993, *Consciousness Explained*, Penguin, London.

Dictionary of Caribbean English Usage, 1996, edited by Richard Allsopp, Oxford University Press, Oxford.

Dictionary of Jamaican English, 1980 (rev. edn), compiled by Frederic G. Cassidy and Robert Le Page, Cambridge University Press, Cambridge.

Dictionary of Lexicography, 1998, compiled by R. R. K. Hartmann and Gregory James, Routledge, London.

Edmonds, P., 2002, Introduction to SENSEVAL, *ELRA Newsletter*, October 2002.

Eggins, Suzanne, 1994, *An Introduction to Systemic Functional Linguistics*, Pinter, London.

Fellbaum, Ch. (ed.), 1998, *WordNet: an Electronic Lexical Database*, MIT Press, Cambridge, Massachusetts.

Firth, J. R., 1957, *Papers in Linguistics 1934–1951*, Longman, London.

Fodor, J. A., 1975, *The Language of Thought*, MIT Press, Cambridge, Massachusetts.

Fodor, J. A., 1994, *The Elm and the Expert: Mentalese and its Semantics*, MIT Press, Cambridge, Massachusetts.

Fodor, J. A., 1998, *Concepts; Where Cognitive Science Went Wrong,* 1996 John Locke Lectures, Oxford University Press, Oxford.

Fodor, J. A. and E. Lepore, 2002, *The Compositionality Papers,* Oxford University Press, Oxford.

Fries, Charles C., 1940, *American English Grammar,* Appleton Century Crofts, New York.

Fries, U., G. Tottie and P. Schneider (eds), 1993, *Creating and Using English Language Corpora,* Papers from the Fourteenth International Conference on English Language Research on Computerized Corpora, Zürich, Rodopi, Amsterdam.

Goody, J., 2000, *The Power of Written Tradition,* Smithsonian Institute Press, Washington and London.

Green, Jonathon, 1996, *Chasing the Sun: Dictionary Makers and the Dictionaries They Made,* Henry Holt and Company, New York.

Haas, W., 1962, The theory of translation, *Philosophy* 37: 208–28.

Halliday, M. A. K., 1994a (2nd edn), *An Introduction to Functional Grammar,* Edward Arnold, London.

Halliday, M. A. K., 1994b, On language in relation to the evolution of human consciousness, in S. Allen (ed.), *Of Thoughts and Words – Proceedings of Nobel Symposium 92: The Relation Between Language and Mind,* World Scientific Publishing, Singapore and London.

Harris, Roy, 1987, *Reading Saussure: a Critical Commentary on the Cours de Linguistique Générale,* Duckworth, London.

Hartmann, R. R. K., 1983, *Lexicography: Principles and Practice,* Academic Press, London and New York.

Hartmann, R. R. K., 1986, *The History of Lexicography,* John Benjamins, Amsterdam and Philadelphia.

Hartmann, R. R. K., 2001, *Teaching and Researching Lexicography,* Longman Pearson Education, Harlow.

Hasan, Ruqaiya, 1987, Directions from structuralism, in N. Fabb, D. Attridge, A. Durant and C. MacCabe (eds), *The Linguistics of Writing: Arguments Between Language and Literature,* Manchester University Press, Manchester.

Householder, Fred W. and Sol Saporta (eds), 1962, *Problems in Lexicography,* Indiana University Press, Bloomington.

Hunston, Susan and Gill Francis, 2000, *Pattern Grammar: a Corpus-Driven Approach to the Lexical Grammar of English,* John Benjamins, Amsterdam and Philadelphia.

Jackson, H. and E. Ze Amvela, 1999, *Word Meaning and Vocabulary: an Introduction to Modern English Lexicology,* Cassell, London.

Johansson, S., G. Leech and H. Goodluck, 1978, *Manual of Information to Accompany the Lancaster–Oslo/Bergen Corpus of British English, for Use*

With Digital Computers, University of Oslo, Department of English, Oslo, available online (http://khnt.hit.uib.no/icame/manuals/lob/INDEX.HTM).

Johnson's Dictionary: A Modern Selection by E. L. McAdam and George Milne, 1995, Cassell, London.

Keller, R., 1998, *A Theory of Linguistic Signs*, Oxford University Press, Oxford.

Kennedy, G., 1998, *An Introduction to Corpus Linguistics*, Longman, London and New York.

Krishnamurthy, R. (ed.), 2003, *English Collocation Studies: the OSTI Report*, University of Birmingham Press, Birmingham (new edition of Sinclair, J., S. Jones and R. Daley, 1970, English Lexical Studies: Report to OSTI on Project C/LP/08).

Lakoff, G., 1987, *Women, Fire, and Dangerous Things*, University of Chicago Press, Chicago.

Landau, Sidney I., 1989 (2nd edn), *Dictionaries: the Art and Craft of Lexicography*, Cambridge University Press, Cambridge.

Langenscheidts Großwörterbuch Französisch (Sachs–Vilatte), 1979, Teil 1: Französisch–Deutsch, Völlige Neubearbeitung, Teil 2: Deutsch–Französisch, Völlige Neubearbeitung 1968 mit Nachtrag 1979, Langenscheidt, Berlin and Munich.

Larousse, Pierre, 1865–76, *Grand Dictionnaire Universel du XIXe Siècle*, 15 vols, Librairie Larousse, Paris. (Supplements published 1878, 1890 and various editions published later.)

Levitt, T., 1983, The Globalization of Markets, *Harvard Business Review* 6 (3), May–June 1983.

Lewis, Charlton T. and Charles Short, 1879, *A Latin Dictionary: Founded on Andrews' Edition of Freund's Latin Dictionary, Revised, Enlarged and in great part Rewritten by Charlton T. Lewis and Charles Short*, Oxford University Press, Oxford. (Various editions published later.)

Liddell, Henry George and Robert Scott, 1843, *Greek–English Lexicon*, Oxford University Press, Oxford. (Various editions published later.)

Littré, Emile, 1863–73, *Dictionnaire de la Langue Française* (Supplement published 1878 and various editions published later.)

Longman Dictionary of Contemporary English, 1978, editor in chief Paul Procter, Longman, London.

Longman Dictionary of Contemporary English, 1987 (new edn), editorial director Della Summers, Longman, Harlow.

Longman Dictionary of English Idioms, 1979, Longman, Harlow and London.

Lyons, J., 1970, *Chomsky*, Fontana Modern Masters, William Collins, London.

Lyons, J., 1977, *Semantics*, 2 vols, Cambridge University Press, Cambridge.

McArthur, Tom (ed.), 1992, *The Oxford Companion to the English Language*, Oxford University Press, Oxford.

McDavid Jr, Raven I. and Audrey R. Duckert (eds), 1973, *Lexicography in English*, New York Academy of Sciences, Annals 211, New York.

McEnerry, T. and A. Wilson, 1996, *Corpus Linguistics*, Edinburgh University Press, Edinburgh.

Macmillan English Dictionary for Advanced Learners, 2002, Macmillan Publishers, Oxford.

Macquarie Dictionary, 1997 (3rd edn), editor in chief Arthur Delbridge, Macquarie Library, Sydney.

Macquarie Concise Dictionary, 1998 (3rd edn), general editors A. Delbridge and J. R. L. Bernard, Macquarie Library, Sydney.

Malinowksi, B., 1935, *Coral Gardens and their Magic*, 2 vols, Allen & Unwin, London.

Martin, J. R., 1992, *English Text: System and Structure*, John Benjamins, Philadelphia and Amsterdam.

Mayr, E., 2002, *What Evolution Is*, Weidenfeld & Nicholson, London.

Millar, S., 2003, The Language of War, *Guardian*, 24 March 2003.

Miller, K. L., 2002, The New Buzzword: Globaloney, *Newsweek*, Special Edition, December 2002–February 2003.

Moon, R., 1998, *Fixed Expressions and Idioms in English. A Corpus-based Approach*, Clarendon Press, Oxford.

New English Dictionary on Historical Principles, 1884–1928, edited by James A. H. Murray, H. Bradley, W. A. Craigie and C. T. Onions, Clarendon Press, Oxford.

New Oxford Dictionary of English, 2001, Oxford University Press, Oxford.

New Shorter Oxford English Dictionary on Historical Principles, 1993 (rev. edn), 2 vols, edited by Lesley Brown, Clarendon Press, Oxford.

Oxford Dictionary of New Words, 1997, edited by E. Knowles and J. Elliott, Oxford University Press, Oxford.

Oxford Dictionary of Sociology, 1998, edited by G. Marshall, Oxford University Press, Oxford.

Oxford–Duden German Dictionary German–English/English–German, 1999 (2nd edn), Oxford University Press, Oxford.

Oxford English Dictionary, 1989 (revised edition of the *New English Dictionary on Historical Principles*), 20 vols, prepared by J. A. Simpson and E. S. C. Weiner, Clarendon Press, Oxford.

Palmer, H. and A. S. Hornby, 1933, *The Second Interim Report on English Collocations*, Kaitakusha, Tokyo.

Pavel, Silvia, and Diane Nolet, 2002, *Handbook of Terminology*, Terminology and Standardization Translation Bureau, Ministry of Public Works and Government Services, Canada.

Pinker, S., 1994, *The Language Instinct: How the Mind Creates Language*, William Morrow, New York.

Putnam, H., 1975, The Meaning of 'Meaning', in *Mind, Language and Reality*, Philosophical Papers vol. 2.

Quirk, R., S. Greenbaum, G. Leech and J. Svartvik, 1985, *A Comprehensive Grammar of the English Language*, Longman, London.

Random House College Dictionary, 1975 (2nd edn), Random House, New York.

Robins, R. H., 1979 (2nd edn), *A Short History of Linguistics*, Longman, London.

Roget, Peter Mark, 1852, *Thesaurus of English Words and Phrases*, Longman, Brown, Green and Longman, London. (Various editions published later.)

Sager, Juan C., 1990, *A Practical Course in Terminology Processing*, John Benjamins, Amsterdam and Philadelphia.

Said, E. W., 1995, *Orientalism: Western Conceptions of the Orient*, Penguin, London.

Sampson, Geoffrey, 1980, *Schools of Linguistics: Competition and Evolution*, Hutchinson, London.

Sampson, G., 1997, *Educating Eve: The 'Language Instinct' Debate*, Cassell, London.

de Saussure, Ferdinand, 1960, *Course in General Linguistics*, Peter Owen, London (translated by Wade Baskin).

de Saussure, Ferdinand, 1972, *Cours de Linguistique Générale*, Editions Payot, Paris (édition critique préparée par Tullio de Mauro).

de Saussure, Ferdinand, 1983, *Course in General Linguistics*, Duckworth, London (translated by Roy Harris).

Searle, J. R., 1983, *Intentionality: An Essay in the Philosophy of Mind*, Cambridge University Press, Cambridge.

Searle, J. R., 1992, *The Rediscovery of the Mind*, MIT Press, Cambridge, Massachusetts.

Searle, J. R., 1998, *Mind, Language and Reality*, Basic Books, New York.

Sinclair, J. (ed.), 1987, *Looking Up: An Account of the Cobuild Project in Lexical Computing*, HarperCollins, London.

Sinclair, J., 1991, *Corpus, Collocation, Concordance*, Oxford University Press, Oxford.

Sinclair, J., 1996, The Empty Lexicon, *International Journal of Corpus Linguistics* 1: 99–119.

Sperber, D. and D. Wilson, 1998, The Mapping between the Mental and the Public Lexicon, in P. Carruthers and J. Boucher (eds), *Language and Thought*, Cambridge University Press, Cambridge.

Strang, Barbara M. H., 1970, *A History of English*, Methuen, London.

Stubbs, M., 2001, *Words and Phrases: Corpus Studies of Lexical Semantics*, Blackwell Publishers, Oxford.

Svartvik, J. (ed.), 1990, *The London Corpus of Spoken English: Description and Research*, Lund Studies in English 82, Lund University Press, Lund.

Tognini-Bonelli, E., 2001, *Corpus Linguistics at Work*, John Benjamins, Amsterdam.

Warburg, Jeremy, 1968, Notions of correctness, supplement to Quirk, Randolph (2nd edn), *The Use of English*, Longman, London and Harlow.

Webster, Noah, 1828, *American Dictionary of the English Language*.

Wierzbicka, Anna, 1980, *Lingua Mentalis: the Semantics of Natural Language*, Academic Press, Sydney.

Wierzbicka, A., 1996, *Semantics. Primes and Universals*, Oxford University Press, Oxford.

Wildhagen, K. and W. Héraucourt, 1963–72, *English–German/German–English Dictionary*, 2 vols, Brandstetter, Wiesbaden.

Wright, Joseph, 1898–1905, *The English Dialect Dictionary, Being the Complete Vocabulary of all Dialect Words still in Use, or Known to have been in Use during the Last Two Hundred Years*, 6 vols, Henry Frowde, London.

Zgusta, Ladislaw, 1971, *Manual of Lexicography*, Mouton, The Hague.

Corpora

The Bank of English, http://titania.cobuild.collins.co.uk/

British National Corpus, http://www.natcorp.ox.ac.uk/

Brown Corpus, manual available at http://www.hit.uib.no/icame/brown/bcm.html

Czech National Corpus, http://ucnk.ff.cuni.cz/english/

IDS (Institut für Deutsche Sprache) corpus *COSMAS*, http://corpora.ids-mannheim.de/~cosmas/

International Corpus of English (ICE), http://www.ucl.ac.uk/english-usage/ice/

London Lund Corpus, http://khnt.hit.uib.no/icame/manuals/LONDLUND/INDEX.HTM

Språkbanken, http://spraakbanken.gu.se/

WordNet, http://www.cogsci.Princeton.edu/~wn/

Index

(words in bold can be found in the Glossary)

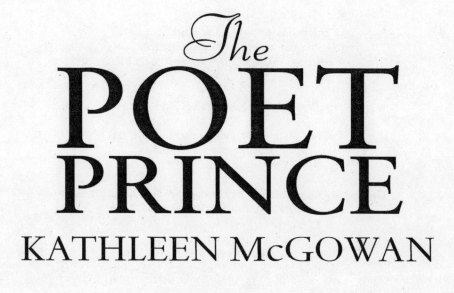

The POET PRINCE

KATHLEEN McGOWAN

SIMON &
SCHUSTER

London · New York · Sydney · Toronto

A CBS COMPANY

First published in the US by Touchstone, 2010
A division of Simon & Schuster, Inc.
First published in Great Britain by Simon & Schuster UK Ltd, 2010
A CBS COMPANY

1 3 5 7 9 10 8 6 4 2

Simon & Schuster UK Ltd
1st Floor
Gray's Inn Road
London WC1X 8HB

www.simonandschuster.co.uk

Simon & Schuster Australia
Sydney

A CIP catalogue record for this book
is available from the British Library

Hardback ISBN: 978-0-74329-537-6
Trade Paperback ISBN: 978-0-74329-538-3

Printed in the UK by CPI Macka~~   ~~TD

C46046251/

For Lorenzo,
to fulfill a promise
500 years in the keeping.

And for all of you
who recognize your own promise
and are committed to bringing about
the Golden Age of a new Renaissance.

The Time Returns

We honor God while praying for a time
when these teachings will be welcomed
in peace by all people
and there will be no more martyrs.

THE PRAYER OF THE ORDER OF THE HOLY SEPULCHER

PROLOGUE

Rome, AD 161

*T*he Roman emperor Antoninus Pius was not a butcher.

A scholar and philosopher, Pius did not want to be remembered by history as one of Rome's cruel and intolerant tyrants. Yet here he stood, literally up to his ankles in the blood of Christians. While alive, the four brothers had been exceptionally beautiful young men. But after their terrible deaths brought about by beatings and torture, they were unrecognizable masses of blood and flesh. The sight made him want to retch, but he could not appear to be weak before his citizens.

Pius was, for the most part, tolerant of the irksome minority who called themselves Christians. He even found it stimulating to participate in debates with those who were educated and reasonable. However odd he personally found their beliefs—about the single messiah who rose from the dead and would come again—their ideas did appear to be spreading at an unnervingly steady pace throughout Rome. A number of Roman nobles had converted to Christianity openly, and their participation in Christian rituals was tolerated by his government. This growing sect was also finding particular popularity with highborn females; women were included as equals in all its rites and ceremonies. They could even be priests in this strange new world of Christian thought and practice.

Prologue

The priests who held court in the temples of Jupiter and Saturn were up in arms that these Christians were allowed to offend the gods with their ridiculous concept of a single deity. Emperor Pius generally ignored the priests' wailings, and thus life in Rome went on in relative peace during much of his reign. It was only when some aberration developed to endanger lives in the Roman republic, some tragedy or natural disaster, that the Christians found themselves mortally threatened. The Roman priests, and their followers, were quick to blame the Christians for any and all misfortunes that might befall Rome. Surely it was their monotheistic insult to the true gods of the republic that caused divine retribution to fall on the other innocent and obedient citizens?

Emperor Pius had himself discovered in his debates that there were two types of Christians: the wild-eyed fanatics who often seemed anxious to die to prove their great piety, and the truly reasonable and compassionate adherents who were more devoted to helping the poor and healing the sick than they were to preaching and converting. Pius definitely preferred the latter type; they were making a positive contribution to their communities and were valuable citizens. These Christians, whom he called the Compassionates, were fond of telling stories of their messiah and his great healing ability and of quoting his very wise words about the need for charity. Most often, they spoke passionately about the power of love and its many forms. Indeed there were even some Christians here in Rome who claimed direct descent from their messiah himself, through his children who had settled in Europe. These claimants were the same Compassionates who worked tirelessly to help the suffering and the poor. Their undisputed leader was a stunning and charismatic noblewoman called Lady Petronella. The flame-haired Petronella was beloved by the people of Rome, despite her openly Christian practices, as she was the daughter and heiress of one of Rome's oldest families. She used her wealth generously for the highest good of the republic and preached only of the need for love and tolerance. If Petronella and her Compassionates had been the only kind of Christian in Rome, this onslaught of terrible bloodshed would likely never have begun.

But the group of Christians that Pius referred to as the Fanatics were another story altogether. In contrast to the Compassionates, who spoke of their messiah in warm and devoted tones as the great teacher of a spiritual path they called the Way of Love, the Fanatics screeched of the one true God who would eliminate all others and bring about a reign of terror for the unbelievers at a time of final judgment. The Romans were deeply offended by this perspective, and the Fanatics compounded the offense by insisting that life on earth did not matter and that only the afterlife was of importance. Such a philosophy, such a craven disregard for the gift of life that the gods bestowed upon mortals, was absolute sacrilege to the Roman priests and their followers. It was incomprehensible to a culture of people who celebrated the experience of the physical senses in their countless spiritual and civic festivals. To most Romans, the Fanatics were an enigma born out of madness, a group to be shunned if not feared.

Thus it was the Fanatics who raised the ire of the Roman people, even when there were no natural disasters to contend with. But when a deadly influenza outbreak struck an affluent Roman suburb, the priests of Saturn began to cry for the blood of Christians to appease their god.

In the center of this growing drama was a wealthy Roman widow, the Lady Felicita. Felicita had converted to Christianity when, overcome by grief following the sudden death of her noble and beloved husband, she had turned her back on the Roman gods. It was said that, left alone to raise seven sons without a father, she went mad with the anguish of her loss. Felicita was visited by Christians who offered her comfort in her mourning, and she ultimately found strength and solace in the Fanatics' extreme perspective on the absolute importance of the afterlife. In this ideal, Felicita was consoled that her husband was in a better place where she would join him one day, and they would be together with their children as a family in heaven.

While Felicita burned with the passion of the newly converted, most of the nobles in her community were not overly upset by her behavior. Felicita would spend hours each day on her knees in prayer, but most felt that this was her own business. In addition, Felicita was charitable and generous, donating portions of her dead husband's fortune to the building of a hospital and compelling her older sons to contribute physical labor to help the infirm. As a result, Felicita's strong and beautiful children were very popular with the people of the Roman suburb in which they dwelled. The boys ranged in age from the golden-haired youngest, called Martial, who was in his seventh summer, to the tall and athletic eldest, Januarius, who was twenty years on earth.

The world in which Felicita and her sons lived remained relatively peaceful until the influenza swept into their town. It struck intermittently and at random, but those who were afflicted by it rarely survived the extreme fevers that accompanied the retching and convulsions. When the firstborn son of a Saturnian priest succumbed to the illness, the distraught man rallied the population to join him in accusing Felicita and her sons of bringing down the wrath of the gods upon them. Clearly, Saturn had punished his own priest to make his point clear: the Romans would need to be strong in their opposition to these Christian people who dared to regard their true gods as obsolete. The gods would not stand for it, and certainly not a god such as Saturn, who was the domineering and ruthless patriarch of the Roman pantheon. Hadn't Saturn even devoured his own son when he found him to be disobedient?

Felicita and all seven of her children were subsequently brought before the regional magistrate, Publius. Because of Felicita's noble status, they were not shackled by chains or tied but were allowed to enter the court of their own volition. Felicita was a handsome woman, tall and well built, with flowing dark hair and the walk of a queen. She stood straight and proud before the court, never wavering and showing no fear.

The proceedings began calmly and were carried out with due order. While Magistrate Publius was known to have a harsh streak when provoked, he was not as monstrous as some of the local jurists were known to be. He read out the charges against Felicita and her sons in measured tones.

"Lady Felicita, you and your children have been brought to this court today under suspicion. The citizens of Rome have grave concerns that you have angered our gods, most specifically, that you have offended Saturn, the great father of the gods. Saturn has taken vengeance upon your community, claiming the lives of a number of your neighbors, including innocent children, as a result. The laws of our people state that 'refusal to accept the gods angers the gods and disrupts the forces of the universe. When the gods have been angered, those culprits who have caused their consternation must beg forgiveness by making sacrifices to them.' Therefore you and your children are commanded to worship in the Temple of Saturn for eight days, making appropriate sacrifices as designated by the priests until the god has been appeased. Do you accept this as a fair and just sentence?"

Felicita stood mute before the court, her children standing in a line behind her equally silent.

Publius repeated the question, adding, "You do understand that the alternative is death? Failure to appease the gods puts our entire nation at risk. Thus you will perform your sacrifices or you will die. The choice is yours."

Publius' exasperation grew as Felicita made him wait for what seemed an interminable amount of time. When it became clear that she did not have any intention of speaking, the magistrate eventually snapped. "You offend the authority of this court and the people of Rome with your silence. I demand your answer, or it will be beaten from you."

Felicita raised her head to look directly at Publius. When she finally replied, it was with the fire of conviction in her eyes and in her words.

"Do not threaten me, heathen. The spirit of the One God is with me and will overcome every assault you make upon me and my family, as he can take us to a place where you will never go. I will not enter a pagan temple nor make sacrifices to your powerless gods. Nor will my children. Not ever. So do not waste your breath further with this request. If you would punish us, do so and be done with it. But I do not fear you, and my sons do not fear you. They are as strong in their conviction as I am, and will remain so."

"Woman, do you dare to bring the lives of your children into jeopardy over your misguided ideals?"

Publius was dumbstruck by her response. The sentence he had passed upon this Christian family was unprecedented in its leniency by all Roman standards. He was certain she would breathe a sigh of relief and guide her brood of boys quietly to the temple to begin their shared penance. Was it possible that Felicita would risk the lives of her entire family over an eight-day temple requirement?

Publius continued, less measured now. His shock and growing irritation crept into his voice. "Beware before you speak again, as this court has the power to see all of you punished most severely for your crimes."

Felicita very nearly spat her reply. "I said, do not threaten me, foul pagan. Your words are empty. You cannot punish me in any way that will change my mind, so spare your breath. If this means you must put me to death, then do so and be quick about it so that I may reach my God and be reunited with my husband. If my children must die with me, they will do so gladly, as they know what awaits them in the afterlife is far greater than anything you can imagine on this terrible earth."

Publius was now utterly outraged. It was unnatural, even monstrous, for any mother to offer up her children for sacrifice. What twisted god was this that the Christians worshipped who would require the lives of seven children to appease his bloodlust?

The magistrate's voice boomed through the court. "Unhappy woman, if you wish to die, so then die, but do not destroy your children in the process! Send them to the temple so that they may live."

Felicita's reply was a scream that shook the stones of the courtroom. "My children will live forever no matter what you do to them! You have no power over them or over me."

Publius spluttered at her audacity before ordering Felicita to be placed in chains and sent into a holding cell. As she was dragged out of the court, she shouted to her sons, "My children, look up to heaven where Jesus Christ awaits you with the only true God. Be faithful and courageous so that we may all be united in heaven. If one of you falters, all is lost! Do not fail me!"

Once their mother had been removed, the magistrate spoke to the children. The youngest two were in tears but trying hard to keep them in check, chins buried in their chests and little bodies nearly convulsing with sobs. Publius, himself a father of boys, felt pity for these small ones, innocent victims of their mother's madness. He addressed Felicita's children as a group.

"Your mother is a misguided woman who would threaten the lives and security of all Rome with her offenses. You do not have to follow her terrible example. This court recognizes each of you individually and promises leniency and pardon to you. All you must do is renounce these words of your mother and agree to accompany the priests to the Temple of Saturn and make appropriate reparations to that god for having offended him. This will restore peace to the land and abolish the plague that has killed your innocent neighbors."

He watched the silent seven, the younger ones all with eyes downcast, and addressed the final question to the elder four. "Do you not wish to see the end of suffering in your community? For this is in your power. Your actions have brought plague and death to your neighbors. You now have the opportunity to correct that and set things to right."

The eldest son, Januarius, answered for all of them. He was the image of his mother both physically and spiritually. Januarius replied with her same fervor. He stated, voice steady and strong, that he would gladly die before entering a pagan temple and that he would take his brothers with him to heaven rather than see them corrupted by heathens. Further, he defended the honor of his pious mother, punctuating his last sentence by spitting on the shoes of the magistrate.

That final act of disrespect turned the heart of Publius to stone. He made his deadly decision in that moment. If Januarius was intent upon dying for his mother and her monster god, then he would be given the opportunity to do just that. Perhaps if Felicita was made to witness the gruesome death of her own firstborn son, she would recant and save the others.

This kind of flagrant disobedience to the Republic and its gods could not be allowed to go unpunished, particularly as it had been witnessed in a public forum. A bloody spectacle to warn other Christians against such crimes was most assuredly warranted and in the best interest of the peace and prosperity of Rome.

*

Januarius was dragged into the public forum and shackled to a whipping post. His mother and three older brothers were given seats near enough to be splattered by his blood with every blow that split his flesh. The younger children, still seen as victims by Publius and the other magistrates of the court, were held in custody away from the execution.

The first executioner was a huge man whose arm muscles bulged as he brought the whip down with all his strength across the prisoner's back, over and over again. At intervals during this flogging of Januarius, the magistrates ordered the executioner to pause. They first asked the condemned if he would like to recant and accept his punishment—and live. Januarius spit on them the first three times. The fourth time he was closer to death than to life and was unable to respond. Thus the final appeal went out to his mother.

"Woman, this is your oldest child, the blood of your union with your husband. How can you watch his torment and not recant? If you accept your penance, he may still live and you will save your other children."

Felicita refused to acknowledge the magistrates. She spoke only to Januarius, but her voice was loud and sure. "My son, embrace your father for me, for all of us, as he awaits you at the gates of heaven. Think no more about this earthly life which means nothing. Go to where God awaits, my child!"

It did not take many more lashes to end the life of Januarius. His blood seeped away into congealing pools as the lashes tore open what was left of his body. When he was declared dead, the executioner unshackled the corpse and dragged it just far enough to be out of the way yet still in sight of Felicita and her three elder sons.

This spectacle of horror repeated itself three more times as each of

Felicita's elder children refused to accept the judgment of the court. Several executioners had to be brought in, as the effort needed to flog each young man to death was too exhausting for any single man, regardless of his size and strength. By the fall of darkness, Felicita had watched as four of her children were flogged to death. She had, in fact, encouraged their deaths by torture. There was no indication that she was going to recant, no matter how gruesome the methods used to kill her children. With each child lost, she appeared to be gaining strength in her twisted version of faith.

The magistrate Publius was now faced with a terrible dilemma. He had no desire to execute the younger boys, who were innocent victims of their mother's madness. And yet Felicita, strangely, appeared to be winning in this battle. She had not broken during the execution of her children, not once. There were no tears and no wincing. Her condemnation of the court and of the pagan priests grew louder and more emphatic with each death. That she was mad was not in question. No mother in her right mind could endure what had occurred here today. Even the executioners were as horrified as they were exhausted by what they had done in the name of their father god, Saturn, and for the security of Rome.

But allowing Felicita's three remaining little ones to live would show weakness. It would demonstrate that her will and faith were stronger than that of Rome and the gods.

This was how the emperor himself, Antoninus Pius, had come to be summoned to this affluent suburb for consultation, had come to be standing in the blood and gore that had once been Felicita's elder sons. This matter had the potential to become a state crisis, and Magistrate Publius did not want the blood of the innocent younger children on his hands if such a thing went against the emperor's will. Antoninus Pius was, himself, at a loss to determine the correct course of action in this hideous case. He considered the now infamous moment, generations earlier, when the Roman prefect Pontius Pilate had ordered the execution of Jesus the Nazarene, thereby creating the martyr around whom this strange cult was built. Pius did not want to create more martyrs whose ghosts would serve to weaken the might of Rome. He also did not want the blood of little children on his hands. But he was not certain how to avoid it. Indeed, the matter had already gone too far.

It was no doubt the most benevolent goddess of beauty and harmony, Venus herself, who smiled on him that evening by sending him an answer. When the alluring and graceful Lady Petronella arrived requesting an audience, Pius breathed a sigh of relief for the first time on that terrible day.

*

Lady Petronella did not have to plead her case with the emperor, although she had been fully prepared to do so. She was stunned that he seemed relieved to see her and to concede to her plan. Petronella was the popular wife of a senator, yet her status as an unapologetic, albeit gentle Christian could have made this mission difficult. Her beauty and elegance had gone far to win over the more hardened nobles of Rome, including this emperor, who was a great lover of attractive women. She came dressed in a simple cream gown, but one made from the highest-grade silk from the Orient. Her hair, the color of burnished copper in the sun, was plaited elaborately, strands of pearls woven through the coiffure. Around her long and delicate throat was an exquisite pendant with a large central ruby from which dangled three tear-shaped pearls. A smaller brooch, etched with the symbol of a rooster with ruby eyes, decorated one shoulder of her gown. To the uninitiated, Petronella's adornments were merely the trappings of a rich woman. But those who knew her intimately understood that these precious stones were the symbols of her esteemed family. The rubies and pearls indicated descent from the ancestor they referred to as the Queen of Compassion—Mary Magdalene. The rooster emblem was the symbol of the other strand of her blood, that of her sanctified great-great-great-grandfather, who was no less than Saint Peter, the first apostle of Rome. She had, in fact, been called after the apostle Peter's only child, given the name that was a feminized version of Peter.

According to the sacred family legend, Saint Peter's only daughter, the first-century saint known as Petronella, had married the youngest son of the holy family. Mary Magdalene had been heavily pregnant at the time of the crucifixion, and was spirited away to safety in Alexandria immediately thereafter. In Egypt she gave birth to the son of Jesus, Yeshua-David, whose own life was wondrous and powerful. It was said that on the day that Yeshua-David and the original Petronella first met as children, they became inseparable. They married and had many children, thus creating a legacy of pure Christian strength that preached the Way of Love throughout Europe. The women in this lineage subsequently married into powerful Roman families to protect their line. Staying alive to preserve the Way was their sole mission. It was their family legacy, as it had been delivered to their patriarch by Jesus Christ himself.

Jesus had given Peter his name, Petrus, meaning "the rock," because he believed his friend the fisherman to be solid and unwavering in his commitment. He was the rock upon which Jesus could build a strong foundation for growth, one of the chosen successors to ensure that the teachings of the Way would not die. Jesus had *commanded* that Peter deny him so that he would escape persecution and live to preach another day. Sadly, Peter's triple denial of Jesus was now infamous and often used to illustrate his weakness of character. It was just one of many injustices manufactured by the scribes who would twist Christian history for their own purposes. But Peter's descendants knew the truth and remembered it with pride, adopting the rooster proudly as their family emblem. That Peter would deny Jesus three times before the cock crowed was their Lord's own request. Contrary to the derogatory legend, Peter was showing his strength in following the sacred orders that Jesus had given to him.

The exact words, spoken privately by Jesus to Peter on that blessed night in Gethsemane, had been passed down and memorized by all Petrus children:

Live to preach another day. You must remain. Only then will the Way of Love survive.

The words of Jesus to Saint Peter, spoken in the Garden of Gethsemane, had been distilled into the sacred family motto:

I remain.

Lady Petronella was the remaining "rock" of the Christians, and as such she must now face this predicament that could prove dangerous to their Way of Love.

Indeed, Petronella hoped to represent the legacy of her most steadfast and compassionate ancestors today with this mission to the emperor to save Felicita and her remaining children. What concerned the lady now was how much confidence Pius appeared to have in her ability to reach Felicita and to turn this situation around for Rome. While she was determined to try, Petronella had deep reservations about the outcome of this venture. Felicita's fanaticism was legendary among the Compassionate Christians, even before her inconceivable act of offering her children up for sacrifice. Would Felicita listen to her? It was hard to know. Petronella's pedigree among Christians was pristine to the point that most nearly worshipped her. And beyond all else, she was the current guardian of the Libro Rosso, the sacred book that contained the true teachings and prophecies of the holy family. Her authority could not be argued by any reasonable Christian. But a woman who would cheer on the unspeakably brutal executions of her children as an act of faith was not a reasonable Christian.

Before requesting an audience with the emperor, Petronella had prayed long and hard for guidance. She prayed to her Lord for his strength and for the clarity to understand his will through the teachings of love. She invoked the Queen of Compassion and asked to be guided by her remarkable grace. She rubbed the central ruby of her pendant and said a final prayer.

"I remain," she whispered aloud, then steeled herself for the inevitable confrontation to come.

*

"Good evening, sister."

Petronella had been allowed, through intervention of the emperor, to meet with Felicita in one of the magistrates' offices. It would have been unseemly for a lady of her status to descend into the depths of the dank, fetid cell where Felicita had been held. While the prisoner had been given a clean shift to wear during the visit, she was filthy and her skin was stained with the blood of her children. Petronella winced inwardly and prayed that her horror was not immediately apparent on the surface.

The two women greeted each other as all Christians did: as siblings of the spirit. After the formalities, Felicita asked with suspicion, "Why have you come?"

Petronella's gaze was steady, her melodious voice soft. "I have come to offer my condolences for your loss and see if there is any comfort your community can provide for you in your time of grief."

Felicita appeared not to hear her at first. Then she looked at the elegant woman in surprise. "Grief? What grief?"

Petronella was taken aback. The woman must surely have lost whatever was left of her mind after what she had witnessed.

"Lady Felicita, we are all heartbroken over the loss of your beautiful boys."

Felicita was looking past Petronella now, as if she were not there—or as if it didn't matter if she were. She shook her head slowly and replied as if entranced, "Heartbroken? Why, sister? I am joyous on this day as my brave children did not deny their God. Our Lord Jesus Christ will welcome them into heaven and celebrate their strength and faith. Don't you see? This is a day for rejoicing! I can only hope that tomorrow the magistrates will give orders to take the rest of us, so that we may all be together in heaven by the time the sun goes down."

Petronella cleared her throat to give herself a moment to think. This was worse than she had anticipated.

"Sister, while I understand your great faith in the power of the afterlife, if I may say so, Jesus taught us that we must celebrate the joy of life that we have here on earth. That it is God's great gift to us. Your three youngest sons can and should be spared so that they may grow and live in this world that God has created for them."

"Get thee behind me, Satan!" Felicita shrieked with a venom that caused Petronella's head to snap back as if slapped. "You . . . ," she spit at the calm woman standing before her as she continued to rage, "you stand here in your Roman finery, married to a foul pagan, and yet you dare to judge me? I will not betray my God for anyone or anything, and neither will any of my children. We are righteous and God will reward us for our courage. Our reward will be togetherness in heaven in the sight of that God."

Petronella, praying inwardly that Magdalena would send her both patience and compassion, tried a different tactic. "Felicita, your death and the deaths of your remaining children will remove powerful voices from this earth, voices that can spread the good news of our teachings and serve to educate others. Do you not think that God wants this? These young boys will grow knowing that their brothers died for their beliefs, and it will make them strong in their resolve to continue our teachings. They must remain. They will be heroes for the Way. This is what God wants from them, and from you."

"How dare you presume to tell me what God wants? I hear him clearly, and he tells me that he wants my children to be martyrs, not heroes. He requires them as a sacrifice to his greater glory. Just as Abraham was told to sacrifice Isaac."

Petronella took a breath and explained patiently, "Yes, but Abraham was stopped before he could kill his own son. The Lord was testing him to determine his obedience, and yet once he was convinced of it, he sent the angel of mercy, Zadakiel, to stay the hand that was holding the sacrificial knife. For it is never God's wish to see any of his children suffer. Felicita, the Lord is begging you to be that merciful angel who stays the hand of the executioner. Please, do not kill your remaining children. If you do, you will not be choosing the Way of Love. If Jesus were here with us now, he would not allow you to murder your babies. Of this, more than anything, I am most certain."

Felicita turned feverish eyes on Petronella. "Jesus is waiting for me at the gates of heaven, waiting to embrace me and to reward my courage. It is you he will reject, you who married a pagan and who concedes to your heathen neighbors at every turn."

"I love and honor my neighbors as his commandment instructs. It is not concession, Felicita. It is the Way of Love. It is tolerance."

"It is weakness!"

"There will be no Christians left if we do not embrace tolerance. Our Way will not survive if we do not learn how to live it in peace with others. The Way bids us to be patient with those who have not yet seen the light. Jesus tells us we must forgive those who do not see."

"Then I pray he will forgive you, sister." Felicita hissed the last word, making it clear that she no longer believed that Petronella was her sister. "I pray that God forgives you for your weakness and for your evil intent in coming here tonight. Only a devil would try to stop me from carrying out this ultimate sacrifice for the extreme glory of our Lord!"

Petronella had run out of patience, and there was no further need for it. It was clear that Felicita was too immersed in her twisted sacrificial fantasy to hear anything that resembled reason, or even sanity. How could she be anything else but completely invested, after sacrificing four of her children to that idea on this day?

Petronella stood to take her leave, saying quietly as she moved toward the door, "Then I shall pray for all of us, Felicita. And for everyone who dares to believe in the Way of Love."

*

The following morning dawned dreary with a haze that covered the sun. The priests of Saturn were declaring it an evil omen even before the news came that the plague of influenza had continued to spread through the night, killing five more. Two of the dead were children of the temple priests.

The emperor Antoninus Pius was accosted by a cadre of angry holy men even before breakfast. They were certain that Felicita had caused this increased plague through her refusal to acknowledge the gods. She must be made to change her mind. They demanded that her surviving children be brought into court and threatened with execution one by one.

The pressure on the emperor grew more extreme as the day wore on, coming now from many regions of the republic as the legend of Felicita and her reign of terror began to spread. He finally succumbed to the weight of it, reconvening that terrible court of execution.

Felicita and her three remaining sons stood before the magistrate. She was a wild-eyed Medea now, completely diseased by the fevered fantasy in her brain, which had been fed by the blood of her eldest. The little boys were terrified, and the youngest cried openly, blond curls sticking to his wet cheeks. Pius had called Publius to his home and instructed him privately that these children must not suffer in death. If it was unavoidable for them to die, then so be it. They would die. But the torture of babies would not be his legacy.

One by one, each of the boys was called before the magistrates. Publius coaxed them, in his most gentle voice, to turn their backs on their mother and follow the priests to the temple. Felicita was chanting now, a terrible, high-pitched wail of a chant, over and over again. "Be not afraid, children. Your father and brothers await you in heaven." One by one, the children shook their heads at the magistrates, as if under their mother's hypnotic spell. As each was led forward to the chopping block, Felicita was asked if she would recant and save this child. Her response each time was a hideous laugh, a terrible parody of the sound of joy.

In the space of a single hour, three beautiful children, including one who was little more than a baby, lost their heads to the executioner's sharpest sword. He was swift with each, ensuring that the boys did not feel any pain. But when it came to the death of their mother, he was not so lenient. He used an axe instead, and it took three blows to separate the lady from her head.

Emperor Antoninus Pius fled the hideous suburb that had been forsaken by the gods that same night, never to return to it. Felicita's reign of terror was over. But he was certain that he would be forever haunted by the sound of her insane laughter and the images that accompanied it as that last, tiny, golden-haired child died on the chopping block under his command.

*

That evening, an exhausted Lady Petronella called a meeting of her closest brethren, the core group of Compassionates, in order to relate the terrible events of the day. She would need at least one to volunteer as a messenger, to be dispatched to Calabria. The Master of the Order of the Holy Sepulcher was in residence there, and they would need his sage guidance to navigate the storm that was inevitably about to descend upon the Christians in Rome.

Petronella explained to those gathered that she feared that Felicita's reign of terror was just beginning, that it would mark danger to Christians throughout the empire and begin the terrible persecutions of previous generations anew. All the progress her family had made over a hundred years to be accepted as upstanding Roman citizens, to preserve the safety of Christians, may have just been washed away by the blood of Felicita's children. The Fanatics would feed on it and become more outspoken, and the Romans would quash their uprising with the savagery that is born of fear.

She could see at the edge of her vision that something had been put into play here through these events, some terrible distortion of the teachings of their Lord that would take on a life of its own and grow into the future. It was a wicked vision, one that terrified her with the force of its darkness. She recounted it to the other Compassionates, all of whom shivered with the ring of truth in her sad prophecy.

"I fear it is the one we have called sister who has proven to be our greatest adversary. She has unleashed an unstoppable force for evil with these actions. The blood of those children will be used to rewrite the true teachings of our Lord. And words written in blood can only come from a place of utter darkness. The teachings of the Way of Love will drown in the blood of those innocents."

Petronella shuddered as the words poured out, unbidden, from some secret place where the truth of the future is held in keeping. On a terrible night such as this, her family's legacy of feminine prophecy was a most unwelcome gift.

PART ONE

The Time Returns

There exist forms of union higher
than any that can be spoken,
stronger than the greatest forces,
with the power that is their destiny.

Those who live this are no longer separated.
They are one, beyond bodily distinction.

Those who recognize each other
know the unequaled joy
of living together in this fullness.

THE BOOK OF LOVE,
AS PRESERVED IN THE LIBRO ROSSO

I am not a poet.

And yet I have been blessed to live among the best of them. The greatest of the poets, the most gifted of the painters, the loveliest of women . . . and the most magnificent of all men. Each has inspired me and there is a piece of the soul and essence of all of them in every image I paint.

I can only hope that my art will be remembered as a type of poetry, for I have tried to make each piece lyrical and full of texture and meaning. I have long struggled with the thought that perhaps it is against the artist's laws of conduct to reveal the inspirations, symbols, and layers beneath the works that we create. And yet Maestro Ficino has found evidence as old as ancient Egypt that such artist's codes were kept in secret diaries, so I will instead say that I am part of this timeless tradition.

As I am a humble member of the Order of the Holy Sepulcher, all that I paint is done with the inspiration and glory of those divine teachings. They are intrinsic to every figure I paint; they infuse the colors, the textures, and the shape of my work. Every piece of my art, regardless of its patron or its worldly purpose, serves the teachings of the Way of Love. Every image is produced to communicate the truth.

In the pages that follow, I will reveal the secrets behind my work that they may one day be used as a teaching tool, for those with eyes to see.

So while I am not a poet, here is what I am: I am a painter. I am a pilgrim. I am a scribe.

Most of all, I am a servant of my Lord and my Lady, and of their Way of Love.

Our Master is fond of repeating the words of the first great Christian artist, the blessed Nicodemus, who said that "art will save the world." I pray that this is so, and I have endeavored to play some part, no matter how small, in that very worthy venture.

I remain,
Alessandro di Filipepi

FROM *THE SECRET MEMOIRS OF SANDRO BOTTICELLI*

New York City
present day

MAUREEN PASCHAL HAD planned her schedule in New York City carefully. Having worked tirelessly in preparation for the release of her new book, she hoped to reward herself with a few blissful hours of recreation at the Metropolitan Museum of Art. Art was her second-greatest passion, trumped only by history, which was why the books she authored were colored so richly by both. To spend even limited time in one of the world's great museums was a balm to her spirit.

Spring was alive in its most glorious form on this early March morning, rewarding her for making the rigorous walk along Central Park to the Met. Maureen loved New York. She decided to enjoy it to its fullest today, trying not to rush despite her crammed schedule. Walking up Fifth Avenue, she took a detour into Central Park. At the northern edge of the sail boat pond stood the enormous bronze sculpture from Lewis Carroll's masterpiece *Alice in Wonderland*. There was a whimsical magic and beauty to this piece of art that touched the eternal child in her. A larger-than-life Alice was depicted at her unbirthday party with her friends from Wonderland gathered around her. Quotes from the children's classic, the most beloved piece of literature from Maureen's childhood, surrounded the base of the sculpture. Walking the perimeter of Alice's party, she read the quotes from the book and from the poem "Jabberwocky." Her own favorite quote from the book, the one that Maureen displayed on a plaque over her computer at home, was not represented here.

> *Alice laughed. "There's no use trying," she said; "one can't believe impossible things."*
> *"I daresay you haven't had much practice," said the Queen. "When I was your age, I always did it for half-an-hour a day. Why, sometimes I've believed as many as six impossible things before breakfast."*

Like the White Queen, Maureen had learned to believe as many as six impossible things before breakfast. And now, with the arrival of Destino in her life, the number was often far more than that. Maureen mused on this, laughing a little at the sculpture as she stood in admiration of it. Her life had become something to rival Alice's most fantastic adventures. Here she was, a savvy and educated woman of the twenty-first century, about to embark upon a trip to Italy—to take lessons from a teacher who called himself Destino and who claimed to be immortal. And yet like Alice before her, she accepted this extraordinary character as an almost natural part of the strange landscape that her life had become.

Maureen allowed herself a few more precious minutes at the sculpture before heading back toward Fifth Avenue and the entrance to the Metropolitan Museum of Art. Her time was limited at the Met, as she had to prepare for her book launch, so she would focus on one area of the museum and give that her full attention rather than try to see as much as possible.

After purchasing her ticket and attaching the Met button to her collar, she made the determination that today she would focus on the medieval gallery. Her research into the grand contessa, Matilda of Tuscany, had instilled within her a new fascination for the Middle Ages. Further, her prolonged excursions to France had given her a strong appreciation of Gothic art and architecture.

It was a sublime choice. She took her time, really giving each piece its due. She was particularly taken by the extraordinary wooden sculptures from Germany with their unequaled craftsmanship and delicacy. A number of the treasures reminded her of the life-changing experiences that had shaped her destiny while in France. Maureen sighed deeply her contentment, taking in the beauty of it all and enjoying the brief respite that art brought to her life.

As she entered the second large gallery, dominated by an enormous Gothic choir screen, something drew her attention to the far right of the room. While most of the artwork in this gallery was sculpture, one painting was displayed at the far right from the corridor entrance. Moving to get a closer look, Maureen gasped as she found herself standing, transfixed, before the most beautiful life-sized portrait of Mary Magdalene she had ever seen.

Notre Dame. Our Lady. *My* Lady. For Maureen, there was no escaping her. Not now, not ever.

Her eyes welled with tears, as they often did when confronted with a beautiful image of this extraordinary woman who had become her muse and master. As Maureen stood eye to eye with her, she realized quickly that this was no ordinary religious icon. This Magdalene sat enthroned, majestically beautiful in her crimson robe and flowing red-gold hair. In one hand she held the alabaster jar with which she was said to have anointed Jesus; the other, cradled in her lap, held a crucifix. She was surrounded by angels, trumpeting her glory. Moving closer, Maureen bent her knees to better view the lower portion of the painting. Kneeling at the Magdalene's feet were four men in pristine white robes. Hoods covered their heads completely, with only the narrowest slits where the eyes should be. There was something cultish and bizarre about their appearance. The kneeling figures were strange characters at best, sinister at worst.

Maureen could feel her heart racing and that strange sensation of heat around her temples that she had come to recognize when something pricked at her subconscious, something that should not and could not be ignored. This painting was important. Terribly important. She scanned her memory for any mention of this work in her research, but none came. While writing her books she had become familiar with dozens of paintings of Mary Magdalene in the world's major museums. That such an important work could exist in the Met—and that she had never heard of it—was fascinating.

Maureen bent to read the title card. The picture was identified as "Luca Spinello—Processional Banner from the Confraternity of Saint Mary Magdalen."

The official Met description, displayed to the side of the work, read

During the Middle Ages laymen often joined religious confra-ternities in which they met for devotions and performed charitable acts. Their hooded robes rendered such acts anonymous, in confor-mity with Christ's injunction that good works should not be done for vain praise. This extremely rare work was commissioned in about 1395 by the Confraternity of Saint Mary Magdalen in Borgo San Sepolcro and would have been carried in religious processions. It shows the members of the confraternity kneeling before their pa-tron saint, who is serenaded by a choir of angels. Mary's ointment jar decorates the sleeves of their robes. The lightly drawn features of the face of Christ are modern. The original was removed and is now in the Vatican. The banner is otherwise remarkably well preserved.

Something was wrong with that description; Maureen could feel it instinctively. It was very clean, very pat, for a painting that looked and felt so mysterious. The hooded men surrounding their saint's feet weren't merely anonymous, they were downright unsettling. The hoods they wore seemed a most emphatic statement, as if it were a life-or-death matter that their identities be concealed. When she looked very closely, she saw that some of the men had openings in the back of their robes. Penitents. The openings were there so they could flog themselves and draw blood as part of their penance and to wash away their sins.

Maureen had always found the penitential practices of the Middle Ages disturbing. She was relatively sure that God did not want us to flog ourselves for his—or her—greater glory. And given her extensive study of Mary Magdalene, the Queen of Compassion and great teacher of love and forgiveness, she was certain that she would never have condoned such practices.

The composition of the painting made it all the more provocative, as it appeared to be an imitation of some of the more famous Holy Trinity images from the early Renaissance. These images depicted God the Father enthroned, holding the crucifix in his hands and on his lap to represent the son. The Holy Spirit was usually present as a dove above the other images. This icon of Mary was painted in an identical way, only in this case she was the enthroned figure holding Jesus, denoting a place of extraordinary authority. Thus the hooded figures appeared to be worshipping Mary Magdalene on her throne as the Queen of Heaven, which would be a heretical concept even today. In the Middle Ages, such worship would likely have been punishable by death.

Then there was this curious phrase within the description: "The lightly drawn features of the face of Christ are modern. The original was removed and is now in the Vatican." There was evidence of destruction to the banner: a patch covered the cut where the face of Christ had been on the crucifix, ostensibly the original piece that was surgically removed and taken to Rome. But why? Why would anyone deface a rare and exquisitely beautiful painting by an Italian master?

If there was one thing Maureen had learned in her search for the truth about the secret aspects of Christian history, it was to never take anything at face value—and never trust the first and most obvious explanation, particularly in the symbolic world of art history. Removing her cell phone from her bag, she switched it to camera mode and photographed the painting in segments, storing them for future reference.

The digital readout on her phone was a harsh reminder that her time at the Met was coming to a close. Maureen slipped the phone back into her bag and stood before the painting in quiet appreciation. The questions that had run through her head so many times while following the clues left in religious art repeated themselves with resounding force.

What stories can you tell me, Lady? Who painted you like this and why? What did you really mean to those who carried this banner? And finally, the question that haunted Maureen every day of her life: *What do you want from me now?*

But today Mary Magdalene was silent, gazing back at her with quiet authority and an enigmatic expression that would have made Leonardo da Vinci weep with envy. The Mona Lisa had nothing on this Magdalene.

Maureen returned to the official description again and gasped. In the second reading, she caught this reference to the banner's origins: "commissioned . . . by the Confraternity of Saint Mary Magdalen in Borgo San Sepolcro."

Borgo San Sepolcro. An easy translation from Italian. It meant the Place of the Holy Sepulcher.

Maureen glanced down at the ancient ring on her finger, the one from Jerusalem with the seal of Mary Magdalene. It was the symbol of the Order of the Holy Sepulcher—the Order that gave Matilda to the world, the Order in which the purest teachings of Jesus and the Book of Love were preserved, and the Order of which Destino was the Master—and into which she was about to be indoctrinated. Was it possible that there was an entire town in Italy devoted to the Order of the Holy Sepulcher with Mary Magdalene at its center?

Maureen had often described her research and writing as similar to the process of creating a collage. There were many different little pieces of evidence, which individually didn't amount to much. But when you began to arrange the pieces together, see how they all could fit, which complemented the other, then you began to develop something beautiful and whole. And here was what appeared to be a central piece of the stunning mosaic Maureen was crafting.

She looked around at the visitors wandering the gallery. Only a few passed by to give the processional banner a cursory glance before continuing on. Part of her wanted to scream at them: *Don't you see this? Do you have any idea that this painting may hold one of the keys to history and you're walking right past it?*

But she wasn't perfectly sure of that yet. Where was Borgo San

Sepolcro? What other attachments did this artist, Spinello, have that might connect him and this masterpiece to the heretical cultures of medieval Italy? After doing her own due diligence, she would call the experts in France and Italy to get their take on it. Beginning, of course, with Bérenger.

After all these weeks apart, the thought of Bérenger Sinclair suffused her body with warmth until she tingled. Maureen missed him so much. She closed her eyes and allowed herself to get lost in that rich, delicious sense of remembering the last time they were together. She sighed heavily and then shook it off. There were new discoveries looming here, and sharing them with him would make them that much sweeter.

She bid farewell to the artistic glories of the medieval gallery and made her way to the front of the museum, stopping briefly in the gift shop to see if there was a postcard of the fantastic Magdalene banner. There was not even a mention of the rare work in the Met visitor's guide. Searching through a vast assortment of art books, she found one that contained a brief mention of the banner's artist, referring to him as Spinello Aretino. The passage explained that "Aretino" indicated that he was from the town of Arezzo. In Tuscany.

Tuscany. If there was one place Maureen was certain was rife with heretical secrets in the early Middle Ages, it was Tuscany. She smiled, knowing it was not a coincidence that she was currently in possession of a plane ticket to Florence and the following week would be on her way to the heart of the heresy.

*

Nothing.

There was nothing on the Internet about the rare and wonderful Magdalene banner at the Met. Even on the Met's own website it took a concerted effort to find information, and there was nothing other than the description Maureen had read earlier at the museum.

Two hours of searching through Magdalene art pages were fruitless. No amount of Googling brought up anything new on the piece itself, so

Maureen went after it from a different angle, looking up other details from the description: the artist, the locales. She found some general information online about the artist and also on Borgo San Sepolcro that might prove helpful later. She made the following notes:

> SPINELLO ARETINO—*given name Luca (Luke), as was his father's, also a painter, after the saint for whom the painter's guild was named. The name "Aretino" means "from Arezzo" which is a province in Tuscany. Primarily a fresco painter, he worked in Florence at Santa Trinità.*

Maureen paused. Spinello painted at the church in Santa Trinità, which was a sacred location for the Order of the Holy Sepulcher and had been one of Matilda's strongholds. This was a good sign that she was on the right track. Her mosaic was beginning to take shape. She read on.

> BORGO SAN SEPOLCRO—*now known as Sansepolcro, it was founded in the year 1000 by pilgrims who had returned from the Holy Land with specific reverence for the Holy Sepulcher and with priceless relics. One of these pilgrims was known as Santo Arcano. It is in the province of Arezzo and is the birthplace of the master fresco painter Piero della Francesca.*

Maureen squirmed with pleasure at this discovery. She was right! There was an entire town in Tuscany dedicated to the Holy Sepulcher. But there was one sentence that gave her a more immediate rush of excitement:

> *One of these pilgrims was known as Santo Arcano.*

Santo Arcano. Maureen laughed out loud. It appeared here that the Church was saying that there was a saint named Arcano. Her Latin wasn't fluent, but it was serviceable, and she had certainly used it to read between the lines many times in her research. Santo Arcano was not a reference to an obscure Tuscan saint. It meant "Holy Secret." If she were to translate all this into English and make sense of it, what the description really said to Maureen was, *This town, named after the Holy Sepulcher, was established based on the Holy Secret!*

Now she was getting somewhere.

She contemplated the rest of this discovery for a moment and made notes. Maureen was familiar with the work of Piero della Francesca, as his iconic Magdalene was among her favorites. He had created one for the duomo in Arezzo, a very strong and majestic image from which her power and leadership emanated. There was nothing penitent about this Magdalene. It was not painted by a man who believed for one minute the sixth-century propaganda of Mary Magdalene as repentant sinner. It was a fresco created to emphasize leadership. Maureen had a framed copy of this image hanging in her office. She had studied Piero della Francesca during her art research and always found him interesting. His frescoes in Arezzo were very alive, very human and full of narrative. When she looked at his art, she felt kinship with him; Piero was a story-teller. He painted *The Legend of the True Cross* in rich and elaborate detail, he infused *The Coming of the Queen of Sheba to King Solomon* with profound sanctity, and all his artwork represented the most sacred teachings of the Order of the Holy Sepulcher.

Reading about the Order reminded Maureen that she needed to make arrangements for her return to Europe, as she had meetings with her French publisher in Paris to prepare for the release there. Paris was never a hardship; she loved the city, and her best friend, Tamara Wisdom, an independent filmmaker, had been hounding her to spend some time there with her. Maureen's cousin and spiritual adviser, Peter Healy, was also living in Paris at the moment. He had once been known as Father Peter Healy, but he was a refugee from the Vatican at the moment, possibly forever, and was no longer referring to himself as a priest or wearing his collar. Maureen was anxious to catch up with him.

She decided she would fly into Paris, do her business there, then drive down with Tammy to where both of their beloveds awaited them at Bérenger's Château des Pommes Bleues in the southwest of France. Tammy was also blissfully in love, engaged to the gentle Languedoc giant Roland Gelis, who was the childhood best friend of Bérenger. They all lived together in the beauty of the Aude river valley, a magical part of the Languedoc region where the château was located, just outside of Arques. Bérenger, the heir to a Scottish oil fortune, had inherited the château from his grandfather. It had been built in the Languedoc as the exclusive headquarters of a secret society that protected dangerous and heretical secrets. Bérenger had inherited these secrets along with his French castle.

It was too late to call Bérenger tonight, but first thing in the morning—her morning, his afternoon—she would talk to him about accompanying her from Arques to Florence. Destino sent her a letter advising them that he was leaving Chartres to return to Florence, stating it was "once and for all." The letter had felt very final, as if he were preparing to die in Italy. It had upset Maureen immensely at the time. Destino was ancient—literally—and his death was inevitable. But to lose such a treasure, now that she understood and accepted what he was and the extraordinary wisdom he had to offer the world, would be hard to take.

Destino's letter indicated that he had much to teach Maureen in a limited time and that it would be her responsibility to be conversant in the Libro Rosso prior to her arrival. He did not have time to teach the basics of the Order's tenets. He had very specific lessons for them and tasks that must be carried out in preparation for the mission they would all embark upon together. Destino was emphatic when referring to "the mission."

In preparation for her trip to Florence, Maureen reaffirmed her commitment to study the teachings of the Libro Rosso, which she currently had in her possession, as Destino had given all of them a translation as a gift: Maureen, Bérenger, Tammy, Roland, and Peter were all currently studying the English translation of the sacred red book that held the greatest secrets of Christianity.

She had used these sacred pages to craft *The Time Returns: The Leg-*

end of the Book of Love. But it was time to study them and commit certain passages to memory. Maureen pledged to start from the beginning and work all the way through, studying a few segments a night.

It wasn't a chore. Maureen had thought from the first moment she had been exposed to the Libro Rosso teachings that they were the most beautiful words she had ever read. She recognized them as truth, and it had been a celebration for her to write a book about the brave souls who risked everything to preserve these astonishing teachings for two thousand years.

Maureen settled into bed with her book. The teachings always returned to the understanding of love as the great gift given to us by God. But as simple as such an idea should be, it was here that the controversy began. For within the Book of Love, God was not viewed as a patriarch; he was not simply Our Father. God was Our Father in perfect union with Our Mother. The first pages contained Maureen's favorite passage:

*

In the beginning, God created the heavens and the earth. But God was not a single being, he did not reign over the universe alone. He ruled with his companion, who was his beloved.

And thus in the first book of Moses, called Genesis, God said, "Let us make man in Our image, after Our likeness," as he is speaking to his other half, who is his wife. For creation is a miracle that occurs most perfectly when the union of male and female principles is present. And the Lord God said, "Behold that man has become one of Us."

And the book of Moses says, thus God created man in his own image, male and female created he them.

How could God create female in his own image if he did not have a female image? But this he did, and she was called Athiret. Later Athiret became known to the Hebrews as Asherah, our heavenly mother, and the Lord became known as El, our heavenly father.

And so it was that El and Asherah desired to experience their great and divine love in a physical form and to share such blessedness with the children they would create. Each soul who was formed was perfectly matched, given a twin made from the same essence. In the book called Genesis, this is told as Adam's twin being created from his rib, which is to say his own essence, as she is flesh of his flesh and bone of his bone, spirit of his spirit.

Then God said, "And they shall become as one flesh."

Thus the hieros-gamos was created, the sacred marriage of trust and consciousness that unites the beloveds into one flesh. This is our highest gift from our father and mother in heaven. For when we come together in the bridal chamber, we find the divine union that El and Asherah wished for all their earthly children to experience in the light of pure joy and the essence of true love.

For those with ears to hear, let them hear it.

EL AND ASHERAH, AND THE HOLY ORIGINS OF HIEROS-GAMOS, FROM THE BOOK OF LOVE AS PRESERVED IN THE LIBRO ROSSO

Since meeting Bérenger, Maureen had become committed to understanding and experiencing the *hieros-gamos* in all its forms. Her eyes had been opened to a kind of love that she had previously never realized could exist outside fairy tales and legends. But this kind of epic union, this all-encompassing, nurturing love, was possible. If Maureen could experience it, be transformed by it, then she was certain that everyone could. She and Bérenger realized that this was part of their destiny: to help others find love as they had been blessed to find it themselves.

Maureen closed the book, content to sleep with visions of El and Asherah dancing in her dreams.

*

Maureen's dreams did not obey her desires.

Her dreaming was usually lucid and clear; complete sequences and coherent images came to her unbidden in her sleep. Always, they contained important messages for her or provided urgent clues to be followed. Until tonight. This dream was chaotic, frenetic, with flashes of image, sound, and emotion, moving through time and space. Some of the images seemed to relate to each other; others did not. But there was one constant factor through the entire dream. No matter the image, no matter the time frame, each flash of vision contained one unifying element.

*

Fire.

The fire burned hot in the town square, the pitch that had been poured upon the kindling to make it ignite faster and burn hotter was effective. Hundreds of people surrounded the stake and its victim. Or victims? Sweat poured down the faces of onlookers as hell appeared to rage before them. In one flash the crowd was weeping, in another jeering. Two different fires. Two different cities. One, then another, then back again. In the first city, she saw the faces in the crowd. They were shocked, terrified, saddened. She did not see the victim, only the flames, which leaped high in the center of the square, enveloping in their terrible embrace what was once a human being. Maureen saw the faces of weeping men and women in the crowd, and one man in particular came into focus for her. He was dressed plainly enough, as a merchant perhaps, but there was something in his demeanor that marked him as different. He stood tall, and despite his obvious distress, he had the presence of a king. As she watched a single tear roll down his cheek, she felt the man's terrible grief—and guilt—over the tragedy unfolding before him. Then another bright flash of fire moved her attention away from the man and back to the space where the stake had been. But it wasn't flame she saw now; rather it was a blinding white light that burst into the sky and rose to heaven. The sky appeared to darken all around them, turning nearly to black, as the white light against it took form for the briefest instant before fading away.

Maureen was then plunged into the fire of another city, another time, and another victim.

The faces in this crowd were angry, in contrast to the previous vision. And they all belonged to men, at least it was only men who were immediately surrounding the scaffolding. These men were the source of the jeering she had heard when the dream began. The riled mob threw things into the fire, objects Maureen could not identify, shouting in anger as they did so. A strange word she did not recognize, chanted over and over again. For a moment she thought they were saying "pig nose," but it seemed absurd to her, even in the surreal dream state. Again, she could not see the victim as the flames here burned even higher than in the first vision. But the atmosphere in this city was markedly different. This victim was despised and those who turned out for the execution were determined to watch the hated one die in this terrible way. This was controlled chaos, but it appeared to be on the verge of getting out of control as the flames grew hotter and higher. Just as Maureen felt the images start to fade, began to feel her consciousness calling her out of the dream state, she had one last vision of the final, terrible execution. At the edge of the square, far enough away to be safe but close enough to be scarred forever by what she was witnessing, was a little girl. Her dark eyes were enormous as she watched the fire and the angry mob that surrounded it. She was a fine-boned little thing like a tiny bird, no more than five or six, and desperately undernourished. And yet for all her fragile physical appearance, this child did not appear weakened or even afraid. It was the look in the little girl's eyes that Maureen would be left with long after the dream was over, as there was nothing of fear in them. Her eyes reflected the flames before her, and in them Maureen saw something she could not quite identify, yet she knew that it was something she did not like.

In the child's eyes was something terrible, something not so far away from madness.

Confraternity of the Holy Apparition
Vatican City
present day

"YOU ALLOWED THIS to happen!"

Felicity de Pazzi hissed at her granduncle as she threw the book across the desk at him. Her heavy black eyebrows were a harsh frame to huge dark eyes, which flashed with the heat of anger in her narrow face. She didn't care that he was old, ill, and feeble. He was supposed to stand for something. And he had failed, failed miserably when they needed him most.

"Calm yourself, my dear." Father Girolamo de Pazzi held up one trembling, palsied hand in an effort to reach his outraged niece. He loved her like a daughter and had played a strong role in raising her to be the power behind the confraternity now that he was no longer physically able to deal with day-to-day operations. Her unbridled passion for their cause made her an unstoppable and infinitely holy force. It also gave her an extreme temper. She had been well named, as inspired by God. Her mother had had a dream of the great Saint Felicita while pregnant with this, her only daughter. Throughout her pregnancy she had had further visions of that blessed saint who had been brave enough to sacrifice all seven of her sons to prove her unwavering faith. It was clear to everyone in the de Pazzi family when this child was born on the tenth of July, the feast day of Santa Felicita, that she had brought her name and her identity with her.

At boarding school in Great Britain, she adopted the English version of the name, Felicity. It had stayed with her, even after she was expelled from several British establishments for "aberrant behavior." While in her early teens, she had begun to have visions that possessed her totally, events that proved deeply problematic for the staunch British schools. She was brought back to Rome and placed in a convent school where her progress could be monitored by those closer to her family and faith. When it was determined that she was indeed seeing authentic apparitions, the confraternity adopted her as their living patron saint. Felicity had become a prophetess in her own right, a visionary who fell to the ground in ecstasy, writhing as she was struck by visions of Jesus Christ and his most Holy Virgin Mother. The fanaticism around Felicity and her visions had grown through the ultraconservative movement over the last two years, and she had begun to develop stigmata as the visions descended. Attendance at the confraternity meetings when Felicity was featured had become standing room only as a result. To watch her as the visions possessed her was eerie, yet powerful. There would be one such meeting tonight at the confraternity meeting hall, and she intended to make her appearance count.

Father Girolamo de Pazzi had given the girl a plaque as a gift upon her return to Italy, something she could use to bolster her strength while she made the transition to the harsher convent environment that would ultimately prove nurturing for her. The plaque was made of wood, inscribed with a quote from the blessed Saint Augustine regarding the sanctified actions of Saint Felicita. It was a quote that the modern Felicity had not only memorized but taken to heart as her model for faith. She would use it tonight during her appearance.

Wonderful is the sight set before the eyes of our faith, a mother choosing for her children to finish their earthly lives before her, contrary to all our human instincts. She did not send her sons away, she sent them on to God. She understood that they were beginning life, not ending it. It was not enough that she looked on, but she encouraged them. She bore more fruit with her courage than with her womb. Seeing them be strong, she was strong; and in the victory of each of her children, she was victorious.

To the de Pazzi family, Santa Felicita was an extraordinary woman of faith, possibly the greatest of all Christian martyrs when the total of her sacrifice was taken into account. This faith in the saint's righteousness was shared with an unequaled passion by the younger Felicity. In all his eighty-plus years of life devoted to the Church, Girolamo de Pazzi had never met anyone with the religious fervor of the woman who stood before him. She was shaking with it now, unable to control her self-righteous anger over the offending book that had brought her to this confrontation. He pleaded for her understanding.

"What could I have done to stop it? It was . . . out of my control, Felicity."

The book sat between them on the desk, a silent enemy. *The Time Returns*, by Maureen Paschal. *The Legend of the Book of Love.*

"You could have stopped her while you had her there."

Girolamo de Pazzi shook his head. He knew when she said, "You could have stopped her," she really meant that he should have killed her. There was a time when he would have been prepared to give that order. But he had discovered that he could not take a life in the presence of the Book of Love, and certainly not *that* life. Not after he had seen the book opened and realized definitively what it was. What *she* was.

What he had witnessed that evening in the crypt of Chartres Cathedral was not something he could readily describe to his grandniece, or to anyone else. He had lured Maureen Paschal into the crypt, sure enough, to bring her into the presence of the Book of Love, the ultimate treasure of anyone who revered the name of Jesus Christ. It was a gospel written in his own hand, and yet one which could not be simply read by scholars and theologians, many of whom had tried over the nearly five centuries that it had resided secretly within the Vatican walls. It was written in a polyglot of languages and there were layers to it, encoded teachings that average humans and traditional Christians had long forgotten how to access. The book was "locked," and as such was a mystical treasure that required a unique key to unveil all the teachings within it.

That key was Maureen Paschal.

It was apparent to everyone in the Confraternity of the Holy Apparition that Maureen Paschal was a prophetess with extraordinary ability and clarity. They had all studied how she had found the Arques Gospel of Mary Magdalene by following her visions, a feat no one else could accomplish. Even within their confraternity, where they had cultivated the greatest visionaries of all time for almost eight centuries, no one had been able to track that treasure successfully. Once she made her discovery in France, it became infinitely clear that Maureen Paschal had a special destiny. Then they knew that she was the "Expected One" who would also be able to unlock the secrets within the Book of Love. This infuriated Felicity de Pazzi.

Felicity had been brought into the presence of the Book of Love on several occasions, and each time the confraternity members prayed fervently that she would be able to unlock the Book and reveal its contents to them. But the Book remained silent, despite Felicity's stigmata, which bled so profusely when in the presence of the Book that she had to be hospitalized after the last session.

Felicity de Pazzi had suffered and bled for *all* her visions. This is how she knew they were authentic. God required pain from his holy ones to test their faith. Anyone who claimed visions but did not suffer for them was a false prophet who had not been tested. Felicity lived to share this understanding with others. Her mission was to tell the truth of the terrible prophecies that were given her about the End Times and the sinners who would be boiled alive in their own blood if they did not repent. The Holy Mother was very specific about the nature of the death that would come to the unbelievers and to those who were not willing to make profound sacrifices to show their love of God.

And Felicity did indeed sacrifice. She wore a *cilicium*, the medieval-style hair shirt that scratched and tore the flesh, beneath her loose-fitting clothes. She was remarkably thin and fine-boned, and she tied the instrument of torture tightly against her skin so that it did not show beneath her blouses. Felicity wore long sleeves at all times, so the scars from her cuttings were not visible. She had been taking a blade to her own flesh since she was in her early teens, carving images of crosses, thorns, and nails into her arms and legs until they bled and scabbed. Felicity knew that pain, suffering, and ultimately martyrdom were the greatest gifts one could give to God, and she could therefore not abide the knowledge of Maureen Paschal's continued grace as a visionary. That woman was an aberration, a heretic and blasphemer who did not deserve the gifts that God had bestowed upon her. She abused them for her own personal gain, exploiting her faith for money and profit. She was worse than the Whore of Babylon, more wicked than Jezebel; she was the serpent Lilith who would destroy Eden.

Maureen Paschal had to be stopped. And if she could be—if the unworthy life of such a demoness could be successfully terminated—then perhaps Felicity would finally be able to fulfill her own destiny. It was clear to her that the Paschal whore had stolen her rightful place. If God would only allow one prophetess at a time to unlock the Book of Love, then eliminating this unworthy one was a necessity. As long as Maureen

Paschal lived, the role was taken. But if she died, Felicity would then be able to step into that place, which was rightfully hers.

Felicity continued to rant. "She was the only one who could unlock the Book of Love, and you brought her there to do it. To prove once and for all that it was not what the heretics claimed it to be. And then . . . put an end to her."

The old man found some strength in the truth as he pulled himself up in his chair. "But it *is* what the heretics claim it to be, my dear. It is everything we feared it could be, and more. And that, unfortunately, is our predicament."

"All the more reason to end her."

"Felicity, God has chosen her. Whether we like it or not, whether we understand his reasons, it does not matter. If God has chosen her, we must accept that."

"You have lost all your wits along with your faith, Uncle!" Felicity looked as if she would strike him, and the old man recoiled as she leaned across the desk to make her point. "Don't you see? It is a test for me. God is waiting for me to show that I am worthy of this place by eliminating the imposter, the usurper. This is a great treasure, to be his prophetess, to speak his truth as it is told to me by the Holy Virgin. Such truths cannot come through the corrupted channels of a fornicator. It is through my chastity and my suffering that the truth will be revealed, and we will save the sinners who would repent. And the unrepentant will die and be condemned to hell, as they must."

Father Girolamo looked at his niece helplessly. He had attempted to explain the events in Chartres to her, but she did not care to listen. The leaders of the confraternity had known that Maureen would never cooperate with what was considered a radical fringe element within the Church—or more accurately, just outside the Church. This was why she had been lured into the crypt of Chartres Cathedral on false pretenses. The plan was to offer her a deal, to persuade her through financial and other means to come to their side and work for the confraternity. They wanted Maureen to recant, to turn her back on her research and deny her discovery of the importance of Mary Magdalene.

Maureen had published her findings to a fascinated audience of millions, claiming as she did that Magdalene was not only the wife of Jesus but also his chosen successor and arguably the founder of Christianity following the crucifixion. Truly, Mary Magdalene was the apostle of the apostles, but to allow her such power—with evidence to support the claim—would diminish the authority of the Church. Maureen's work challenged many long and deeply held traditions in Catholicism, including the refusal to allow women to become priests. But perhaps most controversial of all was Maureen's assertion that sacred sexuality was not only practiced by Jesus and his lawfully wedded wife but that this tradition, known as *hieros-gamos*, was a cornerstone of early Christianity. For an institution that had required vows of celibacy from its clergy for a thousand years, this idea of sex as sacred and holy was completely offensive, if not blasphemous.

The confraternity was not going to allow an American upstart—and a female at that—to challenge their traditions without a fight. Deciding that the most effective course would be to get the heretic herself to recant, they set into motion their plan to entrap Maureen and to blackmail her into changing her story. They knew it was a long shot and were prepared to eliminate her if she did not comply with the terms.

But that was before Maureen Paschal was brought into the presence of the Book of Love, in the holy ground of the Chartres crypt on the summer solstice. That was before the Book opened and revealed itself, surrounding Father Girolamo in the most exquisite blue light, infusing him with the perfect expression of love, a physical experience of what God felt like on earth. That was before Girolamo de Pazzi came to realize that the Book of Love was the true message of his Lord, and that to destroy the one woman who understood what it was and what it said would be a sin too great for him to commit.

"But why did you allow her to leave to tell this tale?" She gestured contemptuously at the book that lay between them. "*That*, Uncle, was not the plan. There is not a man—or woman—in the five hundred years of our people who has been as weak as you were in that moment. After all this time . . . *ahhh!*" She screamed her frustration, unable to put the words together through her rage. "It is inconceivable! And now look what she has done! Her blasphemy infects the world, and you along with it."

It had been a cruel blow. Father Girolamo de Pazzi had to be carried out of the Chartres crypt on a stretcher after his encounter with Maureen Paschal and the Book of Love. That same night, he suffered a stroke from which he had been recovering for two years. His speech had returned, but he was feeble and partially paralyzed as a result of the ailment. He had no doubt that the stroke was God's punishment, his way of warning Girolamo that there must be no further attacks on Maureen's life. He had tried to explain this to Felicity and the other more rabid members of the confraternity, but his reasoning fell on the deaf ears of fanatics who appeared to be growing more rabid rather than less.

There had been two other members of the confraternity with him that night in the crypt, henchmen of the darkest order who had been chosen for their extremism. Both men were committed fanatics, like Felicity, and had been fully prepared to eliminate Maureen if necessary to protect the secrets of the Church—once they were certain of what those secrets were. But they too were changed by the events of that evening. One, the crueler of them, had died in his sleep within a week of the events. His heart merely stopped beating in his chest, despite his youth and physical health. The other man lived still, but he had simply ceased to function and had not uttered a word in two years. He was currently residing in an institution for the mentally handicapped in Switzerland.

No, those who were not present would never comprehend what happened that evening.

"You cannot understand, Felicity. But I beg you to leave this alone. It is . . . far bigger than you can imagine. And I fear for you, fear that you will be the one hurt if you attempt to harm the Paschal woman in any way. God does not wish her to be harmed."

Felicity spat at her uncle, dark eyes glazing over as she channeled the holy Felicita's ire. There were moments when the saint appeared to take possession of her namesake and speak through her with an unearthly fervor, as she did now.

"How dare you presume to tell me what God wants?" the ancient Felicita growled through her vessel at the cowering old man before her. "I hear him clearly. And I pray that God forgives you for your weakness and for your evil intent. Only a devil would try to stop me from carrying out an ultimate example of sacrifice for the extreme glory of our Lord!"

Father Girolamo de Pazzi sat back in his chair, exhausted and deflated by the encounter. His niece appeared to have taken possession of her own body once more, though her eyes were still feverish. Felicity grabbed the offending book from his desk and turned to storm out as he called out weakly after her.

"What will you do now, Felicity?"

She turned to face him one final time, a small, satisfied smile on her lips.

"I have an appearance tonight, Uncle. Don't tell me you are so feeble you have forgotten. And I have no doubt that Our Lady will have much to say about this fornicator who would commit blasphemy in the name of her chaste and holy son." Felicity spat on the book she held in her hand. "And so I shall ensure that the confraternity knows full well who the enemy is."

He nodded sadly, knowing there was nothing he could do to stop what was about to happen.

"And then? Where will you go then?"

"Florence."

"Why Florence?"

"Savonarola," she said first, knowing he would understand that. Her uncle had been named after their infamous ancestor, after all. His full given name was Girolamo Savonarola de Pazzi. It was a name that, until his grand failure of two years ago, he had lived up to brilliantly.

"And because Destino is there." She hissed his name with a venom that she normally saved for her red-haired American nemesis. Destino had been the enemy of the confraternity for centuries, and she had a special desire to stop him as well. However, putting an end to the Paschal creature once and for all would be the greatest blow to Destino, so that remained her sole focus. Eliminating Maureen would destroy everything Destino had ever hoped to build.

And as Felicity turned and stomped out without a glance back, Father Girolamo watched her leave with more trepidation than he had ever felt in his long and troubled life.

Someone would soon die. He had no doubt of that. He just wasn't entirely sure who it would be—or at this stage, who he wished it to be.

The villa of Careggi, outskirts of Florence
July 4, 1442

COSIMO DE' MEDICI paced in anticipation of the arrival of his esteemed guest. The coming of René d'Anjou to Florence was an affair of state, and the members of that republic's council, the Signoria, had been preparing for months. There were political preparations to be sure: René was extremely popular in France, where he held a number of exalted titles, each bearing witness to the tremendous power he could wield when necessary. He was the duke of Provence and the titular king of both Naples and Jerusalem—all territories that would be very valuable to have in alliance should the Florentine republic require foreign aid in times of crisis. The military power of Naples, specifically, was of utmost importance in Italian alliances.

Yet for all his benevolent reputation, and that he was known as "Good King René," those were honors bestowed by his French countrymen. Florentines were, by nature, skeptical of all outsiders, but they were particularly wary of the acquisitive hands of French nobility. The fact that Naples was in French hands was grating enough on many Italians, and yet Florentines also realized that it could have been worse: the more politically aggressive and spiritually restrictive Aragon family from Spain was also vying for control of Naples. At least King René was a charming young man of education, taste, and progressive humanist ideals, all qualities that the cultured people of Florence held in high regard. Still, handling the multititled nobleman would require expert diplomacy and negotiating tactics.

The political potentials and detriments of an alliance with Good King René were argued in the Signoria at the same time that the coffers were opened to create a lavish spectacle of welcome worthy of the Republic of Florence. Cosimo de' Medici observed all of it but did little to participate in the public and political machinations. He was the most powerful and influential man in the Republic of Florence, but his interest in René d'Anjou was entirely personal—and gravely secret. Regardless of the outcome of the grand political posturing that would occur over the next weeks, Cosimo knew that René would never fail him if he ever truly needed him. Their meeting today in the privacy of the Medici villa of Careggi, beyond the watchful eyes that lurked within the city walls, would attest to that. While King René's official entrance and reception into Florence would occur ten days later, he had entered the region today under heavy disguise on a secret mission. It was a visit that was completely unknown to the citizens of Florence, a meeting that would have no witnesses save the chosen few and the ancient stones that formed the walls of Cosimo's elegant retreat.

*

"Cousin! It is a joy to reunite with you." The high-ranking French nobleman, known for his warmth, embraced Cosimo heartily once the door was safely closed behind them.

Cosimo smiled broadly at René's use of the familial greeting, and returned it. "The joy is all mine, cousin. Thank you for coming."

Any Florentine observing this meeting would have been deeply perplexed. René d'Anjou carried the highest royal French pedigree; he was the son of the two most pristine royal bloodlines in Europe, the French Angevin dynasty and the Spanish Aragonese, and the holder of multiple hereditary titles. Conversely, Cosimo de' Medici was a commoner, one of the most wealthy and influential commoners in all Europe, but from a merchant class all the same. How a prince of these exalted and elitist dynasties came to call the Italian banker his cousin was a secret worth more than gold, a secret of life and death for all involved.

René recounted his recent journey as Cosimo ushered him into the elegant *studiolo*. The doors to his private library were opened only to the most intimate and trusted friends and family members. As was traditional in many wealthy Florentine families, even wives were not allowed within the walls of their husband's private studios. Cosimo had kept this tradition, even through his long marriage to a woman he loved, and his secrets were well contained within these walls.

"I have just come from Sansepolcro. I am told that you have secured that territory completely?"

Cosimo nodded. He had purchased Borgo Sansepolcro to add it to Florentine territories in Tuscany, yet he had used private Medici money to do so. This was not merely a strategic political purchase for Florence. It was a personal one. The medieval walled city, established in the tenth century, was sacred ground for the Medici as it had been the dwelling place of the Magi for five hundred years.

"How is our beloved Master? Is he on his way?" Cosimo asked.

"Fra Francesco is well and is not so far behind me. It is astonishing to see that he has not changed a bit since I was a boy."

Cosimo smiled knowingly before replying; the crooked smile transformed his often serious and sardonic face to a landscape where wit and understanding shared space. Memories of their Master and the sacred time spent with him always made him smile. The old man known as Fra Francesco had taught both of these men and instilled in them the understanding that they were cousins of a very ancient blood and spirit. Fra Francesco was entirely unique. He was the gentle yet formidable Master of an ancient society to which both men had pledged fealty until death, the Order of the Holy Sepulcher. The Order and its teachings were firmly ensconced just a day's ride from Florence in the tiny walled city that shared its name and was now a Medici possession: Sansepolcro.

"I dare say he will never change, as you well know," Cosimo responded. "But I am grateful that you have agreed to come on this, the specified date. There is much to discuss, and to plan for."

"How could I refuse? This date is written in the stars, and we must ensure that we honor it appropriately. It is a matter of great excitement for everyone in the Order, and I will do my duty as it has been decided. When is this child destined to arrive?"

"We have assembled all the forecasts from the Magi, with Fra Francesco's counsel. They all agree that the stars clearly indicate 1449 because of the positioning of Mars in Pisces that occurs that year. If properly timed, he will be born on the first day of January, so he can then be baptized five days later on the Feast of the Epiphany. It will require great planning, but as you know, it has been done before with success. And this time . . . we must succeed exactly. Such a birth will give him the stellar influences that satisfy the prophecy most completely. This is why we must begin preparation now, far in advance, to ensure our success. It may take several years to find the perfect woman to mother this child."

No one knew the power of this ancient foretelling more personally than René d'Anjou. He was the reigning Poet Prince, the golden child recognized by the Order for his divine birth and destiny. His path had been predetermined by his bloodline and birth date, and he had done his best to fulfill it. Cosimo's reference to "succeeding exactly this time" caused René to flinch a little. It was a reference to his own birth, which had missed the timing when he arrived two weeks too late. While the position of the stars at René's birth was still in keeping with the prophecy, he had known from his earliest days that he would always be a bit of a disappointment. Yes, he was a Poet Prince. But he was not *the* Poet Prince. And this unfortunate aspect of his birth haunted him each time he made an error or was seen to fall short in his duties to the Order and their divine mission.

René closed his eyes and recited the prophecy of the Poet Prince, which had colored his life in shades of extreme light and dark since his own birth had been predicted by the Magi:

The Son of Man shall choose
when the time returns for the Poet Prince.
He who is a spirit of earth and water born
within the complex realm of the sea goat
and the bloodline of the blessed.
He who will submerge the influence of Mars
And exalt the influence of Venus
To embody grace over aggression.
He will inspire the hearts and minds of the people
So as to illuminate the path of service
And show them the Way.
This is his legacy,
This, and to know a very great love.

Good King René looked up at his old friend with eyes that blurred with tears. "As you know, I have not been the most perfect prince. I have indeed been blessed to know a very great love, I have fathered an equinox-born daughter who fulfills a prophecy of her own, and I have tried to complete all the tasks set out for me to benefit the Order and preserve our ways. But I will admit it does not grieve me to relinquish the title. I shall sleep better once this boy is born, and born perfectly to the plan set forth by God through the schedule of the stars. Perhaps I shall sleep once and for all."

"Do not speak so, René," the elder Cosimo chided. "You are such a young man. There is much greatness awaiting you in this life."

King René d'Anjou had come to Florence at the request of Fra Francesco, known by the exalted title of Master of the Order of the Holy Sepulcher, to surrender his title as the reigning Poet Prince in preparation for the baby whose coming was now foretold. The date of this meeting had been carefully calculated by the astrologers within the Order, who were known as the Magi in honor of the three priest-kings who foresaw the birth of Jesus. Indeed, the legacy of the Magi spanned the fifteen hundred years since the appearance of the Star of Bethlehem. These modern Magi were highly educated in the way of the ancients, conversant in teachings from Zoroaster and the Kabbalah, and were experts in the study of the Sibylline Oracles. They were masters of Egyptian mysticism, Chaldean numerology, and above all, the workings of the planets on the fortunes of mankind. The Magi understood that astrology was a gift from God, meant to be a scepter of power when enhanced by the intellect, spirit, and free will of those who were enlightened enough to utilize it properly. It was the ultimate tool that could be used to accomplish the will of God.

The current Magi were on constant watch for the special children who had been predicted in this generation. In the Order, "The time returns" was the ancient motto that they lived by, and the stars indicated that the coming decades would bring together the most significantly gifted and divinely blessed men and women. There were specific cycles of greatness in history, eras which were predetermined by God, through the stars, to bring forth angelic and evolved souls to improve the state of mankind. The Magi, along with the elders of the Order, were not content to leave all this to chance—nor had they ever been. Through the careful use of astrology they could ensure that certain children were conceived at the appropriate time and in the immaculate way that would dictate divine blessings in birth and through life. With specific guidance and wisdom, this new generation would create a golden age, a rebirth of mankind that would combine ancient wisdom with progressive thought to catapult humanity into a shining time of peace and prosperity. It was a divine vision of unity, of a time when all men and women would understand what it meant to be *anthropos*—fully realized and fulfilled humans—as defined in the Order's most sacred text, the Libro Rosso.

The Libro Rosso, the great red book, was a protected text passed down through the Order. It contained within it a perfect copy of the stunning lost gospel written by Jesus, referred to as the Book of Love. Legend within the Order told that Jesus left this priceless document to Mary Magdalene so that she might teach his words from it after he was gone. While the original gospel written in the hand of the Lord himself had disappeared to history, a perfect copy was made by the apostle Philip in the presence of the first book. That copy was now bound within the gilded leather cover of the Libro Rosso. Also in the sacred red book was a history of the Order, including lives of the saints, many of whom were not recognized by the traditional Church, and others with very different stories to tell than those which were now "accepted" by Rome. Finally, the book contained a series of prophecies, including that of the Poet Prince. The Libro Rosso had been in the possession of French royalty for centuries and was now kept by Good King René as the reigning heir to the prophecy.

René ran his hands through his hair as he settled back in one of Cosimo's plush velvet-covered chairs. He sighed heavily before continuing. "Ah, this child, this child . . . you must know that it is a curse as much as it is a blessing, Cosimo. It is . . . not an easy thing to live with this prophecy. And yet for those of us who do, we must remember at all times that we were chosen for it by God. It is a responsibility that we can never, never lose sight of."

The portents showed that the next child to fulfill the prophecy, the Poet Prince who would usher in this new era of enlightenment, was destined to be the child of Cosimo's oldest son, Piero. Their focus now would be to choose the appropriate "Mary" to wed to Piero, to carry the child—and to raise him properly in preparation for his destiny.

"This grandchild of yours must be taught carefully, by our Master, in the same way that we were—only with even greater focus. We must learn from our mistakes."

Cosimo nodded. "Any advice you choose to impart to prepare us as we raise this child to fulfill his destiny will be considered the most valuable counsel."

René had thought about this while traveling north from Sansepolcro the previous day. Once the Master had told him that the new Poet Prince was expected to be born into the Medici family, he knew that it was time to pass on the mantle he had worn for so many years. And he would, in all honesty, be relieved to be rid of it. He was a young man still, and yet at times he felt ancient and exhausted by the responsibilities of his heritage. The burden had grown far too heavy, and he would enjoy stepping back from it. And while his life had been filled with the blessings of the highly privileged, René d'Anjou had also endured his share of tragedies. One, above all others, haunted him every day of his life and would until he took his last breath and could then beg her forgiveness in heaven.

Jeanne.

She was known by many names now as her legend continued to grow since the terrible day of her execution eleven years earlier. She was the Maid of Orléans, she was Jeanne d'Arc; even the English crossed themselves when speaking of her, calling her Joan of Arc and the Daughter of God, while whispering that the Church had made a dreadful mistake in her execution as a heretic. But for King René, Jeanne had been so much more: she was his spiritual sister, his family's protégée, the Expected One, the hope of France . . . and his greatest failure. That he could not protect her in the end was unforeseeable; that he did not have the courage to do so was unforgivable. And this was the source of the self-loathing that tortured his sleepless nights since that wretched day in May of 1431 when Jeanne had been burned alive for the crime of hearing the voices of saints and angels too clearly.

If René was truly honest with himself, with his brethren in the Order, and with his God, it was his courage that had ultimately failed him—with a fair amount of help from his ego and his love of worldly comforts. He blamed his youth for this ultimate failing; he had only been twenty-two at the time, just three years older than Jeanne. He had been young enough to falter under such a weighty burden. He had not been willing to risk everything he had, everything he was, to try to save the girl he loved more than a sister, the prophetess who had been an angelic being in a girl's body. He knew she had been both conceived and raised to be the Daughter of God, and yet he had allowed her to die through his absolute passivity when she most needed him to save her.

Good King René now lived in a self-imposed hell every day of his life. He would not wish that on the innocent child who would be born into this terrible prophecy.

René cleared his throat. "Tell this future grandchild . . . that he must

have the courage of ten thousand lions, and most of all he must not fear
Rome and their threats. The angels and the innocents who live among
us must be protected at all costs." René grew silent for a moment remembering his own failure once again. "As you know, the Magi say that
more angelic beings and special ones are coming now as the time returns. They must be cared for. Your young prince will be born to lead
them, and he must never waiver in what he knows to be right action, for
one misstep can be the ruination of all that is in God's greatest plans.
I have seen that.

"For while God provides us with the outline of our destiny . . ."

Cosimo finished the sentence, a tenet of the Order's teachings,
". . . he also gives us the free will to fulfill that destiny—or not."

As his old friend continued, Cosimo listened carefully, committing
it all to his sharp memory. He saw the deep lines etched in René's face,
once a place where only laughter and witticisms reigned. But eleven
years of terrible regret had aged him brutally and prematurely.

"I buckled under the pressures of the jackals in Rome, Cosimo, and
to their henchmen priests in Paris. I despised their corruption, recognized it for all that it was and always has been, but in the end I feared
their power more." His voice cracked as he spoke, safe in the presence of
one of his oldest friends, and a man with whom all shared secrets were
sacrosanct. "I . . . I could have saved her. I . . ."

He could not continue. The years of guilt and agony came out in a
flood as the king of Naples and Jerusalem buried his head in his hands
and wept openly. Cosimo remained silent and waited with respect for
his friend, his cousin of blood and spirit, to move through his pain.

René raised his head after another minute, wiping his eyes while
he spoke. "I failed her, I failed the Order, and I failed God. Fra Francesco says that I have already been forgiven. But I do not accept that,
for I have yet to forgive myself. You can help me to make amends for
my failings, old friend, by raising this child to be the true Poet Prince
of our prophecy. Let him learn from my mistakes and vow that he will
not repeat them. And as my gift to all that he can become, I will leave
him with a great legacy of treasure, including our most sacred Libro

Rosso, for it belongs in the hands of the worthy. And I want him to have this."

René reached behind his neck to unfasten the clasp of a long silver chain that hung out of sight and beneath his clothes. As he removed the necklace, Cosimo could see that it was a pendant, a small reliquary locket made of silver. René rose from his chair to place it in Cosimo's hand, then paced the room as he explained.

"It was Jeanne's," he said simply, allowing the import of those words to land before continuing with his explanation. "It was her protective amulet, passed down through the Order and given to her at her equinox birth when it was determined that she was . . . who and what she was. Jeanne wore it every day of her life once she was old enough to understand its purpose. On the day that she was taken, it had fallen off and was later found on the floor where she had last been dressed. The chain was broken. She must not have known it fell off, as she would never have left without it. I contend that she would not have been arrested if she had been wearing it; she would be with us today. Its powers of protection are said to be unlimited. God knows that she wore it into heated battles where she could not possibly have survived, and yet she always emerged from those victorious and unscathed."

René walked over and put his hand over Cosimo's for emphasis. "There is great power in this amulet, Cosimo. See that the child understands it, and that he wears it always. It is a greater shield than armor. One day it may save his life, as it should have saved Jeanne the Maid."

Cosimo moved toward the lantern on his desk to look at the amulet more closely.

It was oval and made like a locket, but with a cover that slipped over the top, like the lid on a tiny box. The lid covered the red wax seal that was used to both protect and authenticate religious artifacts. In this case, the seal was so ancient and deteriorated that it was impossible to determine what the original image had looked like in its entirety, but there were tiny stars visible in what appeared to be a circular pattern embedded in the wax.

While smaller than Cosimo's thumbnail, the casing was, conversely, highly detailed and well preserved. Embossed into the silver cover was a miniature crucifixion sequence. At the foot of the cross, a long-haired and kneeling Mary Magdalene clung to the feet of her dying beloved. Strangely, the only other element—carefully crafted—was a columned temple perched on a hill behind the crucifixion. The temple looked distinctly Greek in style, resembling the Acropolis in Athens, the shrine built to honor feminine wisdom and strength.

Cosimo turned the case over to see the relic itself. It was minuscule, so tiny as to be nearly invisible, but it was there. A speck of wood was held in place by some type of resin, adhered into the center of a golden flower. Beneath the relic was a sliver of paper, handwritten in painstaking script:

V. CROISE

It was an abbreviation that the learned Cosimo understood, even written as it was in the antiquated French of the troubadours. *Vraie Croise.* He looked up at his friend. "This is a piece of the True Cross. The most sacred relic of the Order."

"It is. And it will protect your grandson in a world that is most often hostile to those of us who would strive to change it."

Cosimo took the amulet with gratitude, aware as he did so that René's final words on the subject sounded a little too much like a prophecy of their own.

"It will save his life, no matter how determined others will be to take it."

*

It would be several hours before the others arrived and the official meeting of the Order came together. Cosimo, in anticipation of René's potential melancholy over the day, had planned a diversion for his friend that he knew would be greatly appreciated. He led René through the grounds of Careggi in the golden heat of a Tuscan afternoon, toward an apple cellar beneath the stables. René was perplexed at the destination but followed with interest. No doubt Cosimo de' Medici had something extraordinary in that apple cellar. And René was relatively certain it was not apples.

"Art will save the world," Cosimo said with a smile, and René returned the sentence. Passed down through the Order, it was believed to have been spoken by the holy Nicodemus, who was the first man to create a piece of Christian art. His breathtakingly beautiful sculpture of the crucified Christ was the stuff of legend in Tuscany and remained on permanent display in the ancient city of Lucca. Both Nicodemus and his patron, Joseph of Arimathea, were present at the crucifixion and aided in the removal of the body of Jesus from the cross. After witnessing the events of Good Friday, Nicodemus carved the first crucifix, in this case a life-sized version of the image he could not erase from his mind. The face of Jesus he carved was considered so sacred that the artwork was referred to only as the *Volto Santo*, the Holy Face.

On the day of the original Easter, Joseph of Arimathea and Nicodemus, along with another revered artist who would be known to history as Saint Luke, founded the Order of the Holy Sepulcher. They pledged through their Order to preserve the teachings of the Way as Jesus instructed through the gospel written in his own hand, the Book of Love. When Jesus announced his resurrection to Mary Magdalene on that sacred Sunday, the three men knew beyond any doubt that she was the chosen successor of their messiah. The teachings of the Book would endure under her guidance, and the newly founded Order would be sworn to protect this woman, her children, and her descendants through time. Most of all, they would be sworn to protect the true teachings, the Way of Love as Jesus had set it out most specifically for his followers. Often the Order would preserve these teachings through secret symbolism and encodings in art and literature.

As a result, like Cosimo and all nobles of the Order, René was a keen patron of the arts. He was looking forward to a time when he could focus more completely on art, music, and architecture and less on politics. Because art was the language members of the Order used to communicate the truth, both Cosimo and René were constantly seeking new ways to see the beauty of the secret teachings expressed in art.

As the men approached the apple cellar, René stopped to listen to the deeply melodic sound emanating from behind the door. He looked at Cosimo, amused. "Singing? Do you have magical apples here in the wilds of Tuscany, Cosimo, which have the power of song?"

Cosimo laughed in return. "No, I have wayward artists who are delinquent in their commissions, who have the power of painting."

René was taken aback. Cosimo was renowned as the most benevolent of patrons, giving generously to his artists, even supporting them and their families completely, while lecturing other patrons to be more magnanimous. "You, of all patrons? *You* lock up your artists in a cellar?"

"Well, not normally. But Lippi is the exception to all rules."

René gasped. "Lippi? You have *Fra Filippo Lippi* locked in there?"

Cosimo nodded nonchalantly. "Yes, I do. He doesn't sound distressed to you, does he?"

René shook his head with no small degree of amazement. The booming voice from the apple cellar sounded positively—and inexplicably—ebullient. That the sound was coming from Filippo Lippi, who was the most impressive artist working in Florence, was astonishing. Lippi's frescoes were considered so divinely inspired that even the king of France was interested in sending for him. But Lippi would never leave Cosimo de' Medici or Florence, not for anything: not for the king of France, the king of the world, or a king's ransom. For all his eccentricities, Fra Filippo Lippi was unerringly loyal to the patron who protected him against the perils of the world.

Much of what made Lippi's art transcendent was his extraordinary ability to capture the divine by communicating with it directly. He was a member of what Cosimo referred to as his "army of angels," an elite group of supremely gifted artists who had the talent to translate divine inspirations and teachings into canvas and marble. Within the Order, they were called "the angelics." The coming of these scribes of a new era had also been predicted by the Magi. Cosimo had a passion for locating and cultivating these artists, and he had succeeded most exceptionally with the discovery of Lippi, as well as the remarkable sculptor known in Florence by the name Donatello. They were geniuses possessed by divine inspiration, and consequently, both were rarely impressed by any earthly authority. The angelic qualities they embodied did not always make for the most harmonious lives here on earth. Lippi and Donatello were both notoriously difficult and temperamental. Indeed, no Florentine patron but Cosimo had ever been able to work successfully with either. But then again, no patron but Cosimo truly understood who, and what, they were.

As a member of the Order of the Holy Sepulcher, René d'Anjou did understand and was fascinated. He had not thus far in his life had the luxury of cultivating such talent and working with artists of this nature, and he wanted to know more.

"Lippi is one of the foretold angelics?"

Cosimo nodded. "Of course. And I am hoping to give him some much-needed discipline so that one day he may teach some of the younger artists who show that same promise—without also imbuing them with his bad habits."

Cosimo fished the key to the solid iron lock out of his pocket. "His minor incarceration here is for his own good and he knows it. Lippi must be protected from himself."

René saw immediately that the apple cellar was no dank dungeon. Light filtered in on all sides through well-placed skylights, and Lippi painted happily, surrounded by everything he could possibly require while performing a day's work. The artist grinned as the two men entered and he addressed his patron.

"Ah, perfect that you have come now, Cosimo. See here, what I have done. I have added some touches here to the angels, and see how I have placed the book here carefully? No one will be the wiser."

Cosimo introduced René to Lippi, but the artist was far too single-minded, completely absorbed in his current masterpiece, to show much concern for the fact that the king of Jerusalem and Naples was in his presence. He continued his questions to Cosimo.

"What do you think? Do I dare paint the book's cover red? Make it a true Libro Rosso?"

"At this stage, Lippi, I don't care if you paint it violet with rosy stripes, just as long as you finish it quickly. The archbishop is howling for your head. I will not be able to protect you from his wrath much longer."

Cosimo turned to René and explained. "Lippi is notoriously late on all his commissions, distracted as he is by wine and women."

"Oh no, no!" Lippi held up a hand. "*One* woman, Cosimo. Not women, plural. Woman, singular. There is only one perfect woman for me, created by God at the dawn of time from my own being, my own soul's twin, and yes, she distracts me utterly . . ."

Cosimo continued with René as Lippi lapsed into more ecstasy over his one true love.

"Meanwhile, Lippi is no less late with this altarpiece for Santa Annunziata, for a clergyman who is already carrying a grudge about Lippi's abandoned vows. If he does not deliver it on time, the archbishop will withdraw his commission and lock him up—in a real cell. So you see, what I do here is quite humane."

Lippi shrugged and nodded, with an afterthought. "It is. Although you could be more generous with the wine."

"That's enough out of you." Cosimo's smile was affectionate for all his harsh words. "You will have nothing but bread and water in a dark cell if you don't finish this commission, so stop complaining."

As Cosimo turned to go, he said over his shoulder, "And *of course* you should make the book red. That is the point, isn't it?"

Lippi winked at him and returned to his masterpiece, bursting into a ribald song about making love on the banks of the Arno in the springtime, as he mixed the russet pigments to create the perfect, heretical red for the unsuspecting archbishop's book cover.

The Poet Prince

Florence
1448

IN THE FIRST of many things that Lucrezia Tornabuoni de' Medici would accomplish to absolute perfection, she conceived a son during the sacred ceremony of Immaculate Conception with her husband, Piero, in the spring of 1448.

The challenge faced by Cosimo de' Medici, along with the female hierarchy within the Order, had been to find the perfect woman from a Florentine family to mother the child of their prophecy. This was not simply an issue of lineage but one of temperament and spiritual potential. The young woman chosen to mother this special child would require rigorous training in the ways of the Order, and it was critical that she not be resistant to the sometimes extreme heresy represented by the teachings found within the Libro Rosso. The suitable girl from an acceptable family would recognize the beauty and the truth of what the Order was teaching and therefore embrace her role as the new Mary for the dawning of the golden age. Just as the golden child would come as predicted, so would the "Mary" who would give birth to him become apparent when the time was right.

Lucrezia Tornabuoni emerged as the unanimous choice to marry into the Medici dynasty and mother the Poet Prince. The adored and highly educated daughter of an exalted Florentine family, Lucrezia was renowned both for her brilliant intellect and for her extraordinary common sense. She was also recognized in the elite literary circles of Florence as a gifted poet, a valuable characteristic for the mother of this future prince to possess. The ultimate benefit of this arranged marriage was that Piero and Lucrezia managed to fall completely in love with each other while the preparations were under way to unite them.

Piero and Lucrezia de' Medici had been married for almost five years when this ritual to conceive their Poet Prince was invoked. They had married early in 1444, their wedding date and time chosen by the Magi to ensure the greatest fortune. The year itself was considered a great blessing as it contained within it the number 444, called "the manifes-

59

tation of the angels" in ancient numerology. Indeed, the union had appeared to bring angelic blessings thus far to the growing Medici family. During the course of their peaceful and contented marriage thus far, Piero and Lucrezia had blessedly conceived three beautiful and healthy daughters.

Lucrezia and Piero de' Medici followed the rite of Immaculate Conception exactly as they were instructed by the Mistress of the Hieros-Gamos. This approach to coupling within the bedchamber was the ultimate sacrament within the Order, and the two of them had been through intensive instruction in sacred union. They understood that Immaculate Conception was the conscious conception of a much-desired child. The beloved couple entered the bedchamber in an atmosphere of absolute love and trust for each other, and with the understanding that they were about to engage in a holy act that would bring forth a child to them, if God was so willing. During the act of coupling, each was to pray for the admission of the child into the woman's body.

It was a beautiful ceremony, one in which the senses were invoked to create an environment of heaven on earth within a bedchamber transformed into a sacred space. White candles reflected soft shadows on the walls, and the bed was draped with the softest and finest white linens and silks. The room was filled with vases of enormous and fragrant white lilies, as it was believed that the scent of lilies stimulated the senses as a reminder of the divine. For centuries, lilies had been the symbol of the Immaculate Conception and were often found in paintings representing the blessed moment of Mary's conception, but none outside the Order understood that this was a reference to the *hieros-gamos* ritual of sacred coupling. Lilies represented the scent of heaven.

Lucrezia Tornabuoni came to her husband that night dressed in a silk gown of white trimmed with threads of gold. Together they invoked a prayer to the angels for the protected guidance of the soul of this child into Lucrezia's body. The invocation asked that a special gathering of angelic beings come together to watch over this little soul, to guide and protect him so that he might carry out the bidding of God during all his days on earth.

Outside the bedchamber, a musician strummed a lyre and sang low chants the couple could hear during their union. The songs were meant to invoke angelic presence through sound, stimulating yet another sense in a divine manner. In the corner of the room an altar had been erected, and upon it sat the holy book of true teachings, the Libro Rosso. It had been René d'Anjou's ultimate gift to the Medici family in anticipation of the prophesied prince who would usher in a rebirth of truth and enlightenment. The return of the Libro Rosso to Tuscany heralded the recognition of the Medici by the French royal family, including René's cousin King Louis XI, as legitimate heirs to European power. Louis XI also granted Piero and his descendants the right to use the French royal fleur-de-lis emblem within the Medici crest in perpetuity as part of this gift from within the spirit family of the Order.

And so it was to the lovely sound of angelic music, amid the bliss-inducing scent of lilies, and in the presence of this most sacred book that Lucrezia de' Medici conceived a son at the precise moment determined by the stars and instructed by the Magi.

In keeping with Lucrezia's reputation for flawless execution of every task given her, she delivered the little prince, healthy and wailing and with a finely shaped head covered with glossy black hair, precisely as scheduled on January 1, 1449. The parents named the child in honor of the saint who had inspired their family's basilica and was one of the greatest inspirations in the history of the Order, Saint Laurence. Within the archives of the Order, it was known additionally that Saint Laurence had been conceived immaculately; he was one of the first to bear the title of Poet Prince. His name was an important clue to this legacy: Laurence came from the root Laurentius, in reference to the laurel tree. From ancient times in Greece and later in Rome, the leaves of the laurel tree were used to create crowns in honor of the greatest poets of their times, thus leading to the term *poet laureate*. Great poets were crowned with laurel leaves. They were, in this way, declared as poet princes.

Therefore this saint could be the only namesake for such a blessed child. He would bear a name that invoked both poetry and power, courage against the greatest odds, and an unstoppable determination to carry out a mission for the highest good under God. That name was Lorenzo, and this blessed child of Piero and Lucrezia de' Medici would carry it into the future in a way that even they could not have imagined on the glorious day that he first drew breath.

Lorenzo de' Medici, the great Poet Prince, had arrived as scheduled by God to herald the rebirth of a golden age.

Château des Pommes Bleues
Arques, France
present day

TAMARA WISDOM WAS in a creative frenzy. As a filmmaker, she had so many possible subjects to choose from that she didn't know where to start. Her documentary about Maureen's work was something she had been outlining for months now. But there were so many directions in which to take it that she was having trouble settling on just one. Trying to find just the right way to present this story to the cynical world so that others might understand the beauty and the magic of it was going to be the challenge.

And while studying the Libro Rosso over these last weeks, Tammy had come up with another idea.

Destino.

Surely there had never been a more extraordinary documentary subject in history. But would he allow her to tell his story? And what, exactly, was his story? Could it be possible that the wise and gentle man with the fearsomely scarred face really was what he claimed to be? Or was he just a crazy old Italian with a great sense of drama and history? That was precisely what would make Tammy's film amazing, if she could get him to concede to going on camera with her. Let him tell the story, and let the viewer decide just how real—or how crazy—this Destino really was.

Tammy picked up her copy of the Libro Rosso translations and read through the legend one more time, making notes as she went.

*

And so it was that on the darkest day of our Lord's sacrifice upon the cross, he was tormented in his final hour by a Roman centurion known as Longinus Gaius. This man had served Pontius Pilate in the scourging of our Lord Jesus Christ and had taken pleasure in inflicting pain upon the Son of God. As if this were not crime enough for one man, this same centurion pierced the side of our Lord with his deadly spear at his hour of death.

The sky turned black at his moment of passing from our world into the next, and it is said that within that moment the Father in heaven spoke directly to the centurion thus:

"Longinus Gaius, you have most offended me and all people of good heart with your vile deeds on this day. Your punishment shall be one of eternal damnation, but it will be an earthly damnation. You shall wander the earth without benefit of death so that each night when you lay down to sleep, your dreams will be haunted by the horrors of your own actions and the pain they have caused. Know that you will experience this torment until the end of time, or until you serve a suitable penance to redeem your tarnished soul in the name of my son Jesus Christ."

Longinus was blind to the truth at this time in his life, a man of sadistic cruelty beyond redemption, or so it would seem. But it came to pass that he was driven mad by the pronouncement of his eternal sentence to wander in an earthly hell. Therefore he sought out Our Lady Magdalena in Gaul to beg her forgiveness for his misdeeds. In her unlimited kindness and compassion she forgave him and instructed him in the teachings of the Way, just as she would any new follower, and without judgment.

What became of Longinus Gaius is uncertain. He disappeared from the writings of Rome and from those of the early followers. It is unknown if he ever truly repented and found release from his sentence by a just God, or if he wanders the earth still, lost in his eternal damnation.

THE LEGEND OF LONGINUS THE CENTURION,
AS PRESERVED IN THE LIBRO ROSSO

It was a haunting legend, made all the more astonishing by the fact that the old man named Destino claimed to be Longinus, a living witness to the history of the world for the last two thousand years. While he claimed that Mary Magdalene had forgiven him, it was only the forgiveness of God that would release him from his terrible curse. He became the Master of the Order of the Holy Sepulcher on the day he took his vow to Mary Magdalene that he would devote his eternal life to teaching the Way of Love. This was his penance, and he would serve it for two thousand years. Destino spoke of training Matilda of Canossa, who lived a thousand years ago, as if she were his student just last year. And he talked often about their blessed Magdalene, in tones of hushed reverence.

Tammy was constantly asking herself, Was Destino, as he claimed, the eternal soul who pierced the crucified Christ with his spear and was cursed by God to wander the earth? Or was he a madman with an extraordinary sense of storytelling? The beauty of it was that she was perfectly torn. At times she was absolutely convinced that he was one thing, and then he would do or say something that swayed her in the other direction.

Like the Roman centurion who had scourged Jesus, Destino had a terrible, zigzag scar across his face. As part of her research, Tammy had been tracking this idea of the scar-faced man carefully through history. She had found references to him in art and literature throughout centuries, references that were certainly interesting if not convincing. Of course there were more plausible explanations than immortality: the scars on these men through history were a coincidence, or perhaps there was some kind of cult, or there was a ritualistic reason for men who called themselves Masters of the Order to inflict such a scar upon themselves.

Tammy felt that it would be her job as a filmmaker to take a neutral position, to simply present what Destino claimed and allow the viewers to make up their minds. The more she thought about the possibilities, the more excited she became. And now Destino was begging them to come to Florence. He promised that he would introduce them to the deepest secrets of the Renaissance and the hidden stories behind the greatest works of art in human history, proving once and for all that he was precisely what he claimed.

She put down her copy of the Libro Rosso and picked up an obscure, nineteenth-century British academic booklet about Botticelli that she had found in a storage box in the château's expansive library. No artist moved her quite like Sandro Botticelli. An enormous copy of his masterpiece known as *Primavera* hung in the entry of Bérenger's château. This *Allegory of Spring*, with its beautiful spirit of rebirth and celebration of life, never failed to inspire her. The great goddess of love, Venus, garbed in red and blessing the world, stood at the center of a lush garden where the three Graces danced beside the figure of Mercury. Flora, the goddess of spring, dropped flowers all about her, as the nymph Chloris was chased by the wind called Zephyr. Cupid fluttered at the top of the painting, preparing to shoot his arrow at one of the unsuspecting Graces.

She began to read about it:

> *Art historians disagree bitterly about the meaning of Botticelli's ultimate masterpiece, which was not called* Primavera *during the Renaissance. It was likely not given this title until the eighteenth century when it appears documented as such, although the first use of it is uncertain. There are possibly more theories about its origins and intentions than there are about any single piece of Renaissance art.* Primavera *is an enigma, challenging every viewer to judge its meaning based on individual conclusions. Because Botticelli did not leave us with any notes as to his inspirations,* Primavera *shall remain one of the greatest unsolved mysteries of the art world for all time.*

Tammy prepared to skim the rest of the chapter until an unexpected sentence returned her focus.

> *The renowned Renaissance humanist Giovanni Pico della Mirandola said, "Whoever understands deeply and with intellect the reason for the separation of Venus from the trinity of Graces while studying Botticelli will find the proper way of advancing their*

understanding through this unequaled painting, known to us as
Le Temps Revient."

Le Temps Revient. Tammy jumped up with excitement and ran through the château in search of Roland and Bérenger. That Botticelli called his masterpiece *The Time Returns*, according to a contemporary from the Renaissance, just might be the most important—and most overlooked—detail in the history of Renaissance art.

*

Bérenger Sinclair held the tiny reliquary in his hand, running the chain through his fingers. It had captivated him since the day that Destino had given it to him as a gift. He had been skeptical at first, knowing that there were so many relics purported to be pieces of the True Cross.
With this little locket Destino had enclosed a card:

> *This once belonged to another Poet Prince, the greatest who ever lived. You are charged to wear his mantle. Do so with grace and God will reward you just as the prophecy promises.*

Bérenger was relatively sure that the greatest Poet Prince referred to was Lorenzo de' Medici, the godfather of the Renaissance. Bérenger was a bit ashamed to say that he didn't know as much about Lorenzo as he perhaps should, although he was very willing to learn at Destino's instruction. He had, however, studied the man revered by the French heretics as their great Poet Prince, the Renaissance heir to the dynasty of Anjou known as Good King René. Bérenger, whose birthday fell on the Feast of the Epiphany, had been raised to understand that his bloodline family expected him to inherit the title bestowed by ancient prophecy. Whereas Bérenger's brother, Alexander Sinclair, remained in Scotland to learn the oil business, he was sent to France at a young age to live with his grandfather in preparation for a different destiny. His grandfather had founded the Society of Blue Apples here in the

Languedoc at the time he purchased the château. The property and society were devoted to the heretical teachings and legends that existed
in this part of France, specifically the understanding that Mary Magdalene brought the true teachings of Jesus here following the crucifixion.

Bérenger's knowledge of French heretical tradition was unparalleled, but he was a novice at Italian history. And while he was aware that
there had been Cathars in Italy, it was not until Maureen discovered the
astonishing life of Matilda of Tuscany that he came to understand just
how much secret teaching had come from—and remained in—that region of Italy.

And now Destino was insisting that they all come to Florence, as he
wanted to instruct them in the history of the Order pertaining to that
place and Lorenzo's time period. And he was emphatic that time was of
the essence.

Bérenger raised the locket to his lips and kissed it, while praying to
God to keep his Maureen safe in absentia.

Florence
spring 1458

DONATELLO WAS IN trouble again.

The brilliant and prolific Florentine sculptor, born Donato di Niccolò di Betto Bardi and known by the name Donatello, had achieved
extraordinary fame in his lifetime. There was no artist to equal his
skill or accomplishment anywhere in Florence, or arguably anywhere
in Italy. The vast number of commissions he received was a tribute
to his genius, but for all his supernatural skill, Donatello was notoriously temperamental and impossible to deal with. Cosimo de' Medici
favored and protected Donatello, and in the general interest of peace
for the Republic of Florence, he warned all potential patrons of the artist's extreme temperament. The Medici patriarch was often called in to

mediate between his pet sculptor and the latest patron who had been offended by one of Donatello's outbursts. Or worse.

Cosimo was recounting Donatello's most recent escapade to the young Lorenzo, who had listened wide-eyed and amused at the legends of the artist for as long as he could remember. Lorenzo's most important lessons of governance were learned in moments such as these, from the wisdom of his grandfather.

"You see, Lorenzo, the more gifted the artist and the closer to God he is, the more difficult it is for him to function in our earthly environment. But this is why you must protect your artists against the philistines who would exploit them. Wealthy Florentines want Donatello to sculpt for them because it gives them prestige to have one of his originals in their palazzo. It is beneath him to take vanity commissions, and yet it is necessary for him to do so in order to avoid offending the spiteful members of influential families. But such men do not understand what these artists are and why they are. You and I do. These artists are our special army, our angels who are able to convey the purest teachings of the divine through their work. They are the priests and scribes of our Order, providing as they do our newest translations of the oldest and most important gospel. *Our* gospel. So when they are attacked by those who do not have the ears to hear or eyes to see, it is your mission to defend and protect them."

"Is it true that Donatello hurled one of his own busts off the balcony of the Palazzo di Signoria?"

Cosimo laughed. "Yes, yes. He did that just last week and it is one of the reasons he is in so much trouble. Scared the citizens below in the piazza near to death as the bust shattered into a million pieces. I only wish I had been there to see it!"

Lorenzo laughed, but his nine-year-old mind was constantly inquiring. It was not enough to understand that Donatello was capable of such high jinks; he also wished to understand what motivated them. From his earliest days, Lorenzo had been supremely fascinated by human behavior and had strived to understand it. Certainly a character study such as Donatello was a great learning tool.

"Why did he do it, Grandfather?"

"The patron was a vainglorious fool and a skinflint," Cosimo explained. "First, he insisted that Donatello bring the bust to the Signoria and cart it up the stairs. Then, after the successful unveiling, where everyone agreed that it was yet another masterpiece of sculpture, the idiot of a man took our Doni aside and complained that there were flaws in the work! Now mind you, there were not, and everyone knew that there were not. The idiot believed that if he could convince Donatello that the work was imperfect, he could default on the rest of the commission payment. In short, he wanted to cheat an artist out of the payment he richly deserved."

"That's a terrible thing to do!" Lorenzo was scandalized.

"Not only is it terrible, it's theft. No different from highway robbery, stealing what rightfully belongs to a man through force. And this is your next lesson as a defender of the arts, my boy. Artists are forever taken advantage of, cheated by those who do not understand how much of their heart and soul and essence goes into a work of art. All art is priceless, Lorenzo, and we diminish it every time we apply a monetary value to it. But this is the world that we live in, and why we must set an example as patrons. If Dante were here today, I believe he would create a special level of the *inferno* for men who cheat artists."

Cosimo could see that Lorenzo's fine mind was taking it all in. The child missed nothing.

"And so Donatello feigned that he wanted to see the sculpture in the light, to inspect the flaws that the man claimed he had discovered." Cosimo stopped for a moment to laugh at what he knew was coming next. "The bust was brought to the balcony for inspection, and Donatello moved it to the edge, claiming that the best sunlight was right there . . . and then he tossed it over the edge and watched it shatter! He then turned to the wretched man and said, 'I would rather see my work in a million pieces than in the hands of an undeserving swine such as you.'"

Lorenzo joined Cosimo, erupting in laughter at Donatello's insult to the horrid man who tried to cheat him.

"Of course, now the man wants his money back, which I, of course, will pay him as a means of protecting Donatello and keeping him out of a cell in the Bargello. But he is making enemies quickly, and after we defend him to the council today, we shall pay him a visit and ask that he try to behave himself for a while—before he breaks the Medici bank with restitution payments!"

Lorenzo set out on the walk to the Palazzo Vecchio with his grandfather, who continued to fill him in on the adventures of Donatello and the reason this particular mission today was of such great importance. Several of Donatello's outraged patrons had banded together to file a formal complaint about him, which now required diplomatic intervention.

"I don't understand what they are accusing him of, Grandfather."

Cosimo considered his explanation carefully. He had insisted that Lorenzo, as young as he was, accompany him today so that he could see the importance of standing up for the truth, even when it was very unpopular. Perhaps most of all when it was very unpopular. This case was delicate for one so young, and yet as always, Lorenzo was capable of understanding things well beyond the grasp of an average child.

"Donatello, as you may or may not have noticed, has a grand appreciation of beautiful young men. He is inspired by them. As he was when he created our magnificent *David*."

Lorenzo nodded. Donatello's bronze sculpture of David was the centerpiece of the Medici courtyard in the Via Larga. All agreed it was a masterpiece, a sculpture of extreme beauty and daring, the first fully sculpted nude figure in the round to be executed since antiquity.

"Well, there are men in the Signoria, closed-minded and spiteful men, who do not appreciate our *David*, or the fact that Donatello's inspiration comes from other men. Remember, my boy, that the reason we chose David as our central theme is that he is the pure shepherd who conquers the corrupt and mighty against all odds. And that is what we must do today. Defend the pure against those who would use their might to defeat him."

Cosimo, renowned in Florence for his measured temperament, was much beloved by the common folk and the nobility alike. The majority of sitting members of the Signoria were in awe of his influence and his brilliance. And so while he had to be patient with the order of the proceedings in the council chamber, he was quick to control the room and move them along to the issue he needed to address. Lorenzo watched his grandfather's every move in awe and committed each moment of that day to memory.

The men who had complaints against Donatello each said their piece against the sculptor, who was significantly not in attendance. This absence was another stroke of genius by Cosimo, who knew that Donatello's presence in the council chamber would be disastrous. Cosimo held his tongue in annoyance as he listened to the accusers. Each proposed that Donatello's "immorality" was a negative influence on the Republic of Florence and that he flaunted his homosexuality in such a way as to encourage others to become sodomites. They knew that accusing the artist on a morality charge would likely create the harshest sentence against him.

Then Cosimo stood and addressed the Signoria. They awaited a measured and intelligent speech. But Cosimo de' Medici stunned everyone in the council that day. He had a point to make—for Florence and for his grandson, who would one day rule in his place—and there was nothing measured about Cosimo's defense of Donatello.

"How dare you!" roared the Medici patriarch, as he slammed his hand flat against the heavy table before him. "How dare you—any of you—take the position that you are experts on whom a man can and cannot love! How dare you be so presumptuous as to say what may or may not inspire a man to create art!"

There was shocked silence in the room as Cosimo lowered his voice. He began pointing at individuals in the chamber. "You, Poggio. And you, Francesco. You have both dined in my home and admired the sculpture of David that graces the center of the loggia. Tell me, what was your reaction to that piece of art?"

The first man, Poggio Bracciolini, was an ally whom Cosimo had planted in the Signoria that day. Poggio was a devoted humanist and patron of the arts, and not incidentally a high-ranking member of the Order. His response was precisely what was expected of him. Later Cosimo would explain this strategy to Lorenzo: never ask a question in public unless you already know for certain that it will be answered in your favor.

"It is a masterpiece of sculpture. I have never seen anything as flawless as the *David* that was created for your palazzo," Bracciolini replied perfectly.

The second man gave a similar response, with several other members of the council nodding in agreement. Florentines, for all their flaws, were ardent art lovers. Cosimo seized the moment and continued.

"Yes, Donatello's *David* may even be the premiere work of art that we see in our time. Not since Praxiteles has there been such divinity in sculpture. And so I say to you all, who are you, who am I, who are any of us to question this man's inspiration? If Donatello is able to create the most sublime works of art because he is inspired by love, then this is a gift from God that none of us has the right to question. Whom he chooses as his muse is not my business, nor yours. And how he chooses to love that muse is even less for us to consider or judge. Love is love. It is God-given, and a sacrament. It is not for any man to judge. I stand by that pronouncement, and I stand by the fact that I thank God every day for any man who can love so deeply that he is able to create art that is so very obviously divine!"

Only silence greeted the end of Cosimo's speech, for what man could argue with the eloquence of what had just been invoked within that chamber?

Donatello was pardoned and Lorenzo was left with one of the most powerful lessons of his life, along with a piece of wisdom that rang in his ears for the rest of his days.

Love is love. It is God-given, and a sacrament. It is not for any man to judge.

*

Lorenzo accompanied his grandfather to Donatello's studio to advise the artist of the positive outcome. The door to his workshop was opened not by the temperamental artist himself but by a calm and friendly face, a man Lorenzo had met on other occasions and liked tremendously. He was Andrea del Verrocchio, a master sculptor and art teacher in his own right, but more important, he was a key member of the Order and one of Cosimo's most trusted artists. Verrocchio had once been apprenticed to Donatello and was one of the few who ever survived the maelstrom.

"Andrea, what a wonderful surprise!" Cosimo embraced the tall man with the gentle demeanor. "What kind of torment do you inflict upon yourself that you return to be abused by your former master?"

"I heard that!" The unmistakable voice of Donatello rang out from the adjacent room.

"You were meant to," Cosimo shouted back. "And do let us know if you intend to grace us with your presence, will you? I have a commission for you, but I can give it to Andrea here if you prefer."

They could hear the grumbling and scurrying in the other room. For all Donatello's temperament, he worshipped Cosimo and would never keep him waiting too long.

Verrocchio turned to call forward a young man, a teenager who was grinding pigments across the room. The youth was beautiful; covered in golden curls and with deep-set amber eyes, he had the appearance of a young lion. The young man stood up and smiled a crooked, endearing smile at the visitors. He came forward, bowed gracefully in obvious recognition of the esteemed company, but then looked down at his hands apologetically. "Vermilion. It is messy, so I dare not touch anything or anyone."

Verrocchio made the introductions. "Cosimo and Lorenzo de' Medici, I present to you Alessandro di Mariano Filipepi. We call him Sandro. You shall be hearing more from him and soon, as I can say with absolute certainty that I have not before seen such raw natural talent in an apprentice, perhaps ever."

Sandro, well aware of his talent yet determined to appear humble, made a face at Lorenzo and shrugged. It was a self-effacing yet strangely confident gesture for one so young. Lorenzo laughed, liking him immediately, and asked Sandro to show him how the messy vermilion pigment was made. Lorenzo had grown up splattered with paint, watching in awe all the great artists who were integral to the Medici household and protected by Cosimo and Piero alike. He had always been fascinated by the pounding of minerals and the elaborate mixing that went into the creation of the paint and was excited at the prospect of getting his own hands a little dirty.

Cosimo raised a questioning eyebrow in Sandro's direction as the boys wandered off. Verrocchio explained in a lowered voice. "He's extraordinary. I've never seen anything like it. It's not just his talent but his understanding. He is a natural."

"An angelic?"

Verrocchio nodded. "He may be *the* angelic we have been waiting for. His abilities are unnatural. Supernatural. I will work with him on the preliminaries, but then if all goes as I believe it will, he will need greater training. He is worthy of the Master, I think."

Cosimo watched where the two boys were working in the pigment, Lorenzo happily grinding and crushing with the mortar and pestle, as Sandro guided his technique. There was an aura around the two of them, a sense of fate hanging in the air that was not lost on either Cosimo or Andrea. These boys were destined to be friends. Indeed, it appeared that they already were.

"If he is what you say he is, then I shall move him into the palazzo and raise him as a Medici."

The conversation was interrupted by the loud and dramatic entrance of Donatello.

"Ah, my patron, my savior. Tell me you have come to bring news of your poor, humble artist's exoneration from the tyranny of the Florentine philistines."

Cosimo replied, "You are neither poor, thanks to me, nor humble, thanks to your talent. But what you are is free. Yes, you have been exonerated and shall live to sculpt another day."

Donatello threw his arms around Cosimo. "Thank you, thank you! Never has there been a kinder or more beloved patron than my magnanimous Medici."

"You are welcome, Doni. But now I think we must agree that you will take no more vanity commissions, as they are not in anyone's best interest. Further, I have decided to monopolize your time with a commission of my own. I want you to create a sculpture of Our Lady, the Queen of Compassion."

"Maria Magdalena?"

"Yes. Life-sized. It will be a gift to the Master from all of us."

Donatello nodded. "And what are my parameters?"

"You have none from me, other than to use your heart as you sculpt her and pour your love of Our Lady into the piece. I do not care what medium you use and will leave all artistic decisions up to you. Just make her magnificent and memorable, a true symbol of the Order and what we all stand for. And of course, I will pay you in advance so you are not tempted to take any other commissions, which will distract you and end in certain disaster. Do we have an agreement, Doni?"

The artist threw his arms around Cosimo again. "Yes, sweetest patron! I shall sculpt Our Lady as she has never been seen before. Leave everything to me!"

*

Donatello spent the better part of a year sculpting Maria Magdalena. He made the decision to create her out of wood, a remarkable challenge for a life-sized creation. He chose white poplar for its pliability, and finding the piece of wood large enough to fulfill his vision was in itself a task that took several months to accomplish.

He sculpted in absolute solitude and secrecy. No one, not even his closest assistants, were allowed to enter the room where he carefully whittled and carved away at the figure of his Maria Magdalena. When Cosimo inquired as to his progress, Donatello merely smiled, with a faraway gleam in his eye. "You shall see," he said simply.

The day came for the unveiling, and Cosimo had the sculpture moved under Donatello's guidance to the villa at Careggi for a meeting of the Order. The Master would be in attendance tonight, and the creation would be presented to him and the others. Donatello was giddy with excitement, while at the same time slightly apprehensive. Although he was renowned for his enormous faith in his own talents, which was more than justified, this particular commission had arguably been the most challenging of his artistic life. He had poured his heart and his soul into this piece, and like all artists of the Order used the technique called "infusion" to transfer his intention for the piece directly into the materials. If the infusion was done properly, the effect went beyond the visual, and the art transferred the artist's emotional and spiritual intention to the viewer. It was an artistic alchemy, something which could only be achieved by masters such as Donatello, who had perfected the process.

And so his Maria Magdalena was infused with all the devotion and understanding that he had of her. He knew, if given the chance, that she would convey her essence to those who viewed her. But first they would have to overcome what they saw with their eyes, because his Magdalena was unlike anything that had been created before.

He had not set out to depict her this way. But she had insisted. He could feel it every time his hands went to touch the wood; it all but screamed to him what it was, precisely, she wanted to look like. And he had taken a vow, like every artist of the Order before him beginning with Nicodemus himself, to protect the legacy of Madonna Magdalena at all costs. He did just that, creating art that was purely expressive by listening to exactly what she demanded of him as he sculpted her.

The gathering was brought to order as Fra Francesco, the Master, opened with a blessing, followed by the prayer of the Order of the Holy Sepulcher:

We honor God while praying for a time
when these teachings will be welcomed
in peace by all people
and there will be no more martyrs.

Following the prayer, Cosimo made a short speech, dedicating this new work of art to Fra Francesco, while praising Donatello for his commitment and his genius.

But as Donatello feared, there was absolute silence in the great dining hall of Careggi when the sculpture was unveiled. If the attending members of the Order were expecting to see their Queen of Compassion depicted in all of her luminous beauty, they were to be thoroughly disappointed and more than a little shocked.

In Donatello's sculpture, Maria Magdalena was utterly wretched.

Her body was emaciated and naked underneath a mass of hair, which covered most of her, as it flowed nearly to her feet. It was extraordinary that even in the carving of the wood and without paint, the artist had conveyed perfectly that Magdalena was unwashed, her hair matted to her head. Her eyes were haunting in their hollow stare, and she was mostly toothless.

"She looks like a beggar woman!" a female voice whispered.

"It is blasphemy to the Order!" came a male whisper, slightly louder.

The Master of the Order of the Holy Sepulcher rose from his chair and approached the sculpture. He ran his fingers lightly over the intricately carved hair of this terrible, tragic sculpture. After considering it for a long moment, he turned to Donatello.

"It is perfect. It is art. Thank you, my son, for this unequaled blessing you have given all of us."

Donatello began to weep openly under the love of the Master. The pressures of the last year, the need to perfect this sculpture, had weighed heavily on his spirit. He knew that there was a tremendous chance of its being misunderstood, and from the initial whispered comments, he feared that it had been.

It was the child among them who ultimately came to his rescue. Using his remarkable intelligence and sensitivity of spirit, it was the nine-year-old Lorenzo de' Medici who interpreted the art for those who did not have eyes to see. He moved toward the sculpture as if mesmerized and stood before it, tilting his head a little as he looked at Maria Magdalena, to whom he was deeply devoted. The assembled Order watched

Lorenzo in absolute silence. He was their Poet Prince, and his interpretation would be critical.

Donatello, standing closest to the sculpture, whispered to Lorenzo. "You hear her, don't you?"

Lorenzo nodded, never taking his eyes off the sculpture. He walked around it, looking at every side of her, all the while appearing to listen to some phantom voice that no one else in the room heard. Finally he stopped and turned to face the assembly. A single tear slid down his cheek.

"Tell us what you see and hear, Lorenzo." It was the voice of the Master, warm and encouraging.

Lorenzo cleared his throat, not wanting to cry in front of the assembled Order. He began haltingly at first but then found his voice as he continued.

"She is . . . presented here as she asked to be. For this is how she truly is. Not to me or to you. To us she is the most beautiful woman who ever lived; she is our queen. But this is not how the world sees her. It is not how the Church would have the world understand her. They call her terrible names, tell lies about who she was. They take away her life, her love, and her children. They make her a sinner. They take this woman who would save all of us with her courage and wisdom and love, and they turn her into a beggar.

"The Magdalena that Donatello has sculpted here is wretched, because that is what has been made of her by those who do not have eyes to see and ears to hear. It is for us to change that, to restore her to the throne of the Queen of Heaven. And to do that, we must remember how others see her and not how we see her."

Lorenzo was choking back the beginnings of a sob now, as devotion overcame him. Still all eyes were focused entirely on him as he made his final pronouncement, solidifying what most in attendance already knew: Lorenzo de' Medici was growing into a more remarkable prince than any of them could have imagined.

"I think . . ." Lorenzo choked back the tears and looked over at Donatello. "I think she is the most beautiful piece of art that I have ever seen."

And to punctuate that pronouncement, Donatello fell to his knees and sobbed with relief. The infusion had worked. His art had been understood. Most of all, *her* message had been delivered.

Headquarters of the Confraternity of the Magi
Florence
January 6, 1459

"How DO I look, Mother?"

Lucrezia de' Medici looked at her son, who had just celebrated his tenth birthday, and fought back the tears. They were tears of joy and pride as she straightened the gold-embroidered coat so that it hung perfectly over the breeches worn by her growing boy. She would always think that her eldest son was absolutely perfect, for all that he had inherited the squashed nose of the Tornabuoni family and the infamous underbite of the Medici. While Lorenzo was not a traditionally beautiful child, there was a radiance about him that was undeniable. Further, he was unerringly polite and almost unfathomably responsible for his age.

And it was that sense of responsibility that was gnawing at him as he squirmed in the elaborate silk and damask costume, which he would be wearing in today's parade of the Magi. It was the Feast of the Epiphany, the day when the three kings came to adore the infant Jesus in the manger. Each year in Florence, this blessed event was reenacted by the Confraternity of the Magi, with a magnificent procession through the streets of the city, followed by a festival. The celebration would be grander than ever this year, more elaborate and lavish: Cosimo had demanded it and seen to the more extreme details. Because the Medici family were the founders and leaders of this particular confraternity, Lorenzo would today be playing the role of the young king, the golden one known as Gaspar. He took his task very seriously, knowing that there was a heavier weight on his slender shoulders. This was not simply a part to play in a parade; he knew it, and the people of Florence knew it. No, this was Lorenzo's coming-out party, the announcement to the world by the Medici that Lorenzo was preparing to take on the exalted mantle of the Poet Prince. The crown he wore today was very heavy on his head. No doubt it would leave marks on his skin for days to come.

In Tuscany, the confraternities had become an integral part of society, the spiritual heart of their towns. In a number of major cities—Florence chief among them—the confraternities became distinct forces of political power as well as social welfare. The type of confraternity one belonged to could tell much about a family and where its interests and loyalties were. The first confraternity founded in Florence was devoted to the archangel Raphael, and its members performed acts of charity related to healing. Other confraternities were founded to represent the acts of a specific saint. The more extreme were based on penitence and required acts of mortification of the flesh.

The Medici had co-founded the Confraternity of the Magi to give them a vehicle in which to openly and publicly display their belief in the esoteric without offending the Catholic population. For all their secret heresies, every Medici family leader since the days of Charlemagne had been an expert at appearances. Cosimo belonged to no fewer than ten confraternities and had recently had a cell installed for himself within the Dominican monastery of San Marco. Periodically, he would retreat there for meditation and prayer with the brethren. That he spent a fortune expanding the buildings and hiring the quiet yet brilliant monk Fra Angelico, to fresco the place to perfection was not lost on the grateful Catholic population of Florence. For all public purposes, Cosimo de' Medici was the most devout of Catholics, and he was only too willing to prove that devotion through his extraordinary generosity.

But the Feast of the Epiphany was not a day to be solemn or penitent. It was a day to celebrate the coming of the Prince. Cosimo had made generous donations to guilds and committees throughout the city in honor of the event—and in his grandson's name. At the age of ten, Lorenzo was now one of the most generous donors in Florence.

His generosity was not lost on the common people, to whom he was rapidly becoming beloved.

Lucrezia de' Medici straightened Lorenzo's jewel-encrusted crown one final time and kissed him on the forehead before turning him over to his father, who would escort him to the elaborately caparisoned white stallion who awaited the young King Gaspar. She sighed as she watched him depart, his growing body awkward under the massive silks that weighed him down. For all that he was the child of a divine prophecy, he was still her little boy.

"Lorenzo, my son," she called after him. "Don't forget to have fun!"

*

Florence, a city known for its elaborate, even decadent festivals, had never seen the equal of the Feast of the Epiphany as it occurred in 1459. The procession of the Magi itself was stunning, with Cosimo leading it on a pristine white mule as the old king Melchior. A train of wagons laden with bejeweled chests and colorful silks followed him, as did a camel brought over from Constantinople on a cargo ship. An entourage of Medici supporters, all of whom were secret members of the Order, followed as Cosimo's attendants. Cosimo's most loyal friend, the renowned writer and humanist Poggio Bracciolini, led the entourage. His son, Jacopo Bracciolini, was the same age as Lorenzo and as such had been chosen to walk in the parade alongside the Medici prince. The two boys were friends and had been tutored by the same great men of Florence. Jacopo was a beautiful child, golden-haired and fair, with features so delicate that they were almost pretty, and a lithe agile body. His was a marked physical contrast to the swarthy, sturdy Lorenzo.

Jacopo had been petulant about being cast in the procession as Lorenzo's servant, so to appease his ego he was given the role of the Keeper of the Cats. As such, he was allowed to walk one of the exotic African servals, an ill-tempered wild cat that looked like a shrunken leopard.

"Hey, Lorenzo, look at what I can make the cat do!" Jacopo yelled up to where Lorenzo was perched on a huge white stallion. He pulled up sharply on the cat's velvet lead, which was attached to a bejeweled collar. The cat growled but rose up to walk on his two hind legs. He took a few steps as if walking upright. Jacopo burst into delighted laughter.

Lorenzo laughed to appease his friend but was inwardly concerned that the cat was suffering discomfort as well as indignity. He attempted to distract Jacopo by pointing out some of the other animals in the procession, but to no avail. Jacopo was finding an audience for his antics with the serval and was clearly loving the attention. He began shouting, "Behold! I am the Master of the Cats!" each time he pulled on the poor animal's lead.

Lorenzo stayed the course, riding as tall and proud as a young king, and left Jacopo behind to play jester. He was the undisputed star in the parade, the figure who drew the cheers of the Florentine people. As Lorenzo passed by, astride the white horse and dressed in his finery as the golden young king, the crowds erupted with adulation. Lorenzo, at first very serious in his role, was swept away in the excitement and pageantry of the moment. He smiled at the people, his people, with the infectious grin for which he would one day become famous as an adult. He waved at the Florentines, and they waved in return, shouting blessings and throwing roses.

"He is magnificent!" a woman in the crowd screamed, and the others began to take up the chant: *"Magnifico! Magnifico!"*

By the time the procession had reached its destination at the monastery of San Marco, where a living nativity had been created, Lorenzo's position in the hearts of the Florentine people was secure.

He would forevermore be known by the name that was as much a prophecy as it was praise, for he was destined to grow into it spectacularly: *Lorenzo il Magnifico.*

Lorenzo the Magnificent.

New York City
present day

THE BEEPING OF a text message woke Maureen Paschal early on the morning of the twenty-second day of March. She reached blindly to the bedside table until she felt the source of the offending noise. She wasn't really annoyed, despite her sleep-deprived state. No doubt it was one of her beloved friends in Europe, anxious to be the first to contact her on her special day and miscalculating the time difference. She hit the button on her phone to read the message. It said:

HAPPY BIRTHDAY. I HAVE A GIFT FOR YOU.

Maureen sat up in bed now. She rubbed the sleep out of her eyes and wondered who had sent the message; she didn't recognize the number. The text message had come from Europe; it was attached to an Italian phone number.

Maureen padded out to the little kitchen to make coffee. Caffeine first; all things must happen in order. She searched sleepily through the cupboards. Dark-roast coffee beans, a grinder, and a French press would at least get her started, and she was certain that all those things would be here.

Maureen smiled to herself as she thought about it. There were two things that Maureen would bet her life Bérenger would have on hand at all times, and those things were great coffee and better wine. She was right on both counts. The night before she had taken a quick look at the small but exquisite wine selection that he kept in a custom-built cooler off the dining room. Not surprisingly, there were bottles from several private vineyards in the Languedoc, elegant and limited vintages that were not exported under normal circumstances. But the owner of this wine collection was nobody's average customer.

Bérenger had purchased the apartment on Fifth Avenue years ago because of its extraordinary location: the front door of the apartment complex faced the entrance to the Metropolitan Museum of Art.

Bérenger was a devoted art connoisseur, and he had made a sport of acquiring properties all over the world within easy reach of magnificent museums. He owned property on the Rue de Rivoli across from the Louvre and had a little place in Madrid, around the corner from the Prado. But Bérenger had a special passion for the Met. His schedule rarely allowed him to get to New York anymore, so he was delighted to turn his keys to the Fifth Avenue pied-à-terre over to his beloved Maureen—who was equally happy to accept them. Her career as an author brought her to New York regularly, and the apartment would provide her with a perfect place to call home.

Maureen opened the bag of imported Italian coffee beans that she had found in the second cupboard and inhaled the rich scent. The smell of coffee alone was enough to awaken her senses and she was already able to think more clearly. Whom did she know in Italy who would know that it was her birthday? Could it be her spiritual mentor, the enigmatic teacher known as Destino? Back in Florence now, he was inclined toward mysterious messages and secretive behavior.

She put water on to boil and grabbed her cell phone. She hit the reply button and sent a text message in reply.

THANK YOU. WHO IS THIS?

Maureen picked up the remote control for the television and turned on a national morning show. There was the usual offering of pop culture and daily news, and she left it on as she made coffee. She was momentarily distracted by a gossip piece that had all the women in the studio buzzing. Supermodel and socialite Vittoria Buondelmonti was going to make an announcement today that the tabloids were drooling over in anticipation. The Italian catwalk queen was the mother of a two-year-old boy who, until now, she had kept sheltered from the press. The paternity of the boy had been the cause of speculation since the earliest days of her pregnancy, and Vittoria had remained adamant that she wasn't going to reveal who had fathered the child. She had been involved in a string of high-profile relationships before the birth of her

son, and the rag papers had speculated endlessly on the paternity issue as they presented photographs of Vittoria with the many men she
had dined out with: an international soccer star, a rock-and-roll icon, a
race driver, a Greek billionaire, an oil tycoon, her childhood sweetheart
from Florence.

Tomorrow Vittoria Buondelmonti was going to reveal the identity
of her child's father to the international press. Why she had decided to
do this now was unclear. But as Maureen clicked around the networks
to see if anything more interesting or important was happening in the
world, she found that Vittoria and her love child were the hot topic on
all the morning shows. Maureen hit the off button on the remote with
a grunt.

She forgot all about Vittoria's paternity drama as her cell phone
beeped with a text message response to her question.

I AM A FRIEND OF DESTINO. AND BERENGER.
I WILL SEE YOU TONIGHT.

"Curiouser and curiouser," she said out loud. Maureen had been
quoting Lewis Carroll often these days, because she felt she had fallen
down the rabbit hole herself, perhaps never to return to reality again.
Reality, it seemed, was a thing of the past. She wasn't sure that she would
ever get used to the surreal turns that her life had taken.

The journey had begun a few years earlier when Maureen first met
Bérenger Sinclair, who introduced her to the mysterious world of heretics and history that he presided over in the southwest of France from
his ancestral home. Her life had exploded when she discovered an ancient manuscript in a French village called Arques, a legendary gospel
written in the hand of the apostle Mary Magdalene herself. While others
had been searching for this document for nearly two thousand years,
many believed it had been Maureen's sole destiny to find it. Within this
world of hidden Christian history, which was unfolding for Maureen
as she delved deeper into the secret societies of Europe, were a series of
prophecies that had been passed down for countless generations. The

prophecy of the Expected One told of a woman who would rediscover the true, unedited teachings of Jesus and his descendants and would share these with the world when the time was right.

Maureen was the Expected One.

It was a dizzying, electrifying, and often perilous experience. Maureen's discovery of what was now known as the Arques gospel had led her to write her first international best seller about the legacy of Mary Magdalene. The manuscript was an explosive document that alleged that Magdalene was legally married to Jesus and was the mother of his children. But perhaps the most important revelation within was not about blood or marriage but rather about a spiritual legacy. The Arques Gospel of Mary Magdalene proclaimed that she was the chosen successor of Jesus, the apostle to whom he entrusted his most sacred teachings. And before his death on the cross, Jesus had given Mary Magdalene a manuscript of his own. He called it the Book of Love.

That Jesus had written a gospel in his own hand was the most controversial revelation that Maureen had ever stumbled upon. How was it possible that Jesus had written his own book, with his teachings indisputably preserved in his own hand, and yet no one had ever heard of such a thing? As she researched this question, Maureen discovered that the Book of Love was so controversial, so earth-shattering, that it was necessarily kept secret by those who revered it—and by those who despised it. Her search for the book took her through Inquisition records and deep into the histories of France and Italy. Maureen discovered that a secret society called the Order of the Holy Sepulcher had protected the Book of Love and those who were sworn to preserve the lost gospel of Jesus Christ and teach from it. It was her discovery of this shadowy Order—which still existed today—that had led her to discover Matilda of Canossa, a Tuscan countess who had lived in the eleventh century.

Matilda was a child of this secret legacy. Born into the prophecy of the Expected One at the vernal equinox, she possessed the same powers of prophecy and vision that had haunted Maureen since her childhood. And Matilda was raised on the heretical message of the Book of Love. She was the devoted keeper of a version of this gospel, a copy made in the first century by the apostle Philip and then brought to Italy. To Matilda and subsequent generations of heretical Italians, the gospel was known as the Libro Rosso—the Red Book. The Libro Rosso also contained a series of prophecies passed down through the women of the bloodline, as well as their personal histories and lineage documents. The Libro Rosso, with its spiritual teachings of love and its prophecies for mankind, its preservation of the dynastic details of the bloodline descendants of Jesus, was arguably the most valuable book in human history. Matilda had once possessed it, and she used it to change the world.

While she researched Matilda, there were times when Maureen felt that they were blending into the same person. She felt Matilda's pain and joy, observed her life in vivid detail as she wrote. It was almost as if she were writing her own memoirs, remembering intimate moments of her deepest loves and closest friendships, understanding Matilda's most private longings and fears firsthand. Their consciousness and memories had somehow combined, merged to become one, as Maureen wrote.

And it was not the first time she had had that feeling. Maureen had had the same exhilarating yet troubling experience while writing about Mary Magdalene in her first book. Viewing the first century through Magdalene's eyes had nearly driven her to the edge of sanity. She was certainly not claiming anything as grandiose as having walked in Mary Magdalene's exalted sandals in a past life. No, what she experienced was something very different, some strange yet magical gift of storytelling that had been passed down to women in her lineage for thousands of years. She understood it as a type of genetic memory, a collective consciousness that existed in the DNA of these women to whom she was so blessed to be connected, a memory that she could tap into. As such, it was exalted in its own unique way. It made the passage of time simply not matter, as if all periods could be accessed simultaneously, as if they were happening all at once.

It was a miracle, and yet it was a terrible beauty at the same time, a daunting responsibility. She could not curse the experience, God-given as it appeared to be, but she had spent the better part of the last four years trying to understand it all. Maureen hesitated to discuss this with anyone but Bérenger, as he alone understood it—and everything about her—perfectly. In this way she had discovered that he was her one true soul mate, the other half of her heart and spirit, and there was an effortlessness in their communication that she still marveled at and completely cherished. Bérenger had become her ultimate sanctuary in a world that could not understand her gift and therefore often sought to destroy it.

Matilda of Canossa had obsessed Maureen for the better part of the last two years, possessing her first when Maureen read the autobiography of the controversial countess, and then as she wrote her latest book in honor of this remarkable woman. *The Time Returns: The Legacy of the Book of Love* detailed Matilda's adventures and accomplishments. Today, her birthday, was the official release date for the North American edition, which was what brought Maureen to New York. There was a launch party tonight at the Cloisters, the medieval department of the Met, in honor of Maureen and Matilda.

*

Reigning over the north end of Manhattan with unequaled views of the Hudson, the Cloisters is the uptown, elegant sister of the Metropolitan Museum of Art. Its stunning display of art and architecture from me-dieval Europe is preserved in a magnificent and unique building, one created through the use of authentic architectural elements imported from medieval French monasteries. Though there are many treasures to be viewed among the nearly five thousand artifacts on display in the Cloisters, the unparalleled attraction was the unicorn tapestries. The seven magnificent wall hangings, created in Flanders during the Re-naissance, depict in vivid details the story of a determined hunt—and the ultimately brutal killing—of a majestic unicorn.

Maureen had seen replicas of these tapestries while in France, when she first met with the enigmatic spiritual teacher known only as Destino at the headquarters of the Order of the Holy Sepulcher. For the Order, the unicorn was a symbol of the pure teachings of Jesus Christ as passed down to his descendants through the Book of Love. *The Killing of the Unicorn* series was a type of textbook for the Order, a particularly beautiful teaching manual woven in woolen threads to illustrate the terrible tragedy that occurs when pure beauty is destroyed and truth is lost. When writing the truth in plain language was heresy and meant certain death, the Order found other means of communicating through symbols and secrets—for those with eyes to see and ears to hear. *The Killing of the Unicorn* represented the destruction of the authentic teachings of Jesus, the Way of Love, as told through symbolism.

Maureen took some time to view the exquisite Cloisters tapestries before stepping into her public duties as the guest of honor for the launch party.

Her thought, as she was collected by her publicist and brought back to the reality of the work she had to do this night, was that this series of priceless, exquisite tapestries was a tragic reminder that we live in a reality where love is not honored as it should be—and men are all too inclined to kill unicorns.

*

Maureen sensed her before she saw her. It was part of her life, the strange intuition that had saved her on so many occasions. The shiver that caught her attention as she was signing a book for an avid reader alerted her that something significant was about to happen.

The line of people waiting for Maureen's signature wrapped through the cloister and through the stunning gardens, which contained the same flora and fauna depicted within the unicorn tapestries. Beyond the queue, she saw the woman who was different from the rest.

Easily six feet tall before donning four-inch stilettos, the woman was stunning, a goddess incarnate. She walked with the grace and authority of one who knew that the entire world stopped and stared as she approached—always had, always would. Sleek black hair hung to her waist and framed a face of angular perfection. Perfectly lined amber-colored cat's eyes stared at Maureen across the room, unblinking, as she approached.

Maureen caught her breath as she recognized the woman who was the current darling of the media. Vittoria Buondelmonti glided regally past the gawking commoners who waited in line for Maureen's autograph. Everyone recognized this celebrity of the moment, and several people dared to photograph her with their cell phones. Vittoria ignored them all, and with a flourish she presented Maureen with a large manila envelope. Her Italian accent dripped like honey from her words.

"Happy birthday, Maureen. Here is the gift I promised you. But I recommend you do not open it until you are alone later."

Maureen saw that the envelope was sealed with heavy tape. She couldn't open it now without a knife or scissors, although she was filled with curiosity about it. Her question was inspired by the earlier text message: "You are a friend of Destino? And of Bérenger?"

"Of course. I know them both very well. They will find this gift as interesting as you will." She gestured with her elegant, long arms to the queue. "Congratulations on all of your success. Bérenger tells me you are . . . the real thing." She sniffed at this, as if to indicate her skepticism, before pivoting perfectly to make her exit. "*Buona sera* and *buon compleanno*," she tossed over her shoulder as she slinked toward the door without ever looking back.

*

The envelope screamed at Maureen to open it for the two excruciating hours that she remained in her place to sign books and talk to readers. It was impossible not to be distracted by what the contents might represent. Vittoria hadn't exactly been warm or sincere with her birthday wishes, and yet she claimed friendship with both Bérenger and Destino—the love of her life and her trusted teacher.

Once the final book had been signed, Maureen rushed to the awaiting Town Car, which would take her back to Fifth Avenue. She used the nail scissors in her purse to cut open the top of the envelope. Carefully she extracted what appeared to be a doubled-up newspaper. She unfolded it to discover that it was an advance copy of a British tabloid, due to go on sale in the morning, judging by the date. The headline screamed:

Vittoria Declares: Sinclair Oil Heir Is the Father of My Baby!

A photograph splashed across the remainder of the front page. It depicted Vittoria, wrapped in the arms of Bérenger Sinclair.

*

"It's a lie, Maureen."

Maureen tried not to cry over the transatlantic connection as she explained the gut-wrenching events of her birthday to Bérenger. He denied everything.

"I know Vittoria, but I did not sleep with her. And you may not believe this, but I have no desire to do so. I love *you*. I want to be with *you*."

Maureen sighed, still holding back the tears. "That may be true *now*. But we were separated for a long time . . ."

"We were separated because you requested it. I gave you that space— and waited for you."

Maureen couldn't argue that point. She had been the stubborn one, determined to keep Bérenger at a safe distance in the early days of their relationship. Then, she was still afraid of the powerful bond that was building between them. It threatened to overwhelm her, and she bolted. They were apart for almost a year.

"The timing is perfect in terms of the age of that child," she continued. "He would have been conceived when you and I were separated."

Bérenger snapped with the stress, more than he meant to. This revelation of Vittoria's had blindsided him and he was still reeling from the shock. "You are so ready to condemn me over this, even though I am telling you as emphatically as I can that Vittoria means nothing to me and never will. *You* are the only woman in the world for me. The love of my life. My heart and soul."

"What about the photos on the cover of the *News of the World*? And the *Daily Mail*?"

Bérenger answered with exaggerated patience. "First of all, there is only one photo, and I am *hugging* her in it. I am not having sex with her. It was taken in Cannes in front of about five hundred people. I was there with my brother representing the family's interests in an independent film about Scotland's mystical heritage. Vittoria was there too; our families are long acquainted. She's bloodline."

"She's *what*?"

"Didn't you know? Vittoria is a bloodline princess. Her mother is an Austrian baroness, from the Hapsburg lineage. The baroness was the one who secured my access to the museum in Austria for my research on the Spear of Destiny. Her father is of the Buondelmonti, an ancient and very wealthy family, originally from Tuscany. Vittoria and I have run in the same esoteric and social circles in Europe."

His explanation just made things worse. Much worse. Not only was Vittoria one of the world's most beautiful women, she was also the daughter of a fascinating noble heritage. Both sides of her family belonged to bloodlines that claimed descent from the union between Jesus and Mary Magdalene. Not incidentally, these families—including the Sinclairs—were some of the wealthiest and most influential in the world. Bérenger and Vittoria had more in common than not. The fact made Maureen feel like a common outsider.

"Vittoria claims to know Destino." It was gut-wrenching to think that this woman had a claim on Maureen's beloved teacher too.

"That's entirely possible. I didn't know about Destino when I last saw her, so I can't tell you that. Maureen, listen to me. I have had no contact with Vittoria since that photo was taken, which leaves us with several important questions."

"Which are?"

"Why is she lying about this? And why did she make such a show out of coming personally to you?" Bérenger paused for a moment, and Maureen could hear him breathe heavily as he thought about it. He continued.

"I don't know the answer to either of those questions, but I swear to you, I will find them as soon as I can. And I am so sorry that you have been dragged into this. But in the meantime, I need you to believe in me. I love you. And I'm not going to let anything come between us, and I pray that you won't either."

"Okay." Maureen whispered the weak reply. She was exhausted and hurt by the events of her birthday and needed time to think. The following afternoon on the airplane, she would torment herself all the way across the Atlantic with possible scenarios, most of which featured the love of her life entangled in the impossibly long legs of the world's most sultry supermodel.

Headquarters of the Confraternity of the Holy Apparition
Vatican City
present day

FELICITY DE PAZZI gritted her teeth as she drove the sharpened nail deeper into her left palm. It was bleeding more profusely now, which would give her the dried crust and the scabbing she would need tonight. Timing was everything with the stigmata. They required a few hours to scab over, so that the wounds would bleed anew when she ripped them open during her public appearance. The left hand would need an hour or so before she could wrap it and begin the process of impalement on the right hand.

Felicity saw the first traces of stigmata when she was in school back in England. She had been having visions more regularly, falling to the ground in ecstasies when the Holy Spirit would take over her body. The headmistress, however, was neither convinced nor amused by what she referred to as Felicity's fits. It was after she had been sent to counseling and was being threatened with expulsion that the stigmata first made themselves known.

On the day that the bloody wounds began to appear in Felicity's palms, she wept with the joy of it. Finally, here was physical proof that she was born to be God's instrument. Everyone would be forced to believe her now; how could they deny it? It was there for anyone with eyes.

And yet, when Felicity showed her classmates, the headmistress, and subsequently the counselor, they all looked at her with a mixture of pity and horror. No one was able to see her stigmata.

Felicity was devastated at first and sobbed until she choked with the violence of her rage and disappointment. How could God have betrayed her so? How was it possible that she saw the wounds of Christ so clearly on her own hands, but the others did not?

And in the darkest hour of her most agonizing night, Felicity understood. The people around her were mostly godless; they were certainly not gifted with the holy sight as she was. Of course they could not see a vision of something so sacred that it was bestowed upon her specifically by her Lord Jesus Christ. It was her own special gift, shared between her and her savior. And yet these common people were the ones she would have to reach if she was going to assume her place as the Lord's special child. And it was in that realization that she knew what she would have to do.

She would have to help the ignorant masses to see the bleeding wounds left by sharpened iron nails so that there would be no further doubt from any of them.

Felicity began that night in the bathroom of her dormitory. She did not have access to any nails immediately, so instead she stole the blade from a razor out of the toiletry kit belonging to one of her roommates. The razor wasn't optimum as it required some work and artistry to create the look of a hole left by a nail, but she made decent work of it. Unfortunately, she also fainted in the first attempt. This led to her expulsion from the school, followed by her hasty return to her family in Italy.

She had perfected her technique now, after more than ten years of practice, perfected all of it. When she appeared before the growing crowds who were coming to see her, the passion poured from her and she commanded the attention of all in the room without fail. When she spoke as herself, she was charismatic and convincing. Fanatical, yes, but it was hard to turn away from her if you were inclined to believe that God was to be feared and that there was limited time to be saved. But it was when she spoke directly to the Holy Spirit that the drama began, making her infamous throughout Rome and causing lines to form at the door of the confraternity for hours before the meetings began. It was when she engaged the Holy Spirit that Felicity fell to the ground and writhed horribly, when the stigmata opened in her hands and began to bleed. At other times, the voice of Santa Felicita herself poured from her in a type of ecstatic possession.

There were even a number within the confraternity who referred to her as Saint Felicity, so convinced were they that this little prophetess was the true messenger of God.

Felicity, now expert in what it took to gain the attention of those who came to hear her, could manipulate a crowd within minutes. And she knew just how to make the ragged holes in her flesh so that the godless ones could finally understand how she suffered with her visions. For Felicity, this suffering was all-important. To be a prophetess for God was the task of a martyr, one that required agony and constant penitence. It was only through mortification of the flesh, total chastity, and an absolute commitment to the physical experience of suffering that one could be certain that the visions were pure.

People needed to understand just how much pain was required to hear God clearly.

Maureen met Tammy at her hotel in Paris, a quiet little boutique inn that was Maureen's home in the French capital. She loved this hotel, which existed in what was once an outbuilding on the eastern edge of the Louvre palace complex. It was charming, untouristed, and within walking distance to nearly anything that mattered to her.

With the picture windows of her hotel room open, the gargoyles appeared to be jumping from the neighboring medieval church and into the room. Each gargoyle had a unique personality—some fierce, some comical. All of them were her friends, and she felt strangely protected by them as she slept under their gaze. The alley that separated the buildings was so narrow that she could very nearly reach out and touch her Gothic watchdogs. This was Maureen's favorite feature of the rooms on this side of the hotel.

She sat on the bed on the afternoon of her arrival, looking out the window at a springtime shower in Paris. She was waiting for Tammy, who was in her adjacent room getting dressed.

When it rained, the gargoyles spit. Maureen marveled at the engineering of the medieval architects who created the gargoyles not as decoration but as drainage systems. The drainpipes flowed from the roof, with openings to expel the rain that ran through the gargoyle sculptures and ended in their gaping mouths. She had learned that the word *gargoyle*, from the French, was related to *gargouille*, which meant "gullet."

The knock at the door startled her, and she rose to let Tammy in.

Tammy was clutching a file folder in her hand as she strolled gracefully through the door. Her long black hair was pulled back into a sleek ponytail, and she was dressed casually today in jeans and a white T-shirt that spelled out in black letters Heresy Begins with HER. The two women could not have been more different: Tamara Wisdom, the statuesque, olive-skinned beauty who was brash, outspoken, and vivacious; Maureen, the fair-skinned redhead who, while feisty in her

Irish way, was more reserved in her expression. But spiritually, they were sisters of the highest order who shared a great love, both for their work and for each other.

"Do you want to talk about Bérenger first?" Tammy was never one to mince words or avoid conflict. "Because I have a perspective."

"I'm sure you do, and I'm guessing it's his."

Tammy and Roland lived at the château with Bérenger, and they considered one another to be family. She was fiercely protective of Bérenger, as he had been extremely generous with her, financially and spiritually, throughout their friendship. It was rare when she didn't defend him, which is exactly what Maureen was expecting from her now.

"Stop it. He loves you. And only you. Totally, eternally, completely. You *know* that. God made you for each other, and you know that too. If he slept with Vittoria during the time when you two weren't together, so what? He's a man and a healthy one. It happens."

Maureen considered this for a moment. "Yes, but . . . he *loved me* at the time he did this. If it had happened before we met, I could accept it easily. But he was already certain I was his soul mate, said repeatedly that I was the only woman he would ever want. Apparently he forgot to mention the exception about Italian supermodels."

"You hurt him, Maureen, remember? You insisted on separation from him, and he was destroyed when you did."

"Uh-huh. He was so destroyed that he fathered a child with Vittoria during those months apart as an act of consolation. Must be a European custom I am unfamiliar with."

Tammy looked annoyed. "He made a mistake. And there's a child as a result of that mistake, which isn't the kid's fault."

Maureen shook her head. "No, of course it isn't. If the baby is Bérenger's, he needs to take responsibility for it and be a father to him."

"And what are you going to do?"

Maureen shook her head. "It depends on what Bérenger does. He is denying that he ever slept with Vittoria at all, but I don't believe it. I know him too well and I can tell when he is lying to me. I would rather he was honest and just owned up to his mistake. And incidentally, why would Vittoria lie about it?"

"Are you kidding? I can think of over a billion reasons why she would lie about it."

Maureen shook her head. "She's an heiress on both sides, and she has a career that pays well on top of that. Money isn't her motivation. And if you had seen her . . . I can't explain it, Tammy, but there was something in the way she looked at me when she delivered that envelope. It wasn't evil, exactly, but it was the look of a woman who was very determined to accomplish a mission. And at that moment, hurting me was her only mission. Otherwise, why choose my birthday and a very public place to make her appearance?"

"That bitch," Tammy snapped. "I'm so sorry you had to endure that. But you're right, it was carefully calculated. Sounds like jealousy to me. Half the socialites in Europe despise you for snagging Bérenger out from under them. Don't take it too personally."

"I'm trying not to . . ." Maureen stopped midsentence when she noticed that a strange look had come over Tammy's face. Without another word, Tammy dashed past Maureen and into the bathroom, closing the door behind her. Maureen could hear Tammy retching, suddenly and violently. Worried, Maureen knocked after a moment.

"You okay?"

She heard the water running and shortly thereafter Tammy emerged, face wet.

"What is it the old wives say when they tell their tales? That the sicker you are, the more likely it is to be a boy? Or is it a girl? I can never remember."

Maureen screamed and threw her arms around her friend.

"Why didn't you tell me!"

"The timing didn't seem to be so great. I didn't think the word *baby* was one you needed to hear at the moment. But . . . I am telling you now."

The two women embraced warmly as Maureen showered Tammy with questions, which she answered patiently. Yes, she and Roland were extremely happy even though the pregnancy was unplanned and unexpected. Yes, Bérenger knew and he had been instructed not to say a word to Maureen, which was killing him, but Tammy had wanted to tell her in person. And yes, Tammy felt this sick pretty much all the time but hoped that once she entered her second trimester, she would feel better.

And yes, they had a wedding to plan for the early summer, before Tammy got too big to wear a suitably fabulous dress.

*

Maureen left Tammy in the hotel to nap and walked up the Rue de Rivoli in the rain. She passed the Louvre and the souvenir shops on her way toward the hallowed, book-filled halls of Galignani. The first English-speaking bookstore established on the Continent, in 1801, Galignani had been Maureen's literary addiction since her first visit to Paris as a teenager. Here she was able to find treasure within pages devoted to great European characters throughout history, often coming across rare jewels for research that were unavailable to her in American bookstores.

As she approached Galignani, Maureen pulled up short with a little, involuntary squeal. There in the window of the most elegant English-speaking bookstore in continental Europe was the British edition of her latest book, *The Time Returns*. Her own novel was on a shelf adjacent to an annotated version of *The Collected Works of Alexandre Dumas*, and just below Emily Brontë's romantic masterpiece, *Wuthering Heights*. Hoping that the rain would mask her unexpected tears, she stood before the window for another minute to take it all in. To be on a shelf with Dumas and Brontë in this place . . . well, it was more than she could ask for, the perfect realization of her dream to become an author since she won her first writing competition as a child. Dumas was one of her literary heroes; Maureen had cut her teeth on the adventures of D'Artagnan and the Musketeers, the Count of Monte Cristo, and the unfortunate Man in the Iron Mask. And Emily Brontë had made her weep for hours at a time, as she had so many young women since the publication of her classic romance. Maureen had even memorized pieces of the heart-wrenching story of Heathcliff and Cathy, wondering if that kind of undying and epic passion could ever really exist in the modern world we live in.

> *He shall never know how I love him . . . because he's more myself than I am. Whatever our souls are made of, his and mine are the same. . . . He's always, always in my mind—not as a pleasure . . . but as my own being. . . . Haunt me, drive me mad. . . . Only do not leave me in this abyss, where I cannot find you! . . . I cannot live without my life! I cannot live without my soul!*

So beautiful, yet so heartbreaking. Why was love so often accompanied by pain? Why were the tragic romances the ones that we remembered and cherished above all others? It was the star-crossed who resonated somewhere in the deepest places of our spirit.

Maureen had the briefest vision then of Bérenger Sinclair's aristocratic face, accompanied by the fleeting knowledge of something more, something about the past and a promise, something sacred and eternal.

> *Whatever our souls are made of, his and mine are the same . . .*

"Yes, they are," she whispered to herself. That was the one thing of which she was certain. No matter what Bérenger may have done in the past, she knew with all her heart and soul that he loved her and that she loved him. This would be her challenge, and she knew it: could she allow love to matter above and beyond the challenges that they were going to face in the spotlight of this new scandal?

She closed her umbrella and turned her own face up to the sky, allowing the light rain to come down on her for a moment. There were times in our lives when we simply needed to surrender to the power of something that is greater than our limited humanity. God had a plan, and he was kind enough in his love and grace to give Maureen signs along the way that she was on the right track. Today was one of those days, and this was one of those moments that kept her going when faith in many things still so unknown and unknowable was all she had.

"Thank you," she whispered up to the sky, as a ray of sun broke through the clouds. Maybe it was a trick of the light, but it appeared to specifically illuminate the cover of her book about love, where it sat in the window on a Parisian street.

Château des Pommes Bleues
Arques, France
present day

THE SPEAR OF Destiny.

It was the legendary weapon of Longinus the Centurion, used to pierce the side of the crucified Christ. Bérenger Sinclair had devoted a portion of his library to this artifact, as it had obsessed him since he was a teenager. He possessed every book that had ever been written about it in multiple languages, had participated in research teams to authenticate items claimed to be authentic pieces of the spear, and even had multiple replicas created and displayed.

It was one of the greatest legends in Christian history, and now he had a chance to go directly to the source to find the truth. Destino could tell him what had happened to the real Spear of Destiny. But would he divulge such a secret after all this time?

The spear had become an object of questing through history, in the same category as the Holy Grail and the Ark of the Covenant, only the spear was believed to have extreme powers of negative influence; some even said that it was possessed by an evil demon. Evil or not, it was coveted by military leaders who believed that ownership of the weapon would bring them victory in their battles. Legend claimed that Charlemagne had used the spear as his secret talisman to win more than forty battles, until the greatest of all European emperors dropped the spear on the battlefield during his forty-eighth skirmish. It was lost to him underfoot in the melee. It was a fatal loss, as Charlemagne died in that same battle. His fate enhanced the legendary status of the great artifact. It was now understood that possession of the Spear of Destiny could lead to unlimited victory, even conquest of the world. But to lose it would prove fatal to the man who allowed it to slip through his hands.

Most famously, Adolf Hitler had coveted the spear and had been committed to obtaining it for the Nazis. Hitler told a story about viewing the artifact for the first time while visiting the Hofburg Imperial Palace in Austria. He was literally entranced by it, feeling as if he were losing consciousness as the power of the spear reached out to him. Hitler had been quoted as saying, "I felt as though I myself had held it before in some earlier century of history. That I myself had once claimed it as my talisman of power and held the destiny of the world in my hands."

Following that experience, Adolf Hitler had become obsessed with the Spear of Destiny. He believed that possession of it was necessary for him to succeed in his goals of domination. Some said that acquiring the spear was his single greatest personal fixation. Immediately after bringing Austria under Nazi control in 1938, Hitler demanded that the spear be brought to him in Nuremberg. As the Allies gained ground in Europe, he had the spear moved into an underground bunker built specifically to protect it and the rest of his collection of artifacts. In 1945, American forces took control of the bunker and confiscated the Spear of Destiny. Within two hours, Adolf Hitler was dead.

The American military leader of the time General George Patton became convinced that the power of the spear was real, and he studied it in depth, tracing its history and telling its tales. He even wrote poetry about it. But the Spear of Destiny was eventually returned with the rest of the Hofburg collection to the museum in Austria, where it remained.

Bérenger Sinclair had been part of a research team in Vienna that worked to evaluate the age and authenticity of the Spear of Destiny in the Hofburg collection a decade earlier. That research had been financed by Vittoria Buondelmonti's mother, the Baroness von Hapsburg, who had also secured Bérenger's participation on the team alongside her daughter. It was where they first met; in fact Bérenger and Vittoria had become quite close during that summer in Austria. Despite the twenty-year age difference between the young beauty and the Scottish oil billionaire, Vittoria's family was more than eager to broker a wedding between the two. It was a match made in secret society heaven, one which would combine the wealthiest and most pristine bloodlines—and help to contain some of the deepest held secrets— in Europe. Further, there was real compatibility between Bérenger and Vittoria, at least on the surface. She was deeply immersed in the research and they shared a passion for religious artifacts and their potential application to family histories.

There had been high drama around the results of the scientific testing, as it was ultimately determined that the Hofburg spear was not old enough to be the authentic weapon once wielded by Longinus the Centurion. The metal could not have been forged prior to the seventh century. No one was more bitterly disappointed than the baroness herself, who held it as a point of honor that the Hapsburgs had been in possession of this spear for hundreds of years. Bérenger remembered that Vittoria had been emotional about the results as well; she had wept when it was determined that the Hofburg spear was a fake at worst, a replica at best.

When the research project had ended, Bérenger returned to France and Vittoria to Italy. He had no interest in pursuing a relationship with the girl, as that was what she was—a girl. He appreciated her beauty and spirit, but she was half his age at that time. He had watched with interest as her career in the fashion industry catapulted her to the covers of magazines worldwide, but he did not see her again until that fateful meeting in Cannes almost three years ago.

He was thinking about that encounter as his phone rang.

"What the hell are you playing at, Vittoria?" Bérenger snapped as he recognized the phone number. He had been trying to get her on the line for hours and had barraged her with messages since his upsetting conversation with Maureen.

"I'm not playing at anything. It's true. Dante is your son."

"I am not an idiot. The dates don't match. He was born on the first of January, two years ago. The last time you and I were together was that previous May in Cannes. Nice effort, but it doesn't add up. It means you were already pregnant when you seduced me."

Vittoria clucked at him, completely unfazed. "Seduced you? Come now, Bérenger. You make it sound like it was a strategy, an effort. Difficult even. Don't pretend there hasn't always been chemistry with us."

"Stop avoiding the issue. Dante was born too early to be my son."

"You're right about one thing. Dante was born early. He was premature. I have the birth certificate that proves it by showing his birth weight at four pounds. But the real proof will come when you see him, Bérenger. There's not a person with eyes who would not recognize the Sinclair blood in this child instantly. I have protected you from it for as long as I can. But he is getting older and he will begin asking questions about his father. It was time for you to know, and for him."

"Then why didn't you come to me in a civilized way? Why drag Maureen into this? Do you have any idea what you have done to her?"

Vittoria sniffed. "*She* is the reason I did it this way. I did you a favor. She is all wrong for you, Bérenger. She isn't like us. She wasn't born to the life and world that we share. You and I are the same. We belong together." She lowered her voice to a purr. "If you remember, we have had some very good times. My family adores you and always hoped we would marry. There is no reason we can't try to make this work and raise Dante together."

"There is a very good reason. I'm in love with somebody else, regardless of what you think of her, and I will never let her go. Vittoria, if Dante is my son, I will take responsibility for him. But you are going to have to prove it. I want DNA tests, and I want them outside of Italy."

"Why?"

"For the same reason you want to have them within Italy. Results can be bought. And in Italy, your family can buy anything."

"I don't need to buy results. I know Dante is your son and I will prove it. But when I do, Bérenger, what then? Has it occurred to you that a child of ours brings all three of the holy bloodlines together? Hapsburg, Buondelmonti, Sinclair. Our son has the bluest blood in Europe at this moment in time."

Bérenger stopped, momentarily speechless at the potential implication. He asked his next question carefully. "What are you saying? Are you telling me that this was intentional? That you set out to create a child who would combine our bloodlines?"

"Stop pretending you didn't enjoy it. You weren't exactly complaining at the time of conception. Think, Bérenger, think. Dante is a very special child. He is both beautiful and brilliant. And he is a prince."

She waited for a moment before delivering her final piece of news. "In fact, he is a Poet Prince. That is why I named him Dante, after our great Tuscan poet. Check your mail, Bérenger. I sent you something via FedEx from New York. Call me after you've had a chance to look at it."

Bérenger was rarely speechless, but Vittoria had stunned him into silence with this final piece of news. She lowered her voice to the honey-dripping growl that the Italian media devoured. "You do know what that means, don't you, my darling? A Poet Prince who is the son of another?"

She did not pause long enough for him to answer. "Now if you will excuse me, I have to go and feed *our* son, whom you may hear shrieking in the background. He may look like a Sinclair, but in terms of temper, he is all Buondelmonti—and every inch a prince."

*

Bérenger sat in his study with his closest friend, Roland Gelis. Roland loved Bérenger like a brother, but he was clearly irritated with him as he ran one giant hand across his forehead in exasperation. "So in addition to everything else happening here, you lied to Maureen."

Bérenger nodded lamely. God, he hated this.

"Why?"

"Why? Because I love her beyond reason and I am terrified of losing her. I knew that the dates couldn't match and the child was born too early to be my son. So because I was certain that DNA would vindicate my position, I decided that the best strategy to take with Maureen was to tell her I never had sex with Vittoria. She didn't need to know if it couldn't be proven. It would hurt her unnecessarily. Besides, now we are solid, together, and I will never cheat on her again. Never."

"But you did have sex with Vittoria."

"Yes. And . . . if she is telling the truth about Dante being premature, then he could actually be mine. She says he looks just like me, but I haven't seen photos yet. No doubt Vittoria is saving photos as one of her aces with the press. God only knows when and where those will surface."

Roland glared at his friend as he gestured to the table. "And now . . . we have this to deal with."

Laid out between the two of them on the study table were the contents of Vittoria's FedEx package. It contained the birth certificate confirming the baby's low birth weight, ostensibly from premature arrival, and an astrological chart for the baby with an analysis attached. Bérenger cringed when he saw the heading at the top of the page: "Birth Information for Dante Buondelmonti Sinclair."

The two men read through the results again. Within the ancient prophecies of the Order, the astrological qualifications for a Poet Prince were specified:

He who is a spirit of earth and water born
within the complex realm of the sea goat
and the bloodline of the blessed.
He who will submerge the influence of Mars
And exalt the influence of Venus.
To embody grace over aggression.

According to this document, if anything from Vittoria was to be believed, Dante fulfilled every requirement of the prophecy in exactly the same way that Bérenger did. He was born under the astrological sign of

Capricorn, the sea goat, and his chart was a mixture of earth and water elements. The planet Mars was "submerged" in the water sign of Pisces, and Venus was in an "exalted" position at the time of Dante's birth. And he was born on the first day of January, as was the greatest of all known Poet Princes—Lorenzo de' Medici.

"Bérenger, I don't have to tell you how serious this is. You are a servant of the Grail. You cannot ignore this, no matter what it costs you personally."

Bérenger Sinclair shook his head miserably. He could not possibly ignore a child of his own blood under any circumstances. But if Dante indeed proved to be his son and if this birth chart accurately reflected the position of the planets when the baby was born, matters were complicated in a new and unexpected way. Bérenger Sinclair was the heir to more than a huge oil empire; he was also the heir to a powerful spiritual tradition that dated back to Jesus and Mary Magdalene and ran through the greatest families in European history. His devotion to the teachings of the bloodline was absolute, and he had sworn to protect and defend those traditions with his life when he took the vows of a Grail knight under the guidance of his grandfather. It was a vow he had taken in this very castle as he knelt beside Roland when they were both teenagers.

If baby Dante was a child of this prophecy, Bérenger would need to be actively involved with raising the boy to fulfill his promise. His involvement would be a moral and spiritual imperative.

Was it possible that he was being asked to make the sacrifice of his own happiness in order to do the right thing? He wasn't even sure he knew what the right thing was at this point. But the churning in his stomach was leading him to a wretched realization: that it was quite possibly his duty to marry Vittoria and raise Dante to fulfill his destiny as a Poet Prince.

Because there was one more thing at play here that had not been discussed—an element that Vittoria was clearly aware of and that Bérenger feared more than anything else. There was a second part to the prophecy of the Poet Prince, an additional prediction about how the future of mankind rested upon the shoulders of this little boy—and upon Bérenger Sinclair.

Bérenger didn't have time to contemplate the wretched possibility further, as his phone rang. He instantly recognized the number of his family seat in Scotland and picked up the phone.

The Marais district
Paris
present day

THE CARD WAS standard-issue Destino—the stationery he preferred was embossed with the A&E design in celebration of Asherah and El— as was the message, which was something of a riddle. In a scrawling hand the Master had written

Are you as wise as Solomon?

If so, the Golden Age awaits you. Come to Florence, one and all, while the Primavera is at its most beautiful.

Come one and all, he said. Peter had no doubt that his cousin, Maureen, and all her comrades in this grand adventure that life had become would heed Destino's call. Maureen's role was clear and central, and Bérenger's as well. They had much to explore together and separately about their destinies. Each was the child of an ancient prophecy in a modern world; each had a great desire to unveil the truth and improve the state of humanity through their work. Tammy and Roland shared those passions, and the four of them had become a dynamic force of research and exploration together.

But Peter was still a little uncertain where he belonged in this adventure.

Destino, in his remarkably intuitive way, addressed Peter individually in the next line, knowing that he might need additional encouragement to join in this particular gathering.

Come, Peter, and walk in the footsteps of Lorenzo, and see where his path may take you.

Where, indeed, would his path take him?

His life had changed drastically in the last two years, and he was still in a state of uncertainty. After a lifetime devoted to his work in the Church and as a teaching Jesuit, Peter was now a refugee from the Vatican. Two years earlier, he and a small team of Italian cardinals had stolen the Arques Gospel of Mary Magdalene from the vaults of their own Church. They feared that the current forces in Rome would attempt to discredit Mary Magdalene's gospel or, worse, try to destroy it. Peter had been present when it was discovered and was the first to translate it. He knew it was authentic and he knew what it contained. Most of all, he understood exactly what Maureen had endured to discover the gospel and bring its message of love and forgiveness to the world. In good conscience he could not stand by and allow yet another cover-up, not as long as he was physically capable of doing something to stop it. So he took a vow to preserve the truth no matter the cost, as did the other men who joined him.

And it cost them plenty.

Peter had spent eighteen months in a French prison for grand theft. His companions in the crime, much older men whom Peter revered, did only six months; Peter had agreed to take the harshest charges solely upon himself to save the others. The sentences had been much heavier initially. There had been intense negotiating, and perhaps a little bit of implied blackmail, to reduce their punishment. Peter knew where quite a few bodies were buried around Vatican City. And while the Church had been determined to make him pay for his crime, it ultimately did not dare to push him too far. Most important, the Arques Gospel of Mary Magdalene was safe, currently under the quiet protection of a family in Belgium with ties to the Order going back a thousand years.

Since his release from prison, Peter had spent the last six months working to help Maureen and Bérenger as a researcher while they continued on their quest to uncover and preserve the truth of the lost teachings of Jesus. He had thrown himself into this task, playing watchdog for Maureen in preparation for the release of the controversial new book. He smiled as he thought of his cousin, who was more like a sister to him. She was sometimes so naïve. Did she think she would really get away with publishing a book that claimed to contain secret teachings of Jesus and not feel the repercussions? It was at times one of the things that he loved most about her: she was so singularly dedicated to telling the truth, no other option ever occurred to her. Maureen wasn't capable of comprehending why someone would find such teachings to be dangerous or offensive. They were beautiful lessons about love, faith, and community. Why would anyone find those ideas harmful?

Why indeed. But Peter had been a priest all his adult life, and he knew the answer personally and viscerally in a way that Maureen could never fully grasp: because those ideas challenged more established values. They represented a potential earthquake that could serve to tear down two thousand years of empire founded on money, power, politics, superstition, ego. And Maureen's work threatened everyone who had a stake in such institutions—institutions like the Vatican.

As a result, Maureen was threatened, far more than she even knew herself. Peter had tracked nineteen separate death threats against her just in the last six months. Most appeared to be hoaxes without merit, but there were a few that needed further investigation.

He was relieved that she was on her way here, happier still that they would likely all be heading off to Florence together. If Maureen was flanked at all times by Peter and Bérenger, chances were they would have an easier time keeping her safe. And while the greatest threats seemed to be coming from the United States at the moment, Maureen was never really safe in Italy, and everyone knew that.

Peter had the television tuned to the CNN broadcast in English. He had not been paying much attention to it until he heard the commentator utter the name "Sinclair." Looking up, he saw video footage of a man in handcuffs being led away from what appeared to be an elegant office building.

"It has been a difficult week for the Sinclair Oil family in Scotland," the announcer said. "Today Alexander Sinclair, the president of Sinclair Oil, was arrested on charges of corruption in the United Kingdom. This is a breaking story and details regarding the alleged criminal activity are scarce. We will fill you in as we follow this one. You may remember that the elder of the Sinclair brothers, Bérenger, found himself in hot water yesterday when Italian supermodel Vittoria Buondelmonti announced that he was the father of her baby boy."

Peter couldn't move for a moment; he was stunned. Bérenger worshipped Maureen, would die for her. Or so he had thought. Peter, who had committed to a life of celibacy, didn't always understand the affairs of men in such matters. He had his cell phone in his hands within seconds, but he could not reach Maureen. He tried Bérenger next, but the call went immediately to voice mail.

He went to pick up Destino's invitation again, contemplating the question "Are you as wise as Solomon?" His immediate answer was an unqualified no. At times like this, he was at a loss about what to do and how to be of help to the people he loved. The priesthood had not prepared him for many of life's most complicated problems, including those surrounding relationships and sexuality.

But Peter also knew that where Destino was concerned, every question was a trick question.

The Confraternity of the Holy Apparition
Vatican City
present day

"The Holy Virgin Mother allowed her only child to die in pain! And he died for all of you, in that pain!"

Felicity screeched at the packed crowd in the confraternity's meeting hall. There was higher attendance tonight than there had ever been. It was so full that the confraternity had to turn people away for fear that the fire brigade would come and shut down the meeting. She extended an arm and pointed at the assembly. "How many of you would do the same? How many of you would suffer for God?"

There was no time for audience response. As Felicity screamed the last question, her eyes began to roll back in her head. The crowd was silent, waiting to see what would happen next. This was what they had come to see—this great drama of possession by the saints and the Holy Spirit.

Felicity began to babble in a strange, harsh type of gibberish.

"She's speaking in tongues!" someone shouted in the crowd but was hushed by the rest, who waited for what would come next. In their anticipation of the spectacle, no one noticed that the voice came from Sister Ursula, the elder nun responsible for the Confraternity of the Holy Apparition. She, alongside Felicity, had resurrected the organization after Girolamo de Pazzi proved incapable following his illness. Sister Ursula had been Felicity's guardian since the day she returned to Italy. She had protected the girl and nourished her visions under careful supervision for a decade now. At the public appearances, she played a key role in ensuring that the crowd was steered in the right emotional direction. Other members of the confraternity were well placed in the room for the same purpose.

A visceral growl rose from Felicity's throat, followed by a scream so heart-wrenching and full of agony that it rattled the windows of the meeting hall.

"My children!" she wailed again, and the excitement within the hall was growing. Here is what they came for, here was the arrival of the holy Santa Felicita, speaking through the vessel she had chosen for her message.

"My children did not die in vain! I gave my children to God as sacrifices to his holy name. Each one suffered and bled for the honor of being martyred to the name of Jesus Christ!"

She fell to her knees, wailing, ripping her hair out now from the scalp as she continued her tirade.

"Mothers among you, do you weep for me?"

There were murmurs and cries through the crowd of "Yes! Of course!" and "God bless you!"

"Do not!" she roared at them all. "I was joyous on the day that my brave children chose to suffer rather than deny their God. Like the Virgin Mother before me, I was in rapture over the death of my sons. My children will live forever!"

Felicity's eyes rolled back again and she fell to the ground, thrashing. Her back arched and her hand came down hard on the cement floor, splitting open the wounds of her stigmata. The crowd gasped as droplets of blood splashed those who were nearest to her. When her thrashing died down, she was possessed with a new voice.

"All of you, you must begin your preparation. Think no more about this earthly life, which means nothing! The afterlife is far greater than anything you can imagine on this terrible earth."

Sister Ursula cried out, "It is the voice of the Holy Spirit. Praise God for this blessing. Praise God for this saint who suffers for us!"

The crowd was with her now, caught up in the frenzied atmosphere that had followed Santa Felicita. They began to shout out, "Praise God! Praise his saints!"

Felicity rolled over on one side, exhausted and bleeding now, but still preaching in her strange growl.

"You may preserve your place in heaven, but you must show God that you are worthy. You must defend him and his holy truth. All of you who fight to defeat evil and destroy blasphemy will be given your reward. But there is a great evil which threatens our holy way, a heresy which must be stopped . . ."

The energy was seeping from her as she prepared to leave consciousness and faint into blackness. She whispered, just before her head rolled back, "Stop the blasphemer. Stop the fornicators who would lie about the chastity of our Lord. You must . . . stop . . ."

Felicity lapsed into unconsciousness before she could finish her sentence. Members of the confraternity, well rehearsed in this circumstance, brought a stretcher to the front of the room and carried her out amid the frenzy and excitement that remained in the room.

Sister Ursula seized the moment and grabbed the microphone from the podium at the front of the room.

"My brothers and sisters, do not leave without understanding the warning which was given us by the Holy Spirit! There is a great blasphemy which threatens us, an evil, a demon of lies and deceit which must be destroyed."

On cue, a group of volunteers from the confraternity began to hand out leaflets to everyone in attendance as Sister Ursula continued to shout in the microphone over the din.

"I urge you to take this information, and take action! Your place in heaven depends upon it. Stop Satan from spreading more lies! Help us to stamp out the devil! We will be meeting here every night this week to discuss the action plan laid out here for you."

The leaflets were snatched up greedily by the members in attendance, more motivated than ever to find their way into heaven.

The leaflets bore the bold command "Stop the Blasphemy!"

Below that was a photograph of Maureen Paschal's new book, *The Time Returns*, and another one of the demon fornicator herself.

Careggi
spring 1463

THE SUN WARMED the stones of Careggi to a tawny gold as Lucrezia Tornabuoni de' Medici watched her elder son ride away from the villa. She paused at the window until he rode out of sight, his glossy black hair flying behind him. As if sensing his mother's gaze, Lorenzo turned in his saddle and waved back at the house with a dazzling smile before cantering off into the forest. At fourteen, Lorenzo had grown into a fine young man. He was tall and well built, athletic, and utterly charming.

He was possessed of the rare combination of a brilliant mind and a loving heart, and Lucrezia kept a close watch on his education to ensure that those attributes were both protected and developed.

Lucrezia had grown into a deeply pious woman, although in her own words, "Not a tedious one." She wrote devotional poetry that sprang from her heart and her spirit, for she was deeply indebted to the Lord for the gifts he had bestowed upon her family. She had embroidered in her own fine hand a quote from Psalm 127, which graced the bedchamber she shared with her husband, Piero.

Children are a gift from the Lord; they are a reward from him.

They were indeed, and God's rewards to her had been bountiful. She had five thriving children: three daughters, Maria, Bianca, and Nannina, each more beautiful and intelligent than the next, and two utterly remarkable sons. Lorenzo was the elder of the boys and the more like her in appearance and intellect. Lucrezia Tornabuoni was not herself a beautiful woman, but she had a grace and presence that transcended any shallow ideal of physical perfection. She had passed on her most unfortunate family trait to Lorenzo: the scooped nose with the flattened bridge that deprived both of them of a sense of smell and any hope of a singing voice. But Lorenzo had also gained some of her greatest characteristics, including her physical height and regal posture combined with the extraordinary mental acuity that made her the most accomplished of Florentine matriarchs. Intellectually, Lorenzo was unequaled by any child she had ever seen. His love of learning was unsurpassed, his linguistic skills were nearly supernatural, and his ability to memorize and comprehend the most complex lessons was astonishing. His first teacher, the renowned intellectual Gentile Becchi, once said that "there were not enough superlatives to describe Lorenzo as a scholar."

Like his mother, Lorenzo was also possessed of an extraordinary charisma that overcame any of his physical deficits. There was an animation to his face, born from his sheer passion for life, that was entirely enchanting. He was immensely popular among the otherwise cynical people of Florence, who referred to him fondly as "our prince." Even at this young age, Lorenzo had already carried out important diplomatic missions for both the family and the Florentine state.

"Mama, where is Lorenzo going?"

The voice from the doorway caused Lucrezia to turn with a smile. Her younger son, Giuliano, four years junior to Lorenzo, was petulant. Tears welled in his huge brown eyes.

"The equerry came to the house to tell Lorenzo that his spoiled horse was restless and would not eat from any hand but his master's. Lorenzo has gone to feed the beast and give him some exercise."

"He said he would take me riding today." Giuliano pouted. "He promised! Why didn't he take me?"

"I'm sure he will come back for you if he promised. Lorenzo never breaks a promise." This was the truth. Lorenzo was entirely trustworthy and never broke his word, particularly to his baby brother, whom he doted upon unconditionally.

Lucrezia ruffled the younger boy's dark curls with affection. Giuliano had been given all the physical blessings of which Lorenzo had been deprived. He was a beautiful child and gifted with a sweet, if overly sensitive, nature. Yet Piero was fond of saying to her in the privacy of their chambers, "God knew what he was doing when he gave us Lorenzo as our prince. Lorenzo was made for this purpose. Giuliano, on the other hand, will never have the disposition for leadership of any kind. He is too sweet, too soft."

They would watch Giuliano closely to see if he had a vocation for the Church, which would suit the Medici purposes well on a multitude of levels. Yet while Lucrezia was a key decision maker in the most powerful family in Florence, she was also a devoted mother who wanted her children to find happiness in what was often a harsh world. She would not force Giuliano into the Church but rather allow him to make that decision on his own if he had such a calling. Again, this was the privilege of being second-born and free of the burden of an enormous, looming prophecy. Giuliano would have far more say over his personal destiny than his elder brother. Yet Lucrezia saw Lorenzo more clearly than did his father, which frightened her sometimes. She recognized the tender heart beneath the sense of responsibility; she saw and understood that there was truly a delicate poet beneath the powerful prince. While God had a plan for Lorenzo, Lucrezia feared for his happiness. Would he be able to fulfill the role of Medici ruler, of banker, politician, and statesman—and find peace and personal joy in the process?

But above all there was the other responsibility, one that was spoken of only to the most trusted members of their intimate circle: the awesome and daunting holy prophecy that Lorenzo had been chosen by God to fulfill. That he was the Poet Prince was without question from the day of his perfect conception and January birth, under the sign of the sea goat and with Mars submerged in Pisces, just as the Magi had specified. Lorenzo, sixteen now, was in the process of becoming fully indoctrinated. Cosimo de' Medici, the family's legendary patriarch and Lorenzo's grandfather, was finalizing that plan with the Order imminently.

Even at such a young age, the weight of his destiny was beginning to settle upon Lorenzo's broadening shoulders. Cosimo was dying and his heir, Piero, was also unwell, indeed had never been particularly healthy, living up to his unfortunate nickname throughout Florence of Piero the Gouty.

Lucrezia sighed as she ushered Giuliano out the door. Giuliano would never know how fortunate he was to be born into all the privilege with little of the responsibility. But the same could not be said for Lorenzo. *Ah, my poor prince.* She looked toward the window where she had last glimpsed him. *Enjoy your freedom now, my son. Before the reality of who you are and what you must accomplish engulfs you completely.*

Turning back to Giuliano, she grabbed his hand. "Come, my little one. It is time for you to sit with Sandro so that he may finish our beautiful painting. And no squirming this time!"

*

Lorenzo de' Medici placed the slightest pressure on his heels, urging Morello into a canter. He never kicked or whipped his horses. Indeed, he revered them, and some said he even had the ability to communicate with them. Marsilio Ficino, Cosimo's physician and astrologer, credited Lorenzo's birth chart with this talent. Lorenzo was an earth sign, governed by the mythical sea goat called Capricornus. Ficino said that this sign, combined with other auspicious elements of Lorenzo's chart, gave him an extraordinary affinity for animals, adding that they would figure into his destiny in unexpected ways.

With horses, particularly, Lorenzo was comfortable, and they appeared to return his love. The Medici horses were known to neigh and whinny when they sensed Lorenzo approaching the stables. His favorite mount, the high-spirited Morello, refused to take oats from any hand but Lorenzo's if he so much as sensed the presence of his young master at the family's country retreat here in Careggi.

Urging Morello into the woods, Lorenzo followed a path that he knew well. He had promised to take his little brother riding this afternoon, so he mustn't stay out too long. He knew it would break his brother's heart if he did not keep his promise, and that was something he could not bear. Giuliano worshipped him, and he would not give him any reason to do otherwise. But Lorenzo needed this time alone, to ride in the sun and feel the warmth on his hair, to listen to the sounds of spring coming alive in the forest. He was secretly composing a sonnet to the season, and he wanted to savor it a bit more before he finished his piece. Spring, the season of new beginnings, the time of promise. Florentines celebrated the New Year with the coming of spring, their calendars beginning on the twenty-fifth of March, the Feast of the Annunciation. That was three days away, and Lorenzo would have his sonnet ready for the celebration that was to come.

What was that sound?

He pulled gently on Morello's reins to slow him to a stop and listened. There it was again, a sound on the wind that was unfamiliar in this place. Lorenzo stiffened in his saddle, completely alert now. These were Medici lands, and while he felt safe here most often, a family of such wealth and power had many enemies. He could not be too careful. He heard the sound again—definitely a human sound—but he relaxed a little in his saddle now as he listened. The sound was small and sad, not threatening. Moving Morello slowly toward the noise, he stopped sharply when he heard a gasp.

Sitting in the leaves and looking up at him was the most beautiful creature he had ever seen.

Close to his age, perhaps slightly younger, the girl looked like one of the nymphs that Sandro sketched for him when they discussed the great Greek legends that they both loved so dearly. The most beautiful heart-shaped face set with delicate features and a perfect Cupid's bow mouth were framed by a cloud of chestnut-colored ringlets that were streaked with a coppery gold. There were leaves in that hair and her clothing was disheveled, but it was clear that her attire was new and expensive despite her current state of disarray. The girl's eyes were bright with tears that magnified their extraordinary light hazel color. Lorenzo would later come to know that these eyes changed color depending on her mood, sometimes amber, then the lightest sage green. But at that moment, she was the most exquisite mystery.

"Why are you crying?"

She moved to show him that she was holding something, something that fluttered and cooed, scattering white feathers.

"A dove? You have caught a dove?"

"I didn't catch it," she snapped, surprising him with her shift to anger. "I rescued it. It was caught in a trap, up in that tree. But it is injured. I think his wing is broken."

Lorenzo sized up this spirited wood nymph as she stood, holding the dove against her fine-boned frame as she brought it closer for his inspection. That the bird was caught in a poacher's trap was information he would have to turn over to his father later. But there was a more pressing matter at hand. He dismounted gracefully and put his hand on the struggling bird, gently stroking its neck.

"Shh, little one. It's all right."

KATHLEEN McGOWAN

To the girl's surprise, the bird calmed and allowed Lorenzo to stroke it.

"Lorenzo de' Medici," the nymph said, with a touch of awe in her lyrical voice.

It was the most beautiful sound he had ever heard—his name on her lips. "Yes," he said, suddenly and uncharacteristically shy. "But you have an unfair advantage, as you clearly know me and yet I do not know you."

"Everyone in Florence knows you. I saw you during the procession of the Magi, riding that same horse." She paused for a moment before asking, "Will you have me arrested for trespassing on your lands?" She looked most earnest in her question.

Lorenzo stopped himself from laughing out loud and maintained a most serious demeanor, asking, "And does everyone in Florence say that I am a tyrant?"

"Oh, no! I didn't mean that. It's just that . . . oh, I am sorry, Lorenzo. Everyone in Florence says that you are . . . magnificent. I just know that my father tells me to stay in our own lands, yet your forest is so much more inviting that I sometimes walk here when no one is watching, and . . ."

He interrupted in an effort to alleviate her obvious discomfort. "Would you like to enlighten me as to who your father is?"

"I am a Donati. Lucrezia Donati." She curtsied slightly, while juggling the dove. Clearly, this was a girl of extraordinary breeding.

"Ah. A Donati." He should have guessed by the quality of her attire. The Donati lands backed up to the Medici, even exceeding their own in terms of usable acreage. They were the nearest thing to royalty in Tuscany, with an illustrious heritage traceable all the way to ancient Rome. The revered Tuscan poet Dante had married a Donati, adding further cachet to that already exalted family name.

"Well, Your Highness." Lorenzo gave a deep bow as he smiled at her. "Given that your family is one of the most aristocratic in this part of Italy, it doesn't appear that this mere Medici has a hope of arresting you. Much as I might like to. Instead, your punishment is to give that dove to me."

"But . . . what will you do with it? You won't eat it, will you?"

"Of course I won't eat it! My lord, what must you think of me? I shall take it to Ficino. He is one of my teachers, but also a doctor. He is a maestro, a master of many arts. If anyone can mend this wing, Ficino can. And he lives just over the ridge in Montevecchio, behind our house."

Lucrezia considered him thoughtfully before stating rather than asking, "I'm coming with you. After all, I did go to all of this trouble to fall out of a tree to rescue him. I'd say I deserve to go. Besides, it's my birthday today and you would be terribly cruel to deny me."

Lorenzo laughed again at this spirited, enchanting creature. "Mistress Lucrezia Donati, I doubt that I would ever have the strength to deny you anything. You didn't hurt yourself when you fell from the tree, did you?"

"Not nearly as much as my mother will hurt me when she sees what I have done to my new dress." She brushed at the dirt and the leaves, straightening herself as she did so. Lorenzo inspected her, using the excuse to circle and take in every inch of her beauty.

"I think you got very lucky this time," he observed with mock seriousness. "It will brush off and nothing is ripped." His tone lightened as he added, "And if Mona Donati asks, tell her that your clumsy neighbor Lorenzo de' Medici fell from his horse and you came to his aid. I will tell my father the same, and everyone will shower you with gifts on your birthday!"

It was Lucrezia's turn to laugh now, revealing her delicate dimples. "A good plan, Lorenzo, except that you have forgotten one thing. Your skill as an equestrian is legendary, and no one will believe for a moment that you fell from your horse—particularly that horse. No, I must take the blame for what I have done. Besides, I am a terrible liar. Honesty suits me better."

"Then you are a noble woman in every sense of the word. Can you ride?"

She tossed her chestnut hair and raised her chin at him. "Of course I can ride. Do you think yours is the only family in Florence that educates its daughters?" But the dove flapped in her arms again and she deflated. "Although it may be difficult while holding our little friend."

Lorenzo devised a solution. He helped Lucrezia up and onto Morello, who was very cooperative. Mounting behind her, he kept his arms around the girl's shoulders to steady her as she clutched the dove to her body. Together, they rode off slowly in the springtime sun, looking very much the way that teenagers in the throes of a first crush have looked since the beginning of civilization.

*

Marsilio Ficino watched Lorenzo carefully, if surreptitiously, as he examined the wounded bird. He had been charged with Lorenzo's intellectual and philosophical well-being since his infancy, and he knew and loved the boy like his own child. He had never seen him like this, as giddy and self-conscious as he was in the presence of the Donati heiress. At least she was worthy of him and not some farmer's daughter from Pistoia. On the other hand, this pairing posed its own complications. How would the Donati patriarch feel about his treasured daughter frolicking in the forest with the Medici heir? While Lorenzo's family was the wealthiest and subsequently the most influential in Florence, they were not nobility. To the regal elite of Italy, the Medici were merchants who had struck it rich, whereas the Donati were of an ancient and storied lineage. Merchant class versus the aristocracy: it was unlikely that the Donati would ever approve of anything beyond the friendship of these children. Perhaps not even that.

"His wing is broken, but I have seen worse," Ficino declared in his gentle voice. He watched Lucrezia's face light up at this pronouncement.

"Can he be saved? Can you heal him?"

The hope that radiated from the girl was infectious. Ficino, in spite of himself, was softened by her warmth. He smiled at her.

"It is up to God's will if the creature is healed, my dear. But we will do our best to use our human skills and see what comes next. Lorenzo, hold him for a moment while I gather some supplies."

Ficino handed the bird to Lorenzo, who took him gingerly, cooing to the dove all the while. He looked up and caught Lucrezia's eyes, seeing them bright again with tears. He rushed to reassure her.

"He will be all right, I know he will. The maestro will help him, and you and I . . . we will pray together for his healing."

Ficino returned with two small sticks and some linen strips and bound the bird's wing to his body. Lorenzo held the dove while his teacher ministered to it, Lucrezia watching both with wide-eyed fascination.

"I will keep him here, but he will need to be fed by hand," Ficino explained, feigning irritation. "I do not have the time to play nursemaid to this bird, so it will be up to the two of you to be sure that he is fed."

Lorenzo glanced at Lucrezia, who nodded solemnly. "I will come every day, if I am able." Her father spent his days in Florence proper, and her mother was lenient with her free-spirited daughter when they were here in their country villa. Lucrezia was able to get away on most days, provided she gave her family no cause to worry by staying away too long.

"I will come too," Lorenzo promised. "I will meet Lucrezia at the edge of her lands and bring her here on Morello."

Ficino nodded, emitting a grunt. "Good enough. Now away with the two of you, as this old man has work to do. I am translating something of great importance for your grandfather, and his legendary impatience has not been diminished by his illness. And don't get into any more trouble for today, at least."

Lorenzo took Lucrezia lightly by the arm and escorted her out the door. "This way," he whispered.

"Where are we going?"

"Shh. You'll see."

He led her along a winding, overgrown path, pushing aside the low tree branches that threatened to obscure the way. But Lorenzo could find this place with his eyes closed. It was his favorite place in the world and would remain so for the rest of his life. They turned a final corner and he escorted her through the opening in a wall.

"What is this place?"

They were on the edge of a large and enclosed circular garden. In the midst of the tangled flowers was a temple in the Greek fashion: a dome supported by columns. In the center was a statue of cupid mounted on a pillar. A plaque on the pillar carried the motto *Amor vincit omnia*.

"Love conquers all," Lorenzo translated. "Virgil. The inscription, that is. And . . . something else too. But the temple was built by the great Alberti."

"It's pagan!" Lucrezia exclaimed, shocked.

"Is it?" Lorenzo laughed. "Come over here."

Lorenzo took her to one side of the garden, where an altar in stone had been erected. It was the base to a stunning marble crucifixion scene.

"From Master Verrocchio's hand. Now this *is* Christian."

"It's amazing." Lucrezia was awestruck. "But . . . I don't understand it."

Lorenzo smiled at her. It was absolutely forbidden to bring anyone here who was not indoctrinated into the Order, but Lorenzo wanted to share this magical place with her. He knew instinctively that she would learn to love it as he did—and that somehow she belonged here. She was a part of this place just as he was. It was something that he knew, from the first moment he laid eyes on her. She belonged in every place that he loved, at his side.

"Ficino teaches that the wisdom of the ancients and the teachings of our Lord can and should live together in harmony. That all real divine knowledge comes from the same source and should be celebrated together so that we may become better humans. *Anthropos.* That's a Greek word. It means to become the best human you can be. Similar to *humanitas* in Latin. My grandfather has dedicated his life to that belief, and I hope to do the same thing."

Lucrezia giggled. "*My* grandfather would say it is heresy."

"And my grandfather would say it is harmony. But this is where I come to pray, so it is actually very holy. It is why I brought you here. To pray for our dove. I thought it would be . . . appropriate."

Lucrezia admired the beautiful sculpture before her. She ran one hand along the cold marble base and up the side of the cross as high as she could reach, then back again. She began to speak but was overcome with shyness suddenly. Lorenzo, who would be acutely attuned to her moods for the rest of his days, noticed. "What is it?"

She looked up at the achingly beautiful face of Our Lord as sculpted by a master artisan. She whispered, "I have dreamed about it."

"About what?"

"The crucifixion. I see it as if I were there. It is raining, and I watch it all happen through the rain. I have had the dream three times that I can remember."

Lorenzo looked at her strangely for a moment but didn't respond immediately. "Come with me," he said finally. He led her through bushes flooded with fragrant white roses to another small altar, this surmounted by the marble statue of a woman. A dove rested on her outstretched hand.

"She's beautiful," Lucrezia gasped. "Who is she?"

"Maria Magdalena. Our Lady, the Queen of Compassion."

Lucrezia gasped. "Oh! She is in my dream too!"

"You dream of our Lady Magdalena as well?" It was Lorenzo's turn to gasp.

She nodded solemnly, then asked, "Is that bad?"

"No," Lorenzo laughed. "It is, I think, very, very good!"

Lorenzo took her hand again and knelt before the statue, indicating that she should do the same. Lucrezia obeyed, without letting go of his hand. She didn't understand the strange mixture of pagan and Christian symbolism, but she was nonetheless enchanted by this place. There was a sense of magic here, of the harmony of which Lorenzo spoke. And if he came here to pray, surely it couldn't be a bad place.

"Lorenzo, will you teach me about all of this? About what it all means?"

He smiled at her and nodded. "Pray with me. First we will give thanks that God has spared our dove thus far. And then . . ." He paused for a moment, overcome with shyness. When he continued, the words came out in a rush, so he could not stop them. "We will give thanks that God has brought us together."

"I will gladly pray for both of those things, and to thank God for loving me so much that he brought you to me on my birthday."

Lucrezia Donati blushed prettily as she squeezed his hand, and then she lowered her head in prayer. Lorenzo did the same, and at that moment the sun struck the marble, illuminating the statue before them. Somewhere in the distance, they both heard the cooing of a dove.

✻

Lucrezia Donati was true to her word. She found a way out almost daily, running to meet Lorenzo on the edge of their property and to ride with him on Morello to see Ficino. There they would feed the dove gingerly by hand; it appeared to be recovering well under their care. They finished each day with a trip to the secret garden, the Temple of Love as it was known to the Medici.

Each day, Lorenzo shared with her some piece of his classical education. Lucrezia was an apt and eager pupil, memorizing everything Lorenzo taught her and asking many questions.

It was on such a day that Lucrezia surprised him with a request.

"Lorenzo, I want you to teach me Greek."

"You want to learn Greek? Really? Why?"

"Yes, really. And I have had much education for a girl, and you will find I am a good student," she said with a haughty little tilt of her head, which Lorenzo thought was the most beautiful thing he had ever seen. She continued, "I want to learn because you love it, and I want to know about all the things that you love. I want to experience them and share them with you. Will you teach me Greek, Lorenzo?"

"I will teach you anything your heart desires. We will start tomorrow after visiting our feathered foundling."

The following day Lorenzo was prepared with a gift of a Greek primer wrapped with a red silk ribbon. He was rewarded with one of Lucrezia's dazzling, dimpled smiles and her contagious excitement. The lessons began in earnest, and he found that she was, indeed, an astonishing student. At the end of the fourth week, Lorenzo presented Lucrezia with some Greek letters he had written on a parchment.

"What's this?"

"Today's lesson. I want you to translate the question for me, and then I want you to answer it. In Greek, of course."

Lucrezia wrinkled her brow in concentration. She was studying very hard, but it had only been a few weeks. She stumbled over some letters but allowed Lorenzo to correct her gently. Finally, she realized what the parchment said and squealed with delight.

The words spelled out "May I kiss you?"

She replied in Greek, with one of the few words she knew well, "*Nai.*" Yes.

*

At the end of the third week, Ficino advised the two of them that he was certain the dove had healed and could be released into the wild. Lorenzo and Lucrezia were giddy with the excitement of their success. In a duplication of their first meeting, Lucrezia rode ahead of Lorenzo, encircled in his arms, the dove clutched to her breast. Morello took them to the edge of the forest, where they dismounted. Lorenzo unwrapped the linen strips from the bird delicately while Lucrezia held him in place. The sticks fell away, and the dove exercised his wing, cooing up at them as he did so.

"He is expressing his gratitude," Lorenzo observed with wonder.

Lucrezia stroked the bird on the back of his neck, tears filling her eyes, "Good-bye, my little friend. I shall miss you so." Her tears fell on his repaired wing. When she looked up, she saw that Lorenzo's eyes were also bright with tears.

"Are you ready?" he whispered.

Lucrezia nodded, and together they lifted the dove into the air. He flapped several times, stretching his healed wing, cooed again, and then flew off in a cloud of white feathers. They watched him fly, a little unsteady at first, but then straighter and stronger. Finally he alighted on a tree branch, cooing back at them.

"Lorenzo, look! He landed on a laurel tree!"

Lorenzo shook his head in amazement, both at the bird's choice of perch and at Lucrezia's acute perception of the symbolism. The laurel tree was his personal emblem, as the word *laurel* and the Latin version of his name, Laurentius, had the same root.

"He is honoring you for saving his life."

Lorenzo turned from the bird to the beautiful young woman standing before him. "It is you who saved him. There is much of your spirit in that dove." He cupped her chin in his hand and kissed her very gently. He stopped himself after an instant and straightened.

"I have just thought of something."

"What?" she asked, breathless as she always was when he kissed her.

"I have been thinking of what I shall call you. My mother's name is Lucrezia, and it does not suit you for me. But the dove has settled it. I shall call you Colombina. My little dove."

"It is the most beautiful name ever," she whispered.

This time, it was she who kissed him, standing on her tiptoes to find his lips. In that moment in the forest, with the promise of spring and the renewal of life all around them, they spoke their love for each other aloud for the first time. It was a love that would endure through their turbulent lives and the often difficult path that God would present to them, separately and together.

It was a love that existed for eternity. From the beginning of time, to the end of time.

*

Regarding The Madonna of Humilitas, *also called* Madonna of the Magnificat

Madonna Lucrezia commissioned me to create a portrait of her family, as a gift to honor the twenty years since she and Piero entered into their union.

I have painted her as the Madonna. Which Madonna? Does it matter? Are they not all one, in the end? The eternal mother, our lady of compassion and humility. And yet this is a celebration of motherhood in a way that cannot be accomplished with a virgin, and indeed this Madonna is our lady Lucrezia portrayed as Mag-

dalena. She writes the Magnificat, a hymn of praise to God, because Lucrezia is herself a grand poetess, and there is a great legend surrounding Magdalena's own writings. I have layered the Madonna's hair in pure gold, that the world may know the brilliance of the women who inspired the work.

It is good to have the Medici as patrons!

Of the angels who surround Our Lady, I have painted Lorenzo as the one who holds the inkwell, as he is the Poet Prince whence the new inspiration will flow. I sketched Lorenzo in profile for this painting during one of our lessons when he didn't know I was watching. He was gazing up at the Master as he told us the legend of Longinus the Centurion. I wanted to capture Lorenzo in a devotional moment, so that the energy of this emotion was infused into the work. And in profile, Lorenzo is most beautiful.

The angelic Giuliano helps to hold the book and gazes at his elder brother for guidance. This will always be Giuliano's role: he will help Lorenzo, and he will look up to him. If he is wise, he will learn from him. Giuliano has the face of an angel, and thus I have depicted his full face. To achieve his stillness long enough to capture him from this angle is no easy task, and required some bribery and the help of Madonna Lucrezia. He is at an age when stillness is most unnatural for a boy.

The eldest Medici sister, Maria, has her hands on each of her beloved brothers, protectively, as this is her loving nature. The other two girls, Nannina and Bianca, are the angels who hold the crown over the Madonna's head. The first grandchild of Piero and Lucrezia represents all the golden children of the flourishing Medici line. The child's hand rests on the word "Humilitas." It is one of the great virtues according to the Libro Rosso, the opposite of pride and hubris. It is the message that Madonna Lucrezia has chosen as the most important at this time for her children to embrace. To be a truly great leader is to know humility.

The child holds a pomegranate. As the master has taught us, and Ficino confirms through his deep studies of the Greeks, the pomegranate is the symbol of indissoluble wedlock. It is the emblem of a marriage that cannot be destroyed. For what God has put together, let no man separate.

The marriage of Piero and Lucrezia is the most indissoluble of any I have ever seen. They walk in the footsteps, truly, of our Lord and Lady.

It was a joy for me to paint the features of Madonna Lucrezia as our beloved Magdalena. I have taken liberties with her coloring and softened her a bit, showing

Lucrezia de' Medici as she appears to those of us who revere her: she is radiant, she is golden, she is "perfected."

In the background I have painted the underground stream as it flows directly to Careggi, as that place is the home of the greatest learning and a refuge for those who would learn to open their eyes and attune their ears to the great truths. It emanates from the women of the bloodline as an artery of life and beauty to all of us with eyes to see and ears to hear.

I remain,
Alessandro di Filipepi, known as "Botticelli"

FROM *THE SECRET MEMOIRS OF SANDRO BOTTICELLI*

Montevecchio
1463

DURING HIS STAYS in Careggi, Lorenzo brought Lucrezia with him to Ficino's adjacent retreat in Montevecchio, the small villa that Cosimo had built for him as the headquarters of the Platonic Academy. The academy was flourishing under Ficino's guidance, becoming a solid educational facility for their Florentine colleagues who cared to study the classics in a relaxed social setting where true dialogue and debate could occur. Poets, philosophers, architects, artists, and scholars flocked to Ficino's retreat each time he announced that he would hold a meeting of the academy. In between those events, Ficino used Montevecchio as a school for Lorenzo and sometimes Sandro, when the latter wasn't in Florence apprenticing with Verrocchio. Sandro would be spending more time in Careggi, at Cosimo's insistence, as the elder Medici wanted to expose Sandro to Fra Filippo's particular techniques of artistic infusion. And while Sandro was being pushed to new levels of artistic achievement, Cosimo felt the time was right to add to his classical education as well.

Lucrezia Donati, whom they were all now referring to only as Colombina, had convinced her parents that she was staying behind in
Careggi so often to learn embroidery from Madonna Lucrezia along
with the Medici daughters. Mona Lucrezia was renowned for her skill,
and to have such an illustrious teacher was a feather in the cap of the
Donati heiress. Her parents were far more concerned with their social
status in town to worry overmuch about their daughter's whereabouts.
As long as they believed she was engaged in a suitable feminine pastime with other influential and respectable women, they would leave
her alone.

Lorenzo, Sandro, and Colombina had, in fact, become quite the
trinity, and they often spent time together before and after lessons. Sandro adored Colombina—everybody did, it seemed—and he sketched
her often as inspiration for the various madonnas he was working on in
the studio. Ficino's own earlier resistance to Colombina had long since
melted in the warmth of her own brilliance and interest in the classics.
Most of all, she was a natural at language. And Colombina brought out
the best in Lorenzo, who worked even harder at his studies to impress
her. To his credit, Lorenzo never ceased to encourage the girl and show
his pride in her achievements, which were many and growing more
frequent.

Ficino was fond of telling Colombina that if she had been born a
man with such a quick mind and bold spirit, she would have ruled the
world. Still, as one of Lorenzo's unofficial guardians, he was careful not
to encourage their commitment to each other beyond what was literally platonic. He referred to them as Apollo and Artemis, emphasizing their connection as brother and sister, as a duo who could bring
light to Florence through the masculine sun and the feminine moon.
He hoped that this continued emphasis would aid them in the future,
when they would ultimately face the harsh realities of arranged marriages and political alliances that awaited wealthy Florentines. If they
could find joy in their role as spiritual brother and sister, perhaps that
energy could be channeled into their continued work together for
their common cause in the Order, which he had no doubt that Colom-

bina would embrace with extraordinary zeal once she was introduced to it.

Sometimes Jacopo Bracciolini joined in the lessons. Lorenzo had known Jacopo since they were little boys, had jousted with him on ponies, wrestled in the mud while playing knights of the Crusades using broom handles as lances, and marched with him in parades. Jacopo had been the Master of the Cats in the Magi procession when the boys were both ten years of age; he had continued to develop his wicked sense of humor and insatiable need for attention through his teen years.

Sometimes he was truly funny, and at other times he was simply annoying. Sandro barely tolerated Jacopo, but Lorenzo valued him as a brother in spirit and defended him against Sandro's barbs. Not only was Jacopo one of his oldest friends, but the boy's father, Poggio, was a high-ranking member of the Order, after Cosimo. This fact alone made him family, and Lorenzo was highly protective of all aspects of family.

Colombina was kind to everyone, and despite the fact that Jacopo was forever the prankster and always up to some trick or joke at another's expense, she had a soft spot for him. He craved attention, but he was also possessed of a brilliant mind and was capable of deep and insightful conversation. Jacopo once stuffed a tiny frog into the inkpot and exploded in laughter when the poor creature finally broke free, trailing little frog-shaped inkblots across Master Ficino's important translations. But Jacopo could be entirely serious when discussing the glory of Florence and its importance in European history. The Bracciolinis were a storied and noble Florentine family, and Jacopo was proud of his heritage.

His presence, however, changed the chemistry of their little trinity, which was one of the reasons Sandro was annoyed by it. It was particularly noticeable today during Ficino's lesson on Virgil's *Eclogues*.

"Love conquers all things; let us too surrender to love." Ficino quoted the most famous of Virgil's lines and asked each student to provide an interpretation of the idea behind it. Colombina explained that love was the greatest source of power in the universe. Lorenzo, not surprisingly, agreed with her and further discussed the contrast between conquest and surrender. Jacopo, however, was having none of it and began twisting the words.

"Love conquers all fools; let us too surrender to nothing," Jacopo quipped.

Young Bracciolini seemed particularly disruptive, as if the lesson on love were a thorn in his side. Ficino grappled with him briefly but decided he was in no mood for the boy's antics today. There were stacks of translations waiting for him from Cosimo. Thus he dismissed his students early and took note as Jacopo dashed out past them all, without even looking back or saying good-bye.

*

Lorenzo was not so easily dismissed, however. He had been hounding Ficino to bring Colombina to meet the Master of the Order of the Holy Sepulcher for approval. Ficino knew it was inevitable, but with Cosimo growing weaker by the day, he had little time for anything other than completing the outstanding translations of ancient manuscripts for his patron and teaching Lorenzo. Cosimo had opened the Medici library to the scholars of Florence, the first time any private library had been opened to the public. And he wanted to add more manuscripts, translations of some of the rare Greek documents that had been unearthed on the many Medici missions of discovery through the Near East. Ficino was under pressure to accomplish these translations for Cosimo. The unspoken sentence between them was that Cosimo wanted to see them and read them himself, before he left this life for the next.

Lorenzo had had an astrology lesson before the Virgil debacle, and it led him to ask Ficino to look at the aspects of his birth chart together with Colombina's. Ficino grumbled about it good-naturedly but retrieved a valuable ephemeris while doing so, a gift from Cosimo. He paged through the enormous book, an encyclopedia that detailed the placement of the planets, taking note of where the heavenly bodies were in the sky when both children were born. Scribbling the squiggles and analyzing the numbers for some time, he finally made his pronouncement.

Ficino cleared his throat and grew very serious. Astrology was his passion, and his natural intensity increased when he discussed it in detail. A man of utter integrity, he also knew he must speak the truth of his findings despite his personal hesitation to do so.

"I see something here that is . . . unique. Your love for each other will only grow through time and last . . . an eternity. It is divine love. God-given. You were made, one for the other, by God. And no man—or woman—will ever be able to take that from the two of you."

Lorenzo grabbed for Colombina's hand and brought it to his lips, kissing her beautiful, long fingers impulsively. "I could have told you all of that without the aid of the stars."

Colombina smiled at him but turned back to Ficino, suddenly serious. "You give us such beautiful news. Words about God, and about divine love that lasts forever. And yet you deliver it with sadness. Why, Maestro?"

Ficino reached out his hand to place a finger under her chin, tilting her head, like a sculptor preparing to work, before answering in his thoughtful, halting way. "Because, dear child, your love will not be supported by the circumstances you have both been born into. It—and you—will face many challenges in your lives. Lorenzo's destiny . . ." He stopped as he looked down at one of the squiggles on the paper, then smeared the ink across it with the tip of his finger. "There are others who would make such decisions for you."

Lorenzo's earlier giddiness evaporated as he looked at his love with a new sadness.

"My father," Colombina said simply.

"You are correct. And yet . . . I urge you to remember one thing, my children: what God has put together . . . no man can separate."

With a heavy heart, Marsilio Ficino watched his most beloved pupils leave. He knew so much more than what he had imparted to the young lovers. But even in all his wisdom, he understood that there was something happening here that was larger than his education and experience. There was only one man alive who could help them now, the only man who truly deserved to be called the Master.

Ficino grabbed his lightweight cape and went in search of Fra Francesco.

*

Marsilio Ficino did not have to search very far for Fra Francesco, as he was installed in his own little wing in Montevecchio and rarely ventured beyond the gardens, where he had installed an elegant labyrinth made of paving stones. Fra Francesco used the labyrinth as a walking prayer tool and also taught lessons within it. But today he was indoors in his study, as if he had been anticipating Ficino's arrival.

"How is it possible that we did not know of this Donati girl?" Fra Francesco's question to Ficino was not a reprimand, as that was not in his nature. It was a sincere, curious question.

Still, it irked Ficino that he hadn't seen it earlier. Why hadn't he thought to look at her astrological chart before? The stars were very clear.

"The Donati are traditionalists," he replied. "They are not of our beliefs and would not welcome our teachings. They're solid Catholics and would think that what we do is a serious aberration."

"More's the pity, given that their daughter is likely an Expected One. Are we sure they can't be swayed?"

Ficino pulled himself up, surprised that Fra Francesco had made that pronouncement without even meeting the girl. The Master noticed and continued.

"It stands to reason that she is, given Lorenzo's obsession with her. She is of a noble Tuscan family, an ancient one, and one that Dante married into. All ancient Tuscan families are bloodline, Marsilio; never forget that. All three of the great holy blood dynasties settled in Tuscany and Umbria, and it is the only place in Europe where that ever occurred. That is why this place is more exalted than any other."

"It's also why there are so many blood feuds and family rivalries," Ficino observed.

"Yes, yes, that is sadly true. But it is also what we are working to repair with all the intermarrying that we have sponsored. Whoever would have thought that the Albizzi and the Medici would ever unite into one family through marriage? And the Pazzi? But it is happening. Perhaps we can convince the Donati to give their daughter in marriage to Lorenzo."

Ficino shook his head sadly. "We can try, but I do not have much optimism for success. Not because it is a blood feud. The Donati and the Medici are peaceful enough as neighbors, though the Donati are untrustworthy, I think. But it is their status that is the problem. They are elitists as well as Catholics. That is a difficult combination. For all that the Medici are one of the wealthiest and most influential families in Europe—"

"And the *true* royalty of this land," Fra Francesco reminded him, making reference to the ancient and storied lineage of the family, as well as Lorenzo's exalted birth.

"Yes, but you would not get the aristocratic Donati to agree with you. From their perspective, the Medici are merchants and many layers beneath them on the hierarchy of mankind."

"This girl. You say she is intelligent as well?"

Ficino nodded. "She is Lorenzo's equal, Master. I would say that to no one but you, but she is. Aside from her horoscope, I can see that she is his own soul's twin through the way that she learns and the subjects in which she excels. They are so similar sometimes that I find it disturbing. There is a symmetry there, a perfection in their togetherness. And yet . . . I can also see that it is not their destiny to be together. Such things make me ask questions of God and of faith."

Fra Francesco nodded. "Fair enough, my boy, fair enough. I have seen many things in my long life that would make me question the will of God, and most of them pertain to the course of love. Why are two souls made for each other but then kept apart? It is the strife of love, Marsilio. The strife of love in the dream we call life. But it all has purpose, and that purpose is to seek union. We are tested to see if we have the mettle to battle the illusion and find the love at the end of the dream. And when we do, the dream becomes a reality. Then nothing is more beautiful."

Ficino, who had never been in love in all his years, merely nodded, as he had nothing to add. He was a singular soul, happiest when immersed in his studies and his books, and not one to be distracted by longings of love. It was simply something he did not crave.

"Earthly love is not the mission for everyone, of course," Fra Francesco continued. "There are a number of angels, like yourself, who have come here to work in singular purpose. You do not crave love because you were not incarnated with a mate. You do not search for anyone, because there is no one here for you."

"I am happy as I am, Master."

"Of course you are! Our mother and father in heaven do not make mistakes, and they are never cruel. They would not send you here without a mate and then give you the terrible longing to find one. Instead, they send you here alone so you can focus on your work, which is your one true love. And it makes you completely happy, as it was meant to."

The Master laughed now, the jagged scar beneath his beard bobbing up and down. "And this is why it is your mission to teach the classics and linguistics, while it is my job to teach about love. Which brings us back to the subject at hand. What shall we do about this delightful new Expected One who is Lorenzo's one true love? Have you discussed her with Cosimo?"

Ficino shook his head. "Cosimo's health is a concern and I do not wish to burden him with this yet until you are certain that she is what we think she is."

"Well then, there is only one thing left to do. Bring her to me as soon as you can so that we may decide this, once and for all."

*

Colombina joined Lorenzo in Montevecchio the next day, where she was brought into the presence of the Master for the first time. She had heard many stories of him, of course, and Lorenzo worshipped him absolutely as the wisest and kindest man who ever lived. He had warned her of his ancient and rugged appearance, but such things did not affect her at all. Colombina was a pure spirit, and she saw others for what they were in their truest selves and not what they were on the surface.

They spent the first hour together in the drawing room of Ficino's house, the four of them. The Master watched Colombina interact with Lorenzo and Ficino, interested in observing her in her most natural way. He realized as he watched her that there was no other way to view her: she was entirely without artifice.

The Master smiled at the little gathering but then announced that it was time for him to speak to Colombina on her own. Ficino excused himself and dragged Lorenzo with him. They had plenty of preparation to do for the Platonic Academy meeting later in the week.

When Ficino and Lorenzo had gone, Fra Francesco asked, "Now, my dear. Lorenzo tells me that you have had dreams of the crucifixion and of Our Lady Magdalena. When did these begin?"

Colombina nodded obediently and told him. "The first time was last year, the night before I met Lorenzo. And I remember because it was the eve of my birthday and I woke up crying. My mother was most vexed. 'Why are you crying when it is your birthday and the beginning of spring?' she asked me. I told her that I had a nightmare, but I did not tell her what it was. My mother is very religious, and I have no doubt that if I told her about the dream I had, she would send me off to a convent!"

"Will you tell me of the dream?"

"Oh yes. I do not think that *you* will send me to a convent!" She laughed.

Fra Francesco laughed with her. "I can assure you that will never happen."

"Well, I see Our Lord upon the cross, and it is raining very hard. And I see Maria Magdalena at the foot of the cross, and she is weeping terribly, and I begin to cry with her. I see other women there as well: the Holy Mother and the other Marys. All of them are weeping, but none of them can I feel so much as Magdalena. I . . ." She paused for a moment, looking down at her hands in her lap, hesitating to discuss the part of the dream that could land her in a convent with no means of escape.

"Go on, my dear. You have nothing to fear from me."

She smiled at him then, the dazzling dimpled smile that enchanted everyone who came in contact with her. "I know that, Master. I have known that since the moment I walked in the door. It is just that the next part of the dream is not so easy to explain. But . . . I feel what Magdalena is feeling in the dream, as if I am her, and yet I know that I am not really her. But it is as if she wants me to know her mind and her heart, and so she somehow shares them with me. It would be strange enough if I had the dream just once, but I have had it three times."

Fra Francesco nodded at her. "It is a remarkable dream, little dove. A blessed dream. Do you see any of the Roman soldiers in the dream, by chance? See their faces?"

She shook her head. "No, not very clearly. I am aware that they are there, but I do not see them. I am mostly aware of Magdalena."

The Master nodded, satisfied. Colombina was indeed having the identical dream of the crucifixion that all the Expected Ones who came before had experienced. And if she was unable to see the face of the centurions, so much the better: it kept him from having to explain why the face of Longinus Gaius was a younger version of his own face, with its terrible scar across the left cheek.

There was no doubt that Colombina was authentic, a daughter of the holy prophecy. And like all the bloodline prophetesses, she wasn't just seeing Magdalena, she was feeling her. But how would they get her away from her parents and into proper Order training? What role could this girl play if she was not able to marry Lorenzo, which was highly unlikely?

Fra Francesco embraced the girl, then released her to spend the rest of the afternoon with her beloved Lorenzo. He smiled as they wandered off to the garden, hand in hand. To watch the two of them together was a blessed thing. It gave him hope and filled his ancient heart with love, in spite of Marsilio's dire predictions.

"Love conquers all, my children," he whispered after them. "Love conquers all."

PART TWO

The Miracle of the One Thing

Truly, without Deceit, certainly and absolutely . . .

That which is below corresponds to that which is above,
and that which is above corresponds to that which is below,
in the accomplishment of the Miracle of the One Thing . . .

Its Father is the Sun. Its Mother is the Moon.
The Wind has carried it in his belly.
Its nourishment is the Earth.
It rises from Earth to Heaven,
and then it descends again to the Earth,
and receives Power from above and from below.
Thus you will have Glory of the whole World.
All obscurity will be clear to you.
This is the strong Power of all Power.

In this way was the world created.
From this there will be amazing applications,
because this is the Pattern.
Therefore am I called Thrice-Great Hermes,
having the three parts of the wisdom of the whole World.

THE EMERALD TABLET OF HERMES TRISMEGISTUS

AT THE EDGE of the river Arno lies a district known as Santa Trinità, an area named for the Holy Trinity. A secretive and somewhat mysterious community of monks with ties to the Order built a monastery there in the tenth century, under the patronage of Siegfried of Lucca, Matilda of Canossa's legendary great-great-grandfather. The monks were not only sympathetic to the origins of the Order, some of them were descended from the most powerful bloodline families themselves and were sworn members. Here, the teachings of the Libro Rosso were preserved, the sanctity of union and the truth of the Trinity were understood as cornerstones to the true teachings.

The antique towers of the Gianfigliazza family had stood guard over the edge of the neighborhood known as Santa Trinità for almost eight hundred years. Today, both towers existed in perfect restored condition, straddling either side of the fashionable shopping street named for the family of Lorenzo de' Medici's mother, the Via Tornabuoni. One tower had been converted into a fashion museum as well as the flagship store of the ultrachic Italian designer Salvatore Ferragamo. The other tower contained a hotel as well as a series of private apartments. On one floor of the south tower were the living quarters of Petra Gianfigliazza; the apartment was also the current headquarters of the Order of the Holy Sepulcher.

A stunning and stylish blonde, Petra had purchased this apartment in the tower in an effort to reclaim her family's ancestral property in Florence using the money she had saved while working as a fashion model in Milan. She was too old to model now, although still more

beautiful than most of the girls half her age who were working the run-
ways these days. The fashion world had changed too much for her taste
over the years with its unhealthy emphasis on girls who were encouraged to starve themselves and use artificial stimulants to stunt their
appetites. She had worked in it for as long as she could stand. Thus
Petra had been delighted when Destino had phoned to tell her that he
wanted to return to Florence from France. She had not seen him in a
few years, although they kept in close contact and had since she was a
child and his devoted student. Her family still owned some of the property not far from Montevecchio, where Destino stored the artifacts of
the Order and had last lived while in Florence.

Since his return to Italy, Destino most often stayed in Montevecchio. Petra worried about him out there on his own in that old house.
He had aged tremendously since she had seen him last and was indeed
looking very frail. She was relieved when he had decided that staying in
the city was a better idea once Maureen and her friends arrived. There
would be many sights in Florence to show them pertaining to the Order, and it would be far easier if they were all here in one place. Petra
was just glad that she could keep an eye on him at the same time.

And now, after Vittoria Buondelmonti's latest rogue antics, Petra
was feeling more protective of Destino than ever. She had attempted
to reach Vittoria after her outrageous behavior in New York and her
tawdry public claims that Bérenger Sinclair had fathered her child. Vittoria had not returned her calls. Yet. But she would eventually. Petra
had been Vittoria's mentor on the runway but also in the Order, as they
both came from ancient Tuscan families with related heritage. Their
relationship made Vittoria's erratic actions of the last week all the more
upsetting.

Meanwhile, Petra had protected Destino from the news. Her beloved teacher's health was more fragile than ever, and she didn't want to
send him into shock over recent events. Destino loved all his students
as if they were his own children, so when one went off the rails, as it
appeared Vittoria had, he was extremely distressed. Petra feared that
Vittoria's obvious attempt to destroy Maureen and Bérenger's relation-

ship would have a profound effect on Destino. She knew she couldn't keep it from him much longer, as Maureen was certainly bound to ask him for advice in the matter, if Bérenger didn't. Petra would have to alert him before that happened, but she needed to have this out with Vittoria first.

Destino currently shared Petra's spacious apartment, while Maureen and her friends were installed in the adjoining hotel. They were able to hold meetings either in Petra's living room or on the roof deck of the tower, with its stunning views of the Duomo on one side and the Ponte Vecchio on the other.

It was here, on the roof deck, that Destino and Petra, the modern leaders of the Order of the Holy Sepulcher, first met with Maureen's little group, which included Tammy, Roland, and Peter. Bérenger was conspicuously absent, having flown to Scotland to investigate the allegations against his brother. No one had heard from him in the last twenty-four hours, and they were all getting anxious about the events within Sinclair manor.

The group, sans Bérenger, was assembled now in the Florentine sunshine. The little church of Santa Trinità, where Countess Matilda had trained a thousand years earlier—trained with the same man who sat before them, if he was to be believed—was visible immediately below them.

Petra, a flawless hostess, had selected local wines and cheeses to provide for her guests. She introduced herself quite humbly as Destino's secretary and for the moment appeared very content to stay in the background. But for all her deference, she was a powerful presence of whom everyone in attendance was very aware.

Destino opened their meeting in the same way he had done for two thousand years—with the prayer of the Order:

We honor God while praying for a time
when these teachings will be welcomed
in peace by all people
and there will be no more martyrs.

He then began the lesson.

"My children, the fully realized man or woman, the *anthropos*, knows what his or her promise is and works consciously toward fulfilling it. Less enlightened beings wander the earth with a spiritual aimlessness. They do not realize that they made a promise, so they cannot keep it. But you all do realize it, whether consciously or not, which is why you are here.

"Our mission is to keep our promise, which was to restore the golden age by returning the true teachings to the world. Lorenzo and his own 'family of spirit' prepared the way for us. Despite the greatness and beauty that emerged from their lives, they were unsuccessful in fulfilling the mission completely. We will study the life of Lorenzo and we will learn from it. We will understand what failed and what succeeded, so that we may continue the work of restoring beauty to the world.

"That you have all come sends the message to our mother and father in heaven that their children are grateful and obedient, and fully prepared to carry out their mission on earth. I am certain that heaven is rejoicing today. The time returns."

"The time returns," they all said in unison. And as Peter Healy raised his glass to participate in the toast, he was aware of Petra Gianfigliazza's brown eyes examining him very, very closely.

*

Peter opened his copy of the Libro Rosso translations, paging through it until he found the passages that Petra had instructed them to study. He thought about her for a moment, about everything that had happened in the last few days. Petra Gianfigliazza was an impressive woman, and her devotion to Destino was a beautiful thing to observe. As a man who had spent most of his life in the priesthood, he had never had a female teacher before.

And make no mistake, Petra Gianfigliazza was a teacher. She may have been introduced as Destino's secretary, but it was immediately clear to everyone that she was a force within the Order for the new millennium.

He opened to the pages about Solomon and Sheba, and read.

*

And so it was that the Queen of the South became known as the Queen of Sheba, which was to say, the Wise Queen of the people of Sabea. Her given name was Makeda, which in her own tongue was "the fiery one." She was a priestess-queen, dedicated to a goddess of the sun who was known to shine beauty and abundance upon the joyous people known as Sabeans.

The people of Sabea were wise above most others in the world, with an understanding of the influence of the stars and the sanctity of numbers that came from their heavenly deities. The queen was the founder of great schools to teach such art and architecture, and the sculptors that served her were able to create images of gods and men in stone that were of exceptional beauty. Her people were literate and committed to the written word and the glory of writing. Poetry and song flourished within her compassionate realm.

It came to pass that the great King Solomon learned of this unparalleled Queen Makeda by virtue of a prophet who advised him, "A woman who is your equal and counterpart reigns in a faraway land of the South. You would learn much from her, and she from you. Meeting her is your destiny." He did not, at first, believe that such a woman could exist, but his curiosity caused him to send an invitation for her, a request to visit his own kingdom on holy Mount Sion. The messengers who came to Sabea to advise the great and fiery Queen Makeda of Solomon's invitation discovered that his wisdom was already legendary in her land, as was the splendor of his court, and she had awareness of him. Her own prophetesses had foreseen that she would one day travel far to find the king with whom she would perform the hieros-gamos, the sacred marriage that combined the body with the mind and spirit in the act of divine union. He would be the twin brother of her soul, and she would become his sister-bride, halves of the same whole, complete only in their coming together.

But the Queen of Sheba was not a woman easily won and would not give herself in so sacred a union to any but the man she would recognize as a part of her soul. As she made the great trek to Mount Sion with her camel train, Makeda devised a series of tests and questions that she would put to the king. His answers to these would help her to determine if he was her equal, her own soul's twin, conceived as one at the dawn of eternity.

For those with ears to hear, let them hear it.

THE LEGEND OF SOLOMON AND SHEBA, PART ONE,
AS PRESERVED IN THE LIBRO ROSSO

Peter paused before reading on to part two. There was that phrase at the end, "her own soul's twin, conceived as one at the dawn of eternity." It struck him and tugged at something deep within him. He had never allowed himself to consider this concept of soul mates and predestined love. As a priest, all his love was for God, and for God's son and his holy mother. He had taken vows of celibacy at a very early age and kept them completely. For most of his life, Peter felt that he was one of those singular people, created by God for a purpose and to complete specific tasks. It was very rare that he felt otherwise. But in the deepest reaches of his soul, if he was to be completely honest with himself, he did have moments of doubt. They were brief, but they were there. They cropped up when he saw the happiness of a couple strolling together hand in hand across the Pont Neuf in Paris, or a young family playing in the park. Those moments made him question if he was missing out on something, some aspect of life that God may have wanted him to experience.

But God couldn't have it both ways, could he? If it was Peter's calling to be a priest, then it was not his calling to fall in love or have a family. At least, that was what he had believed for most of his life.

Spending eighteen months in a French prison had given Father Peter Healy a lot of time to think. The Arques Gospel of Mary Magdalene, the document he had risked his life and freedom for, proved that Jesus knew human love and celebrated it. Peter believed that completely and had believed it even when he was still firmly committed to his vocation and his Catholicism. He wrestled with it, certainly, but had found a way to live with the idea that did not infringe upon his vows. However, these teachings of the Libro Rosso, which included a gospel asserted to be written in Jesus' own hand, were emphatic that the primary reason for human incarnation was to experience love in all its forms, human and divine, platonic and erotic.

The more he read, the more the teaching resonated with him.

Over the last four years, almost everything that Peter had once held to be the truth had crumbled. Was he even a priest anymore? The Vatican hadn't stripped him of his collar, but he hadn't worn one since he was released from jail and did not have any desire to do so. He was not interested in teaching at the moment, and certainly not in a Catholic environment. Peter Healy was now a man without a vocation. He had followed Maureen and the others because they were not only his family in blood and spirit, they were also his colleagues in a greater endeavor.

Peter was still trying to determine what his own role was in that larger mission that Destino spoke of earlier today. The mission that Petra obviously embraced with joy and intensity. He understood that he had made a promise, and he was here to keep it—but what, specifically, was that promise? He would continue to study what she had assigned him, more intrigued by the moment in where this story was taking him at this pivotal time in his turbulent life.

He read on:

*

Makeda, the Queen of Sheba, arrived in Sion with gifts to the great King Solomon. She came to him without guile, for she was a woman of purity and truth, incapable of pretense or deception. Thus it was that Makeda told Solomon all that was in her mind and her heart. She knew upon coming into his presence and looking in his eyes that he was a part of her, from the beginning to the end of eternity.

Solomon was mightily taken by Makeda's beauty and presence and disarmed in total by her honesty. The wisdom he saw in her eyes reflected his own, and he knew immediately that the prophets were correct. Here was the woman who was his equal. How could she be else, when she was the other half of his soul?

And it was then that the Queen of Sheba and King Solomon came together in the hieros-gamos, the marriage that unites the bride and the bridegroom in a spiritual matrimony found only within divine law. The Goddess of Makeda blended with the God of Solomon in a union most sacred, the blending of the masculine and the feminine into one whole being. It was through Solomon and Sheba that El and Asherah came together once again in the flesh.

They stayed in the bridal chamber for the full cycle of the moon in a place of trust and consciousness, allowing nothing to come between them in their union, and it is said that during this time the secrets of the universe were revealed through them. Together, they found the mysteries that God would share with the world, for those with ears to hear.

Solomon wrote over a thousand songs following the inspiration of Makeda, but none as worthy as the Song of Songs, which carries within it the secrets of the hieros-gamos, of how God is found through this union. It is said that Solomon had many wives, yet there was only one who was a part of his soul. While Makeda was never his wife by the laws of men, she was his only wife by the laws of God and nature, which is to say the law of Love.

When Makeda departed from holy Mount Sion, it was with a heavy heart to leave her one beloved. Such has been the fate of many twinned souls in history, to come together at intervals and discover the deepest secrets of love, but to be ultimately separated by their destinies. Perhaps it is love's greatest trial and mystery—the understanding that there is no separation between true beloveds, regardless of physical circumstance, time or distance, life or death.

Once the hieros-gamos is consummated between predestined souls, the lovers are never apart in their spirits.

For those with ears to hear, let them hear it.

THE LEGEND OF SOLOMON AND SHEBA, PART TWO,
AS PRESERVED IN THE LIBRO ROSSO

Peter closed the book and stood up. He needed to think, and he needed to walk. The layers within the story of Solomon and Sheba were deep—and for him, somewhat disturbing. They inspired him to question everything he had ever believed about himself. He remembered the fixed stare he received from Petra Gianfigliazza at the moment she had also given him his homework assignment. She knew that she was challenging him with these passages, knew that she had given him something to think about that he had never focused on before. No doubt Destino had briefed her well on all the personalities that were coming to Florence, but it was an intuitive choice all the same.

Peter put on his shoes and decided to take a stroll along the Arno. Florence at night was stunning, and perhaps it was just what he needed to help him assimilate.

*

Peter pushed the enormous wooden security door that kept the outside world away from the private residents in the Antica Torre. As he opened the door, he saw a young woman running across the street toward him, waving.

"Hold the door, please!"

She was out of breath but managed to smile at him as she grabbed the door to keep it open. "I forgot my key," she explained, pointing at the magnetic lock that secured the entrance. "The magnets. They demagnetize my credit cards so I cannot carry the key in my handbag. I have to keep it separate. It's such a nuisance!"

Peter nodded at her, preoccupied by all that was swirling through his head. "Good night," he said politely, as the young woman waved at him and entered the building, headed toward the elevator.

Had he not been so distracted, Peter might have noticed that the door where the woman had held it was covered in blood.

*

It was a magical night in Florence. The air was silky with the essence of late spring, and a slight breeze blew in from the Arno. Tamara and Roland sat on the roof deck of the Antica Torre, breathing in the atmosphere as the iconic rooftops of Florence came to life under the full moon. If ever a place had been created for two people in love to spend a quiet evening, it was this special terrace.

Roland had spent the last few days helping Tamara with her work, investigating aspects of the Longinus legend. They were still trying to determine whether they would ask Destino to discuss his claims or wait for him to bring it up.

"What is the etiquette for dealing with a man who claims to be two thousand years old?" Tammy asked.

Roland laughed with her. As the heir to a secret society legacy himself, he knew a few things about decorum. "We wait, and see where he takes us. He will trust us more if we do not push him or appear to be plying him for information. And he brought us here for a reason, so I am happy enough to watch that reason reveal itself."

"Do you think Bérenger will ask him about the spear?"

Roland considered for a moment before nodding. "I hope he does. He needs to. And I think that will be hard to resist for him, not just for the purposes of esoteric knowledge."

"But because Bérenger is being confronted with his own personal destiny now," Tammy completed Roland's thought, as she often did.

Roland nodded. "He is. I have always believed that the Spear of Destiny was a symbol for whatever struggle a man had within himself. It carries some kind of energy or vibration that amplifies what is in the heart of the man who possesses it. A good man is made great, like Charlemagne, and a man with evil intentions can become a monster, like Hitler."

"Bérenger is a good man, who could be made great."

Roland nodded, but his brow was wrinkled with the difficult thoughts that filled his head. "But what is the path to greatness for him, Tamara? What should he do? Should he put his own happiness first, and Maureen's? Or should he take responsibility for this little boy who appears to have been born under very special stars?"

Tammy's jaw dropped. She loved Roland, and though she knew and understood him intimately, he still had the power to shock her. He had been raised in the strange and complex world of European secret societies. His own father had been the leader of the clandestine Society of Blue Apples and had been brutally murdered as a result of related secret intrigues. The world in which Roland lived was one where such intrigues were not games or empty rituals; they were life-and-death secrets that impacted history and humanity. Sometimes it was hard for her as an urban American woman to completely grasp the depth—and dangers—of his world. She had witnessed plenty over the recent years through Maureen's search for priceless lost gospels, and yet each day seemed to bring still greater mystery. Sometimes this was an exciting element of her new life with Roland; sometimes it was frustrating and even frightening.

Tammy stuttered for a moment before getting the question out. "You . . . you can't possibly be saying that Bérenger should marry Vittoria?"

Roland's gentle eyes bored into hers. There was pain in them, but also an understanding of something deep and ancient that she did not yet understand.

"Tamara, I love you. And Bérenger loves Maureen in the same way, so know that it tears my heart to pieces to say this. But . . . you have not been raised in the ancient ways of our people. You understand them, yes, and you have learned to love them and adopt them as your own. But you did not grow up with the legends of massacred relatives, martyrs who died for our beliefs. In the Languedoc, those are our bedtime stories. We are raised with the legends of our Cathar leaders who were brave enough to walk into flames, to suffer and die for their belief in the love of Jesus and Mary Magdalene, to risk everything to keep the teachings of the Way of Love alive."

Tammy protested. "I know all of that. But I don't see how it matters here."

Roland continued in his patient way. "Bérenger was raised in the Languedoc, as the heir to this legacy. And what is at the center of our traditions? How did Bérenger and Maureen meet? What is it that they have in common?"

The light of understanding was beginning to dawn on Tammy, and she answered accordingly. "The prophecies."

"Yes, the prophecies. The prophecies of the Expected One and the

Poet Prince have guided our people for two thousand years. We have always lived by them, chosen our leaders by them, and they have never failed us. Every day of Bérenger's childhood, he was reminded that he was the golden prince of this prophecy by his grandfather. It has haunted him all his life. He lives in fear of not fulfilling his destiny, of letting his people down, of failing. And now, added to all this is the responsibility of a child who is born of the same prophecy. And there is something else that you do not yet know . . ."

Tammy was listening, but the insistent beeping on her cell phone distracted her momentarily. She clicked it to check the text message that had just arrived and read it to Roland.

"Message from Destino via Petra. We are meeting everyone at the Uffizi tomorrow morning at nine a.m. for a lesson in Botticelli. Now, you were saying?"

So immersed were Tammy and Roland in their conversation that they never noticed the young woman who sat not far away from them, writing in what appeared to be her travel journal. They did not see that she wrote down everything they said, nor did they see the palm of her right hand dripping blood onto the page of her notebook.

*

"Master, are you all right?" Petra spoke softly as she entered Destino's room, where he sat on his simple bed in deep contemplation, eyes closed. Destino did not use electric lighting, preferring only candles and oil lamps. He insisted on living simply, despite the wealthy followers who were willing to provide for him any material items he would ever require. But he required very little. Part of the penance he had inflicted upon himself all those years ago was to live in an austere manner, and he had always kept this vow.

Because Destino sometimes fell asleep following his prayer, Petra checked on him each night to ensure that the candles were blown out and the lanterns safe.

"Enter, my dear. And stop worrying about me. I knew this was coming, and I welcome it."

Petra smiled at him in the semidarkness. Of course he knew. "But what do you welcome, Master? The child himself? The Second Prince?"

Destino opened his eyes slowly. "I welcome the opportunity. I welcome the tests. I welcome the teachings that can and will come from it all."

"But Vittoria—"

"Vittoria is playing a role, the role of adversary, the role of challenger."

Petra understood and replied in a matter-of-fact tone, "Get thee behind me, Satan."

Destino nodded. "*Satan* literally means adversary, as you well know, and in that regard she is now Bérenger's personal Satan. But do not think of Vittoria as wicked. She is misguided and her intentions are corrupt, but what she is doing has merit to our people. No hero has ever achieved his crown of laurels without facing strong and dangerous opposition. If Bérenger comes through this with an understanding of the true lesson, he will be worthy of that crown. He will deserve to become Lorenzo's spiritual heir."

"And if he does not?"

Destino's eyes, colorless and rheumy with age, clouded over still more as a deep and ragged sigh escaped him. "Then I shall have to stay alive for as many more generations as it takes to find the prince who is worthy of that prophecy."

*

Bérenger had phoned Maureen from the airport in Edinburgh to say he was on his way to Florence in the Sinclair Oil private jet. His brother, Alexander, was in a type of legal seclusion as a result of his arrest. Because there were conspiracy charges pending that involved the government, he was being held under special circumstances and without bail. Bérenger was still unclear as to what the charges were but had been told by the judge that he would not be allowed to see Alexander for another three days. There was no use staying in Scotland and sitting on his hands in frustration. Not when he had to repair his relationship with Maureen.

Now he sat on her little terrace at the Antica Torre, the Duomo shining behind him, as he made his confession.

"I lied to you."

"I know."

Bérenger nodded, looking deep into her eyes. He knew that he would never be able to lie to her face-to-face. It was impossible. They were too close, too connected. She would always see straight into his soul with her piercing green eyes, and he would always want her to. This was the realization that had overcome him while he was home in Scotland; he never wanted to hide anything from her again. He wanted them to become so unified as a couple that nothing could come between them. Bérenger had hurried to Florence to be with her, to explain, and to beg her forgiveness.

But she did not make him beg.

Maureen too had come to a realization over the last few days. Sitting on the terrace with Destino today, she had missed Bérenger desperately. He was integral to this wild, unpredictable, blessed journey that they had embarked upon together. Being without him was like missing a limb. She had read and reread the pages in the Libro Rosso that detailed the relationship of twin souls, of beings created from the same essence, one for the other. It was the most beautiful teaching of the Order, and she had discovered the truth of it through the way that Bérenger loved her. She didn't just believe it, she knew it: knew that Bérenger was her twin soul, knew that their destinies were as intertwined as their minds and spirits. And if she knew that to be true, how could she walk away from it? She could not. It would be an offense to the gift of love that God had given to them both.

"Maureen, you have taught me the meaning of love. You have transformed me, changed me from someone who was existing to someone who is alive. I am sorry, more than I can ever say, for what has happened with Vittoria. And . . . I must tell you that it *is* possible the child is my son."

"I know that too," Maureen said. She walked from the terrace back into the bedroom to retrieve an envelope from the dressing table. "Vittoria left this for me today."

Bérenger opened the envelope and removed the three eight-by-ten photographs from within. They were all pictures of a beautiful little boy, a toddler just over two years old. Bérenger caught his breath as he went through the photos one by one. The boy in the photographs, with his long, curly dark hair and his blue-green eyes, looked like a tiny version of Bérenger Sinclair.

"You've never seen him." Maureen realized as she watched his unexpected, emotional response to the photos.

"No." His voice was choked as he looked at photos of his son for the first time.

"What are you going to do?"

Bérenger was stunned into silence for a moment. The photos of Dante had instantly diminished his previously held determination. Nothing could have prepared him for the impact of seeing this perfect, tiny version of himself. What stirred in him as he gazed at the child in the photograph was something close to grief. In that moment, he realized that his life had changed indelibly. He had lost all control of it. Dante was his, and he would not deny him.

Bérenger's voice cracked as he ultimately replied. "He's my son, Maureen—just look at him. I don't need a DNA test when I have eyes. And . . ."

"And what?"

"He is a child of the prophecy. I don't have to tell you what that means, and I cannot turn my back on the importance of that. And there is something more, something you do not know yet."

Maureen steadied herself in preparation for his explanation. She was shaking. Her entire world was crumbling around her, and she was certain that the final wrecking ball was about to shatter whatever was left of her castles in the air.

"The prophecy. Maureen, there is another piece to it. It is rarely recited because the event of which it speaks has never happened before. It is called the Second Prince." He paused to breathe for a moment before reciting it for her.

> *The Son of Man shall himself return*
> *as the Second Prince.*
> *When the time has come and the stars align,*
> *a Poet Prince will be born to a Poet Prince*
> *and become once again the King of Kings.*

Maureen, so familiar with the power of prophecy as it had worked within her own life, was terrified. She did not wish to take the risk of misinterpreting what he was trying to say to her. After a terrible silence between them, she asked in a whisper, "What, exactly, are you saying to me, Bérenger?"

He took both her hands in his, grasping them so tightly that she flinched, as the tears welled in his eyes. "No Poet Prince has ever been born to another. It has never happened in the history of our people that a father and son both shared all the qualities of the prophecy. Therefore the Second Prince . . ."

"Is the Second Coming." Maureen finished the sentence with a dull finality, in a voice she did not recognize as her own.

"Maureen, I know it sounds crazy, but think of what we have all been through together. We have seen so much that is impossible. The prophecies have never failed. If there is even a possibility that Dante is . . ." Bérenger paused. He was not even able to say it out loud yet, so disturbing was the concept.

He continued, "If Dante is truly special, then he needs me. And not just to visit him occasionally or to send him money, but to be his father. He will need constant guidance, and he will also need someone to keep his mother's ambitions in check. That will require my constant presence."

Maureen felt the lump burning like a hot coal in the back of her throat as she repeated the question she knew she would never want to hear answered.

"What are you going to do?"

"The right thing. I'm sorry, Maureen. I am so sorry. But I have to prove myself worthy of this position that I hold. I have to pass this test." He shed the tears he had been fighting, then said in a voice that seemed to come from somewhere else, "Perhaps it is our obligation to be noble before it is our obligation to be happy."

Maureen rose as if in slow motion, trying to grasp how a moment so blissful had turned into a nightmare in a matter of seconds. In one instant, they were affirming the undying and eternal nature of their love for each other; in the next, Bérenger was dumping her for a life with Vittoria and their child.

She choked back a sob as she turned from him, found her feet, and ran from the terrace.

Arezzo, Tuscany
July 21, 1463

ALESSANDRO DI FILIPEPI was feeling very grateful for his life. At the age of eighteen, he had been apprenticed to the greatest artists in Italy and was proving to be the equal of anyone painting in Florence. Perhaps more important, he had been adopted into the Medici family in everything but name, living and working under the roof of Piero and Lucrezia de' Medici, and acting as an elder brother to the Poet Prince himself and the younger Giuliano. Lorenzo and Sandro had become inseparable, and it was with great excitement that both of them accompanied Cosimo on this pilgrimage to Sansepolcro, the spiritual home of the Order of the Holy Sepulcher. Cosimo was weak, but he had rallied with the idea—his own—of bringing the boys to Sansepolcro. It was likely to be his last excursion, as the gout made it nearly impossible for him to mount a horse. He rode his gentle white mule at a slow pace beside the equally challenged Fra Francesco. They were perfect company for each other on the journey. And while the boys were itching to move faster, both revered Cosimo and the Master far too much to rush them.

The date was not random, of course; nothing ever was with the Order and those who orchestrated it. Tomorrow, July twenty-second, was the feast day of Mary Magdalene, and it would be celebrated by the official confraternity that carried her name. Lorenzo and Sandro would witness the procession in honor of the woman that both revered as one of their great spiritual leaders. They would follow the feast with a week of intensive study at the hands of the Master and in the presence of the great relics of the Order upon which Sansepolcro had been founded.

But that was the future. Today, the boys were with Cosimo and Fra Francesco on their way to meet with the official artist in residence of the Order: the great Piero della Francesca. This was the source of Sandro's awe and gratitude. Piero della Francesca was the greatest living "angelic," discovered as a boy personally by Fra Francesco; he had been predicted by the Magi and born in the strange and holy little town of Sansepolcro. Piero was a fresco artist without equal, and he was finishing a cycle within the ancient church of San Francesco, the home of the Order in Arezzo. The elaborate frescoes, floor to ceiling and covering an enormous chapel behind the altar, depicted the legend of the True Cross and the meeting of King Solomon and the Queen of Sheba. For members of the Order, this latter was the holiest of stories. It was from the union of Solomon and Sheba that some of the greatest teachings in human history had been handed down, teachings of love and wisdom that were thoroughly transformational. The Order preached that many of the secret teachings that Jesus shared with his followers had been passed through the holy branches of the Davidic lineage, of which Jesus was the heir.

The Order's sacred practice of *hieros-gamos*, the understanding that God is found in the bridal chamber when a man and woman are unified in a place of trust and consciousness, was traced to the union of Solomon and Sheba. Indeed the Old Testament Song of Songs, the ultimate poem of life-affirming passion and sacred union, was attributed to Solomon.

The Master spoke to the boys as they entered the Romanesque

church, built here in honor of Saint Francis of Assisi in the thirteenth century.

"Although we look at the prophecy of the Poet Prince as a Christian concept now, as the coming of men who will restore and protect the true teachings of Christ, it was not always so. The prophecies are ancient. They are timeless. They are from God, and they relate to men and women across time and distance who will come and do God's work—whether they be Jew or Christian or Muslim or Hindu or pagan. It matters not. Solomon and David were both Poet Princes. Think on this for a moment: David wrote Psalms, his son Solomon wrote hundreds of poems, including our most exalted Song of Songs, and both changed the world in their own way. Jesus was indeed a Poet Prince, but he was by no means the first. He was just one in a long line of them and the most exceptional of them all, no doubt, but certainly not the first or the only—or the last." He smiled at Lorenzo.

He stopped the boys, as they were in the center of the nave now. "Look up, toward the altar. Pause here to view something very important that our Piero has created. Before you allow your eye to see the magnificence of the frescoes, look first on either side of the altar."

On both sides of the huge altar space were long, narrow columns. Painted in a twinned manner and perfectly matched were larger-than-life portraits of Jesus on the left and Mary Magdalene on the right. They had been painted perfectly as equals, but also clearly as a pair.

"The portraits of true beloveds. Equals under God," came a soft male voice from behind them.

Piero della Francesca, holding a paintbrush and covered in pigments, smiled kindly at the boys as he explained his work. "I did not create the original portraits of Our Lord and Our Lady. They were done by another native of Arezzo, a great painter who preceded me here, called Luca Spinello. Sadly his work has deteriorated, but I have restored it. I can only hope to have done him justice. He was a genius, who learned from Giotto." Piero nodded toward Fra Francesco as he continued. "Perhaps I should say that he learned to paint from Giotto. He learned all else from our Master."

Piero paused to greet Cosimo with the respect due to the Medici patriarch. While a native of the southernmost regions of Tuscany, Piero della Francesca had trained extensively in Florence under the patronage of Cosimo. While the Medici family wanted to keep Piero in Florence, they understood the Master's need for him in Arezzo and Sansepolcro. It was fitting that as the official scribe of the Order, he should establish lasting works of art in this holy region to preserve the teachings.

This would be part of Sandro and Lorenzo's training over the next week. They would gain a greater understanding of what Piero had accomplished with his unequaled storytelling through fresco painting. Arezzo was the testing ground for these types of "hiding in plain sight" teachings for the Order. Now it would be up to the Florentines to expand on this approach, to bring these same types of powerful, symbolic masterpieces to a larger and more difficult audience. The Order was taking bold steps to conquer Florence through the Medici and their angelic army of artists. If they could achieve their goals in Florence, they would then expand throughout Italy—and ultimately look toward Rome.

Together, the powerful brotherhood created by Lorenzo and Sandro would begin the revolution into a golden age of art and education. The mission was the restoration of the true teachings of the early Christians through epic works of art.

Ficino was fond of reminding his students, when they became a little too inflated with the importance of their mission, that they didn't start it. They were the blessed heirs to a grand fortune, earned by the blood and sacrifice of the astonishing men and women who came before them. He quoted the great scholar and leader of the Order in the twelfth century, Bernard of Chartres:

"Remember, we are but dwarves standing on the shoulders of giants."

"REMEMBER, WE ARE but dwarves standing on the shoulders of giants."

Peter Healy often quoted Bernard of Chartres, keen as he was to remember the greatness of those who came before and gave everything, so that we would not be in the darkness. But the quote seemed particularly applicable as he stood before the statues depicting *Cosimo Pater Patriae* and *Lorenzo il Magnifico* adjacent to the Uffizi Gallery.

Peter and Maureen had walked along the river before making the turn toward the Uffizi, one of the greatest art museums in the world. The approach to this treasury of Renaissance art was lined with the statues of the artists who shaped Florence: painters, writers, architects. They passed Donatello and Leonardo, and up toward the far end of the entrance toward the piazza was the statue of Cosimo, looking very wise and surprisingly warm, standing alongside his grandson. The statue of Lorenzo was equally well crafted and alive. Il Magnifico was depicted with his hand on a bust of Minerva, the goddess of wisdom.

Maureen stood before the stone image of Lorenzo on the pedestal and studied it for a moment, silently. A chill ran through her body as she looked at his face; it was sculpted with the strange feature he was famous for, the nose flattened at the bridge. Yet despite the fact that he was often referred to as homely or even ugly, Maureen was struck by how absolutely beautiful he was. There was extraordinary nobility about him, palpable even from this piece of stone, which had been fashioned hundreds of years after his death.

He was, without question, magnificent.

She shivered, although the sun was well on its way to creating a scorching May day in Tuscany.

Peter saw the shudder. "What is it?"

Maureen swallowed hard, feeling choked up suddenly. "It . . . it looks like him. I mean, I have seen portraits of him and had no reaction, other than to think he was odd-looking. But this . . . this is Lorenzo. It's as if he is trapped in that stone. The image of him. Perfect."

Maureen was transfixed on Lorenzo, trying to get a grasp on how she was feeling. "I can't explain it, really, but when I look at this man I feel utterly committed to him. Like I would follow him into a battle against the devil himself. There is nothing I wouldn't do for him. But that's not the only meaning of the word 'committed' that I am feeling. He was committed. To his cause, to his mission. And that is what inspired such loyalty from so many. Lorenzo would never ask anyone to do something he wasn't prepared to do himself. I look at this and I just *know* that."

"He is one of the giants upon whose shoulders we stand," Maureen added, reflecting in that moment about the meaning of Poet Princes, commitment, and duty.

*

Maureen and Peter entered the Uffizi, walking up the massive flights of stairs, which challenged even the most physically fit tourists, all of whom panted at the top as they reached the ticket takers.

Maureen noticed another bust of Lorenzo de' Medici to the right, just at the entrance to the painting gallery. This sculpture was also a powerful portrayal of a great man. It was strange that as she stood before all these images of Lorenzo, she felt as if she was looking at someone she knew well. While she had connected to the subjects she had written about before, it was usually in the dream state or when she was deeply immersed in her writing. It had never occurred in such a visceral, fully conscious way.

Looking at images of Lorenzo de' Medici made Maureen feel as if she were in mourning over her lost love.

She noticed that Destino, who was waiting just ahead of them with Tammy and Roland, was now watching her. He gestured for her to stand with him, gave a little half smile, and said, "Once you come inside, you will understand far more than ever before. This is an art museum, yet it is also a library of most important volumes. The walls of the Uffizi contain some of the greatest secrets in all of human history."

Borgo Sansepolcro, Tuscany
July 22, 1463

THE OFFICIALLY SANCTIONED legend of the foundation of Sansepolcro states that the town was formed by two saints, one called Santo Egidio, who arrived with Santo Arcano, who returned to Tuscany in 934 from the Holy Land. With them they brought important relics from the Holy Sepulcher and they built the first oratory here to protect the relics. It was a strangely remote place to bring relics of such grand importance and meant to be venerated by the Christian faithful throughout Italy.

Or was it? The secret legend of Sansepolcro said precisely the opposite—that this tiny town tucked away in the southernmost hills of Tuscany was chosen precisely because it was remote and difficult to find. It would be easy to defend and protect, a place only those who knew it existed—and what it contained—would know how to access. And the nature of the holy relics brought from Jerusalem had never been exposed to the public.

It was a fitting place to learn secrets, and Lorenzo and Sandro were both vibrating with the energy of the promise that awaited them. They were in the home of Piero della Francesca, who was examining the processional banner that would be carried at the front of the parade tonight.

"Isn't she magnificent?" Piero shook his head as he stood before the life-sized image of Mary Magdalene, majestic, beautiful, and enthroned. Lovingly cradled in her lap was a crucifix, but it was by no means the focal point of the banner. "I think she is one of the most important pieces of art ever created. No one has ever captured Our Lady so perfectly. The great Luca Spinello Aretino created her for the Confraternity of Mary Magdalene, which as you likely know is a public profile of the Order in this part of Tuscany. Sometimes I just sit before her for inspiration. Look at her face, the expression of serenity—and yet power. There is nothing penitent about this Magdalene! No, this is the portrait of a queen. Our queen."

"Do all in your confraternity wear hoods such as this?" Lorenzo was curious now, as the men worshipping at Mary Magdalene's feet appeared to be penitents. And yet the Order was very clear that Magdalena was not to be viewed in such a way. It diminished her true status and was an invention of the Catholic Church.

"Allegory, my brothers. And important for you to remember as you paint, Sandro," Piero explained patiently. His calm, measured manner made him a most natural teacher. "Spinello, and all the great master artists, used layer upon layer of symbolism to keep our message clear. See the jars on their sleeves? A reminder of who Magdalena really is. She is the woman who anoints Jesus because she is bestowing his kingship upon him, and because she is his wife. She is exalted. But they are hooded to remind us that the truth of her is still veiled, and that it is still heresy for us to identify ourselves as her followers in public.

"Now, see here where the backs of their robes are open, as if they were going to flog themselves in an act of self-mutilation? That is a reference to what our Spinello has created on the reverse of the banner."

He moved the boys around to see the opposite side of the banner. It was a sequence of the flagellation, with Christ tied to a post and being beaten by two Roman soldiers.

"The flagellation is allegory as well, one which Spinello uses to great effect, and I hope to emulate. The message was created by him while working with the Master. They determined that the flagellation was an appropriate symbolic representation of what happened to Jesus every time we denied the truth of his life and his teachings. He is tortured all over again. The true flagellation of Christ was the disinheritance of his family and all that they had to give to the world.

"The same is echoed on the front of the banner with the 'penitent' robes, which provide space for the whip to come down in the act of self-mutilation. The message here is that we are hurting ourselves by not acknowledging this beautiful queen for what she came here to teach us. Beautiful, isn't it?"

Sandro Botticelli stood before the red-robed Magdalene in awe of her beauty and overwhelmed by the rich layers of symbolism that the artists before him had worked so hard to integrate into their work. But Piero wasn't finished.

"Sandro, I see that you are as transfixed by her as I am from the perspective of a painter. You stare at her in awe and wonder why she evokes such emotion from you, aside from her obvious beauty. Do you know why?"

Sandro hadn't been a student of Fra Filippo Lippi and Andrea della Verrocchio for nothing. He nodded with a smile as he gave what he knew was the correct answer. "Because she was created using the process of infusion."

"Well done, brother. She was indeed. And Spinello's approach to infusion was very, very special. If you want your madonnas and goddesses to leap from the work and tell their stories as this one does, you shall need to learn this technique. I don't suppose you have any interest in taking that lesson today?"

They all laughed, knowing the answer. Lorenzo prepared to take his leave and allow the two artists to get on with the more specific nature of the lesson. He was going to meet his grandfather and the Master, to make final preparations for the night's festivities.

*

A low drone of chanting swirled in the darkness as the solemn procession wound its way through the narrow, cobbled streets of Borgo Sansepolcro. The men who marched in the procession carried torches. They were covered head to toe in their robes, with separate hoods that covered their heads completely. The robes were pristine in their snow white fabric. On the sleeves of each robe was an emblem, embroidered in scarlet thread—the alabaster jar to symbolize their devotion to Maria Magdalena and the Order.

The procession wound through the streets. At the center of the parade, two hooded figures carried the majestic Spinello banner, painted with the life-sized image of the Magdalene enthroned. She was truly depicted with grandeur as a female aspect of God and was cheered as such as she was paraded through these streets.

"Madonna Magdalena! Madonna Magdalena!"

Lorenzo watched the procession with his grandfather. For all his youthful excitement, it was a solemn occasion for him. Cosimo was dying, and Lorenzo knew that this would be the last major event he would ever have the opportunity to attend with the old man. It was why he had elected not to march in the procession with Sandro—because he did not want to leave Cosimo during the sacred procession. It was something he wanted to share with his most beloved grandfather, a memory he wanted to keep forever.

Lorenzo was moved by the emotions running through him now: grief for the pending loss, which would shatter the world as he knew it; deep religious devotion for the woman they called their queen. These things combined into the pledge that Lorenzo made to Cosimo that night. Tears streamed down his face now as he watched the procession approach them. There was a light in his eyes as he spoke his promise aloud.

"I will not fail you, Grandfather. Nothing will stop me. I will not fail our Lord or our Lady, and I will not fail the legacy of the Medici."

Cosimo put an arm around him and pulled him close for a moment, realizing as well that this was an ultimate moment for them. "I know that, Lorenzo. I know that more than I have ever known anything. You will not fail because it is your destiny to succeed. You will be the savior of us all. You will be the greatest Poet Prince that has ever lived. You already are."

The banner now came to stand before them, and Lorenzo saw that Sandro was marching directly behind it. Their eyes met, and Sandro began to gesture wildly for Lorenzo to join him and march in the rest of the procession. Lorenzo looked up at his grandfather, who was smiling at him.

"Go!" He pushed Lorenzo playfully toward where Sandro was positioned. "Go show your devotion to our Queen of Compassion by marching in her parade!"

Lorenzo smiled back and moved through the crowd to reach Sandro and march beside him. As they began to move forward again, one of the torch bearers came closer, illuminating the rear of the banner. Looking up at the Spinello masterpiece depicting the flagellation of Christ, Lorenzo noticed something he had not seen earlier that day. The light had caught the image of one of the Roman centurions just right. Luca Spinello had painted a jagged scar across the left side of his face.

*

Colombina.

She was my first muse. The first real woman who inspired me to paint her over and over again. She was beauty in its active principle—a force to be dealt with and never underestimated. From the time she was sixteen to now, I have never known a woman with such fortitude. And yet . . . she is Beauty as Fortitude. It is a strength that is not aggressive, but rather it flows from her goodness. When the history of these golden days is written, I fear that Colombina's name will not be recorded in the annals. She will be like so many women before her who have been lost in this cycle of history where, somewhere, somehow, the women were abandoned. In that way, and others, she wears the exalted sandals of the holy bride, our Lady, Magdalena.

Half of our spiritual nature and legacy as human beings has been eradicated by the omissions of history.

But I will not allow Colombina to be lost. I have painted her, using infusion techniques, to preserve her unique strength and dedication to our cause—and to our prince—so that the world may one day know her.

Thus it was a great day filled with a delicious sense of synchronicity when I was chosen for the commission to paint the personification of Fortitude.

The judges who make up the great Tribunal of the Merchants have commissioned paintings of the seven virtues to decorate the walls of their courtroom, hoping that such art will inspire them to make wise judgments as they preside over the squabbles of their trade, small and large. The commission for all seven of the paintings went to Piero del Pollaiuolo originally. While he is often a competent painter, his name indicates that he is descended from chicken farmers. There are certainly moments when I look upon his work and think that perhaps we would be better served to have more chickens on the table than paintings from Pollaiuolo.

Some would say I am too harsh. Yet as fate would have it, Piero of the Poultry was unable to deliver all seven of the paintings. I was called in—by the grace of God and the Medici—to execute the seventh virtue, the one he was not inspired enough to attempt: Fortitude.

And so it was that Colombina modeled officially and formally, sitting in that position that so inspires me, with her head tilted on her long neck, with her lovely face, so wise beyond its years, in contemplation of the great tasks awaiting her. Having Colombina in front of me, I found it was most important to capture her exquisite eye color, which I was determined to duplicate. The light was reflecting off her gown that day, which was a golden velvet, and her eyes were the color of amber in the sun. And yet, as we always do, we laughed so often and so hard that I could not always hold the brush steady enough to paint her.

In honor of our Order, and in a reference to the great Piero della Francesca, I executed the draping of her red gown in a manner similar to his Arezzo Magdalene. It was subtle enough that only those of us with eyes to see would understand the nod, but I find great amusement in such things—as does Lorenzo.

Lorenzo was so delighted by the likeness of Colombina that he threatened to commit constant acts of offense as a merchant just so he would be brought before the tribunal and have the opportunity to view the painting! I told him it would be far simpler if he would commission me to create a greater work for him.

What began as a joke between me and my brother of the spirit evolved into a serious discussion of what, in fact, the ultimate painting would be—the perfect collaboration between art and wisdom, beauty and energy. We contemplated the possibilities then, excited by the ideas as they began to expand and spiral between us. It was a discussion that led to the greatest painting I have ever laid brush and heart to, the perfect depiction of le temps revient . . .

But that is another story for another day, as it deserves its very own telling.

I remain,
Alessandro di Filipepi, known as "Botticelli"

FROM *THE SECRET MEMOIRS OF SANDRO BOTTICELLI*

THEY ALL MOVED together through the halls of the Uffizi, Destino leading the way with his funny, ancient gait, Maureen by his side, listening closely, with Peter, Tammy, and Roland never far behind. The museum was overwhelming in terms of the sheer volume of extraordinary Italian masterpieces collected in one place. It was laid out according to epoch, starting with the Middle Ages gallery, where an enormous Madonna by Cimabue greeted the visitors in the primary room. From there, it was a labyrinth of chambers and corridors, each leading to the next era in art.

"I am very sorry to rush you through this, as each piece in this museum deserves careful consideration," Destino said. "But we have a very specific destination for a reason, and very particular paintings within that destination as well."

He brought them through the final room representing the Middle Ages until they reached a chamber dominated by seven similar paintings, each of them larger-than-life portraits of an enthroned, majestic woman.

"The virtues." Maureen recognized them immediately from the iconography of each. Justice carried her sword; Faith held a chalice. But it was clear that six of the paintings were identical in terms of style and execution. The seventh virtue was the standout, utterly different in essence from her six sisters.

Tammy whistled as she looked around the room, then sang a song from her childhood. "Uh, 'One of these things is not like the other.' "

Of the seven paintings in the room, six had been painted by the same artist. And while they were lovely in their own way, they were eclipsed in total by the seventh.

The painting of Fortitude shone like the Hope diamond set among agates in the rough. This artist had used more vibrant color and elaborate detail, and there was a grace in his execution that was absolutely breathtaking to behold. But what really elevated the painting was the model. The young woman depicted was an extraordinary combination of ethereal beauty and steel-in-the-spine strength. She was stunning.

"Botticelli's first commission," Destino explained, pointing at the painting of Fortitude. "He was determined to prove his output was of an infinitely higher quality than that of the artists who were getting all the commissions in Florence. He threw himself into this work. Poor Pollaiuolo. When he saw how the light of Colombina as Fortitude obscured all six of his paintings, he went into a deep depression and didn't paint for months."

"That's Colombina?" Maureen stood before the image, breathless. Destino had prepared her with the stories of Colombina and Lorenzo as children, beginning over dinner last night and lasting well into the early hours of the morning. Maureen was enthralled with their story and that of Sandro interacting with them as one of their siblings. The Renaissance was coming to life in a way she had never imagined—so human, so real. It was easy to think of these astonishing characters from history as iconic, while forgetting that they were flesh-and-blood humans who laughed and loved and lost. Destino was changing history for her in a most delightful and unexpected way.

"That is most definitely Colombina," Destino said, his eyes tearing up as he looked at the painting. "And Sandro did what he set out to do. He captured her. And while he painted her many times—the most famous version of her awaits you in the next salon—this is the portrait that makes me miss her above all."

Maureen stood transfixed before Colombina. The woman was already "talking" to her. She could feel herself slipping deeper into that state in which she merged with one of her subjects. She began to experience what Colombina felt during this time in her life when Sandro captured her on canvas. It was a beautiful time but also painful. She felt love but also deep heartache. Maureen's own recent pain blended with the strains of Colombina's that reached out to her across time and space, through the magic of Botticelli's art. Maureen knew that she was only just beginning to understand the complexities of this "little dove" who was the unsung muse of the greatest men of the Renaissance.

Maureen realized further that her destiny was somehow intertwined with the beautiful yet enigmatic woman who called to her from the canvas.

Careggi
Summer 1464

"THE TIME RETURNS."

Fra Francesco started the lesson with that statement, delivering it today to Lorenzo, Sandro, and Colombina. He was particularly happy to be teaching when the three of them were together. There was a harmony, a sense of family and community that occurred when these three spirits occupied the same space. They had a love for each other that was beautiful to behold. Yet they also challenged each other in a way that only those who completely trust each other are able to do.

Ficino was their primary teacher, drilling them in Greek grammar and quizzing them relentlessly on the allegories and lessons of Plato, but they all thrived under the Master of the Order of the Holy Sepulcher when he came to present a teaching. It was on these days that Colombina made certain that she was able to find a way out of the house to meet Lorenzo and join the lessons.

As their teacher, Fra Francesco had to be particularly creative and bold when he had all three of them. It was his greatest and most joyous challenge, which was why he chose the core of the Order's philosophy for their lesson today.

"Now, my children, we start. Give me 'the time returns' in the language of the troubadours."

"*Le temps revient,*" Lorenzo repeated in French. While his French wasn't fluent, he had learned a fair amount while reading troubadour poetry and studying the ideals of courtly love.

The Master nodded, then expounded on the theme. "'The time returns' is our most precious teaching because it has many layers, and each of those layers applies to the different type of love. For all of us, it is an understanding that earthly love returns ultimately to divine love, and then divine love recycles again to give us the gift of earthly life. This is the cycle of the soul."

Whereas Colombina and Lorenzo took notes, Sandro sketched through the lessons. This is how he learned, how he remembered, and ultimately how he would express these teachings through paint. As the Master talked, Sandro was drawing a landscape with characters that moved in a type of circle—cyclical, moving from heaven to earth and then back again.

"Now, shall I teach you something that you do not yet know? 'The time returns' pertains to the series of incarnations, from the beginning of time to the end of time, in which souls will incarnate in the quest to be reunited with their 'family of spirit,' and specifically with their one true mate, who, as it is said in the Book of Love, is 'their own soul's twin.'"

Colombina asked, "Master, are we a family of spirit?"

"Do you believe that we are, my dear?"

She nodded. "I love my blood family, of course, but it is different. When I am with Lorenzo and Sandro and Master Ficino and you, I feel something very deep and beautiful. I love you all so much, and I know in my heart that we are a true family."

" 'The only thing sweeter than union is reunion,' " Lorenzo quoted from the Book of Love.

"Yes, my son. And it is clear to any with a heart that this is the truth for the two of you. And as one of the great troubadour poets once wrote, such love is created *'Dès le début du temps, jusqu'à la fin du temps.'* Say that with me now."

He instructed them again in the French, and they repeated it until they all had the pronunciation down. And from that day forward, the words of an unknown troubadour who had once sung songs of perfect love for his own lady fair became the truth of Lorenzo and Colombina's bond:

From the beginning of time, until the end of time.

*

Sandro later showed Colombina and Lorenzo the sketches he had made during their very special lesson. The first was of Colombina: he had captured her head tilted just so on her beautifully long neck as she contemplated the lesson. He had carefully sketched her lovely long fingers as they intertwined around her pen.

"It is a position I have seen you take before, and one that I have attempted to paint from memory," Sandro said. As a masterful artist with an eye for sheer beauty, he adored Colombina as the muse that she had become. Indeed, she was a muse for all of them; in each she inspired a different aspect of love as taught by the Order. For Lorenzo she was both *eros* and *agape*, inspiring love of the heart, soul, and body. For Sandro, she was the muse of beauty in its active principle, a force, like Venus herself, that transforms everything around it. But she was also his sister of spirit, the essence of the love known as *philia*. For the Master of the Order of the Holy Sepulcher, she was becoming a special muse in the model of the bloodline women who had come before—the prophetesses and scribes who would not only preserve the true teachings but contribute to them in a new world. And she was his daughter, who therefore inspired the love in him known as *storge*.

Together, teacher and pupils shared the love that transforms the world through action and compassion, which was called *eunoia*.

"You are the ultimate muse, Colombina. You are all things to all of us. You are our Magdalena." Sandro kissed her on the cheek. He rarely showed this softer side to anyone, but his artist's soul had been very moved while watching her in the lesson today.

Lorenzo was teary watching both of them. He took the drawing from Sandro and admired it closely. "May I keep this? It is beautiful."

"Afraid not, brother." Sandro snatched the drawing back. "I shall be using this as inspiration for the face of future madonnas and goddesses of fortitude. But I assure you, I will paint our Colombina many times—in this pose and in others."

Careggi
1464

"LORENZO, WE HAVE an enemy."

Colombina had come to meet Lorenzo in the usual place, where they came together to travel to Ficino's villa for lessons. But he could see that she was not herself today as he rode up on Morello. Lorenzo dismounted and put his arms around her as she buried her face in his shoulder and began to cry.

"My love, what is it? What has happened?"

She was hiccuping a bit with the sobbing. Lorenzo would have found it quite adorable under other circumstances, but at the moment he was completely preoccupied with identifying and weeding out the enemy.

"Someone—I cannot begin to guess who it may be—has gone to my father and told him about us."

"Told him what?"

The hiccuping resumed, more intense now. "Oh, Lorenzo, it is horrible. My father asked me today if I had given myself to you completely. Can you imagine hearing such a question from one's own father? He was told that you would make me your whore just to prove the Medici might, just to show that you could do anything and have anything you desire."

"What did you tell him?"

"I told him the truth—no! I have not given myself to you completely, although there is nothing more in the world that I long to do. But Lorenzo, he will forbid me to see you anymore. He is sending me into the city to stay, so that I cannot be tempted by you and our forest. What will we do? I cannot bear to be without you and Sandro and the Maestro . . ."

He hugged her hard and allowed her to cry, stroking her hair as he soothed her. "It's all right, Colombina. You will never be without me. I will think of something."

At the moment, he was at a loss for what that something might be. But he wasn't born into the Medici family for nothing.

*

"Lorenzo, it is out of the question." Piero de' Medici was firm in his assertions to his son. Madonna Lucrezia looked on, distressed, as the confrontation continued. "We cannot make enemies out of the Donati family. They are powerful and revered, not only in Florence but throughout Italy."

"Then allow me to marry her."

"It is impossible, my son." Piero was exasperated. He too was a Medici and as such did not like to lose in any endeavor, and this was one they were sure to lose. "The Donati will not even consider it. Do you not think I raised it as an option? He all but spit on me. We are merchant class to them and always will be. They will not allow their daughter to marry any man who does not carry a noble name. They are narrow people of the old ways."

"She is an Expected One," Lorenzo pressed his case. "And you know what the Libro Rosso says. 'When the Expected One and the Poet Prince are reunited, they shall alter the course of the world in their coming together. Just as Solomon and Sheba, they shall discover the secrets of God and man and work tirelessly in their mission to bring heaven to earth.'"

"Her family does not believe that. They do not even understand what that is, and if we attempted to explain it, they would be at the doors of Careggi with torches demanding our heads as heretics. Think, Lorenzo, think. We have too much to lose, and not just for ourselves. We must protect the Order and our mission. We cannot risk those things even if they mean sacrificing your happiness."

"Then what use are the teachings of the Order?"

"Lorenzo!" Madonna Lucrezia could not hide her shock. She had never seen him be disrespectful of their spiritual traditions.

"I want an answer, Mother. If the Book of Love teaches that Colombina and I were made for each other by God at the dawn of time, and that what God has put together no man can separate, then why? Why are we being separated?"

Piero attempted to answer. "The teachings of Our Lord also tell us to love our neighbors above all, and the Donati are our neighbors. They threaten war upon us and all we hold dear if we do not honor them by keeping you away from their child. And so we must."

Lucrezia tried a softer tactic. "Lorenzo, I understand that you believe the Donati girl is your soul's own twin. Young love can feel very strong. But—"

"I *know* she is my soul's own twin, Mother. And she knows it. And Fra Francesco knows it. So someone needs to make me understand why, through time, so much true love has been kept apart. Why are all the great love stories about pain and separation? I don't want to be one of those stories. I want to change them. I want to shift the model for the universe. Isn't that what I am meant to do? Isn't that why I was born under this gilded prophecy that imprisons me each day of my life?"

"Oh, Lorenzo! How can you say that?"

"Because it's true, Mother."

"Sometimes, my son, it is our obligation to be noble before it is our obligation to be happy. Keeping peace with the Donatis affects every single family in Florence. We cannot return to the blood feuds that we have spent so many years trying to eliminate. If we go to war, the city will be divided and there will be bloodshed and strife among Florentines for generations to come. You and I both know that we cannot allow that to happen."

They all stopped talking when they saw that Cosimo had appeared at the doorway, looking gray and deathly. And yet even though he was days away from dying, he stood unaided and his voice was strong. He dismissed Piero and Lucrezia kindly but firmly, indicating that he desired to speak to his grandson privately. He moved Lorenzo to the settee and sat beside him. His bones cracked as he did so, but he did not seem to notice. As always, Cosimo was singularly focused when he had a mission.

"Lorenzo, I want you to think of some of the great leaders of the Order from our history. The great Matilda was secretly married to the pope! They could not be together publicly, ever, throughout their eventful and important lives. And yet they found ways to nurture their love away from the eyes of the world."

"What are you saying, Grandfather? That I should make Colombina my mistress just as her father fears?"

"I am saying that true love finds a way, Lorenzo. I ache for you, my boy. It breaks my heart to know that you may never understand real happiness and contentment because you cannot be with the woman you believe was made for you by God. So I am saying that you must find a way to be with her. And she with you. And you must look outside the rules that society has created for you. God didn't create these rules. Men did. The Church did. And whose rules will you choose to follow? God's? Or man's? You say you want to break the outmoded patterns and create a new model? Then do it. That is part of your destiny, boy."

Cosimo paused for a moment to catch his breath, contemplating for a moment before continuing. "I realize today that I have never told you the story of my own Magdalena, the beautiful woman who is Carlo's mother."

Carlo was Cosimo's illegitimate son, born of his scandalous liaison with a Circassian slave girl. Cosimo's wife, Contessina, had taken the boy into her household and treated him with great kindness so that he could be raised as a Medici and carry the family name. She had never once complained or been seen to treat Carlo poorly. But it was an un-spoken law within the household that Carlo's origins were not dis-cussed. The fact that he was darker of skin and eyes than the other boys was a constant reminder that he came from a different origin.

"I do not speak of it within the family, as it is a great upset to your grandmother. But it is time for you to know the truth, my boy. Carlo's mother is my greatest joy, and my greatest pain. She is the love of my life; she is my perfect mate. And yet she is a foreign-born slave whom I can never acknowledge. Tell me, Lorenzo, what was God thinking? Why would God create someone for me so perfect, and then make it impossible for us to be together?"

Lorenzo was stunned. He had thought he understood Cosimo more deeply than anyone else, and yet he was discovering now that there was an entire layer to his grandfather's life, and character, that he had never suspected.

"I met her while staying in Lucca on a negotiation many years ago. She was a house slave for a noble couple there. While she was the most beautiful thing I had ever seen, I was relieved to see that the man of the house did not seem to notice. I believe, at the end of the day, that he preferred men to women. As a result, the girl had never been abused by a man, at least not since she had been sold into this family. She was well treated and of good humor. And as she had been in Tuscany for a few years, her command of the language was good. Excellent even. I realized quickly that this was no ignorant slave. She had a mind and a spirit for learning unlike any I had ever seen in a woman. There was a humor that flashed in her eyes and a wisdom that was beyond her years and her origins.

"I stayed in that house for a week but later continued to find reasons to go back there. It was after doing this for several months that I realized I was hopelessly, completely, and utterly in love. Worse, I also understood that this woman was 'my own soul's twin' as is spoken of by the Order, and taught in the Book of Love. But how? Why? And I realized, ultimately, that it didn't matter. God had put her here and I had found her, and now it was up to me to determine whether or not I could be with her. And the rules of the game—the noblesse, the politics, all of it—said that I could not. I was married to Contessina. I had children. And I was Cosimo de' Medici."

He paused to let the enormity of these revelations sink in for Lorenzo before continuing.

"But what God has put together, let no man separate. And so, I purchased the girl from the family in Lucca for three times the price she would have been worth on the open market. I bought her a house in Fiesole, and I installed her there as my mistress, where she is to this day. And I refused to refer to her by the name of a slave and began to call her Maria Magdalena, as she was my Queen of Compassion. When the strife of Florentine politics closed in on me, I could escape to my Magdalena and find comfort.

"It killed me to take baby Carlo away from her. Do you not think that she wanted to raise our son? But she also wanted what was best for him and knew that giving him to the family was the greatest gift she could bestow upon him. And so, Lorenzo, my Magdalena and I have known great pain and suffering, and yet . . . I wouldn't trade my moments with her for anything in the world. She is my muse, and my greatest love. And one day, when the time returns, we will be together in a different way, if God wills it and it serves the mission."

Lorenzo was speechless for a moment. He chewed on his lip as he considered everything Cosimo had just revealed before asking, "What would you do if you were in my place, Grandfather?"

Cosimo's answer was quick and utterly without hesitation. "I would find her a husband."

"What?" Lorenzo practically screeched his response. Cosimo looked annoyed.

"Stop thinking like a broken-hearted boy and start thinking like a prince. Like a Medici prince. You must outplay your enemy. Yours must always be the strategy that looks a year ahead—two years, five years. The Donati will not allow you to see their daughter, and as long as she is under her father's control, he may dictate every step that she takes. This is a fact. How do you change that fact? By altering the circumstances to suit you better. Parental control is nonexistent once she becomes a married woman. A Florentine matron, particularly one of the Donati's social stature, can make her own decisions about how she spends her time. And while she will not be able to frolic with you in Careggi any longer, there is no reason that she cannot become the closest of all friends with the noble Gianfigliazza family. Indeed, that lovely Ginevra is always putting on some kind of charity event, which is a very acceptable pastime for a young, rich married woman the likes of Lucrezia Donati. And this would require her to spend ample time at the Antica Torre in Santa Trinità. Are you hearing me, my boy?"

Lorenzo nodded. He didn't like it, but it was beginning to sink in. He was learning every day to think and act more like a Medici.

That night, Lorenzo went home and put ink to page, working

through his sadness through his art, which was his poetry. He wrote the early lines of what would become known as one of his greatest works, a poem called "Triumph."

> *How sweet is youth*
> *But it does quickly speed away!*
> *Let he who would be happy, be so*
> *Because tomorrow is so uncertain.*
> *Tomorrow is so uncertain.*

*

Cosimo had been ailing for a very long time. The gout, which was the great curse of Medici men for many generations, had taken its toll as it invaded his body during the last year, making movement of any kind difficult. He was irritable with his discomfort, but more with the idea that there was still so much to do and so little time left in which to do it.

When Cosimo knew that the end was very near, he gathered his family around him at the villa in Careggi, one at a time, to say his good-byes—and to issue his final instructions. Cosimo's dearest and most trusted friend, Poggio Bracciolini, was a co-creator of the Platonic community in Florence as well as a key member of the Order. He and Cosimo had spent countless hours together over two decades, influencing Florentine society to become more learned, more tolerant, and more artistic. Together they were the essential humanists, and the inspiration of a new world, which was approaching through their leadership in Tuscany. Poggio came to read to him from the history of Florence that he had composed himself, in Latin.

"I have included you and your father in the book," Poggio said. "And I shall dedicate this first edition to you, as you are the living history of Florence. It has been my joy to call myself your friend for all these years."

Cosimo put a hand on Poggio's as he replied, "The pleasure is all mine, as you have been a most loyal friend and brilliant companion in humanism and heresy. I pray that you will continue to encourage the friendship that grows between your Jacopo and my Lorenzo. I would have Lorenzo know the blessing and power of a Bracciolini friendship in his own life."

Poggio Bracciolini promised to watch over the boys and encourage their education together, that they might one day lead Florence under the human principles taught by both the Order and the Neoplatonists. Losing Cosimo would not only be personally painful for the Bracciolinis, it would be hard on everyone in the Florentine community who cared about social and artistic progress. Lorenzo would have to don quickly the mantle of the Medici if he wanted to preserve the legacy of his grandfather. Poggio hoped that his own brilliant son, Jacopo, would be at Lorenzo's side as the young Medici assumed the leadership role in Florence.

Poggio nodded to Marsilio Ficino, who was waiting at the door for his turn with Cosimo, and took his leave after kissing his dying friend on both cheeks, fighting the tears as he did so.

Ficino visited daily to read from the recently translated *Corpus Hermeticum*, the book of Egyptian wisdom that Cosimo loved so much. His body had failed him but his mind never would; until the last moment that Cosimo drew breath, he was gifted with extraordinary mental acuity. Following the readings with Ficino, they would discuss Lorenzo's future and the plans for their greater mission to merge the teachings of the ancient world with the lessons of the Order and bring them into the dawning golden age.

Cosimo spent the most time in his final days with Lorenzo. Some days their discussions were serious lessons on banking, politics, and the Medici agenda for the future. Other days, Cosimo wanted only to hear Lorenzo read from his latest writings. Even at this young age, his poetry was lyrical and substantive. He was growing into the poet aspect of his title. He was certainly the product of a gifted mother who had passed on her own talents and knew further how to nurture them in her child.

"No man has ever been more proud of a child than I am of you, my

Lorenzo," Cosimo whispered on his last day of life. "You have already brought me so much joy. And I see your promise. But I also fear that you will need to become a man very quickly. Your father will need you immediately to become a Medici in full. He will handle the banking, but you . . . it is for you to handle everything else, as he will no longer have the time. Work with Verrocchio, keep the school going, and guide the angelics. You have quite a stable building there now. Art will save the world, my boy. With Medici patronage."

Verrocchio's workshop was currently filled with brilliant and promising artists, all of whom had been identified and recruited by Cosimo and Piero. Sandro was, of course, the star of the Medici art roster, but there were some promising new additions. The young Domenico Ghirlandaio was showing great skill in fresco, and a lively rivalry was growing between him and Sandro. Together, with Lippi's son, Filippino, they were the terrible infant trio of the art world. A gifted new artist from Umbria had just been brought up, Pietro Vannucci, who was called Perugino after the town of his birth. And there was a boy in the southern town of Vinci who was getting some attention; Leonardo was his name. Lorenzo was going to have much to work with.

Taking his grandfather's hand and holding it in his, Lorenzo thanked him for all he had been given. He smiled at Cosimo, through dark eyes that filled with tears. "Grandfather," he began, choking on the sadness he held inside these final days. "Of all the gifts you have given me—the name, the teachings, the great education from the best teachers, all of it—do you know what I cherish above all? The times we have been together, just you and me. Taking walks in Careggi, talking about books, reading poetry. It is having you as my grandfather that I love above all things. And that I will miss above all else."

And with that Lorenzo wept uncontrollably as Cosimo pulled his beloved grandson close, stroking his sleek dark hair and weeping with him until he finally lost consciousness and slipped away.

*

The funeral of Cosimo de' Medici was an affair of state, with dignitaries arriving from all across Europe to honor the great man. Every citizen in Florence was in the streets that day, following the funeral procession that moved from the Medici palazzo on Via Larga toward San Lorenzo. The people chanted *"Palle, palle, palle"* in reference to the raised circles, or balls, that graced the Medici crest. Liveried servants wearing that same crest heralded the arrival of Cosimo's casket, which Lorenzo and his father shouldered as pallbearers, along with Medici cousins.

Andrea Verrocchio, who had been called in to quickly design the funerary monument to Cosimo de' Medici, presented drawings of a beautiful inlaid marble mosaic in the Order's official colors of red, white, and green, which would bear the simple yet remarkable epitaph:

PATER PATRIAE. FATHER OF THE COUNTRY.

For the first time since Cicero, an Italian citizen had been given the formal right to use that title.

Verrocchio would begin construction of the monument immediately following the interment of Cosimo de' Medici beneath the altar in San Lorenzo. He would work alone, as his old friend and great teacher, Donatello, was so distraught at the loss of his patron that he vowed he would never work again.

"I wish only to be buried at the great Cosimo's feet," Donatello wailed that day, falling to his knees. He sobbed in the basilica as the casket holding his patron's remains passed by him on the way to the final resting place. "I will find a way to serve him in heaven, to serve him for all eternity."

True to his word, Donatello never sculpted again, and he appeared to lose all interest in his life, so deep was his devotion and mourning for his patron. Within two years of Cosimo's death, he simply wasted away. In keeping with Donatello's ultimate wish, he was buried beside his patron and friend, the great Cosimo de' Medici, in the basilica of San Lorenzo.

LORENZO HAD FIRST seen the boy on the road from the Medici villa to Ficino's retreat in Montevecchio but gave him little thought as he passed with a wave. Lorenzo was kind, of course, as he always was to the servants. And the boy had to be a servant, as no simple peasant would trespass this far into private Medici land. He did notice that this particular boy, close to Lorenzo's own age if maybe a year or two younger, had a sweet face and a shy smile, but he must not have been hired by the family officially as yet. His clothes were shabby and he had clearly not been outfitted with the livery worn by the others within the Medici household. But a new stable boy was not something with which Lorenzo could occupy his busy mind, at least not today. He had far too many things to discuss with Ficino, not the least of which was the sublime poetry he had just discovered by a new and as yet unknown Tuscan writer.

A messenger had arrived in Florence the day before with a manuscript from the hilltop village called Montepulciano. In it was a letter of praise to Lorenzo and the Medici household from a man called Angelo Ambrogini, who claimed that his father had died in the service of Cosimo some years earlier. The man indicated, with remarkable elegance in the writing, that he wished to come to Florence to serve the family as his father once did. While Lorenzo processed many such requests claiming undying loyalty to the Medici, this particular one arrested him like nothing had previously. Enclosed with the letter was a collection of poems, the quality of which he had never seen. The poet, this Angelo, was well named; he was clearly one of the angelics, a being with supernatural talent in a human form. He wrote in both Latin and the Tuscan dialect, as did Dante and Boccaccio—and Lorenzo. He made references to Greek, linguistically and allegorically, that were fluent and literate and completely novel in their approach.

Lorenzo had never been so excited by a single letter before. For while his family and the Order searched for angelic contributors who would

preserve truth and beauty through art, they had not encountered anyone truly special within the field of literature. There had been no new
Dante appearing on the horizon. Until now.

Discovering who this angel from Montepulciano was, where he had
obtained such a stellar education, and how to bring him into the fold
was Lorenzo's primary objective today. As he dismounted, carefully extracting his treasured new manuscript from his satchel, he heard the
sardonic voice of his childhood friend behind him.

"Did you study?"

Jacopo Bracciolini had continued to share Lorenzo's lessons with
Ficino, whenever their schedules allowed. But since his father, Poggio,
had promised Cosimo on his deathbed to encourage the friendship between his son and Lorenzo, they had been together more frequently. A
rivalry had grown between the two boys, as both were naturally brilliant, competitive, and raised in the households of men who were renowned for their academic genius.

Lorenzo smacked his own forehead with the heel of his palm. He
had forgotten that Ficino was expecting them both to recite the text of
The Emerald Tablet of Hermes Trismegistus today. And while Lorenzo
loved the Hermetic studies, he hated memorization for its own sake.
And he had been so distracted by the elegant poetry that arrived the
night before, he had completely forgotten that they would be examined
today.

The Emerald Tablet was a legendary artifact from antiquity, believed
to contain the encoded secrets of the universe. These were inscribed on
a large slab of green stone by the great god Hermes himself. There was
a tale from antiquity that the Great Pyramid of Giza was built to house
the teachings of Hermes, known to Egyptians by another name, Thoth.
This fabled artifact of untold power was once kept there within the
King's Chamber. The original tablet had been long since lost to humanity, although Cosimo sent messengers around the world, in vain, to see
if there was any trace of it. He spent the equivalent of several fortunes
in search of the lost treasure of Hermes.

The closest Cosimo ever got to the legendary green tablet was a document from the tenth century discovered near Constantinople, a translation in Latin of the original writings. What language Hermes inscribed into the original Emerald Tablet was also one of history's lost mysteries. It was likely a symbolic language, something ancient and lost to mankind. And yet some of the text had been handed down as an oral tradition for untold centuries.

It was this tenth-century Latin translation of the oral tradition that the boys had been charged to memorize in advance of today's lesson. It was a beautiful afternoon, and the sun shone on the paving stones leading to Ficino's cottage. They sat on a carved wooden bench beneath an arch of white roses framed by potted orange trees; the symbol of the Medici, these trees appeared in profusion on every property owned by the family. Today they were in bloom, and the sweet smell of orange blossoms gave the air a hint of magic.

Lorenzo laughed. "Uh, no. I didn't study. But I think I know it well enough to get by without too much of Ficino's frowning. You?"

Jacopo began the memorization test, to see if Lorenzo could, indeed, keep up with the lesson today.

" '*Tabula Smaragdina. Verum, sine mendacio, certum et verissimum . . .*' "

Lorenzo translated instantly. " 'The Emerald Tablet. Truly, without deceit, certainly and absolutely . . .' " He threw the next line back at Jacopo. " '*Quod est inferius est sicut quod est superius, et quod est superius est sicut quod est inferius, ad perpetranda miracula rei unius.*' "

Jacopo smiled smugly as he translated. " 'That which is below corresponds to that which is above, and that which is above corresponds to that which is below, in the accomplishment of the miracle of the one thing.' "

He began to toss the next lines back to Lorenzo, never hesitating. " '*Pater eius est Sol. Mater eius est Luna. Portavit illud Ventus in ventre suo.*' "

" 'Its Father is the Sun. Its Mother is the Moon. The Wind has carried it in his belly.' "

Lorenzo stopped short, suddenly realizing that he couldn't remember the next line. He paused, reaching hard in his memory to find the missing line and win the game. He was chewing on his lip, deep in thought, when a third voice entered the challenge. It was an unknown voice, of a younger boy, causing them both to jump as he spoke from behind them.

" '*Nutrix eius Terra est.* Its nourishment is the Earth.' "

Lorenzo gasped when he saw that the voice—and the flawless Latin—came from the lips of the dusty stable boy he had passed on the road as he traveled here today. The boy lowered his eyes shyly but managed to add, "I love that line. It is so beautiful. Such a reminder of how the Earth nourishes us with her beauty."

Lorenzo held out his hand and introduced himself to the boy, who took it and grasped it gently. His huge bright eyes, eyes that had seen so much for one so young, filled with tears as he said, "I know who you are."

Lorenzo did not release the boy's hand. Instead, he clasped his shoulder with his other and said, "Then I am at a disadvantage, as I do not know who this brother is facing me, who has such a gift of knowledge and poetry for one so young."

The boy was in tears now and fell to his knees weeping at Lorenzo's feet. "I have come to serve you, Lorenzo. And to study with the maestro Ficino if he will have me."

Jacopo Bracciolini rolled his eyes in exasperation at the sycophant. "Get up, boy. He's neither king nor pope, but mere Medici." He took one arm and Lorenzo the other as they raised the young man gently to his feet.

"What is your name, brother? And where do you come from?" Lorenzo asked gently.

Pushing his heavy hair out of his face and wiping his eyes, the young stranger answered softly.

"Angelo. My name is Angelo Ambrogini, and I come from Montepulciano."

*

"Ah, I see you boys have met. Wonderful. Now we can get started in earnest. A good thing too, as the great Hermes does not like to be kept waiting."

Marsilio Ficino, just out of sight, had been watching the exchange between the newcomer Angelo Ambrogini and his elder charges. He was pleased that Lorenzo immediately accepted the boy, and he hoped that Jacopo would do so too, as he needed the stimulation of equally brilliant minds. And there were few minds that could claim equality with this young man. Ficino had been watching Angelo for years now, at the suggestion of Cosimo. His father had been murdered in a blood feud killing, stabbed brutally in front of Angelo when he was a little boy. The Ambrogini family had been devoted servants to the Medici for two generations. At a time when Cosimo was in exile and the feuds were raging in Florence, the Medici patriarch had stayed with the family in Montepulciano. While there, he had an opportunity to observe the shy yet obviously brilliant little boy who was already showing a prodigal intellect. Cosimo discussed the child's aptitudes with his father and was stunned to learn that he was already conversant in Latin and a natural with Greek. It was as if Lorenzo had a twin brother, born a few years later across Tuscany.

Following the brutal execution of his father, Angelo received an education secretly provided by Cosimo—and supervised by Ficino. Before falling ill, Cosimo had intended to bring the young Angelo to Florence and integrate him into the Medici household. Circumstances interfered, and the brilliant young intellect began to languish in the wilds of Tuscany. When Angelo wrote to Ficino in desperation, the tutor had the letters forwarded to Lorenzo. Ficino spoke nothing of it in advance, preferring to watch how Lorenzo filled Cosimo's shoes as the ultimate patron of the arts. Would he recognize angelic talent from the outset? Was he truly the equal—if not the superior—to his grandfather when it came to discovering and cultivating talent?

Ficino was thrilled to see that, at the tender age of fifteen, Lorenzo was well able to fill the unique role that he alone could aspire to. He was, indeed, growing to become the Poet Prince in every sense of the title.

Lorenzo and Jacopo were staring at Ficino now, blinking at his revelation that he had been expecting Angelo all along. Ficino smiled and ushered them through the door, as Sandro Botticelli joined them for the lesson, nodding to Jacopo as he entered and introducing himself to Angelo. Sandro knew that every minute he could spend with Ficino made him a better painter, as he acquired more storytelling elements to weave into his artwork. He attended the lessons with Ficino whenever possible. And while Sandro wasn't especially fond of the arrogant Bracciolini heir, he could feel from the electricity in the room that today was a lesson not to be missed.

"Come on, then, boys. The Tabula Smaragdina awaits us."

Ficino ushered them all into the larger antechamber that served as his lesson hall. He repeated the memorization test that Jacopo and Lorenzo had been practicing in the garden. While both boys passed the exam, neither was as quick or as fluent as Angelo Ambrogini, either in memorization or in understanding the context.

" 'That which is above is also below,' " Ficino said. "What is another way in which we can—and often do—say those words?"

Lorenzo answered this, immediately. "On earth as it is in heaven."

"Precisely," Ficino replied. "And what does this tell us, about the correlation between the teachings of our Lord Jesus Christ and the teachings of the ancients?"

"That it is all correlation and no separation," Jacopo replied. This was Ficino's favorite theory, and all his students knew it well.

"And?" Ficino looked to Angelo. He was curious with anticipation to see where the boy would take these two in discussion. While Jacopo and Lorenzo were both brilliant, they had developed a pattern of interaction between the two of them that was often more about their rivalry than about the lessons. Sandro was a quiet student and rarely spoke during the lessons. An extra intellect added to the mix would be just what Lorenzo needed to push him to the next level of learning.

Angelo looked at his classmates and hesitated. He was the newcomer, and the youngest. He was also heavily outranked socially and was highly unsure of his position. Lorenzo sensed this and encouraged him.

"Go on. Tell us what you think, Angelo."

"I think it doesn't matter." He spoke softly but firmly, and the others, teacher and students, were silent with shock at his eloquence as he continued.

"All wisdom comes from God and is the truth. It matters not if it comes from Hermes or from Jesus, or who said it first or in what language it was spoken. This is why the Emerald Tablet opens with the words 'Truly, without Deceit, certainly and absolutely.' Because that is the nature of all divine law."

Ficino questioned him. "And does this mean that Jesus was a student of the Emerald Tablet? That he was aware of Greek teachings? And is such a thing heresy?"

"I am not a priest and I cannot tell you what is or is not heresy," Angelo replied simply. "But I say again that it does not matter if Jesus obtained his wisdom from a Hellenist philosopher or from God himself. The pure and perfect truth of life is that we are here to create heaven on earth, to bring the perfection of what is above down to us, and in doing so to become transformed as human beings into something great and beautiful."

Lorenzo was leaning toward Angelo now, completely attuned to what he was saying. He jumped in. "To become fully *anthropos*." He explained quickly to Angelo, "Fully human, our most perfected state. To become fully realized is to know who you are and what you are here to do, to consciously and actively fulfill your promise to God and yourself, and to find the others in your soul family and help them to do the same."

"It is a Greek word, *anthropos*. I know it," Angelo replied. "But I do not know it in the context in which you use it."

"Then we shall have to teach you," Lorenzo said. "Just as it appears that you must teach us."

Sandro had been silent through the lesson, although it was clear to Lorenzo, who knew him better than anyone, that he had been sketching all along. Sandro turned the page to reveal his pencil drawing to Angelo. He had sketched the boy as Hermes himself, looking up to heaven.

In one hand he held a staff, and he appeared to be stirring the clouds with it.

Angelo blushed at the beauty of the drawing. "You honor me by comparing me to Hermes."

"I sketch what I see, brother. And what I see is your brilliance, alerting us below about the truth of the above, but I also see you stirring things up a bit in flaccid Florence! That, incidentally, is a delightful element."

Jacopo Bracciolini appeared annoyed at all the fawning over the newcomer but held his tongue. The Medici were famous for adopting stray poets and philosophers as pets.

"Welcome to our family of spirit, brother," Lorenzo said, grasping Angelo's hands. The younger boy was determined not to weep again, but for the first time since the death of his father, Angelo Ambrogini felt something akin to joy.

As the lesson continued, Marsilio Ficino felt a thrill run up his spine. He was not a prophet, but he had seen enough of the world to know that, in the presence of these three shining lights—the prince, the painter, and the poet—he was truly on the threshold of a new era. Florence was about to be reborn, and all of Italy would follow, and perhaps even the rest of the world.

It was not lost on Ficino that Jacopo Bracciolini, as brilliant as he was, stood apart and separated from this stunning trinity by his own choosing. Jacopo, despite his noble family and exceptional father, did not share in the special sense of family that was growing here. He was a young man of great cerebral gifts, but Ficino had watched him carefully over the years. He had noticed that while Jacopo fully engaged his agile brain, he seemed completely unable to connect with his heart.

Florence
1467

COLOMBINA RUSHED TO the entrance hall, her heart in her throat. Her sister, Costanza, had been breathless in her announcement that the mysterious Fra Francesco had come calling to the Donati town house. What was he doing here in her parents' house? Surely this was not official Order business? Could something be wrong with Lorenzo?

"Maestro! You honor us with your presence here. What brings you?"

"I was in the neighborhood."

His relaxed demeanor relieved her, and she smiled warmly at the old man. "You are far too great a man to be a good liar."

He returned the smile and shrugged simply. "And you are too young to be so wise. But as you are, I shall tell you the truth. Did you know, that when you stand on the Ponte Santa Trinità at precisely midday, the sun shines perfectly on the center of the Ponte Vecchio? And what a coincidence; it is almost midday now."

Colombina winked at him. "A good Florentine girl must know such things. I shall get my cape, and you can show me."

*

Colombina and Fra Francesco strolled along the Arno, through the Lungarni district that lined the river, toward the bridge at Santa Trinità. Santa Trinità had become a code for the Order, given its associations with the earliest days of the Order in Florence: it was where the current members attended secret services that celebrated their precious traditions. When Santa Trinità was mentioned, there was surely secrecy to be kept.

The Master gently approached the delicate subject. "I have heard that your father wants you betrothed. Soon."

Colombina nodded simply. "Yes, and not to Lorenzo."

"You expected as much."

"Yes, Maestro. I have always known that I would not be allowed to marry Lorenzo. It is not . . . our destiny."

"Mmm. And what have we taught you about destiny, child?"

"That the stars guide us, but they do not compel us. It is our free will that determines the outcome of all things. God does not impose his will on us, rather he makes it known and allows us to choose if we will follow it."

"And what is the Latin phrase that represents this idea?"

"*Elige magistrum.* Choose a master."

"Correct, and well spoken. So who is your master? Your heart? Lorenzo's destiny? God's will? The future of Florence? Where are you in this situation?"

Colombina gazed out at the river. The midday sun was indeed sparkling off the river and shining toward the venerable Ponte Vecchio, just as Fra Francesco had said it would. Even in such details, he was never mistaken.

"God has made his destiny for Lorenzo known since the day he was born. Since before he was born. My own parents have been straightforward with their attitudes about my future. They believe that I can only marry into an equally aristocratic family, and the Medici must stay out of the way. Our free will is to determine if we can live with that decision or not. We must choose."

Fra Francesco nodded sagely. "Yet Lorenzo speaks to me—quite seriously—of eloping. He would choose love and abandon his destiny. He would throw away everything he has and is to be with you."

"No, he would not. And I wouldn't allow him to do so, even if he meant it, which he doesn't."

Her tears came fast, hot and unbidden. She pulled her cape over her face and wept for a moment.

"Oh, Maestro, it is so hard. I want to be strong for Lorenzo, but the idea of him wed to another woman makes me want to leap from this bridge. We dream of being together, of escaping the responsibilities of his destiny, but we both know that we would never do such a thing. He will follow in the steps of Pater Patriae, as certain as he is Cosimo's grandson and a January-born prince."

"Both circumstances you mention are God-given, and therefore part of divine will and Lorenzo's destiny. What does that dictate for his nature as a result?"

Lucrezia wiped her face as she composed herself, ever mindful of pleasing her teacher.

"He is ruled by Saturn, the planet of obedience and sacrifice, the planet of the father and fatherhood. His first priority is and will always be his family and related obligations. And as Cosimo's heir, he has . . . all of that to carry on, in addition to the ruling of Florence. Lorenzo will always sacrifice his personal happiness to fulfill his responsibilities. *Semper.* Always."

"Yes, my child. He will. God knew what he was doing when Lorenzo was born on that date and at that time. He gave Florence a prince who would certainly not fail his destiny. But I can see that he also gave us a princess who would be equally strong and brave in fulfilling her own.

"For you see, my sweet child, this is as much about your destiny as it is Lorenzo's, and why you were born on the equinox, on the cusp of Pisces and Aries, the alpha-omega point of the zodiac, the beginning and the end. Pisces gives you the deep subconscious awareness to hear clearly and to feel at uncommon depths. Aries gives you the strength, determination, and fearlessness to move forward with your mission, even when it is very difficult to do so."

Colombina nodded the acceptance of her own role in this grand drama that belonged to God. "I will not fail him. I will not fail Florence, and I will not fail . . . our beliefs." She looked pointedly back in the direction of Santa Trinità, and the stone tower of the Gianfigliazza family that stood beside the monastery with its beautiful church, before finishing her thought. "The work of the Order means more to me than anything now. It must come first. But Maestro, there are days when all of this hurts very, very much."

"I know, my dear. I know. And I came here to tell you what Cosimo's final words were to me, regarding you."

Colombina gasped. "Pater Patriae? Mentioned *me* when he was dying?"

"Oh yes, my dear. He said to tell you and Lorenzo that what God has put together, no man can separate. And so while you are unable to marry within the laws of man, you are free to do what you wish within the laws of God."

Colombina was stunned. Surely he wasn't suggesting . . .

Fra Francesco looked in the direction of Santa Trinità. "Ginevra Gianfigliazza has the key. I can deliver Lorenzo there to you tomorrow night. Secret marriages are something of a tradition in the Order, after all."

Of course he referred to the most infamous of the secret weddings, that of Matilda of Tuscany to Pope Gregory VII. It was a legend in Tuscany, and one of the sacred stories of the Order.

Colombina sputtered, not knowing what to say. She threw her arms around him and began to cry, thanking him profusely.

"You are welcome, my dear. And for the future, on the days when it looks very dark, I want you to know that I will always be there for you. For both of you. *Semper.* And remember this most of all: when it is darkest, that is when you can see the stars most clearly."

Santa Trinità, Florence
1467

THE CHURCH THAT had served as a secret center of the Order since the days of Matilda glowed in the dim light of a dozen candles. They had chosen to perform the ceremony quietly in one of the small side chapels, the one with the glorious depiction of Jesus crowning his beloved, Mary Magdalene, as his wife and his queen. Lorenzo and Colombina stood together in the central space facing each other, joined together by outstretched hands, while the Master stood to one side, with the Libro Rosso open to a page from the Book of Love. He appeared to read from it, although he did not need to, as he knew these words by heart and had for more years than he could remember.

Having been instructed in the ceremony earlier by the Master in an impromptu rehearsal on the way into Florence from Careggi, Lorenzo recited to Colombina the poem of Maximinus with all of his love.

> *I have loved you before*
> *I love you today*
> *And I will love you again.*
> *The time returns.*

Tears streamed down Colombina's porcelain face as she repeated these same words to Lorenzo, in a whisper. No matter what happened from this day forward, the two of them were united by God.

Once the vows were completed, Ginevra Gianfigliazza, an esteemed teacher of the Order who was known as the Mistress of the Hieros-Gamos, began to sing a French troubadour song about love that the legendary Matilda had included in her own secret wedding ceremony to Pope Gregory VII. Ginevra's voice was sweet and clear as she sang:

> *I have loved thee a long time*
> *I will never forget thee. . . .*
> *God has made us one for the other.*

When Ginevra finished the song, the Master invited the two to exchange the traditional nuptial gifts: small gilded mirrors, which had been found quickly by Ginevra in time for the ceremony. Fra Francesco recited one of the sacred teachings of union as they did so.

"In your reflection, you will find what you seek. As you two become One, you will find God reflected in the eyes of your beloved, and your beloved reflected in your own eyes."

The Master concluded the ceremony with the beautiful words from the Book of Love, those that are also included in the gospel of Matthew. "For no longer are you two, but you are one in spirit and in flesh. And what God has put together, let no man separate."

He turned to Lorenzo. "The bridegroom may now gift the bride with the *nashakh*, the sacred kiss that blends together the spirits in union."

Lorenzo was weeping as he wrapped Colombina in his arms and pulled her tightly against him. What should have been their most joyous moment was one filled with deep sadness. For while he knew that no one but Colombina would ever be the bride of his heart, he also knew that the dawn would come too soon, and they would be separated by the cruel realities they had been born into. Their marriage would be valid only to them, in their hearts. It would not matter when they left this room. It was a secret for them alone, a little bit of rebellion wherein they could hold on to the truth of their love for each other: no matter what fate forced them into, they would know that they were secretly joined in a spiritual union that only God could undo.

But there was still some bliss awaiting the young couple. They would spend the night in the Antica Torre, the home of the Gianfigliazza family, where the Mistress of the Hieros-Gamos would instruct them both, before closing the door and leaving them to their privacy. The Gianfigliazza were one of the wealthiest and most esteemed families in Tuscany, therefore Colombina's parents did not hesitate when Ginevra had requested that Lucrezia stay with her in their legendary family home for a night. It was a coveted social invitation that the savvy Donatis would never deny.

And so it was that Lorenzo and Colombina joined together that night, married in the eyes of God and each other, combining their spirits through their flesh. Both wept with the joy and the ecstasy of their love, swearing through their tears that nothing would ever separate them.

The Libro Rosso was very clear on the teachings of Solomon and Sheba: "Once the hieros-gamos is consummated between predestined souls, the lovers are never apart in their spirits."

The Uffizi Gallery, Florence
present day

MAUREEN GASPED AS she entered the enormous salon known as the Botticelli Room, the centerpiece of the Uffizi collection. It was overwhelming, filled as it was with the most exquisite and iconic paintings of the Renaissance. In the middle of the room was an island of ottomans, providing a place to sit in awed contemplation.

"Remember, today we are not tourists, and we will not try to take in and understand each and every painting in this room. That is a fool's errand. Each of these paintings deserves many days all on its own, filled as they are with knowledge, intention, and emotion. So as much as you are tempted to wander and take it all in, I beg you not to do so. I promise that we will return every day that you are here and continue the lessons with new paintings each day. You will be better off for this approach. You must believe me."

Tammy gulped and nudged Maureen. To be in this room and not see every work of art, even peripherally, would be a type of torture for all of them.

Maureen said, "In this room you get an awesome sense of how accomplished the man must have been, how committed. To create this much art in one lifetime is astonishing. It seems impossible."

"And it is only a portion of what Sandro created," Destino answered. "He was more prolific than most people know. A truly angelic being in a man's body. In his life he created close to two hundred paintings. In contrast, Leonardo da Vinci completed perhaps fifteen. And yet the average person will throw Leonardo's name around as the greatest Renaissance artist! It is a crime."

Destino was rarely emphatic, so they all were stunned to hear him disparage Leonardo in this way. "It is our duty to right the wrongs of history, and the lack of appreciation of Botticelli's true genius is one of them," the ancient one responded to their incredulous expressions. "I will tell you—and show you—more on this. Come over here."

He moved the group to stand before Botticelli's *Annunciation*. Annunciation paintings were very popular in medieval and Renaissance Italy, capturing the moment in the gospel of Luke wherein the archangel Gabriel appears to tell the Holy Mother that she is going to give birth to the Son of God.

The Madonna in Botticelli's masterpiece was graceful beyond reason—elegant and strong, yet clearly filled with humility at the moment of divine annunciation. The archangel Gabriel, exalted though he might have been in heaven, was on his knees before Mary in honor of her grace and position.

"Stand in front of this painting, just here." Destino guided them all to the best place in which to feel the essence of the image. "Allow yourself to feel the power of this moment. Don't admire this art with just your eyes. Admire it with your heart and your spirit. Let it whisper to your soul. It was created in such a way as to do all of those things, for those with ears to hear."

They all stood before the *Annunciation*, experiencing it in this new way. Destino watched them all closely, noticing that Roland and Maureen immediately connected. Both of them had tears in their eyes as the enormity of the moment, captured perfectly by Botticelli, began to move through them. Tammy and Peter were not far behind. In a matter of two minutes, all of them were in different stages of weeping.

"Art is experience. When it is created by an angelic force, it transcends the visual and becomes entirely visceral. Yes?"

"Yes," Maureen whispered, still caught up in the moment expressed in the art before her, the moment when a woman accepts the enormity of her promise to bring forth the savior of the world and all that will mean to her—and to mankind.

"Now while you are in this state of bliss, follow me carefully into this next room. We shall perform a comparison."

They moved across the Botticelli salon and into the adjacent Room 15. On the far wall was another annunciation painting. It was beautiful, undoubtedly, but of a very different nature than the Botticelli piece.

"Now stand here, before this painting, and tell me what you feel."

They all admired the beautiful piece but were unable to reclaim the sense of bliss and connection they had felt from Botticelli's art.

"I feel nothing," Peter said. "Intellectually, I see that it is beautiful and I can admire it as an accomplishment, but it evokes no feeling in me."

The others nodded. Maureen added, "It lacks emotion. The Madonna here is beautiful, but she appears to be made out of marble. She is cold, disconnected. I don't feel anything from her."

In this version of the annunciation, Mary had a book before her in a stand, and her hand was resting on it as if to hold her place in the passage.

Tammy observed, "It looks as if she is more concerned about losing her place in the book, as if the angel interrupted her and she is just waiting for him to leave so she can finish her reading!"

"It is also missing the reverence for Our Lady," Roland commented. "Here, Gabriel appears to be a stronger character, or at least her equal. There is no sense of Mary as the focus of grace here."

Destino nodded. "One cannot communicate what one has never felt. This artist did not revere women and did not have any kind of emotional attachment to the idea of the annunciation. And so while it is executed perfectly in terms of technical merit, it does not teach you anything, it does not affect you emotionally or spiritually, nor does it move you."

"Whereas with Botticelli," Maureen interjected, "you feel his love for the subject and for the woman he is painting."

"Sandro loved and revered women. He was passionately committed to celebrating the divinity of femininity. This is part of what you feel in his work, but why this other artist's work leaves you cold."

"Who is this artist?" Tammy and Maureen asked at the same time.

Destino delivered the point he had begun to make in the Botticelli room. "I have shown you the art of Sandro Botticelli and the work of Leonardo da Vinci. One was a technical genius, the other was an angelic master. Now you know the difference."

Destino shepherded them all back into the Botticelli room and now took them around the perimeter, indicating a series of different Madonnas, all of which had the similar tilting of the head, porcelain skin, and light hazel eyes. A glass case in the center of the room contained two small paintings of the life of the Old Testament heroine Judith, after she had slain and decapitated the giant called Holofernes who terrorized her people. The same beautiful girl had clearly modeled for the fierce Judith in this work.

"All Colombina?" Maureen asked. When Destino nodded, Maureen asked, "Why is it that we never hear of her? Someone who inspired so much of Botticelli's work—and these paintings obviously depict the same model when you look closely at them."

"Two reasons," Destino replied. "The first is that everything about our Colombina was too controversial for history to record. The second is that Botticelli later discovered another, more famous muse who overshadowed all others."

He moved them all to stand before one of the most famous, iconic paintings in the history of art. In *The Birth of Venus*, a naked goddess of beauty arrives on earth, emerging from a scallop shell as her golden hair floats over her body.

"My friends, allow me to introduce you to a sister from the past, Simonetta di Cattaneo Vespucci. But you may call her Bella, as we all did back then."

Genoa
1468

IN A FAMILY renowned for the beauty of its women, the young Simonetta Cattaneo was the crowning glory. There had never been a girl so lovely, so exquisite of both feature and coloring. Her hair was the one element of her appearance that everyone remarked upon: by the age of ten, it hung to her waist in thick, apricot waves, a stunning golden peach color, not quite red, yet not blond in any traditional sense. Like all else about the young woman who was known by the nickname of la Bella, "the Beauty," her eyes also complied with God's command that everything about Simonetta be unequaled by any woman alive. They were a nearly translucent blue with coppery flecks, and they sparkled with the sweetness of her good humor.

Simonetta's skin was uncommon for an Italian woman, even one of such storied lineage. It was the color of rich cream, dotted gracefully with soft freckles in strategic places on her body and face. Her family referred to these as "angel kisses," for they were like sweet punctuation marks that highlighted the beauty bestowed upon her by the divine. She was tall, even as a child, lithe of limb and slender, moving with the grace of a willow tree in the first breezes of spring.

And yet for all her physical perfection, Simonetta was equally flawless of character. She was a gentle girl, and deeply sensitive. For many years into the future, her mother would tell the story of hearing her daughter crying on a spring afternoon, then searching for her with rising desperation as she heard Simonetta's sobs increase. She found her daughter weeping uncontrollably in the rose garden, as she sat amid a sea of colorful blooms. Roses in sunset shades of reds and oranges blossomed all around her, set against a sea of smaller white blossoms. There were butterflies in the garden this day, large yellow wings with black patterns flitting over Simonetta's head. The scene was idyllic and beautiful, and the lovely young woman with the gleaming apricot hair had her face lifted to the sun. She wept uncontrollably.

"What is wrong, my child?"

Madonna Cattaneo ran to her daughter, wrapping her arms around her as the girl's body shook against her own. The girl fought through her tears to speak.

"Is . . . isn't it so beautiful?" Simonetta cried, pulling away from her mother to gesture around the garden. "The flowers, the butterflies. All that God has created for us. Could anything be more beautiful than this? How blessed we must be for God to love us so much!"

The child Simonetta wept with the joy of God's creation, and for the beauty of the world. She remained pure in her appreciation of the precious nature of life on earth, every day of her existence. That loveliness from her inner being radiated, shining forth as a beacon of light that would one day touch the world, influencing millions for centuries into the future. But on that day in the garden, Simonetta's role as the future muse who would represent the Renaissance was being decided for her.

Her parents had just the night before been weighing their options for their daughter's marriage. She was a Cattaneo, which was enough to command a strong match anywhere in Italy. But that she was exquisitely beautiful with it was a benefit beyond florins and jewels. Beauty was necessary for landing a marriage within one of the strategic Florentine families. Marrying into Florence was no easy task for a foreign family; it was a culture that demanded beauty, intelligence, and wit in their women, in addition to hefty dowries and family connections. It was easy enough to marry off a plain girl into Rome or the outer regions of Lombardy if the money and paternal influence were there. Not so in Florence.

The Cattaneo family was the royalty of the ancient city of Genoa. They were descended from a storied Roman dynasty, one in which the women played a secret yet powerful role. They were teachers and healers, prophetesses with a hidden legacy of prayer and traditions that harkened back to the earliest days of Christianity. The Cattaneo women wore a symbol woven into their clothes and etched into their jewelry to represent this legacy. It was a pattern of stars set in a circle, dancing around a central sun. It was the symbol of Mary Magdalene, called the Magdalene's seal, and it had been used by women in the Order of the Holy Sepulcher for almost fifteen hundred years.

The family were storied members of the Order descended from the legendary early Christian leaders, Saint Peter and his many granddaughters named Petronella. It was this element of their family lineage that influenced the Cattaneos' decision. Simonetta's husband must come from Tuscany, where the Order was strongest, but more specifically from Florence. The Master had been consulted, of course. And while they had all considered marrying Simonetta into the Medici dynasty, Lorenzo was on the verge of a betrothal and Giuliano was being held in reserve for possible leadership within the Church. Thus it was determined that Marco Vespucci, the soft-spoken son of a wealthy and noble Tuscan dynasty, would be the best match for Simonetta. He was gentle, as she was, and a scholar. His family fortune and properties would ensure that this unique Cattaneo treasure would be well cared for and protected. Any children from the pairing would be of the most noble combination of bloodlines and likely to be both beautiful and intelligent.

And so it was that on the day that Simonetta Cattaneo wept for the beauty of God's creation, her parents made the decision to send her to Florence. She would study there with the Order and with the Mistress of the Hieros-Gamos, Ginevra Gianfigliazza, in preparation for her marriage to Marco Vespucci. The Cattaneo family were happy to discover that Simonetta would not be entirely alone during her preparation. A daughter of the Donati family, also renowned for her beauty of both body and spirit, would be waiting to greet their Simonetta as a "sister." With the grace of the Father and Mother in heaven, the girls would become friends and the Cattaneos' precious daughter would not be lonely so far away from the flowers and butterflies she loved so much.

*

La Bella Simonetta.

Even her name is art, one that I whisper as I paint even all these years after she has left us.

Will I ever capture her as she deserved? Perfectly and totally as the pure, yet real, living example of beauty that she was?

I remember the first time I saw her, at the Antica Torre, in the celebration that the Order created to welcome her to Florence. I could neither breathe nor speak when I looked upon her for the first hours that I was in her presence. Surely such ethereal magic could not exist in flesh and blood. And make no mistake, this was not mere physical perfection, although she was all of that and more. It was her radi-

ance, her divine sweetness, that I knew would haunt me until the end of time, until I captured it perfectly.

It is a quest without end. Capturing Simonetta is the goal I will never accomplish and will never cease to pursue.

And yet that night in the castle built by the Gianfigliazza family, I saw her not as singular perfection but as the completion of a trinity of the divine feminine essence that I had come to worship. On that magical evening I watched as Simonetta danced with Colombina and Ginevra. I sketched them as they moved together, more grateful than I had ever been in all my years to have my sketching tools with me.

I saw that these three women each represented an aspect of female divinity and then sketched them as such: Simonetta was purity, Colombina was beauty, and Ginevra was pleasure. Together, they were the three graces, dancing hand in hand as sisters, representing love in its earthly forms.

I would never forget that night for as long as I lived, and I vowed to paint the three of them together like that in some way that would capture the magic these women bestowed upon us. Lorenzo was in attendance, as was Giuliano, and both were equally entranced by the beauty that surrounded us. We were a family of spirit, immersed in the mission we were devoted to, while delirious with gratitude for the perfection of the world.

How fleeting such beauty is, how temporary. All the more reason for us to love it, revere it, and celebrate it in any way we can while it is with us.

I remain,
Alessandro di Filipepi, known as "Botticelli"

FROM *THE SECRET MEMOIRS OF SANDRO BOTTICELLI*

The Uffizi Gallery, Florence
present day

"No *PRIMAVERA*." DESTINO was firm. "Not today. Later."

Maureen, Peter, Tammy, and Roland were rebellious. They were here, in the Botticelli salon, where one wall was dominated by the enormous, mural-like masterwork of Botticelli's career known most commonly as *Primavera*, or *The Allegory of Spring*. It was a painting they all loved so much that Bérenger had a replica of the same enormous size installed in the château. To tell them that they were not even permitted to go and look at it up close seemed almost cruel, if not silly. How could it hurt?

"Find your spiritual discipline, my children. If this is the harshest task I ask of you on this path, you should all be grateful."

There was humor in Destino's voice, but the point was made. If their greatest spiritual trial was that they couldn't get an up-close look at a painting, they needed to count their blessings.

"You do not yet have all the information you need to appreciate what *Primavera* truly is in its entirety. I assure you it will mean far more and have the lasting impact that it was meant to have if you will allow yourselves to wait. Some things are sweeter for the waiting, and this is one of them.

"But to take away the sting, let us look at the *Madonna of the Magnificat*."

They followed Destino to the painting, which had been commissioned by Lucrezia Tornabuoni for her twentieth wedding anniversary with Piero de' Medici. Destino pointed out the various angels and explained which of the Medici children had posed for each as they all listened intently. On Maureen's left, a young woman was inching up, clearly trying to hear the commentary. She was young and striking, with close-cropped dark hair and huge doe eyes. She was extremely thin, which was the fashion at the moment with younger people in Italy, and wore jeans and a long-sleeved black shirt. Maureen also noticed that she wore black leather gloves and carried a notebook—or possibly a sketchpad—and a pen. *She must be an Italian art student*, Maureen thought, but paid little attention, as she was listening to Destino.

Destino was answering a question for Roland when the girl in the gloves tapped Maureen lightly on the shoulder. She surprised Maureen by speaking to her in excellent English, with a slight British accent.

"I have heard that some believe this is Mary Magdalene and not the Virgin Mary," the girl said.

Maureen smiled and shrugged, noncommittal. "Well, she is the most beautiful Madonna I have ever seen, regardless of which one she is," Maureen replied.

She was very careful in public not to become engaged in controversial conversation with strangers. This girl appeared harmless enough, and was very possibly one of her readers, given that Maureen was the author who had, in her first book on the subject, put forth the theory that this Madonna was, indeed, a representation of their Magdalena.

"The most beautiful Madonnas I have ever seen are Pontormo's, from his deposition mural in the Church of Santa Felicita. Have you seen those?" The young woman gushed. "His Magdalene wears a pink veil, rather than a red one. She is stunning. And it is one of the few deposition paintings that contain Saint Veronica at the foot of the cross. You really should go see it if you have time. It is just across the river over the Ponte Vecchio, ten minutes' walk from here."

Maureen thanked the girl, always interested to discover some new and beautiful piece of artwork. No doubt Destino would know a few things about the Pontormo painting too. But the mention of Veronica was the most interesting to Maureen. Veronica was an important character in the legends of the Order, and yet she was often overlooked.

The young woman was ripping out a page of her notebook now, where she had written the address of the Church of Santa Felicita. She handed it to Maureen, who thanked her.

"My pleasure. Enjoy your stay in Florence," she said sweetly, and with a wave of her gloved hand, she walked out of the Botticelli room without looking at one single piece of art.

*

Felicity de Pazzi's hands were shaking in her gloves as she ran out of the Uffizi. She had done it, she had forced contact with the wicked usurper, with her nemesis. It had been a strange sensation to be face-to-face with the woman she had conjured in her head as the Whore of Babylon, to see her as a flesh-and-blood person. Felicity was disappointed in retrospect. What had she been expecting? Something more . . . demonic? No, Maureen Paschal was just an average woman, other than the hair color, which marked her as a part of the tainted bloodline.

But that was the trick, wasn't it? Satan was crafty. He would not put his spawn in the body of a recognizable demon. He would create her in the image of the everywoman, someone whom people could relate to so that she would be able to lure them in with her facile lies. Felicity must not, even for a moment, allow herself to underestimate the evil inherent in the Paschal bitch. She was a blasphemer, the tool of Satan.

Felicity hurried down the stairs and out the door into the heat of an early Tuscan afternoon, toward the bridge and Santa Trinità. She did not know if Maureen would take the bait, but she hoped she would. Meanwhile, there was a meeting of the Florentine chapter of the confraternity in the rectory there this afternoon. They would vote today to determine whether to pursue reopening the case to beatify the holiest monk of the Renaissance, or any time period as far as she was concerned, Girolamo Savonarola. Felicity intended to control that vote. When she was present, none in the organization would oppose her. And it was time to redeem the sacred name of their ancestor, the greatest reformer ever to live in Italy.

Felicity sighed as she stepped up her pace, correcting her own thoughts. The greatest reformer ever to live in Italy—so far.

Ognissanti District
Florence
1468

THE HAND OF God was often seen to work in the affairs of Lorenzo de' Medici. Fra Francesco taught that when one was living in harmony with one's promise to God, opportunity would appear and doors would open most effortlessly. This night was to be no exception in the life of Lorenzo.

The Taverna was an eating house in the Ognissanti district, not far from Sandro Botticelli's *bottega*. It was a regular meeting place for Lorenzo and Sandro, an escape where the two great friends could relax and talk about art and life in a vibrant, if somewhat tawdry, atmosphere. Lorenzo preferred it to the more elegant Florentine establishments, where he was constantly under the microscope of political and social behavior. Here, he wasn't Florence's first son; he was just another patron. And the otherwise refined Lorenzo had an earthy side that gave him a secret taste for the bawdy and the ribald, one that he indulged in places such as this.

His little brother Giuliano, now fifteen, had tagged along with him today. It was his first experience in such a place, and no doubt Lucrezia de' Medici would be unhappy with Lorenzo for bringing her baby here. But Lorenzo felt that it was his duty to school Giuliano in the ways of the world. Besides, he was entirely safe with Lorenzo and Sandro at his side. Both men were tall, sturdy, and highly respected. Together, they were a formidable combination that no Florentine with any wits would ever cross.

A commotion at the bar drew the attention of all three in the Medici party. A darkly handsome man, preening and strutting from a cocktail of alcohol blended with attention, was being celebrated by his friends. The gaggle at the bar were getting louder as the time went by, the evident effects of too much drink. The peacock at the center of the group was telling a story with great gesticulation, punctuated by throwing money on the table in an ostentatious display of wealth, good fortune, and utter lack of taste. Lorenzo watched him carefully for a few minutes, eavesdropping on the boisterous conversation while his brother listened to Sandro discuss the details of his latest commission.

"A very typical Madonna and child. Not particularly interesting, but lucrative enough. I will add a forbidden element here or there to spice it up, a red book perhaps." He smiled wickedly, winking at Giuliano.

"The tediously pious Catholics who commissioned it will never know the difference."

"You wouldn't!" Giuliano was in awe of Sandro and worshipped him as a god. He hung on every word, and Sandro embellished his stories to please his young audience.

"I would. I do it all the time. No one is any the wiser and it amuses me. Why do you think I dress them all in red? When I am amused in my work, I paint with more passion and perseverance, so in the end it is all the better for the client. Everybody wins."

Giuliano nudged Lorenzo, who was paying no attention to a conversation that he normally would have enjoyed immensely—art and heresy, a delicious and favored combination for all in the Medici household. Lorenzo shushed him and nudged Sandro. "Who is the braggadocio at the bar?"

Sandro craned his neck to get a better view, then grimaced with a theatrical shudder and grunted as he recognized the character in question. "The monumentally annoying Niccolò Ardinghelli. He was insufferable even before he went off on a trade adventure with his uncle, but now he has the distinction of being completely unbearable. You would think he was one of the Argonauts and that he found the Golden Fleece, the way he goes on."

"Well then, let's call our pretentious Jason over here."

Sandro pulled a terrible face. "Tell me you're jesting. Please."

"No, I'm not. Call him over."

Seeing that Lorenzo was serious, Sandro conceded, grumbling. For all their fraternal friendship, Lorenzo was his prince and patron. The Medici had given him an order and he would obey it. Sandro bowed with a great mocking flourish. "As you wish, Magnifico. But you will owe me for this one."

Sandro approached the crowd and was greeted by some of the men who recognized him, including Ardinghelli, who cried out, "Well, if it isn't the Little Barrel himself!"

Sandro swallowed his irritation but corrected him quickly. "My brother is called Little Barrel, not me."

Sandro's brother, Antonio, was known by this unflattering nickname due to his physical stature, which was short and stocky. The younger of the Filipepi brothers, Sandro was far more gifted in the appearance department—tall, well built, with finer features and fairer hair. He had also grown terribly vain and intolerant of fools on top of it, so it rankled him that the moniker of Little Barrel, or Botticelli, appeared to be sticking firmly to him as well.

"How goes it with you, Little Barrel?" Niccolò extended his hands to grasp Sandro's in greeting, a little too vigorously. Sandro cringed.

One of the men, worse for drink, shouted, "Hey, watch his hands! They paint the most delectable nymphs! I would that I were a painter and could invite naked women to lounge about in my *bottega* under the guise of labor. What a life you must lead!"

"You have no idea," Sandro muttered.

Niccolò Ardinghelli, aware only of what concerned him, jumped in with a thought. "Sandro, you must paint my latest encounter with Barbary pirates! It will be a most handsome commission!"

Another compatriot chimed in, slapping Niccolò on the back. "Yes, and he will commission you to do so with the money he stole from their treasure chests once he vanquished the sea serpent, ravaged Aphrodite, and wrestled with Poseidon!"

The men burst into raucous laughter again, but Niccolò was only encouraged by the attention.

"More drink for everyone! And give the Little Barrel here a big barrel! He needs to stop being so serious!"

Sandro turned back to where the snickering Medici brothers watched his misery with no small degree of amusement. He glared at Lorenzo pointedly and rolled his eyes before returning to his task. "Niccolò, there is a friend of mine who wants to hear about your adventures in more detail."

"Well, by all means, call him over!"

"I think he would prefer that you came to him."

Niccolò began to protest, plumping his chest like an overfed pigeon on market day, as he turned to see whom Sandro was seated with. Upon recognition of the company, he deflated, but only slightly.

"Ah, I see. And are the Medici brothers too good to join me and my friends?"

Sandro turned to walk back to their table, delivering the clipped answer under his breath as he did so.

"Yes. As a matter of fact, they are."

*

Niccolò Ardinghelli was a braggart and a show-off, but even with too much wine in his system, he was not a complete fool. He was a Florentine and recognized a summons when he was presented with one. He excused himself from his friends at the bar and approached the table where the Medici held court.

Sandro made the introductions. Lorenzo spoke first, welcoming Niccolò warmly. He clasped the man's shoulder with his left hand as he shook the right, looking directly in Niccolò's eyes as he spoke. It was a diplomatic trick Lorenzo had learned from Cosimo. "Connect physically with both hands when you first meet, and stay completely focused on the person you are speaking with," his grandfather had taught. "Hold his eyes and let him know that you care about every word he says, as if he were the only person in the city that mattered at that moment. And always use his name. It is such a small thing, but this kind of connection is rare and will win the loyalty of a man in a matter of seconds."

Lorenzo never failed to follow this advice. For Lorenzo the humanist, these actions were sincere. He did turn his full attention to the citizens he spoke with, and in those minutes they were the most important person in the city. He had learned that in doing this, he not only earned the loyalty of men but also gained great knowledge of human nature. Like a chameleon on the summer stones in the Tuscan hills, he could change his colors to match his surroundings. With refined company, the scholars and poets, he was both a scholar and a poet. With ambassadors he became a statesman, with artists he was their brother in art, and he could even outdo the worst of scoundrels if necessary by becoming as debauched as they were in the moment. The result was that men of Florence from all walks of life felt completely comfortable with Lorenzo. It was one of the reasons that, at such a young age, he was already called "the Magnificent."

"Ardinghelli. It is a venerable name, my friend. You are practically royalty."

"One of the oldest and greatest in Tuscany. You honor me by recognizing it."

"The honor is mine, Niccolò. Tell me something: do you plan on leading this life of an adventurer forever? It sounds . . . superb. Please, tell us more about it. I cannot wait to hear your remarkable stories."

Sandro kicked Lorenzo under the table. Hard. Giuliano stifled a laugh by spilling his drink a little. Niccolò, delighted to have an audience, didn't notice, and Lorenzo stayed focused on his prey, smiling benevolently.

"There is no better life for a real man!"

Niccolò continued to weave his great yarns until Lorenzo, completely in control of the conversation, stopped him with another question. "How is it, friend, that with such a noble lineage, your father does not demand that you marry and carry on the family name?"

"Ach, marriage." Niccolò made a dismissive gesture to accompany the distaste on his face. "I have no interest in it at all, and yet you are right, of course. It is our noble obligation. I shall be forced to wed eventually, there is no way around it. But I will return to Florence just long enough to get sons on my woman, and then off to the sea I shall go again!"

Lorenzo nodded thoughtfully. "But Niccolò, what if your wife was shockingly beautiful? Could not a marble-skinned goddess of love keep you in Florence if she waited in your bed? Wouldn't that be enough to keep you from the sea?"

"Never! You read too much poetry and are still young, Medici. You need to remember this: women are sirens, luring men from their adventures. And Florentine women are the worst of all, with their ideas and their prattle. I much prefer the fast and furious tumble with a Circassian slave girl. Have you ever had one of those, Lorenzo? Black hair and blacker eyes and lips like pomegranates. Delicious and wild. And they know their place and don't annoy me with their chatter afterwards! I shall take you to Pisa when the next slave ship comes in and we can find one for you. You'll thank me for it, I promise you."

"You are too kind, Niccolò."

"Bedding beautiful women is a necessity for men like us, Lorenzo. It is our birthright. But it is a brief enough thrill and I dare say one that can be replaced. The sea, on the other hand, is eternal." His eyes began to glaze over as he set off on another rhapsody. "An unequaled adventure that no woman, even Aphrodite herself, could ever take me away from."

Lorenzo smiled at him, a sincere and bright expression. "Perfect," he said, realizing that there was no fear of Niccolò listening to him, as he was already off on a tangent about the color of the Adriatic Sea at sunset.

Lorenzo turned the smile to Giuliano and Sandro. "My God, he is absolutely perfect."

*

The engagement of Lucrezia Donati to Niccolò Ardinghelli was announced within a few weeks. The Donati family was pleased to find an equally esteemed and noble house to wed their daughter into. And as an engagement gift, the benevolent and generous Lorenzo de' Medici provided a highly lucrative seafaring commission to his great new friend, Niccolò, one that would take the man out of Florence for the better part of a year, immediately following his marriage.

True to his word, no woman—even the most desirable woman in Florence—would keep Niccolò from his adventure.

Lorenzo was right: it was absolutely perfect.

*

"He's insufferable."

"He's temporary. And necessary. Colombina, once you say your vows, it's over. He is on a ship and you are free once more."

Lucrezia Donati turned from him, moving to the window of their room in the Antica Torre. She was furious with Lorenzo for his hand in arranging her betrothal. Although the Medici were famous for brokering marriages throughout Florence, she had not expected Lorenzo to be so completely involved in her own. How could he bear to do such a thing?

"But . . . how could you?"

Lorenzo joined her at the window, where they looked out over the Vallambrosan monastery, the cross of Santa Trinità shining in the sun. He placed a reassuring arm around her and explained patiently.

"How could I not? If I am forced to share you, it is my greatest desire to find the least oppressive circumstances. A husband who is absent for years at a time is a perfect solution. I dare say a God-given solution. I am grateful for it, Colombina."

"But Lorenzo, how will I bear that one night?"

"We will get your husband raging drunk, which I dare say is not hard to do, and it will be over quickly. If we're very successful, it may not happen at all. I did try to send Niccolò off to sea first and marry you by proxy, but he would not concede. At least he is not completely blind. The best I could do was to ship him off the following day. I'm sorry, love, but there is no way around it."

"Then you best get me very drunk too."

He kissed her on the forehead. "Do you not think that this kills me? I am brokering the marriage of the woman I love to another man. I would rather rip out my own teeth. It is perhaps the most heinous task I have ever carried out, but it must be done, for both of us. We should be grateful that God gave us this option, put the one man in our path who would both please your family and get out of the way, all in one package. And he is not a hunchback or a villain, merely a braggart. And some of the women envy you, I am told. They believe he is quite handsome and dashing."

"The women of Florence do not envy me over Niccolò Ardinghelli." Lucrezia ran a finger over his flattened nose before leaning up to kiss it. "They envy me over you."

"Nonsense. I will never be as pretty as Niccolò, with his perfect nose."

"Stop it. You can't possibly be jealous of him. Besides, you are the most beautiful man in the world."

"As long as you think so, I don't care about anyone else."

Lorenzo paused for a moment before asking her, with sincere curiosity, "Does everyone know, then? About us? Really?"

Lucrezia gasped at him, incredulous. "Lorenzo, please. For such a brilliant man you sometimes miss the most obvious things. The whole city knows about us. Except perhaps for poor Niccolò!"

They both laughed at this, but Lorenzo's mind was on to something else.

"That could be a good thing, Colombina."

"Why?"

It was his turn to tease her. "For such a brilliant woman, you sometimes miss the most obvious things!"

He grew serious as he looked out the window again, this time pointedly in the direction of Santa Trinità.

"Because if people think you and I meet secretly only because we are lovers, they will not be looking at our more dangerous endeavors together."

Antica Torre, Florence
present day

"WHY ARE YOU doing this?" Petra Gianfigliazza, known for her cool patience, was trying not to lose her temper with the arrogant beauty who confronted her. "What is it you want, Vittoria?"

"I want Bérenger," Vittoria replied. "I always have. He is my soul mate and I have loved him since I was a girl. You know that."

"No, I don't." Petra shook her head. "I don't believe it for a second. I have known you too long and too well. You are not in love with him. You are not in love with anything except your career and your power. That's why Destino stopped teaching you."

Vittoria spat at her. "I am the one who brought Bérenger to Destino's attention, the reason he discovered his precious Poet Prince and that wretched redhead in the first place. And this is how he thanks me."

"What is it you are really after, Vittoria? You will save us both time and trouble by being honest with me."

"Dante is Bérenger's son and he is a Poet Prince," she hissed. "I want my son to have his father's name, legitimately. He is the Second Prince, Petra. *The Second Prince.* Do you understand what that means? For all of us? For the world?"

Petra nodded, taking it all in. "I understand that you want Bérenger to marry you."

"It is his duty as Dante's father and as the heir to the prophecy. And I want my son to be recognized for who and what he is by Destino."

"Why do you care about whether or not Destino recognizes him?"

"Because Dante is the true heir to the power of the Order. The artifacts should be his when Destino dies."

The artifacts. So that was the real prize that Vittoria was after.

Petra asked the next question without even attempting to keep the incredulous tone out of her voice. "You think Destino will give *you* the Libro Rosso?"

"It belongs in the hands of the reigning Poet Prince," Vittoria replied. "It is the law of the Order."

Petra considered this for a moment. Vittoria may have been delusional, but she wasn't stupid. She countered, "The law of the Order is that Destino makes the law of the Order. That said, Bérenger is the reigning Poet Prince. By your logic, he should have the Libro Rosso."

"But Dante will be his legitimate heir. Everything should go to Dante as both Bérenger's son and as the first child in two thousand years to fulfill the prophecy completely. Perfectly."

"Why? Why do you want this so badly that you are willing to risk so much to attain it?"

"Why?" Vittoria was the one who was now incredulous. "Have you lost your wits, Petra? Dante will then be the highest-ranking blood prince in Europe."

"So what? It's the twenty-first century. There is no monarchy in Europe anymore."

"That's because there has been no one worthy to restore the monarchy. Don't you see? My Dante changes all of that. We can concentrate the power of all the noble bloodline families behind Dante: Hapsburg, Buondelmonti, Sinclair. With our unified fortunes and power combined within this one perfect child, *my* child, we can rule Europe."

Petra was stunned. She had not expected this. For hundreds of years, secret societies had been breeding grounds for half-baked plots to restore monarchy in Europe. The strategy always involved proving that some heir of one of the bloodline families represented a "lost king" who would unify Europe as a superpower. But Vittoria's scenario, while far-fetched, had some chilling possibilities. While Dante might not ever sit on a recognized throne, he could potentially unite billions of dollars and great power under one agenda, but what would that agenda be? And who would control it? And while she had not mentioned the messianic aspect of this master plan for her son, it was implied in her speech. Petra was chilled to the bone as she considered that Vittoria was likely not smart enough to have concocted this herself. How big was this conspiracy? How much wealth and power was behind this terrible idea?

"Vittoria . . ." Trying a new tactic, Petra modulated her voice to that of mentor. "Help me understand what it is you want to do here. The Order isn't a political organization, it is a spiritual one. Temporal power is not our agenda."

The light of fanaticism grew in Vittoria's eyes as she reacted. "Destroying the Church is our agenda, and we can do that if we are unified. We can return the teachings of the Libro Rosso to the light, and to Europe once and for all. We can defeat the lies that have ruled in Rome for too long. It is a blessed mission, *sister*." Vittoria addressed Petra intentionally using the sibling definitions of the Order. "We can all make this happen together—you and me, Bérenger and Destino, and Dante. Let us bring about this new era of rebirth. The time returns. Let's finish what Lorenzo started. *That* is the mission."

Petra shook her head sadly. How had Vittoria become so misguided? "Destroying the Church has never been our agenda. Living in peace with other belief systems is what we aspire to, and what we have always tried to achieve. That is the Way of Love."

Vittoria growled her frustration. "You are the Mistress of the Hieros-Gamos, the leader of a dying tradition, possibly the most powerful tradition in human history. Are you going to sit back and let it die, Petra? Because I say we stand up for it and let it live. We restore the true teachings with all the power and money of Europe behind them. Bérenger and I rule together, with Dante as our heir, protecting the Order as our highest priority. If Dante is ultimately in possession of the Libro Rosso, as well as the—" Vittoria stopped herself before completing the sentence, but Petra, knowing her too well, understood.

"In possession of the Libro Rosso as well as the *what*, Vittoria? The spear?"

Vittoria was in too deep to deny anything now. She snapped "Of course. The Spear of Destiny is the ultimate weapon of power on Earth. He who wields the true spear cannot be defeated. We need it to ensure our victory. Dante needs it."

Petra took a deep breath and answered carefully. "The spear is not meant to be used as a weapon of war or pain ever again. To do so would be a tremendous mistake and tragedy. Destino will never part with the authentic spear, at least not until the day he selects an heir who is worthy of its power."

Realizing her words were falling on deaf ears, Vittoria turned to storm out of the apartment in frustration. She stopped at the door to make her final point. "Destino needs Dante. The Order needs Dante. He is that heir. You cannot deny his birth chart or what he is. The sooner you and Destino understand that, the easier this will be on everybody."

Petra, for all her grace and diplomacy, had not become a leader in the Order through a lack of spine. She shot back, enunciating each word clearly and with authority. "Remember who I am, Vittoria, as you said it yourself. I am the Mistress of the Hieros-Gamos. It is my mission and my destiny to teach the power of love and to recognize twin souls. Bérenger and Maureen are twins. They belong together. And what God has put together, let no man separate. That is the law that rules above any other."

Vittoria slammed the door in response; Petra considered the situation as she did so. Destino had ceased to teach Vittoria because she had always been fixated on power and never on love. She was the product of a family that had lost the true meaning of the Order along the tumultuous path of history. This perverted strategy she was presenting made that clear. Fanaticism on any level was a dangerous thing.

And yet there was the question of the child. Dante Buondelmonti Sinclair was, indeed, a Poet Prince, and as such his presence and destiny could not be ignored by anyone in the Order. Whether or not he was the legendary Second Prince was still to be confirmed.

But what if he was? What then?

Florence
spring 1469

"SHE IS THE closest thing to royalty that exists in Rome, this girl from the Orsini family. They have the greatest number of cardinals in their line, and several popes. They are rich and influential, and will bring a prestige and influence to the Medici we have never had before."

Lucrezia de' Medici knew that Lorenzo would hate this discussion, as did she, but it had to happen. She had just returned from Rome, where she had gone in search of an appropriate bride for Lorenzo. That the Medici were reaching outside Florence was controversial; that they were going to Rome to find Lorenzo a wife was unheard-of.

Lucrezia, who had become a true Medici in her years of marriage, continued. "She is not beautiful, but she is not ugly either. And she is not Florentine, so she is neither cultured nor terribly merry in her demeanor."

"Does this get worse, Mother? Because if it does, let me go drinking with Sandro, then come back to hear the rest of it when I am appropriately numb."

"Stop it. Think of this as Order business. That's all it is, Lorenzo. Business. A bride from the most noble family near the papacy is the next step for you. For all of us, and for what we wish to create. The girl is a broodmare. Her purpose is to give you children with Roman blood who will help us to secure our place in the papal circle. With the help of the Orsini family, we shall get our Giuliano into the center of that circle and establish a Medici cardinal. If this Orsini girl breeds well, your sons will follow the trail Giuliano will blaze to Rome. Keep your eye on the outcome, my prince."

Lucrezia grabbed her elder son by the shoulders and kissed him soundly on both cheeks. She did not release him as she made her point. "Understand this, Lorenzo. We are after nothing less than a Medici pope. Your own father is too ill to give you guidance and emphasize our strategy. It falls on my shoulders now as the Medici matriarch to carry out the grand plan, until you step into your grandfather's shoes and rule Florence.

"A Medici pope, Lorenzo. Imagine it. It will give the Order access to all that is held in secret in Rome, all that has been kept from us that is rightfully ours. It may even give us the power to change the Catholic Church. And you shall be the patriarch that brings this to pass."

Lorenzo was listening in a new way. An arranged marriage had been inevitable, so what did it matter whom he married? Anyone who was not Colombina would be abhorrent to him, so it might as well be a woman who could further the ambitions of his family and his Order.

He responded calmly. "This girl whom you and Father have chosen is fine with me, Mother. Do whatever has to be done to make it official.

But know this: I will not participate in a formal vow-taking ceremony with her. I will never stand before God and proclaim devotion or loyalty to any woman who is not Colombina. Marry us by proxy. Throw whatever party or spectacle you must in order to appease this Roman family and show them honor, just do not force me to take vows. Tell the Orsini that I am too busy with affairs of state to participate in a vow ceremony, particularly now that Father is so terribly ill. Of course they will understand."

Madonna Lucrezia knew better than to push Lorenzo too far. He had accepted their choice for his bride, and that had been the objective of this discussion. She had accomplished what she needed for the further glory of the Medici dynasty.

"Of course they will understand, my son. I will make the arrangements immediately."

*

Lorenzo went in search of Angelo the next morning after a long and sleepless night. Sandro was with Verrocchio this week, working hard on a number of important commissions, so Angelo was his port for this storm. He and the little poet from Montepulciano had become immediate and inseparable friends. Angelo was as sweet as he was smart, as loyal as he was shy. He was utterly devoted to Lorenzo. And in Angelo, Lorenzo had more than just a trusted new confidant; he had a writing partner, a poet of such talent and discernment that he pushed Lorenzo's own writing to new levels.

It was the second great sadness of Lorenzo's life that he did not have time to pursue his writing. He was remarkably gifted, and when his poems were entered into the highly competitive Florentine writing competitions, he always won some kind of mention. Lorenzo entered these contests under assumed names so that the organizers would not simply award him medals because he was a Medici. He wanted to have his poetry judged on its own merits. Each time that it was, the result was the same: he was a poet of exceptional gifts.

But when Angelo Ambrogini came to Florence, there was no one who could best him for the perfect turn of phrase or most lyrical use of language. Lorenzo wasn't the least bit jealous—far from it. He had been the one to cultivate his friend's abilities and support him as he continued to write. Angelo's skills as a poet had become so renowned, so quickly, that he was now known by a new name throughout Florence. It was a tradition to honor the most gifted artists with a professional name, which consisted of their given names followed by a reference to their hometown. Thus was born the poetic name Angelo Poliziano, which meant "Angelo from Montepulciano."

Lorenzo found Angelo in the *studiolo* he had prepared for him in the palazzo on Via Larga, working on a Greek translation.

"Angelo, I am tormented. I am to be wed to a homely Roman girl who is apparently completely without culture. What am I to do?"

Angelo smiled at him. "Use your misery in your poetry, as all great writers have in the past."

"I tried. I was awake all night in the effort, but I cannot judge it for myself to know if it is worthy or just self-indulgent."

"This is the beauty of the gift we have been given, Lorenzo, the purpose of our art—to express emotion through poetry. Even if it isn't worthy and you have to throw it out, at least it served a purpose in getting you through the night. And besides, how dull would it be if the only reason we created poetry was to celebrate springtime and flowers and rainbows? All those things are lovely, but they are not art unless they have a contrast. Let this new wife from Rome provide you with some contrast. What is her name?"

Lorenzo stopped for a moment, thinking. He shook his head and replied, "I don't know. I didn't ask." Lorenzo groaned aloud. "I do not care. Angelo, I cannot write poetry about a woman because she does *not* inspire me."

Angelo was brilliant, but he was young and had never been in love. Clearly. Lorenzo continued, "I can only write about someone who does inspire me. And while thinking of this tormented mess I find myself in, I realize that it will hurt Colombina even more to know that I am getting married. So I chose to write a poem to her and about her, so that she would always know my true feelings no matter what circumstances fate put upon us. I shall read it to her to soften the blow of the terrible news. Will you look at it and tell me what you think?"

"Of course," Angelo nodded, then read Lorenzo's latest offering. He was quiet for a moment, causing Lorenzo to panic with insecurity.

"You hate it?"

"No, Lorenzo. It is stunning. Beautiful. I was just thinking that if this is how you write when you are miserable, then apparently God knew exactly what he was doing by delivering an unpleasant wife to you!"

*

Regarding Lorenzo's banner.

The Medici chose to produce a spectacle in honor of the marriage of Lorenzo and Clarice Orsini that would be so elaborate, so memorable, that the people of Florence would be talking about it into the next century. Lorenzo wanted nothing to do with it, of course. He was miserable over the entire idea of arranged marriage, and it was my duty as his brother to cheer him from the dark hole he threatened to fall into. We devised secret ways to incorporate our heresies into the tournament as a means of amusing ourselves.

There would be a joust and a series of games in which the young noblemen of the city would square off against each other in combat, just as in the times of chivalry. Each knight would have colors and a banner and carry the favor of one of Florence's beautiful women. In this case it was determined that there would be an official Queen of Beauty who could sit on a throne in an elaborate gown and preside over the events as the goddess Venus herself. Of course our queen was Colombina. Who else? And no one in Florence could argue against her unparalleled beauty. Only Simonetta could compete with her, and she was still too new a presence in the city, and a foreigner at that. And she did not belong to Lorenzo.

It was given to me and the apprentices in Verrocchio's studio to create the banner that Lorenzo would carry in the joust. Thus I created the sketch from which we would work, using Colombina as our model for Venus and incorporating the dove symbol into the imagery as a nod to the name by which we all called her. Lorenzo and I both determined that we would use the Order's motto of "Le temps re-vient" *in its French form as our ultimate act of heresy.*

And so Colombina would sit on a throne, from where she would crown Lorenzo with flowers, the violets which had been symbolic of her family since ancient times, and tie the ribbons of her chosen colors to Lorenzo's armor. He would joust behind a banner painted with her image and the ancient motto of the Order, in his own way declaring that what God has put together, no man can separate. It was a daring public statement given that Colombina was now married to Niccolò Ardinghelli, so all of it was done under the auspices of the troubadours, emphasizing the notion of courtly love and the ideal of untouchable beauty.

And thus would Lorenzo de' Medici usher in his new bride from Rome.

I remain,
Alessandro di Filipepi, known as "Botticelli"

FROM *THE SECRET MEMOIRS OF SANDRO BOTTICELLI*

Florence
June 1469

CLARICE ORSINI HAD been married to Lorenzo de' Medici by proxy in Rome, where a stand-in from the Medici party had spoken Lorenzo's vows for him, carrying a document emblazoned with the Medici seal giving him permission to do so. The papers were signed and notarized by an envoy of the pope himself, and the wedding was declared legal. It was a very tidy business transaction. Clarice was then escorted from Rome to Florence with the elaborate entourage of a princess. Giuliano de' Medici was a member of the escort, and he tried very hard to calm the nervous bride and make kind conversation with her on the long ride north.

It was not easy going. Clarice Orsini de' Medici, his new sister, was not much of a conversationalist at the best of times, and at the moment she was terrified. It didn't help that some of the Florentines in the wedding party said ribald things in praise of Lorenzo's legendary prowess, indicating the pleasures that the bride had to look forward to. Clarice was beside herself with fear and embarrassment and refused to speak for most of the journey.

*

The wedding reception was held in the Medici palazzo on Via Larga, and no expense had been spared. Meat had been roasting for days in preparation. There were sweets from the Orient and a hundred barrels of wine. Orange trees in terra-cotta pots, the symbol of the Medici family, were beribboned and strewn throughout the property.

The bride was brought through the main portico in her elaborate lace and damask dress, moving very slowly through the property in an effort to balance the heavily jeweled headdress that had been a gift from her parents for this occasion. Clarice may have been denied a traditional vow-taking ceremony, but the Orsini were at least determined that she would make a fine appearance on the day of her reception. The Florentines would be forced to accept that this Roman girl was every bit their equal and worthy of her place as the Medici bride and the First Lady of Florence.

Clarice stopped short with a gasp as she saw the statues that dominated the central courtyard: Donatello's *David*, in all of his glorious nakedness, stood beside Donatello's *Judith*, who was in the process of separating Holofernes from his head. They were the symbols of male and female power in an exalted form, put here by one of the world's greatest artists as commissioned by the most legendary patron.

Lucrezia de' Medici, who was escorting her new daughter-in-law into the reception, stopped, worried that the sheltered Roman girl was going to faint. "What is wrong, Clarice?"

Clarice gestured to the statues in horror. "Those . . . horrible images! Why are they here on my wedding day?"

"They are always here, Clarice. They are great art, and part of the Medici collection."

Clarice shuddered and looked like she was going to cry. "They are vulgar!"

Lucrezia gathered her patience, took Clarice more firmly by the wrist, and propelled her forward into the reception. Integrating a conservative Roman girl into the glorious artistic culture of Florence just might prove to be more of a challenge than anyone had anticipated.

*

Clarice de' Medici was seated with a group of young, married women, as was the custom for the bride at a Florentine reception, in which the men and the women sat separately. Clarice was grateful to be sitting beside a sweet, dimpled young noblewoman who had been introduced to her as Lucrezia Ardinghelli. The woman was very beautiful, Clarice couldn't help but notice, and quite kind to her. She appeared to know a great deal about Lorenzo as they had been friends since they were children. Here was an ally to have, Clarice thought. And as this poor Lucrezia Ardinghelli was the wife of a seafaring man, she was often home alone for many months at a time. Perhaps this would be her first true friend in Florence.

Clarice dared to be optimistic about finding new friendship until the defining moment of the evening, when Lorenzo approached their table and greeted all the women there. While he was unerringly polite to each of the young matrons, he never took his eyes off Lucrezia Ardinghelli, nor she him. There was a bond between them that was palpable.

Clarice Orsini de' Medici may have been young and inexperienced in the ways of the world, but she was not blind.

She had identified the enemy.

*

In the nuptial chamber, Clarice was dressed in her nightgown by female attendants from the wedding feast, as was customary. Lucrezia Ardinghelli was notable in her absence. The women who were present teased her good-naturedly and chattered giddily about Lorenzo's legendary masculinity, nudging Clarice and reminding her that she was the luckiest woman in Italy to be on the threshold of such an experience. While a Florentine girl would have joined in the frivolous fun, this kind of talk was nothing but scandalous to the sheltered Orsini princess. The women began to take notice that the bride was flushed to the point of fainting and reduced their commentary. They finished their ministrations quickly and left the Roman girl alone, shaking their heads as they left the Medici bridal chamber.

"What a waste of a magnificent man," one of them whispered, and the others burst into laughter in agreement. There would be much gossip about the frigid Roman bride for years to come, resulting in plenty of offers from Florentine women who were more than willing to show Lorenzo the appreciation they knew he did not receive from his wife.

Clarice was left alone, perched on the edge of the bed, rigid with dread. Here she was, married to a man whom every noble woman in Europe envied her for, and she wanted nothing more than to run away, as far and as fast as she could, back to the safety of Rome. For all that she was the daughter of one of the noblest and most storied families in Italy, she was still a sixteen-year-old girl who found herself under immense pressure while surrounded by strangers and a culture she did not comprehend. Florence was as exotic to her as Africa or the Far East. And now she would be confronted with the terrifying physical realities of this virile young man who was spoken of in such mythical terms.

By the time Lorenzo entered the chamber, Clarice was sobbing with the fear of him.

He approached her with genuine concern. The events of the evening would have been overwhelming for anyone, but he had great sympathy for her circumstances under the tremendous scrutiny of Florentine observation. It would take some getting used to for one so young and sheltered in her ways.

"Are you unwell, Clarice? Was this too much for you tonight?"

Steeling herself for what would come next, she raised her chin with some hint of her Roman pride intact as she responded. "No. I am an Orsini. I am not afraid of your Florentines. And I will do my duty to you as a Christian wife, Lorenzo. I have sworn before God to do so, to be obedient to you, and I will."

He approached her with the same slow gentleness he would use with a fawn in the forest. He touched her hair delicately as he began to remove the pins that held it back so severely. "You have lovely hair, Clarice. I would see it down."

Her hand flew up to stop him. "Don't!"

He stopped, pulling his hands away from her quickly. "What is wrong?"

Her heart was beating like a trapped fox surrounded by hounds on all sides. She was trying to forestall the inevitable. "Loose hair is the sign of wanton behavior."

"Clarice, I am your husband now. You can show yourself to me without fear."

She recoiled when he reached out for her again, as if he had struck her.

Lorenzo inhaled deeply, finding his patience. He explained slowly, "You know, some women actually find this pleasurable. The time may come when you do as well, which is as it should be. If you can give me a chance to be a good husband to you, our years together as man and wife will be much improved. Even enjoyable."

Clarice straightened again, spine as stiff as steel. "My confessor says that it is a woman's lot to suffer, first in the marital bed and then in childbirth. It is the curse of Eve."

Lorenzo made a mental note to send her confessor back to Rome at first light. On a fast horse.

"It does not have to be so, Clarice. Let me show you."

Her response was haughty. "Do your duty, my husband. And I will do mine. But do not expect me to enjoy it."

Lorenzo stunned her by standing up quickly and turning to take his leave.

"Where are you going?"

"I will not take you against your will, Clarice. Wedded or no, I am a decent man. I will never force a woman under any circumstances. When you can welcome me into our marriage bed as your husband, I will return to it and do my duty as you say. I assure you, this is no more pleasant for me than it is for you. And I will not allow my own wife to turn me into a rapist. It is not in me."

Clarice was shocked by his coarse language and terrified now that she had done something unforgivable. "You cannot leave! You will shame me, and my family." She was screeching now. "Tomorrow they will come for the sheets, and they will see no blood on them. Your people will think I did not perform my duty to you. Or . . . worse. You must stay and I . . . I must do this."

Lorenzo looked at the door longingly, and then back at the terrified virgin who sat trembling on his bed. He allowed himself a brief thought of the teachings of the Order. The Book of Love emphasized that conceiving a child where there was neither trust nor consciousness in the bridal chamber could condemn it to a difficult life. He could not allow such a curse to afflict his children. Somehow, he would need to reach this woman whom destiny had chosen for him to take to wife, for whatever reason of God's indeterminate will.

He took a very deep breath before turning to her with patient finality. He knelt beside the bed and took her hand. "Clarice, you must trust me as a man and as your husband. I will never harm you, and I have pledged to protect you and provide for you with all my strength. I will do all of those things, and more. You are a Medici now, and you are my family. Every child we conceive will be loved and cared for with my heart and my soul. And you will be likewise, as their mother. This is my vow to you."

Her brown eyes were full of tears, but there was more softness in her expression than before.

"Look at me, Clarice. Tell me, if nothing else, that you will learn to trust me as your husband." He brought his hand to her face and smiled at her, stroking her cheek with his thumb to wipe away the tears.

She attempted to smile back. "I . . . trust you, my husband." And she reached out to take his other hand in her own and squeezed it with all her strength, willing the fear to leave her body.

He approached her with great tenderness and infinite patience, careful not to hurt her or frighten her, praying all the while that this would perhaps get better as their days as man and wife stretched into the future. He knew that she would tear as he entered her, causing the bleeding that would be much analyzed on the sheets in the morning. He was as gentle as he could be, but there was no way to spare her that particular pain. Clarice winced and turned her head from him, then lay very still and kept her eyes shut tight. Lorenzo, for his sake and hers, withdrew from her quickly. He was inside her just long enough to fulfill the obligation of consummation, as he was as horrified by the circumstance as was his new wife. Before taking his leave, Lorenzo asked her, quite kindly, if she was all right. She nodded mutely, trying very hard not to sob with the indecency of what had just occurred. She could not imagine how any woman would ever find such a thing to be tolerable. Her confessor had been right. It was a woman's lot to suffer.

Lorenzo sighed heavily, replaced his breeches, and left their chamber without looking at her again or saying another word.

Left alone in her marriage bed, the young woman who was now Clarice Orsini de' Medici, the wife of the most magnificent man in Italy, allowed herself only one more thought before crying herself to sleep: never, at any time, did her husband try to kiss her.

*

Lorenzo had insisted that Colombina spend the night in the Medici palace following the wedding banquet. She had demurred, not wanting to be in the same building where he would be forced to bed another woman who was now everything that she had ever wanted to be in his life. But he had begged her, and she relented, as she always did when Lorenzo was truly insistent. It was there, to the chamber where she was installed as a guest, that he headed immediately after the nightmare with Clarice.

He threw himself with a fierce desperation into the arms of the only woman he would ever love, nourished and reinvigorated by the answering passion he found within her.

"My Colombina," he whispered, as he kissed her neck and lost himself in the mass of her hair. Lorenzo began to recite to her from their sacred scripture, the Song of Songs, as he whispered in her ear. He needed the respite of their tradition, the only escape he ever found from the weight of his responsibilities. His mouth trailed kisses across her collarbone between the words. "How beautiful you are, my love. How beautiful you are. Your eyes are doves." His voice caught on the words, so lost was he in the rawness of this night.

Colombina knew, as she always did, what a toll such responsibilities took on his poet's heart. She knew that what had transpired in his marital bed had been more difficult for Lorenzo than it was for Clarice— infinitely more difficult. It would always be her own place as his beloved to allow him the freedom to release his most deeply held feelings and to escape within her. It was a role she cherished. She responded to the holy song, holding Lorenzo to her as she sang the verse that spoke of spring and of renewal in her lilting, sensual voice:

Come then, my love,
For see, winter is past
The rains are over and gone.
The flowers appear on the earth
The season of glad songs has come,
The cooing of the dove is heard
In our land.

She stroked his hair as she whispered the last line with emphasis, and through tears, "My beloved is mine and I am his."

Lorenzo wept openly as he caressed her in this, the only respite of trust and consciousness he would ever know. His stolen hours with her would always be bittersweet. Why God had created someone so perfect for him, and yet did not allow them to be together, was the issue that would challenge his faith and serve to torment him every day of his life.

He held her face in his hands, gazing into her eyes as he entered her.

"It is always spring when I am with you," he whispered as they moved together in the perfect rhythm of destined lovers. "You are my only beloved, Colombina. My only wife in the eyes of God. *Semper.* Always."

And then the time for words was finished as lips, soft and searching, blended their shared breath in a way that matched their bodies and ultimately their souls, souls which had been joined together since before the dawn of time.

*

The parents of Simonetta Cattaneo would have indeed been pleased with the friends who awaited their cherished girl in Florence. Lucrezia Donati, known to her loved ones as Colombina, the Little Dove, took the beautiful, shy young girl under her protective wings. She integrated the lovely Simonetta into their community and watched with no small degree of humor as the men of the Order fell to her feet in a heap each time she entered the room.

Colombina shared with Simonetta the ways of the Order as she had learned them, the beautiful teachings of love and community that had enhanced her own life beyond any imaginings. She sat and held her friend's hand during the sacred lessons of union as they were taught by the Mistress of the Hieros-Gamos, Ginevra Gianfigliazza. Such lessons of the deeper physical interactions between a man and a woman were daunting, even terrifying, for one as delicate as Simonetta Cattaneo. She was a romantic creature and gentle of spirit; she was equally delicate of body. While tall, Simonetta was extremely thin and wan, even weak. She did not eat well or often and was sometimes overtaken with fits of coughing, which required her to retire to her bed. And while she had consummated her marriage to Marco Vespucci, Colombina and Ginevra knew that this was the sole time in which there had been any kind of physical union between the couple. Simonetta simply wasn't well enough to take the chance of getting with child. Thankfully, her husband was gentle and patient, willing to try every possible doctor in Tuscany to heal Simonetta and work toward making her healthy first and foremost.

For another woman of a different character, the presence of such physical perfection as Simonetta would have been threatening, or at least irksome. But Colombina did not know or feel jealousy. In her studies with the Master, she had learned well the dangers of the Seven Patterns of Deadly Thought, and most corrosive of these was envy. Envy was an affront to God. To feel envy was to believe that you were not created perfectly as you were meant to be by your mother and father in heaven. To feel envy was to accuse God of caring for another more than yourself, which was not the nature of a loving parent. Parents were meant to love their children equally, and this was certainly true of our divine mother and father.

No, Colombina felt no envy of Simonetta's beauty or of the attention she received from men. She knew full well what it was like to be the object of intense male admiration, and it was not always an easy role to play. For beautiful women, no matter how virtuous, were often the subjects of scrutiny and gossip. Colombina had snapped at more than a few Florentine matrons whom she had overheard casting aspersion on her friend's virtue. It infuriated her that the narrow-minded—and certainly jealous—women of Florence must immediately jump to the conclusion that Simonetta was Giuliano de' Medici's mistress, simply because he paid court to her loveliness during a joust. The Medici men, indeed all men of the Order, honored the troubadour traditions of celebrating beauty. During Giuliano's *giostra*, the festival of jousting that celebrated his coming of age, Simonetta was chosen to represent the Queen of Beauty, just as Colombina had once been chosen for Lorenzo. It was symbolic, a festive and mythical throne occupied by the woman judged by the young men of Florence to be the closest embodiment of Venus.

And from the day that Simonetta was introduced to Sandro Botticelli, the rumors in Florence became more vicious.

Sandro was besotted with her. He stopped sleeping at night, so tormented was he with her physical perfection. She became his only muse, the model for every nymph and goddess he painted. He drew her face endlessly through the night, trying to capture its contours and the magical way that her hair flowed around it in a frame of shimmery golden curls. He imagined her body beneath its heavy Florentine gowns, knowing that the lithe perfection beneath it was more beautiful than any he had seen before. He never meant to create such scandal, but the whispers began throughout Florence that Simonetta was posing nude for Sandro. Those who were enemies of the Order poisoned these rumors further, embellishing them to create legends of orgies where Simonetta shared her body with Sandro first, then the Medici brothers later.

Colombina was disgusted by it. The rumors challenged her belief that she could act only through love: there were times when it was very difficult to love those who reviled your family. And make no mistake, the members of the Order were her family, more than any blood relations had ever been. She loved Simonetta as a sister and wanted to protect her from the acid nature of the jealous and intolerant. And yet one of the many lessons Colombina would learn in her life came to her through the beautiful girl from Genoa.

After hearing a particularly vile rumor about Simonetta in the marketplace, Colombina had taken the two spiteful Florentine girls who were its source to task publicly. She was infuriated that the sweet Simonetta was a constant source of gossip. Further, she was particularly sensitive as someone who had been victimized for years by those who whispered about her, referring to her by the title she carried behind the closed doors of Florence, "Lorenzo's whore."

Simonetta heard the story, which was turning into legend across the city, and came to visit her friend and defender.

"The little dove has claws, it is said," she joked gently with her friend.

Colombina hugged her. "I could not help myself. Those girls were so poisonous in their jealousy, so hateful in the unfair things they said about you. I could not allow it to pass."

Simonetta's eyes were bright, but she did not shed tears. "It disturbs me less than you think, my sister, and certainly less than it does you. I know what those women say about me—and about you. But it matters not. As the Master has taught us, it is the struggle of all elements of beauty to be recognized and protected in this world. We mustn't allow it to hurt us or turn us to anger. Wasn't our own blessed Magdalena called a whore by so many?"

"She still is," Colombina replied. That Maria Magdalena, the beloved of Jesus and the apostle of the apostles, was referred to as a repentant sinner and even as a prostitute was an injustice that rankled Colombina. It was in studying Madonna Magdalena that she had first come to understand the terrible struggle that the teachings of the Way of Love had encountered over the centuries. Maria Magdalena had become dangerous to the established Church in Rome in the early days of Christianity. She represented a shadow side of Christianity, a set of teachings not beholden to the political strategies or economic goals of the Roman Church. The Way of Love was pure, taught as it was from the Book of Love and its later editions of the Libro Rosso—and taught most often by women.

Colombina had a special role in the Order. She was the new scribe, committing the old prophecies of the Magdalene lineage to writing under the guidance of Fra Francesco. It was Colombina's responsibility to ensure that the oral traditions of the Order did not die. Her current task was recording the story of the French prophetess called Jeanne, who had been executed at the stake for heresy a generation earlier. Colombina felt a special connection to the little maid from Lorraine, whom she dreamed about periodically. Sometimes Jeanne visited her in dreams and spoke to her of truth and courage, but Colombina only discussed these things with Fra Francesco and Lorenzo.

Along with Ginevra, Colombina was evolving into a very powerful and devoted force in the cause of absolute heresy in Florence.

"CLARICE DE' MEDICI is pregnant—again. Can you believe it?"

Costanza Donati, Colombina's younger sister, couldn't wait to deliver the news. Costanza was a pretty girl but a gossip, made all the more malicious by the jealousy she felt for her more beautiful sister.

"How I envy her," Colombina sighed. "Does she appreciate it, I wonder? That she carries his name and wakes in his arms each day, as naturally as the sun rises. That she . . . bears his children." Her throat caught at these last words, as they represented a terrible and private pain she had never expressed to anyone, and certainly not to Lorenzo.

"You don't know that she wakes in his arms." Costanza's tone turned conspiratorial. "You know what they say, don't you? His personal apothecary mixes a tincture that makes Lorenzo more potent so that when he is forced to bed his wretched wife, he impregnates her immediately. Then he can be free of her for the next ten months."

"That is idle gossip, sister. Lorenzo is the most noble man I have ever known. He treats his wife as a queen. She is the mother of his children, and he reveres her for that."

"Oh, of course Madonna Clarice wants for nothing," Costanza said dramatically, before adding, "but she is colder than a slab of Carrara marble, that creature, and dull as dishwater. She is as far from you as it is possible to be, and Lorenzo worships at your altar. So to speak."

Colombina indulged the inane giggling for a moment and then continued with her original thought. Costanza was hardly the perfect audience, but she was family and generally loyal, in spite of her petty nature. And Colombina needed to talk.

"But do you know what I am saying, 'Stanza? Clarice lives in his house and his crest is engraved in their marriage bed. What I wouldn't give to know how that feels."

Surprisingly, Costanza actually appeared to be listening. Her next comment was even insightful.

"Do you know what is tragic? I am certain that she envies you even more. Can you imagine what it is to have such a magnificent man for a husband and know that you will never satisfy him in any way? That his eyes are closed and he thinks of another each time he touches you? I bet he never kisses her."

Colombina's expression was wan. Costanza would never understand just how accurate she was, or why. Kissing was considered a great sacrament in the *hieros-gamos* tradition, known as the sharing of the sacred breath. It was an act that blended two spirits together by combining their life force energies, and was not to be shared by anyone except one's most beloved. "No, I'm quite sure he does not kiss her."

"Well, that would be torture for any woman married to a man like Lorenzo, even one as heartless as that Roman Medea."

"She's really not so bad, you know." Lucrezia felt real sympathy for Clarice, who was, in her way, just as much a victim of circumstance as she and Lorenzo. "Clarice is quite kind beneath all that Roman coldness. And I don't think she really cares that much how Lorenzo feels or whom he beds so long as he is discreet and provides for his family. And he is expert at both those things. Lorenzo says Clarice is happiest when he leaves her alone, which suits him perfectly."

"What do you think of her being pregnant again so immediately? You must admit, il Magnifico is shockingly fertile where his *wife* is concerned." Costanza look pointedly at Colombina, who conspicuously had never become pregnant during her lengthy affair with Lorenzo. What Costanza did not know was that the same apothecary mixed an equally potent tincture for her, which she had used many times to bring about her courses and force bleeding. It was the same potion used by the high-market courtesans in Venice, who could not afford to allow pregnancy to interfere with their trade. Their clientele, ranking nobles and more than a few cardinals of the Church, paid handsomely for their ladies to remain beautiful and unmarred. Colombina tried not to fixate on this detail, on the idea that she was viewed by many in Florence as Lorenzo's personal courtesan, albeit a highly pedigreed and exquisite one. No one dared speak it for fear of the Magnificent wrath that it would invoke, but she was not a fool. Colombina knew what was said of her by those who had no love of the Medici. And yet, she allowed it little time to disrupt her. She had taken an oath to belong to Lorenzo for eternity, and nothing mattered to her more than that. Jealous and malicious Florentines be damned.

Yet on early mornings when the mist covered the Arno and Florence was peaceful before the bustle of the day began, she would take walks along the river and allow herself to weep at the injustice of it all.

Each time she bled, Colombina prayed to Maria Magdalena to forgive her for violating the laws of the Order and sobbed over the loss of a child she would give anything to bear.

*

Niccolò was back in Florence, home from his latest excursion. These were always the hardest times for Colombina.

When he was away, she was the absolute mistress of her own destiny, spending most of her time with Ginevra and Simonetta, and with the Master when he was in the city pursuing the business of the Order. And her sweetest, most secret stolen moments came about when Lorenzo was able to meet her at the Antica Torre. Here they were alone in their own world, together as the most intimate of friends and ardent of lovers. It was blissful.

But when Niccolò returned from his seafaring adventures, she was expected to be home with him as a proper wife should be. It was wretched.

On this particular night, Colombina had thought she would be safe enough keeping her meeting with Lorenzo, as Niccolò was going out to the tavern with his friends to regale them with his latest tales of pirates and lost treasure, and likely a few ribald details about slave girls and harlots in Constantinople. None of these details bothered or even interested her, so long as they meant that Niccolò wasn't around to demand her attention physically or emotionally. When he did decide he wanted to take advantage of his marital rights, he was relatively quick about it, for which Colombina was grateful, although it had given her cause to grieve for all her sisters in the world who would never know any other kind of husband, never know what it was like to have a man make love to them with all his heart and soul, as well as his body, in the way that Lorenzo did with her. So many women only knew arranged marriages to the Niccolòs of the world, who might just as well have had a hole in the bed as a flesh-and-blood wife.

She was thinking about this as she made the walk home from her all-too-brief evening with Lorenzo, about how blessed she was to have found him and how enriched her life had become through the teachings of the Order. How she wished she could share these understandings of love and equality with women who would never know anything of the kind. That was one of the objectives of the Order, and certainly Colombina's dream—to bring about a time when arranged marriages were seen as a crime committed upon women, and female children would no longer be treated as pawns in a family's game of wealth and power.

As Colombina rounded the corner to their city house, she stopped. There was a light on in Niccolò's study. Why was he home so early? She would have to think of something, quick, to explain away her absence in the night like this. She knew it was risky to see Lorenzo during the periods when Niccolò was home, but it was far more painful to be separated from her beloved for too long. She was willing to take the chance, always. She gritted her teeth and entered her house, praying he would be preoccupied with some new map or idea for a voyage.

"Where have you been so late into the night?"

Niccolò was waiting for her, and he was drunk.

"I was with the Gianfigliazza women, preparing for the Saint John's Eve carnival. We have so much to do that I lost track of the hours passing. I'm sorry, Nico. Can I get you something? More wine? Come, have some wine with me and tell me of your evening."

It was usually easy enough to distract him, but not this night. Something—or someone—had gotten to Niccolò Ardinghelli.

"You . . . are . . . a liar!" Niccolò yelled as he slapped her, hard enough to make her stumble as he continued his tirade, stalking her across the room. "Do you think I don't know where you are? Where you go when I am not in Florence? Do you think I don't know that you whore for the Medici every chance you get and have done so for years?"

He slapped her again. She fell to the ground this time with the force of the blow.

Colombina picked herself up, her expression reflecting a blend of dignity and contempt. She faced her husband and said with quiet strength, "I do not whore for that Medici. I give myself to him freely. I always have and I always will. Lorenzo has my heart; why shouldn't he also possess my body?"

Her husband was incredulous. He blinked at this, trying in his drunken state to grasp the reasoning. "Because . . . because you are my wife."

"You just said I was a whore."

"You behave as one!"

Lucrezia allowed the bitterness of her enforced years with him to flow from her lips for the first time. "Perhaps you're right on one account. A whore beds a man because she must for her very survival. It is an act of empty rutting, done by a woman with no choice. So if I am a whore for anyone, it is for you."

Niccolò sputtered for a moment, taken aback by a defiance he had never before seen in a woman, much less his wife. Blinded by rage, he swung, hitting her full in the face with his fist. Horrified by what he had done, he ran from the room and closed himself in his studio. Colombina picked herself up, gingerly touching the place where his fist hit the mark. Moving to the mirror that graced her entry hall, she examined her face. Niccolò's blow would leave a welt and a deep black bruise on her cheekbone for days to come. And there was a meeting of the Order in three days' time.

*

Colombina arrived three days later for the gathering of the Order at the Antica Torre. Niccolò had avoided her since the night of her beating, out of a combination of guilt, anger, and humiliation. The positive side effect of this was that she was able to attend this meeting without asking for his permission.

She had done her best to conceal Niccolò's mark on her face, rubbing it with ice and with an oil from the apothecary. While it was less vivid than before, there was still a purplish shadow, which was impossible to disguise completely. She knew that Lorenzo would notice instantly and demand an explanation. She had prepared one; not because she cared about protecting Niccolò, but because she cared about protecting Lorenzo. He had enough worries without her victimization adding to them. And she believed that her husband had felt real remorse. While he was a braggart, Niccolò wasn't inherently evil, and she was convinced that this was a singular incident and he would never hit her again. Colombina had to forgive him, as that was the Way of Love. Besides, Niccolò would be leaving again soon enough. She just needed to be patient.

Careful to enter the Torre in the presence of others so that she would not have to answer Lorenzo privately, Colombina knew that she could not avoid the issue indefinitely. As he came to kiss her in greeting, he stopped suddenly and raised one gentle index finger to run it lightly over her face. His questioning of her was deceptively gentle.

"What happened here, Colombina?"

She could not look at him and lie. Lowering her eyes, she replied, "It's nothing. A careless cleaning woman did not dry the floors properly after washing them. She left water on the marble for me to slip in. I hit the side of my face on the stairs."

Lorenzo said nothing. Instead, he used that same gentle finger to lift her chin and forced her to look at him. He held her eyes for a moment, and Colombina shuddered at what she saw in them. In all their time together, they had never truly quarreled. Their love was so strong, and so selfless, that there had never been any lie or betrayal between them. But Lorenzo's dark eyes were like burning coals as they bored into her. He released her, gently, and walked away. For the remainder of the evening, he sat on the opposite side of the room and refused to speak with her.

He was morose and contributed very little to the evening's conversation. When he did speak, it was in clipped tones and short phrases. It was clear to everyone that il Magnifico was in a difficult mood, and the meeting was cut short with little of the usual socializing at the end.

As the gathering dispersed, Colombina looked at him across the room, her eyes full of tears. She hated seeing him like this, and hated even more that she was the cause of it. She could see his chest heave with a sigh as he walked deliberately toward her. Pulling her aside to a corner of the room, he finally spoke to her. His voice was soft, almost a whisper, incongruous with the harshness of his words.

"Lucrezia . . ."

Lorenzo's use of her given name was a more painful blow to her than anything she had endured at Niccolò's hands. Since their days as children in the forest, he had never called her anything but Colombina, even in public. The lines were etched in his face, and he spoke slowly and with emphasis, not in his characteristically clipped tones.

"While I understand why you have lied to me, I pray that you will not do so again. There are few left alive whom I trust completely, and I do not think I could bear it if you ceased to be one of those."

With a lover's instinct, she reached for him. "Lorenzo, please . . ."

There would be no tenderness this night, not from a man wrestling with the mighty demons that were threatening to close in on Lorenzo de' Medici. He held up his hand, gently but firmly, to stop her from coming any closer.

"I am not finished. I have a message for your husband, and I ask that you deliver it exactly. Tell Niccolò that you were with me tonight—it is clear that he already knows that we are still together—and tell him that on this night Lorenzo took a vow before God. Tell him that I vow, if he ever strikes you again, I will kill him with my own hands."

MAUREEN WEPT AS Destino related the story of Lorenzo and Colombina and the terrible heartache of their enforced separation. He had summoned her to Petra's apartment to spend time with him after watching her connect so deeply with Colombina's images in the Uffizi.

"The time returns, right?" she asked him. "Colombina and Lorenzo could not be together in any traditional way because of their circumstances. And the same is now true of Bérenger and me. Over and over again, the cycle happens. Jesus and Magdalene, Matilda and Gregory, Lorenzo and Colombina. And now Bérenger and I are not going to be able to be together as we dreamed, just another couple separated by circumstances that they must honor. So is this my test?"

"What do you see as your test?"

"Can I be as selfless as Colombina? Can I accept that Bérenger's destiny is to be a Poet Prince—and raise another—and that this is more important for the world than our own happiness?" She fought the tears as she continued. "But why? That's what I want to know, Master. Why?"

Destino had heard this question many times over the centuries, a question he was never allowed to answer directly. It was not for him to give his struggling students the answers that they needed, for there was no learning in that, no permanent change to the soul. They would have to find the answers on their own and make their own choices. Over and over he had endured the pain of watching those he loved fall, and he prayed it would not happen again.

"But you see, my dear, that is precisely the point. The time returns. But it doesn't have to. It is a choice."

Maureen shook her head, confused. "You've lost me."

Destino explained in his wise way, always careful to share the wisdom, yet equally determined not to give away the answers. "If I had to choose the one factor that caused our grand plan for the Renaissance to fail, more than any other, it was the enforced separation of Lorenzo and Colombina."

Maureen was shocked at this. "Really? More than the politics, power, and religion?"

"Yes, because their separation was caused by all those things. If the Medici had fought to allow Lorenzo to marry for love, rather than power and alliance, the world might look very different now. Yes, the Donati opposed the union, but I believe they could have been bought. Piero was weak, and Cosimo was ill, so we did not push for the marriage as hard as we might have. We are all to blame for that failure. We did not stand up for the power of love."

Maureen listened, fighting through the circumstances, the concepts, her own pain and frustration. "So what are you saying? That the time returns, but it shouldn't? That it returns precisely because we keep getting it wrong?"

"I'm saying that what God has put together, no man should separate."

*

The morning was bright and beautiful as Tammy and Maureen turned left at the Ponte Santa Trinità to walk along the Arno. They would cross the river at the Ponte Vecchio, the picturesque and storied merchants' bridge, which was one of Florence's most beloved landmarks.

The women decided to take the walk across the river to visit the Chiesa di Santa Felicita, the church that the art student had told Maureen about yesterday in the Uffizi. Maureen had spent most of the night with Tammy, talking through her session with Destino and trying to make sense of it all. Bérenger had called five times yesterday, but she had not spoken with him yet. Maureen needed to be very clear about the right course of action before she did so. She was still unsure of exactly what that was. A walk along the river seemed like a good way to start the day as she continued the discussion with Tammy.

"Colombina was content to be Lorenzo's mistress, to be with him in any capacity available to her no matter what. I don't know that I have the same selflessness."

Tammy replied, "Colombina didn't have to cope with the insufferable bitch who is Vittoria."

Maureen stopped and looked out to where the sun sparkled on the river, gilding the reflection of the Ponte Vecchio in the Arno.

"Nor did Colombina have to compete with the Second Coming."

"Neither do you."

"What do you mean? You don't believe in the prophecies?"

Tammy shrugged. "I do believe in the prophecies. I don't believe in Vittoria. Something is rotten in Florence, but I can't put my finger on it. It's just a hunch."

They put their conversation on hold as they approached their destination. Santa Felicita was the second-oldest church in the region, originally built in the fourth century and dedicated to a saint from Rome who was martyred in the second century. Maureen was always fascinated by stories of the women in the early Church: there was usually much to learn beneath the surface legend if you were able to dig long enough and deep enough. The case of this Saint Felicity seemed particularly tragic: she was a mother who lost all seven of her sons to Roman persecution before being executed herself. Maureen wanted to read more about her to find the details; she would put it on her agenda for further research if the church they visited today inspired her.

During the Renaissance, the Church of Santa Felicita was decorated with artworks from greats like Neri di Bicci, and *The Deposition of the Cross* by Pontormo was considered one of the most significant works of the early Mannerist style. It was amazing to Maureen that so many of the most important artworks in Italy were readily available to view in the churches that dotted the city every few hundred yards. Each church she entered was a like a miniature world-class museum.

Santa Felicita was no exception. The Pontormo artwork covered the chapel designed by the great Brunelleschi, the genius responsible for the majestic and unequaled Duomo. Surrounding the window, a fresco, also by Pontormo, depicted the popular annunciation scene, with a beautiful and welcoming Mary receiving her joyous news from the angel Gabriel. But the standout was the fresco that covered the entire wall, encapsulating the moment when Christ's body was removed from the cross. Pontormo's version was indeed unique; the colors were bright and vibrant, women draped in deep blues and vibrant pinks. In the early Mannerist style, they were long-limbed and graceful, and the characters appeared to merge into each other in a strangely lyrical dance of mourning. Mary Magdalene, veiled in pink, held Jesus at his head and shoulders, supported by other characters less easily identified, while his mother swooned with her grief. Saint Veronica was present, back to the viewer, and appeared to be reaching out to the blessed mother with one hand, and holding the veil of her legend in the other.

It was a beautiful and worthy piece of art, and yet after spending a day in the presence of Botticelli, Maureen and Tammy were not as inspired by it as they might have been on another day. They explored the church a bit, walking along the nave and admiring the rest of the art and architecture that graced the building. Tammy, walking ahead of Maureen, now stopped in front of an enormous painting on the right wall. She had a look of utter horror on her face.

"What is it?" Maureen asked, as she approached her friend and the painting.

"Maureen, meet Saint Felicity."

The painting was majestic, tragic, and horrifying. Felicity rose like a phoenix from the bodies of her dead sons, which lay scattered around her in various poses of death. They were bloody and twisted; some were decapitated. Felicity herself stood in the midst of it all, arms outstretched to heaven. Her pose was one of defiance rather than grief. Over her knee was the body of her youngest son, a beautiful golden-haired boy who was limp and lifeless.

Maureen was nauseated by the painting. Tammy was horrified. But neither of them could turn their eyes away from it.

"Beautiful, isn't it?" They both jumped at the English accent, which came from behind them, and turned to see the art student from the Uffizi. Maureen noticed that she was still wearing the leather gloves, despite the hot weather. The girl looked down at her hands self-consciously for a moment and said by way of explanation, simply, "Eczema." She then continued, explaining her appearance. "I work here as a volunteer, for the Confraternity of the Holy Apparition. The Florentine chapter meets here. Felicity is one of our patronesses. Although she wasn't a visionary as such, she heard the voice of God clearly enough to sacrifice her children for him. Do you know her story?"

"Other than the fact that her seven sons were slain before her, no. I don't know the rest."

Felicity launched into the story of Santa Felicita, providing the details of how the saint encouraged the deaths of her children, even cheered them on. She concluded by reciting the quote from Saint Augustine:

> Wonderful is the sight set before the eyes of our faith, a mother choosing for her children to finish their earthly lives before her contrary to all our human instincts.

Tammy could take no more. She wasn't skilled at holding her tongue at the best of times, but as she stood there with the new life of a beloved child growing within her womb, everything within her spirit rebelled. Unconsciously, her hand moved to cover her belly, as if to shield it from the horror of Felicity's story.

"Sorry, but everything about that is wrong in so many ways that I wouldn't even know where to begin. No sane woman allows suffering or death to come to her child. No mother watches while her son is murdered before her, if she has the power to stop it. Nor do I believe that this is what God would want from any of us."

Felicity narrowed her eyes as she looked away from the painting and then at Tammy. "You believe you know what God wants?" she asked softly.

"I believe that God does not want us to allow death or injury to come to our children, and he entrusts us to become mothers and protectors of the innocent. I do not believe that God wants a blood sacrifice of innocents. Ever."

Felicity refused to look at Tammy or Maureen and fixated again on the horrific sight of Felicita draped in the corpses of her babies. When she spoke it was in a strange cadence, a mantra repeated by rote.

She did not send her sons away, she sent them on to God. She understood that they were beginning life, not ending it. It was not enough that she looked on but that she encouraged them. She bore more fruit with her courage than with her womb. Seeing them be strong, she was strong, and in the victory of each of her children, she was victorious.

Tammy appeared outraged and Maureen was speechless. Was this young, twenty-first-century woman saying that she thought this was not only acceptable but exalted behavior? It was unconscionable.

Before either of them could speak again, Felicity turned to take her leave. She said over her shoulder, "We are having an event here in honor of one of Florence's greatest heroes later this week, on the twenty-third of May. It is the anniversary of the death of the holy brother Girolamo Savonarola, and it promises to be quite an event. There are fliers at the front of the church if you are interested in more information. Enjoy your stay."

Tammy leaned against one of the pews, both hands holding her belly now, as Felicity walked away, disappearing somewhere into a gated area of the church that was not open to the public. She exhaled deeply and said to Maureen, "I think I am going to throw up."

Maureen nodded. The encounter had been very disturbing for both of them. "This"—she pointed to the painting of Felicita surrounded by the massacred innocents—"is everything that is wrong with religious fanaticism. This is the example of how the teachings of the Way of Love were abused and corrupted. This, my friend, is the enemy."

They were walking toward the front of the church now, both anxious to get out of there and into the healing rays of the Florentine sun. Tammy stopped at a little table near the holy water font, where church bulletins were scattered alongside a stack of fliers for the event Felicity had mentioned. Tammy picked one up and gasped.

"No, my friend," she said to Maureen. "I believe *that* was the enemy." Tammy gestured to where Felicity had disappeared before handing Maureen the offending flier. Beneath the details of the commemoration in honor of the martyrdom of the holy brother Savonarola was a photograph of Maureen's latest book, *The Time Returns*, along with the bold command to "Stop the Blasphemy!"

Florence
1475

THE TAVERN IN Ognissanti was calmer than usual this night. The weather was glorious, the kind of Florentine evening in which the air caresses the skin like a silk coverlet. For Tuscans, it was criminal to be indoors on such a perfect night. And yet for Lorenzo, these opportunities for unbridled relaxation with Sandro were sacred, stolen moments. And Sandro was in fine form, having come from an eventful day in the studio with Andrea del Verrocchio and his brother artists.

Sandro Botticelli was caught up in a magnificent creative spiral: the more he painted, the more he wanted to. He was devoted completely to his mission as an artist. For all his cynicism, Sandro was a man of deep and abiding faith. He thanked God every day, and often many times a day, for the talent he had been given and for the means with which to express it. He also thanked God for Lorenzo and the Medici family and prayed for their safety so that the mission of combining art and faith would endure.

Verrocchio's studio was the training ground for the angelics, and Sandro operated as the eyes and ears of the Medici from within it. He reported to Lorenzo regularly on the progress of the members, some established well within the Order, others still being tested for their mettle.

"Domenico is clearly the most gifted. Aside from me, of course," Sandro began. He was many things; humble was not one of them. Yet he did not exaggerate his talents. He was unequaled anywhere in Florence now in terms of technique and output. No one could dispute that. But as a result, Lorenzo knew that he could trust every word that Sandro uttered about the other artists they were grooming for the Order.

They were discussing the work of Domenico Ghirlandaio, a darkly handsome, soft-spoken family man from an accomplished Florentine art dynasty.

"His fresco technique is unmatched. The frescoes he is working on for your mother's family at Santa Maria Maggiore are stunning. You must get over there to see them in these early stages, for to watch him while he is working is very inspiring. And he has the face and bearing of an angel himself, which adds to the pleasure of observing him as he creates. I would use him as a model if he wasn't already so inclined to paint himself. He is a bit of a peacock. A quiet peacock, but one who struts all the same. That said, he's not insufferable like that strange bird from Vinci."

"Leonardo?"

Sandro nodded and signaled the serving girl to bring more ale. "Mm-hm. Leonardo. I'm not sure about him, Lorenzo, even though his sketches are remarkable and he has a technical precision that is something special to observe. I haven't quite figured out how to describe him. He's . . . off. He is not one of us."

"You don't think he has angelic talent?"

"I don't think he has angelic temperament."

"Neither do you, most of the time."

"Ha. Very funny. And it's a good thing you're buying the ale or I wouldn't put up with you. Leonardo is different from the others, different from me, to be sure. He is a loner. That in itself isn't a crime. Donatello was a madman as well as a loner, and yet he was still angelic. The difference becomes apparent when you watch them create. When Donatello stood before a piece of wood or stone, you could see the divinity pouring through him as he made that initial contact with the source of his art. Fra Lippi is the same, as you well know. God works through him when he paints, so tangibly that you can almost see it pouring from his fingers. But most of all, I know how it feels myself. It is something that engages the heart and spirit in combination with the mind, before flowing into the hands."

"And Leonardo doesn't do that?"

"He can't. I watch him, and he works only from the neck up. He also has a very high opinion of himself and listens to nobody."

Lorenzo was slightly irked that Sandro might be brushing aside Leonardo's talent too readily because of personality conflicts—or jealousy. He responded, "Andrea says that Leonardo creates the most technically perfect sketches he has ever seen. We need that kind of talent, Sandro. We must work with him. The Master needs that kind of talent for what we are creating."

Sandro snapped at his friend, "*I* can and will create whatever Fra Francesco needs. He does not require the services of someone who has no reverence for our Lord."

"What does that mean?"

"I told you. Leonardo is not one of us. He cannot engage his heart when he is given tasks that involve our Lord or our Lady. He's from Baptist country, Lorenzo. The extreme side. He believes that John was always the true messiah."

"He did not say so when we interviewed him to come into our studio."

"I said he is odd, but he is not a fool. He knows that there is more opportunity here for him than anywhere else in Italy, and he also knew that he would never be admitted to the Guild of Saint Luke if he did not please you."

The Guild of Saint Luke was the artists' enclave responsible for overseeing all the great painting commissions in Florence. To truly make a name for oneself, and a good living as an artist, one had to be a member of the Guild. And given that it had ties to the Order and the Medici, being within the good graces of both was necessary for membership.

"But it will have to end somewhere, I'm telling you. He may be brilliant, but he is not one to produce quickly or proficiently when the subject matter isn't to his liking. He has been working on a Magi sketch for months. And while he continues to add figures to it, it is going nowhere. I would bet every florin I have ever made that it will never see paint. Such genius is of no use to us, Lorenzo, if it cannot be channeled to our purposes. I can paint ten times what he sketches in a month."

Lorenzo nodded. Sandro was full of his own abilities, but he had every right to be. He was not only a creative genius, and one who truly understood the teachings of the Order, but he was also unequaled in his productivity. He was prolific beyond any other artist Lorenzo had ever seen. And this was a tenet of the Order: to create for God, as often as possible, and with as much passion and commitment as could be channeled into the art. Angelic artists were not only gifted in terms of quality, they were able to produce in quantity without sacrificing the art.

"Leonardo is not a producer. While the rest of us pour out frescoes and major works, he is still drawing bizarre machines on his sketchpad—gigantic tools for excavating dirt, or weapons of war to chop a man to bits. Perhaps those are useful and even interesting, but they do not serve our mission. Further, he has no interest in the teachings of the Order and isn't hearing Andrea when he conveys certain secrets."

Sandro had Lorenzo's full attention now, as he knew he would. That Leonardo wasn't connecting with the teachings of the Order, and was perhaps even in opposition to the true teachings, was important. The purpose of cultivating these artists was not merely for art's sake; it was to create a stable of divinely gifted scribes who could translate the sacred teachings into masterworks for the future.

"Do you think he is dangerous? Or a spy?"

Sandro shook his head. "I don't see guile in him, necessarily. But that doesn't mean he can't be used by those who have plenty to spare. I simply don't think he has the capacity to be loyal to you or to the Order. We are not his priority, nor do I think we can ever be."

Lorenzo considered this and added, "Jacopo tells me that Leonardo is the greatest artist who has ever lived."

"Bracciolini said that?" Sandro did not attempt to hide his disdain. "He would. They are similar types. Cerebral. Mental geniuses who are completely cut off from anything higher than what is in their own heads."

"So you do not think that Leonardo should be moved to the next level, just to see how he fares?" Lorenzo asked. "I was going to send him to a private meeting with the Master for evaluation."

Sandro shrugged. "It wouldn't hurt to see what Fra Francesco has to say about him. He is the greatest judge of character on God's earth. But I would not hold out great hope for this Leonardo. Did I mention that he writes backwards? As if in a mirror? While it is an interesting feat, what is the point of such an endeavor other than a parlor trick? I would like to see what would happen if he put that mind of his into something more diverse."

Lorenzo nodded, taking it all in. He was disturbed by this report. Leonardo da Vinci was a rare talent, an extraordinary genius. Lorenzo had great hopes of bringing him into the fold. And on the occasions when they met, he always found Leonardo to be elegant and polite, a well-spoken young man with extraordinary intelligence and insights. To learn of these unexpected challenges was troubling. He would need to discuss them with Andrea as well as Fra Francesco.

"Oh, and there's one more thing I haven't told you. He hates women."

"What do you mean, he hates women?"

"Despises the female sex. Can't stand the sight of them. Told me he thinks they are all deceitful whores and tricksters. He speaks as a man who was abandoned in the cradle, and perhaps he was. He has not known maternal love, which is clear when you see that he is incapable of drawing a Madonna who is connected to her child. He has no understanding of the mother-and-child bond. And he won't stay in the room if the model is female. So I do not think he is going to be overjoyed with the teachings of the Order once he is further immersed into the requisite devotion to our Lady.

"So while you might get a few decent John the Baptist paintings out of him, I'm thinking that he may not be the best portrait artist for our beloved Madonnas."

*

There was an air about Leonardo da Vinci, a controlled yet tangible energy that radiated from the young man. Lorenzo, after spending several hours with him in the studio, had no doubt that Leonardo was an angelic. His talent was staggering. To look through his sketches was to be stunned by the exquisite precision with which he worked. And like the others who had been identified by Lorenzo and his grandfather before him, Leonardo had a certain charisma that was found in all the divinely gifted artists. On the surface, there was nothing about this man that should not be exciting and promising to all who valued artistic talent. And he was unerringly polite to both Lorenzo and the Master. While Sandro and the other artists had complained that Leonardo's temperament was often one of well-displayed hubris, Lorenzo did not witness this himself.

"You honor me, Magnifico," Leonardo said in a warm voice with a southern Tuscan inflection. "I wish to create in a way that is pleasing to you."

Lorenzo thanked Leonardo as they worked through his sketches. The infamous *Adoration of the Magi* sketch, which Sandro had complained about, was the focus of their discussion. It was indeed a very busy sketch, but also a grand one. The scope was magnificent, and there was an elaborate narrative woven through the work. It was beautiful and powerful, and yet as Lorenzo examined it, he was beginning to understand what Sandro meant when he said it would always be incomplete.

"You do not like it, Magnifico?"

Leonardo da Vinci was genuinely concerned. Again, Lorenzo was not witnessing the grand pride that the other artists accused him of, nor did Leonardo appear to be playing the innocent for his patron. And yet there was something happening here with this artist that Lorenzo had not experienced with any of his other angelics. With the other artists, even the extremely temperamental ones, there was an ease of communication. It amounted to a sheer passion for art and the process of transmitting the divine into the work that they all shared and all celebrated. That passion could not be seen in Leonardo, for all his extraordinary talent.

Lorenzo stared at the *Adoration of the Magi*, willing his mind and spirit to work together to help him to identify exactly what was missing in the sketch. As Sandro had pointed out, there was no feeling of relationship between the Madonna and her child. But there was something else here that was disturbing, and Lorenzo was trying to grasp it. Leonardo was waiting for him to reply, and it was cruel to leave an artist to believe his work was not appreciated.

"Actually, Leonardo, I like it very much. What you have created here—this background with the staircase, the horses here and how they help create perspective, the use of the kings spaced across the foreground on either side—it is stunning. Truly magnificent. It's just . . ." Lorenzo ran his finger along the edges of the paper as he considered, then jumped when he cut himself on the corner, drawing blood. He sucked on the offended finger for a moment to stop the bleeding, and as he did so, the realization came to him.

"It's just that . . . all of these figures appear to be *afraid*. Here is a scene of the most sacred event in human history, the birth of our Lord, the prince who will show us the most divine love. And yet you have given all those in attendance of the holy event an expression of fear."

Leonardo was quiet for a long moment before responding. "I do not see it as fear. I see it as awe."

Lorenzo considered this for a moment before responding. "Awe? Really? But look at this figure here, the king who is Balthazar," Lorenzo pointed out, animated with both the realization and the challenge now. "He is cowering from the infant Jesus. Clearly, that is fear rather than awe. And this figure above the holy child. He appears to be recoiling, almost as if in horror. I'm afraid, my friend, I do not get the sense that this is a *celebration* of our Lord's birth."

Leonardo shrugged, his mouth twitching a bit, as he let his careful guard down for the first time. Perhaps it was Lorenzo's honest assessment of the work that allowed him to slip, but slip he did. When he replied, Leonardo's voice was soft but sure, although he could not look Lorenzo in the eyes as he spoke.

"Perhaps not everyone believes that the birth of Jesus was something to be celebrated. Perhaps for some it was an event to be feared, or even despised. If art is meant to be truth, then I would paint it as such."

Lorenzo was taken aback by the harshly heretical statement. He glanced up at Fra Francesco, who was utterly silent, an observer of what he sensed to be a grand drama playing out quietly before him in the studio of Andrea del Verrocchio.

"You do not believe that the birth of Jesus is an event to be celebrated, Leonardo?" Lorenzo kept his voice calm and casual. He wanted a true answer, and not a reaction.

"It does not matter what I believe, Magnifico. If you are my patron, and you want figures who are smiling at the birth of Jesus, then it is my job to please you. I can assure you that when these images are translated into paint, I shall adjust the facial expressions to provide you with whatever it is that you require."

It was a careful answer, and a brilliant one. Leonardo did not answer the question of what he did or did not believe. He avoided it completely, giving the correct reply to please a patron.

Lorenzo smiled and thanked him, assuring Leonardo again that he was an artist of consummate skill and that he, Lorenzo, would look forward to seeing what he produced in the future. He then called for Andrea to meet with him and the Master later that afternoon back in the Via Larga for dinner to discuss what was now being called the Leonardo problem.

*

Andrea del Verrocchio had been unerringly loyal to three generations of Medici, but he was not going to lose the greatest sketch artist he had ever trained without a fight.

"Leonardo's is a rare talent, Lorenzo. He is a genius."

"I'm aware of that. I have eyes, Andrea. I also have ears. Did you hear what he said about the birth of our Lord being an event to be feared and despised? He may be a genius, but unfortunately, he is not *our* genius."

"Give me more time with him. We work well together. Perhaps he can be brought around . . ."

"You cannot make a man what he is not." Lorenzo smiled wanly at the man whom he loved and trusted so completely. "Even you, my friend, as brilliant a teacher as you are, cannot transform a man who does not want to be thus changed. No man ever achieved true greatness using just his mind. One must also engage the heart. I do not think Leonardo will do that, because he does not desire to do so."

Andrea looked at Fra Francesco, who had taught them both the meaning of love as it had been brought to them all through the teachings of Jesus Christ. "And what do you think, Master?"

Fra Francesco answered carefully. "What do I think? Or what do I feel? Because that is what this comes down to, isn't it? Leonardo knows how to think, but he does not know how to feel, and he chooses to stay in that place of isolation. I do not think anyone will draw him away from that choice, as he holds it too close. There is great darkness in that heart, a darkness that comes from sadness. It is not of his own making or of his own doing, but it is there all the same."

"Do you think he is an angelic?" This was Lorenzo's question.

"Undoubtedly," the Master answered, startling both men with his certainty. Never before had any artist, no matter how difficult, been dismissed if it was determined that he was born with the angelic gifts. Would Fra Francesco insist on keeping him, then?

"But I think he is an angel who has been damaged by his human experiences, and this happened at a very young age. It would take great love to crack him open and release the pure divinity that is trapped within his spirit. I do not foresee that happening. However, we are taught through the greatest of prayers that forgiveness must be for all men, and we must therefore allow Leonardo to continue awhile longer under Andrea's tutelage. We will treat him with love, tolerance, and forgiveness, as our Lord has taught us through his commandments, and see if that brings about a change in him."

"And if it does not?" Lorenzo asked.

"If it does not," Fra Francesco said with a little smile, "then we find him a new patron, elsewhere in Italy, some noble family whose favor you wish to secure who will celebrate the name of the Medici for selflessly surrendering their most talented young artist as an act of friendship."

Lorenzo raised his glass to the ancient man with the scarred face. Now *that* was genius.

*

The year 1475 was turning out to be an important one for Lorenzo, one in which the blessings of God were being showered on all of Tuscany through the arrival of several children, deemed to have potentially angelic gifts, based on their parentage combined with the position of the stars at their time of birth. The astrological and numerological predictions of the Magi had foretold that this would be an exalted year. Indeed, Clarice was expecting again, due in December, and the Magi were predicting a son with a destiny to carry the mission of the Order into the future. Lorenzo had great hopes for this expected child, as his elder son, little Piero, was already showing signs of being a product of his mother. He was sullen and spoiled, and Lorenzo argued with Clarice regularly about the boy's pending education. He was still too young for these battles to matter overmuch, but in the next few years Lorenzo would have to be firm in guiding the direction of Piero's education. Clarice wanted him schooled from the Psalter, learning to read and write only from the sanctified teachings of the Church. Lorenzo, of course, wanted him immediately immersed in the classics.

Lorenzo's greatest joy as a parent came from his daughters. The elder, named after his mother, Lucrezia, was a sweet girl who loved to sing for her father. But his baby, the joy of his life, was little Maria Maddalena. Madi was precocious and playful and had her father wrapped around her pudgy little finger. The first thing Lorenzo did when he entered the palazzo after a day away was scoop her up and toss her about until she squealed with delight. Maddalena was special, not just for her sunny, feisty personality—she was a born under the star sign of Leo, on the twenty-fifth of July—but because she had healed Lorenzo's broken heart after the loss of the twins. In the previous year, Clarice had given birth to twin boys, but they were tiny and weak and did not survive longer than a few days. He was shattered by the loss, as was Clarice. But the arrival of Maddalena restored him. Strangely, Clarice had the opposite reaction and seemed less inclined to favor Maddalena than she was the other children. This caused Lorenzo to pamper his Madi even further.

Still, the Medici dynasty required boys to continue with their grand plan, particularly one whom they could devote to the Church. Piero was not shaping up to have the personality, temperament, or intelligence of his father. He was young enough to change, perhaps, but he was Clarice's child so completely that such a thing seemed unlikely. What Lorenzo needed was a son with Maddalena's intelligence and temperament. He prayed daily for the safe delivery of this new son. And he prayed for the other baby.

Colombina was also expecting.

They no longer bothered with the charade where Niccolò was concerned, but for the rest of Florence and for the sake of this baby's name and future, it had been necessary to ensure that Niccolò Ardinghelli was in Florence long enough to appear to have impregnated his own wife. Then Lorenzo shipped him off again. He had an agreement with Niccolò now, which was very lucrative for the Ardinghelli family. As a result, Niccolò maintained the appearance that he and Colombina were man and wife and did exactly as Lorenzo bid in public. Most of all, Lorenzo insisted that Colombina have absolute freedom to live any way she pleased.

Still, it was widely rumored in Florence that the Ardinghelli marriage was a sham. Supporters of the Medici defended it, but their detractors were quick to gossip and point out the various pieces of evidence that indicated that Lorenzo and Madonna Ardinghelli were engaged in adultery and had been for years. Sandro was nearly imprisoned for breaking the nose of one of these loose-lipped men, an old drinking partner from Niccolò's bachelor days, in the Tavern at Ognissanti. The lout had shouted in response to the news that Colombina was expecting, "The Medici balls really are everywhere in Florence—but particularly in Lucrezia Ardinghelli!"

The loudmouth had it coming, Sandro said simply in his own defense. Besides, it was a great risk to the hands of any painter to punch someone that hard. Sandro had suffered enough for the offense. The judge, from a long line of Medici supporters, agreed and let Sandro go with no penalty and chastised the plaintiff for attempting to sully the good name of Madonna Ardinghelli. The judge was later given a lovely portrait of his wife by the grateful Sandro.

Lorenzo's commitment to his one true love never wavered, and it was devastating for him that he could not be with her during her pregnancy. Colombina, heavy with his child, was the most beautiful thing he had ever seen. Lorenzo sent Sandro over to sketch her, as he wanted her captured in this ripe beauty, looking like Venus incarnate. The drawings Sandro returned with were stunning, and Lorenzo and Sandro pored over them for hours, trying to determine precisely how they would want to include them in a painting that would grace Lorenzo's private studio.

But the abundance of blessed children was not limited to Florence alone. The Magi had been giddy with their predictions for a child who was due to the Buonarroti family in southern Tuscany. The Buonarroti, as the descendants of the great Matilda of Tuscany, were watched closely by the Order, as their children were often highly gifted in some way. There was a Buonarroti among the Magi, and it was in fact this same astrologer who cast the birth chart of the baby boy who entered the world on March 6, 1475, near Arezzo. The horoscope of this infant was so exalted that the Magi recommended he be given a special name to identify him as an angelic from the moment of his arrival. Thus the baby had been called by the unusual name that evoked the Archangel Michael.

Michelangelo.

It would be interesting to keep an eye on this boy, and Lorenzo and the Order had compensated the Buonarroti family handsomely to secure their move north to Florence, where he could be educated and observed. Lorenzo was excited about the prospects. Surely a boy named for the greatest of the archangels had extraordinary promise for the future Order.

*

Le temps revient.

For years, Lorenzo and I had been discussing the merits of creating an ultimate work of art that would encapsulate all the teachings we held so dear, one which we would entitle The Time Returns. *It would need to be large enough to capture all the concepts that we laid out, and thus he ultimately commissioned a mural that would cover the majority of the wall of his private studiolo.*

It was the pregnancy of Colombina that inspired this painting. She was unspeakably beautiful in her fullness, the essence of the mother goddess in flower. When I sketched her, I wept with the beauty that was so evident in this state of impending motherhood. Thus I placed Colombina, as the female aspect of God, in the center of the work. Call her what you will, and it matters not. She is Venus, she is Asherah, she is our mother who guides and nurtures us by any name. She is Divine Beauty. I have cloaked her in the red of Our Lady Magdalena, which is embroidered with the diamonds of divine union, and she is wearing the sandals referenced in the Song of Songs: "How beautiful are your feet in sandals, my love," says the sacred bridegroom to his eternal bride.

Our Lady presides over the cycle of souls as they experience the beauty of human love here before ascending to the love of God and then returning back to earth as it all begins again. Her garden is lush and magical, filled with the symbols of the Medici family and the flowers and plants that grow around the gardens we all love so much in Careggi. She blesses us with her right hand, and yet also signals that we move our attention to the dance of the three Graces. This is the dance of life, a celebration of earthly love in its three guises: purity, beauty, and pleasure. Purity, or chastity, does not and should not remain once true love has come into the mix, and thus the figure of Cupid hovers above the scene, with his bow aimed squarely at Chastity. Soon she will become Beauty and then Pleasure as she moves through the threefold cycle of love.

Of course I have used the sketches I made of Ginevra, Simonetta, and Colombina, on the night they all danced together like this in the Antica Torre.

Another sketch I have used for this family portrait of sorts was the one I made of our Angelo, on the day he arrived in Careggi, depicting him as Hermes, stirring things up for all of us. I used this idea of Angelo but combined it with the face and figure of Giuliano de' Medici, who is the more beautiful model for a god. Here, Mercury/Hermes is stirring the weather, but he is also acting as the conduit between heaven and earth. He is the embodiment of his own teachings within the Emerald Tablet: that which is above is also below, as we all come together to accomplish the miracle of the One Thing.

And what is that One Thing? It is creating heaven on earth through the utter appreciation of Beauty in all its forms, through the veil of love. This is the Way.

To the right of the painting I continued to pay tribute to the Emerald Tablet of Hermes with the image of the wind, Zephyr. "The wind carries it in his belly" is an allegory for the miracle of life, returning the soul to earth. Here Zephyr is giving birth to Chloris, who was his true beloved. According to the Greek masters, Zephyr and Chloris were souls twinned by God to rule over the weather together, and thus I used them to illustrate this concept of one twin giving birth to the other, which is the essence of what occurs when true beloveds are reunited. They are reborn. As Chloris, she is making the transition from the heavenly realms to the earthly realms. She ultimately incarnates as Flora, showing the full cycle of incarnation as she steps into her role as the fully realized human woman. Flora is anthropos, she is humanitas, she is all that is beautiful about flesh-and-blood mankind. The flowers in her apron are held over her womb to indicate fertility, for she is lush with life. She throws the blooms about, scattering joy through the understanding and celebration of Beauty in its most exalted form.

Simonetta, of course, was my model for Flora, her delicate beauty inspiring me as it always does. I have taken artistic license in her figure, making her full and vibrant with health while hoping that somehow my painting will create the alchemy of healing magic and turn our Bella into the same image of radiance. But alas, she had to return to her bed after a few short hours with me. Her strength is yet to return, but our hope for her is as eternal as the spring in the painting.

And so it was that I completed the masterwork of my life, the one into which I poured my heart and soul; it depicted the people I loved most enacting the teachings I revere. Lorenzo was overjoyed with it, more than I have ever seen him with any other piece of art. He had it installed in his studiolo *immediately and told me that nothing, other than Colombina herself, has ever brought him such an understanding of the nature of Beauty.*

I remain,
Alessandro di Filipepi, known as "Botticelli"

FROM *THE SECRET MEMOIRS OF SANDRO BOTTICELLI*

Florence
present day

"WHAT IS GENIUS?" The Master posed the question to all of them as they drank Chianti on the roof terrace. "Was Leonardo a genius simply because he was technically proficient over and above other artists? Does that make him a genius? Certainly, he had a mental capacity that has rarely been seen among men in any time in history. So perhaps that is enough to be called such?"

Having been through the Botticelli-versus-Leonardo challenge in the Uffizi earlier in the week, no one in this company was going to speak up for Leonardo as a genius. Petra added to the lesson, "No man ever achieved greatness using just his mind. One must also engage the heart."

"True, of course. Leonardo's output was sporadic and incomplete. He was incapable of finishing most of what he started, and yet no one ever talks about that aspect of his character. Does a genius or a great man abandon the majority of his projects long before completion? I do not think so. Leonardo could not produce to the levels of Ghirlandaio and Botticelli, not even a fraction. And yet he is given more credit for genius than the two of them put together and multiplied, as the greatest mind of the Renaissance. It is one of history's most notable injustices."

"What happened between Leonardo and Lorenzo?" Maureen asked.

Destino continued the tale. "Lorenzo kept his promises as he always did, in this case both to me and to Leonardo, by allowing him to stay in Florence for a number of years. This was in spite of the fact that he was never really productive for the Medici and created nothing that we would ever be able to use within the Order. Ultimately he was extremely disloyal to Lorenzo, although Lorenzo was never disloyal to him. In fact, Leonardo had great reason to love the Medici, although he never found it in his heart to do so.

"It became clear that Leonardo was no longer benign. Even Andrea, who defended him for years, could no longer tolerate the vitriol he was emitting on a more regular basis. He lasted a long time, but in fourteen eighty-two it became necessary to get him out of Florence once and for all. We sent him to Milan, as a gift to the powerful Sforza family. They were solidified as allies for the duration of Lorenzo's life as a result of this most generous gift of his greatest artist to Milan!"

"And the story ends there?" Peter asked.

Destino's eyes became cloudy with the disturbing aspect of this memory. "I'm afraid it does not. We discovered, years later and far too late, that Leonardo had been a true enemy in our midst. He was spying for Rome, leaking secrets of the Order to the Vatican. What his motivation was, I will never know for sure. Whether he did it for money, for spite, or more likely for some twisted idea of religious conviction, intending to bring about the downfall of our Order, I do not know to this day. Perhaps Leonardo's greatest genius was that he remains a tremendous enigma.

"Leonardo da Vinci is a great lesson for all of us. For years I did penance for the night in which I insisted that Lorenzo keep him. Had we sent him away when he was first identified as a danger to us, perhaps the terrible thing that happened next would not have happened at all. Perhaps that villain Sixtus would not have had the ammunition he needed to attack the Medici as he did. What I felt was forgiveness turned out to be lack of judgment. And this is the lesson, my children. You must always forgive, and treat others with love. But this does not mean that you need to keep a snarling wolf among the lambs.

"For Leonardo, while treacherous, was not the ultimate traitor. There was one far greater and far more dangerous in our midst."

Florence
December 1475

CLARICE COULD NOT locate Madonna Lucrezia and was in a panic. She had given birth enough times to know that this baby would be coming soon and they would need the midwife. It was a festival week and members of the regular staff had the week off, so there were fewer people around to aid her with the children and the household. Lorenzo was too generous with the servants, and she was always the one who acquired extra work as a result. She rarely complained about it, knowing that it was a wife's lot to suffer, but in her ninth month of pregnancy Clarice was entirely without patience.

She knew that she was forbidden entry into Lorenzo's study. It was a Florentine tradition that wives were not permitted in their husband's private spaces, and Clarice had observed this rule without question until now. But in her panicked state of early labor, she needed assistance and was desperate to find Lorenzo. She ran to his *studiolo* and flung the door open without knocking.

She stopped in her tracks and blanched at the sight before her: an enormous image of a pregnant Lucrezia Donati dominated a mural of such foul paganism that Clarice was certain they would all go immediately to hell as a result of its presence in the house.

Lorenzo looked up from where he was auditing books from the Medici Bank in Lyon. He was surprised to see his wife here, and concerned. "Are you all right, Clarice? Is it the baby?"

Clarice held her hands on her swollen abdomen and nodded, but she had not taken her eyes off Sandro Botticelli's showpiece, as it covered the wall. When she finally spoke, her voice shook. "Lorenzo, I will not have that in my house."

"This is *my* house, Clarice." Lorenzo was annoyed, as he usually was with her, but he didn't snap as he could have. "And this is my private study. I will determine what I will or will not have in it without anyone else's perspective or assistance. I allow you to decorate elsewhere. This is the only space I control completely. Let me."

"But it is not fair, Lorenzo!" She was shrieking at him, her condition increasing her growing hysteria. "You ask too much, for me to endure such a thing. It is cruel. You pride yourself on your sense of justice and humanity. Why is it that you have never been able to apply those same principles to me, to your own wife?"

There was passion in her outburst, an emotion that Lorenzo had never seen in his years with her, as she continued.

"There is not a day of my life that I do not endure the torment of knowing you will never love me. There are three people in this marriage, and I am the least important of them. I know that, I live with it, and I try not to wilt from the constant winter that I live in as a result. Instead, I find the sun in my children. Our children. I do not ask for much, Lorenzo. But if you do not remove that horrible, pagan piece of furniture, I am going back to Rome and taking your children with me. Including your precious Maddalena."

Lorenzo was not one to be moved by threats or coercion, yet Clarice's words about justice had found their mark. He had never thought about her pain in all these years. It hadn't even occurred to him that she cared much, so indifferent had she been through their marriage. She endured the need for their coupling so that they might populate the Medici dynasty in exactly the same way that she approached preparing lunch or mending a cushion: each was a task to be carried out by a wife.

But with this outburst he saw that she was wounded, and he had wounded her. His remorse was sincere.

"I'm sorry, Clarice," he replied softly and with some tenderness.

The tears came unbidden as she stood before her husband, willing him to come to her, to hold her, to provide the warmth and comfort that she had dreamed of finding in him when she came to Florence as a terrified foreigner to marry a stranger. But they were too far gone for such displays; their silent war had been waging for too long. The best Lorenzo could provide for her was concession as she stood before him, heavy with the exhaustion of pregnancy. His reply was gentle, if not warm.

"I will have the piece removed in the morning. Good night, Clarice."

In the bravest moment of their married life, Clarice took a chance that cost her dearly. "Lorenzo, will you not . . . can you not give me just one word of love?"

Lorenzo was truly puzzled. "Love, Clarice? In all our time as man and wife, I have never heard you use the word. Duty, yes. Love . . . never. Forgive me if I have no context for this request from you."

"Lorenzo, you are my husband . . . and I . . . I do love you."

Lorenzo sighed, feeling a mixture of pity and sadness for the role he played in the unhappiness that fate had dealt to her. She was not, for all her flaws, an odious woman. She was merely a product of her family and her faith. His answer, while not pointedly cruel, was all that he could summon.

"Then, Clarice, I truly am most sorry."

She ran from the *studiolo*, sobbing now, and back into the main house, where Madonna Lucrezia found her and returned her to bed to wait for the midwife.

The next day, Lorenzo had the masterpiece he and Sandro referred to as *The Time Returns* removed from the palazzo on Via Larga. Lorenzo had it reframed and made into the backing of an elaborate piece of furniture that he determined to present as a gift for the wedding of his cousin, Lorenzo di Pierofrancesco. This other Lorenzo was also a student of the classics and would certainly appreciate the mythical elements of the work. Lorenzo asked Sandro to personalize it somehow, so that it would appear that the painting had been created for the Pierofrancesco side of the family. As their family emblem was a specific kind of sword, Sandro merely painted this weapon slung across the waist of Hermes.

Lorenzo di Pierofrancesco and his bride were delirious with the generosity of this grandiose wedding gift from their exalted cousin and the greatest living artist in their midst.

Lorenzo de' Medici, on the other hand, was devastated by the loss of the greatest piece of art that Sandro Botticelli had ever created. His consolation was that Clarice gave birth to a healthy and alert baby boy on the eleventh day of December. They named him Giovanni.

*

Colombina gave birth to her son in the company of her sister, Costanza, and Ginevra Gianfigliazza. Niccolò was away at sea.

The child's biological father was unable to attend.

Colombina wept through the pain of the birth, but she cried harder as she cuddled the beautiful little boy against her body later that night. He had a perfect nose and fine features, looking most of all like a male version of herself. Blessedly for all of them, the child had not been born with the Medici overbite or the smashed Tornabuoni nose. He would not be labeled as the bastard son of Lorenzo's whore through a misfortune of features. Colombina was grateful that he would be spared that.

And yet as she looked at him she wished, just a little, that there was more of Lorenzo to be seen in the child.

Florence
April 1476

GINEVRA GIANFIGLIAZZA SAT in the window seat, staring out across the Arno. It was stormy today, dark and gloomy, and she felt the dampness in her bones. She did not rise to leave her place when Colombina entered. The women were too close for formalities, and each understood the moods of the other in the way that young women who have shared many secrets are uniquely able. Colombina did not greet her friend verbally, merely kissed her on the cheek before taking a seat opposite, with a similar vantage point overlooking the river.

Ginevra looked up finally, eyes red and swollen. She saw, without surprise, that Colombina's were the same.

"You see it too," Ginevra said simply.

Colombina nodded and then burst into tears. She put her head in her hands for the moment it took to let the worst of the emotion work through her body, before trying to speak.

"She is so ill, Ginevra. And she knows but does not speak of it. Why does she not tell anyone that she is dying? How can they not see it?"

Both women had visited the Vespucci household separately to look in on Simonetta, who had been bedridden for the last few days. Her coughing had increased and was producing blood. Still, her family seemed oblivious to the fact that Simonetta was clearly gravely ill. They were treating her condition as if it were just a little setback and to be expected, given that she was so weak of constitution.

"Because she hides it so well. And Simonetta is such a thing of beauty that in her, the shadows on her face just serve to make the rest of her skin more translucent. The brightness in them does not look like fever; rather it enhances the unlikely color of her eyes."

Colombina nodded. "I do not know what to do about Sandro. Or Lorenzo and Giuliano for that matter. They will be distraught, as will we all. But at least you and I are prepared for it. We have watched death stalk her for the last years, watched as it came closer and closer to our sweet girl. But the men in our midst are unprepared. They know she is

fragile, but I don't think any of them have actually accepted that we will
lose her."

"And soon." Ginevra shivered.

"How long, I wonder? I need to hug her against me one more time
and tell her that she is my sister of spirit and let her know just how
much I love her."

"Then I suggest you do so immediately, Colombina. After seeing
her today, I do not think we have much time left with her. Perhaps we
should send a messenger to Lorenzo and Giuliano. They will want to
see her as well."

Colombina paled. "Oh God, they aren't here. They're in Pisa on
business, both of them. But they'll be back in a few days, and I will have
a messenger waiting for them as soon as they return to Florence. You
don't think . . . we will lose her that soon? Oh, please don't say so."

Ginevra, usually the pillar of strength, began to sob. Simonetta was
like her little sister, and she had grown to love her in these years. Losing
her would be challenging to all of them, to everything they believed.
What was God thinking, giving the world such beauty and then taking
it away like this?

*

The messenger Colombina had prepared to send to Lorenzo and Giuliano ultimately made the long ride to Pisa with the message that she
had most dreaded: Simonetta Cattaneo de Vespucci had died suddenly
that same day, April 26, 1476.

No one had a chance to say good-bye.

Lorenzo and Giuliano took a long walk together that night, to
talk about Simonetta and to share their grief over the young woman
who had moved all of them with her purity and sweetness. They all
loved her completely; she had become the official little sister of the
Order.

"April twenty-sixth. It will forever be a day of sadness in our world,
Giuliano. We must always honor her on this day."

Giuliano nodded and pointed to the sky. "See that? The star that is brighter than the others? Is it Venus?"

"Perhaps," Lorenzo answered. "Or perhaps our Simonetta is with God, and the light of her soul has merged with that star to create something as beautiful and bright as she was."

"I will never have your gift of poetry, my brother. I can only say that I loved her and I will miss her, and I will pray that she is surrounded now by the same beauty and grace she brought to all of us."

Lorenzo smiled at his little brother. "Who said you weren't a poet?"

Returning to his room that night, Lorenzo wept at the loss of their beautiful little sister. As Angelo always prodded him, Lorenzo used his pain to inspire a poem, which would become a favorite of the Tuscan people, "O Chiara Stella," Oh Beloved Star.

Simonetta was a piece of heaven now.

*

The funeral of Simonetta Cattaneo de Vespucci was an elaborate and somber occasion. Her casket was carried from her home to the church in Ognissanti by the Vespucci and Medici men who loved her. Thousands turned out in the city of Florence to mourn her. Perhaps the enormous attendance at her funeral was an indication that at the end of her all-too-short life, the people of Florence did indeed understand that they had lost a unique treasure.

Marco Vespucci did mourn her, but he remarried quickly. His new bride was homely but sturdy, a woman of the earth with whom he could lustily mate and actively procreate. While drinking in the Tavern at Ognissanti one night, he was overheard saying, "Goddesses are to be worshipped, but they are not meant to become wives. Simonetta was never meant for me. She belonged to the world. Ultimately, she belonged to God, and he called her back home, as heaven was incomplete without her."

*

La Bella Simonetta.

She was the most exquisite thing I have ever seen. She was the troubadour muse—perfect, untouchable, divine.

People say that I was in love with her. Of course I was. So was everyone in the Order. Simonetta embodied love, and anyone who knew her experienced that love. But it was not something as simple as Eros would define it. It was not a physical yearning to possess something so lovely. Simonetta moved all of us beyond that and into an understanding of the nature of the living female aspect of God on earth. I truly believe, with all my heart and soul, that Simonetta was the true incarnation of Venus. And I painted her as such.

In Lorenzo's garden there is a statue from ancient Rome that is called the Medici Venus. She is naked perfection, her right hand covering her breasts in part, and her left draped over her most personal female area. I used that statue as the model for Simonetta's body, but the rest is all her: lengths of golden hair, creamy skin, copper-flecked eyes. She arises from the sea in a scallop shell, symbols of Asherah, our mother in heaven who is Beauty, and who is later known by the Greeks as Aphrodite and the Romans as Venus.

To the left, Zephyr and Chloris blow life into her, helping her to incarnate while moving from heaven to earth. She is surrounded by touches of real gold, a reminder to the viewer that what they are seeing here, True Beauty, which is also Love, is priceless and to be treasured.

To her right, a woman arrives to cover her with a red cloak draped in flowers. The woman is Colombina, who here represents the sister who would protect her against the harshness of the world. Though Colombina knows she is beautiful in her nakedness, she also knows that the world will not understand it and will abuse her for it, and she seeks to cloak her from the eyes of a world that does not deserve her.

I have draped Colombina in Lorenzo's symbol, the laurel leaves, and given her a girdle of pink carnations. Those flowers are a pun, carrying as they do the root of the word incarnation *within their name.*

The Birth of Venus is my tribute not only to Simonetta but to the beautiful sisterhood that exists within the Order. It is love personified.

I have asked to be buried at Simonetta's feet, in the same way in which Dona-tello chose to spend eternity alongside Cosimo. I shall submit the request in writing to Marco Vespucci to prove that I am indeed serious. I have no doubt that even her bones will be beautiful and will inspire me into eternity.

She was, indeed, the Unparalleled One.

I remain,
Alessandro di Filipepi, known as "Botticelli"

FROM *THE SECRET MEMOIRS OF SANDRO BOTTICELLI*

Florence
present day

"The arrangements are made, Bérenger. Meet me tomorrow after-noon at two in the Palazzo Vecchio," Vittoria informed him from her cell phone. "We will be married by the magistrate in the Sala Rossa. The Red Room. It was once Cosimo de' Medici's bedroom. He conceived his children there. Appropriate, no?"

"Vittoria, why the mad rush? Why must we do this tomorrow? I need time. For the love of God, my brother is in jail and my family in chaos."

"I told you, Bérenger, that this is just a civil ceremony at the town hall. Just between you and me. I need to see your commitment to our son and his destiny. No one else even has to know. Yet. We will plan a so-ciety wedding that the entire world will talk about for later in the year. October is beautiful in Tuscany."

"Vittoria, please. I need—"

She wasn't listening to a word of it. "I am not going to allow you to buy me off—or attempt to take my son. We are a package, Bérenger, and you will get both of us together. Which you should be grateful for. Do you know how many men would kill to have the chance to marry me?"

He tried another tactic. "Vittoria, I want to see you tonight, before the wedding. Just to talk. May I come over to your place? Some time after ten?"

Vittoria was delighted by the implication of a late-night rendezvous with Bérenger in her apartment. He was finally coming around, as she knew he would. Men always did. Always.

*

The time returns. That was the heretic's favorite catchphrase, wasn't it? It was their sickening motto that dated back even beyond the anti-Christ spawn Lorenzo de' Medici and his adulteress whore. There was once a time when her uncle, Father Girolamo, could not even utter the name of Medici without choking on his own bile, so abhorrent was the legacy of that family to him and his ancestors. And combating that heretical legacy was the reason this sacred confraternity had been created in the first place all those years ago in Florence, created by his namesake, Girolamo Savonarola.

The diminutive Dominican friar came to Florence in 1490, somewhat ironically, through the invitation of Lorenzo de' Medici himself. History was unclear as to why Lorenzo would have welcomed the fire-and-brimstone preacher, installing him at the head of the monastery in San Marco, the retreat so beloved of Cosimo de' Medici. Savonarola's sermons against sin and frivolity were shocking to Florentines, who were not used to having the wrath of God rain down upon them in the way that Savonarola called upon it. Lorenzo would come to regret his decision, as soon Savonarola would condemn the Medici as tyrants, all the while preaching the evils of art. The Madonna was painted as an overpriced whore, he shrieked, taking Botticelli to task for his elaborate and beautiful *Madonna of the Magnificat*. He would escalate this campaign with the infamous bonfires of the vanities, mockeries of the elaborate festival events that Florence and the Medici had once been famous for. In Savonarola's Florence, the "festival" consisted of his followers knocking on doors and demanding items of vanity—luxury goods of any kind—to be donated to the enormous bonfire that would take place in the Piazza della Signoria. But the real treasure for Savonarola's followers, who were called by the cowed people of Florence the Piagnoni—meaning "the snivelers"—was art and literature. Nothing fed Savonarola's flames like paintings and poetry. These instruments of heresy had to be weeded out at any cost. And Girolamo Savonarola had been expert at destroying hundreds of pieces of art, which would be worth countless millions today.

Good riddance to bad rubbish, Felicity thought. As it stood, too much of it had survived.

Now that her uncle had lost his faith, it was up to Felicity to carry on the holy war against those who would continue the blasphemy started here by the Medici five hundred years earlier. She would be the one to continue Savonarola's work. There would be a new Renaissance, to be sure, but this rebirth would not be one of Lorenzo's heresy through the Paschal witch's blasphemy. It would be a resurrection of the great Savonarola's efforts to cleanse Florence of sin. She would recreate the bonfire of the vanities, beginning with the commemoration the confraternity was hosting this week in honor of the anniversary of Savonarola's death.

Having gained permission to create a bonfire in the courtyard behind Santa Felicita, Felicity was challenging confraternity members to gather vanity items, specifically books considered heretical and blasphemous, to feed the flames. She would supply copies of everything Maureen Paschal had ever published. She had versions in English and Italian.

Meanwhile, the American campaign had worked brilliantly. The confraternity members here in Italy had mobilized their sister organizations in the States to attack Maureen Paschal online in every possible forum. Some were hired guns, others were merely faithful followers who were willing to do whatever it took to stamp out such blasphemy as she created. But they had been quick and effective in spreading the rumors created in Rome against Maureen—and inspiring the death threats. The death threats were the icing on the cake, the final, sweet element. When the media ran with the story that Maureen had been threatened, the confraternity's team hit the Web again with the rumor that Maureen's publicist had manufactured that rumor to gain more publicity and sympathy. It was a beautifully vicious circle, which appeared to be effectively chipping away at Maureen's reputation. And it was only the beginning. There was much more to come.

After Felicity's last encounter with the blasphemer and her cohort, she was more determined than ever to step up her campaign against their godlessness. Unfortunately, the Antica Torre, where they were living in Florence, was relatively impenetrable. She was still formulating the second half of her plan, the means by which she could eliminate the blasphemy permanently—by eliminating the blasphemer.

The time returns? she thought. *You bet it does.*

Confraternity of the Holy Apparition
Vatican City
present day

FATHER GIROLAMO DE PAZZI was making his final preparations for his departure to Florence. He was tired, so tired, and wanted nothing more than to stay in the sunny sanctity of Rome for the rest of his days. But there were too many pressing issues to be dealt with in Tuscany, and he could no longer sit idle when he knew so much.

Felicity would certainly have to be dealt with, but that was not his first priority. He knew that action was about to be taken to eliminate the Buondelmonti problem, and he would need to be in Florence to deal with the repercussions. The Confraternity of the Holy Apparition had existed for nearly five hundred years, and while its public purpose was to study and celebrate visions of the Blessed Virgin Mary, it had a deeper, private purpose. The confraternity had become a rogue element operating outside the Vatican, one that made its own determinations about protecting the Church. If a threat was perceived, that threat was systematically eliminated.

Before his stroke, Girolamo de Pazzi had been the most effective and ruthless leader of the confraternity in the last century. There was a time when signing off on the death sentence of any enemy of the Church was effortless. Protecting the faith was necessary, a holy mission that he would not abandon. And while he still believed passionately in his Church, the events of the last three years had changed him. He was no longer willing to take lives quite so quickly or easily. This was what had caused the rift between him and Felicity, indeed between Girolamo and the rest of the confraternity. He had been put out to pasture, essentially, once it was determined that he had been too soft on Maureen Paschal during the Book of Love debacle.

He was a still a venerated elder who was worthy of respect, but he had been retired from making operational decisions for the confraternity. Still, the confraternity's new leaders in Rome had approached him for urgent consultation on this matter of Vittoria Buondelmonti. Father Girolamo was an expert on the bloodline families, the Order, and all their secrets. Did he believe that Vittoria Buondelmonti was dangerous to the established Church? What was she proposing to do with all this public posturing about her baby? Why was the paternity of this child so important? Their intelligence underground was effective enough to understand that she posed a threat to them, but they didn't understand the nuances of her plot.

The report Girolamo de Pazzi gave was distressing. It appeared that there was a high-level conspiracy among several of the noble families of Europe to unite behind this child, who they claimed was a messiah—perhaps even the Second Coming of Christ—and there was a clear threat to the Church within that strategy. It appeared to be a very serious threat, as the families involved had access to a great many secrets about the origins of Christianity. They were also in possession of priceless holy relics. Forces within the confraternity had tried for hundreds of years to get their hands on the Libro Rosso and the Spear of Destiny. Their goal was to stop them from ever becoming known beyond the secret societies, to keep their authenticity from ever being proven. The Libro Rosso was the most damaging single piece of evidence against the Church's authority that existed, whereas the Spear of Destiny held the power of victory over all opposition. Both were priceless and worth fighting for, regardless of the collateral damage.

The Buondelmonti threat was real, and it was therefore determined that Vittoria and her child must be removed from the game board. Vittoria had been followed and monitored by the confraternity since she made the announcement about her son. When it became known through their advanced intelligence operations that Vittoria was meeting with Bérenger Sinclair in Florence later that night, a plan was put into action.

They could kill three birds with one stone.

Girolamo de Pazzi would not give the order to harm Bérenger, Vittoria, and the child. Those days were over for him. But he knew that there would always be someone within the confraternity leadership who was willing to do whatever was deemed necessary to ensure the safety of the status quo and eliminate any threat. That was what the confraternity attracted, after all: the most fanatical element, the self-appointed soldiers for Christ who would take any action they felt protected their Church.

Vittoria Buondelmonti had gone too far, and she would die as a result, as would the baby and his father. He had no doubt of that, nor could he stop it.

They were deemed to be an unholy trinity that threatened the Church, and they would be eradicated accordingly.

LORENZO SIGHED HEAVILY and took another large gulp of the strong wine from the elegant goblet on his desk, careful not to spill on the official document that currently absorbed his complete attention. This particular piece of parchment represented one of the most challenging diplomatic puzzles of his life.

In his role as the head of the Medici Bank, now the most profitable and powerful banking institution in the world, Lorenzo was often petitioned to provide loans that were risky or otherwise unusual. Most often, these requests came from powerful personages: kings, cardinals, or influential merchants who knew how to wield their weight. Lorenzo had learned well by watching his grandfather handle these difficult problems masterfully. He had learned equally from witnessing his father botch these negotiations and create formidable enemies in the mishandling of these requests. Lorenzo understood that balance in such negotiations was critical. And this particular request, from no less than Francesco della Rovere, was going to be the most difficult he had ever considered.

There was nothing regal about Francesco della Rovere. He was a large man, uncouth and almost completely toothless, and fat in the manner that comes only from massive self-indulgence. There was little about his speech that could be called eloquent, despite the fact that he was well educated. He was clever in the way that all the della Rovere family was renowned to be: shrewd, manipulative, excessively ambitious, and entirely self-serving. This cleverness had lifted them out of the poverty-stricken fishing village where they originated and into the exalted place they currently held in Roman society. And none of the della Rovere clan had raised themselves up quite as high as the gruff, unpleasant, and enormously narcissistic Francesco della Rovere.

In fact, he was no longer known as Francesco della Rovere. Since 1471, he had been known as Pope Sixtus IV.

During his climb to the throne of Saint Peter, the man now known as Sixtus had bribed, traded, finagled, and promised his way through the maze of Roman politics. No others benefited as well as his own family, most specifically his sister's relatives, the Riario family. Within a few months of attaining the title of Pope Sixtus IV, he bestowed the title of cardinal upon six of his nephews. This action coined a phrase that would be used for centuries into the future to illustrate the corrupt practice of rewarding unworthy family members with positions and power that were far better suited to others. From the Italian word for nephew—*nipote*—evolved the word *nipotismo*. Nepotism.

It was one of these "nephews" that was the source of Lorenzo's current predicament. There was much smirking when Girolamo Riario was mentioned. While he was recognized as one of the huge brood of Sixtus' nephews, it was whispered that Girolamo was, in fact, the illegitimate son of the pope. Unlike the other Riario boys, who had some charm and culture, although each was ostentatious and boastful, Girolamo was brash and uncouth, also given to corpulence in a way that showed a tremendous resemblance to his "uncle" the pope. It was often remarked, albeit in Roman whispers, that Girolamo's appearance and mannerisms proved that the apple did not fall far from the tree.

That his sister had kept his scandalous secret by claiming Girolamo as her own was one of many reasons that Sixtus was in debt to her and eager to hand out favors to his nephews.

And now the convoluted and often dirty family politics of the della Rovere and Riario family had landed squarely on Lorenzo's doorstep. These people and their corruption made him shudder with revulsion, and yet they were now the first family of Rome. Lorenzo had made the trek to the Vatican when Sixtus had ascended the throne, to pay his respects and to reaffirm the position of the Medici as the primary bankers to the Curia. They had been so for three generations, since the days when his great-grandfather, Giovanni, had first influenced papal politics by providing strategic loans to the Church. Pope Sixtus had embraced Lorenzo, welcoming him and assuring him that the Medici position was as strong as ever in Rome.

Lorenzo needed it to stay that way. Banking with the Church was a cornerstone of Medici profit. It also strengthened his position in other areas of Europe.

All these factors weighed heavily on Lorenzo's mind as he considered the papal request before him, which had arrived via messenger from Rome this morning. Pope Sixtus IV was requesting a loan of forty thousand ducats—a huge sum—for his so-called nephew Girolamo. It was a type of real estate loan, as the acquisitive Girolamo wanted to buy the town of Imola to add to his holdings.

The money wasn't the issue here. The bank could easily afford the loan, and it would be guaranteed by papal authority, so in that regard there was little risk. The complicating factor was the location of Imola and the unstable, aggressive nature of Girolamo himself. Imola was in a strategic position, just outside Bologna, therefore between Florence and the rich Emilia-Romagna region. It was the perfect base from which to expand one's holdings, if one were inclined to begin conquering and acquiring territories. And from what Lorenzo knew of Girolamo Riario, this was precisely what he was intending. Further, the largest road connecting Florence to the north ran through Imola and would be entirely controlled by the lord of Imola.

Essentially, if Lorenzo gave this loan to Girolamo Riario, he was endangering surrounding territories, which were under the protection of Florence. His Florence. And that was something he would never do, even under threat from the Curia.

Lorenzo denied the loan. He sent a messenger to Rome with a carefully drafted letter, indicating that the Medici bank was currently undergoing a series of changes in structure, and as a result loans of that amount were on a temporary hold. He was stalling, and everyone knew it—including Pope Sixtus IV.

Rome
1477

"THAT MERCHANT SON of a gout-stricken idiot and a Florentine whore!"

Pope Sixtus roared with anger when Lorenzo's reply was brought before him. He disrupted the bowl of fruit before him, grapes and cherries flying across the table as he gesticulated wildly. "How dare he refuse me!"

Girolamo Riario was petulant. He picked up one of the grapes and threw it in a fit of pique. "I want Imola. I *need* Imola!"

"I know that, you ingrate," snapped the pope. "Can't you see I am working on it? The Medici aren't the only bankers in Italy. Send for the Pazzi. They are always happy to pick up Lorenzo's scraps."

The Pazzi, whose name translated from Tuscan to mean "madmen," were a rival banking family from Florence who had deeply held jealousies toward the Medici monopoly. No doubt the Pazzi bankers would jump on an opportunity to ingratiate themselves into the papal circle. They were a family possessed of rogue personalities, exacerbated by their envy and their greed. A perfect match for what Sixtus needed at the moment.

"I will get the Pazzi here, then," Girolamo grumbled in his high-pitched whine of a voice. "But that's not enough. I want Lorenzo punished for his offense to me . . . er, to you. How dare the Medici put himself above Your Holiness?"

"How dare they, indeed," Sixtus said to himself as Girolamo left on his errand. The pope contemplated the current situation carefully. While it would have been so much simpler if the Medici had simply conceded and played the game according to plan, there were some benefits to be achieved from this turn of events. Lorenzo was far too powerful throughout Europe, enjoying the same respect as his grandfather before him. The expansion of the Medici banks into Bruges and Geneva, and now with talk of London, was proof that their wealth was becoming seriously problematic. And that wasn't the worst of it. There was that great Medici secret that protected them across the continent, those royal ties they had that reached from Paris to Jerusalem and as far as Constantinople. Even the king of France referred to Lorenzo as "cousin," and the damnable merchants from Florence had been allowed to use the royal fleur-de-lis in their family crest. It was the French royals' way of showing their undying loyalty to the Medici. But why?

Pope Sixtus IV knew why. He had made it his business to know why. You didn't reach the most powerful throne in the world without becoming a master of intelligence networks.

Pope Sixtus had spies in the Order of the Holy Sepulcher.

In the great morass of family feuds and extreme jealousies that darkened Florentine history, finding someone to turn on the Medici had not been difficult—or even terribly expensive. Sixtus would use his knowledge of the great Medici heresy as his ultimate weapon against them when the time was right, and when he would most benefit from its use. He would bring Lorenzo down, and in doing so, he would accomplish his larger goal: to bring the arrogant, independent Republic of Florence to its knees and acquire it as a papal state. There would be no greater acquisition in the history of the papacy thus far. Florence would be the shimmering jewel in his papal tiara. He would possess it, and no Medici would stop him.

And he knew exactly where to start. He would hit Lorenzo in a very personal place, just to get his attention and remind him who held the real power in Italy.

Florence
1477

ANGELO POLIZIANO WAS out of breath as he burst through the door of the *studiolo*.

"Lorenzo. A messenger. Sixtus . . . he is trying to take Sansepolcro."

Lorenzo ushered his friend in, placing a calming hand on his shoulder as he guided him to a chair. "Sit down, Angelo. Breathe. Now, start from the beginning."

Angelo nodded. "A messenger has come from Sansepolcro. The pope has sent forces to Città di Castello. He has excommunicaed Niccolò Vitelli for heresy and has announced his intention to place his own man there. He is claiming it as a papal property now."

"He doesn't want Città di Castello," Lorenzo stated the obvious. "And he has no real quarrel with Vitelli. This is revenge on me, and on Florence because of me."

The town of Città di Castello, while of strategic interest, sitting as it did at the southern border of Tuscany, was more important to Lorenzo for another reason: it was the nearest outpost to Sansepolcro. Sixtus was firing a warning shot at the Medici by threatening the Order. He didn't dare invade Sansepolcro directly, which was a Florentine possession, as that would be an all-out act of war. But to claim the nearest outpost, and to insult the commander of that region, who was a Medici ally, was a highly calculated attack.

"What are you going to do?"

Lorenzo didn't even have to think about it. If Sixtus was going to declare war so early in his reign, so be it. Florence would not allow bullying within its territories, or to its allies. He would convince the council to defend Vitelli and the town of Città di Castello. Six thousand Florentine troops seemed like a good start.

*

Despite the best efforts of Lorenzo and Florence to defend Vitelli, the Città di Castello fell to the forces of the pope. The defeated Niccolò Vitelli was welcomed into Florence as a hero, which was viewed by the papacy as a further act of war. It no longer mattered. Nothing that Lorenzo, or Florence, could do would serve to repair the seething hatred of Pope Sixtus IV. Lorenzo de' Medici had become an almost singular obsession for him. The arrogant banker from Florence continued to flaunt his wealth and power in ways that Sixtus was certain were meant as intentional and repeated personal insults against his holy person and his esteemed family.

The divide between Florence and Rome deepened into a grand chasm when one of the Riario nephews died quite suddenly. Piero Riario, who held the position of archbishop of Florence, had been the last della Rovere foothold in the republic. His death was a shock, and an unexpected blow to the plans of Pope Sixtus IV. Before Rome could interfere in the affairs of Florence, Lorenzo moved to have Clarice's brother, Rinaldo Orsini, appointed as the new archbishop of Florence. It happened so quickly that an Orsini was installed and holding the title before the intention was ever announced.

The pope was outraged that he had not been consulted. He appointed his own man, Francesco Salviati, as the new archbishop of Pisa in retaliation. But the lucrative port city of Pisa was a Florentine stronghold, and the laws of the republic indicated that the pope could not affect affairs in their democracy without express consent of the Signoria. That consent was refused, and the pope was told in no uncertain terms that Francesco Salviati would not become the archbishop of Pisa anytime soon. In fact, the Signoria decreed that the pope's man would not be allowed into Florentine territory at all.

Lorenzo had just added another venomous enemy to the mix. Francesco Salviati, denied the ability to take up his position as archbishop of Pisa and show his faithful service to Pope Sixtus, simmered in his own bile in Rome. The Medici upstart had gone too far. Surely there was something that could be done to punish him for his effrontery.

But Lorenzo did not feel he had gone nearly far enough. After the papal threat to his beloved Sansepolcro, it became clear to him that Sixtus understood the workings of the Order. Finding the traitor in Florence who was supplying information to Rome was one of the many items on Lorenzo's agenda. But first and foremost, he must protect his republic and its democracy from further papal incursion. Calling a meeting of the leaders of Milan and Venice, he proposed a dominant and intimidating Northern Treaty. The agreement was signed, and the message was clear: the northern Italian republics of Florence, Milan, and Venice would stand together against any further threat of papal tyranny. And there was a subtext to the message, one that was not lost on Pope Sixtus IV: Lorenzo de' Medici was more important to the rulers of Europe than he was.

*

The Pazzi were one of the oldest families in Florence, and one of the richest. They had created their fortune in banking in the same way the Medici had but were not as successful in leveraging that fortune into political power and social influence. They were rather infamous squanderers, spending outrageous amounts to build monuments to the family glory. This was in contrast to the successful Medici model, which instead invested in the Florentine community in a way which inspired civic pride, stimulated the economy, and protected the arts.

Jacopo de Pazzi, the current patriarch of that family, had no great love for any of the Medici, although he had known both Cosimo and Piero well and had never been in any kind of real feud with them. There was little point. It was better to be a Medici ally than a Medici enemy. Jacopo was not an overly ambitious man; he did not seek to expand the Pazzi fortunes beyond what he currently possessed, as long as he remained comfortable. And he was a notorious gambler, a pastime that took a significant amount of his energy.

Thus when his nephew Francesco de Pazzi arrived in Florence with reports from the Pazzi bank in Rome, old Jacopo was not at all interested in listening to his ranting about overthrowing the Medici. It was a ridiculous idea, born out of Francesco's youth and inexperience.

"But Uncle, don't you see?" The younger man, wiry and fidgety, was pacing wildly around the room. "We can unseat the Medici once and for all. Rid Florence of Lorenzo the Tyrant."

Jacopo shrugged. "Lorenzo isn't a tyrant and you know it. Nor do the people of Florence believe that he is. This is a fool's errand, Francesco. And a dangerous one. We have secured the business of Sixtus for our bank, and I am very content with that."

Francesco blanched at this. "I secured the business of Sixtus! I did, because I am in Rome and I know the temperature there. I know what Sixtus wants, and what he wants is the end of the Medici. This is the greatest opportunity we will ever have."

"To do what?"

"To kill Lorenzo."

Jacopo spit out the wine he had just raised to his lips.

"You want to murder Lorenzo de' Medici? That's madness. And even if it weren't, if I should consider this even for a moment—which I will not—he has a brother. If you kill Lorenzo, Giuliano will inherit, and do so with the sympathy of the people of Florence. And those people will *not* support you."

"We'll kill them both. We will ensure that there will be no more Medici menace."

"I will hear no more of this talk in my house. Go back to Rome, Francesco. Such plotting does not belong here in our republic."

"Our family will never have any power in this state as long as the Medici rule. And as Catholics, we must defend the pope. Lorenzo has deeply offended our Holy Father. He is a heretic who offers insult to the Curia at every turn and keeps the rightful bishop of Pisa from taking his position to minister to Tuscan souls."

Jacopo got up to usher his nephew to the door. He had heard all he cared to on this day. Besides, there was a game of dice waiting for him at his favorite tavern in the Oltrarno.

"Save your self-righteous speeches for someone who has not known you since you were born, Francesco. I will not support any conspiracy for assassination, not because I bear any great love for the Medici, but because it is doomed to failure. Speak no more of this to me, and I will pretend I did not hear any of it."

"But Uncle—"

"Go!" Jacopo pushed his nephew out the door and slammed it shut. He hoped that was the last he would ever hear of such a ridiculous idea as a coup d'état against the Medici.

Private chambers of Pope Sixtus IV
Rome
1477

GIAN BATTISTA DA Montesecco was uncomfortable. To begin with, he was a huge man sitting on an undersized chair, and he was forced to squirm every minute or two to rearrange his bulky frame in a way that would not unseat him. But his discomfort extended beyond the physical and had now permeated his mind and his spirit.

Montesecco was a hardened warrior, a mercenary who never knew anything other than battle and blood. He had been in the service of the Curia for all of his adult life, having inherited the needs of the della Rovere family with the accession of Sixtus IV to the throne. Most of the last few years had been spent in the service of the pope's sniveling and demanding nephew, Girolamo, who was now the lord of Imola and never let anyone forget that. It was this particular "lord" who was whining at him now.

"My rule in Imola is not worth a pile of Tuscan beans as long as Lorenzo is alive! He opposes me at every turn; he ensures that no one in the Romagna will deal with me."

Montesecco stayed silent. As a condottiere, a military commander, he knew that the only strategy in such an environment was to determine what the position of each man in the room was before speaking a word. What would a man die for? What would a man kill for? Until you knew the answer to those questions, no speech was safe. He looked to the two others in attendance here in the small antechamber outside of Sixtus' private apartment. One, Francesco Salviati, was the shunned archbishop of Pisa. It was no surprise to Montesecco that there appeared to be little about this weasel of a man that was potentially holy. Salviati's beady eyes, set too close together over a hooked nose and prominent overbite, gave him a rodentlike appearance that was somewhat distracting when he spoke.

"The people of Florence will rise up against the Medici tyrants if we lead them! We will liberate them from Lorenzo and his hordes!" This was the rodent speaking.

Montesecco was a soldier, but he was not an ignorant one. He knew that Lorenzo was largely beloved of his people, who had called him il Magnifico since he was a teenager or younger. The Medici had always worked the common folk effectively and donated generously to those causes that supported the needy. What hordes was Salviati speaking of, that he thought Florentines would rise against? Artists? Philosophers? Poets? But the weasel-man was still ranting. Finally, an annoyed Montesecco interrupted.

"Beware of taking on the entirety of Florence. It is . . . a large and unruly place for those who are not on the inside. And no one is more inside than Lorenzo de' Medici."

Salviati wrinkled his nose in disgust, exaggerating his rodent face. "You dare to challenge me on the affairs of Florence? I am the archbishop of Pisa! A Tuscan! I know Florence better than any man in Rome, and I speak for the people when I say I am certain they will view us as liberators if we destroy the Medici."

Montesecco nodded but said nothing. He would bide his time now until they were called in to the papal chambers for their meeting with Sixtus. At the end of the day, he was the pope's mercenary, and he would carry out the will of the Curia. If Sixtus told him to kill Lorenzo, then Lorenzo was as good as dead. However, given the caliber of men in this chamber who would acquire power if the Medici were destroyed . . . well, God help the Florentines.

The three men were escorted into the papal chambers, where Montesecco was exceedingly happy to stretch his legs and settle onto a more comfortable, and certainly wider, upholstered bench. Girolamo Riario sat in the chair closest to his uncle, slumped in his typically petulant posture, while the archbishop Salviati took the bench adjacent to Montesecco. Pope Sixtus IV sat behind a gilded desk, pulling apart a pomegranate, which he ate throughout the interview, spitting the seeds into a silver dish between sentences.

"And so, gentlemen, on to this affair of Florence. Montesecco, I am exceedingly anxious that we should find a way to . . . shall we say . . . neutralize that terrible threat that the pernicious heretic Lorenzo de' Medici has made to me and to my holy office."

Pomegranate juice dripped from his chin as he turned to Salviati. "Archbishop, what say you?"

"I say, Holy Father, that there is only one way to neutralize the Medici family and that is through the death of both brothers."

Pope Sixtus IV dropped his pomegranate and pounded his chest dramatically with his open hand. "I cannot condone murder, Archbishop. It does not become my sacred office. And while Lorenzo is a terrible villain, and his family are all heretics, I cannot ask for anyone's death. I ask only for a change in the government of Florence."

Girolamo, sitting up in his chair now, chimed in with his high-pitched whine. "Of course, Uncle, we realize that you are not telling us to kill Lorenzo. Don't we, gentlemen?" He waited for the obligatory nodding of heads before continuing. "But we're just asking, really, that if such a thing were to happen—accidentally, in the course of attempting to change the government in Florence—would you pardon anyone who was directly or indirectly involved in Medici death?"

Pope Sixtus IV looked across at the man who looked a little too much like a younger version of himself. The expression on his face was one of absolute disgust, as if he wanted nothing more than to hurl the remainder of the pomegranate at Girolamo Riario.

"You are a fool, and I will insist that you do not say another word about this in the presence of my holy person." He turned his gaze to Salviati and Montesecco. "You gentlemen have heard me clearly. Under no circumstances have I, the heir to the throne of Saint Peter, condoned murder. I have only said that a change in government to remove the poisonous Medici family from power would be extremely pleasing to your Holy Mother Church. Montesecco, I have great faith in your abilities to make that happen, and will leave those details in your capable hands. I will provide all the troops you may require to back up such an endeavor. That is all. Now out with you." He glared pointedly at Girolamo. "*All* of you!"

*

The three conspirators moved to the apartments of Archbishop Salviati to begin planning the attack on the Medici in earnest. All three agreed that they had heard the same thing in the papal chambers: kill Lorenzo and the necessary members of his family if you must, just as long as that blood never leads to the back door of the Vatican.

Montesecco was dispatched to the Romagna region to begin assembling troops to back up their attack on Florence, in the event that Salviati wasn't entirely accurate in his assessment that the citizens of the republic would enthusiastically support the cold-blooded assassination of their favored prince. In his desire to gain the measure of the man he was to murder, Montesecco would carry a letter to Lorenzo from Girolamo Riario, extending his hand in friendship and forgiveness as the lord of Imola. This would give the condottiere the opportunity to see Lorenzo in his home and sum up the character of his target while taking stock of his potential weaknesses.

Lorenzo was at his villa in Caffagiolo with members of the Orsini family, as one of Clarice's brothers had passed away suddenly. Despite the somber mood in the household, Lorenzo welcomed this unexpected visitor and was the most gracious and hospitable host. He invited Montesecco to join him for dinner and engaged the man in long and interested conversation about his military history. In doing so, Lorenzo was just being himself: his interest in human nature was one of the great qualities of both a poet and a prince. For as long as he lived, his philosophy was that every single human being one encountered presented the opportunity to learn something unique through the eyes of that person. Lorenzo, like his grandfather before him, collected people and their experiences.

Montesecco was completely taken aback by his unexpected reaction to Lorenzo de' Medici. Hardened soldiers who killed for a living were not easily charmed. But this man, this Florentine prince, was unlike any other he had ever encountered. None of the so-called holy men he had ever worked for in the Curia had such elegance, grace, and impeccable hospitality. During his evening in Caffagiolo, Montesecco watched Lorenzo play with his children, show affection to his beloved brother, treat his mother with extraordinary love and respect, and handle an entire household of guests and servants seemingly without effort. Throughout the course of the evening, the condottiere had to remind himself repeatedly: this man is the enemy. His weakness is his family. He has no weapons at hand and is relaxed and comfortable in his own environment. Clearly, killing him—and the shy, kind younger brother, Giuliano—would be best accomplished within the false security of their own home. He could easily get weapons into a Medici dinner party, given what he had witnessed here tonight.

And yet for all the plotting, Montesecco could not release himself from the regret that he had been chosen to kill a man such as this. Lorenzo was full of humor, approachable, and a brilliant conversationalist; when he spoke of the people of Florence, there was no hauteur or scorn, there was only true concern—even love. He was, in short, worthy of the title his people gave him.

Lorenzo was magnificent.

*

Montesecco was a soldier and a mercenary, and that combination of obedience and materialism moved him through his uncharacteristically emotional state of regret about murdering Lorenzo. He had to push on and do what he had been charged by his pope to do, which was bring about a change in Florentine government. That could only happen through the elimination of Lorenzo de' Medici and his brother.

A series of meetings was carried out in the Pazzi household, with the old patriarch Jacopo in attendance. He had continued to resist the idea of murder for the personal gain of his family, until Montesecco convinced him that the endeavor had the blessing of the pope. This fact was given evidence by the number of troops that were being moved toward Florence in anticipation of containing the expected rioting that was sure to erupt in the early stages of chaos as the coup was staged in the republic.

Jacopo de Pazzi finally gave in and threw his hat in with the conspirators. While he wasn't precisely enthusiastic about the idea of murder, he was opportunistic enough to go along with the plot if it was indeed sanctioned by the pope. The deaths of Lorenzo and Giuliano would enable the Pazzi family to take over the majority of important banking in Italy and establish themselves as the first family of Florence under the guise of "liberators." He even allowed his nephew Francesco to convince him that they might deserve that title. Surely the people of Florence would realize that they had been under the heel of a despot once they had been released?

Jacopo recommended the first of several failed plans to kill the Medici brothers. He was of the opinion that murdering Lorenzo in Rome was far more efficient and less likely to inspire rioting in the streets of Florence. Also, in separating the brothers and using two teams of assassins, there might be less chance of missing one of them. Unfortunately for this idea, Lorenzo declined all invitations to go to Rome. There was too much pressing business at home, and the last thing he needed was to trek south to a place he more often than not found tedious.

Following the implosion of this divide-and-assassinate approach, Montesecco reiterated his observations that the Medici family were completely unprotected on their home territory, and he recommended that both brothers be taken out simultaneously in the middle of some grand entertainment at one of the villas. Knowing Lorenzo's reputation for hospitality and having experienced it firsthand, he recommended creating a scenario that would require the Medici to play host to a significant crowd.

It was the once reluctant Jacopo de Pazzi who created a new scenario. He suggested inviting the pope's youngest nephew, seventeen-year-old Raffaelo Riario, to Florence to celebrate the fact that he had just been made a cardinal. The title was ridiculous for one so young, but apparently it was impossible to be a nephew of Sixtus IV and not possess it. Raffaelo was studying at the University of Pisa, so he was conveniently located in Tuscany. He was also too young and innocent to understand that he was the bait for a poisonous trap. The youngest Riario came to

Florence gladly, excited to be the center of such esteemed attention. Once comfortably installed in Jacopo de Pazzi's home, he sent a letter of introduction to Lorenzo de' Medici.

True to form, Lorenzo immediately invited Raffaelo to the villa in Fiesole, where he was staying with Giuliano for a few days, at his brother's request. The plot to murder the Medici was now in place. All the conspirators had to do was determine the means of murder: arsenic, or daggers to the heart?

The Medici villa at Fiesole
1478

LORENZO WAS WORRIED about his brother. Giuliano had been acting strangely and for the first time in their lives together would not confide in him. He had begged Lorenzo to come to Fiesole, promising to explain once they were both in the house there together and away from the gossips in Florence. But so far, Giuliano hadn't revealed anything. In fact, strangely, he had disappeared at dawn without a word to anyone but the head groom, who had prepared his horse.

Lorenzo would wait patiently for a day or two and enjoy the air of tranquility—and the unparalleled views of Florence, with its magnificent Duomo in the distance. Cosimo had been the primary force behind financing the masterpiece of architecture that brought nobility from all over Europe to view its magnificence. Indeed, the great works of art in the center of the city were all tributes to Cosimo's vision. The magnificent bronze doors of the Baptistery, the expansion of the cathedral, and the unprecedented dome, which was the largest and highest ever built, had all been instigated and at least partially financed by Medici money.

Lorenzo, happy to leave Clarice and the children in town with his mother, brought Angelo along for further company. Perhaps they would find time to work through his latest pieces of poetry. Lorenzo's poetry was suffering of late as a result of the complex politics he was forced to navigate, and he longed for the time to focus on his own art form. And while Lorenzo had also hoped to find a way to get Colombina out to Fiesole for a day, he had not been successful in that venture. He was missing her desperately, but it had become nearly impossible to get her away from Florence now. She was committed to her work with the Master, who was living in the city near her, in addition to the duties she had with her son.

He felt the catch in his throat each time he thought of the little boy with the dark eyes who was now three, and by all accounts precociously intelligent. Lorenzo had little time to consider the great sadness of his personal life, on this day or any other, but it hung as a constant haze that covered his otherwise privileged existence.

He was in search of Angelo when he first heard the commotion in the stable yard. Yelling, lots of it, and the whinnying of horses.

Running out toward the commotion, Lorenzo's heart skipped several beats as he saw Giuliano being carried on a litter, perfectly still, by two of the stable hands and another man he did not know.

"What has happened?" he yelled at anyone and everyone.

"He fell from his horse," said the unknown man, who then introduced himself as the majordomo of a neighboring family. "I was out inspecting the lands and I found him. He is breathing, and nothing appears to be broken, but he must have hit his head quite hard, as he has been unconscious all the while. There is a doctor in the village who has already been summoned, but I suspect you will want to call in your own."

Lorenzo began shouting orders to send for the best physician in Florence, to get a message to his mother, and to prepare the house for Giuliano's comfort. Once his brother was settled into bed, Lorenzo sat beside him, wiping his head with a damp cloth and speaking to him gently. Giuliano began to stir, groaning with pain as his consciousness began to return.

"Giuliano, are you in there?" Lorenzo teased him gently as he saw his brother's eyelids flicker. Even though Giuliano had been twenty-five years on earth, he would always be Lorenzo's baby brother.

"Hmm . . . I fell. I was riding too fast and it was . . . not full light. Ow, my head!'

Giuliano clutched his head in pain and squirmed in the bed.

"What else hurts?"

"My leg. Left. I fell on it." Giuliano, coming to full consciousness now, reached down to feel around his left thigh to his knee. "I can bend it, and I don't think it's broken, but it is well twisted."

"Well, you won't be riding anywhere for a few days, so you better get comfortable. And maybe now that you have nothing better to do, you can tell me why you are acting in such an odd way."

"Fioretta," Giuliano said simply.

Ah. A woman. Lorenzo had suspected as much but had been unsure. While Giuliano was the object of desire of all Florentine girls, he had never shown any real interest toward one in particular and had resisted all attempts to marry him off. Again, he was blessed with the privileges of the second-born: all the benefits and none of the responsibilities. Giuliano was free to play, and play he did. His was a carefree life compared to Lorenzo's, and yet there was no envy on either side. Both brothers were living the lives they were created for, and they were content to do so.

"Fioretta Gorini. She lives just up the hill. Daughter of a shepherd, Lorenzo. Penniless. Little education. I could never be with her. But she is sweet beyond words. Innocent, lovely . . . like an angel. She has eyes the color of amber . . ." He drifted off for a moment, and Lorenzo wasn't sure if it was the fall or if Giuliano was actually in the throes of real love.

"At first, I thought it was just passing fancy. But it is not. When I am not with her, I think of nothing else. After I have been with her, it is worse." Giuliano tried to sit up as he described the feeling, but his brother's strong hands returned him to a supine position. "Oh Lorenzo, I never understood entirely about Colombina, but I do now. And I am sorry for all that you have been kept from, my brother."

Lorenzo nodded, surprised at the tears burning behind his eyes as his brother talked about experiencing real love for the first time.

"Do you know that feeling, Lorenzo, after you have been with the woman you love? You can still feel her on your body; she is present in every pore. You can smell her skin on yours and feel the silky creaminess of her still beneath you . . ." He closed his eyes for a moment, lost in the magic of love, before continuing.

"That's Fioretta. And I came here . . . I brought you here . . . because she is with child. My child. And she went into her birthing pangs last night, and I was riding at first light to see if she was delivered safely. Lorenzo, you must send someone to her immediately. Please. I must know if she is safe, and I must know if my child is born."

The doctor from Fiesole arrived as Giuliano completed his revelation. Lorenzo brought the physician to his brother, and as he left the room, he offered, "I am sending someone now to gather the news that you require, dear brother. Try to sleep and do not give the doctor any trouble."

Lorenzo knew exactly whom he was going to send, but first he had an errand to run.

*

The Gorini home was small and certainly modest, but it was beautifully kept, showing touches of love. Carefully planted spring flowers absorbed what was left of the afternoon sun. Lorenzo's errand had taken longer than anticipated, but he was satisfied that he had been able to attain what he was searching for.

A child played in the garden, a little girl about ten years of age. She smiled at Lorenzo as he dismounted.

"Is your horse nice?" She was just bold enough to speak to him, though clearly somewhat shy.

"He is particularly nice if you rub his nose." Lorenzo smiled at the girl. "Here, I will hold his rein and you can pet him very gently, right there. His name is Argo."

The girl, who was fine-boned and delicate, like a tiny bird with long black hair, approached Argo carefully. She reached out to touch the stallion's velvety nose as Lorenzo steadied him. After a moment she turned dark eyes to Lorenzo.

"Have you come to see the baby?"

Lorenzo nodded. "Has the baby arrived?"

The girl smiled, excited to discuss the new arrival. "He came this morning. I have only seen him for a moment. He was covered with blood and sticky, but he cried very loud and Mother said that is good. Fioretta was sleeping, so I came out here."

The sound of the front door opening startled both of them. An older woman called to the girl sharply, "Gemma! Who are you talking to . . ." The woman's voice trailed off when she saw the face of the visitor. The most famous man in Florence was standing in her garden.

"Il Magnifico . . ." She wiped her hands on her apron—which appeared to be covered in birthing blood—but didn't move from the doorway. She appeared to be stunned as she tried to continue. "I . . . Oh! Have you come to take the baby?"

Lorenzo wasn't sure what she meant. His reply was simple. "I have come to see Fioretta and to send her my brother's love. He rode out here this morning to be with her but fell from his horse."

The woman raised her hands to her face and gasped. "Is he—"

"He will be fine, Madonna Gorini. He is bruised and hit his head badly but appears to be coming around nicely. No bones broken. But he is most distressed that he has no news of Fioretta and his child."

The woman began to speak but then burst into tears. She ran out to where Lorenzo was standing with Argo. "Oh Magnifico, please forgive me. I . . . I told Fioretta that your brother would not come. That he would never care about a poor shepherd girl and her bastard child. I did not want her to have expectations that any Medici would care about the likes of us . . ."

Lorenzo wrapped Argo's reins around the fence post and moved to put his hand on Fioretta's mother's shoulder, soothing her. "He cares very much. As do we all."

The woman was sobbing harder now. "Then, I saw you here and I thought . . . dear God, he has come to take the baby away from Fioretta. It will kill her. And the birthing was already so hard on her . . . She is so weak."

Lorenzo was now the one feeling shock. It hadn't occurred to him that Fioretta might be in any danger from the birth. "What? Is she all right?"

"She lost much blood, and the baby is large. You Medici men are tall, and my Fioretta has fine bones . . ." Lorenzo flashed for a moment on the news of Colombina's delivery of his own child three years earlier. That baby had been hard on his mother's tiny frame as well. He had been worried to death for weeks that Colombina would not recover.

"There are two doctors at our home in Fiesole now. I shall send both to Fioretta immediately. Is she well enough that I may speak to her? And may I see the baby?"

Madonna Gorini nodded, wiping her hands on her apron nervously, and ushered Lorenzo the Magnificent into the tiny shepherd's cottage where she lived with her beloved daughters.

*

Lorenzo reached out for the tiny bundle and laughed out loud as the infant was placed in his arms. "He is the image of Giuliano! Lucky boy. He got the best of the Medici blood without the worst of it." Lorenzo was forever referring to himself as the ugly Medici, while Giuliano was the beautiful one. But this baby was definitely a Medici—strong features, long nose, piercing dark eyes, lots of glossy black hair.

A tiny voice from the next room interrupted him.

"Giuliano?"

The voice was weak and tired. And so hopeful.

Lorenzo looked at Madonna Gorini, who took the baby from him and indicated he should go into the bedchamber to speak with Fioretta.

"I am sorry to disappoint you." Lorenzo smiled as he entered the room. This was probably the only woman in Florence who would be disappointed to see Lorenzo de' Medici enter her bedchamber.

"Oh!" Fioretta was struggling to sit up. "Lorenzo! I . . ." She gave up, too weak to do so. Lorenzo came to the edge of the bed and knelt beside it.

"Rest yourself, sister." He smiled at her, and she looked at him strangely. Even though she was extremely pale and weak from the delivery, Lorenzo could see what his brother was so taken with here. The girl was beautiful in a way that was absolutely pure. Her skin was like milk, and he could tell that her mass of dark hair, tied behind her though it was, was glossy and very long. But it was her eyes that totally arrested him. Giuliano was right, they were the color of the amber that came from the Baltic Sea. Huge and clear, she stared at him with those eyes now.

"Sister . . . ," she whispered. "How I wish I could be."

"You already are," Lorenzo offered gently, stroking her hand. "You are the mother of Giuliano's son, Fioretta. That makes you family. But more than that, my brother loves you."

"But he did not come."

"Yes, he did." Lorenzo explained the events of the morning, assuring Fioretta that Giuliano would recover. Her distress at the idea of his being injured was profound.

Amber eyes filled with tears as she looked at Lorenzo. "He is my life. My heart, my soul, everything I am. It is all Giuliano. I love him so. I wish that he were not a Medici. Do not hate me for saying so, Magnifico. But if he were simple, like me, we could be together. We would marry and raise our child . . . our children, perhaps." She stopped as the tears flowed harder. "It can never be, I know."

Lorenzo's own eyes were stinging. How he knew this feeling of wanting to die more than to be separated from the one person in his life who represented the sun, the moon, and the stars. There was no light without her. No life.

"Fioretta, Giuliano sent me something to give to you. Here."

Lorenzo removed a heavy velvet pouch from the deep pocket within his doublet and handed it to the exhausted girl. He helped her as she raised herself up on one arm to release the drawstring. A cascade of amber spilled out onto the woolen bed sheet.

Fioretta gasped as she held up the gift between her fingers. It was a chain crafted entirely of amber beads and flawless pearls, the necklace of a queen. It was worth a fortune.

"Giuliano said that the amber beads are the color of your eyes, and the pearls represent your eternal beauty, like that of Aphrodite, and that his love for you is deeper than the sea itself."

Fioretta cried as though her heart would break and clutched the beads to her breast.

Lorenzo continued. "It is his promise to you, Fioretta, his promise of love, which will not be forsaken. And with it I give you my own pledge. You are my sister, and your child is as beloved to me as my own son. Come what may, sweet one, you will be a part of the Medici family forever."

And to punctuate Lorenzo's pledge, the baby—who would be named Giulio—cried out for his mother, in need of his dinner.

＊

Madonna Lucrezia de' Medici was firmly in charge at Fiesole by the time Lorenzo returned. She was clucking over Giuliano, ever her baby. But Lorenzo saw the strain in his mother's face. For all her strength, she was the most tender-hearted woman in the world where her family was concerned. She worried for her sons now more than ever.

"Yours are still babies, Lorenzo," she said to her elder son. "You know the natural fears that a parent has when children are small. But do not think it gets better, my son. It is only harder as your children grow. The world gets harsher for them and there is more to fear. All I have ever really wanted was for all of you to be safe and happy. And yet, those two qualities are very difficult to provide, even for the most devoted parents."

Lorenzo was pleased that his mother was thinking and speaking of the health and well-being of children. He wanted to approach a difficult subject with her, and she had given him an opening.

"Mother, I know you have given me everything in your power, and what you could not give me was out of your hands ..." He did not need to finish the thought. His mother was well aware of the anguish Lorenzo had endured as a result of his separation from Colombina. He had developed a compatible relationship with Clarice overall, and she was a very competent wife and an excellent mother. But Lucrezia de' Medici knew that she and her husband had sentenced their elder son to a loveless life when they arranged that marriage.

"What I am saying to you is that you have a chance to give that happiness to Giuliano. Let him marry Fioretta. Let us bring her into the family and raise little Giulio as a Medici, which he is."

Lucrezia flinched. When she had been told about the shepherd girl and her newborn bastard grandchild, she wasn't entirely surprised. It wasn't uncommon that well-born boys would tumble the occasional peasant girl. The countryside was filled with nameless children as a result. And even Cosimo had had a bastard son with a Circassian slave girl. That child, Carlo, had indeed been raised as a Medici and had even been accepted by Cosimo's wife, Contessina. Lucrezia often referred to her mother-in-law as Saint Contessina as a result.

"Lorenzo, I am happy to raise the child in our family. He has Giuliano's blood. But there is no need for him to marry the girl for that to happen. We will adopt him and educate him and see to it that he has all he needs."

"You're missing the point, Mother," Lorenzo snapped, more harshly than he meant. His deep-seated anger from his own past was creeping into the conversation now. "He loves her. She isn't just a girl he tumbled when he came upon her in the fields one day while hunting. And she isn't a trollop. They are in love. And just once, wouldn't it be glorious if someone in this family was actually allowed to marry for love? To completely participate in and fulfill the ideals and beliefs which we all hold so dear?

"I have done everything you want. I married whom you wanted and have secured heirs for both the family and the Order. Giuliano does not need to do any of those things."

"But he is destined for the Church, Lorenzo!"

"Is he? Really? He is twenty-five years old, Mother, and he has not taken vows because he does not want to. And he will not be able to take a position in the Church as long as that criminal Sixtus is on the throne of Saint Peter. So perhaps it is time we were all honest here. Let Giuliano live his life in a way that makes him happy. Shouldn't one of us at least get to do that?"

Madonna Lucrezia was speechless. Lorenzo rarely raised his voice to the mother he adored to the point of worship, so when he did, it had an impact. But he had spoken his piece and now needed to get out of the oppressive atmosphere of the villa. He left his mother to think about what he had said and went to take a walk under the stars of Fiesole.

Lorenzo remembered as he did so that he was supposed to host a dinner here the next night for the pope's young nephew and some of the Pazzi family. He would have to send a messenger into Florence to cancel it. Giuliano would not be well enough for visitors for at least a few more days.

*

Gian Battista da Montesecco had a sore head, a heavy heart, and a bad temper.

He had spent the previous evening drinking in a tavern in the Ognissanti district. Hoping to drown all his reservations about what he had come to Florence to do, he had ducked into one of the seedier-looking dives to divert his attention in the way that soldiers did best—with too much wine and inexpensive women.

It was as if God were laughing at him. It seemed that everyone within the tavern, from the old man nursing his drink in the corner to the saucy bar wench who lifted her skirt for him in an upstairs room, had a story to tell about Lorenzo de' Medici. Each was a grander tale of magnanimity than the one that preceded it: Lorenzo never called in my father's loan, Lorenzo rebuilt our church when the ceiling collapsed, il Magnifico funded the confraternities which allowed the poor boys of our district access to a fine education, the Medici were the reason that Florence was the most beautiful city in Europe. It went on and on—for hours. The men worshipped him and the women swooned over him. It was nauseating. And depressing.

What cards had he been dealt, what terrible destiny was in play, that he had been chosen to kill someone like this? Why was it that his hand was the one selected to plunge a dagger into the heart of the man whom these people called their prince? A man who by all accounts— including Montesecco's own observation—was in truth a rare, noble, and generous servant of the people?

And by whom had he been chosen? Who was it who wanted to murder this prince? A fat, nasty, arrogant, acquisitive son of a fisherman who manipulated his way to the throne of Saint Peter, and his fatter, nastier bastard of a son. A bitter, rabid weasel of a man who thought that possessing the title of archbishop somehow made him immune from the laws of God and men, and a twerpy, unscrupulous banker who had more ambition than sense. These characters were supposed to stand for something noble, perhaps even holy, in their leadership. Leadership was something that a soldier looked for—the ability to inspire people and be uncompromising and fearless. He saw this quality in Lorenzo de' Medici, certainly. But not in Pope Sixtus IV or any of his entourage. None of those men would ever inspire by leadership. They would only manipulate through fear.

As the night wore on and Montesecco fell deeper into his cups, he had entered into a conversation that was somewhat hazy to him now, in the harsh light of day and with a head that felt as if his horse had stepped on it. The old man in the corner had called him over. A strange old man, ancient in appearance, he had been sitting alone all night as if waiting for something. Montesecco stumbled to his table and sat as instructed, asking the old one, "Are you a soldier?"

The old man smiled slightly and nodded; the left side of his face puckered up when he smiled, as there was a huge scar that covered his cheek.

"That looks like a battle scar, old man."

"Indeed it is, my friend. For I have done terrible battle with myself and my conscience, just as you are doing now."

Montesecco was drunk, but he was still conscious enough to be taken aback.

"How do you know what I am thinking, ancient one?"

"Because I *am* ancient. And because I know the look of a soldier in turmoil. You are wondering if you have chosen wisely, aren't you? If you are on the right side of your battle? Remember, warrior, that while you are a soldier and you follow orders, God gave you a mind and a heart and a conscience so that you could make such choices of life and death for yourself. In the end, the only real battle is between you and your soul. Choose wisely, friend. Choose wisely."

"I am a mercenary. There is only one side, and that is the side where the money is."

"Really? And what will that money bring you if you gain it all and lose your soul? Or even if you die in the attempt?"

"All war has risk. Dying in the attempt is a part of what I do."

"Yes, but the odds are against you this time, friend. This is not a battle you can win. You are on the wrong side. Your opponent is stronger than you can ever know."

Montesecco, too deep into the wine to be discreet, was wrestling with his own demons. He banged his hand on the table for emphasis. "But I am employed by the pope himself! I fight on the side of the Church! Who could possibly be stronger than that?"

The old man shook his head at the war-torn soldier and sighed, the ragged and ancient sound of a man who had seen too much of this particular battle.

"God is your opponent. You cannot win this battle, soldier, because your opponent is a man who is under the protection of God."

Montesecco had heard enough, and what he was hearing from this disconcerting old man was causing him to squirm. He laughed in the old man's face as he rose to leave the table. "God, is it? And I suppose next you are going to tell me that Lorenzo de' Medici is one of the archangels!"

And as the condottiere turned his back on the aged stranger with the scarred face, he thought he heard the old man say after him, "You have no idea just how right you are."

*

And now here was Montesecco in the early afternoon, back in the house and company of Jacopo de Pazzi and his annoying nephew, looking at the ratty face of Archbishop Salviati as he raged.

"The Medici escape us again. Damn Giuliano and his ineptitude on horseback! I wanted them both dead tonight!"

Montesecco thought about the old man in the tavern. Maybe God had pushed Giuliano de' Medici off his horse yesterday so that he would escape his assassination. He shook the thought from his head, groaning inwardly at how much that effort still hurt.

"We need another plan," said Francesco de Pazzi. "I still think we use young Raffaelo Riario as bait. Lorenzo has a weakness for students—he likes to talk their ears off about all his Plato nonsense—and this one is the pope's nephew. We send Lorenzo another letter from Raffaelo, saying that he wants to see their art collection at the Palazzo Medici. Raffaelo is set to attend his first Mass here next Sunday, so we can suggest a banquet in his honor, to coincide with the High Mass next week."

Montesecco realized at that moment that he wanted nothing more than to hit Francesco de Pazzi in the face. He said more calmly than he felt, "Next Sunday is Easter. You would murder the Medici brothers on the feast day of the resurrection of Our Lord?"

Archbishop Salviati snapped back, "We are doing God's work, freeing Florence of a tyrant for the protection of the Holy Church. Choosing a holy day for our task will only bring us Godspeed in accomplishing our goals."

Jacopo de Pazzi looked at Montesecco across the room, with a hard and knowing glance. The two men locked eyes long enough to know that each had deep reservations about this plan. It was not what they signed up for. And each day, it appeared to be getting worse.

*

A week later, the conspirators were back in the Pazzi palazzo and frustrated once again. Francesco de' Pazzi had gone to the Palazzo Medici on the Via Larga to check on the arrangements for the banquet in the young cardinal's honor. They had decided on poison, arsenic being the quickest, and as such it was necessary to discuss seating arrangements with Mona Lucrezia de' Medici. Lorenzo's wife, Clarice, was never consulted on entertainments. Her Roman customs had never been welcomed in Florence and she preferred to run aspects of the household that dealt with her children. Thus it was still Lorenzo's competent and hospitable mother who ran the Medici entertainments. Francesco fussed about protocol and seating preferences with Lucrezia. He insisted that because Montesecco had been so taken with Lorenzo, he wished to be seated beside him for the dinner conversation. Furthermore, Archbishop Salviati wanted to discuss Church matters with Giuliano, who he knew was well versed in such things. Of course, what the Medici matriarch did not understand was that Francesco was positioning the two assassins—each of whom would be carrying arsenic—next to her beloved sons and their wine goblets.

But Madonna Lucrezia stunned Francesco by advising him that Giuliano would not be attending the banquet the following evening.

"His leg is still quite sore, and further, he has now come down with an inflammation of the eye, which appears to be contagious as he has passed it on to little Piero. So it is best if he stays in bed for another few days, I think."

Francesco de' Pazzi tried not to let his panic show. This plot only worked if both Medici could be murdered on the same night.

"But ...," he spluttered, trying to think fast, "the young cardinal is anxious to meet him and will be so disappointed if he is not there."

Lucrezia de' Medici smiled. Giuliano was so likeable and charming, it was natural that many would be disappointed if he were not in attendance. But, truth be told, he was a bit vain, and the inflammation of his eyes was something he did not want to show off at a banquet. She hoped to appease Francesco with her reply.

"The cardinal will have the opportunity to see Giuliano at High Mass. He would not like to miss the Easter service, given that he has much to be thankful for and wants nothing more than to celebrate the glorious resurrection of Our Lord. But he will return to the palazzo immediately afterward, no doubt exhausted and sore, as he has yet to be out of bed since his accident."

Francesco de' Pazzi had stopped listening. Everything had changed yet again. There was now only one thing to be done; the path was clear. The Medici brothers would have to be assassinated in the cathedral during the Easter Mass the following morning.

*

"You are mad, I tell you. *Mad.*" Montesecco's bellowing shook the walls of the Pazzi palazzo. "I will have none of it. You have pushed me too far. I will not add sacrilege to my crimes under God. I will not murder a man—any man—during Mass. In a cathedral. On Easter Sunday. Do you not hear yourselves? Is there no decency left in any of you?"

Salviati wrinkled his rodent nose. "How dare you speak to us like that? We have no choice, and as it appears that God has forced our hand, we must assume that it is his will."

Jacopo de' Pazzi was tired. He was too old for this, and none of it was to his taste anymore. "Montesecco is right. This goes too far."

Francesco de' Pazzi was nearly hysterical. "You don't understand. This is our only chance! Montesecco, you said yourself that the troops from Imola and the surrounding regions of Romagna were on the march and will be at the walls of Florence tomorrow by the end of Mass. We must time this so that those troops can come to our defense immediately. You will cover Lorenzo in the basilica, and I will cover Giuliano."

Jacopo de' Pazzi blinked hard at his nephew as if seeing him for the first time. "You? You are going to wield the dagger that kills Giuliano de' Medici?"

"Of course." Francesco said it as if it were the most natural thing in the world. "I will be hailed as a hero, as one of the men who was brave enough to take on the Medici menace and free Florence of the tyrants."

Oh dear God, Jacopo thought, shaking his head. *Francesco really is mad.*

And in that moment, each of the men involved in what would be known to history as the Pazzi Conspiracy was forced to make a decision. For Francesco de' Pazzi and Archbishop Salviati, both blinded by greed, envy, and unbridled ambition, there was only one course of action. They were determined, even excited, about killing the Medici brothers on Easter. And while Salviati would not be wielding any daggers, he had his own role. He would be the one, when given the signal from the cathedral, to march into the Signoria and seize the government. He would be aided by a co-conspirator whose duty was to give the signal to let the troops into the city, while marching with the archbishop to demand control of the Signoria. They would be accompanied by mercenaries from Montesecco's troops, all of whom would be prepared to kill any member of the council who tried to stop them. This was a revolution. This was war. People would die. It was the way of the world.

But for Gian Battista da Montesecco, the plot had irrevocably dissolved into sacrilege and insanity. He had been searching for a way to remove himself from it. Even before meeting the old man in the tavern, he knew he was on the wrong side. He did not want to kill Lorenzo de' Medici. His would not be the hand that ended so noble a life. In fact, it crossed his mind at that moment to kill Francesco de' Pazzi and Archbishop Salviati instead, ensuring the safety of the Medici brothers for a while longer. Later he would have much cause to wish he had acted on that particular instinct.

"I'm out." Montesecco looked at the other three men in disgust. "Jacopo, I think you are beyond this too, but you are a man and must make your own choice. As for the two of you,"—he spat on the ground as he prepared to take his leave—"you will be good company for each other in hell. Give the Devil my best, and tell him I will not be too far behind you."

And before anyone could object, Montesecco was out the door and out of Florence. He didn't look back as his horse carried him as fast as he could ride back to Romagna.

*

Jacopo Bracciolini had fallen from grace.

He had once been Lorenzo de' Medici's partner in Hermeticism and heresy when they were younger, but he had grown into a handsome, self-indulgent, and completely corrupt man. He was tormented by his own insecurities and eaten away by envy over the glory of Lorenzo de' Medici's golden life as the most respected and desired man in Florence. The younger Bracciolini had all of his father's mental acuity but none of his nobility; he was a cerebral genius, but the dangerous kind— a man completely disconnected from his heart. While he was capable of extraordinary feats of intellect, he had no desire to use his mind for anything that wasn't immediately amusing or entertaining for him. He had stolen from his father to save himself from his gambling debts, had sold off his mother's jewelry and pilfered his sisters' dowries to protect himself from the trouble he was constantly embroiled in. Giving himself the title Florence's Ultimate Hedonist, he hosted wild, underground orgies where he indulged the darkest elements of the city in nights of unruly—and often unthinkable—pleasures. There was nothing he wouldn't try, no risk he wouldn't take, and he was fond of saying that he experienced all the deadly sins on a daily basis. So when he was first approached by Francesco de' Pazzi to participate in the coup d'état to overthrow the government of Florence, he was delighted by the prospect.

"What's in it for me?" had been his first question, had always been his first question in any circumstances. Francesco de' Pazzi initially offered Bracciolini a ridiculous sum of money to gain his attention. He then rattled off a number of additional incentives that he knew would appeal to the heathen hedonist: a country house, Circassian slave girls—virgins, of course—and various treasures to appeal to his vanity.

But Bracciolini, while an outrageous narcissist, was not entirely stupid. He had asked the key question.

"Why me? I am not skilled in war and politics. I am a scholar by trade and a hedonist by practice. The only time I ever held a sword was in one of Lorenzo's tournaments, and that was for show. Why do you want me to lead this rebellion with you?"

"The Order of the Holy Sepulcher," Francesco de' Pazzi said, looking his prey square in the eye.

Bracciolini had stopped smiling then. God, how he hated the Order, and everyone involved with it. The mere mention of it made his stomach turn.

"I see. And as Lorenzo is the Poet Prince, the golden boy of the sanctimonious Order, you know I have no qualms about seeing him dead," Bracciolini guessed. He didn't mention what was foremost in his mind at that moment: nothing would make him happier than to see that little bitch they all called Colombina throw herself into the Arno in grief over Lorenzo's murder. That alone was worth more to him than all the money he was being promised.

Francesco nodded. "Yes, I know. But there's more. And there are far greater riches in your future than you can dream of should you choose to help us. The pope himself is asking for your assistance."

Ah, now we were getting somewhere. To be on the payroll of the pope was to ensure that the future was paved with gold.

"What does he want from me?"

"Intelligence. He wants you to come to Rome and tell him everything you know about the Order and about the Medici as its leaders. He wants any relics or documents that your father may have kept pertaining to the Order, and any book or paper given to your father by Cosimo."

Bracciolini's father, Poggio, had been Cosimo de' Medici's closest friend and ally. He had been instrumental in the Order. In fact, the

Bracciolini family had been connected to the Order of the Holy Sepulcher for many generations, and Jacopo had been raised in their sacred traditions. He had even spent some time in the presence of the Master with Lorenzo when they were children. But he was always different, never quite able to focus on or grasp the lessons of love and community that were the central elements of the Libro Rosso. It didn't help that he was constantly compared to Lorenzo and Sandro, who were stellar pupils and devoted initiates. Bracciolini was jealous of Lorenzo's position and Sandro's talent, neither of which he had in equal measure. He had once wanted to be a painter, but his time in the workshops proved that he was best suited for crushing minerals to mix pigments.

When Lucrezia Donati—known only in the Order as Colombina—had come into the fold and joined the Order at the age of sixteen, something snapped in Bracciolini's already twisted mind. She was the most beautiful creature he had ever seen. He could actually believe the Order's teachings about the divinity of women when he looked upon Colombina. But his adoration was short-lived when it became obvious that she belonged to Lorenzo. Here was yet another great privilege that Lorenzo possessed that was out of Bracciolini's reach. His envy, and his hatred, simmered. Bracciolini went to the Donati home and informed Colombina's father that the merchant Medici intended to make his treasured, noble-born daughter into his lowly mistress, if he hadn't ruined her in that way already. His informing had been the reason the Donatis had forbidden Lorenzo to have further contact with their daughter. Later, Bracciolini would also be the informer who brought the news of Colombina and Lorenzo to Niccolò Ardinghelli's doorstep. Repeatedly. His information, which included cruel goading with invented graphic details, had led to Colombina's beating at the hands of her enraged husband.

One night after getting very drunk, he waited outside the Antica Torre for Colombina. She was the new princess of the Order, their precious Expected One, the Master's golden student. But he knew what she really was. She was Lorenzo's whore. And Lorenzo was in Milan on a diplomatic mission for his father at the time, so it seemed logical to Bracciolini that Colombina would be in need of a stand-in while Lorenzo was away. He grabbed her as she passed the little alley that separated the Antica Torre from Santa Trinità and put his hand over her mouth before she could scream. She bit him, drawing blood. And she wasn't finished yet. Sweet, fine-boned Colombina, it turned out, was a fighter. She pulled the brooch out of her mantle and stuck him with it hard, the pin digging deep into his flesh. Bracciolini screamed, loud enough to bring a member of the Gianfigliazza family out of the tower and to Colombina's rescue.

Bracciolini threatened her, blackmailed her, came up with every foul idea he could invent to shut her up, but to no avail. Colombina, the voice of truth, demanded that he pay for his attack upon her and refused to allow him to turn it on her and somehow make it her fault. She would not be the victim of his lies, nor would she allow him to go free and do this to another woman. He had not only disgraced the good name of Bracciolini, he had violated every possible rule of the Order. And for his kindly, devoted father, this was the greatest crime imaginable. Jacopo was ostracized from his family and disinherited as a result.

Every second of pain Jacopo Bracciolini had ever experienced in his life had come from Lorenzo de' Medici, his little whore, and their blessed Order.

And now he considered his good fortune for a moment. Was it possible? Was he actually being offered to be paid handsomely to destroy Lorenzo and the Order?

"What are the pope's intentions?" he asked de' Pazzi. "Is he going to declare them heretics?"

How delicious that would be. Maybe he would burn Lorenzo at the stake like that crazy French bitch they always yammered on about. Maybe Lorenzo's whore would burn too, and he would get to watch. Perhaps he would recommend this to the pope. Certainly he would emphasize the hated Colombina's role as both heretic and adulteress while informing His Holiness of the crimes committed against the Church regularly by the Order.

"It is not for me to say what the Holy Father does with the information," de' Pazzi answered. "But I would assume that it is his greatest desire to eliminate heresy in all its forms."

"As it is mine, Francesco. So consider me your partner, and tell the pope that if he will prepare appropriately comfortable accommodations for my arrival, I will deliver all the evidence he desires. And perhaps far more than he even expects!"

*

Jacopo Bracciolini paid an unexpected visit to the Palazzo Medici on Via Larga shortly after his secret meeting with Francesco de' Pazzi.

While Lorenzo was aware of the younger Bracciolini's roguish reputation and would never forget what he had done to Colombina, he agreed to see his childhood friend privately in his *studiolo* for the sake of the old family connections. However, he wondered how long it would be into the conversation before Bracciolini asked to borrow money from him.

"Lorenzo, my old friend." Bracciolini embraced him and kissed him on both cheeks before continuing. "I have come to make amends for the events of the past. It has been many years since I treated your Colombina in that unforgivable manner. I would apologize to her myself, as the events of that night haunt me all these years later, but I know that she would not hear it from me. I was hoping you might tell her how sorry I am. I assure you, I am a changed man."

Lorenzo nodded graciously. The apology seemed sincere enough. He would not judge it yet but rather see where this meeting was headed. He remained silent and let Bracciolini talk.

"I know you are wondering why I am here. I bet you are even waiting for me to ask for a loan from you. Well, you are incorrect if that is what you think. I have come asking for nothing but your forgiveness. And to present you with a gift."

Bracciolini removed a beautifully bound book from his satchel and presented it to Lorenzo with ceremony.

"*The History of Florence*, as written by my father, Poggio Bracciolini. As you know, he wrote it in Latin. But inspired by your love of the Tuscan language, I have translated the entire book into our vernacular. I have been working on it for years. And I have dedicated this Tuscan version to you, for encouraging our language and because you are now as much a part of the history of Florence as your grandfather."

Lorenzo was stunned. The last thing he had expected from this now notorious member of the Florentine nobility was a gift of this magnitude. Lorenzo paged through the beautiful book, which was a masterwork of translation and history. Perhaps there was real hope for Bracciolini yet. He was still capable of extraordinary feats of academia, despite his increasing dissipation, and he was gracious enough to add passages about Lorenzo's accomplishments to the text.

Lorenzo thanked him and brought out several bottles of his best wine. The two men drank into the night, talking about the good times when they were younger. Lorenzo relaxed as they discussed Plato and their early days with Ficino and laughed about some of their antics as boys. He was so convinced that Bracciolini was sincerely trying to change his life that he even brought his childhood friend up to date on the Order and their plans for the future.

Despite his years as a leader immersed in the dangers of Florentine politics, Lorenzo always wanted to find the best in people. He was not naturally skeptical, and he believed in giving every man a chance to atone for his past and redeem himself through his future. The trait was part of his spiritual education, but it was also essential to his character. It was how he was made. That Lorenzo was so noble and forgiving was what made him great. It was also what made him vulnerable.

*

Jacopo Bracciolini kept his word to the Pazzi conspirators, providing Sixtus IV with more evidence than he could have ever imagined for Lorenzo's heresy. He had strategized his visit to Lorenzo perfectly and knew him well enough to be certain he would fall for the book. It had gone exactly to plan, and Lorenzo had spilled all kinds of secrets when he let his guard down. Everything Bracciolini knew about the Order he verified in that evening's conversation. He embellished a bit when sending the report to Pope Sixtus, just to make it that much more valuable. Then he demanded double the original payment as reward for such perfect evidence of heresy against the Medici and their supporters. His money was paid in pieces of silver as a little joke from the Curia.

Bracciolini was firmly committed to storming the Signoria with Salviati, the archbishop of Pisa, during the assassination. It would be a dramatic piece of theater, and one he would enjoy playing a leading role in. He almost hoped there would be resistance so he could kill a member of the council as part of the spectacle. He had never plunged a sword into a man; it was a new and exciting experience he was looking forward to.

With Bracciolini firmly committed to the plan, Francesco de Pazzi now needed to find a few more assassins. Losing Montesecco was an enormous blow, but it was not insurmountable. He consulted with Archbishop Salviati, who came up with a solution. It was imperfect, perhaps, but a solution nonetheless. The archbishop had found two priests who were willing—even excited—to kill Lorenzo de' Medici. The first was Antonio Maffei. He was a scrappy little man from Volterra, a Florentine possession that had endured a civil war. The bloody uprising there had left more than half the population dead. Maffei had lost his own mother and sisters to the marauders who came into Volterra. The marauders were paid mercenaries, brought in by the Medici family to quell the rioting there when the Florentine army was spread too thin on other frontiers. While it was not Lorenzo's fault that the mercenaries turned out to be brigands and criminals, their devastation of Volterra was often blamed on him. Lorenzo visited Volterra on many occasions, offering personal restitution to the people there following the bloodshed. He spent a fortune of his own money to restore the town and its remaining citizens. And his guilt haunted him; Lorenzo had nightmares about Volterra regularly. It was the greatest regret of his political career.

But for the young priest Antonio Maffei, Lorenzo de' Medici was a villain of the highest order. If he could play a part in the death of such a man, he would be a hero for Volterra. He agreed to wield the dagger for no compensation other than pardon from the pope once the deed had been accomplished.

Maffei would be joined by another priest, a man who was deeply in debt to the Pazzi family bank and looking for a way to clear his ledger. Stefano da Bagnone agreed to assist Maffei in the event that it took more than one man to take down Lorenzo. As Easter Mass was a formal state occasion, it was to be expected that Lorenzo would be dressed for it. Full formal attire in Florence included a sword. And Lorenzo, the accomplished athlete and sportsman, did not wear a sword simply as an ornament. He knew how to use it. Therefore the plan was for the two priests to take him from behind, before he was able to unsheathe his weapon.

Together with the archbishop, the two priests came upon a brilliant plan to ensure their success. The signal to attack the Medici brothers would come during Mass, when the host was raised up on the altar in preparation for Holy Communion. Not only was it a signal that could not be missed, marked as it was by the ringing of bells, but devout Florentines would all be looking down in their prayers at that moment. It would give the assassins time to strike from behind without being immediately witnessed. Two daggers in Lorenzo's throat in that instant would guarantee the success of their venture.

That there were now two priests and an archbishop in the service of the pope planning the bloody murder of two brothers on Easter Sunday—to be accomplished as the holy host was raised on the altar of a basilica—never bothered the conscience of any of the conspirators.

Nor did it strike anyone involved as the least bit ironic that the only man to make the determination that such a plot was utterly diabolical, the only man to walk away from what he determined was absolute evil, was the professional killer.

320

Palazzo Medici, Florence
April 25, 1478

LORENZO'S SMILE WAS broad as Giuliano limped into his *studiolo*.

"It lives! It walks!" Lorenzo got up from his desk and bounded over to his brother, embracing him in a bear hug. "How do you feel?"

"Much better. Sore. Getting downstairs was hard. It will require more healing before I feel like myself again, but I am on the mend overall."

Giuliano stopped talking for a moment and Lorenzo saw that his eyes, still red with the inflammation, were also unnaturally bright. Concerned now, he put his hand against his brother's forehead. "Do you have a fever? Do your eyes hurt from this inflammation?"

Giuliano laughed, brushing his brother's hand away as he moved to sit on the red upholstered settee that had once rested beneath Botticelli's masterpiece, *The Time Returns*. "No, no. I'm fine. That is what I am here to tell you, brother. I have just come from the chapel, where I prayed before the Libro Rosso for the last hour as you advised me to do. I listened to the angels, and they have spoken to me. They tell me to marry Fioretta, to choose only love. To acknowledge and raise my child as my own."

Lorenzo could feel the lump building in his throat as he listened. It took him a moment to speak. "I am so happy to hear you say this. And I believe that you have heard the angels correctly. What else would angels say, other than that love conquers all?"

"But you have not heard the best of it yet! You will not believe it, but it is a miracle. Mother . . . she does not object! She was waiting for me when I was finished in the chapel, and she told me that she had been searching her heart and wanted only my happiness. Can you believe it? I shall marry Fioretta!"

Lorenzo embraced his little brother and hugged him tightly. For a moment, they were children again. Innocent, happy, playing out their roles of protective older brother and sweet, indulged baby. There were tears in Lorenzo's eyes as he pulled away from Giuliano.

"I am . . . so happy for you both. I can only imagine how Fioretta will feel when you tell her."

"I have decided to propose to her tomorrow, if my eyes are better. It will be her Easter surprise. I shall ride up to Fiesole first thing in the morning and surprise her. And my son."

"You aren't going to the High Mass tomorrow? The young cardinal is coming, and he is the pope's nephew. He has asked to see you there specifically, as you will not be at the banquet tomorrow night."

Giuliano considered for a moment. "Perhaps I will, and then go to Fiesole afterward. It depends on how I feel. I'm not sure how my leg will feel after walking to the cathedral and back; it may be too sore for me to ride. But now I must go and apply the compresses to my eyes that the doctor has given me so that I may celebrate the most blessed Easter of my life!"

Florence
Easter Sunday 1478

THE CATHEDRAL BEGAN to fill hours early, as Florentines arrived to get a seat for the High Mass on Easter Sunday. Seats were always saved in the front pews for the ruling elite, of which the Medici were the highest in rank. Lorenzo's space was reserved at the front right, facing the altar. He would attend today with his closest friends and his brother, rather than his family, as the Mass here in the center of Florence was something of a state occasion. His mother, wife, and children would attend a separate service at their "home" basilica of San Lorenzo.

Francesco de Pazzi watched Lorenzo enter the cathedral with Angelo Poliziano. He looked around for Giuliano and began to panic when he didn't see the tall, unmistakable form of the youngest Medici brother. De Pazzi approached Lorenzo, who advised him that Giuliano was feeling very sore today and had decided that the walk to the cathedral wasn't in the best interest of his ailing leg.

Sprinting the long blocks from the cathedral and down the Via Larga to the Medici palace, Francesco de Pazzi was admitted by Madonna Lucrezia, who was preparing to leave for her own local service with her grandchildren. De' Pazzi told her breathlessly that the young Cardinal Riario was asking for Giuliano and that there was still time for him to attend the Mass so as not to offend the family of the pope. Lucrezia allowed the man in to speak with Giuliano about it directly. Her son was a grown man and perfectly capable of making his own decisions.

Francesco de' Pazzi knew the character of Giuliano de' Medici well. Everyone in Florence did. He was known for the sweetness of his nature and his unfailing manners. De' Pazzi preyed upon this quality, pushing Giuliano hard.

"The cardinal is the youngest of powerful brothers, at seventeen. He is certain that you would give him invaluable advice about filling such grand shoes and living up to an exalted family name. And I have no doubt that the pope would feel far more kindly disposed toward Lorenzo in the future if you would grant his favorite nephew this small audience. Just a few minutes following the Mass, and we will have you back in bed in no time."

Giuliano sighed. In truth, his leg was feeling much better today and he was capable of walking to the cathedral, albeit with a limp. But he had hoped to get up to Fiesole early, as he was so excited to be with Fioretta and the baby. But if what Francesco was asserting here was true, if the pope's nephew really wanted to spend some time with him, then he should go to the Mass. It would benefit Lorenzo, above all, to have an ally within the pope's family. And it wouldn't delay him so very much, really. And after all, he did have much to be grateful for, and therefore an hour on his knees in honor of the Lord's resurrection was the least he could do. He had actually been feeling rather guilty about skipping the service. Perhaps God sent Francesco de' Pazzi to ensure that Giuliano went to church today!

Further, Giuliano remembered as he dressed that today was April twenty-sixth. It was two years ago to the day that their lovely Simonetta passed away. What was it that Lorenzo had said? "April twenty-sixth will always be a day of sadness for us"? He would go to Mass today to pray for the soul of Simonetta as well, and for the Cattaneo and Vespucci families, who still mourned her.

He dressed quickly and was a little surprised when Francesco hugged him tight around his waist as he emerged from his chambers, exclaiming his joy that the younger Medici was feeling well enough to accompany him on this fine day. What the unsuspecting Giuliano could not have known was that Francesco was checking for weapons and for armor. But because he had dressed so quickly and did not want any extra weight on his recovering body, Giuliano had decided to forgo the formal attire and leave the military dress items at home. Lorenzo would be wearing them, no doubt magnificently, and he would represent the family, as he always did.

Giuliano limped down the Via Larga toward the magnificent basilica, the pink and green marble facade gleaming in the sunlight. The masterpiece of the red brick Duomo was an inviting sight, welcoming all Florentines in to worship on this holy day.

They entered through the cathedral, but it was getting late and the spaces around Lorenzo had already filled. Giuliano would need to sit elsewhere, further back in the cathedral. His brother spotted him and raised an eyebrow to question his presence at the Mass, to which Giuliano just shrugged and pointed to de' Pazzi. Lorenzo smiled at him and waved as if to say "explain it later" and turned back to prepare to take his seat. He adjusted his sword and scabbard so that they would lie across his lap during the Mass and not knock against the pews. As he did so, Lorenzo noticed that there were two priests sitting behind him. He didn't recognize them, but he smiled politely and wished them a blessed Easter before turning back in readiness for the service. He commented to Angelo that the pope's nephew, the most recent Cardinal Riario, looked very young and very nervous from his place on the altar. No doubt he had never experienced High Mass in such an enormous place as their beautiful cathedral of Santa Maria del Fiori.

Giuliano followed Francesco de' Pazzi back toward the northern side of the cathedral, near the choir, and sat beside him. He was trying hard to focus on the service, but in truth all he could think about was seeing Fioretta. When the sacristy bell rang to signal the arrival of the host, he bent his head in reverence, as did the majority of the congregation.

Giuliano de' Medici, about to begin a prayer in honor of the Lord he loved so much, never saw the dagger coming. Francesco de Pazzi struck hard with the power of adrenaline, plunging the first blow into the younger Medici's neck with such force that it split him open.

Bloodlust seized Francesco de' Pazzi, and he continued to stab Giuliano de' Medici as hard and as fast as he could, grunting with the effort of it. He was so frenzied in his attack that he sliced open his own thigh, mistaking it for Giuliano during one blow.

There was chaos in the cathedral now, screaming as the blood splattered the congregation on the north side, and people began to scatter. Simultaneously, the two priests in place behind Lorenzo had attacked, but the priest-turned-assassin Antonio Maffei had made a tactical error. As he pulled his dagger from the sleeve of his robe with one hand, he steadied himself for the first blow by grabbing Lorenzo with his other.

Lorenzo de' Medici had lightning-fast reflexes, well honed from years of hunting and athletics. He jumped the moment he was touched from behind, causing Maffei's blow to land with less force. While the dagger sliced into Lorenzo's neck, it was not a fatal wound. The intended victim was able to unsheathe his sword and defend himself before the other assailant could get a blow in.

For Angelo Poliziano, this was the moment of his life when everything he had ever been or ever would be was crystallized. His father, the most significant source of love and wisdom in his life, had been stabbed to death before his eyes when he was a little boy. Now Lorenzo de' Medici, the most significant source of love and wisdom in his life twenty years later, was similarly threatened by knife-wielding assassins. But this time Angelo would intervene.

He wasn't a big man, and his years as a poet had not given him an athletic build or any physical strength to speak of, but Angelo Poliziano had something else—determination. He hit one of the assassins with the heel of his right hand, hard enough to knock him off balance, and then seized Lorenzo by his free arm to pull him back and out of harm's way. The two priests, stunned and terrified by the quick reactions of both Angelo and Lorenzo, turned and ran out of the cathedral before anyone could stop them.

"Come on! Now!" Angelo yelled over the chaos at Lorenzo, who was now bleeding profusely from his neck wound and was in no condition to do anything but obey. Lorenzo's party pulled him immediately through the huge bronze sacristy doors, slamming them shut against any further attacks. Lorenzo was momentarily stunned, but then the true terror hit him and he began to scream for his brother.

"Did you see Giuliano?" he asked Angelo desperately. But Lorenzo's friends had no answer for him. His little brother had been sitting behind them and to the left, too far to see what was happening in the madness of the attacks and the haste to protect il Magnifico. Until that moment, it hadn't even occurred to the others that Giuliano would be a target. Who, really, would want to assassinate the nonpolitical, sweet-natured Giuliano? It made no sense. Lorenzo's loyal entourage was focused only on their leader at that moment. His young friend Antonio Ridolfi sucked the wound on his neck. If the assailants had been truly skilled, their daggers would have been poisoned. Ridolfi would gladly take the poison if it meant saving the Magnificent One. One day, perhaps, Florence would be grateful for his sacrifice.

"Giuliano!" Lorenzo was weak now from blood loss and Angelo was trying to keep him still while wrapping his throat with his own cape. "Is he safe?" Lorenzo was frantic. He had to know about his brother.

Another longtime Medici companion, Sigismondo Stufa, jumped up on a ladder and climbed into the choir loft to get a better look at the chaos that had transformed Easter Sunday into a bloodbath. Someone screamed that the dome was caving in, and people were now being trampled in the effort to escape the basilica. It took Sigismondo a long minute of searching to set his eyes upon the terrible sight that he would remember in his nightmares for the rest of his life.

Giuliano de' Medici, nearly unrecognizable in a mass of his own

The Poet Prince

blood, lay lifeless in the northern corridor. He had been torn to pieces, stabbed with the most vicious blows nineteen times.

There was no time to mourn. No one knew who or how many the attackers were. They must get Lorenzo to safety. And if Lorenzo knew that Giuliano had been massacred on the cathedral floor, they would never get him out of there. Sigismondo said that he had not seen Giuliano from the choir loft, giving Lorenzo false hope that his brother had escaped. The lie broke Sigismondo's heart, but it was the only way he could ensure that Lorenzo would leave the basilica and get back to the safety of the Palazzo Medici as quickly as they could carry him.

Later Sigismondo would claim that he hadn't lied when he said he didn't see Giuliano in the cathedral. In the terror of the moment, he could hardly fathom that the terrible mass of flesh and blood on the floor was his childhood best friend and jousting partner. That mess was not Giuliano de' Medici. How could it possibly be?

*

The second element of the Pazzi conspiracy launched as Archbishop Salviati and Bracciolini marched toward the Signoria in preparation for their coup. They were joined by a team of ruthless mercenaries from Perugia. The approach of this ragtag bunch of soldiers raised the hackles of the Signoria, despite the fact that they were led by an archbishop. The current *gonfaloniere*, the commander in chief of the republic, was a hard and fearless man named Cesare Petrucci. Petrucci was having lunch when the archbishop and his brigade arrived and demanded audience. The savvy Petrucci allowed them in but separated Archbishop Salviati and Bracciolini from the band of villainous Perugians, requesting that this "honor guard" wait in an adjoining room. What the archbishop didn't realize was that the room where the mercenaries were asked to wait was a cleverly disguised holding cell. There was no way to exit that room once inside unless a member of the Signoria released them.

Archbishop Salviati advised Petrucci that he had a message from

327

the pope. He began to deliver a somewhat nonsensical speech about liberating Florence, but his nerves got the better of him and he stumbled over the words. But Petrucci had heard enough. Words like "overthrow" and "tyrant" were all he needed to hear to know that there was trouble brewing. Besides, there was commotion in the square and he could already hear chaos in the streets outside. He shouted for the Signoria guards and, as he did so, was attacked suddenly by an erratic Bracciolini, who was awkward and late pulling his sword.

Petrucci, a burly man and a skilled warrior, didn't bother with a weapon. He grabbed Bracciolini by the hair and wrestled him to the ground in a matter of seconds. Guards from the Signoria piled in the room and further subdued him, at the same time getting a few good kicks in at the archbishop of Pisa, who was also taken into custody.

"Toll the *vacca!*" Petrucci shouted.

The *vacca* was the enormous bell in the Signoria tower, given that name, the "cow," because of the odd and deep mooing sound the bell made when rung. It was a sound of grave importance to Florentines. The *vacca* was only tolled when there was a crisis in the city. It was a call to order, and it brought the citizens of the republic rushing into the Piazza Signoria to discover its purpose.

As the *vacca* tolled its lowing sound, riders wearing the livery of the Pazzi family charged into the square shouting, "Liberty! Death to the Medici tyrants! For the people of Florence! For the people!"

If the Pazzi conspirators were hoping that the citizens of Florence would chime in with them, they were to be sorely—and dangerously—disappointed. The word of Giuliano de' Medici's terrible murder at the hands of Francesco de Pazzi was spreading wildly, causing outrage throughout the city. As more Pazzi shills rode into the square shouting for liberty, the populace of Florence poured into the square shouting in return, "*Palle! Palle, Palle!* For the love of the Medici!" The Pazzi horsemen were pelted with rocks as the crowd became progressively more unruly. Details of Giuliano's murder continued to spread and were exaggerated.

"He was cut into a hundred pieces! He was scattered all across the altar! His eyes were torn out and his nose cut off by the Pazzi scum!"

The terrible butchering of sweet Giuliano de' Medici would not go unpunished in Florence this day. The palace guards had already killed the Perugian mercenaries and were hacking off their heads to place on spikes as a warning to all who would threaten the peace in this civilized republic. The first official conspirator to see retribution was the stunned Bracciolini. This was not how he had anticipated his involvement in the coup d'état to end Lorenzo's life and Medici reign. He began to talk fast, to promise complete intelligence on all the conspirators if they would spare him. Petrucci listened for less than a minute before he was interrupted with the news of Giuliano de' Medici's murder on the altar at High Mass. He spit on Bracciolini and nodded to the palace guards.

"Make an example of him. And make it count."

Within seconds, the guards had found a sturdy rope and tied one end of it around the transom beam across the window. The other end went quickly around Bracciolini's neck. They hurled him out the window, not even bothering to watch as he smashed against the side of the Palazzo Vecchio, breaking his neck and his teeth all in one motion. He was left to dangle out the window as the first example. But he was only the first.

They grabbed the archbishop of Pisa next. He was screaming and kicking and invoking papal protection until one of the guards broke his jaw to shut him up. The guards sent him to join Bracciolini, in precisely the same way. He did not die as quickly, and the gruesome details of his slow and agonizing death would be recorded later by Angelo Poliziano. As the archbishop swung violently from the rope and smashed into the cold body of Jacopo Bracciolini, his last living act was to sink his teeth into the dead man's flesh. Why he did it was a mystery, and a macabre one that was speculated upon by Florentines for years. Most speculated that the archbishop somehow believed he could save himself with this final, gruesome act. If that was his plan, it failed as had his others.

The mob was now screaming for Pazzi blood, and there was a surge toward their palazzo. Francesco de' Pazzi was in hiding there, but not very effectively. The wound in his thigh was bleeding profusely, and it was easy enough to follow the blood and find him where he was hiding under a bed. The mob stripped him naked and dragged him through the streets, turning him over to the Signoria so that he would join his companions in their instant execution. Like those who preceded him, Francesco de' Pazzi was left to dangle out the window of the Signoria from an impromptu but effective noose.

As the mob ruled and rumors spread, the people of Florence demanded to know if their magnificent Lorenzo was still alive. Hundreds of people now marched in the streets, on their way to the Palazzo Medici, chanting, "Magnifico! Magnifico!" The crowds swelled, with more shouting, more demands for proof that Lorenzo was alive.

Inside the Medici home, immediate plans were being made to get Clarice and the children out of Florence to one of the villas as quickly and quietly as possible. Lorenzo did not want his family in the city for the chaos that would clearly continue until the truth was known about this terrible day and its origins. He was praying that his mother would consent to leave with them, and yet he knew she would not. Lucrezia was in shock, unable to speak since hearing the news that her baby, Giuliano, had been brutally slain.

Lorenzo's personal physician, having been rushed in through a back door of the palazzo, examined the neck wound carefully.

"You are truly beloved of God, Lorenzo," the doctor said, shaking his head. "There is no way you should have survived a direct stab wound to the neck. But look at this."

The doctor held out the piece of silver chain he had cut away from the wound. Still attached to it, albeit covered in blood, was the necklace with the relic of the True Cross that Lorenzo had been given as a child. It had been held for him until he was old enough to appreciate it, a priceless gift from King René d'Anjou, which had once belonged to Joan of Arc.

"It looks as if the knife cut the chain, but that as a result, the blow was deflected and hit further up your neck, above the artery. This pendant quite possibly saved your life."

*

Florence was in chaos. There was rioting and mayhem as the citizens reacted to the conflicting rumors swirling through the charged Tuscan air. Hundreds were surrounding the palazzo at Via Larga, demanding to know if Lorenzo was dead or alive.

Angelo became liaison between the street and the palazzo, reporting to the people of Florence that Lorenzo was in the care of the doctor and asking that they continue to pray fervently for Lorenzo's survival. But as the afternoon progressed and the crowds swelled, there was no appeasing them. They wanted Lorenzo. They demanded Lorenzo.

As the doctor wrapped Lorenzo's neck, Colombina and Fra Francesco were admitted into the room. Colombina fell to her knees at Lorenzo's feet when she saw him, grabbing his hand and weeping.

"Oh, Lorenzo, thank God. Thank God you are alive."

He stroked her hair and wept as he asked, "Do you know about Giuliano?"

She nodded but could say nothing, too overwhelmed by her grief over Giuliano's death and relief over Lorenzo's salvation.

Lorenzo's next question was for his Master. "How do I reconcile all of this, Master, through the teachings of the Order? Where was God today, when my brother went to worship, to celebrate the resurrection of Jesus and to give thanks for his life? Why was my beautiful, innocent brother taken?"

Fra Francesco, who had seen more tragedy and violence than any single soul should ever have to witness, placed his hand gently on Lorenzo's shoulder. "My son, I can only say this: it is easy to have faith on a day when all is well. It is very hard to have faith on a day when we are surrounded by tragedy. I cannot tell you why God did not save Giuliano, but it is clear that there was divine intervention to save you. And so rather than cursing God for what he did not do, I prefer to give thanks for what he did do. I am grateful that Madonna Lucrezia is not mourning both her sons on this day. And so is most of Florence, by the sound of it."

Lorenzo nodded. He whispered, "I am grateful for my life, Master. But . . . it will take some time for me to apply the teachings of love toward the men who did this."

"But that is exactly what you must do, Lorenzo, and you must do it now. It has taken over fourteen hundred years for men with a purpose to unravel the true teachings of Jesus and to destroy the Way of Love. You will not be able to restore them all on your own in your lifetime. But what you can do now is set an example for your people and the future by giving them a message of peace."

Colombina clenched his hand and looked up at him. "The people of this city are terrified that something has happened to you, and it is mob rule out there now. Innocent Florentines are getting hurt, and in the current climate, there may even be more slaughter. But they love you, Lorenzo, and they will follow your lead. Talk to them and they will listen."

Lorenzo nodded. His first attempt to stand up was unsuccessful. He was dizzy from blood loss and shock. The three in the room—Colombina, the Master, and the doctor—helped him to try again and held him up while he gained his balance. Angelo came in panting, announcing that the mob was more restless and uncontrollable than ever. He had told them that Lorenzo would deliver a statement through him, and he had come to craft one.

"I will deliver it myself, Angelo. But you may have to repeat it for me if I cannot be heard over the din."

*

"Look, Lorenzo lives!"

The swelling mob outside the palazzo had been waiting for more information from Angelo when the window on the second story, just left of the main door, opened and Lorenzo appeared. His neck was dramatically bandaged and his clothes were caked in blood; his face was white with shock. Even from a distance it was clear that il Magnifico had been gravely injured in the attack. There was a collective intake of breath as the crowd watched Lorenzo struggle to remain on his feet and deliver his message. Angelo was visible beside him. What the mob below could not see was that Colombina and the doctor were propping him up from behind so he would not fall.

"My brother and sister citizens," Lorenzo summoned all of his strength to be heard, as the people of Florence hushed each other in an effort to listen. "A terrible crime has been committed this day. An affront to God, a scar upon our republic, and a crime against my family. As some of you may know, my brother Giuliano . . . is dead. He was . . . murdered in the cathedral during Mass on this, of all holy days."

The crowd erupted with the official announcement of Giuliano de' Medici's murder. Lorenzo, who was failing fast, continued with only the slightest pause, forcing the crowd to silence itself in order to hear him.

"But we are a civilized people. As such, we must not add to the crimes that have been committed on this terrible day. We, the Republic of Florence, are viewed by citizens all across Europe as leaders of a progressive and independent state, one known for its culture, learning, and most of all, its law. And as such we must continue to set an example by allowing a just system of law and order to take effect and ensure that the perpetrators are brought to justice."

There was more screaming at the word "justice," before Lorenzo continued. "Let me stress that we cannot take this justice into the streets, no matter how much we may feel the need to right these wrongs. It is not the way in which a civilized republic operates. Our freedom comes from our commitment to justice. So let us remain free by also remaining just.

"While my family appreciates your outpouring of love and loyalty more than I have words to express, we must also beg that you do not commit acts of renegade retribution in an attempt to prove that loyalty. Those of you who knew my brother know that he was a kind and gentle man. He detested violence and would never want to see bloodshed carried out in his name.

"Most of all, I ask that in this time of terrible trial, you stay together as a community. Take care of each other. Cherish each precious moment that you have with your family . . ."

Lorenzo was choking up now, the reality of losing Giuliano setting in as he spoke. He had to cut it short. "That really is the only message that matters now. Love one another. And thank you. Thank you all for your loyalty and support."

The crowd gasped as Lorenzo collapsed against Angelo. He was carried to his bed as the citizens of Florence cheered him, chanting "Il Magnifico" and "*Palle, palle, palle*" through the streets. The sympathy toward Lorenzo and his family had never been greater. Pope Sixtus and his closest family and followers were reviled as the criminals they were. The citizens of the Florentine Republic would stand with Lorenzo on virtually every decision he would make. Traditional councils were abolished or simply became obsolete as a council of ten Medici supporters was convened as an emergency measure during the tumultuous period immediately following the cathedral massacre. That council, never meant to be anything but temporary, became the ruling force in a city that took its mandate from the Medici.

For the next ten years, Florence belonged exclusively to Lorenzo as he became the most powerful man in Europe to never hold an official title.

*

In one of the many strange twists of fate in the history of the Medici family, Fioretta Gorini died of fever and blood loss in her bed on the same morning that Giuliano was murdered in the cathedral. Blessedly, she never knew about the massacre. Fioretta's last communication from Giuliano was an excited message of love and hope, telling her that his family had consented to their union. She fell asleep shortly after receiving the correspondence, dreaming of the beautiful future she would have as Giuliano's wife and the mother of Medici children. She never woke up from that dream.

Had Giuliano gone to Fiesole that morning, he would have arrived just in time to hold the hand of his beloved as she slipped away from him and returned to God.

Now they were together in heaven, taken on the same day.

Lorenzo de' Medici adopted the baby, Giulio, with the permission and blessing of Fioretta's parents and sister. For the rest of their days, the Gorini were treated as members of the Medici family and wanted for nothing. Baby Giulio was raised with Lorenzo's favorite son, Giovanni, and the two boys became as close as twins. They played together, learned together, challenged each other. They finished each other's sentences and spoke their own shorthand language. And like many sets of natural twins, they were opposite personality types: Giovanni was sunny and sweet where Giulio was serious and sullen. Although Lorenzo always treated Giulio with the same affection that he showered on his own children, the boy seemed to have an innate resentment for the world that had deprived him of his natural parents. It was often necessary for his half brother, whom he called Gio, to cheer him out of his moods.

The destinies of these two boys were as intertwined as if they had shared a womb.

*

The Church is a hybrid monster.

For centuries, it has been the tradition in art to depict the Church in such a way, most often as a minotaur, the creature who lived in the center of the labyrinth in Crete and devoured the innocent. For that describes the Church, does it not? A mysterious type of hybrid monster, half horrible and half redeemable; half based on truth and half based on lies. A hybrid of love and hate, good and greed. This monster lives at the center of an impenetrable fortress and feeds on the blood of the innocent.

I have painted my hybrid monster as a centaur. He is a wretched one, and stupid, as he represents Sixtus and the brood of hideous inbred creatures who would carry out a plot to butcher the innocent on Easter Sunday. He clings hopelessly to his weapon, as he knows it has already failed him. He is caught. The truth is known.

The centaur is being controlled easily by the hand of the great Pallas Athene, who represents the goddess of eternal wisdom. It is in this way that I assert she will triumph, for she represents the truth. I have clothed her in a gown that is made up entirely of Medici devices, Lorenzo's interlocking wedding rings, while also draping her in laurel leaves. It is clear to any who have eyes to see that this wise and mighty goddess favors our Lorenzo. May it always be so. I create this painting as a talisman of protection for him and the entire Medici family.

I remain,
Alessandro di Filipepi, known as "Botticelli"

FROM *THE SECRET MEMOIRS OF SANDRO BOTTICELLI*

Florence
present day

"POPE SIXTUS IV excommunicated Lorenzo shortly after murdering Giuliano in the cathedral."

Destino was giving the lesson to all who were assembled in Petra's living room that evening: Maureen and Peter, Roland and Tammy, and Petra.

"Excommunicated him for what reason?" Peter wanted to know.

"For surviving. Laugh, please, because it is ridiculous. But this is the truth. Sixtus was so outraged that Lorenzo had dared to survive his attempt to murder him that he excommunicated Lorenzo for the act of survival. And when the citizens of Florence would not acknowledge the act of anathema against il Magnifico, Sixtus excommunicated the entire Republic of Florence."

"What?" This was said in a unison of disbelief.

Peter, the former priest who had once worked inside the Vatican, added, "You cannot excommunicate an entire city! And certainly not because of one citizen in that city!"

"Yes, I know it is absurd, but everything that pope did was rather unbelievable. And he always got away with it. Papal authority being what it was, and the pope being infallible, he could do whatever he wished, and so he did. You can understand why Lorenzo became more and more fixated on the elimination of absolute papal authority while at the same time he was always seeking ways to destabilize the structure of the Catholic Church."

"What happened?" Roland asked. "Did the citizens of Florence accept their excommunication?"

"Of course not. For Florentines, Sixtus was a criminal and therefore nothing he said or did held much weight with the average citizen. The council in the Signoria sent a letter back to the pope, telling him that they would much rather follow Lorenzo than him, thank you very much. It was the ultimate affront! I wish I could have seen the face of Sixtus when he was faced with that letter."

"The story of Giuliano and Fioretta is so sad," Tammy said. "And yet, there is something poetic about their dying on the same day."

"They were twinned souls, of course," Petra said. "They left this world together, and I have no doubt that they were instantly reunited in heaven, to become as one again."

Peter had been analyzing the material from the Libro Rosso on this idea of each soul having a twin. It fascinated him, confused him, and most of all, it disconcerted him.

"So are you saying that all people have soul mates? In reading the legends of Solomon and Sheba in the Libro Rosso, I see reference repeatedly to one's 'own soul's twin.' Are all souls twin souls?"

Petra looked at him for a long and careful moment, a slight smile on her lips. When she answered, it was with a softness that they had not yet seen from her. "Yes, Peter. All souls are twinned and perfectly mated. All of them. However, we do not incarnate together in every lifetime, depending on what the mission requires. Let us take Sandro Botticelli as a perfect example. Sandro was a singular character. He did not exist to find his soul mate, as he was singularly devoted to the mission. Sandro's true love and authentic passion was creation, which is why he was so prolific. This was true for many of the greatest angelics: Donatello, Sandro, Michelangelo.

"Commitment to the love of another is a very specific task unto itself, and for some it is part of their mission—or even the mission itself. For others, it is a distraction. But the beauty of it all is that those who desire to find their soul mates do so because they have one to find. Those who have no interest do not because it isn't their mission. Destino will tell you that Sandro was one of the most contented men he has ever known, and he was entirely alone. He liked it that way, because anything else interfered with his art."

"So, I'm not entirely getting this. Sandro didn't have a twin soul? I thought everyone did." This was Peter, still trying to stay with the concept.

"Angels are not so easily understood, are they?" Destino asked. "But this is true about many of the angelic ones. Everyone does, and therefore Sandro did, indeed, have a twin soul. But such a person was not alive during the Renaissance, as it was necessary for him to channel that love and passion solely into his art."

"But," Petra continued with emphasis, "and this is critical to understand, he did not feel that terrible sense of longing that one feels when one is searching for someone. This is because his twin soul chose to remain in the angelic realms and help him from above. He tapped into the energy of his other half each time he worked, and his mate was right there with him. This is why his output was so extraordinary—because he was in essence working as two people, one above and one below, to accomplish the miracle of the one thing! And this is also why he felt such ecstasy while painting, which led to his unequaled output. He experienced no longing or loneliness. That particular pain happens only when soul mates are incarnate at the same time and unable to reunite; then there is an increased desire to find each other."

Peter watched her with fascination. She was mesmerizing: brilliant, intense, completely aware of herself and her surroundings. He wondered as he watched her, *Is she one of these angelics? Is she so committed to her mission that she has not allowed herself to know committed, human love?*

Maureen was curious about this, thinking of various friends who were still alone and still unhappy. "So in other words, anyone who feels lonely is actually sensing that there is someone out there for them?"

"Precisely. God is all good all the time, Maureen. He would not allow us to incarnate in pain, feeling loneliness for a companion we can never find."

Peter pointed to Roland and Tammy. "I can certainly believe that they were born to be together. But are they just fortunate? Are some more blessed than others? Am I to believe that everyone has the potential for their type of bliss?"

Petra took a deep breath and sat up very straight, preparing her answer. She was a natural teacher. Peter, who had been teaching for twenty years, recognized the gift in others.

"We are all meant to find our twin souls, just as we are all meant to achieve our highest destinies. But we don't always do either, and the two are connected. Now, what I mean is this. It is useless to go out in deliberate search of your soul mate, because you will never find him or her in that way. There is only one way to find your twin soul, and that is to find yourself first."

Petra continued the lesson. "I will tell you something about me personally. I have not experienced their blessing of divine love in this lifetime, and yet I have all faith that it awaits me. I know that by teaching the lessons of *hieros-gamos* and making it readily understandable for those who have found their beloveds, as well as those who have not, I create the path for my own soul's twin to walk through the door. But had I stayed in the fashion industry, which was not my true calling, I likely would have remained alone or ended up with someone other than my truest mate."

Peter considered this for a moment. It was all so new to him. Foreign, but also exciting. "Will you know him when you see him? Will it be love at first sight?"

"There is a veil over these things, Peter," Destino answered the question. "Often one partner recognizes the other far earlier."

*

As they were preparing to take their leave for the evening, Petra approached Tammy and asked, "May I place my hands on your abdomen? I want to see if I can feel the baby."

"Sure," Tammy said. "But it's too early to feel anything yet."

"It isn't if you're Petra," Destino said.

Petra leaned over and placed her hands gently on Tammy's abdomen, closing her eyes. Moving palms very gently, she paused, breathed deeply, and then moved again. She repeated this motion for another minute before opening her eyes. She shook her head slightly, as if to clear it and return to the here and now.

Smiling warmly at Tammy, she said simply, "*Serafina.*"

"Serafina?"

Petra nodded. "It is a girl. Did you know?"

Tammy shook her head and looked at Roland excitedly.

"I told you it was a girl!" he said.

"It is. A golden one. An angelic. She is of the seraphim, the shining angels who surround the throne of our mother and father in heaven. The word *seraphim* means 'fiery one,' which if you study your Libro Rosso, you will recognize as the original name of the Queen of Sheba. Makeda, the fiery one. For she was one of the seraphim come to life on earth, to change the world with the twin of her soul. Just as this child will do."

"Are you telling me that my baby is the reincarnation of the Queen of Sheba?"

Petra laughed. "Something like that. A similar energy, anyway. In Italian, a female angel of this order is called a *serafina* and is a very blessed thing."

"Serafina . . ." Tammy smiled back at Petra as her hands moved to her belly, and she burst into tears of joy.

*

As Petra escorted the others out, she stopped Peter at the door.

"For the others, this conversation about soul mates is entertaining but not useful. They have found each other, after all! But for you, I think, it is far more important. If you would like to continue it, we should grab a bottle of wine."

Peter laughed. "How can I say no to such an offer?"

"I was hoping you couldn't," Petra said.

*

Maureen entered the roof deck and inhaled at the panoramic beauty of the Florence skyline, which surrounded her. She stopped short as she saw the figure standing at the far corner. His back was to her as he faced the Duomo, but she did not need to see his face to know who he was. The warm breeze rustled his dark curls, and his broad shoulders under his shirt tapered into a perfectly formed back and waist.

"Hi." It was all she could think of to say as she approached him from behind and ran her hand up his back.

"Good Lord!" he cried out with surprise, as he had not felt her coming up behind him. Maureen was confused at first as he drew back from her sharply. She looked at him and blinked, shaking her head for a moment. The man standing before her looked like a nearly identical copy of Bérenger. But . . .

"You're not Bérenger," she said, embarrassed. "I'm sorry . . ."

The man laughed now. "Don't be. It has happened all my life. I'm Alexander Sinclair, Bérenger's brother. You must be Maureen."

Maureen was still in shock. "You could be twins."

"Bérenger is two years older, but we have always been mistaken for each other. We used to play that game as kids until Bérenger realized that he got the worst end of the deal, as I was the one who was always getting into trouble."

"Does he know you're here?"

"He does now," said a similar voice, as Bérenger walked out onto the terrace.

*

"The charges were trumped up, totally fabricated," Alexander explained to his brother. Maureen had left them to speak privately on the roof deck after Alex's surprise appearance. Bérenger was dying to speak with her, but the appearance of his brother was completely unexpected. Exhausted, Maureen went to bed with the promise to have breakfast with him in the morning. She needed to try to get some sleep before making critical decisions about her future.

"It is clear that they won't stick, which is why they released me so quickly. I should never have been arrested, and they know that. Now we just need to determine who was responsible for creating that chaos. And who had the power to have me arrested."

"And why." Bérenger was listening carefully, trying to put the pieces together. Alexander was the president of Sinclair Oil, but he was a far less controversial figure than Bérenger. While Alex was powerful in industry and society, he was not known for making enemies. And to arrest a leader in the British business world was no easy task; it required airtight evidence, which was clearly not present here.

"Do you have any idea of motive, Alex? There has to be someone who would want you out of the way, even temporarily. Who?"

Alexander looked down at his shoes for a moment, clearly embarrassed. "There is, which is why I came here. Not just to see you, but to clear things up with Vittoria."

"Vittoria? I don't understand."

Alex squirmed a bit before blurting it out. "Vittoria and I slept together three years ago. In March, after a party in Milan. Bérenger, it was forty weeks to the day before Dante was born. And two months before she seduced you."

"What are you saying?"

"I'm saying that Dante is indeed a Sinclair but he isn't your son. He's my son. Vittoria was two months pregnant in Cannes, and I think she seduced you because she wanted to force you into marrying her and accepting Dante as your heir."

"But you're a Sinclair too."

"Yes, but I'm not *Bérenger* Sinclair. You're the glamorous man of mystery, not me. I'm the boring businessman. She has always been infatuated by you, and in fact I know that the only reason she wanted me was because I was a substitute for you. And of course, you are the esoteric heir, aren't you? The Poet Prince."

Bérenger sat back for a moment and allowed the reality of this to wash over him. If Dante wasn't his, everything changed. The child was a Sinclair and a Poet Prince, but he was not the heir to a far more disturbing element of prophecy.

"But the baby . . . he was premature. He could be mine in that case."

"He wasn't premature. He was underweight. Vittoria is a model. She starved herself and smoked when she was pregnant. Dante was small and ill when he was born, but he was full-term."

"How do you know all this?"

"I'm not an idiot and I can add. I knew when Dante was born that he was mine, but Vittoria wouldn't return my calls and never has. And I think she is the reason I was arrested."

"I'm not sure I follow you."

Alexander explained patiently. "I was arrested the day she announced that you were Dante's father. Vittoria knew that I would call you immediately and tell you the truth, so she had to create a scenario that would immediately remove me from her game. I have no doubt that her family pulled some strings to make that happen. They're capable of it."

Bérenger nodded his agreement. "But they didn't anticipate your getting out this quickly. Certainly not before tomorrow after two o'clock." Bérenger thought of the fate that awaited him in the Red Room of the Palazzo di Signoria and shuddered.

"Clearly. So I came here because I knew you were here, and therefore it was also likely Vittoria was as well. Have you seen her?"

"No," Bérenger replied. "She has barraged me with requests to meet, but I have put her off. I wanted a few days to consider my strategy. But I have an appointment to see her tonight."

"Where?"

"She has an apartment just down the street, off the Via Tornabuoni."

Alexander smiled at him conspiratorially. "Do you mind if I keep that appointment in your place?"

"Not at all. But what is it that you plan to do?"

Alexander hesitated for a moment. "I know this is crazy after all that has transpired, but I am going to ask her to marry me."

"What? Have you lost your mind? That woman is poisonous. Deadly."

Alexander shook his head. "No, Bérenger, I don't believe that, even after what she has done to me. I think she is lost, and I think she has been brainwashed by her parents and is in her own way a victim of this secret society madness that we all know so well."

Alexander did not share Bérenger's passion or commitment to their heretical family heritage. He never had. Alex had watched as Bérenger was spirited away to France every summer of their childhood for "training" that he neither understood nor received himself. Bérenger was the golden child, the Poet Prince, and Alex was just a normal little boy. And while he had never blamed his brother for his lesser treatment, it had left an indelible impression upon him.

"Vittoria is also the mother of my son. I want to be in his life, and the best way to do that, to ensure he has the education and upbringing that is best for him, is to marry Vittoria. I want to protect him from the madness and provide him with a normal life. And, as sick as this may sound, I am completely besotted with her. Always have been. I could do worse than to marry the most beautiful woman in the world."

Bérenger spent the better part of the next hour attempting to talk Alexander out of this idea, but it was useless. He was snared in Vittoria's web and could not be saved. How many times had he watched otherwise brilliant men lose their wits over a woman's physical beauty? And he understood here that there were other elements in play for Alexander. Perhaps Bérenger had never entirely understood the depth of his brother's jealousy. This was a way for Alex to get something back on the bloodline side of the family. His son was now the prince with the bluest blood in Europe. Marrying Vittoria and raising Dante, while nightmarish for Bérenger, was a dream come true for Alexander.

Bérenger gave Alex the address and the scheduled time for the rendezvous. Alexander would go in his place, at eleven p.m., and surprise Vittoria.

Bérenger Sinclair hugged his brother and wished him luck. But as Alexander left him, he could not help thinking that this was a very bad idea.

*

Maureen had a headache and was exhausted from days of sleeplessness and turmoil. She was too restless to truly rest, sleeping in small bursts and waking often. She was also a vivid dreamer and always had been. Many of Maureen's dreams were prophetic and had led to amazing discoveries in her life, so there was a blessing to be found within this curse of restless sleep.

It looked like tonight was going to be no exception.

"Oh!" Maureen squealed and sat up in bed. She ran her hands over her face and looked for the clock. It was 10:50 p.m. She had been in bed for an hour. Her cell phone was on the nightstand next to her, and she grabbed it and hit the speed dial for Bérenger.

He answered the phone on the first ring, clearly excited that she was phoning him. But there was no time for lengthy discussion.

"Nightmare. Bérenger, something is wrong and it involves Vittoria."

"Why? What did you see?"

"Fire. An explosion of some kind. I thought it was you at first; I saw him from behind. But he turned and I knew it was Alexander there with her."

"And you think it is happening now? Here? In Florence?"

The dream had an intensity to it, an urgency, that Maureen had never experienced before. "Yes. Call them. Now. We have to warn him. And Vittoria. Do you have her number?"

Bérenger said yes and immediately dialed Alex. He was hopeful when the phone rang, but after four rings it went to voice mail. He sent a text message to Alex, hoping that would get to him more quickly. It was often difficult to get cell phone reception behind the heavy stone walls of ancient European buildings, which the Palazzo Tornabuoni happened to be.

He tried Vittoria next. She was notoriously hard to reach, as she only turned her phone on if she wanted to call someone and never, ever answered. He dialed her number, but the phone went immediately to her bilingual voice mail.

"Dante," Bérenger said suddenly, realizing that the boy would be in danger as well.

He speed-dialed Maureen. "I'm going down there. It's just a few blocks down the street. I have to get to them." He never doubted Maureen or her visions. Believing in her was as natural to him as the instinct to save his brother and his nephew. And Maureen didn't know about Alex and Vittoria yet, which made her dream that much more chilling in its accuracy.

He was out the door before hanging up.

✳

Bérenger Sinclair passed the chic shops, then crossed at the old church with the enormous Medici crest as he ran down the Via Tornabuoni. The old palazzo, which had once been the home of Lorenzo de' Medici's mother, was now being converted into very expensive apartments. The construction was still under way, and only a handful of the posh dwellings were completed. Vittoria Buondelmonti was one of the first to buy in the complex, as an investment for the future. She rarely stayed there because the construction noise was so annoying, but was still more convenient and private than dealing with hotels. Vittoria lived for the paparazzi, but she also liked to control them. There were times, particularly with Dante, when she wanted to escape her celebrity and become less visible. She had told Bérenger this as she described the building and gave him directions to the hidden entrance off the street, which was why he knew exactly where to turn as he passed the first sets of construction scaffolding.

He didn't get any closer. The ball of fire exploded into the night sky, illuminating Florence in a gaseous yellow glow as debris rained down upon Bérenger Sinclair.

Florence
1486

LORENZO WAS IN the library in Careggi working through a particularly tricky sonnet when Clarice entered. He sighed, hoping it wasn't too audible, and removed his spectacles. He could see by his wife's face that this was going to be a struggle.

Clarice spoke to him in her formal Roman manner, which she rarely shed even after seventeen years of marriage and seven living children.

"Lorenzo, do you agree that I am a dutiful wife and devoted mother to our children?"

He knew it was a trap of some sort, so he cut right to the chase. "Of course, Clarice. What is this about?"

"Let me finish, Lorenzo. It is not what you think."

Lorenzo said nothing and allowed her to continue.

"No, I have long learned to live with the constant specter of Lucrezia in our bedroom. She is a wound that will never quite heal and yet bleeds no longer. You know, I cannot even hate her. She loves you. What woman does not? But I have not come here to speak of her . . ."

Clarice was hesitating now, which made Lorenzo a little edgy. What could be so dangerous that she was clearly unwilling to broach the subject with him? He was too tired to be patient. "Then what is it about?"

Clarice took in her breath sharply, then blurted, "Angelo."

Lorenzo thought he had heard her incorrectly. "Angelo? *My* Angelo?"

His incredulity seemed to feed her resolve. "Yes, and he may be *your* Angelo, and so be it. I cannot determine whom you call your friends. But I can and will determine who educates my children and lives in my home. I will not have that man filling my children with any more of his heretical ideas. Today, our little Maddalena advised me that she was named after the wife of Jesus."

Lorenzo shrugged. "She was."

"She was not. She was named for my mother, who was a pious and noble woman of impeccable Roman blood. And my mother was named for a saint, Maria Maddalena, the penitent saint and redeemed sinner, as she is recognized by the Holy Church."

"Why this, Clarice? Why now?"

"Because I will not have that taught to my children. If you want to play with your secret missions and your heresies, I cannot stop you. But I will not allow my children to be a part of it any longer."

What was left of Lorenzo's patience snapped. "Unless there is something you have been hiding from me, I believe they are also my children."

"Lorenzo! How dare you." She was stunned momentarily at the insult. Lorenzo was rarely cruel, but she sometimes tried his patience beyond bearing.

"My children—our children—will not be subjected to blasphemy."

"It's not blasphemy. The definition of blasphemy is taking the Lord's name in vain. What it is, is heresy. If you're going to accuse me of something, at least get the charge right."

"I will not have that man teaching any more heresy to the boys. Giovanni is destined for the Church!"

"Yes, he is. But which Church, Clarice? Yours? Or mine?"

"I'm serious about this. I will have Angelo out of our house."

"You go too far, my dear."

"No, I have not gone nearly far enough. Lorenzo, do you not think that I fear for you as well? Do you not know that I pray for your immortal soul, pray that you will not go to hell?"

Lorenzo sighed, a deep and anguished sound.

"You're too late, Clarice. I am already in hell."

✳

The battle between Clarice de' Medici and Angelo Poliziano raged on. It was fueled by Lorenzo's eldest son, Piero, who had no love for his teacher. Angelo was impatient with him and pushed him in his studies. Piero was indulged by his mother and lazy; he had little interest in applying himself, so he complained to his mother about real and imagined insults to worm out of working with Angelo.

Lorenzo, fed up with Clarice's nagging, found a compromise. He moved Angelo to another villa, where Clarice rarely visited, and freed Piero from further instruction at his hands. Angelo was relieved, as having any responsibility for Piero's education was a dodgy business. And while Lorenzo was aware of the shortcomings of his eldest, Piero was still the Medici heir. Angelo could only be partially forthcoming with Lorenzo about the boy's utter uselessness.

But Lorenzo would not have to intervene between the two for very long. Clarice de' Medici became ill early the next year, deteriorating rapidly into weakness, and then coughing up blood. She died quite suddenly at the age of thirty-four. Lorenzo was away at the western edge of Tuscany when she passed away, and he remained away during her funeral. Still, in spite of the sadness of their years together, he indicated in his journal that he was distraught over her death. For all that she lacked as a wife and companion to him, she was a devoted mother to his children. He grieved for her loss as a result and felt no small degree of guilt for his own hand in giving her a life that was not as happy as it could have been.

Lorenzo moved Angelo back into Careggi to focus on the education of Giovanni and his half brother Giulio. Now, with literally the greatest teachers in the world—Angelo, Ficino, and the Master—available to them, they were receiving exactly the education Lorenzo wanted for them. And the "twins," as Lorenzo referred to them, were not alone. He had adopted another thirteen-year-old boy, a special angelic whom he and the Order had been watching from birth. Michelangelo Buonarroti had grown into the most extraordinary talent anyone had ever seen at such an early age, and it was determined that he must be raised as a Medici.

Michelangelo joined Lorenzo's family hesitantly. He was painfully shy, but the boisterous brood welcomed him and he quickly learned to fit in. The older girls adored him and waited on him, and the younger ones annoyed him with requests to sketch horses and flowers. When they sat down for meals, Michelangelo was placed at Lorenzo's right. He was treated as a son from the moment he walked through the door.

"He is an astonishing student," Angelo informed Lorenzo. "In everything. Ficino is working with him on Hebrew and the study of the Old Testament, and he is thriving. His language skills are strong and he can retain almost verbatim stories told to him once. And the Master is over the moon about Michelangelo's spiritual understanding. Says he was born with innate knowing of all these teachings. He knew them coming in. It is as if he truly is the incarnation of the Archangel Michael."

"Maybe he is," Lorenzo said. He wasn't kidding.

*

Michelangelo was in the garden sketching when Lorenzo came to find him. He stood back, watching for a moment, as the boy held up a small statue. It was the statue of what appeared to be a saint, about a foot tall and very old. He held it to the light, turned it, then put it down and sketched. He held it again, looking very closely at the face, then resumed his sketching.

"Who is your muse, my boy?" Lorenzo asked him, pointing at the statue.

Michelangelo looked surprised to see him. "Good morning, Magnifico. The statue is of Saint Modesta. It is the treasure of my family, as it belonged to the grand contessa, Matilda of Tuscany."

Lorenzo was impressed. "May I see it?"

"Of course."

Lorenzo picked up the little statue and examined it. He understood why Michelangelo was so fixated on the face. It was beautiful. The features were delicate and sweet; they conveyed a wisdom and yet also a sadness.

"What is it you are sketching?"

"A pietà. It is our assignment from Verrocchio. Only I wished to create one that is not traditional but rather celebrates the teachings of the Order. See . . ."

Michelangelo showed Lorenzo the drawing. His beautiful Mary, whom he sketched with the sweet face of Modesta, sat with Jesus draped over her lap in a classic pietà style. But there was something different about this piece. An elegance and a sadness that Lorenzo had never seen before.

"Stunning, my son. And her face is perfection. Yet . . . she is quite young to be the mother of Jesus, is she not?"

"She is, Magnifico. But that is because she is not the mother Mary. She is Mary Magdalene. I have created a pietà that represents our Queen of Compassion in mourning for her lost love. Her pain is our pain; it is the pain of love when it suffers separation, the way that most humans feel it on earth. I would capture that feeling through this new way to interpret the story. Someday I would like to sculpt this in stone and make it come to life completely."

There was a light in his eyes when he spoke. Such an inspiration would have been extraordinary in an adult with a lifetime of education and experience, but coming from the lips of a thirteen-year-old boy, it was completely unexpected. And utterly divine.

Lorenzo's reply was simple. "Thank you, Michelangelo. Thank you."

THE NIGHT AIR was particularly silky as the moonlight bounced off the red tiles of the Duomo. Petra and Peter sipped the Brunello as they continued their discussion.

"Are you still a priest, Peter?"

Surprised at the direct question, Peter hesitated, then put his glass down. "Hmm. I paused because I have yet to actually say this aloud, to myself or anyone else. But no. I'm not a priest. I no longer believe in any of the things that I originally took vows for. And while I am a more devoted Christian than I have ever been, I am not a Catholic any longer. At least, not a blind one. I have many questions for my own Church."

"And when you were a priest, did you ever question your vocation?"

"You mean did I feel lonely? Like I was missing out by not having a relationship? If I am truly honest, yes. I did. But I refused to think about it and simply chalked it up to the doubt of the devil talking."

"Were you ever tempted?"

"No." Peter shook his head. It was not as if he hadn't had countless opportunities. He had. Peter was a very handsome man with his "black Irish" looks: dark hair and deep blue eyes. He was the priest that the female students always fought over. If you had to take Latin or Greek, at least you could sit in Father Peter's class. "I just never considered it. I have a lot of self-discipline, and when I commit to something, I commit all the way."

"Commendable and rare," Petra said. "But now that you are no longer a priest . . ."

"Am I tempted?" His question was soft, pointed.

As was her answer. "Yes."

He nodded, looking at her over his wineglass. "You already know the answer."

Her huge brown eyes were suddenly very bright. "I . . . knew before you arrived, and it was confirmed when you walked through the door. We were both teachers who were forced to leave our original occupations and find ourselves through the Way of Love. There were other clues." She laughed, a little with nervousness now, and a little with the wonder of life. "God has a sense of humor and he leaves such things for us, knowing we are so often asleep. You are a linguist. You know that Petra is the female version of Peter. That . . . I am the female version of you."

He smiled at her. "I do, and it already occurred to me. I have thought of nothing else since arriving in Florence. I've been quite tormented about it, to be honest."

She reached over and took his hand. "There is no need to rush anything, Peter. This is all new for you and I expect you to have doubts."

"Oh, but I don't." He stunned her with certitude. "None whatsoever. The Arques Gospel and the Book of Love have led me to understand that there is another way, and I know that it is the way that Jesus truly taught. And it is the Way of Love. That is the way of God, the reason we are here. And I need to continue to understand it so that I may teach in a new way, to a new world."

"I am happy to be your teacher. So that we may teach in this new way together, to what is becoming a new world."

"Then I am happy to be taught. But you will have to be patient with me. Not because I have reservations, but because I am inexperienced. I have no personal frame of reference for a relationship with a woman."

"Then I shall have to give you one," she said, moving closer to him now. "After all, I am the Mistress of the Hieros-Gamos."

But as Petra moved closer to begin Peter's instruction, the roof deck was illuminated by an explosion and a flash in the near distance.

*

The explosion at the Palazzo Tornabuoni Apartments rocked the city of Florence. It was a tragic accident, and the cause would be under investigation for some time. It appeared that a gas line had been cut during the construction earlier in the day, causing a leak. That the majority of apartments were not yet occupied was a blessing in this terrible tragedy.

Supermodel Vittoria Buondelmonti and a visiting friend, originally reported in the news to be Bérenger Sinclair, had been injured in the explosion. Later the reports would be amended to reveal that it was Alexander Sinclair, the president of Sinclair Oil, who was in critical condition at the hospital, along with Vittoria.

While Bérenger had been nearly buried by debris, he had been able to take shelter beneath the entry of the neighboring palazzo. He was treated for minor injuries and a concussion and then released into the waiting arms of Maureen.

In a strange little twist, the hospital in Florence where all the victims were treated was in Careggi. It was, in fact, the Medici villa where Cosimo and Lorenzo had lived such full lives, now renovated as one of Florence's hospitals.

There was one more twist that would reveal itself in the events of that night. The child, Dante Buondelmonti Sinclair, was not in the building at the time of the explosion. The construction noise had made him irritable, and a nanny had taken him to visit his grandparents at their villa in nearby Fiesole several hours before the tragedy.

Careggi
April 1492

THE DIMINUTIVE DOMINICAN friar Girolamo Savonarola was becoming increasingly problematic. He openly cursed Lorenzo from the pulpit now, calling the Medici tyrants and predicting their downfall at the hands of an angry God.

Savonarola had arrived two years earlier, when he had been invited to Florence by Lorenzo and installed most comfortably in the beautiful monastery of San Marco, which had been restored and decorated under the guidance of Cosimo Pater Patriae. When Lorenzo first made the decision to invite Savonarola, he knew it was a gamble. The monk was renowned for his heavy-handed preaching style as he raged against frivolity and corruption. He was troll-like and ugly, and yet charisma radiated from him when he opened his mouth. Even those who despised him and his message were often transfixed when Savonarola spoke, and they had trouble turning away.

Lorenzo had been convinced by his friends in the humanist movement to allow Savonarola to come to Florence for two reasons: the first was that the little monk saved his greatest ire for the corruption of the papacy; they had a common enemy. And while the current pope, since the death of the villain Sixtus, was an ally, there was still much reform needed in Rome. If Savonarola could be controlled, or at least influenced, he could become an effective tool in creating that reform. The second reason was precisely that Lorenzo was not a tyrant. He did not want it to be said outside Florence that he was excluding Savonarola because he was afraid of his message. By welcoming the controversial Dominican into his fold, he could keep a close eye on the message as well as the messenger, perhaps even exerting control over them both.

It is likely that Lorenzo de' Medici would have been successful in his management of the Savonarola problem had his body not been in a state of rapid deterioration. He suffered with the gout that afflicted all Medici men and had killed both his father and grandfather. Lorenzo was only forty-three, and he hoped that if he was careful with his food and his treatments, he might live as long as Cosimo. Besides, he didn't dare die now. Piero was too much of a fool to run the Medici empire, and Giovanni—who had been made the youngest cardinal in history at the age of fourteen—was still too young to take over.

But Lorenzo had little energy or spirit left to deal with Savonarola, and as a result the friar's poisonous preaching continued unchecked— and escalated.

An angry and distressed Angelo returned from the Duomo, where Savonarola had had a packed crowd earlier that morning. "He must be stopped, Lorenzo. He is playing prophet now. And while you and I both know that he is inventing prophecies which we know he can fulfill, the average citizen in Florence doesn't realize that. If Savonarola says tomorrow will come, his idiotic followers will all stand up and cheer the sun tomorrow and say, 'Fra Girolamo was right! Tomorrow did come!' "

Lorenzo was in bed, exhausted. He had been out at Montecatini taking the waters, as they seemed to help his gout in some small way. But the ride back across Tuscany was almost too painful to make it worth it.

"Let him rage, Angelo. I do not care."

"You need to care. He is predicting your death."

"Really?"

"Yes. And soon. He is saying that God is striking you down and that suddenly you will take a terrible turn and die immediately."

"Well, I do not intend to die, Angelo. So we shall prove Savonarola a liar once and for all."

"I hope so, Magnifico. I hope so."

∗

Lorenzo's condition worsened. Like Cosimo, his pain became so acute upon standing that he was confined to his bed. But he was definitely not dying. Of this he and his physicians were certain. Still, they tried every possible cure for gout, including a bizarre mixture of ground-up pearls and pig dung, boiled into spiced wine. It was so vile that Lorenzo insisted he would rather have the gout.

During these bedridden days and nights at Careggi, Lorenzo was entertained by those he loved most. Angelo and Ficino read to him; Giovanni and Giulio practiced their Greek and Latin together. The girls showered him with love. Michelangelo would come and simply sit, content to be with the man who was more like a father to him than anything else. Sometimes he would sketch; at other times he would ask questions about life, art, or the Order. He was easy and welcome company for Lorenzo, who referred to him as "my son."

Colombina came as often as she was able, visiting both Lorenzo and the Master at the same time. She would kiss Lorenzo on the forehead and sing to him and sometimes merely hold his hand while he slept. All the while she was praying as hard as she knew how for God to heal the prince so that they might continue their mission together, and that she might have the chance to love him for as many years as possible.

Sandro would come with new sketches for paintings, and his visits often cheered Lorenzo most of all. Sandro could still make his friend laugh harder than anyone else, and he did it effortlessly.

Sandro had returned to Florence one evening in early April with Colombina, leaving Lorenzo in the hands of his family and Angelo. For the rest of her life, Colombina would wonder what might have happened if she or Sandro had stayed. She knew one thing: neither of them would have allowed Savonarola into Lorenzo's room without supervision.

*

In Angelo's defence, it was a situation he could not have been prepared for. The little friar had arrived completely unannounced, and to open the door at Careggi and see Girolamo Savonarola was not something that anyone expected. The monk traveled with three other friars from San Marco, one of whom was known by Angelo. In retrospect, this was likely part of the plan. Because Angelo had some familiarity with one of the brothers, he ushered them in quickly and submitted to their requests more readily than perhaps he should have.

"I wish to see Lorenzo," Savonarola said simply in his raspy voice. In person and outside the drama of the pulpit, he was far less intimidating. He was small and slightly hunched. Angelo thought if he passed him on the street, he would feel sympathy for him or place money in his cup.

"Why?"

"Because I hear that he is dying."

"He is not. He is ill, yes, but Cosimo lived many years in this state. Lorenzo will too."

"You dare to say you know the will of God?"

"You say it every Sunday in the Duomo."

"I am God's instrument. It is for me to do so. It is not for you, poet.

But I am not here as your enemy, or as Lorenzo's. I would show my lenience, and God's, by offering him consolation in this time of darkness."

Angelo considered this for a moment, as the friars accompanying Savonarola murmured their agreement that they were here only to provide comfort and offer a gesture of peace to the Medici patriarch.

"I believe he will want to see me," Savonarola said. "Why don't you ask him and see what he says?"

Angelo nodded. If Lorenzo was indeed awake, this was the best course of action. There was nothing wrong with il Magnifico's mind, even though his body was failing him. And if he were feeling strong enough, he might find this encounter to be very interesting indeed.

Angelo found Lorenzo awake and restless when he entered the room. "What is happening, Angelo? I sense disorder in the house."

"You could say that. You have a visitor. An unexpected visitor. Girolamo Savonarola."

"Really?" Lorenzo began the painful process of sitting up in his bed. "Well, by all means send him in. I am anxious to show him I am not dying.

"Oh, and Angelo, bring us some wine, please. I cannot fail to be hospitable to my guest."

*

"I need to be alone with him." Savonarola was insistent. "What I need to discuss with Lorenzo is a private matter regarding his soul. It is not to be witnessed by anyone but God."

Angelo led the little monk into Lorenzo's bedchamber and closed the door behind him. If Lorenzo had any concerns about being alone with Savonarola, he didn't show it.

There would be no witnesses to exactly what happened in the room that night, precisely as Savonarola had demanded. At least, no witnesses that anyone was aware of. Students of history would argue these events into the next five hundred years, without benefit of one vital piece of information.

Thirteen-year-old Michelangelo, forever Lorenzo's angel, had been sketching quietly in the adjacent antechamber, separated only by a curtain. Nobody knew he was there.

He heard everything.

*

Girolamo Savonarola stormed out of the Medici villa in Careggi, signaling for his brothers to follow him quickly. He snapped over his shoulder at Angelo, "You'd best send for his doctor. And anyone else who needs to say good-bye. I told you he was dying. You were a fool to disbelieve me."

What no one saw as he rushed out the door to the waiting horses was the wine goblet he carried beneath his clothes, the one emblazoned with Lorenzo's symbol of the three interlocking wedding rings.

Lorenzo was having a convulsion. He was groaning in pain, shaking uncontrollably and unable to speak.

Michelangelo was already ahead of them. The doctor had taken up residence in Careggi, in chambers just down the hall from Lorenzo. The boy had waited, shaking, until that horrible man was safely out of the room; he ran down the hall to fetch the doctor.

The doctor sedated his patient to stop the convulsing and Lorenzo slept. His breathing was heavy, but even enough. Still, the prognosis was upsetting and shocking: it appeared that Lorenzo really was dying.

Angelo sent a messenger into the city to collect Colombina and Sandro. The message said, "Do not wait until sunrise." They did not want to make the same mistake they had with Simonetta, when nobody had the chance to say good-bye. Sadly, there was not enough time to summon the Master. He would not see Lorenzo alive again.

*

Lorenzo awoke, weak and exhausted, before the sunrise. He called his children in one at a time to speak to them, delivering messages to each about their future. He included Michelangelo in this, treating him always as one of his own flesh-and-blood children. Michelangelo would never speak about this day in public to anyone, except to say two things: Lorenzo de' Medici was my father above all else, and I will be haunted until I die by the voice of Girolamo Savonarola.

The "twins," Giovanni and Giulio, Lorenzo addressed together. Their destinies were entwined, and it was fitting that they hear Lorenzo's final instructions to them in unison. Together, the boys made a pledge to their father to carry out his wishes—without flinching and without fear—in the name of the Order. They weren't born Medici for nothing.

The vows taken in that bedchamber would one day alter the course of the Western world.

Once the boys had said their good-byes, exiting the chamber in tears, Angelo, Sandro, and Colombina entered Lorenzo's room together.

"You are the only three people in the world whom I trust. The only three who know everything. I need you all to take a vow, here and now, that our work will continue. I do not know if the mad monk poisoned me or not. I cannot prove it. But we did drink from those glasses there, so we can see . . ." Lorenzo pointed to the table, and when he saw that there was only one goblet, he sank back in his bed.

Sandro slammed his hand on the table and Angelo just looked sick. He would forever blame himself for allowing this to happen.

"I will oppose him to the death, Lorenzo," Sandro hissed.

Lorenzo nodded. "Just be wise about it, my brother." He smiled weakly. "Be the Medici that I have made you."

Colombina had no more interest in talking of Savonarola or revenge. It was clear to her that Lorenzo was dying, and she wanted only to spend his last minutes with him in peace and confessing her eternal love. But before Sandro and Angelo left them, they all joined hands and said the prayer of the Order together.

We honor God while praying for a time
when these teachings will be welcomed
in peace by all people
and there will be no more martyrs.

"Promise me, my most beloveds. Promise me that we will all be together again when God chooses and the time returns. Meet me here, on this beautiful earth, that we may finish what we started. It is a promise we all made in heaven, so long ago, and it is a promise we must keep on earth for the future. On earth as it is in heaven. Promise."

"I promise," each said in unison. Sandro and Angelo both kissed Lorenzo on both cheeks, tears flowing from all three men, as they took their leave.

"You are still the most magnificent woman who ever lived, Colombina," he whispered to her. "I have loved you from the very first day that my eyes rested on your beauty. And now as I die, I love you more than ever, and with God as my witness, I will love you through eternity, you and only you. *Dès le début du temps, jusqu'à la fin du temps.*"

She grasped his hands. Once so strong, there was little strength in them now, just enough to clasp hers gently. Colombina lowered her head, mouth beside his, so that their breath came together as one. She whispered the translation, "From the beginning of time, to the end of time."

She raised his hand to her lips and kissed his fingers and began to weep. "Oh, Lorenzo, please do not leave me. Have we been wrong about God? For how can he be a God of love, when he has kept us apart for so long and now he would take you from me completely?"

"No, no, my Colombina." He used the little strength he had left to stroke her hair. "This is not the time to lose our faith. Faith is all we have, and we must cling to it. I do not profess to understand the trials that God has put us through, but I have faith that there is a reason for them. Perhaps it was a test, to see how strong our love could be through all things. To see if our love had the endurance of our Lord and his own beloved."

She stroked his sallow face and let the tears flow. "Then I believe we have passed his test, my Lorenzo."

"It is better this way, my dove."

Colombina was exhausted and agonized beyond understanding. "Don't say so, Lorenzo. I will never see that losing you will be anything but torment for all of us."

"But it is." He seemed to find a surge of strength in these final words. "In our mortal lifetimes, God has seen fit—for whatever his reasons—to keep us apart. But once I have passed from the restrictions of this world, I am quite sure that God will allow me to be with you always. You see, Colombina, we will never be apart again. Isn't that so much better?"

She couldn't speak through her tears, as he continued. "I would extract the greatest promise from you, Colombina. Promise me that when the time returns, no matter where or when, that you will find me and never give up on me. Just like this time . . . you never gave up, and I gave you so many reasons to do so."

"No, my sweet prince. There is never a reason to give up on love. Not the kind of love that we share. It is deeper than any of the challenges that we will ever face, in any life or any time. It is eternal, it is from God."

"You are my soul. You must promise me, Colombina. I have to know that someday, somewhere, I will hold you again."

"Oh, my Lorenzo, my beloved," she whispered with soft determination, "I will love you again. I will." Her tears blended with his.

He was now too weak to reply, but his eyes told her everything. Very tenderly, she kissed him for the last time. It was the final moment of merging their souls through their shared breath, that he might take a part of her with him, and that she might keep a piece of him with her.

He would hold her in that way until they would be together once again in the spirit or in the flesh, however God would decree it.

*

Colombina walked quietly from Lorenzo's chamber as the sun was rising in Florence. Angelo and Sandro were sitting outside the door, looking drawn and anxious. Opening her mouth to speak, she choked on the sob that shook her body and hurried from the house. She didn't have a destination, she was just running blindly to get away from the place where Lorenzo had died. She found herself in the loggia, and there she attempted to steady herself on a great stone pillar, but there was no stone strong enough to hold her grief. She sank to the ground and let the agony of her sorrow overtake her as the first sob broke through in an unearthly scream.

Her cries were heard throughout the valley. Pitiful and heart-wrenching wails, filled with decades of pain and lost love, they echoed through the forest of Careggi where she and Lorenzo had first met as children all those years ago.

It was Sandro who came to console her finally, after giving her some time alone.

"Sandro, what shall we do? How will any of us live without him? How will Florence?"

"We will live to fulfill his vision, Colombina. As we promised."

"But how will any of us find the strength? Without our shepherd, we are lost sheep."

Sandro looked at her, not without sympathy, and yet his reply to her was forceful as he got to his knees to hold her by both shoulders. "Listen to me. I have painted you many times, and each time for a reason. As Fortitude, because your strength of purpose is unlike that of any other woman I have ever met. I have painted you as the Goddess of Love, not only because Lorenzo desired it, but because your love for him embodies all that Venus should mean to us. I painted you as Judith, because you are fearless and will flinch at no task that is given to you in the name of what you believe. And I have painted you as our Madonna, many times, in celebration of your grace. You have been a brilliant muse, little dove, precisely because you bear all those qualities. And now you must call upon all of them—your strength, your love, your faith, and your fearlessness. You must do it for yourself, for Lorenzo, and for the work we have promised to complete."

Colombina reached up to brush the omnipresent shock of golden hair out of Sandro's eyes. "You are the best brother anyone could ask for, Alessandro."

"*Le temps revient*, sister. Come on, Judith. There is a giant out there who needs decapitating, and you are just the girl to do it."

*

In the early hours of April 9, 1492, as Lorenzo de' Medici was extracting promises from his loved ones on his deathbed, a series of unexplainable events occurred in the city of Florence. An intense electrical storm hit, and lightning struck Giotto's Campanile, causing chunks of stone and marble to fly from the tower and land in the center of Florence. In the midst of this melee, the two male lions who symbolized the emblem of Florence, and who had lived peacefully together beside the Piazza della Signoria for years, began to roar and pace in their pen. They attacked each other and fought viciously. Both lions were dead by morning. So was Lorenzo de' Medici.

The people of Florence saw these things as a terrible omen. Most were Medici supporters who feared the worst with Lorenzo gone. There was no leadership to fill his shoes, and the specter of Savonarola's reign of terror loomed darkly over the city.

Girolamo Savonarola, for his part, manipulated the events of April ninth in another direction, and did so masterfully.

"God has spoken!" he roared the following Sunday. "He has struck down Lorenzo de' Medici, the archheretic and wicked tyrant. He has shown us his wrath and his disdain for the frivolities that Lorenzo indulged. God has shown us the evils inherent in art, in music, in any book that is not his own holy word. He has shown us with his lightning that he will take the entire Republic of Florence down, and he has killed the lions of this city as his first sacrifices. Do you wish to be his next sacrifice?"

The little friar roared his fire from the pulpit of the packed Duomo. The faithful in attendance, full of fear, roared in response, "No!"

"Did I not prophesy that Lorenzo would die before the seasons changed? Did I not tell you that God would no longer allow the Medici tyranny and blasphemy to continue?"

But Savonarola did not stop with fulfilling his own prophecy. He manufactured a tale of his final minutes with Lorenzo, telling of how the heretic refused to recant on his deathbed, despite Fra Girolamo's unselfish trek out to Careggi to offer him the comfort of absolution. Lorenzo de' Medici remained a heretic until he drew his last breath, and he died with the heavy stains of sin on his soul. The monk had no choice but to refuse to administer last rites, as the man was an unrepentant heretic until the end.

The message was clear: heresy leads to death. And the Medici were heretics.

Florence
present day

THE SUN WAS setting over the Arno, turning the rooftops of Florence into a burnished terra-cotta mosaic. Bérenger and Maureen sat hand in hand, enjoying the view, and each other.

"I had come here that afternoon to tell you that I would not marry Vittoria under any circumstances," Bérenger explained. "Even if Dante was my son, even if Dante was the Second Coming as foretold in the prophecy. I had come to the realization—with some assistance from Destino—that the most noble action I could take would be to honor love. The best example I could provide for anyone would be to have the courage to stand up for the one thing that I know to be true in my life: my love for you."

Maureen reached up to kiss him lightly, then said, "The time returns, but it doesn't have to."

"Precisely. It is time to break that cycle, Maureen, and that is what I realized. It is time for a new Renaissance, a golden age of the twenty-first century, a rebirth of the way we think and believe and respond. It is time to be reborn through love, and love alone. By shackling myself to Vittoria I would have been perpetuating the cycle of loss and turning my back on the most perfect gift that any of us can ever have. It would have served only to increase suffering, which as we know is not what God wants from any of us. It would have been a type of martyrdom."

The realization of it hit Maureen hard. She understood in a new way exactly what it was that Destino had been trying to convey to so many of his students across so much time. They said the prayer of the Order in unison:

We honor God while praying for a time
when these teachings will be welcomed
in peace by all people
and there will be no more martyrs.

*

Felicity de Pazzi wrapped her hands tightly. The commemoration in honor of Savonarola's martyrdom had gone beautifully. The confraternity crowd had been even larger than that in Rome, and the stigmata had bled perfectly and on time. The bonfire, while small, was sufficiently dramatic to destroy the books that had been accumulated. Heresy and blasphemy burned bright in the flames, urged on by the gasoline, which Felicity poured on them from a canister.

She picked up the canister now and took it to her car. Her hands hurt, and she would need them for what she planned to do next. They just needed to stop bleeding so she could work with them. But there were a few hours left until it was fully dark. She had time. But not much.

Florence
1497

"She is your daughter, Girolamo, whether you wish to acknowledge her or not."

Fra Girolamo Savonarola could not stand the sight of the little guttersnipe, nor her whore of a mother. This foul wench, who stood in his cell in San Marco with a scrawny, underfed little girl, was an instrument of the devil. She had seduced him in a moment of weakness, and this dirty little thing was the spawn of that horrific mistake. Now this child was the one thing that threatened his future as the ruler of Florence's austere republic. She had to remain a secret at all costs. He had far too much to lose at this point.

In the five years since Lorenzo's death, Fra Girolamo Savonarola had successfully destroyed the Medici. It wasn't hard once Lorenzo was gone. His eldest son, Piero, was one step above an idiot. Unprepared to take over the Medici empire, he had systematically run it into the ground without much help, weakening what was left of the family and making it easy for Savonarola to insist on their exile. He had even been allowed to ransack the Palazzo Medici in Via Larga to search out fuel for his bonfires, and fuel he found. Paintings, manuscripts, all aspects of heresy and foul paganism were confiscated from the palazzo and thrown onto one of the roaring bonfires that burned regularly in the Piazza della Signoria.

Savonarola had become famous for the bonfires, called bonfires of the vanities. His followers now numbered in the thousands. The people of Florence called them the Pignoni, which meant "the weepers," if one was being kind, or "the snivelers," if one was not. It was the job of the Pignoni to collect vanity items to burn in the bonfires. Anything that pertained to physical vanity—perfumes, creams, clothing of any adornment, jewelry—was meant for the fires. All musical instruments were as well, given that they were used only for secular celebrations and led to the gyrations of dancing followed by rutting. All books that were not Bibles or works of Church fathers were headed to the fires, with a special emphasis on the pagan classics.

But Savonarola held a special place in his heart for the destruction of art. It was art that the Medici had cultivated, art that contained the hidden clues to their heresies and their Order. By destroying as much art as possible, he would eliminate the teaching tools of blasphemy.

Within three years of eliminating Lorenzo, Savonarola had the Medici expelled from Florence, although the two he could not control, Giovanni and Giulio, were now cardinals in Rome. The current pope was a Borgia, and a Medici supporter, which was to be expected. The Borgias were the only family in Italy more corrupt than the Medici, from Savonarola's perspective. So while Savonarola seethed that the Medici brothers thrived under Pope Alexander VI, at least they were far away from his Florence. By 1495 Savonarola was the undisputed ruler of the Florentine Republic. He created a new constitution and implemented new laws of morality and austerity. It was now illegal to walk through the streets wearing any kind of adornment. Vanity was the ultimate crime against God.

No one dared to oppose him, and his power grew. But the existence of this child was a problem, which had to be dealt with immediately.

"I have made arrangements for the . . . child to be adopted into the de Pazzi family," he said without looking at the whore of a mother overlong. The sight of her sickened him. The de Pazzi had been his allies in eliminating the Medici, and they were easy to manipulate. They owed him a lifetime of favors, and he had convinced them to take on this girl with no questions asked.

"For your troubles, I will give you one hundred florins to go away and never utter a word of this to anyone, nor are you to ever see this girl again once she becomes a Pazzi."

The woman started to object, but Savonarola produced a sack with gold florins worth a king's ransom.

"Do you concede to this agreement, woman?"

She nodded mutely, reaching out to grab the sack.

He dropped it to the floor and laughed as the coins scattered. The woman was forced to collect them on her hands and knees.

"Leave the girl in the foyer. I will have the brothers take her to the Pazzi."

He left the room and never looked at the girl or her mother again. The little girl, her eyes huge with all that she had seen in too hard a life, stared ahead of her. Had Savonarola stayed to look at her, he might have noticed something disturbing about her, something in her eyes that held the earliest glint of madness.

*

Colombina was sweating with the effort but continued working with her fellow Pignoni. They were loading the items for the bonfire that had been collected during previous days onto the carts. The Pignoni had raided all across Tuscany in search of vanity items and heretical fuel for Savonarola's bonfires. Every manuscript that Colombina prepared for burning made her stomach turn. Every piece of art she loaded onto the carts made her want to weep. But she could not show any emotion other than joy that these terrible offenses to God would see the flames.

It had taken Colombina and Sandro the better part of these last five years to become trusted members of the Pignoni. Savonarola did not trust either of them at first, but as they proved to be some of the most dedicated workers among his faithful, and were particularly involved with the bonfires, he became convinced of the sincerity of their conversion. Sandro Botticelli had even submitted a number of his Madonna-as-whore paintings to the flames to prove his devotion to the cause. Both Sandro and Colombina were considered leaders of the Pignoni now, and as such they saw everything that was being prepared for the bonfires.

They were working together today, preparing for the biggest fire yet in honor of the Lenten season. The hoard was so huge and impressive that Savonarola himself came out to inspect it.

"Ah, will you look at this! It shall give me so much joy to see this go up in the flames. Raise it up that I may see it."

Two of the Pignoni held aloft what appeared to be a processional banner. A woman, a female saint, sat enthroned, surrounded by worshippers at her feet. Sandro swallowed hard as he recognized the Spinello Aretino masterpiece from Sansepolcro. He and Lorenzo had marched behind this banner when they were boys, in honor of the woman depicted so beautifully upon it, their Queen of Compassion, Maria Magdalena.

"But first, I must make an incision," Savonarola declared, reaching into his robe to remove the little dagger he used at meals.

The banner depicted Magdalene holding a crucifix. Savonarola took his blade to the banner's canvas, slashing it. He cut in bold strokes around the painted face of Jesus on the cross, salvaging the image of Christ. "Now, I shall keep this image of Our Lord from burning. But throw the whore into the flames!"

The other Pignoni cheered the piece of theater as Savonarola marched out of the courtyard. Sandro looked at Colombina and then around them. There were three carts, and each had two Pignoni working it. Sandro scurried over to claim the banner for his cart, and no one argued with him. They had perfected this process, but this banner was big and they would have to be careful here. Waiting until the other Pignoni took a break for lunch, Colombina and Sandro made their move. They removed the banner from the top of the pile and slipped it under the cart. A secret shelf space had been built into the carts for just this purpose. Since the implementation of the bonfires, Sandro and Colombina had been rescuing the finest art and literature of the Renaissance, one item at a time.

Once the banner was secured, they both relaxed a little. It was always stressful but worth every bit of risk. And when they were able to save something particularly sacred to the Order, all the better. Colombina looked to heaven and smiled at Lorenzo. He helped her every day, each step of the way.

*

Sandro and Colombina met at the Antica Torre that night to finish preparing the documentation. Rescuing the art wasn't their primary objective, important though it was. They had been building a case against Savonarola for five years, documenting everything that came out of his mouth in his sermons and in his private dealings with the Pignoni. His pronouncements became more extreme as his power grew. His arrogance made him careless.

Savonarola had been censured by the pope, who was threatening to excommunicate him. The only reason Alexander VI hadn't taken action yet was that he didn't have a solid case against the man whom they all now called the Mad Monk. Savonarola, for all his tyrannical madness, was still the power broker in Florence. He controlled much of Tuscany along with it, and Alexander knew that he would require a fair amount of evidence to make the excommunication appear legitimate.

Colombina and Sandro were convinced that the documentation she had been carefully preparing all these years was not only enough to enforce the declaration of anathema but perhaps even enough to have Savonarola brought up on charges of heresy. Achieving his execution, and the absolute abolition of his reign of terror over Florence, was the only acceptable outcome after the republic's five years of near enslavement to the Pignoni.

Colombina summoned her son. While his name was Niccolò Ardinghelli, anyone with eyes would see that he was a Medici. His features were softer, like his mother's, but he had Lorenzo's eyes—and no small degree of Lorenzo's spirit. It was Niccolò who would take this package to Rome. He would present it first to his brothers in the Order, Giovanni and Giulio, and then the three of them would take the evidence gathered over five hard years to Pope Alexander VI.

Colombina hugged him and wished him Godspeed, ensuring as she did that he was wearing the amulet that Lorenzo had left to him—the tiny protective locket with the sliver of the True Cross contained within it. It would keep him safe.

*Florence
present day*

"THE TIME RETURNS, Felicity."

Felicity froze. She was in the rectory at Santa Felicita preparing to leave when her uncle arrived in the doorway. He was walking with a cane, and a younger priest supported him. She was shocked to see him, but more annoyed at the timing. She was in a hurry.

"What are you doing here? And how dare you quote their blasphemy to me!"

"It is not blasphemy, my child. It is truth. Whether you believe it or not, whether anyone believes it or not, it is simply true. And it is happening, Felicity. All around us. The time is returning and it will sweep all of us along with it if we do not learn from the past."

She spit at him, but he stopped her before she could say anything.

"You must hear me out before it is too late. This is bigger than you are, my child. Did you hear me? My child."

Felicity sat down now, as a feeling of dread crawled over her. She knew what he was going to say before he said it.

"I am not your uncle, Felicity. I am your father. Your mother was . . . is . . . Sister Ursula."

It all became clear to her then—the reason for her exile to the boarding schools in another country. The "mother" who never wanted her was, in actuality, a much-burdened aunt. Sister Ursula, the strict yet sympathetic nun who understood her visions and helped her to cultivate them, was her biological mother.

Like Savonarola, Girolamo de Pazzi had committed a sin and there was a daughter born of that. She was the spawn of that sin.

Oh God. *The time returns.* It really was true.

Felicity de Pazzi ran from the rectory room and into the garden. She fell to her knees and began to retch, her body shaking with the turmoil it was in.

Father Girolamo did not go after her. He was too tired and about to collapse with illness and exhaustion. He could only pray that his revelation to Felicity would somehow interrupt whatever it was she had planned.

But when he closed his eyes in an effort to sleep that night, all he saw in his dreams was fire.

Montevecchio
present day

THEY SAT IN the cozy living room of Destino's little wooden house out near Careggi. Destino had invited them all out for the afternoon, indicating that he had some important things to show them, which could not be brought into Florence but which might help to heal them all after the tragic events of the preceding month. It had been two weeks since the explosion that had rocked Florence and injured Vittoria and Alexander.

Destino told them the amazing story of Savonarola, hoping that learning this extraordinary and secret piece of Renaissance history might offer them some distraction. He knew that the greatest balm for the soul was to throw oneself into gratifying work, and so he challenged them to discuss the importance of Savonarola and the perils of fanaticism. It was an important lesson for the future.

"There was a movement to beatify Savonarola in the Catholic Church, around nineteen ninety-nine," Peter told them when Destino had finished this part of the story.

"Someone wanted to make the Mad Monk a saint?" Tammy was incredulous.

Peter nodded. "I remember it clearly because my order, the Jesuits, opposed it vehemently. They knew clearly what Savonarola was. History is fond of remembering him now as the great reformer of the Church, but he was far more of a tyrant than the Medici or any other ruler in Florence."

"He was a villain, and never doubt it," Destino said. "A dangerous murderer. Not only a fanatic but a narcissist. He was out for his own power and nothing else. And would stop at nothing to achieve it."

"Here is something I have always wondered, Destino," Bérenger said. "History books say that Botticelli and Michelangelo became followers of Savonarola and that Sandro even burned some of his own paintings in the bonfires. Given the stories you tell of their involvement within the Medici family, I find that hard to believe."

"History also says that Mary Magdalene was a prostitute," Petra quipped, a wry smile crossing her lips. "Just how accurate are you finding history these days?"

"I have read that Michelangelo said, when he was dying, that he could still hear Savonarola's voice in his ears," Bérenger added. "Now I am beginning to see that differently."

Destino nodded. "Michelangelo was present in that chamber, and he heard the terrible things that Savonarola said to Lorenzo. The names he called him, and Savonarola's vow to destroy Lorenzo's children. The monk was crafty, as always. He began by pouring wine and offering Lorenzo a drink of friendship and amity. They spoke of things in Florence that both knew and cared about, and Lorenzo relaxed more than he should have. It was after Savonarola was certain that Lorenzo had ingested enough wine—wine he had infused with poison—that he began to reveal his true reason for being there, which was primarily to torment Lorenzo as he lay dying. It was sadistic. Evil.

"And so when Michelangelo said at the time of his own old age that he could 'still hear Savonarola's voice ringing in his ears after all these years,' this is what he meant. Sadly, this is how history fails us. That comment has been interpreted to mean that he was a follower of Savonarola, and that his righteous preaching still inspired him! Nothing could be further from the truth."

"And Sandro?" Maureen asked.

"Ah, Sandro. There is one more piece of this story yet to be told."

Piazza della Signoria, Florence
May 23, 1498

"PIGNONI, PIGNONI!" THE crowd jeered as the flames climbed higher.

Sandro Botticelli stood as close as he dared. He was known as a sympathizer, so it was in his best interest to stay out of the mob until after the execution. Later, he would redeem his reputation in Florence. But today he wanted only to appreciate the success of the harsh struggle of the last five years by watching the fruits of his labor.

Colombina was not with him, as women were not allowed in the piazza during the execution. They were kept on the perimeters for their own protection. The crowd was violent and dangerous, and there was too much potential for rioting and more bloodshed.

Girolamo Savonarola burned in the center of Florence, finding death in the same manner and in the same location as the art, literature, and culture he had been destroying for these last five years. There was a delicious irony in it, Sandro thought as he considered the date. May twenty-third. Forever after, he would call it the Day the Art Was Reborn.

Their package to Pope Alexander VI, created with such care by Colombina, had been welcomed with relish. It contained more than enough proof to accuse and convict Savonarola of heresy. And the timing was flawless, as the city of Florence was beginning to erupt with resentment over their oppression. The years of austerity had taken their toll, and a rebellion was brewing against the mad monk who had once been their savior. Mobs were very fickle. Thus when Savonarola was arrested, the divided city erupted into chaos and rioting.

From the look of the mob today, everyone supported the papal decision to declare Savonarola a heretic. Through the jeering shouts of "Pignoni" could also be heard "Florence is free."

The smell of burning flesh sickened Sandro, who was not a violent man. He struggled mightily with his spirit on this day. He would need to get back to his devotions now that his task had been carried out. He would need to find forgiveness and move on. But not today. He would do that tomorrow.

Today he would celebrate at the tavern of Ognissanti, which had re-opened this morning for the first time since Savonarola forced its closure years ago. Today he would sit at the table he had shared so many times with Lorenzo, and he would raise a glass to his friend, his truest brother, for what he had given to him, to Florence, and to the world. Today he would write rather than sketch, write about the brother who had inspired him and the art they had created together. And then, perhaps, he would paint once again. It had been a long time, but today he was born anew.

*

Colombina made the journey to Montevecchio almost every Sunday morning. She would begin her day in prayer in the secret garden of Care-ggi, a place that had been her spiritual sanctuary since Lorenzo had first introduced her to it so many years ago. The statue of Mary Magdalene, the Queen of Compassion, shone with a beautiful patina despite the passing decades, as Colombina cleaned and polished it herself during each visit.

Following her weekly devotions, Colombina joined Fra Francesco, the Master, in his cottage where she performed her duties as scribe to the Order. She wrote as the Master dictated, careful to commit his words perfectly to paper. What they were creating here was sacred and complex, an encoded masterpiece of the teachings and history of the Or-der. It required all her concentration as the Master used a strange polyglot of Latin and Italian words, veering into Greek periodically. In addition to transcribing the allegorical storytelling exactly as he dictated, Colombina used her fine mind to organize the elaborate drawings and architectural data that would become instrumental to the volume's completion. It was growing to an immense size.

Fra Francesco had explained to her, "When we are finished, we will take it to Venice, to a leader of the Order there called Aldus, who will print it for us. For the first time in the history of the Order, we will have a record of our teachings that can be shown in public. The Church will assume that it is heresy, but it will be so carefully encoded that they will never be able to prove it."

And so the work had continued in this way for the seven years since Lorenzo's death: Colombina carefully transcribing the text and inserting the drawings and artwork which had been collected by the Master from some of the great minds of the Renaissance. There was much of Lorenzo and Colombina's own story woven into the allegory: the legend of a man on a journey of discovery through a fantastic dreamscape, who finds the truth of life through love, a love which encounters and overcomes a great many obstacles.

Colombina infused much of her own spirit into the writing and often felt Lorenzo's presence in the room with her as she worked. On the day that they grew very near to completion of the gargantuan work, she asked the Master, "What are you going to call this masterpiece of yours?"

He smiled at her, and the puckered scar at the side of his face twitched over the top of his beard as he answered. "It is not my masterpiece, Colombina. It belongs to all of us, to each of the great minds and lives who have contributed to this story. It belongs to every human being who chooses to claim it, learn from it, and become the hero of their own epic." He paused for a moment, considering. "As such, I think it should have a title that is universal and speaks to the journey of all mankind, reminds us of what is real and what is not. I was thinking of *The Strife of Love in a Dream.*"

Colombina, who had endured the struggle to preserve true love, nodded. "Because love is the only true reality, and the rest is all a dream?"

"Of course." The Master nodded. "And because love conquers all."

*

The Poet Prince.
He was my friend, he was my brother.
I have painted the prophecy, his prophecy, in an allegory of Venus and Mars, using the two people Lorenzo loved most as models: Colombina and Giuliano.

The Son of Man shall choose
when the time returns for the Poet Prince.
He who is a spirit of earth and water born
within the complex realm of the sea goat
and the bloodline of the blessed.
He who will submerge the influence of Mars
And exalt the influence of Venus
To embody grace over aggression.
He will inspire the hearts and minds of the people
So as to illuminate the path of service
And show them the Way.
This is his legacy,
This, and to know a very great love.

Colombina is Venus, of course, and she is awake and exalted in her beauty, as the prophecy states. Mars is shown here sleeping, to indicate that he has been submerged. The little Pan creatures, symbolic of Capricornus, blow from a seashell to allude further to the submersion.

The love of Venus and Mars is epic, and it is clear here that she has given him grace over aggression. She has shown him the Way, and it is a very great love indeed.

I remain,
Alessandro di Filipepi, known as "Botticelli"

FROM *THE SECRET MEMOIRS OF SANDRO BOTTICELLI*

Montevecchio
present day

IT WAS LIKE a museum. But the most magical, extraordinary museum any of them had ever seen. Destino and Petra were positively giddy as they rolled back the antique Persian carpet to reveal the trapdoor in the floor of Destino's little house. It led to a staircase, more like a ladder, which each of them descended in single file.

The house, once Medici property, was built over one of the apple cellars in Montevecchio, similar to the one that Cosimo had once locked Fra Filippo in while he fulfilled his delinquent commissions. But Destino had been storing his treasures here for centuries. There was art—Botticelli paintings and Michelangelo sketches, jewelry and artifacts. There were hundreds of documents. It would take years to sort through the items in this cellar, to catalogue them, to analyze them.

"Dear Lord, Destino. You need a state-of-the-art security system. This collection is priceless."

Destino laughed. "God is my security system. No one will steal from me here. It has not happened in five hundred years and I do not think it will happen now. But come, I have gifts for each of you. Tammy and Roland first."

He moved them to a corner of the room where there was an object on the ground, covered by a heavy blanket. He signaled to Roland to help him, and they carefully unveiled the item beneath the covering. It was a hand-carved cradle, of the most remarkable craftsmanship. It was carved with the Magdalene's seal along the edges.

"This cradle was made for the birth of Matilda of Canossa. It will be a fitting place for your baby girl to sleep. She will be a fiery one, as Petra says, just as our Matilda was. And this will bring her angelic dreams as she makes the transition into our world."

Tammy, who was on her knees examining it, burst into tears. "It's the most beautiful thing I have ever seen."

"How can we thank you for this?" Roland whispered.

"By raising a daughter through love who will fulfill her fiery destiny and change the world the way that she sees fit within her own unique mission. That is the only thing any of us need."

He called Peter and Petra over and handed them a large box, indicating they should open it together. They did, and it contained a set of antique hand mirrors.

"As you rediscover your eternal love, you will see the truth: that be-

loveds are a reflection of each other, always. These were used in the secret wedding of Lorenzo and Colombina. It gives me great joy to know
that your own union will never have to be a secret."

The next box was for Maureen, who was already in tears from the
miracles happening all around her. Each object in this room was alive
with the power of its history. Bérenger teased her, "Maybe you better sit
down for this one."

Destino nodded his agreement. "Yes," he said softly, "I believe that
perhaps she should sit down for this." He motioned to a beautifully
carved chair with velvet cushions, no doubt a piece of furniture with
a history all its own. Destino placed a wooden chest in her hands and
motioned for her to open it. Maureen did and gingerly removed layer
upon layer of red silk fabric, which covered the object within it. When
the silk was clear and Maureen could see the object in full view, she
gasped.

It was an alabaster jar.

She looked at Destino and awaited the explanation, afraid to consider the truth of what she might be holding in her hands.

"You already know what it is, my dear," he said softly. The others in
the room were motionless, silent. Maureen lifted the jar carefully from
its place in the chest. The alabaster appeared to shine from within, giving the jar a pinkish glow. She opened the lid, and though the jar was
empty, it contained the faintest scent of something ancient and spiced
and sacred.

"It is the jar with which our Queen of Compassion anointed her
beloved, first for their wedding and last at his burial. It was handed
down through the female line for many centuries before coming to rest
safely in Sansepolcro, with the relics of the Order. All these were moved
to Florence during Lorenzo's reign, when we were afraid that Sixtus
would take Sansepolcro and confiscate everything. But now it belongs
to you. I am certain that she would want you to have it."

And it all sank in then, for Maureen and for everyone in that room.
Destino truly was what he had always claimed to be: a man tormented
to live eternally in a world that would never understand him. His exis-

tence, his survival, was the greatest of all miracles, a reminder that anything was possible, and that there were untold layers to reality above and beyond what we allow ourselves to understand.

Maureen could see that Destino was growing very tired now, but he had one more gift to give. He walked over to Bérenger and put his hands on both sides of his face. "It is your time now, my prince. Time for you to become what you are, time for you to be the leader you were born to be. I need you to take what I shall give you as a symbolic scepter. You are to become a leader into a new age, a new world of love and enlightenment. Remember that God has given you the most extraordinary blessings that you may devote the rest of your life to this mission of restoring the Way of Love. Can you pledge to do that?"

"I can," Bérenger whispered.

"Then to you I give the one true Spear of Destiny."

Destino removed a heavy iron key from a hook on the wall and opened the lock of a crate that ran half the length of the cellar. He motioned for Bérenger to assist in opening it. As the lid opened, blue light emanated from the box. Pale at first, and then growing brighter, it became an intense indigo, which swirled through the room before returning back to the object from which it had come. *Il giavelotto di destino.* The Spear of Destiny.

"Unlike the false spears, with their legends of evil spirits and death, this, the spear I carried when I committed the greatest crime against humanity, is an object of goodness and positive power. It is an object of transformation. See here, bring it up and look closely. Go ahead, Bérenger. It is for you to wield now."

Bérenger lifted the spear out reverently as Destino pointed to the tip. It was caked with blood.

"His blood transformed me. As did his love. This spear is the emblem of how the most irredeemable soul can be transformed through love. This is the ultimate lesson of the Way, the lesson you must all pledge to remember and to teach to the world."

They were all in tears now, tears of joy and awe at the miracles that were happening in this magical little cellar, when all hell broke loose.

*

"Fire!"

Roland smelled it first, but as he took notice and began to warn the others, they heard the crash of timber falling. The little house was ancient and made of wood, and it would burn quickly. They had to get out of the cellar fast. Roland went up first so that he could haul the women up from the top, with Peter and Bérenger helping to push them quickly from the bottom. The three women scrambled, Maureen wrapping the alabaster jar in her blouse while Petra did the same with the mirror. Tammy glanced back at the cradle; there was no time to save it. Once the women were safe, Bérenger and Roland motioned for Destino to go next.

He shook his head.

"Come on!" Bérenger yelled. "We don't have much time before the whole place caves in." Bérenger was in a panic. He could hear the devastation as the fire crackled through the house. The smoke was getting heavy.

"No!" Destino shouted. "I will go last. You must make sure that Maureen is safe—and the spear. Go. Now!"

Bérenger handed the spear up to Roland and climbed as fast as his legs would take him.

"Maureen!" he screamed, but he could see nothing. The house was engulfed with flames and smoke. He heard her voice, faint, yelling, "I'm here, I'm out, follow my voice."

Bérenger looked down to where Peter was emerging from the cellar and gave him a hand up. They both looked down to grab for Destino, but as they did so, the ceiling collapsed above them. Both men jumped quickly out of the way, but it was clear what had happened: the door to the cellar had been completely covered with flames and burning timber. They would not be able to get to Destino. And he had known it.

Bérenger and Peter could see nothing now, but they ran to where they heard voices calling to them through the chaos. Bérenger, holding the Spear of Destiny in his hand, felt as if it propelled him forward. He followed an instinct, grabbing Peter with the other hand and running in the direction that the spear pulled him. In just a few seconds, they were out in the Tuscan night, where they could breathe. The others waited for them, tears of fear and joy as they counted heads and determined that everyone was safe. Everyone but Destino.

"Oh God," Maureen cried. "We've lost him."

There was no time to mourn. A scream of agony split the air, and they ran around the rear of the house, now a raging conflagration. The little group, each dripping sweat and smeared black with smoke, stopped in horror at the sight ahead of them.

Felicity de Pazzi was in the center of the flames.

She had been on the roof, and as she had poured the little canister of gasoline on the shingles, she had inadvertently spilled some on her clothes and on the bandages that wrapped her damaged hands. The fire spread, too hot and too fast, catching her clothing in it. Dizzy from blood loss and exhausted, she didn't move as fast as she normally would. But this would be her only chance to eliminate all of them— every remaining member of the Order of the Holy Sepulcher—at one time. This was for God's greater glory, the ultimate gift she could give to her Lord. She could not, would not fail him now.

When the roof caved in before she could move away from the center, she was engulfed in the flames. The gasoline on her clothing ensured that her death, at least, would be quick.

*

Destino felt no pain, no fear. He felt only the sadness of leaving the beautiful men and women who had attended him here in the end. They would mourn for him, but he did not wish them to. He was ready. His life had been more extraordinary than most could imagine or even understand. And now his work was done. He was quite certain that the six who remained would fulfill their promises: to God, to themselves, to each other, and to him. They would work toward restoring the Way of Love to the world, and they would do it together.

The time returns.

And his time was returning as well. He was returning to his mother and father in heaven. He was surrounded again by the blue light, and engulfed in a feeling of universal love, as the man known by many names through time—Longinus, Fra Francesco, the Master, Destino—closed his eyes for the final time in his earthly life.

Florence
present day

DESTINO HAD LEFT one final gift behind.

The Libro Rosso, the blessed red book that had held the secret traditions of Jesus Christ and his descendants for two thousand years, had been transferred to Petra's apartment before the fire.

There was one final card wedged beneath the cover of the book, addressed to Peter. It said simply,

You are as wise as Solomon, for you have chosen Sheba.
Restore these teachings
while praying that they will be welcomed
in peace by all people
and there will be no more martyrs.

*

Bérenger Sinclair shook the hand of Pietro Buondelmonti while Maureen spoke soft words of comfort to his wife, the Baroness von Hapsburg. Vittoria was still in a coma. She and Alexander had fallen two stories from her balcony in the explosion. Alexander was in traction with multiple breaks and fractures, and it would be months before he would walk again—perhaps longer. But Vittoria's head trauma had been far more serious. Her recovery was still far from certain. Both had been spared from the fire as a result of the fall, however, and that was a blessing of sorts.

It had been a difficult decision for the baroness and her husband to agree to what Bérenger proposed, but they both knew that it was the best thing for Dante. They signed the paperwork in the solicitor's office after the terms had been drawn up to everyone's satisfaction. Dante Buondelmonti Sinclair would be raised by his uncle, Bérenger Sinclair, at the château in France, until such time as his parents were recovered and able to care for him. He would spend summers with his grandparents in Austria and Italy, as he learned the languages, culture, and heritage of the three noble families from which he was descended.

Dante would become the symbolic big brother to Serafina Gelis, the newborn daughter of Tamara and Roland Gelis. The children would learn together from the Libro Rosso and grow into their angelic destinies together.

The legacy of the Poet Prince would thrive into the future, with only love as its teacher.

Rome
1521

Pope Leo X sat quietly in his study, relieved to be alone after the many days of emergency meetings and councils. He drank deeply from the heavy red wine in the goblet, which was ironically etched with intertwined wedding rings. It was his favorite vintage, from Montepulciano, and he had it brought in from his native Tuscany by the barrel. The pontiff could not stomach the watery swill the Romans called wine and refused to serve it anywhere within his reach. Why drink gutter water when the nectar of the gods was available instead?

He smiled and thought that his teacher, Angelo Poliziano, would laugh if he were here now to witness that pagan reference. Of course

Angelo would be the first to celebrate the events of the last few years, and certainly with the wine that came from his own hometown.

There was a gentle knock on the door, and Leo sighed heavily. He wanted no company tonight, and yet it was inevitable. His gout was bothering him and he did not feel the urge to get up, so he merely called out "Come in" and hoped that the visitor was someone he cared to deal with on a night like this.

God is indeed good, he thought, as the tall figure of his cousin, Cardinal Giulio de' Medici, entered. Giulio was the only person he could stand to see at the moment. He was the only person he could stand to see most of the time. This was the one person alive with whom he could be entirely free with his thoughts and words.

"Come in, come drink with me. We have much to celebrate today."

Giulio nodded, pouring the wine into a matching goblet. He nodded at the portrait on the wall before taking his first sip.

"I could feel him today, Gio." Giulio never called the pope anything but his given name. It was a privilege of those from a close family. "It was as if he were here, watching us, willing us to do the right thing. Just as he always did."

Pope Leo X looked up at the portrait of his father and raised his glass. "This was for you, Papa. All of it was for you." The pope's dark eyes, nearly black, were identical to those of the man in the portrait. They filled with tears as he thought of his father, whom he still missed so much.

"History will not remember me kindly, Giulio, for what was done today. For what has been done these past three years."

Giulio, always the most serious of the children, now did something very rare: he smiled.

"But we did it, Giovanni. We did it."

"Well, we started it. There is much still to do, but we did indeed fulfill our promise today. And if history remembers me as weak, incompetent, and indulgent, then so be it. It was my promise to carry out this deed, and I have done it. I knew what it might cost me, but it is a small price to pay for the ultimate victory."

They both drank, reflecting on the events of the past weeks. Four years earlier, a rebellious upstart priest and professor of theology in Germany, one Martin Luther by name, had declared a type of holy war against the Catholic Church. In an act of genius, he had rallied the common folk by nailing a document to the door of a cathedral in Wittenberg. Luther's document, called *The Ninety-five Theses*, condemned the Church for a number of wrongdoings, several of which had been actively instigated and encouraged by Leo X and his cousin, Cardinal Giulio.

Pope Leo X had come out against Luther for his audacity but had done so very slowly. He took three years to investigate, and ultimately excommunicate the heretic, who clearly had an intention no less grandiose than trying to destroy the Catholic Church.

The pontiff had been heavily criticized by many of his brother cardinals and other Church leaders throughout Europe, who were insisting that he take a harsher, quicker stand against Luther and his growing movement of reformers. But Pope Leo X had been adamant that such events should be carefully considered and dealt with only after much time and thought. He sent papal envoys—all Medici friends and supporters—to Germany to investigate Luther, but these events seemed only to inflame the reformers and add more, and increasingly rabid, members to the movement. By the time Luther was excommunicated, his followers were so swelled in number and strong of spirit that the decree of anathema against Luther was worn as a badge of honor and celebrated throughout the reformist movement.

To be excommunicated by a church one despised was a blessing.

Today, in a series of heated debates, Pope Leo X decreed that no further action would be taken against Martin Luther. He proclaimed that the sentence of excommunication was enough; the reformers would no doubt be disheartened by this act and their little rebellion would diminish. There were other matters at hand that Leo X wished to deal with—the rebuilding of Saint Peter's, his new commissions for Michelangelo and their other favored angelic, Raphael, while an exciting new artist appearing out of the Venetian school, a man called Tiziano, warranted special cultivation.

The conservative cardinals were outraged. Was the pope completely mad? How could he not see that the Catholic Church was faced with a revolution the like of which it had never seen before? Further, he had already squandered several fortunes on art and architectural commissions, solidifying his reputation for frivolity and fueling the fires of the reformers. Did the pope not understand the gravity of the circumstances they were in? Did he not realize that the very future of Catholicism was possibly threatened by these protestors?

None but the most intimate inner circle would ever know that Pope Leo X saw the threat very clearly. Those who mumbled about his ineptitude and railed against his lack of leadership for the Church would never have guessed just how brilliant, committed, and purposeful Pope Leo X was in every single choice he ever made. He had, in fact, carried out a carefully orchestrated plan that had been put in place when he was made the youngest cardinal in history at the age of fourteen. His partner in the plot was his cousin Cardinal Giulio, the sullen child who held a lifetime grudge against the Church that had sanctioned the murder of his father during High Mass on Easter Sunday. But they were not the founders of the plot; they were merely the latest in a long series of operatives.

"Send our most trusted messenger to Wittenberg," the pope said to Giulio, "with a message to Luther telling him that his job was well accomplished and we are most grateful. He has served the Order to perfection.

"But first, come and drink with me—one final toast to the man who put all this into place so fearlessly. To Lorenzo il Magnifico, a wonderful father and the greatest poet prince to ever live. We have kept our promise to you!"

He raised his goblet to Giulio, who returned the gesture. "To Lorenzo," Giulio said, before adding, "and in memory of my father, Giuliano, that such crimes will never be committed in the name of any papal authority again."

And the first Medici pope, Leo X, drank a toast with Cardinal Giulio de' Medici. Once a boy orphaned by the acts of a corrupt Church, he would one day follow his cousin to the throne of Saint Peter, to become Pope Clement VII.

After all, they weren't Medici for nothing.

Epilogue

England, 1527

I seek no other.

ANNE READ THROUGH the letter once again, whispering the words aloud and savoring each passion-filled syllable.

> *Henceforward, my heart shall be dedicated to you alone.*
> *I wish my body was, too. God can do it if He pleases –*
> *and to Him I pray every day to that end,*
> *and hoping that one day my prayer will be heard.*
> *I wish the time to be short, but fear that it may be long*
> *until we see each other again.*
> *Written by the hand of that secretary who in heart, body and will*
> *is your loyal and most devoted servant.*

The lovesick suitor who called himself Anne's *loyal and most devoted servant* signed his declaration with a phrase in medieval French borrowed from the love songs of the troubadours: *Aultre ne cherse.* I seek no other.

She sighed with the beauty of it all, and then once again with the pain. For as much as her passion was reciprocal, the object of her affection was unattainable by the laws of this land. He was a married man and a father, and therefore utterly off limits. Yet his letter indicated

"God can do it if He pleases" as if to reassure her that their love was so strong and surely destined that God would intervene to change their circumstances. In the European courts where she spent her childhood, Anne had been taught that *love conquers all*. Holding fast to that belief, she went to retrieve her Book of Hours from its resting place on her bedside table.

A smile played across Anne's lips as she paged through her cherished prayer book. It was an exquisite masterpiece of Flemish art, an illuminated private volume given to her by her grand teacher, Margaret of Austria. But it was neither the artistry nor the sentimental value of the book which brought the smile to her now. It was the handwritten notes in the margins. Anne and her love had devised a clever method in which to pass secret messages to each other—through her prayer book during church services. His last message had been inscribed on a page depicting Jesus Christ following the flagellation, a man of sorrows, beaten and bleeding. It read, in her preferred French: *If you remember my love in your prayers as strongly as I adore you, I shall hardly be forgotten, for I am yours forever*. His message was clear: I suffer for the love of you.

Anne had given careful consideration to her response. She chose to reply on a beautifully illustrated page of the Annunciation, wherein the lovely Madonna is told by the angel Gabriel that she will bear a son. Composing a couplet in English, she wrote:

By daily proof you shall me find
To be to you both loving and kind.

The symbolism was unmistakable; Anne had chosen wisely. The selection of the Annunciation was an emphasis on the glorious event of God bestowing a son upon a most blessed woman. This was her promise to her lover: she would be both loving and kind to him and she would give him the son he most desired. Whereas her beloved was a married man and a father, his wife had only given him one living child, a girl.

To emphasize her sacred promise, Anne added a final signature to the book, one which she knew he would comprehend immediately. She wrote in French this time, invoking the Troubadour tradition—and something else, a secret vow that only he would recognize—as she inscribed: *Le Temps Viendra.*

The Time Will Return.

She completed her signature with the tiny drawing of an astrolabe, a symbol of time and its cycles, an emblem of time returning, before writing her name with full flourish:

Anne Boleyn

Later that afternoon, as the King's own chaplain droned the words of Mass to the small group gathered in the royal Chapel, Anne Boleyn quietly passed her prayer book to her secret beloved. Anne's father, Sir Thomas Boleyn, acted as her surreptitious messenger. Sir Thomas's importance in the court and as a confidante of the king allowed him the privileged position of sitting beside his sovereign during Mass. He was more than willing to encourage the growing affection between the king and his daughter.

Henry VIII, King of England, received the message intended for him and held the book to his heart. The tears in his eyes blurred his vision as he gazed upon the woman he loved and whispered across the chapel to her, "The time *will* return, my Anne. We will see to it that it is so."

*

How had it all gone so terribly wrong?

Anne had much time to contemplate this question as she sat in her cell, awaiting the moment of her execution. The French swordsman had arrived from Calais prepared for his grotesque mission; he would separate her head from her delicate neck with a single slice of his sharpened weapon. It was Henry's final gift to his beloved. As he had signed her death warrant, the king had also softened her sentence: Anne Boleyn, the Queen of England, would not be burned at the stake as a convicted heretic and traitor. In an unexpected act of mercy, Henry had sent to France for an executioner who could put an end to both her life and his misery quickly, efficiently and as painlessly as possible.

It had been nine years since Anne and Henry had pledged to each other that the time would return. Anne held that same prayer book now, running her finger over the fading ink of that golden promise she had once believed—they had *both* believed—would change the world. Make no mistake, Henry had been as committed to this mission as she was. Their love had been real and it had been an unstoppable force for both good and ill.

Anne paused on the astrolabe to contemplate the passing of time. She had so little left. There was one more thing she must accomplish before leaving this life, one final act of devotion to the mission. She must find a way to protect her tiny, precious, red-haired daughter. Picking up her quill, Anne began to write the letter in French:

Beloved Marguerite,
By the time you receive this letter you will be aware of just how
spectacularly I have failed you. There is so little time for me to
express my sadness and regret. And yet all is not lost. We have
accomplished much toward our goals, and we must not allow my
death to stem the tide that is washing over this great land.

I write to remind you of my deep fondness and admiration
for you, and to entreat as my final wish that you will find a way
to impart your vision, our vision, to my daughter. Let me assure
you that Elizabeth is the golden child of our dreams, conceived
perfectly and immaculately in a place of trust and consciousness
within all rules of The Order.

Epilogue

I beg of you, do not fail her. Even now, she shows a strength and a brilliance that is beyond compare. If Elizabeth is protected, she alone will ensure that the Time Will Return.
Until the day that we are reunited in heaven,
I remain.
Anne Boleyn.

Arques, France, Present Day

Maureen awoke to another dawn breaking over the hills of Arques. She sat up gently, so as not to wake Berenger sleeping beside her, but to no avail. Berenger, so attuned to her moods and energies, opened his eyes as soon as she stirred.

"You okay, my love?"

Maureen looked at him and shook her head. She ran her hands over her own throat and whispered, "And I have a little neck."

"What?" Berenger sat up now, concerned.

"That is what she said, while awaiting her execution. It would be fast because she had a little neck."

"Who said it? What execution?"

"Anne Boleyn."

The realization dawned on him then. "You were dreaming again."

She nodded. This had been the strangest and most vivid dream Maureen had ever experienced. She was not simply observing Anne Boleyn in the Tower of London, she was Anne Boleyn. She was experiencing the thoughts and feelings and memories of the most notorious queen in history as she prepared to die.

Maureen was not an expert on English history, but she had long been fascinated by the story of King Henry VIII and his six wives, the most infamous of whom was Anne Boleyn. Anne had been the catalyst for the Reformation in England as Henry had defied the Pope to be with her.

History did not remember Anne Boleyn kindly. She was most

often portrayed as a scheming adulteress of depraved and unlimited ambition.

But the Anne in Maureen's dream was a very different woman. Maureen could feel the lump rising in her throat and tears stinging behind her eyes as she remembered the excruciating pain and desperation of the tragic queen in the tower.

She knew she would soon be uncovering a new version of history which was waiting for her beneath the layers of five centuries of lies.

To be continued in *Book IV* of The Magdalene Line:

The Tudor Heresy

Author's Notes

While writing this book, I thought often of the old saw about painting the Golden Gate Bridge: it is a task that is never complete. I could spend the rest of my life writing a book about the birth of the Renaissance and never be finished. There were so many characters, story lines, and added pieces of information that could have—and perhaps should have—been included. The vast array of artists and their works, the humanists and patrons, and the histories and anecdotes surrounding them all is as daunting as it is inspiring.

A prime example is the rich and prevalent influence of Dante's work (as well as that of Petrarch and Boccaccio) on the elder Cosimo de' Medici and later on Lorenzo and his circle. They all deserve celebration, if not lengthy analysis, but I had to jettison those elements, as they took me too far afield from what was already complicated storytelling.

The finer points of Neoplatonism in the Renaissance are worthy of volumes, and indeed have inspired them, yet I toned down Plato in an effort to play up heresy. And while I believe that no intelligent person can argue that the Neoplatonist movement wasn't critical to the unfolding of Renaissance art, I stand by my assertion that it was one element of many, and the most important of these was heresy. Neoplatonism was often a front for the true heretical teachings that were preserved in these great masterpieces. The Gnostic concept of becoming *anthropos*—a fully realized and enlightened human—is essentially identical to what we now think of as humanism. The difference is that to be *anthropos*, one must attain a personal connection to God, becoming fully human through that direct connection. Heresy!

There was initially an entire subplot in this book about the fifteenth-century enigmatic literary masterpiece known as the *Hypnerotomachia Poliphili* and how Lorenzo inspired and influenced it. Unfortunately, the *Hypnerotomachia* is such a complicated subject that I have had to save that information for another day, another time, another book! Those familiar with that book may have caught the reference to it when Colombina ends her life writing for Destino.

The bibliography for the books in the Magdalene Line series consists of hundreds of volumes (a partial list of which is posted on my website, www.kathleenmcgowan.com). But the Hope diamond in my library is the volume written by Professor Charles Dempsey, *The Portrayal of Love: Botticelli's* Primavera *and Humanist Culture at the Time of Lorenzo the Magnificent* (Princeton Press). After years of wading through Botticelli commentary, in which each new authority contradicts the previous with astounding vitriol, the discovery of Dempsey was one of the great eureka moments in my research career.

Dempsey's book is brilliant, and I am grateful for the enlightenment that I gleaned from it—and apologize to Professor Dempsey for the more extreme conclusions I have drawn, which are mine alone. While Dempsey never makes a definitive case for Lucrezia Donati as the centerpiece of *Primavera*, as the icon of love personified, he refers to it as a distinct possibility. I would also like to assert that I came to my own conclusions about Lucrezia's esteemed position in Botticelli's work several years before reading Dempsey.

Dempsey is also the only art historian I have found who admits a likeness between the woman in *Fortitude* and the woman at the center of *Primavera*. This was, in fact, my own observation in the Uffizi Gallery in the spring of 2001 as I moved from the room that housed Botticelli's two small *Judith* pieces and the *Fortitude* into the main Botticelli room. Although the Uffizi has altered the collections in those rooms recently, moving *Judith* into the main Botticelli salon, there used to be a magical place in the gallery which I referred to as "the Lucrezia Donati spot." One could stand in front of the case displaying *Judith* and see the full version of *Fortitude* and the central figure from *Primavera* in the same sight line. It was in doing this that I became certain that the same woman was the model for all. Even the tilt of her head is the same, but in a mirror image from *Primavera* to *Fortitude*. And thanks to Botticelli's mastery of the infusion technique, I discovered that I felt something about this woman, experienced some element of her character, when I stood before the paintings. I began to look at those pieces with new eyes, and am convinced that all three are Lucrezia Donati. I believe that Colombina's specific and charming tilt of the head is also found in some of Sandro's early Madonnas.

That said, I am not an art historian and make no claims to be, although I am a most ardent and committed art enthusiast and have been blessed to spend much of the last two decades loitering in the great art museums of the world. And I have eyes. Sometimes it's just that simple.

I find that much of the evidence art historians draw their conclusions from is necessarily circumstantial, and yet their assumptions often astound me in their simplicity and—dare I say it—irresponsibility. For example, many art experts believe that *Primavera* was not commissioned by Lorenzo the Magnificent but rather by his cousin Lorenzo (the Much Lesser) Pierofrancesco de' Medici. The reason for this assumption is that an inventory was done upon il Magnifico's death in 1492, and *Primavera* was in the Pierofrancesco household at that time. Now, there are countless reasons why paintings commissioned by Lorenzo the Magnificent during his life may not have been in his personal collection at the time of his death, so to assert definitively that he was not the patron of such a huge, expensive, and personal piece—simply because his cousin had it in 1492—seems irresponsible to me.

I have made a sport of sitting in front of some of the greatest artworks in the world so that I may listen to the various guides, critics, and experts comment on the masterpiece at hand. I have spent hours in Botticelli's salon, listening to the varied explanations of *Primavera*.

Invariably, each expert asserts a definitive explanation of the painting's meaning. And, equally invariably, these assertions differ—often dramatically. There were times when I delighted in the idea that art is so expansive that it provides us with almost infinite opportunity for interpretation; others when I despaired at the idea of ever really grasping what the artist's true intentions may have been. Once I discovered the concept of "infusion" and learned to feel the art as well as see it, my appreciation of these masterpieces was enhanced beyond measure.

Much of what you read about the Medici in English refers to them in unpleasant terms: tyrants, hedonists, and worse. I mentioned this recently at an event in Italy, and my comments were met with stares of disbelief. Lorenzo de' Medici was the father of the Renaissance, the champion of the Italian language, and a man known for his generosity and enlightened way of living. Most of the Italians I have discussed this with find it unfathomable that history views Lorenzo in any other light. It was in discovering Lorenzo's greatness, and Cosimo's before him, that I became an ardent champion of the Medici. I believe that much of the confusion comes from the generations of Medici who followed Lorenzo and were indeed corrupt. I think Lorenzo himself would have been horrified and sadly disappointed to watch as his descendants lost their way and abandoned the principles of love, beauty, and *anthropos* that he and his grandfather worked to preserve.

I came across references to how the Medici "locked their artists in basements and forced them to paint," but then I would discover these fantastic stories about how Donatello and Lippi were utterly devoted to Cosimo. I use the word *devotion* specifically as it indicates love: these artists loved their patrons, they didn't just serve them. Donatello really did beg to be buried at Cosimo's feet and he really is buried alongside him in San Lorenzo. These are not the actions of an artist who was abused. I can see how Cosimo's often comical relationship with Fra Lippi could be misinterpreted by history, and I was determined to show the beauty of it.

I was stunned to discover in my research that both Botticelli and Michelangelo lived as members of the Medici family in their youth.

Lorenzo adopted Michelangelo at the age of thirteen in everything but name, and the boy was utterly committed to his foster father. There is also an argument that Sandro Botticelli was similarly "adopted" by Lucrezia and Piero and raised as Lorenzo's brother, as I have depicted here. Little is recorded about Botticelli's personal life, but esteemed British historian Christopher Hibbert makes this assertion in his book *The House of Medici*, as well as providing the description of Botticelli's commission to create the *Madonna of the Magnificat* for Lucrezia Tornabuoni de' Medici.

The understanding that Michelangelo and Botticelli were members of the Medici "spirit family" drove me to grasp the Savonarola period. Art and history assert that both these great, heretical artists became followers of Savonarola. I will never believe that, not even for a moment. They were both utterly devoted to the Medici and the mission, and neither would have embraced a man who sought to destroy Lorenzo. I do believe that in the early days Savonarola was welcomed into Florence as someone who could have been a tool to revolutionize the Church and eradicate corruption in Rome following Pope Sixtus and the chaos created by the entire Riario family. It all went terribly wrong. Michelangelo is widely quoted to have said about Savonarola, "I will hear his voice ringing in my ears until the day I die." That quote is interpreted by art and history experts to mean that Michelangelo was a follower of Savonarola. I beg to differ. I think Michelangelo said it because he knew that Savonarola ultimately destroyed Lorenzo and everything they hoped to achieve together.

I realize that my assertion that Savonarola hastened Lorenzo's death is controversial, but I also believe it is possible. Even if he did not physically poison Lorenzo, he certainly did so spiritually. I think the voice of Savonarola haunted Michelangelo, because it took away his foster father and his primary inspiration. The influence of the Order and Lorenzo can be seen throughout the Sistine Chapel, where touches of heresy abound. Who is that woman next to Jesus in the Last Judgment? Does that really look like his mother to you? And of course, Michelangelo sculpted Mary Magdalene as the prominent figure in the

Florentine *Pietà*, which he created for his own tomb, which I think speaks volumes about the artist's beliefs.

Sandro was even further devoted to Lorenzo as his brother and his patron, so I believe passionately that the time in which he was recorded as being a Pignoni was essentially Sandro working as double agent, as I have portrayed it here. His art plays out this theme, time and time again.

The story of Saint Felicity began to haunt me after a more recent trip to Florence. Standing before the painting of the saint and her seven dead sons had the same effect on me as it does on Tammy: it sickened me. Personally compounding the experience was the fact that the youngest child painted as dead on his mother's lap was the image of my own youngest son. Something crystallized for me in that moment, some tragic understanding of how it all went so wrong, how the teachings of love are lost in the fires of fanaticism. I wanted to shriek at that painting, *Everything about this is* so wrong! *This is not what God wants from us!*

I wrote the prologue to illustrate the fanatical version of Felicity's life, rather than celebrate her as a martyr. I wrestled with that prologue for a long time. It is a brutal story, and I considered toning it down—until I went online to investigate Saint Felicity and how she is viewed by followers in the twenty-first century. I was stunned, and further sickened, to discover a suggestion posted by a mother in honor of Saint Felicity's feast day: she advocated taking seven of your child's favorite toys and destroying them in front of the child, emphasizing all the while that this is what Felicity endured, and these are the sacrifices we are required to make for God.

Even writing that last sentence makes me queasy. I cannot believe that any woman of spirit thinks this is a lesson of love that God would want for any of his children. It was the realization that this type of fanaticism is still influencing our children in modern times that doubled my determination to tell Felicity's story in all its horror. I wanted to show it for what it was, and I hope it will make people think. It certainly has made me think, and it became critical to the theme of this book, as Felicity and Savonarola both illustrate the dangers of fanaticism over tolerance. Some of Felicity's words of dialogue were taken verbatim from early Church records.

I became hopelessly devoted to Lorenzo il Magnifico during my research, to the point of what was, at times, a literally feverish obsession. I knew I had to write much of this book in Florence because I needed to have the energy of Lorenzo all around me. Not a day went by in my final stages of writing in Florence when I did not "visit" Lorenzo in some way. My morning walk took me past his statue in front of the Uffizi. Sometimes I went into that museum just to see the Vasari portrait (my favorite representation of him), although it is poorly displayed and behind glass, so I find the glare ultimately frustrating. Still, I love that it is adjacent to a painting of Cosimo. I finally bought a copy of the Vasari, framed it, and kept the Magnificent One on my desk when I wrote (I'm gazing at him right now), even traveling with the more portable post-cards of the image.

I visited the Medici Palace on Via Larga (now Via Cavour) every few days so that I could spend time in the last known repository of the Libro Rosso, the gorgeous Gozzoli Chapel, and in Lorenzo's chambers, which are now the site of a very space-age, multimedia interactive tour-ist attraction. I took issue with this development at first but came to the conclusion that anything that makes history interesting and interactive is a good thing, and that Lorenzo himself would probably really be into it if he were here today. He was, after all, a pioneer in the arts.

My regular trips to the Uffizi really began to feel like I was going to visit my friends, and I would often start with the Lucrezia Donati spot, then work my way into the main Botticelli room to chat with Sandro. I really came to believe that Lorenzo and his Colombina were urging me to tell their story in a most human way, surrounded by the people who loved them most. Those people just happen to be the greatest artists and minds of the Renaissance. And of course, I stay exclusively in the Antica Torre Tornabuoni when I am in Florence, so that I may live in the footsteps of the beloved couple and the Order that inspired them. I swear, their conjoined spirits roam the roof deck of that turret that overlooks Santa Trinità and has the most inspiring view I quite possibly have ever seen. I don't get much sleep when I stay there, but I know that I'll always be in good company.

As for Lucrezia Donati, there is very little known about her life specifically. The lives of women in the Renaissance, unless they were monarchs, were not well recorded. Factor in that Lorenzo himself would have wanted to keep her out of the public eye as much as possible, and I think we have some very deliberate obfuscation. It is the same principle as secret society activity. There is no documentary evidence for most of it because there was never meant to be any! That's precisely the point of it being *secret*. I found Colombina through the art and poetry of the time and tried to see her and experience her through the eyes of Lorenzo and Sandro. But, as with Mary Magdalene and Matilda before her, she became very real and alive to me, and my passion to tell her story took over as I wrote about the period.

I speak of history as a mosaic, and it has been a very beautiful one for me. Little pieces fall into place and begin to clarify the picture. Single sentences from research books have often altered the course of my understanding of these characters and their lives. One book on Lorenzo's art collections speaks of Lucrezia Donati's son searching desperately for a lost painting of his mother—commissioned by Lorenzo and in his private collection. This led me on the path of investigating the boy's parentage. I cannot prove that Lucrezia Donati had a son fathered by Lorenzo de' Medici, but I do believe it to be true.

Another jeweled tile in my mosaic came from an art journal that referred to the original title of *Primavera* as "likely called *Le Temps Revient*." Beautiful! The legend of Lorenzo's banner, and the reason that the great defender and proponent of the Italian language would carry a mysterious motto in medieval French is something that has baffled historians for five hundred years. That is because historians were missing the secret society element, the heretical understandings of the Order, and the Medici connection to these heresies. The banner led me to uncover the connections between Cosimo and René d'Anjou, as well as Piero's and Lorenzo's close relationship with the French king Louis XI, who inexplicably refers to both Medici men as "cousin" in his intimate correspondence to them. Connecting these elements, and watching them come together, is pure joy for me.

Space restrictions demanded that I edit elements of the highly complex Pazzi Conspiracy. I had no choice but to eliminate several villainous characters who were participants in the assassination of Giuliano and the attempt on Lorenzo. I apologise to history buffs who might find this element disconcerting. I chose, instead, to focus on those characters who I felt were the true core of the conspiracy and held fast to my determination to present the crime in all of its horror through their actions. That such an appalling and cowardly attack was carried out during mass in a cathedral, sanctioned by the pope and planned by an archbishop using priests as henchmen, is one of history's great atrocities – and yet it is very rarely discussed or written about outside of Medici biographies. I was struck by the irony of the professional killer acting as the voice of reason, which comes to us historically through Montesecco's confession prior to his execution. And of course, I was deeply moved by the account of the wounded Lorenzo's courage in speaking to the mob and calling for calm in the hours following the murder of his beloved brother.

Renaissance scholars of both history and art will likely throw tomatoes at me for violating all kinds of academic codes, but let them. They can join the biblical scholars who scoff at my version of New Testament events. My role is to show the secret and human side of history, and it is the greatest possible occupation I can think of.

As Destino said, no man ever achieved greatness using just his mind. He must also use his heart. Thus I have endeavored to show you the heart of the Renaissance, and perhaps a little bit of my own.

And *of course* I have taken liberties. I did mention this was fiction, didn't I?

I honor God and pray for a time when these teachings will be welcomed in peace and there will be no more martyrs.

KATHLEEN MCGOWAN
NOVEMBER 22, 2009

Acknowledgments

While I worked on this book in Florence for several weeks over the last few years, I finished it in a quirky little cabin in the mountains outside Los Angeles. It is a house that my grandfather, BB Rhodes, built for my grandmother, Ethel Rhodes, as his own monument of love to her. It is a place of beauty and serenity, but the energy of familial love is so alive within its walls that writing there is the greatest of joys. I want to honor their memory with this book, as their spirits are an integral part of what I delivered. They were twin souls, as were my other set of grandparents, Katy Paschal and W. Joe Harkey, created for each other by God at the dawn of time. How blessed I was to have such influences in my young life.

The unequaled blessing these beautiful soul mates created was that of my parents, Donna and Joe Harkey, who have given everything they have to me—repeatedly—that I might thrive, grow, love, and experience life at all levels. Writing this book made me think about the importance of parents and grandparents, and all that mine have given me, so I dedicate this work to all of them, with much love and gratitude.

While researching this book, I became the devoted fan of Cosimo de' Medici, the great patron of the arts and humanity. He was truly a man without equal. But while writing him, I realized that I was drawing from life: much of Cosimo's character—his warmth, his humor, his brilliance—was informed by my literary agent and friend, Larry Kirshbaum. Larry is a Cosimo for our time, a supporter and defender of the arts and a champion for new voices in literature. Like Donatello and Lippi, I am utterly devoted to him and eternally grateful for his love and generosity.

My editor, Trish Todd, continues to share her patience, insight, and talent with every book I write, and I have to give her much credit for pushing me as hard as is necessary to ensure that these stories are told to their greatest advantage.

Throughout the incredible journey that was this book, where art and life blurred for me as they do for Maureen, I discovered an unparalleled muse in a Belgian-born author and researcher named Philip Coppens. Philip was intrepid, devoted, and unerringly dependable, sharing my love of the Renaissance and my passion for the mission of the Order. He brought my research, and subsequently this book, to life in ways I could not have accomplished without him. He has my love and gratitude. *Dès le début du temps, jusqu'à la fin du temps.*

My own spirit family supported me throughout, and as always I give love and gratitude to them—Stacey, Dawn, Mary, Patricio. And thanks to Larry Weinberg, who is both a great friend and wonderful lawyer, and to Kelly Cole, for her wisdom and support.

Everything I create is for my children, that they may be inspired in their own journey, as they continue to inspire me throughout mine: so to Patrick, Conor, and Shane, know that you are my three most constant muses, who inspire everything I do.

I use Destino's process of infusion in the writing of this series of books. Although it translates differently in print than it does in paint, I find that it still works. The countless letters I receive from my readers around the world, indicating that my work makes them feel something new or exciting or beautiful, is proof of that. Thus, I want to acknowledge the strength and inspiration I receive from those letters in return, from the handwritten to the emails to the guest book posts on my website and Facebook. I cannot respond to each of them individually, but I read them all and they mean the world to me. So to my readers I give my heartfelt thanks. Please know that *you* make *me* feel something magical with every word you send to me. You are my collective muse, the one that keeps me working. Because of you, I have decided to expand what was once a trilogy into a series. There are so many more stories to be told, so many more emotions to be shared. Thank you all for continuing to inspire and support my journey.

Demori!

I remain.